PARLIAMENT THE MIRROR OF THE NATION

The notion of "representative democracy" seems unquestionably familiar today, but how did the Victorian era – the epoch when the modern democratic state was made – understand democracy, parliamentary representation, and diversity? In the famous nineteenth-century debates about representation and parliamentary reform, two interlocked ideals were of the greatest importance: descriptive representation, that the House of Commons "mirror" the diversity that marked society, and deliberation within the legislative assembly. These ideals presented a major obstacle to the acceptance of a democratic suffrage, which it was widely feared would produce an unrepresentative and undeliberative House of Commons. Here, Gregory Conti examines how the Victorians conceived the representative and deliberative functions of the House of Commons and what it meant for Parliament to be the "mirror of the nation." Combining historical analysis and political theory, he analyses the fascinating nineteenth-century debates among contending schools of thought over the norms and institutions of deliberative representative government, and explores the consequences of recovering this debate.

GREGORY CONTI is Assistant Professor of Politics at Princeton University. He has written numerous articles about the history of liberalism and democratic theory, with a special focus on questions of representation and freedom of speech. He has served as a research fellow at Jesus College, Cambridge.

IDEAS IN CONTEXT

Edited by David Armitage, Richard Bourke, Jennifer Pitts, and John Robertson

The books in this series will discuss the emergence of intellectual traditions and of related new disciplines. The procedures, aims, and vocabularies that were generated will be set in the context of the alternatives available within the contemporary frameworks of ideas and institutions. Through detailed studies of the evolution of such traditions, and their modification by different audiences, it is hoped that a new picture will form of the development of ideas in their concrete contexts. By this means, artificial distinctions between the history of philosophy, of the various sciences, of society and politics, and of literature may be seen to dissolve.

The series is published with the support of the Exxon Foundation.

A list of books in the series can be found at the end of the volume.

PARLIAMENT THE MIRROR OF THE NATION

Representation, Deliberation, and Democracy in Victorian Britain

GREGORY CONTI

Princeton University

CAMBRIDGE
UNIVERSITY PRESS

CAMBRIDGE
UNIVERSITY PRESS

University Printing House, Cambridge CB2 8BS, United Kingdom

One Liberty Plaza, 20th Floor, New York, NY 10006, USA

477 Williamstown Road, Port Melbourne, VIC 3207, Australia

314-321, 3rd Floor, Plot 3, Splendor Forum, Jasola District Centre, New Delhi - 110025, India

79 Anson Road, #06-04/06, Singapore 079906

Cambridge University Press is part of the University of Cambridge.

It furthers the University's mission by disseminating knowledge in the pursuit of
education, learning and research at the highest international levels of excellence.

www.cambridge.org
Information on this title: www.cambridge.org/9781108450959
DOI: 10.1017/9781108582469

First published 2019
First paperback edition 2019

A catalogue record for this publication is available from the British Library

ISBN 978-1-108-42873-6 Hardback
ISBN 978-1-108-45095-9 Paperback

Contents

Acknowledgments

I have incurred a tremendous number of debts in pursuing this project – more than I can possibly do justice to here.

This project began as a dissertation, and so the first round of thanks must go to the outstanding members of my committee: Samuel Moyn, Eric Nelson, Nancy Rosenblum, Richard Tuck, and Cheryl Welch. A special word of thanks is owed to Eric and Richard. Eric was invaluable in helping me to see what a fruitful theme the mirror theory of representation was. More generally, he has provided a model of how to conduct one's academic life with grace. Richard was there for me at every turn in graduate school, both at a personal and an intellectual level. My debts to him are so numerous that it would look tacky to attempt to list them.

In the course of writing I have profited from the advice and conversation of a number of people, during graduate school and my postdoctoral stint at Cambridge, as well as at a range of other forums and events. These include Jacob Abolafia, Tom Arnold-Forster, Eric Beerbohm, Duncan Bell, Jocelyn Betts, Eugenio Biagini, Richard Bourke, Jonathan Bruno, Hugo Drochon, Jacob Eisler, Sean Fleming, Michael Frazer, Alex Gourevitch, John Harpham, Tom Hopkins, Emily Jones, Stuart Jones, Duncan Kelly, Rita Koganzon, Jacob Levy, Daniel Luban, Emma MacKinnon, Bernard Manin, Jane Mansbridge, Harvey Mansfield, John McCormick, Zeynep Pamuk, Jennifer Pitts, Arjun Ramamurti, Michael Rosen, Emma Rothschild, Lucia Rubinelli, David Runciman, Paul Sagar, Michael Sonenscher, Laura Valentini, Richard Whatmore, and Bernardo Zacka. I am particularly grateful to the two anonymous reviewers of the manuscript for Cambridge University Press for their wise suggestions and their encouraging words. Benjamin Hofmann provided editorial assistance in the late stages of preparing the manuscript. And I am sure I have forgotten others whose contributions merit mention; all I can do is apologize.

A few individuals deserve special recognition for the mixture of intellectual and emotional support which they have given me over the last half-decade. James Brandt and Madhav Khosla have managed the difficult feat of being both scholarly interlocutors and close confidantes. In addition to being dear friends, Sungho Kimlee, Ben Slingo, and Samuel Zeitlin all patiently read large portions of the manuscript and offered helpful suggestions. Finally, I cannot imagine having gone through the labors of the last few years without Adam Lebovitz and Will Selinger. With Will I had innumerable discussions about representation and parliamentarianism, and it was a boon to have had his intellectual companionship as I worked through these ideas. Adam performed an incredible labor in carefully combing through every page of the manuscript and suggesting a number of changes that much improved its final condition; more generally, he was always ready to assist me with his inimitable energy and erudition.

I am grateful to Cambridge University Press, and especially to the series editors and editorial staff of Ideas in Context. It is an honor to have this book appear in a series which has played such an important role in the development of the field of the history of political thought.

Portions of the first half of the book have appeared, in rather different form, in: "Democracy Confronts Diversity: Descriptive Representation in Victorian Britain," *Political Theory*, 47 (2019); and "Reappraising Walter Bagehot's Liberalism: Discussion, Public Opinion, and the Meaning of Parliamentary Government," *History of European Ideas*, 41 (2015) (co-authored with Will Selinger). My thanks for their permission to re-use this material.

No setting could have proven more conducive to the completion of this project than Jesus College, Cambridge. I owe much to its staff and fellows for having made it such an enjoyable place to live and work. My most earnest thanks are due as well to my new colleagues at Princeton for the warm welcome they have given me.

Finally and most importantly, I must thank those who are closest to me in my life outside work. I have been blessed to have had tremendous friends and family at every stage of my life, but I must limit myself here to mentioning the few people most indispensable to me: Erik, my family, *e Vittoria, senza la quale la vita perderebbe il suo fascino.*

Note on the Text

Note on Translations: For foreign language texts I have used, wherever possible, a modern English translation. For texts with no reliable English edition, and which I have cited in the original language, the translations are my own.

Note on Citations: All citations to Walter Bagehot's texts (with the exception of a few instances which are noted) will refer to *The Collected Works of Walter Bagehot*, 15 vols., ed. Norman St. John-Stevas (Cambridge, MA, 1965–86). Likewise, all citations to J. S. Mill's texts will refer to *The Collected Works of John Stuart Mill*, 33 vols., ed. J. M. Robson (Toronto, 1963–91).

Note on Attributions: For much of the period covered here, it was rare for authors of periodicals to sign their work. For the identity of the authors of these articles I have relied on the attributions provided by *The Wellesley Index to Victorian Periodicals, 1824–1900*, online edition [http://wellesley .chadwyck.com].

Abbreviations

Primary Sources

BM	*Blackwood's Edinburgh Magazine*
CM	*Cornhill Magazine*
CR	*Contemporary Review*
ER	*Edinburgh Review*
FM	*Fraser's Magazine*
FR	*Fortnightly Review*
Hansard	*Hansard Parliamentary Debates*
MM	*Macmillan's Magazine*
NBR	*The North British Review*
NC	*The Nineteenth Century* (from 1900, *The Nineteenth Century and After)*
NR	*National Review*
QR	*Quarterly Review*
SR	*Saturday Review*
WR	*Westminster Review*

Academic Journals and Secondary Materials

APSR	*American Political Science Review*
ARPS	*Annual Review of Political Science*
BJPS	*British Journal of Political Science*
ODNB	*Oxford Dictionary of National Biography*, Oxford University Press, 2004, online version [www.oxforddnb.com/]
EHR	*English Historical Review*
EJPT	*European Journal of Political Theory*
HEI	*History of European Ideas*

HJ	*Historical Journal*
HPT	*History of Political Thought*
HR	*Historical Research*
IPSR	*International Political Science Review*
JBS	*Journal of British Studies*
JPP	*Journal of Political Philosophy*
JHI	*Journal of the History of Ideas*
JMH	*Journal of Modern History*
JP	*Journal of Politics*
PA	*Parliamentary Affairs*
PH	*Parliamentary History*
PS	*Political Studies*
PSQ	*Political Science Quarterly*
PT	*Political Theory*
TRHS	*Transactions of the Royal Historical Society*
VS	*Victorian Studies*

Introduction

In contemporary politics and political theory, democracy is often associated with *descriptive representation*. Whether it goes under this name or such cognate labels as the "politics of presence," "indicative" representation, or simply "group" representation, it has become commonplace to treat concern about the presence of a range of social groups in legislatures and other institutions as intrinsic to a commitment to democracy itself. Today, anxieties about a "democratic deficit" often stem from a worry that the composition of political bodies does not reflect the important divisions within society at large.[1]

However familiar it is at present, the association of descriptive representation with democracy is not timeless. In the Victorian era, a formative period for the development both of the modern state and of democratic theory, the ideal of descriptive representation was at its apex – but it was largely claimed by opponents of democracy. In the famous clashes over parliamentary reform of the period, the impression that democracy was incompatible with a fair and socially inclusive assembly – with a House of Commons that could constitute "the mirror of the nation" – was formidable and widespread.

Instead of these aims being clearly aligned with a democratic self-conception, adherents to the ideal of a *mirroring* parliament tended to subscribe to one of three main paradigms. The first of these schools – and

---

[1] E.g. Anne Phillips, *The Politics of Presence* (Oxford, 1995); Philip Pettit, "Varieties of Public Representation," in *Political Representation*, ed. Ian Shapiro, Susan Stokes, Elisabeth Jean Wood, and Alexander Kirshner (Cambridge, 2009): 61–89; Iris Marion Young, *Inclusion and Democracy* (Oxford, 2000); Pablo de Greiff, "Deliberative Democracy and Group Representation," *Social Theory and Practice*, 26 (2000): 397–415; Will Kymlicka, *Multicultural Citizenship: A Liberal Theory of Minority Rights* (Oxford, 1996). Beyond the confines of academic theory, the purchase of descriptive representation is even greater. In public discourse, appeals to the premises of descriptive representation in assessing the satisfactoriness of assemblies and other governmental bodies have long been ubiquitous; e.g. David Judge, *Representation: Theory and Practice in Britain* (London, 1999), ch. 2.

the one which held sway at the midway point of the nineteenth century – was what I call the *variety-of-suffrages* school. Authors in this camp put forward plans for electoral reform that deliberately varied the suffrage across constituencies in order to ensure seats in the House of Commons for different classes, interest groups, and ideological movements. This variation in electoral regulation was valued for the sake of protecting and including diversity. To these writers, the variety of suffrages was the true *liberal* mode of regulating the vote, because it ensured that all of the "classes, interests, and opinions" that constituted their diverse society had spokesmen in Parliament. These thinkers were not only devoted to an ideal of descriptive representation; they also believed that their proposals accorded with English constitutional history, a major legacy of which was a suffrage variegated across different constituencies and justified on the grounds that this arrangement generated an assembly that was an "epitome" of the diverse civil body. In contrast, a uniform suffrage entailed bestowing an illiberal hegemony on only one part of the body politic. If the requirements for the vote were restrictive (what they called *oligarchy*), only the opinions of an upper class would be included. Conversely, if all property thresholds or special requirements for the franchise were abolished (what they called *democracy*, or "one man, one vote" in equal districts), the working classes or other majority groups, by virtue of their vast numbers, would outvote or "swamp" the other elements in society and lead to their exclusion from the assembly. Beyond simply being unfair to those excluded, such uniform suffrages would impair deliberation in the Commons by diminishing the range of ideas heard, thus rendering debate "partial." And this parliamentary deliberation was of indispensable significance, since they believed that a broader deliberative polity – the only kind in which progress, freedom, sound policy, and the formation of a real public opinion were possible – could not exist unless the highest representative institution itself operated in a deliberative manner.

Against this ascendant outlook, a second paradigm emerged for thinking about the meaning and mechanics of a mirroring assembly: *democratic theory*. Two discrete paths were followed by advocates of a more democratic franchise who attacked the variety of suffrages on its own terms. The first was to affirm either that the working class contained a variety of opinions, or that the demos possessed qualities and characteristics that were in keeping with the preservation of diversity and deliberation. Therefore, its full admission to the suffrage posed no threat of "swamping" other sections of society or of eliminating the contestation among viewpoints that gave the assembly its deliberative character. The second, more radical democratic response was to deny that concern for social and ideological diversity had any place in the evaluation or design of electoral-representative structures. For these democrats, descriptive representation and democracy were opposed and irreconcilable principles. Democracy was, in their eyes, a happy escape from a tradition of mirroring whose prescriptions they judged to be arbitrary and unfair.

The final normative-institutional vision of a mirroring parliament was *the theory of proportional representation* (PR). Neither the motivation for devising the scheme of the single transferable vote championed by Thomas Hare and John Stuart Mill, nor the truly stunning range of moral, epistemic, and social benefits predicted from its implementation, can be adequately understood in isolation from the anxious quest for a reform which would increase the inclusivity of the electoral system without causing the Commons to become unrepresentative and undeliberative. PR was supposed, by many of its backers, to square this circle, to provide an electoral system which could yield an assembly that was a mirror of society in its diversity even under a uniform (and probably at some point, they thought, universal) suffrage. However, PR was not a simple reconciliation of descriptivism with suffrage-uniformity or democracy; in contrast to a current view which sees PR as the form par excellence of descriptive representation, both Victorian supporters and critics of PR were acute about the ways in which Hare and other proportionalists were departing from traditional descriptivism even as they sought to remain faithful to many of the ideas of parliamentarianism that undergirded it. While a delicate give-and-take with rival schools of thought about mirroring went into its theorization, ultimately Victorian PR constituted an integral political theory in its own right, built on the foundations of *electoral liberty* and *voluntary association* and accompanied by a unique moral-political outlook. This outlook, in turn, provoked a cogent set of criticisms from theorists and commentators who came to see the plurality-rule system as essential to a vital, contestatory, and progressive democratic society.

This book aims to reconstruct and analyze the ideal of the mirroring parliament during its Victorian apogee, and to depict the contest among these rival visions about the meaning and institutions of deliberative, descriptively-representative government. As the first history of the theory of mirroring representation in the nineteenth century, it is my hope that this book will allow us to rethink the intellectual-ideological contours of the political thought of the period. The political, social, and economic history of parliamentary reform has been well-studied, but its intellectual history remains underserved. Furthermore, to the extent that the intellectual side of reform has been treated, it is other sets of arguments that have garnered the most attention. The wealth of theorizing and institutional design that took place under the heading of diversity and mirroring has remained strangely understudied. Importantly, some political historians who take the history of ideas seriously have noted that beliefs about the representation of classes and interests, or about the opposition between democracy and representative government, played a significant role in the debates about parliamentary reform.[2] But they have not attempted a systematic analysis of the theory of mirroring representation or tried to give a philosophical reconstruction of these debates. Moreover, such histories have tended to neglect the place of PR. In turn, the few historical treatments of the British PR movement have not been concerned to elaborate how much the invention and theorization of PR owed to the intense conversation around the ideal of a mirroring Commons, but have instead focused on explaining why PR did not win out in the party-political machinations around electoral reform in Britain.[3] As a result, the important ways in which PR both drew from and broke with the conceptual and normative universe of Victorian descriptive representation have gone unexamined. This lacuna is particularly unfortunate, both because PR is a major institution of modern representative democracy on the nature and genealogy of which it is important to reflect, and because its invention and promulgation was a force whose shaping effect on the development of modern political thought has received insufficient consideration.

Restoring mirroring representation to a central place in nineteenth-century political thought adds fresh layers of nuance and context to some familiar political-philosophic themes, such as the tensions between democracy *and* representation and between democracy *and* liberalism. When a conflict between democracy and representation is invoked, what is often meant is that in a democracy the "will of the people" acts in some sense directly, while in a representative system it is mediated by an intervening set of officials and institutions. But historically there was another

---

[2] See the excellent volumes by Robert Saunders (*Democracy and the Vote in British Politics, 1848–1867* [Farnham, 2011]) and Angus Hawkins (*Victorian Political Culture, 'Habits of Heart and Mind'* [Oxford, 2015]). Both have been invaluable resources for me.

[3] As in Jenifer Hart's *Proportional Representation: Critics of the British Electoral System, 1820–1945* (Oxford, 1992). The only work in the history of political thought concentrated on Victorian PR is Floyd Parsons's *Thomas Hare and Political Representation in Victorian Britain* (Houndmills, Basingstoke, 2009). I have benefited greatly from both of these works.

important way of seeing the conflict – namely, as a conflict between a representative government, which contained securities against a "part," however large, speaking for a diverse "whole," and a democracy, which did not. In this respect this book participates in a growing theoretical literature which resists treating representative government as simply a mode of instantiating democracy and instead understands the former as having a distinct historical and theoretical basis which ideas of democracy then came to modify.[4] Similarly, when theorists speak of a tension between democracy and liberalism, what they typically have in mind is that the popular will can conflict with individual rights. Yet there has been another important manner of conceiving the tension between democracy and liberalism, where the clash is wholly internal to the electoral-representative sphere: for many Victorians, the heart of the matter in parliamentary reform was whether "true liberalism" or "democracy" would come to characterize the future of the English representation.

Along related lines, an understanding of Victorian debates about mirroring can offer alternative perspectives on trends and assumptions in contemporary political theory. As I have already noted, democratic theory has witnessed a growth of sympathy for descriptive representation, and the practice of many democratic governments has been to implement descriptivist devices such as quotas or special constituencies for particular groups. And yet little attention has been paid to the fact that descriptive representation has no intrinsic connection to democracy. Depending on one's underlying sociological presuppositions, one may be led to endorse electoral arrangements that are distinctly undemocratic while remaining faithful to the principle of descriptive representation. Indeed, although proponents of descriptive representation today are counted in the democratic ranks, historically this affiliation is the exception rather than the rule. There is a corresponding parallel with the great wave of "deliberative democracy" in contemporary theory: while deliberation has been a core commitment of nearly all theories of representative government for the last two centuries at least, its connection with democracy has been far more tenuous.

---

[4] E.g. Mónica Brita Vieiro and David Runciman, *Representation* (Cambridge, 2008); David Plotke, "Representation Is Democracy," *Constellations*, 4 (1997): 19–34; Bryan Garsten, "Representative Government and Popular Sovereignty," in Shapiro et al. (eds), *Political Representation*, 90–110.

This book was not written in order to exemplify any particular method of doing either intellectual history or political theory – at least not consciously. Nonetheless, the reader is entitled to an account of the basic convictions orienting the author's research and writing. Indeed, I do subscribe to a few notions which might grandly be called *quasi-methodological*, insofar as they shaped how I conceived of this project and motivated me to present it as I have done – although perhaps it would be more accurate to describe them as articles of faith.

Cardinal among these is the belief that that there need be no trade-off between history and theory. That "history is a laboratory for arguments" and can thereby enrich political theory is an old saw,[5] although it is no less true for its familiarity. But I would push the thought even further: the more history, I would suggest, the better the laboratory. The more fine-grained our historical knowledge, the more urgently and clearly the arguments, problems, and debates of the past can speak to current dilemmas and questions. In other words, a major reason to plunge deeply into the historical context of political thought is precisely (if paradoxically) because one is aiming to produce a piece of writing that is *not* solely of historical value.[6] Whether this book itself affirms this conviction about the mutually beneficial connection between historical and theoretical research, only the reader can decide. That such a harmony or synergy should exist, however, is not accidental, but stems from two truths about our political thinking.

The first is that political thought – and especially that political thought which draws heavily from and in turn impacts the surrounding political culture – is an ensemble rather than a star-driven production. Hence, our understanding of political ideas becomes richer by allowing a greater number of actors onto the stage.[7] Without casting our net so widely, it is too easy to imagine that certain canonical ideas were the only ones on offer, or to attribute to them a triumph that they may, in fact, never have achieved; and a certain amount of mischaracterization and lack of nuance in evaluating particular arguments or outlooks becomes almost inevitable. A thicker reconstruction of the public debate of an historical period, featuring a deeper roster of thinkers, therefore serves as an aid to reflection

[5] E.g. Jürgen Habermas, "Popular Sovereignty as Procedure," in *Between Facts and Norms: Contributions to a Discourse Theory of Law and Democracy*, trans. William Rehg (Cambridge, MA, 1996): 463–90.

[6] E.g. Richard Tuck, *Philosophy and Government, 1572–1651* (Cambridge, 1993), vii.

[7] Jan-Werner Müller's label of "in-between figures" applies well to many of the *dramatis personae* of this book; Müller, "The Triumph of What (If Anything)? Rethinking Political Ideologies and Political Institutions in Twentieth-Century Europe," *Journal of Political Ideologies*, 14 (2009): 211–26.

on the relations between different concepts, values, and institutional arrangements.

A second way in which history of political thought can enhance political theory is that it can focus our minds on the shape and significance of specific institutions. Political theory has recently heard calls to be more attentive to the actual institutions by which politics is conducted.[8] History has much to contribute to such a project. In both public discourse and political philosophy it can be difficult not to take for granted the existent institutional backdrop, not to let an assumption of its permanence or naturalness inflect our thinking in myriad ways of which we are seldom fully aware.[9] A richer historicization of political thought is one means by which to avoid being complacent about institutional matters or leaving them in the background of our theorizations of politics, for it forces us to confront the concrete institutional forms in light of which past thinkers developed their views about justice, equality, representation, etc. Historical inquiry often provides, from the perspective of the present, a sense of mismatch – we find institutions unlike those with which we are familiar being justified in the name of values or ends which resonate with us, or, vice versa, we discover institutions similar or identical to our own being defended on grounds not widely known or accepted today – and this sense can be productive of fresh thinking about the nature of our political structures. For this reason, history can mediate between the institutional and the normative, the particular and the abstract, in a way that is productive for political theory; it can open up avenues by which broad normative and conceptual problems can be credibly connected to the nitty-gritty of institutional design and evaluation.

These general rules likely do not apply universally; there probably are historical settings that have no light to shed on certain current questions. But if there are exceptions, Victorian Britain is not one of them. The Victorian era was marked by an extraordinary richness of thought about politics which has been underserved by political theorists, in part out of a too-exclusive focus on John Stuart Mill. A tremendous outpouring of writing about liberty, democracy, the state, empire, and many other issues which remain live today contributed to a highly rationalistic public sphere

---

[8] Jeremy Waldron, *Political Political Theory: Essays on Institutions* (Cambridge, MA, 2016).

[9] E.g. the warning of the pluralist historian and philosopher J. N. Figgis that "nearly every system which professes to be deduced from general philosophical principles will be found on investigation to bear a very close relation to the facts of some existing government"; Figgis, "William Warburton," in *Typical English Churchmen from Parker to Maurice*, ed. William Collins (London, 1902), 215–56, at 232.

in which political and intellectual life were closely imbricated.[10] Spurred on
by a sense that they lived in an age of transition in which the bases of society
and government appeared uncertain and open to challenge, a wide array of
thinkers entered the public fray in self-conscious dialogue with one another
to tackle fundamental questions. Going beyond the relatively thin cast of
nineteenth-century British philosophers (Bentham, the Mills, perhaps
T. H. Green) who are familiar beyond the realm of historical specialists,
this book attempts to bring to the fore a host of intriguing and insightful
figures. On our specific theme – mirroring representation, its institutions
and values – a profound and multifaceted debate was generated through
the manifold contributions of authors from a wide array of professional,
intellectual, political, and socioeconomic backgrounds. The Victorian
period is therefore an excellent proving ground for the proposition that
going beyond the philosophical canon to reconstruct broader currents of
political thought can yield theoretical benefits.

   In addition, the second half of the nineteenth century constitutes
a kind of ideal point from which to take up questions about representation that are still with us today. Victorian thinkers tended to combine
support for many of the values which still loom large in contemporary
politics and philosophy – deliberation, inclusivity, pluralism, responsiveness to public opinion – with a different set of beliefs about what
sort of representative structures and forms of electoral regulation
instantiated these values. Likewise, their sense of how these values and
institutions related in turn to such apparently familiar master-
categories as liberalism, democracy, and modernity is often alien to
our own. Sharing much with and yet departing interestingly from
twenty-first-century politics and philosophy, nineteenth-century
Britain is the right kind of mirror to hold up to contemporary political
theory. In particular, by recovering a world in which descriptive representation was a widely held ideal but the meaning and desirability of
democracy were hotly contested, we are able to gain a critical vantage
point on a number of issues prominent today. The tensions and trade-
offs between rival views of representation are more easily seen in the
light of the more pluralistic normative-political vocabulary of Victorian
controversy than in the flatter, more univocal idiom of contemporary
political theory and public debate, over which democracy looms as

[10] E.g. J. P. Parry, *Democracy and Religion: Gladstone and the Liberal Party, 1867–1875* (Cambridge,
     1986), 48; H. C. G. Matthew, *Gladstone, 1809–1898* (Oxford, 1997), esp. part 2, chs. 2–3;
     Julia Stapleton, *Political Intellectuals and Public Identities in Britain since 1850* (Manchester,
     2001), ch. 2.

a kind of amorphous and all-encompassing presence.[11] At the least, it is in keeping with the striking revival of interest in representation – from its first principles to matters of institutional design[12] – in recent political theory to examine with care a period at once formative for and under-explored by contemporary political theory.

Let me close with a few clarificatory points.

First, a word is due about the scope and limits of this study. This is not a history of British democratization, nor does it attempt causal explanations of political events more generally. Without the research done in such fields as the comparative history of electoral institutions, and without the comparative-politics and formal-theoretical literatures on electoral institutions, this book would not have been possible. But it is not a book in that vein. Nor does this volume attempt a chronological narrative, as is the case with many histories of political thought. Although taken as a whole the book does move forward chronologically, and although it takes account of changes that occurred over the decades covered, its basic organization is thematic rather than temporal. It offers a historically grounded analysis and interpretation of traditions of thought about representation – of normative-institutional clusters, if you will. It aims to map the territory of thought about democracy, diversity, inclusivity, deliberation, parlia-mentarianism, elections, and related themes in the mid-to-late Victorian era. And it seeks to explain how these outlooks and discourses worked: how they both influenced and reacted to the political and intellectual conditions of the time; how their constituent assumptions, arguments, rhetorical strategies, social imaginaries, and institutional proposals fit together or pulled apart.

Another proviso about the book's scope derives from the fact that, given a suitably rich terrain, in the history of political thought there is always more than one story to tell. Consequently, this book should not be taken as a comprehensive account of theories of representation or democracy in nineteenth-century Britain. These are widely ramifying subjects, aspects of which have been examined well by other scholars. *Parliament the Mirror of the Nation* is meant as a complement to, not a replacement for, other studies of the multifarious debates about representative government and parliamentary reform of the era, such as those which have homed in on the

---

[11] E.g. Bernard Crick, *Democracy: A Very Short Introduction* (Oxford, 2002), 1–10.
[12] E.g. Sofia Nässtrom, "Review Article: Where Is the Representative Turn Going?" *EJPT*, 10 (2011): 501–10.

question of the deserving or undeserving character of the working class, the notions of sinister versus legitimate interest, clashes over the existence or nonexistence of a natural right to the suffrage, or ideas about the "capacity" required to qualify for political participation.[13] While I certainly hope that this book will illuminate these issues, they are considered here only as they bear on themes related to mirroring representation.

The third point is terminological. Throughout this volume I use the term "descriptive representation" in a capacious sense, as largely although not entirely synonymous with "mirroring."[14] Put most concisely, I understand a descriptive theory to be one which posits that the representative system is to be judged by the degree to which it reflects salient social cleavages, however these are defined. In other words, it is a view that states that *authorization* alone is not sufficient to establish a satisfactory system of representation because such a system requires a correspondence between the composition of representative institutions (paradigmatically, the assembly) and an understanding of the relevant kinds of diversity in society at large. This manner of conceptualizing descriptive representation departs from some recent usages in political theory, which employ the term only in a narrower way to designate the shared demographic identity between a specific congressman or MP and a body of citizens (hence an American senator of Asian background is said to have a special kind of "standing-for" relationship to Asian-American citizens). Instead, I follow those writers who understand descriptive representation in a way that is broader in two senses: first, by seeing it as a category that can apply to both specific officials (with respect to their belonging to or standing for particular demographic blocs) and to institutions judged holistically (based on the attributes of its membership overall, an assembly as a body can be or fail to be descriptively-representative of the society for which it legislates); second, by leaving open precisely which aspects of social life

---

[13] The leading study of the concept of capacity in this period is Alan Kahan's *Liberalism in Nineteenth-Century Europe: The Political Culture of Limited Suffrage* (Houndmills, Basingstoke, 2003). I accept the bulk of Kahan's account of capacity and have benefited much from it. Where I diverge from Kahan is in this: Kahan treats mirroring representation as merely an offshoot or subset of capacitarian arguments, whereas I see mirroring representation as an integral outlook on representation in its own right, one which interacted with and incorporated notions of capacity in varying degrees across different authors and schemes. Ideas of capacity feature in this book, therefore, insofar as they were one important factor that could enter into the judgments about the nature of society which authors then wished to translate into or reflect in the Commons.

[14] E.g. Hanna Pitkin, *The Concept of Representation* (Berkeley, 1967), ch. 4. I believe it is best to understand these terms in such a way that they can diverge, for reasons examined in Chapter 4: briefly, that PR had a claim to *mirror* opinion accurately, but had in fact departed from a descriptive system as that had been traditionally understood.

are to be accounted for in judgments about descriptive representativeness, such that they might include class, "interests" of both a socioeconomic and other sort, occupation, religion, gender, race, opinions, perspectives, regional and linguistic communities, and more.[15] Indeed, it is a lesson imparted by the study of nineteenth-century Britain that there are as many possible notions of descriptive representation as there are conceptions of the nature of society.

A final point concerns the book's structure, the building blocks of which, as mentioned earlier, are not individual authors or successive chronological periods, but contending *schools of thought* about mirroring representation. The book is arranged around the reconstruction of the three above-named paradigms for the realization of descriptively-representative, deliberative government. Chapters 1 and 2 are devoted to the variety-of-suffrages theory: Chapter 1 covers the different institutional schemes that fell within this family of approaches, while Chapter 2 explores the set of values that undergirded these schemes. Because the variety-of-suffrages was the traditional British "mirror theory of representation," Chapter 1 also includes a brief survey of the historical background of the "unreformed Parliament" out of which this outlook grew. Chapter 3 moves on to depict the reaction of democrats to this school of electoral variegation. Chapters 4 and 5 take up the movement for PR. The first of these chapters analyzes the key technical and conceptual elements of Victorian PR, with a special focus on identifying the continuities and discontinuities with traditional descriptivism; the second examines the broader set of goods which the PR campaign sought to realize, as well as defenses of the plurality-rule system that developed in reaction against it.

From this outline, it might look as if there is an inequality between the treatments of the different schools. Democracy may seem to be given short shrift relative to the other outlooks, receiving only one chapter instead of two (and a shorter one at that). This impression is partly accurate. The familiarity of uniform suffrage under plurality-rule elections to Anglophone readers makes it unnecessary to scrutinize its institutional aspects in the level of detail that I have reserved for the variety-of-suffrages and PR. Moreover, my analysis of Victorian democratic theory has more modest aims than my treatments of the other two schools, which try to convey something like complete approaches to parliamentary reform

---

[15] On the variety of factors that have been the objects of descriptive concern, see e.g. Mark Brown, "Citizen Panels and the Concept of Representation," *JPP*, 14 (2006): 203–25; Gerhard Loewenberg, *On Legislatures* (New York, 2011), 27–9.

in their integrity. What is relevant to this book about the democratic thought of the period is, rather, the more limited problem of how it sought to respond to a longstanding and vibrant tradition of antidemocratic mirroring. In another respect, however, the shortfall in attention paid to democracy is more apparent than real. The question of democracy is as pervasive in this monograph as it was in the intellectual and political life of the Victorian period. It is omnipresent in Chapters 1 and 2 for the simple reason that the variety of suffrages was defined as an antidemocratic program, as a haven from democracy's ills; hence, understanding the kind of political system which its advocates believed democracy to be is of fundamental importance for grasping these authors and their programs. And it is equally salient in Chapters 4 and 5 insofar as the question of the relationship between PR and democracy was a vexed one which stimulated the expression of an array of contending views and which imparted to the debate about Hare's and Mill's scheme much of its dynamism and energy. The issue of democracy therefore runs throughout this book, and it is for this reason that I hope that it can serve to deepen our genealogy of democratic theory.

CHAPTER I

Diversity without Democracy: The Theory of the Variety of Suffrages

Part One: Institutions and Sociologies

In 1914, one Philip Arnold Gibbons of St. John's College, Oxford, won the prestigious Gladstone Essay Prize for a composition in which he surveyed the history of British thought about parliamentary representation.[1] Ironically, *Ideas of Political Representation in Parliament, 1660–1832*, despite earning an award named for one of the statesman most closely associated with the rise of British democracy, opened with a sympathetic description of the "unreformed Parliament" – that is, of the far-from-democratic system which prevailed until the First Reform Act of 1832 and in which the suffrage was both very restricted on the whole and highly varied by the different customs and regulations that obtained in different constituencies.

More interesting, though, than the seeming incongruity between Gibbons's appreciative depiction of the unreformed Parliament and the democratic credentials of the prize was the particular form which his appreciation took. For Gibbons avoided the notes commonly played in apologies for aristocratic government: the nobility, independence, and wisdom of the rulers; the farsightedness of aristocracies in comparison to the fickle and unstable desires of the mob; the concentration upon high objects as opposed to base goods. What he valued most about the unreformed system was, instead, its *representativeness*: "Speaking generally, it may be said that the unrepresentative character of the House has been considerably overrated, and that on the whole it represented fairly well such public opinion as there was in England"; theories of representation from the time had been correct in "generally recogniz[ing] the representative character of the House of Commons." The eighteenth-century parliamentary system "was a good one as systems go, for it allowed free play for effective political forces ... the political machinery provided a sufficient

---

[1] The prize was given for an essay "on some subject connected with either Ecclesiastical History after 461 AD, or the Political and Constitutional History of the British Isles, or Political Theory," and it came with an award of £20 worth of books; *Student's Handbook to the University and Colleges of Oxford* (Oxford, 1913), 216.

channel for the really efficient forces of political thought."[2] His forebears who had boasted of living, in contradistinction to their unfortunate European neighbors, under a "representative government" had not been mere dupes or fools.

Gibbons's remark about the representative character of the unreformed Parliament had a further strange feature. This was its suggestion that he was offering an assessment which would have surprised his contemporaries. But this was hardly the case; like many a scholar since, Gibbons was inflating the novelty of his thoughts. His judgment that Parliament had not needed to await the advent of a democratic franchise to become *representative* was not as original as he implied. For example, on this topic he not merely echoed the spirit of, but bordered on plagiarizing, one of the eminent historical tracts of the period. The opening of the Victorian critic, historian, and essayist Leslie Stephen's epic *English Utilitarians* had made the point in almost identical words.[3] Although the old arrangements wound up, by the second quarter of the nineteenth century, in need of transformation, it would be wrong, Stephen had alleged, to assume that until recently Parliament had simply failed in its mission to represent the nation.

How could such authors as Gibbons and Stephen, writing in a (mostly) democratic Britain,[4] look back on their country's undemocratic past with sympathy for its representativeness? However counterintuitive this apprai-sal may sound to us today, these authors could appeal to a robust tradition of thought about representation, one with centuries-old roots that would reach its apogee in an explosion of institutional designs and constitutional theories during the middle decades of the nineteenth century.

This vision of representation is what I will call, depending on the particular aspect being emphasized at a given moment, the *mirror* theory or the theory of the *variety of suffrages*. The former appellation corresponds to the desired end or outcome for the composition of the legislature – namely, that it should constitute an accurate image of the society for which it made laws. The latter, however, pertains to the level of means or technique – namely, that variation in electoral regulations across

---

[2] Gibbons, *Ideas of Political Representation in Parliament, 1660–1832* (Oxford, 1914), 8, 10–11.

[3] In the eighteenth century "on the whole, the system was a very good one – as systems go . . . It allowed free play to the effective political forces . . . The political machinery provided a sufficient channel for the really efficient force of public opinion"; Leslie Stephen, *The English Utilitarians*, 3 vols. (London, 1900), vol. 1, 16. Gibbons did at least list Stephen's tomes in his bibliography.

[4] Due to the complexities of the laws of enfranchisement and inefficiencies in the registration system, roughly a third of adult men still lacked the franchise between 1885 and 1918; David Butler, "Electoral Reform," *PA*, 57 (2004): 734–43.

constituencies was the proper method for bringing the assembly into descriptive conformity with society. The two labels also correspond to a difference between genus and species; as Chapters 3–5 will show, one could hold that resemblance to the nation at large was a central virtue of the legislative body without believing that electoral differentiation was the best mechanism for achieving it. For the purposes of Chapters 1–2, though, the two sets of terms can be used interchangeably.

It is the goal of this and the following chapter to reconstruct and analyze this approach to representation. The next section sketches the origins and development of the mirroring school up through the First Reform Act. The longer succeeding section of this chapter and Chapter 2 combine to address the climax of this theory in the decades leading up to the Second Reform Act of 1867: the former canvasses and classifies various institutional schemes, most of them forgotten today, to which this theory gave rise during these years, and also interrogates the sociological premises on which these schemes were founded; the latter examines the values which motivated the creation of these schemes, as well as criticisms of and tensions between these values.

1 Mirroring and Electoral Diversity before the First Reform Act

Mirror theories of representation had been a critical element in British political discourse from the time of the English Civil War.[5] As conflict arose between king and Parliament in the early 1640s, supporters of the parliamentary side argued that only an assembly could *represent* the country because only a numerous body, and not the single person of the monarch, could attain a likeness of or resemblance to the "whole body of the State" in "all parts."[6] Because Parliament but not the monarchy had the capacity to *re-present* or capture the people in miniature, government by the former was representative while government by the latter was not, and therefore government by the former but not by the latter could be expected to respect and further the interests of the whole people. This "Roundhead" argument for the supremacy of Parliament based on its representativeness of the manifold of English society was a potent weapon in the theoretical

---

[5] Quentin Skinner, "Hobbes on Representation," *European Journal of Philosophy*, 13 (2005): 155–84 and "A Genealogy of the Modern State," *Proceedings of the British Academy*, 162 (2009): 325–70; Eric Nelson, *The Royalist Revolution: Monarchy and the American Founding* (Cambridge, MA, 2014), ch. 2.

[6] Henry Parker, *Observations upon some of his Majesties Late Answers and Expresses* (London, 1642).

arsenal deployed against personal rule and the royal prerogative in the mid-seventeenth-century's great conflict.[7]

In the following century, continued debates over the prerogative,[8] flaring up in particular at moments of constitutional crisis such as during the American Revolution,[9] were joined by another issue which rivaled it in salience for the microcosmic or societally reflective strand of parliamentarianism: corruption.[10] The main preoccupation of many of those who would defend the independence and representative character of the Commons was now the abuse of royal patronage.[11] The Crown's use of its financial power to manipulate elections (to purchase "Crown boroughs") and its ability to suborn pliant MPs through making gifts of the many offices at its disposal, it was claimed, transformed the assembly from a body in sympathy with the nation and its main interests and ideas into a "dependent" and "instrumental House of Commons" suborned to the "favour of the Court."[12] Reducing the monarchy's electoral interference and the "influence" that came from its financial-administrative power was necessary to restore a correspondence between the House and the society for which it legislated.

These early antimonarchical formulations of the mirror theory of representation were not particularly concerned with the operation of the actual electoral system. Over the course of the eighteenth century, however, the "Old Whig" view, articulated by Burke and other statesmen, of the connection between the descriptive satisfactoriness of the Commons (its status as an "*express image* of the feelings of the nation"[13]) and the traditional,

---

[7] Lorenzo Sabbadini, "Popular Sovereignty and Representation in the English Civil War," in *Popular Sovereignty in Historical Perspective*, ed. Richard Bourke and Quentin Skinner (Cambridge, 2016): 164–86; Quentin Skinner, *Liberty before Liberalism* (Cambridge, 1998), ch. 1.

[8] E.g. J. C. D. Clark, *English Society, 1688–1832* (Cambridge, 1985), ch. 4.

[9] E.g. Bernard Bailyn, *The Ideological Origins of the American Revolution* (Cambridge, MA, 1967).

[10] This is a generalization, of course: warnings about corruption as a mechanism by which the Crown suborned the other constitutional powers to its will had been heard in the seventeenth century: e.g. Andrew Marvell, *An Account of the Growth of Popery and Arbitrary Government in England* (Amsterdam, 1675); Anthony Ashley Cooper, Earl of Shaftesbury, *Two Seasonable Discourses Concerning this Present Parliament* (Oxford, 1675).

[11] On clashes over patronage and the representativeness of the Commons in the second half of the eighteenth century, see William Selinger, *Parliamentarism: From Burke to Weber* (Cambridge, 2019), ch. 1.

[12] Edmund Burke, *Thoughts on the Cause of the Present Discontents, in Select Works of Edmund Burke*, 4 vols. (Indianapolis, 1990), vol. 1, 66. This antiroyalist line was summed up in the famous 1780 resolution of John Dunning that "the influence of the crown has increased, is increasing, and ought to be diminished"; e.g. Betty Kemp, "Crewe's Act, 1782," *EHR*, 68 (1953): 258–63.

[13] Burke, *Thoughts on the Cause of the Present Discontents*, 118 (my italics); Melissa Williams, "Burkean 'Descriptions' and Political Representation: A Reappraisal," *Canadian Journal of Political Science*, 29 (1996): 23–45.

inherited arrangements for the regulation of the suffrage began to appear.[14] These arrangements were in essence a motley and uncoordinated assortment of local customs which had, in Burkean language, *grown* rather than been *made*.[15] This "Enlightenment" variant of the theory, then, consisted of a kind of organicist and ex post facto justification: it was directed toward showing that the country *already possessed* a set of electoral institutions that translated the nation in all its diversity into the Commons. This is how the influential theologian and early utilitarian philosopher William Paley lovingly portrayed the electoral-representative system in 1785: "By annexing the right of voting for members of the House of Commons to different qualifications in different places, each order and profession of men in the community become virtually represented"; in this way "the irregularity in the popular representation," however much it may have offended against the instinct for symmetry and order, guaranteed that "the condition, wants, and occasions of the people ... [in] every quarter" were reflected in the legislature. Consequently, if one could see past the seeming "confusion in which it confessedly lies," one would recognize "the variety of tenures and qualifications, upon which the right of voting is founded" to be a political blessing, for this variety "tends to introduce into parliament a corresponding mixture of characters and professions."[16] Importantly, the organicist appreciation of the existent electoral maze – the way in which the likes of Burke and Paley tied the inclusive, reflective Commons to the array of rules governing elections – gave their formulations an additional critical dimension. Beyond bolstering the case for the curtailments of the Crown that went under the label "economical reform" by suggesting that the Commons would function in a satisfactorily representative way once the former were enacted,[17] this late-eighteenth-century variety-of-suffragism also combated the proto- or quasi-democratic calls for more "equal" representation that began to be heard in the 1770s.[18]

[14] Samuel Beer, "The Representation of Interests in British Government: Historical Background," *APSR*, 51 (1957): 613–50. Also John Burrow, *Whigs and Liberals: Continuity and Change in English Political Thought* (Oxford, 1988), 117–19.

[15] Edward Porritt, *The Unreformed House of Commons: Parliamentary Representation before 1832*, revised edition, 2 vols. (Cambridge, 1909), vol. 1, part 1.

[16] William Paley, *The Principles of Moral and Political Philosophy*, ed. D. L. Le Mahieu (Indianapolis, 2002), 332–3, 342, 345–6.

[17] E. A. Reitan, *Politics, Finance and the People: Economical Reform in England in the Age of the American Revolution, 1770–1792* (Houndmills, Basingstoke, 2007).

[18] On these radical reform movements, see Richard Bourke, *Empire and Revolution: The Political Life of Edmund Burke* (Princeton, 2015), chs. 5, 8. The exemplary text of this outlook was John Cartwright's *Legislative Rights of the Commonalty Vindicated; or, Take Your Choice!*, second edition (London, 1777).

Because the Commons – or, at least, a Commons appropriately purged of monarchical corruption – included the interests of society in their plurality and was responsive to "public opinion," a wider franchise was a solution without a problem to solve.[19]

Despite this long history, however, it was not until 1818 that the archetypal theoretical coupling of the *end* of a composition of the Commons that mirrored society in its diversity with the *means* of electoral variety arrived, in the form of an essay by the philosopher, historian, and MP James Mackintosh. Mackintosh was hardly alone in trumpeting the "Old Whig theory" grounded in the "variety of franchise" in these years.[20] But just as his youthful defense of the French Revolution against Burke's attacks had encapsulated Whig fervor of the early 1790s for the great event,[21] in the second decade of the nineteenth century Mackintosh once again proved to be the mouthpiece of Whig consensus, this time on the themes of representation and electoral regulation. His statement of the view, moreover, was the one that would carry the most weight among the mid-Victorian cadre of authors who occupy the bulk of this chapter. What gave this article a special salience was not only the force of Mackintosh's statement, but also a crucial change in the context in which it was delivered relative to its earlier expressions. As we have glimpsed, although through the eighteenth century the mirroring tradition had been occupied predominantly with threats of royalist authoritarianism or corruption, the antiradical or antidemocratic implications of the discourse had begun to appear. However, this side of the outlook of mirroring electoral variegation did not reach its full conceptual or polemical potential, principally because the push for democracy crumbled

---

[19] See the use made of these "first principles" against democratic notions of consent by William Pitt the Younger, the Tory Prime Minister of the Revolutionary and Napoleonic eras, during his reformist period of the 1780s; Pitt, *The Speeches of the Right Honourable William Pitt in the House of Commons*, 4 vols. (London, 1806), vol. 1, 76, 234–8.

[20] Samuel Beer, *British Politics in the Collectivist Age* (New York, 1965), 18–9. Also John Clive, *Macaulay: The Shaping of the Historian* (Cambridge, MA, 1987), 145. The embrace of a variegated franchise became so identifiable with British Whiggery that some Francophone Anglophiles of the postrevolutionary period – associated with the "Coppet circle" which shared close connections to Whigs such as Mackintosh – endorsed the variety-of-suffrages as among the greatest of trans-Channel blessings. Among these was the Genevan J.C.L. Simonde de Sismondi, the polymathic intellectual and groundbreaking theorist of the cycle of capitalist crises. Sismondi sought to replace the French system of "uniformity of electoral title" with an imported version of the "multiform system of the English . . . which linked the national representation to all the classes of the nation"; Sismondi; *Études sur les constitutions des peuples libres* (Paris, 1836), 80–6. Sismondi had few companions in this opinion, however, and uniformity of suffrage tended to be upheld even by French liberals who most admired the English constitution.

[21] J. C. D. Clark, "Introduction," to Burke, *Reflections on the Revolution in France: A Critical Edition* (Stanford, 2001), 104.

along with much more modest reformist ambitions in the reaction against the horrors of the French Revolution and the Tory ascendancy during the Napoleonic Wars.[22] Mackintosh revived this dimension, and raised it to a higher pitch of sophistication against the return of democratic sentiments under the Benthamite aegis.[23] His most urgent adversary was not royal power, but the philosophic-radical program of universal suffrage championed by Bentham.[24] And after Mackintosh's elaboration of the theory, its antidemocratic valence would never again fall out of prominence.[25]

Mackintosh's rejoinder to Bentham, analogously to Macaulay's more famous "Whig" rebuttal to James Mill the following decade, began with a methodological dissent.[26] Rather than homing in, as Bentham had done, on the matter of accountability and control, of restraining the sinister interest of MPs and aligning their interests with those of their constituents,[27] Mackintosh argued that the primary question for the science of representative assemblies was sociological in nature: "To understand the principles of [the 'representative assembly's'] composition thoroughly, we must divide the people into classes, and examine the variety of local and professional interests of which the whole is composed . . . whether that interest arises from inhabiting the same district, or pursuing the same occupation." From this preliminary sociological inquiry one unavoidably made the discovery that society was a *diverse* entity – "in a great state, even that part of the public interest which is common to all classes, is composed of a great variety of branches" – and from this perception of diversity Mackintosh immediately deduced that "the proper composition of the House of Commons," as well as "the justice of the government," entailed that "each of these classes must be represented" directly.[28] The great Whig's conclusion, in short, was that the chief object of that branch of political knowledge which concerned representative institutions was one to which the philosophic radicals paid scant attention: that the composition of the House match social reality.

[22] Philip Brown, *The French Revolution in English History* (London, 1918), chs. 8–9.

[23] Élie Halévy, *The Growth of Philosophic Radicalism*, trans. Mary Morris (Boston, 1955), book 3.

[24] Bentham, *Plan of Parliamentary Reform, in the Form of a Catechism* (London, 1817).

[25] Mackintosh's greater wariness about the threat of democracy can be seen as part of the pattern Leslie Mitchell has identified whereby democracy replaced autocracy as the *bête noire* of Whiggism; Mitchell, *The Whig World, 1760–1837* (London, 2005), xi, 148–9.

[26] On the Mill/Macaulay episode, see e.g. Terence Ball, "Introduction" to James Mill, *Political Writings* (Cambridge, 1992), xxiv–xxvi.

[27] Michael James, "Public Interest and Majority Rule in Bentham's Democratic Theory," *PT*, 9 (1981): 49–64.

[28] James Mackintosh, "Universal Suffrage," *ER*, 31 (1818), 181, 175.

Fortunately, in this case theory already coincided with practice. The electoral variation that England possessed was superior to what any philosopher-statesman, who would have felt compelled to "act upon some uniform principle," could have devised.[29] Mackintosh's message was to appreciate the arrangements with which history had blessed the country: "we ought not to exchange our diversified elections for any general qualification."[30] From this it did not follow that one had to reject incremental change; Mackintosh believed, rather, that the traditional English principle of representation itself contained a dynamic element: "As every new class arose, it was fastened to the government by those constitutional links. This left no class politically powerful, who did not visibly draw their power from the Constitution." Consequently, in response to Lord John Russell's reenergizing of the Whig movement for Reform in 1820, Mackintosh declared for the "addition of twenty Members ... chosen by the most opulent and populous of the communities which are at present without direct representation; with such varieties, in the right of suffrage, as the local circumstances of each community might suggest, but in all of them on the principle of a widely diffused franchise."[31] But the need for periodic adjustment was itself simply dictated by the fact that "a variety of rights of suffrage" reflecting the body politic's diverse parts was "the principle of the English representation."[32] Or, as the leading Whig of the following generation, then a young MP just beginning to formulate principles of representation, articulated the Mackintoshian credo, it was necessary to avoid the "dark blot" of "uniform suffrage" so that "all parts of the country, and all classes of the people" could be present in the legislature, and "the grand principle ... that the representative body should be the image of the represented" be realized.[33]

---

[29] Ibid., 182. He clarified with a Burkean metaphor: "A builder can seldom imitate, with success, all the fantastic but picturesque and comfortable irregularities, of an old mansion, which through a course of ages has been repaired, enlarged, and altered, according to the pleasure of various owners."

[30] Ibid., 182.

[31] James Mackintosh, "Parliamentary Reform," ER, 34 (1820), 481, 469. The dynamic aspect of the descriptive theory of representation in the nineteenth century will recur as a theme throughout this text. From the examples of Russell and Mackintosh, though, we can already glimpse that the claim sometimes encountered in contemporary democratic theory today – namely, that a commitment to descriptive representation implies a static view of society which precludes openness toward the future – is misconceived (as in e.g. Nadia Urbinati, "Representation as Advocacy: A Study of Democratic Deliberation," PT, 28 [2000]: 758–86.) A view of descriptive representation only posits that one criterion according to which the satisfactoriness of a representative system is to be judged is the degree to which it reflects the salient social cleavages at a given moment, however these latter are defined and however they may have come about.

[32] Mackintosh, "Universal Suffrage," 180; "Parliamentary Reform," 469–71.

[33] John Russell, An Essay on the History of the English Government and Constitution from the Reign of Henry VII, to the Present Time (London, 1821), 247–50. The volume would come out in several editions (1823, 1865, 1866). I will specify the edition in subsequent citations.

The variety of suffrages was vital to the prospect of *representative* government because "the labouring classes" and "lowest classes" so outnumbered the rest of society that a democratic franchise risked allowing the whole of the assembly to be returned by this "perpetual majority." The sociologically satisfactory "representation of *classes*" would give way to the unrepresentative rule of "*numbers*." Mackintosh illustrated his fear of working-class monopoly of the legislature with a (well-chosen, given English antipapist sentiment) thought experiment: he asked what would happen to the "Protestant minority" if "we suppose Ireland to be an independent state." By virtue of the great disparity in numbers between the two religions, the Catholics who comprised "four-fifths of the population" could bar the Protestants from entry into the "House of Commons" and thereby "exclud[e] them from all political privilege." If the reader found the prospect of such Catholic domination in Ireland to be a deviation from "just or equal government," then he was bound to reject electoral democracy in England as well, for even if the groups of "oppressors and oppressed" would differ in the latter instance (namely, not on religious but on socioeconomic lines), the fundamental dynamics of exclusivity and unrepresentativeness would be the same.[34]

Importantly, Mackintosh was clear that his argument, although prompted by Bentham's espousal of democracy and combating most intently the democratic alternative,[35] also had as its target the political orientation at the opposite extreme. In truth, the chief wrong in the Benthamite creed of "uniform universal suffrage" pertained not to the second adjective but to the first: uniform *restricted* suffrage was likewise an evil.[36] The problem with uniform restricted suffrage was that, since it "must incline towards independent property, as being the only ground on which it can rest," it would deny the lower orders access to seats in the assembly; "true popular election" would no longer take place in any constituencies. Instead of a representative legislature, this arrangement would yield "a mere aristocracy" – which, he remarked, might very well suit the "situation and temper of the French nation," but which was unsuitable for British soil.[37] Thus, while the occasion for Mackintosh to

---

[34] Mackintosh, "Universal Suffrage," 184–6. [35] Ibid., 182.

[36] "We prefer this general principle of our representation to *any* uniform right of suffrage"; ibid., 180 (my italics).

[37] Ibid., 181. At the time of Mackintosh's essay France was under the Restoration regime of Louis XVIII which had followed the downfall of the Napoleonic Empire. During the Restoration the suffrage was highly restricted; about 100,000 men were enfranchised out of a population of nearly 30,000,000, and there were notoriously more *fonctionnaires* than voters. Some of the successors of Mackintosh whom we will encounter later in this chapter would likewise contrast their schemes

theorize about representation had been to refute the radicals, the upshot of his theory was broader: to wit, that, regardless of where one drew the line, the uniform suffrage was *en soi* a crucial mark against a government's representativeness.[38] Whatever other virtues it might have, a regime with electoral uniformity would have an objectionably classist and exclusive character.[39]

By the first third of the nineteenth century, then, the mirror theory of representation had traversed a large distance since its inception in 1640s antiroyalism. In the hands of the preeminent Whig intellectual post-Burke,[40] the political salience of the principle that the legislature faithfully transcribe or re-present society in all its parts was not primarily to favor parliamentary over personal rule, elected legislative over hereditary monarchical power. To Mackintosh, the mirror theory was not an instrument for diminishing kings and exalting assemblies, but rather a reason for favoring one set of electoral rules over another; in his hands the mirror theory was a way of proving that representativeness could only be ascribed to a variegated as opposed to a uniform regulation of the suffrage.

Before leaving Mackintosh, two further aspects of his theory of representation should be mentioned. First, it is worth noting explicitly a feature that was implicit in the earlier discussion of religious divisions: namely, that Mackintosh was operating with a wide notion of "class." This feature is important because it will persist in subsequent writers of the variety-of-suffrages school. *Class* in Mackintosh's texts designated any stable community of interest, a category which extended beyond economic groups. This expansive meaning of class comes through clearly, for example, in the plea he made for Catholic emancipation: "The English Catholics are a large and respectable body of men, who do not possess the elective franchise. The class is unrepresented, and possesses no political security for its common interest."[41] Second, in taking the accurate reflection of varied

favorably with the exclusiveness of the French suffrage, but in that case they had in mind the July Monarchy which succeeded the Restoration. While the July Monarchy's electoral regulations were also notoriously restrictive, twice as many men had the vote from 1830–48 as under the previous regime. On Restoration electoral law, see Paul Bastid, *L'avènement du suffrage universel* (Paris, 1948), 20–2; Frederick Artz, "The Electoral System in France during the Bourbon Restoration, 1815–30," *JMH*, 1 (1929): 205–18.

[38] Russell agreed that Whiggism provided an alternative to the opposite evils of "insulated aristocracy" and simple "popularity"; *History of the English Constitution*, first edition, 251.

[39] Vincent Starzinger, *The Politics of the Center, France and England, 1815–1848* (London, 1991), 61.

[40] Patrick O'Leary, *Sir James Mackintosh: The Whig Cicero* (Aberdeen, 1989).

[41] Note also how the "*principle*" of representation is phrased: "that every great community, with distinct interests, ought to have separate representatives"; Mackintosh, "Parliamentary Reform," 494, 475.

interests to be the foundation of parliamentary representation, Mackintosh gave this principle priority *over territoriality* as the basis for constructing constituencies. While Mackintosh does not seem to have recognized this privileging of mirroring over territoriality as an important theoretical moment,[42] this move would prove extremely fruitful in the hands of his mid-century descendants and open whole new possibilities for institutional design – including, most spectacularly, in the original plans for proportional representation, covered in Chapters 4–5. For Mackintosh, as for the more creative reformers of Sections 2b and c and the Victorian PR movement, what was ancient and principled about the British electoral system was not the territorial construction of constituencies, but the variety of suffrages as a mechanism for achieving the goal of the accurate representation of interests.

When the Whigs at last emerged from the political wilderness and formed a government in 1830, however, they promptly ran afoul of Mackintoshian principles. Although it greatly augmented the number of voters (to around 20 percent of the adult male population[43]), the reform bill which they proposed and finally passed in 1832 diminished Mackintosh's cherished electoral diversity. The Reform Act reduced a bewildering mix of voting regulations down to essentially just two: one franchise for all boroughs and another for all counties. A property quali-fication was required to vote in both kinds of constituency, a lower one in the boroughs than in the counties.[44] As may be inferred, though, from the fact that four-fifths of the male population remained without the vote, this reform had the effect of diminishing the electorate in those boroughs which had lacked a property qualification, had had only a very low one, or had granted the suffrage according to some other criterion altogether

---

[42] The subject was merely broached *en passant* as he attempted to justify a plan for allotting additional seats to the interest of "science": "If some representatives were in time to be allowed to learned societies, it would not be a greater novelty than the grant of the privilege to the two universities by James I"; ibid., 490. On James I's initiation of university representation, see Peter Roberts, "The Tudor Origins of the Grant of Parliamentary Representation to English Universities in 1604," *Parliaments, Estates & Representation*, 26 (2006): 35–44.

[43] On the exact electoral figures, see e.g. Philip Salmon, "The English Reform Legislation," in *The History of Parliament, vol. 1: The House of Commons, 1820–1832*, ed. D. R. Fisher (Cambridge, 2009): 374–412; Sean Lang, *Parliamentary Reform, 1785–1928* (London, 1999), ch. 2; Derek Beales, "The Electorate before and after 1832: The Right to Vote and the Opportunity," *PH*, 11 (1992): 139–50.

[44] The First Reform Act set the property requirement in all boroughs at the occupation of a house valued at £10 annual rent and in counties to tenants-at-will who paid £50 annual rent. On the Reform Act's franchise requirements, see Michael Smith, "Parliamentary Reform and the Electorate," in *A Companion to Nineteenth-Century Britain*, ed. Chris Williams (Oxford, 2004): 156–73; John Phillips and Charles Wetherell, "The Great Reform Act of 1832 and the Political Modernization of England," *American Historical Review*, 100 (1995): 411–36.

(such as membership in a guild or corporation).[45] Thus, though 1832 *increased* the total number of electors, it disenfranchised the working-class voters who had previously possessed the vote in the assortment of boroughs with expansive suffrage rules, and it thereby *decreased* the diversity and range of types of electors.[46] In sum, the First Reform Act had the paradoxical consequence of making the electorate both *more numerous* but also, arguably, *less inclusive*, for its standardizing measures cut the working classes off from Parliament in those boroughs which saw their low or nonexistent property requirements raised as a result of this standardization.

In response, Tories adopted the variety-of-suffrages position as their own and turned it against the Whigs.[47] The Tory MP for Oxford, Robert Inglis, opposed the Whig bill in order to defend "the House of Commons [as it] is now," which was "the most complete representation of the interests of the people, which was ever assembled in any age or country." He continued, in a manner that would have fit perfectly into Mackintosh's tracts, "it is the very absence of symmetry in our elective franchises which admits of the introduction of classes so various," because these localized discrepancies allowed there to be "something to please every body, and to catch every body."[48] Similarly, the great Tory statesman and future Prime Minister Sir Robert Peel, in a posture which presages the "Tory

---

[45] "Except that it preserved the personal rights of living voters, and retained the privileges of freemen in towns where they existed [though freemen thereafter could vote only if made such by birth or servitude] it swept away all the old qualifications, and replaced them by a single new franchise based exclusively upon the tenure, or rather the occupation, of land"; A. Lawrence Lowell, *The Government of England*, 2 vols. (New York, 1908), vol. 1, 204.

[46] A striking casualty of the diminution of diversity in the electorate effected by the First Reform Act was women, who in certain circumstances likely could have possessed the vote under the motley assortment of unreformed franchises; e.g. Andrew Reeve and Alan Ware, *Electoral Systems: A Comparative and Theoretical Introduction* (London, 1992), 52. The Reform Act was the first law "explicitly to state that the householder had to be male"; Neil Johnston, "The History of the Parliamentary Franchise," *Research Papers of the House of Commons Library* [https://researchbriefings.parliament.uk/ResearchBriefing/Summary/RP13-14#fullreport].

[47] I do not mean to suggest that the Tory voicing of variegated suffrage was solely an opportunistic maneuver to dish the Whigs. Even the ultra-Tory poet laureate Robert Southey had accepted as early as 1816 (albeit with a tone that was patronizing even by the standards of the era) that it was "exceedingly proper that the mode of election should be purely popular in some places; and that the populace and the ultra-liberty boys should return such representatives" as could champion their sentiments and guard their interests; Southey, "On the state of Public Opinion, and the Political Reformers, 1816," *Essays, Moral and Political*, 2 vols. (London: John Murray, 1832), vol. 1, 385. On the broad appeal of class- and interest-based schemes of representation by this time, see Joseph Hamburger, "James Mill on Universal Suffrage and the Middle Class," *JP*, 24 (1962), 174; Jack Lively and John Rees, "Introduction" to *Utilitarian Logic and Politics*, ed. Lively and Rees (Oxford, 1978), 37, 50.

[48] Inglis, *Parliamentary Reform. Substance of the Speech Delivered in the House of Commons, on Saturday, the 17th December, 1831* (London, 1832), 29–30.

democracy" that would undergird the Second Reform Act,[49] set himself against reform on the grounds that it would "limit the franchise to particular districts and particular classes ... sever[ing] all connexion between the lower classes of the community and the direct representation in this House." In contrast to the present system, which enjoyed "the immense advantage" that there was "no class of people, however humble, which is not entitled to a voice in the election of representatives," after reform the lower ranks of society would lack any "champion within your walls."[50] An anonymous anti-reform tract of the same year eulogized the powers of inclusivity and representativeness of Britain's wild medley of inherited electoral laws with an eloquence that exceeded even these great parliamentary orators:

> with reference to the representation of all the separate orders of the community, the constitution of the House of Commons is peculiarly felicitous. By virtue of the different rules of franchise that prevail in different electoral corporations, – some of which admit of an almost universal suffrage, while others are strictly oligarchical, – there is no class of persons in England who do not find an echo within the walls of Parliament. From the potwalloper of Preston, to the titled proprietor of Aldborough or Gatton, through all the intermediate ranks, this proposition holds equally true ... One advantage is thus gained, which no uniform law of franchise could possibly secure; for at whatever point, short of universal suffrage, we fix the standard of qualification, some of the lower classes must be overlooked; while, on the other hand, if the standard be very far reduced, the franchise of the higher orders will be virtually compromised. Happily, the variety of the electoral qualifications prevalent in England allows us to steer a middle course, – it saves us from the dictation of demagogues, and the dangerous course of innovation which they are uniformly found to pursue; it saves us also from an exclusively aristocratical Parliament, destitute of sympathy with popular feeling.[51]

[49] The Second Reform Act – an unexpectedly generous measure passed in 1867 by the minority Conservative government led by Lord Derby and Benjamin Disraeli after more moderate Liberal bills had been rejected the previous year – would nearly double the electorate, vastly expanding it in the boroughs by extending the suffrage to all householders who paid rates (local taxes) and some lodgers, and more modestly extending it in the counties by lowering the property requirement in the counties. While it did mark a new era of mass politics, its framers did not intend it as a "democratic" measure, and more than three in five adult males remained without the suffrage; Robert Saunders, "The Politics of Reform and the Making of the Second Reform Act, 1848–67," *HJ*, 50 (2007): 571–91.

[50] "The individual right is limited ... but the class is represented,"; Peel, Speech of 3 March 1831, reprinted in *The Emergence of British Parliamentary Democracy in the Nineteenth Century*, ed. J. B. Conacher (New York, 1971), 30–1. In 1867 Disraeli would explicitly reach back to speeches such as Peel's to show that the Tories had historically been the party of the working man.

[51] *Observations on the British Constitution, and on the Proposed Improvement of Our Parliamentary Representation* (Edinburgh, 1831), 39.

Probably the most vociferous of the Tory adopters of the variety-of-suffrages outlook was the Scottish historian Archibald Alison. In an 1831 essay Alison emphasized the treachery of "Sir James Mackintosh," who inexplicably supported "the present Bill" despite his previous convincing proof that uniformization of the suffrage was inconsistent with the goal of giving to all segments of society "a direct and immediate access to the legislature, without being indebted for it to the tolerance or indulgence of the other classes."[52] While he had a constricted notion of the proper place of the lower classes in politics,[53] and was more concerned with what he perceived as the harm the bill would do to the representation of the "commercial, colonial, or shipping interests" than with any harm to the lower classes, even he was consistent enough to admit that "the Radicals, like every other interest in the state, should be fairly represented in Parliament."[54] For the likes of Peel, Inglis, and Alison, as much as for the "Old Whig" of a preceding generation, the extent to which the Commons constituted an "express image" of the nation was a crucial metric upon which the electoral system was to be evaluated; a basic question to be resolved before the future of the suffrage could be decided was whether in fact the composition of the Commons coincided with the diverse society over which it stood.

2 Institutions and Sociologies

Despite the attention that it received during the decades spanning the end of the eighteenth and the first third of the nineteenth century, it was not until the wave of "democratic" revolutions on the Continent and Lord John Russell's reopening of the question of parliamentary reform in 1848 that the theory of the variegated suffrage reached its zenith.[55] In the

---

[52] Alison, "The Reform Bill," in *Essays Political, Historical, and Miscellaneous*, 3 vols. (Edinburgh, 1850), vol. 1, 35, 16. The article was originally published in *BM* in 1831. Alison was one of the most famous conservative intellectuals of the second quarter of the century. In light of his hatred for the Revolution he opposed all constitutional change in Britain; Michael Fry, "Alison, Sir Archibald (1792–1867)," *ODNB*. Mill had a particular distaste for Alison; Letter to Macvey Napier, 15 Oct. 1842, in *CW*, vol. 13, 551.

[53] Alison, "The Athenian Democracy," in *Essays*, vol. 2, 303.

[54] Alison, "The Reform Bill," 24–5. For a correspondingly global list of the relevant interests, see *Observations on the British Constitution*, 40–1, 112. The historian Llewellyn Woodward quipped that "West and East Indian interests were represented, and indeed over-represented" by the existence of patronage boroughs which those who had grown wealthy in the Empire could purchase; Woodward, *The Age of Reform, 1815–1870*, second edition (Oxford, 1962), 26–7.

[55] This effervescence in variety-of-suffrages schemes is in keeping with the character of these decades as (in Robert Saunders's words) a time of "unique constitutional experiment"; Saunders, *Democracy and the Vote*, 26. See also two older articles from Francis Herrick: "The Reform Bill of 1867 and the

1850s–60s the extension of these originally Whig preoccupations regarding a system of franchises adequate to the representation of the polyphonic entity that was British society went even further than in the pre-Reform period; they became truly common property across the partisan spectrum.[56] In this period of ascendance for the theory, an astonishing array of institutional schemes were promulgated which promised to bring the Commons into alignment with the condition of society and public opinion outside its walls.

This section and the following chapter depict this theory in its heyday. The account is not exhaustive; a rendering of the full panoply of pamphlets, essays, and books that treated reform in this vein would fill a monograph on its own. My aim is more modest: to present a representative sampling of (in this section) the major institutional currents into which the theory flowed and (in the following chapter) the values which these authors wished their schemes to realize.

Attempts to perfect the "representation of the country" by apportioning the suffrage such that "every class, every interest, every opinion was represented in exact proportion to its weight and worth" followed a few different paths.[57] For our purposes, it is helpful to divide the variety of positions on the proper form for mirroring or descriptive institutions into four categories, even if the exact boundaries between some of these categories cannot be fixed definitively.

The first of these modes of envisioning a properly variegated suffrage and descriptively accurate Commons can be dealt with most quickly, for it required no new exercises in institutional design. This was the camp of

---

British Party System," *Pacific Historical Review*, 3 (1934): 216–33 and "The Second Reform Movement in Britain, 1850–1865," *JHI*, 9 (1948): 174–92. On the stimulus given by the 1848 wave of revolutions – and the Chartist petition of that year with which they were often linked – to the resurgence of the parliamentary reform question, see Roland Quinault, "1848 and Parliamentary Reform," *HJ*, 31 (1988): 831–51; F. B. Smith, "The View from Britain, I: 'Tumults Abroad, Stability at Home'," in *Intellectuals and Revolution: Socialism and the Experience of 1848*, ed. Eugene Kamenka and F. B. Smith (London, 1979), 94–120.

[56] This transmission across party lines was facilitated by the weakness of party discipline in the period. On the porous and shifting ideological and party scene in the Commons in this period, e.g. Angus Hawkins, "'Parliamentary Government' and Victorian Political Parties, c. 1830–1880," *EHR*, 104 (1989), 669; Robert Blake, *Disraeli* (London, 1966), 270–1. The decades between the Reform Acts experienced "a multiplicity of parties, and English politics resembled the politics of the French Assembly more closely than they have done before or since"; Norman St. John-Stevas, "The Political Genius of Walter Bagehot," introduction to Bagehot, *CW*, vol. 5, 75. Also Philip Salmon, "The House of Commons, 1801–1911," in *A Short History of Parliament: England, Great Britain, the United Kingdom, Ireland & Scotland*, ed. Clyve Jones (Woodbridge, 2009), 265.

[57] Bernard Cracroft, "The Reform Session of 1866," in *Essays, Political and Miscellaneous*, 2 vols. (London, 1868), vol. 1, 48.

supporters of the First Reform Act who defended the Act on the grounds that, although reform had reduced the amount of *formal* variety in the regulation of the suffrage, it had accomplished the *substantive* end of the variety-of-suffragists by increasing the degree to which the composition of the Commons conformed to the condition of society and public opinion outside it. Among other lines of defense,[58] espousal of the alignment of the House with the nation was a popular one among the Whig politicians who made the Act; as the future prime minister and leading architect of the Reform Act, Lord John Russell, stated, 1832 had transformed the Commons into a "mirror of the sentiments of the people."[59]

Such defenders of the descriptive character of reformed politics tended to rely on two arguments to buttress their claims. The first was that the reduction of electoral diversity was dictated by a kind of social flattening. On this view, the middle class which benefited above all from the new electoral regulations was, empirically, so far the predominant force in English life that it warranted a great shift of political power in its favor at the expense of those classes above and below them; to reorient parliamentary life around the middle class was merely to take account of the fact that English prosperity and public opinion had less robustly pluralistic roots than at an earlier time.[60] The second claim was that a sufficient amount of electoral diversity persisted even after the standardization of the suffrage in

---

[58] Other prominent apologies for Reform included that it had brought into power the most intelligent leadership possible, that it had reduced corruption and restrained the power of the Crown, and that it had produced governments which had ended abuses and pursued correct policies; see e.g. Eric Evans, *The Great Reform Act of 1832*, second edition (London, 1994).

[59] Russell, *Letter to the Electors of Stroud: On the Principles of the Reform Act*, third edition (London, 1839), 9. The Whig statesman and intellectual George Cornewall Lewis expressed this thought in typical fashion. "Our representative system has not been a sham," he wrote. It has succeeded in "represent[ing] the feelings and opinions of the people"; "that the existing House of Commons has reflected with fidelity the predominant opinions of the great body of the community, and particularly of the educated and intelligent classes, we hold to be a matter of fact, established by the evidence of general notoriety"; Lewis, "History and Prospects of Parliamentary Reform," *ER*, 109 (1859), 279.

[60] Dror Wahrman, *Imagining the Middle Class: The Political Representation of Class in Britain, c. 1780–1840* (Cambridge, 1995), esp. chs. 9–11; Francis Wilson, *A Theory of Public Opinion* (Chicago, 1962), ch. 9. In this conception of the status of the middle class's preeminence and the notion that Britain had become a "middle-class society" we can glimpse a contrast between English Whigs such as Macaulay and French *doctrinaires* such as Guizot. Of course, English Whigs believed that the middle class embodied certain virtues, but their analysis of the middle class's rise was relatively more hands-off and empirical than the Guizotian school's desire (in a post-Revolutionary context of peasant proprietorship and widespread but small landholdings) to use the state to enforce an aggressively normative conception of the middle class. In justifying the bestowal of political supremacy on the middle class, Macaulay and company saw themselves largely as ratifying historical trends accomplished without top-down imposition. E.g. Pierre Rosanvallon, "Préface: Le Gramsci de la bourgeoisie," in François Guizot, *Histoire de la civilisation en Europe, suivie de Philosophie politique: de la souveraineté* (Paris, 1985): 9–18.

the form of variety in the size and location of electoral districts.[61] And indeed, judged against postrevolutionary France's standard of equal electoral districts, this was a highly plausible claim: the great inequality in size of districts, the maintenance of the distinction between counties and boroughs, and the geographically irregular character of the reformed constituency map all spoke in favor of interpreting 1832 as an amendment of the system that had remained sensitive to the virtues of electoral diversity.[62] In these Whigs' judgment, the difference between a metropolitan borough with thousands of urban voters caught up in the full swing of the industrial economy and a small borough with a few hundred electors engaged in a more local and traditional economic-social life was vast enough to secure a salutary diversity in the membership of the Commons.[63] Hence, depending on the demands of a given debate, it was available to the stalwarts of 1832 either to embrace diminished electoral variety as the appropriate response to the predominant standing of the middle class, or to deny that any loss in the translation of the relevant aspects of social diversity into the representative structure had been suffered at all.

A telling instance of approval of the descriptive integrity of the reformed Commons comes from the political commentary of the essayist, industrialist, and civil servant William Rathbone Greg.[64] In keeping with his

---

[61] Even after he embraced a further measure of reform in the 1860s, Russell would still maintain that the Reformed Commons had great merit as a diversity-enabling device: "the character of our present House of Commons ... is a character of extreme diversity in representation. Elections by great bodies, agricultural, commercial, or manufacturing, in our counties and great cities, are balanced by the right of election in boroughs of small or moderate population, which are thus admitted to fill up the defects and complete the fulness of our representation"; Russell, *History of the English Constitution*, fourth edition. (London, 1866), 237.

[62] Homersham Cox, *The Institutions of English Government: Being an Account of the Constitution ... and Its Departments* (London, 1863), 93–111.

[63] Take, for example, the verdict of George Cornewall Lewis that the mirroring of social pluralism was sufficiently accomplished by the non-uniform system of territorial representation: "the principle of the representation of *classes* ... is, to a considerable extent, involved in the principle of locality. Different classes and different interests predominate in different places; and by multiplying electoral districts, and varying their size and character, we give a representation to different portions of the community – to the weak as well as to the strong"; Lewis, "History and Prospects," 289. Also John Charles Spencer, Lord Althorp, HC Deb 9 Aug 1831, *Hansard*, Third Series, vol. 5, 1060.

In keeping with this view of the contributions to parliamentary pluralism of a variety of constituency types, mirror theorists were highly skeptical of the proposal for equal electoral districts. The principle of equal districts had little mainstream acceptance until late in the nineteenth century (only being enshrined as a practical principle with the 1917 boundary commission), in part due to the stigma of its association with Chartism, which placed equal districts among the Charter's six demands: Philip Norton, "The House of Commons," in A Short History of Parliament, ed. Jones, 271; Julius West, *A History of the Chartist Movement* (Boston, 1920), ch. 3.

[64] Greg is as interesting as any figure from the period. His life was subject to great swings in his personal financial fortunes; he was one of the most controversial Victorian writers on religion due to

intellectual approach in other areas, Greg wrote voluminously but unsyste-
matically on parliamentary reform; it would be an act of interpretive over-
reach to attribute to him anything like a *theory* of representation, since his
writing on the subject really had only one fixed point: the rejection of
democracy as unrepresentative and class-based.[65] Indeed, even his opinion
on the merits of the current system was not steady: he did not consistently
enunciate satisfaction with the representativeness of the reformed Commons.
At times he spoke of the need for further improvement to render the assembly
"as fair and complete an organ as practicable of the various interests and
elements which compose the nation" and to achieve a more "fair and beneficent proportion" for "*all* classes."[66] Yet while the "inadequate admission . . .
of the labouring classes" was a "blot" on the "actual Parliamentary suffrage,"
Greg's considered view seems to have been that it was not an especially serious
one with respect to the *descriptive* properties of the Commons.[67] It was
"beyond dispute" that "the actual electoral law . . . does enable the country
to express its opinion clearly and forcibly"; the Reform Act had brought "fully
and fairly . . . to bear upon Parliament the feelings and opinions – the
prejudices and passions – the well- or ill-understood interests of the
country."[68] "Theoretically imperfect as our actual franchise is," he summed
up, "Parliament yet does, in fact, respond, with very great sympathy and
promptitude, to the ascertained wishes of the country."[69] Despite its warts,
no reasonable analyst could deny that Britain benefited from a legislature that
was a "*bona fide* representative," a "faithful representative" of society properly
understood – an understanding heavily skewed toward the greater "capacity" of
the upper classes even by mid-nineteenth-century standards.[70]

his skeptical theology and importation of German methods of Higher Biblical criticism; he was an
ardent advocate of free trade; he went through an epoch of intense enthusiasm for "animal
magnetism"; and he maintained a rather intimate correspondence with Tocqueville.
John Morley, "W. R. Greg: A Sketch," in *Critical Miscellanies*, 3 vols. (London, 1886), vol. 3,
213–60; Ruth Edwards, *The Pursuit of Reason: The Economist, 1843–1993* (London, 1993), ch. 13.

[65] The opposite of "fair representation – a faithful reflex of all these varieties" was democracy, "the
system of election by numbers" which would "virtually throw the whole representation into the
hands of one class only – the class assuredly the most numerous, the most mobile, the most easily
misled; but neither the most various, the most catholic, nor the most competent"; Greg,
"The Expected Reform Bill," *ER*, 95 (1852), 250.

[66] Greg, "Representative Reform," *ER*, 96 (1852), 471; "Representative Reform," *ER*, 106 (1857), 269.
These two articles will henceforth be distinguished by "Representative Reform [1]" and
"Representative Reform [2]."

[67] Greg, "Parliamentary Purification," *ER*, 98 (1853), 567.

[68] Greg, "Representative Reform [2]," 259; "Expected Reform Bill," 214.

[69] Greg, "Expected Reform Bill," 237. For additional similarly positive judgments, see e.g.
"Representative Reform [2]," 270–1; "Parliamentary Purification," 567.

[70] Greg, "Expected Reform Bill, 214, 240. Greg fits neatly into Kahan's notion of a strand of
the discourse of capacity that was focused on social classes rather than individuals, although

The reformed Commons received such high marks for representativeness from Greg for two reasons. First was that the degree of working-class voicelessness under the current arrangements was exaggerated; the pecuniary qualifications were low enough, Greg estimated, that "many of the more deserving of the lower classes ... are on the register."[71] Second, and more important, was the just-noted rationale of societal flattening. The ascendancy of the middle class was the paramount social phenomenon of the nineteenth century; the "voice of the country" was now indisputably that of "the middle classes."[72] To this great sociological shift the fitting response was a sort of parliamentary compression, and this compression had been the guiding principle of the great law of 1832; it had managed, as no other institutional means could have done, to "curtail the representative power of both the higher and the lower orders in favor of the middle ranks." Hence, in reducing the influence both of the landed aristocracy and of the lower classes – in taking power "out of the hands of these parties and plac[ing] it in that of the *middle* classes" – the Reform Act had improved Parliament qua image of society, for this latter class was by a large margin the leading generator of the ideas and prosperity of England.[73]

Supporters of the status quo were, however, far from possessing a monopoly on the mirror theory. Quite the contrary: the unprecedented energy devoted to arguing for a variety of suffrages as the institutional bedrock of a representative system proceeded principally from dissatisfaction with the mid-century Commons. This dissatisfaction stemmed from two sources. The first was the impression that, however well suited the Reform Act may have been to the state of Britain in the early 1830s, it had become outdated due to social and intellectual developments that had transpired since its passage. This was a potent charge against defenders of the status quo, since many of the Whig architects of 1832 had been fervent

Kahan does not address him explicitly; Kahan, *Liberalism in Nineteenth-Century Europe*, esp. 11–13. Unlike many of even the more elitist variety-of-suffragist authors, the unsystematic Greg could occasionally slip into the nonmirroring, individualistic idioms of capacity which Kahan sees as characteristic of French liberals, as when he called for the enactment of a 50£ savings qualification for the franchise to broaden the current censitary requirements, which were based solely on the value of real estate, because he thought that such a uniform nationwide rule based on savings would cover all of his "fellow countrymen [who] are qualified to exercise." Despite his somewhat disjointed approach to questions of representation, the balance of his sympathies (as we will see going forward) lay with the conception of a diversity of communities translated into the Commons via the "*variety* of our constituencies."

[71] Greg, "Expected Reform Bill," 240. He qualified this pronouncement with: "though confessedly fewer than is desirable." It is important to bear in mind that in the run-up to the Second Reform Act there was a great deal of uncertainty about what the socioeconomic composition of the electorate at present actually was.

[72] Greg, "Expected Reform Bill," 240.   [73] Greg, "Representative Reform [1]," 456–7.

progressivists.[74] As Henry Warwick Cole (whom we will examine more closely in Section 2b) wrote, "the time is ripe for new arrangements which shall bring our political institutions in closer conformity to the altered state of society."[75] John Eardley Eardley-Wilmot (who will return in Section 2a) took the sentiment even further: the fact that the Reform Act had been passed a third of a century earlier sufficed to provoke doubt about its current fitness, for "the Representative System cannot be expected to remain as it stood in 1832."[76] A progressive nation such as Britain continually needed to revise its electoral arrangements in order to maintain the appropriate correspondence between Parliament and the society over which it ruled; having neglected this task after 1832, Parliament had fallen out of step with Britain.

The second source of discontent regarding the unrepresentativeness of the reformed Parliament did not depend on any reading of recent British history or any progressive historical metaphysics. Instead, it directly attacked the provisions of the Reform Act itself; in particular, it fastened onto what is, at least in the eyes of modern liberal democrats, the Act's most paradoxical feature. This was that, although the law increased the size of the electorate, it curtailed the local variation in the franchise and thereby rendered the electorate less socially diverse even as it expanded it in absolute numbers. Like the Tories mentioned in Section 1 who saw the exclusivity of the bill's property requirements vis-à-vis the working classes as a reason to retain the unreformed electoral structures, mid-Victorian reformers of many stripes, including Walter Bagehot, who will appear in Section 2a, would come to lament the Whigs' abandonment in 1832 of the view of the suffrage which Mackintosh had directed against Bentham in 1818.[77] In effect, mid-century proponents of a revived variety of suffrages

---

[74] Ellis Wasson, "The Spirit of Reform, 1832 and 1867," *Albion*, 12 (1980): 164–74.

[75] Cole, *The Middle Classes and the Borough Franchise* (London, 1866), 9.

[76] Eardley-Wilmot, *A Safe and Constitutional Plan of Parliamentary Reform* (London, 1865), 4. Also Saunders, *Democracy and the Vote*, 167–8. In the manner of Gibbons and Stephen in this chapter's opening vignette, Bagehot projected the point about historical change determining constitutional shifts further into the past: "On the whole, the English constitution of the last century, in its best time, and before the occurrence of changes which we shall soon describe, gave an excellent expression to the public opinion of England"; "History of the Unreformed Parliament, and Its Lessons" in *CW*, vol. 6, 274.

[77] "The simplest expedient [for re-admitting the working-class] is to recur to the old English system of different suffrages in different boroughs, which existed down to the Act of 1832 ... There can be little doubt that its abolition was an error. It gave an element of variety to our Constitution, exactly where it was wanted. Sir James Mackintosh and Lord Russell, and other Whig authorities, had written panegyrics on it"; Bagehot, *The English Constitution*, in *CW*, vol. 5, 407. (This passage was present only in the 1867 edition.) He had earlier called Mackintosh's essay the "authoritative exposition of liberal doctrine"; Bagehot, "Parliamentary Reform," in *CW*, vol. 6, 221.

appealed from the later Mackintosh – the one who stood by his Whig brethren as they pushed for the Reform Act – to the earlier Mackintosh – the one who had taken to the *Edinburgh Review* to defend a varied suffrage against illiberal democracy – in the name of a renewed increase of diversity in the franchise and, hence, of the reopening of direct electoral paths for the admission of working-class ideas and interests into Parliament.[78]

Both from the perception of societal change and from a negative appraisal of the exclusivity of the Reform Act itself, then, mid-Victorian reformers sought to put electoral multiformity back in the center of parliamentary representation. These two lines of argument for multiformity-enhancing reform mingled intimately in the works of the authors addressed here, though some emphasized one over the other – an emphasis that could have subtle but significant institutional repercussions.

Thus, in one of those provocative twists of fate that characterize the history of political thought, a way of thinking about representation that had originated for the sake of justifying a condition of the suffrage that had come about in an undesigned and evolutionary manner was embraced, in the 1850s–60s, as a template for the conscious, deliberate improvement of the parliamentary system.[79] Unlike their forebears who had lauded an inherited political tradition and their contemporaries who defended the reformed system, advocates of the differential franchise during the theory's mid-century peak had to devise their own set of institutions which would satisfy the demanding standard of descriptive accuracy.

This task was a difficult one. Because their vision of reform was founded on the value of representativeness, and not on, say, a technocratic or paternalistic conception of good governance, there was necessarily a *sociological* phase as well as a *constructive* phase to their projects. Their institutional recommendations required a grounding in a sociological understanding of the relative importance of the nation's different "classes, interests, and opinions," for knowledge of the social state to be matched or reflected had to precede the construction of institutions whose merit would lie in their matching or reflecting capacity. The argumentative burden on designers of variety-of-suffrage schemes was therefore doubly heavy: they needed both to articulate a convincing sociological portrait and to

---

[78] The Whig-Liberal journalist Bernard Cracroft, who straddled the line between being a variety-of-suffragist and a democratic reformer, expressed this frustration at the parliamentary marginalization of the working class in colorful terms: "At the present moment, railways, beer, sugar, insurance offices, are all more effectively represented in the House than labour"; Cracroft, "The Reform Session of 1866," 47–8.

[79] E.g. Bagehot, "How to Amend the Reform Bill," in *CW*, vol. 14, 87–90.

demonstrate that the institutions which they prescribed were appropriate instruments for translating this sociology into the Commons. Given these hurdles, it was natural that mirroring proponents of increased electoral diversification would form a more divided camp than mirroring apologists of the status quo. Against this latter group, a rejuvenated "old-Mackintoshianism" of the 1850s–60s can be understood as splitting into three broad schools (as outlined in the following three sections), which are treated in ascending order based on the degree to which their prescriptions departed from the then-existent electoral arrangements.

a   Selective Tailoring

From the perspective of political thought as taught today, the best-known of the authors considered in this chapter is Walter Bagehot. His copious writings on representation bear out the verdict that he was an archetypal Victorian – his interventions into the debates about parliamentary reform were typical of the variety-of-suffrages school at its apex.[80]

Bagehot interlaced both reasons for dissatisfaction with the status quo delineated above. First, he charged the Reform Act with betraying genuine Whig-liberalism by diminishing the variety in the franchise. Instead of finding a means to increase the power of the middle classes and counter oligarchic and royal patronage[81] which would have respected the "crazy-quilt pattern" of local suffrage regulations then in existence,[82] 1832 had decreased the multiformity of the suffrage, rendering Commons membership less diverse and cutting the lower classes off from Parliament. The "varying qualification," long embraced by the "more philosophic of liberal statesmen" over any "uniform 'right of suffrage,'" had been sacrificed to the exigency of producing a "simple bill" that would remove the worst "abuses" of the old system and quell the swelling "semi-revolution."[83] Such had been the sad end of a central electoral tenet of liberalism.

Second, while countering the standardization of the franchise was an important undertaking simply as a matter of principle, the urgency of doing so was compounded, on Bagehot's telling, by recent social changes. The tragic irony of the Reform Act was that it had disenfranchised the urban working classes precisely at the moment at which their claims to

---

[80] G. M. Young, "The Greatest Victorian," in *Victorian Essays* (Oxford, 1962): 116–28.

[81] Bagehot, "History of the Unreformed Parliament," 272.

[82] Starzinger, *The Politics of the Center*, 64. For Bagehot's sympathetic description of the suffrage regulations before Reform, see "Lord Althorp and the Reform Act of 1832," in *CW*, vol. 3, 220–3.

[83] Ibid., 220–1.

a parliamentary voice were growing strongest. According to Bagehot, for most of English history the working classes had lacked the intelligence or interest to attend to national affairs, and therefore they had not contributed to the formation of that public opinion which it was the duty of the electoral "machinery" to convey accurately into the Commons.[84] Along with many other liberals – including, importantly, a vocal segment of urban working-class radicals[85] – Bagehot held that this un- or prepolitical condition persisted among the rural laboring population.[86] Yet, he judged, since 1832 there had arisen a segment of the working classes which *did* contribute importantly to the development of public opinion through its distinctive "sentiments on public affairs."[87] This was the advanced, intellectual component of the working classes, the "town artisans" and "the lower classes ... in the larger towns [who have] opinions to state."[88] The social, economic, and intellectual progress of this group entailed an adjustment in the electoral system that would recognize its greater socio-ideological standing.[89]

Provision of seats for the urban working classes thus had to be made for Parliament to fulfill its mirroring function and for parliamentary discussion

---

[84] Ibid., 221.

[85] Eugenio Biagini, *Liberty, Retrenchment, and Reform: Popular Liberalism in the Age of Gladstone, 1860–1880* (Cambridge, 1992), 52. Hence, even working class and proto-socialist figures once associated with Chartism could wind up with a greater affinity toward variety-of-suffragist resistance to democracy than is often acknowledged.

[86] "There are no ideas among our ignorant poor"; "there are not in the enormous majority of country towns any working men who have much opinion about politics"; Bagehot, *English Constitution*, 403. This negative verdict on the political consciousness of the rural lower classes has fallen out of favor in historical scholarship, although see F. B. Smith, *The Making of the Second Reform Bill* (Cambridge, 1966), 52, and John Vincent, *The Formation of the Liberal Party, 1857–1868* (London, 1966), 252. It ought to be noted in this connection that there was no national system of public primary education in England until the Elementary Education Act of 1870.

Similar judgments of the "ruralocracy" were frequently heard across the Channel during these decades, where liberals and republicans (including socialists such as Louis Blanc) decried the peasantry for maintaining Napoleon III's imperial regime out of excessive concern to protect their property and out of incomprehension and indifference toward genuine political sentiments: Louis Blanc, "Du Gouvernement direct du peuple par lui-même," in *Questions d'aujourd'hui et de demain*, 2 vols. (Paris, 1873), vol. 1, 74–5; Roger Price, *Napoleon III and the Second Empire* (London, 1997), 53. The most Francophilic of all Englishmen, J. S. Mill, agreed with this verdict: "The millions of voters who, in opposition to nearly every educated person in the country, made Louis Napoleon President, were chiefly peasants who could neither read nor write, and whose knowledge of public men, even by name, was limited to oral tradition"; Mill, "Thoughts on Parliamentary Reform," in *CW*, vol. 19, 326. Compare with Marx's famously unkind judgments on the basis of Napoleonic power in the "small peasants"; Karl Marx, "The Eighteenth Brumaire of Louis Bonaparte," in *The Marx-Engels Reader*, ed. Robert Tucker (New York, 1978): 594–617.

[87] Bagehot, "Parliamentary Reform," 196.

[88] Bagehot, *English Constitution*, 315, 408; "Note of 18 Feb, 1859, to 'Parliamentary Reform'," *The Works and Life of Walter Bagehot*, ed. Mrs. Russell Barrington (London, 1915), vol. 3, 173.

[89] On the relationship between "political structure" and "social structure" in Bagehot, see Alastair Buchan, *The Spare Chancellor: The Life of Walter Bagehot* (London, 1959), 188.

to possess all the "materials" of sentiment, opinion, and interest needed for it to be truly deliberative. To accomplish this feat Bagehot advocated an updated version of the "old system of representation . . . based on a variety of franchises."[90] His plan of non-uniform representation was simple in comparison to those we will soon see. First, and most importantly, he would introduce universal or near-universal suffrage in a score of major industrial cities,[91] while maintaining the post-1832 property requirements in all other constituencies. In these democratic urban boroughs the electoral roll would be dominated by working-class voters, who would thereby be empowered to put candidates of their own class (or at least of their own choosing) into the House. Second, he demanded a rural-to-urban transfer of seats that would enhance the influence of industrial centers at the expense of the overrepresented "landed interest" in a way that would better reflect the preponderance of the "growing parts of the country" over the "stationary" parts. With these amendments, he boasted, the "general accordance of parliamentary with national opinion" would be restored.[92]

Insofar as Bagehot sought to reintegrate the working class into the political system and to revive the principle of electoral diversity, then, his mechanism for doing so was to *selectively tailor* the suffrage. Following a process of sociological discrimination, he calibrated the suffrage to fit the facts ascertained about the state of society and public opinion, lowering it only in those places where doing so would achieve the admission of "really organic interests and ideas" which were at present excluded from Parliament.[93] Bagehot's method was to note those elements of the social-intellectual order wrongly missing from Parliament and then to target those areas in which they were predominant for a localized revision of the franchise requirements; in the present mid-Victorian moment this meant reducing the suffrage where it could serve to create an inlet for the town artisans, but in future contexts it might involve carrying out this operation in other constituencies to carve out a space for other groups.[94]

---

[90] Bagehot, "Lord Althorp and the Reform Act," 223.

[91] It is not clear if there were to be any minor restrictions; see Paul Smith, "Introduction," to Walter Bagehot, *The English Constitution* (Cambridge, 2001), xxiv. He did write in the *Fortnightly Review* (though he omitted these lines from the eventual complete edition of *The English Constitution*) that he favored "household suffrage . . . with an effectual lodger suffrage besides"; *English Constitution*, 407.

[92] Bagehot, "Parliamentary Reform," 191–3.

[93] Bagehot, "'True Liberalism' and Reform," in *CW*, vol. 6, 360.

[94] On Bagehot's openness to the future expansion of the political order as an instance of the larger Victorian paradigm of growth and evolution, see H. S. Jones, *Victorian Political Thought* (New York, 2000), 70. While there is the crucial difference that today we do not alter the franchise across districts, we might call this method *Bagehot-mandering* to highlight the continuity between it

Before passing to other schemes of this selective-lowering sort, two further features of Bagehot's approach deserve comment, since they bear on themes that will recur throughout this volume. First, he calculated that on his plan there would be forty MPs for "the lower classes." Although forty working-class MPs may seem a modest total, Bagehot was convinced of its robustness. His plan, he emphasized, would produce more working-class MPs than could be expected from the combination of plural voting and proportional representation endorsed by that famous "advanced liberal," John Stuart Mill.[95] While Mill's uniform suffrage would enfranchise a larger number of his laboring fellow citizens across the country – the (not insignificant) Millian exclusions covered only those who could not "read, write, and ... perform the common operations of arithmetic" or those who were receiving "parish relief" (that, is municipal government aid for poverty)[96] – this greater measure of enfranchisement was, Bagehot judged, a red herring. Despite Mill's protestations to the contrary, the plain truth was that his elitist democracy would not "give so *much* power to the working class" as Bagehot's openly nondemocratic system would:

> By the adoption of [Mill's] scheme, you would give to the working classes no characteristic expression in the legislature; you would give them an influence in every constituency in appearance considerable, but which would be of no practical avail to them as a class, because on all characteristic points their voice would be neutralized ... by the more numerous votes given for that very purpose to the more educated classes.[97]

What mattered from the perspective of "real representation" was not votes, but seats – and seats were come by not through a widespread distribution of "votes ... scattered through many constituencies," but by assigning to the working class a concentrated and "preponderant influence in at least some constituencies."[98]

---

and the current American practice of tailoring the boundaries of constituencies to create "majority–minority" districts in pursuit of the goal of fair racial representation.

[95] Bagehot, "Note of 18 Feb, 1859, to 'Parliamentary Reform'," 174. Mill, of course, did not agree with this assessment.

[96] Mill, *Considerations on Representative Government*, in *CW*, vol. 19, 470–2

[97] Bagehot, "'True Liberalism' and Reform," 358; "Note of 18 Feb, 1859, to 'Parliamentary Reform'," 174. Similarly, Cracroft called it a "fallacy" to make "the polling-booth and not the votes in the House of Commons the test of representation"; "The Reform Session of 1866," 67.

[98] Bagehot, "The Defeat of the Ministry and the Prospects of Reform," in *CW*, vol. 6, 306; "The Withdrawal of the Reform Bill," in *CW*, vol. 6, 333. Also "The State of Parties," in *CW*, vol. 7, 168: he rejected plans to give the advanced artisans "an ineffectual voice everywhere, but a real representation nowhere." Bagehot leveled the same charge against the set of reform plans that dispensed altogether with the mirroring mechanism of a "diversity of qualifications in different constituencies" and sought simply to locate the suffrage nationally at the point at which the

This single-minded focus on seats over votes followed from the fact that the locus of concern for mirror theorists was the composition of the Commons; they attended with great regard to the regulation of the suffrage, but only as the *instrument* for bringing about the desired composition.[99] The issue of any given citizen's personal possession or nonpossession of the vote was unimportant[100]; all that was important was that the overall allocation of the suffrage serve the end of accurate mirroring. Bagehot, who followed the logic of his theory of representation to its conclusion, could thus blithely assert that "to have a good Parliament, we must disfranchise some good constituents."[101] Importantly, in this passage Bagehot was employing the term "disfranchisement" not only to indicate the formal denial of the suffrage to an individual, but also more broadly to describe the misfortune of consistently finding oneself on the losing side of elections due to occupying the position of a permanent minority in a constituency (as, he believed, would be the case for "upper-class" voters in the boroughs to which he wished to grant universal suffrage). This usage was far from peculiar to Bagehot; Russell, for example, gave a nearly identical formulation: "It is not necessary, however, although every class ought to have an influence in elections, that every member of every class should have a vote." The fact of a "butcher at Hackney" having the franchise while a butcher elsewhere lacked it was in itself no demerit in a system of representation.[102] Having a good

maximum number of working-class voters could be admitted without creating a working-class majority on the electoral rolls; "Parliamentary Reform," 223; "'True Liberalism' and Reform," 358.

[99] "The suffrage is not so much a natural claim as a civil function – not an indefeasible right, but a means to an end"; Greg, "The Expected Reform Bill," 262. Contrast this with the religious-symbolic significance of the suffrage in French thought at the time, and in American thought at various periods: Pierre Rosanvallon, *Le sacre du citoyen* (Paris, 1992); Judith Shklar, *American Citizenship: The Quest for Inclusion*, (Cambridge, 1995), ch. 1.

[100] This view conformed well to the widespread mid-Victorian conviction (held of course by Mill as well) that the vote was not a private right but a trust for the best achievement of public ends. Bagehot held this conviction consistently, even in his youth when he thought more favorably of democracy: Bagehot, "On the Character of Mirabeau and His Influence on His Age," in *CW*, vol. 14, 18; "Thoughts on Democracy," in *CW*, vol. 14, 15–17.

[101] Bagehot, "Parliamentary Reform," 223.

[102] Russell, *History of the English Constitution*, fourth edition, 180. In the next chapter, we will see how this indifference about the possession of the vote by every individual connected to a sense of the proper functioning of a *deliberative* system of representation. Although they tend to prefer random sampling and lottocratic measures, contemporary epistemic democrats themselves can demonstrate a parallel insouciance about universal suffrage. Compare, for example, David Estlund's openness to the replacement of "universal voting rights" by a form of "democratic regency" with the variety-of-suffragist conception of a deliberatively necessary restriction of the suffrage; Estlund, *Democratic Authority: A Philosophical Framework* (Princeton, 2008), 181–2. Indeed, to claim that selecting a butcher from one town but not another for the franchise in order to achieve a desired condition of the assembly did not constitute a harm for the excluded butcher parallels closely the reasoning in

parliament meant, for Bagehot, empowering the urban working class in a way that did justice to its newfound social-intellectual importance, and this required not the "*sham-representation*" of many votes accompanied by few or no MPs, but rather substantial "direct representation in the House of Commons." To speak of the level of enfranchisement as a political good in abstraction from the makeup of the House was to operate with a mistaken theory of representation. The only relevant metric of a group's participation in parliamentary government was the number of seats it "command[ed]," not the number of votes it counted.[103]

The second aspect of Bagehot's approach that will prove resonant was his recognition of the difficult argumentative burden involved in applying this theory of descriptive representation. Befitting his standing as one of the most self-aware of Victorian writers, Bagehot acknowledged that the sociology which undergirded his reform proposal was, first and foremost, his own, and that it may not have appeared self-evident to his compatriots: "The most difficult thing to establish by argument is an evident fact of observation. There are no statistics of opinion to which we can refer, there is no numerical comparison which will establish the accordance of parliamentary with social opinion"; indeed, this task was even trickier during the frequently recurring "periods" when "public opinion was much divided and strongly excited."[104] The truth about which "interests and ideas" were the "really organic" ones, and how one of these should be weighed against the others, was not indisputably revealed to all Englishmen. Instead, Bagehot would have to convince the public that his plan was the one that would renew the connection between assembly and society, that forty members was the fitting amount for the working classes and that a more general displacement of seats from rural to urban would reflect the present condition of the

contemporary democratic theory for why, in the eyes of those citizens who are excluded, it ought to be acceptable to randomly select members of an assembly in order to maximize its epistemic capacities or avoid the pitfalls of electoral representation; Hélène Landemore, "Deliberation, Cognitive Diversity, and Democratic Inclusiveness: An Epistemic Argument for the Random Selection of Representatives," *Synthese*, 190 (2013): 1209–31; Alexander Guerrero, "Against Elections: The Lottocratic Alternative," *Philosophy and Public Affairs*, 42 (2014): 135–78.

[103] Bagehot, "The Defeat of the Ministry and the Prospects of Reform," 306–7.

[104] Bagehot, "Parliamentary Reform," 188. See also "The Withdrawal of the Reform Bill," 333, on the "difficulty of this task." Hence, he distinguished his own approach to that "true theory of representative government" that was "class representation" – which was focused on the fair representation of a few "really organic" classes and interests – from more intricate plans for apportioning the electoral system to reflect a wide array of more specifically defined groups and social divisions; he denied that it was "possible for a provident legislator" to allot "an exact *quantum* of corresponding representation" to a sprawling panoply of "particular interests"; "Present Aspects of Parliamentary Reform," in *CW*, vol. 6, 250–1.

country. This admission of the difficulty of the sociological inquiry involved in the design of mirroring institutions would have struck home rather literally for Bagehot, since Greg, who looked more fondly on the middle-class near-monopoly initiated by the Reform Act, was his brother-in-law. For Bagehot the compatibility of subscription to the goal of descriptive representation with a multiplicity of institutional recommendations was a lesson learned inside the family.[105] Yet in spite of this difficult lesson, he held on to the hope that his proposal would ultimately be recognized as the proper corrective of the "bias" and "defects" that distorted the parliamentary image of the nation.[106]

Through the reinvigoration of the principle of electoral diversity, representativeness would be restored to the Commons and the specter of rule by "a single class" which loomed over any standardization of the suffrage, be it oligarchic or democratic, would be fended off.[107] Bagehot's conception of the theoretical heritage of his prescriptions was accurate: this was as direct an application of Mackintosh's vision as was possible in the mid-century, and he had indeed effected a kind of Burkean rhetorical maneuver, appealing from the new to the old Whiggism on the representation question.

Bagehot was hardly alone in seeking to remedy the unrepresentativeness of the Commons through selectively varying the suffrage across geographical constituencies: his scheme was exemplary of the slew of plans that sought by judicious alterations of the suffrage to place "a certain body of, say fifty or a hundred, special representatives of the masses" in Parliament.[108] Given that Bagehot's can be treated as a standard type of these plans,[109] it is worth looking at two authors whose projects fitted the selective-tailoring mold in a less clear-cut manner but who nevertheless viewed themselves as operating within the same framework. This will allow

---

[105] For instance, although he does not mention his relative by name, it appears that he had Greg in mind when he criticized proposals for the creation of nonlocal representatives in conjunction with enfranchisement based on personal property for achieving the opposite of the goal of a just reform, namely, of yet further strengthening the representation of the educated and wealthy classes; Bagehot, "Note of 18 Feb, 1859, to 'Parliamentary Reform'," 168–9.

[106] Bagehot, "Parliamentary Reform," 191.

[107] Bagehot, "The Defeat of the Ministry and the Prospects of Reform," 306–7. Bagehot was a critic of oligarchy as well as of democracy, although the former aspect of his position has received less attention; Greg Conti and Will Selinger, "Reappraising Walter Bagehot's Liberalism: Discussion, Public Opinion, and the Meaning of Parliamentary Government," *HEI*, 41 (2015): 264–91.

[108] Dicey, "The Balance of Classes," in *Essays on Reform* (London, 1867), 79.

[109] In the words of a posthumous edition of Bagehot's writings on parliamentary reform: no one had "put so forcibly" the "Whig" perspective during these decades; "Advertisement," in Bagehot, *Essays on Parliamentary Reform* (London, 1883), v.

us to see how flexible and pervasive a norm of institutional redesign it was. For even proposals which appeared quite different at the institutional and rhetorical level could be understood as procedures of reform through selective tailoring. Take one instance, from an author about as far as possible from the "elitism" often attributed to Bagehot:[110] "A Reformer" who took up the mantle of a working-class champion. In his eyes, the national discussion on reform had been polluted by reactionary elements in thrall to an "oppressive nightmare of the disastrous effects it is supposed will ensue from the admission of the working man to the franchise." This fearfulness prevented clearheaded evaluation of the institutional options available. Fortunately, the author himself was under no such dire delusions: he judged the poor to be as politically capable as the classes above them, for they were possessed of a "sound common sense."[111] In light of this bullishness about working-class capacity, it is not surprising to find our "Reformer" among those authors who decried the First Reform Act for severing the tie between Parliament and the lower classes.[112]

And yet, despite these populist leanings, the "Reformer" retained the principle of the variety of suffrages, seeking manhood suffrage in boroughs only while maintaining a requirement of ownership of agricultural land in the counties in order to ensure direct representation for the "rural" interest and character type.[113] While this appears a much greater measure of working-class empowerment than Bagehot's, given that the "Reformer" wished to institute an extensive suffrage in all boroughs and not just a cluster of the largest ones, in fact he predicted from his arrangements an outcome similar to Bagehot's. This was because, where Bagehot anticipated from the town artisans a rapid politicization and a distinctively class-based political

---

[110] C. H. Sisson, "The Case of Walter Bagehot," in *The Avoidance of Literature*, ed. Michael Schmidt (Manchester, 1978): 349–438; David Easton, "Walter Bagehot and Liberal Realism," *APSR*, 43 (1949): 17–37.

[111] "A Reformer," *A View of Parliamentary Reform* (Wallingford, 1867), 10–12. He also promoted the political fitness of the working classes by denying that they were liable to act, by simple force of their numbers, to the exclusion of the interests and opinions of other groups: "few bodies of working men wholly pull together, but are as much subject to diversity of opinion as other classes"; ibid. 9–10. The significance of observations of this sort will be addressed in Chapter 3.

[112] Ibid., 12.

[113] Ibid., 14–5. It is important to note that high Whigs such as Russell could share the same mindset of seeking varied representation while disavowing any particular fears about the working class. Russell was "persuaded" that a "House of Commons exclusively representing working men" would not "instal [*sic*] anarchy, destroy property, or uproot the monarchy." Nevertheless, he objected to a Commons monopolized by the working class on the grounds that "a representation of one class would not give an image of the property, the experience, the knowledge, the wisdom of England"; Russell, *History of the English Constitution*, fourth edition, 237.

style,[114] the "Reformer" rejected both these notions.[115] Consequently, in order to bring the urban working-class voices which he valorized into Parliament he judged it necessary to cast a wider electoral net than Bagehot had done. The "Reformer" enfranchised the working class more broadly to compensate for its minimal energy and distinctness as a political corps; in order for the representatives of the urban laborer to participate meaningfully in the Commons alongside those of rural landowners and of the urban propertied classes many more of the former, in a wider range of districts, would need to receive the right to vote. In the end, although he made different sociological and political-psychological judgments, the "Reformer" shared with Bagehot a basic approach to representation: namely, that if one got one's facts right about the state of the several elements of British society, one could tailor the suffrage across geographical constituencies in such a way that "every class and interest" would be reflected accurately.[116]

A glance at a third entrant, from yet another region on the ideological map, reinforces the appeal that selective, sociologically based lowering of the suffrage had as a framework for reform. The Tory John Eardley Eardley-Wilmot, 2nd Baronet, despite his solid conservative credentials, sought the electoral integration of the working classes as a foundational political goal.[117] In contrast to what we might call Bagehot's *cognitivism* about representation – his concern to delineate the various streams of public opinion, to match the distribution of *beliefs* in the Commons to their distribution outside – Eardley-Wilmot approached the sociological dimension of his reform effort by delving into a maze of statistics on economic matters such as savings deposits and imports and exports.[118] With these in hand, he proclaimed that a "progress in the wealth and prosperity of the country" remarkable enough to warrant a shift in

[114] The artisans have "strong class feelings, strong class prejudices, strong class hopes . . . they have an inherent political aptitude"; Bagehot, "The Withdrawal of the Reform Bill," 332–3.

[115] Many workingmen were apathetic about politics and therefore unlikely to "take the trouble to go to the poll," and even among those who were politically energized there was often found a deferential temperament that was receptive to the voices of "property, social connections, and intellect"; "Reformer," *View*, 16, 21. This point about deference will also be taken up in Chapter 3.

[116] Ibid., 20.

[117] R. J. Smith, "Wilmot, Sir John Eardley Eardley-, second baronet (1810–1892)," rev. Catherine Pease-Watkin, *ODNB*. He had long believed that "Electoral Reform" had finally passed beyond the sphere of party conflict, with "all parties" now agreed on the fundamentals of a "liberal Extension of the suffrage"; Eardley-Wilmot, *Lord Brougham's Acts and Bills, from 1811 to the Present Time . . .* (London, 1857), ii.

[118] Such comparative analyses of classes based on economic data was typical of Gladstone's approach during the mid-1860s; William Ewart Gladstone, *Speeches on Parliamentary Reform in 1866* (London, 1866), passim.

electoral-representative structures had occurred. This progress was, according to his investigations, "due mainly" to the "productive classes." The problem was, then, how to transfer influence to the working class "without handing over a preponderating portion of the power . . . to any particular class, the object being that each section of the community should be fairly and adequately, but not exclusively, represented." His suggestion was to lower the property qualification in counties but to lower it more greatly in boroughs, and to complement this reduction with the preservation of the "small boroughs" in order that Parliament could continue to benefit from the distinctive character of their representatives.[119] This reform, in which variation in constituency types interacted with variation in the suffrage, was devised to save the Commons from the worst fate of legislatures, that of "being too limited and one-sided."[120]

Despite coming from conflicting ideological orientations and propounding different pictures of the institutional future of English parliamentarianism, the "Reformer," Eardley-Wilmot, Bagehot, and others were united in their general approach to the revival of the representativeness of the Commons. For them, the problem of representative reform was the problem of allotting the suffrage across the panoply of constituencies so as to create a more accurate image of society in the assembly.

b Class Specificity

Henry Davis Pochin was in many ways similar to Walter Bagehot. In addition to being only two years apart in age, they were both successful in business (Pochin in chemical manufacturing, Bagehot in banking); they both stood for Parliament as Liberal candidates and failed; and they were both supporters of women's suffrage.[121]

But beyond these biographical affinities, the two shared a general outlook on the basics of the reform question. As was the case for the English Tocqueville,[122] to Pochin it was true both that the reformed Parliament had legislated well[123] and that the progress of the country nevertheless made

---

[119] Eardley-Wilmot, *Safe and Constitutional Plan*, 2–4, 13–14, 22. Small boroughs were usually small market towns in relatively rural areas. Many reformers wished to abolish them in order to transfer their seats to more populous cities.

[120] Eardley-Wilmot, *A Safe and Constitutional Plan*, 1.

[121] Trevor Boyns, "Pochin, Henry Davis (1824–1895)," *ODNB*.

[122] This was how Dicey described Bagehot; Dicey, "Alexis de Tocqueville," *NR*, 21 (1893): 771–84.

[123] "Looking at the history of the House of Commons for the last forty years, and the many important measures framed and passed to promote the well-being of the masses, it cannot fairly be said that

a further installment of reform necessary. Although England was being governed well, the indubitable truth that "the people generally have advanced into a higher stage of civilisation than that for which the Constitution of 1832 was judged adequate" made amendment of the representative machinery an urgent matter. In particular, the most progressive part of the nation was the "Wage-class" of the largest, most economically developed boroughs – in other words, Bagehot's prized category of "town artisans." Again like Bagehot, he took for granted that the benighted rural laborers, who are left entirely offstage in his *Plan of Parliamentary Reform*, were not candidates for entry into the electorate; only those segments of the working class which had "grown in numbers, intelligence, and productive power" such that "their interests and opinions" would be wronged without "recognised and fitting exponents" were of concern to him. Finally, the actual number of seats which these two wished to devote to the "clear and distinct utterance for the opinions and sentiments of the Wage-class" was in the same ballpark, though Pochin was rather more generous (fifty-six in his case, to Bagehot's forty).[124]

Even more revealing of their common mindset was the fact that Pochin ascribed to his views the same provenance as Bagehot had: his reform tract was inspired by "the old principle of variety [which] was preferred and cherished . . . by so eminent a Whig, and so profound a political philosopher as Sir James Mackintosh." Like the editor of the *Economist*, he enlisted in the ranks of the "eminent authorities" who now recognized the uniformization of 1832 to have been "a disastrous departure from the previous course of the constitution." Only by a return to original Whig principles could the representativeness of the Commons be perfected and the democratic tyranny exercised by "a single class with so overpowering a number" be averted.[125] Pochin's conception of the purpose and impact of an updated program of differentiated suffrage, then, could have been inserted seamlessly into Bagehot's voluminous output on the subject.

Yet despite this considerable overlap, there was a fundamental difference between Pochin and Bagehot. This was that Pochin intended to reserve the fifty-six seats in major urban constituencies *exclusively* for "the present

our present system of selecting men suited to the work to be done, and the varied interests to be represented, has not on the whole worked well"; Henry Davis Pochin, *A Plan of Parliamentary Reform* (London, 1866), 4.

[124] Ibid., 7, 9, 17, 11.

[125] Ibid., 20–1, 6. In contrast to Bagehot, Pochin tended toward radicalism politically. But here Pochin departed from his friend John Bright, the famous radical MP: "John Bright's scheme" was one of those which would "launch us upon the steep incline from which the prospectively indefinite view [of universal suffrage] hinted at already, glooms in the distance"; ibid., 6–7.

unrepresented portion of the inhabitants ... those who reside in houses below the value of £10." Bagehot, and all subscribers to the "selective tailoring" model of the variegated suffrage, sought to reduce the property requirement in certain industrially advanced cities in order that the advanced working classes in these districts would make up a majority of the electorate. From their perspective, what it meant to remedy the deficit of working-class representation was to create *working-class-majority* constituencies in which the working class, when united, could be sure to put a member of its choosing into Parliament. For Pochin, on the other hand, the project of granting a "reasonable share of elective power" to the "Wage-class," "a fair share of political power in the National Council" that would fulfill the promise of a government that mirrored society and public opinion, involved implementing *working-class-specific* constituencies. Pochin did not advocate lowering the value of property stipulated for the suffrage in these boroughs. Rather, this provision was to be left constant, so that the constituencies solely of £10 or greater householders would carry on in these cities unaffected; but alongside these currently existing censitary districts he would establish independent constituencies for the poorer electors. As he explained:

> I propose ... that a new [electoral] register shall be formed early in each of these selected large towns; that this register shall be as democratic as may be found workable, not stopping perhaps even at household suffrage. To give an example: – In Manchester, under this scheme, the possessors of the present £10. franchise would continue to retain two members; and the possessors of the new democratic franchise I propose, would by themselves alone return other two members; so that the middle-class and working-class elements of Manchester, would each be represented by two members chosen by each class, under the operation of its own special register. This plan would result in ... *fifty-six* members to be elected entirely by the Wage-class.[126]

Under the Bagehot model, the working classes would gain their own MPs by virtue of winning elections. On the Pochin plan, the working classes would have their own MPs by virtue of possessing their own constituencies.

This divergence from the selecting–tailoring configuration had important implications. For one, it promised different practical effects. In contrast to the contending paradigm, for example, it did not provoke fears that it would introduce working-class voices into Parliament only at

[126] Ibid., 7, 10–11.

the cost of sacrificing the voices of another, particularly important segment of the British population. This was a charge that Mill had leveled against Bagehot's renovation of the variety of suffrages. Bagehot's plan was, in Mill's words, unacceptably "violent" because it would "giv[e] up the representation of the large towns to day-labourers, by establishing, in them, equal and universal suffrage, thereby disfranchising the higher and middle classes of those places, who comprise the majority of the most intellectual persons in the kingdom."[127] The best minds of England were, in the eyes of Mill, disproportionately concentrated among the educated and professional strata of precisely those major urban constituencies in which Bagehot would institute manhood suffrage. Yet the establishment of manhood suffrage in these boroughs entailed the threat that they would be consistently outvoted by the working classes and consequently cease to have representation in the Commons. In a kind of parable of just how complicated to disentangling the various strands of nineteenth-century liberalism can be, the "democrat" Mill decried the "elitist" Bagehot for advancing a vision of the future of Parliament in which the country's true intellectual elite would be silenced.[128] In Mill's alarmed estimate, parliamentary reform à la Bagehot would amount to a simple substitution of the urban lower classes for the urban educated classes, a shift which would reduce the intellectual standard of British politics and diminish the representativeness of the Commons (since the urban elites contributed more to the formation of public opinion than any other segment of society).

No such objections could be brought against Pochin's class-specific scheme for enfranchising the urban proletariat; Pochin was explicit that much of the value of his project lay in the clear demarcation between socioeconomic groups which allowed him to include the working classes while preserving urban upper-class representation in its integrity. Naturally, since he believed that it was not "desirable to increase the present number of seats in the House of Commons," the extension of seats to the urban working classes had to come at the expense of some other set of seats; in Pochin's case, these were seats belonging to the small boroughs.[129] But because, contra Bagehot, he did not accept the commonplace that the small borough voters had a distinctive sensibility that warranted a place in the representative system, he did not equate the

---

[127] Mill, "Recent Writers on Reform," in *CW*, vol. 19, 364.

[128] On Mill's democratic reputation, see e.g. Carole Pateman, *Participation and Democratic Theory* (Cambridge, 1970), ch. 2; Richard Krouse, "Two Concepts of Democratic Representation: James and John Stuart Mill, *JP*, 44 (1982): 509–37.

[129] Pochin, *Plan*, 11.

diminution of these constituencies with any loss in descriptive representativeness. For these reasons Pochin was confident of the superiority of his scheme; it would endow urban wage-earners with a "material and substantial" parliamentary presence without betraying the genius of English representation, which was that it was "spread and divided among *many* classes" with no group of significance excluded.[130]

Pochin was not a political philosopher, so it was on these practical advantages that he dwelt. But there were also important conceptual implications to the difference between his scheme and other models of mirroring. Relative to the reformed system in place post-1832 and to selective-lowering proposals, Pochin's plan had a distinct conception both of the nature of the electoral constituency and of the relationship between the representation of a class and the ideological makeup of that class. Given the theoretical import of these differences, it is worth saying a word about each of them.

First, regarding the unit of representation: Pochin's plan for producing a sociologically accurate Commons involved a rejection of the assumption, operative in Bagehot, that the form of a constituency was a geographical region over which a single rule of suffrage applied. While geographically bounded communities remained for Bagehot and company the almost exclusive instrument of representation, Pochin's class-specific reform dispensed with this singular focus on geography. Separate constituencies could exist over the same territory; and constituencies operating over the same space could be made independent by virtue of an alternate criterion: class. Pochin believed that socioeconomic standing, and not just residency, was capable of defining the boundaries of a constituency. As noted in Section 1, this expansion beyond residency as the criterion for membership in a given electorate was not an invention of Pochin; he was, rather, taking up the baton dropped by Mackintosh decades earlier. And, by the time of Pochin's pamphlet, several other experiments in the construction of nonterritorial electoral demarcation (of which some will be considered later) had appeared; moreover, university constituencies accounted for six seats in the Commons (up from four before 1832) between the First and Second Reform Act (which expanded the number to nine).[131] Although his inclusion of nonresidential factors in the erection of districts was not novel, the theoretical importance of this difference within the pantheon of variety-of-

---

[130] Ibid., 17, 6.
[131] University constituencies, it should be noted, would proliferate further in 1918 before being abolished in 1950; T. L. Humberstone, *University Representation* (London, 1951).

suffrages arguments nevertheless comes out clearly when we observe that on Pochin's approach, but not on Bagehot's, it becomes conceivable that every citizen could be sorted into an appropriate group-based constituency invested with the proper voting power according to sociological observations about the group's societal significance. On Pochin's reasoning, in principle there was no barrier to organizing constituencies according to ever more finely drawn socioeconomic categories (such as profession or union membership instead of merely classes) or other factors (such as religion) should these be judged to have greater political salience.

This insight that the realization of a mirror theory of representation might require constituencies to be understood in ways other than (what the greatest Liberal prime minister and staunch defender of local representation would call) geographical "integers"[132] brings Pochin's class-specific version of the variegated suffrage close to two more radical kinds of electoral machinery for achieving parliamentary diversity: the more intricate and pluralistic sociologically based schemes discussed in the next subsection, and proportional representation, which is the subject of Chapters 4 and 5. Indeed, although Pochin did not believe he had struck out particularly far from the English constitutional status quo, he had in fact entered a conceptual universe in which the quest to accurately translate England's "varied classes" into Parliament might involve mechanisms very distinct from the traditional territorial district. He may even himself have contemplated such further refinements as a consequence of his plan – while he hoped his scheme could settle the present "pressing and urgent" episode in the history of reform, he welcomed any "safe and timely" adjustments that the development of the country might necessitate in future.[133]

The second noteworthy theoretical upshot of the switch to class-specific districts concerned the relationship between the goal of representing a class (or any demographic group – recall the wide sense of class with which these writers were working) and the conception of the ideological makeup of that class. The extent to which socioeconomic classes were ideologically uniform or multiform was, as will be covered in Chapter 3, a hotly debated question in the mid-Victorian period. The ability of a selective-tailoring design to remedy the deficit of working-class spokesmen in the Commons

---

[132] Gladstone, HC Debate 15 June 1870, *Hansard*, Third Series, vol. 4 (London, 1870), 147. Gladstone would maintain this communitarian view of variegated local representation throughout his life, and (importantly for Chapters 4–5) it would have a strong influence on his negotiations for the Third Reform Act; H. C. G. Matthew, "Introduction," *The Gladstone Diaries: With Cabinet Minutes and Prime-Ministerial Correspondence, vol. 10: Jan. 1881–June 1883* (Oxford, 1990), cviii.

[133] Pochin, *Plan*, 6, 17.

was predicated on the answer to this question lying in the direction of uniformity. With majority rather than exclusively working-class districts, the goal of gaining entry into parliament for working-class voices could be accomplished only if working-class opinion was relatively homogeneous, for if the working class was fractured in its beliefs then the victorious candidate could very well hail from a socioeconomic group to which a minority of citizens in the district belonged but which was more politically cohesive. Under a Pochinian arrangement, on the contrary, no assumption of ideological homogeneity was needed in order for the working class to place members in the House. Class-specific constituencies, in other words, held out the prospect of enabling a diverse and conflicted working class, and not just a united one, to have its own parliamentary agents. This method of variegated suffrage, unlike the one analyzed prior, would allow not only the working-class point of view, but working-class *points* of view, to make their parliamentary mark.

Pochin was not the lone reformer during this period to place class-specific electorates at the center of his plan. In the "Year of Revolutions" the celebrated Whig historian Edward Creasy had concluded his popular primer on constitutional history, *The Text-Book of the Constitution*, with a call to implement an arrangement very similar to the one that Pochin would end up adopting.[134] Like Pochin, he wanted to "pare away fifty members" "out of the smaller and most notoriously corrupt boroughs, and the smaller counties" in order to free up seats for "working men." In contrast to Pochin, Creasy did not assign these new "democratic" districts to the most advanced urban boroughs. Rather, he advised for the creation of these new seats that Great Britain be divided into fifty equal electoral districts in which all male residents not currently enfranchised who met certain minimal criteria would be eligible to vote.[135] Creasy was conceptually a very close antecedent of Pochin, though sociologically they differed: in opposition to Pochin and the wider liberal consensus, Creasy did not privilege the urban worker over the rural laborer.

---

[134] Creasy's endorsement of working-class-exclusive electorates testifies particularly well to the degree to which this had become a mainstream position, for Creasy embodied "parliamentarianism at its most typical"; H. C. G. Matthew, "Creasy, Sir Edward Shepherd (1812–1878)," *ODNB*. Revealingly, Creasy cited Mackintosh on the long constitutional pedigree of a "variety of classes" exercising the borough franchise; Creasy, *The Text-Book of the Constitution* (London, 1848), 51.

[135] "Give a vote in the election of the district member to every male aged twenty-one years, who has no vote for any county or borough, who has resided for a year in the district, who has not been convicted of any criminal offence for the last seven years, or received parish relief for the last year, and who is able to read and write"; Creasy, *Text-Book of the Constitution*, 62.

In the same year that Pochin published his *Plan* another close relative of his scheme appeared. This contribution came from the opposite party milieu; where Pochin was a Liberal friendly to the radical wing of his party, in his own reform tract Henry Warwick Cole did not hide that he was writing as a Conservative partisan.[136] Cole took for granted the standard liberal sociology which privileged the urban working classes over their rural counterparts, and therefore devised a "special application" of the electoral law for the "largest towns only." He sought to replace, in urban boroughs, the current arrangement by which electors voted in common for (almost always) two members with a new system in which "separate electoral bod[ies]" would be assigned to affluent (he called them "middle-class") and working-class voters. He explained his scheme as follows: "to take Westminster for an example, we should have one member for the first division of the borough returned by the Middle-Class electors as their representative, and a member for the second division returned by the Working Class electors as their representative."[137] By a half-and-half division of seats Cole would therefore transform an "aggregate of about 68 cities and boroughs returning 138 members to Parliament" into "69 members" directly elected by the working class and the same number by the middle classes; his class-specific constituencies outnumbered the provisions of Pochin (56), Creasy (50), and Bagehot (40). Cole followed these others in considering his increase to be substantial. Like Bagehot, he boasted that his proposal was more inclusive than those of famous figures on what we would now identify as the "left": just as Bagehot went out of his way to stress that his electoral machinery would generate more working-class representatives than Mill's, Cole bragged that his "Tory" plan was more working-class-friendly than that of the great Whig reformer Lord Russell. Unlike Whig oligarchs' reform pitches, his plan alone would place the different classes on a proper "footing of equality."[138] In the manner of the anonymous "Reformer" of the previous subsection, Cole avowed no fear of the lower orders[139]; his was a scheme, he stated flatly, that would honor and satisfy all classes.

For all the similarities between this trio, Cole's contribution diverged from those of Creasy and Pochin in one respect: he wished to preserve the

---

[136] Cole, *Middle Classes*, 68–71.

[137] Ibid., 2, 31, 28. Cole's choice of Westminster here was a symbolically rich one, since Westminster had historically been a bastion of democratic sentiment and had had a very wide unreformed electorate; Marc Baer, *The Rise and Fall of Radical Westminster, 1780–1890* (Houndmills, Basingstoke, 2012).

[138] Cole, *Middle Classes*, 55, 57.   [139] Ibid., 12.

small boroughs.[140] This disagreement did not ruffle Cole's confidence that *his* was the plan that would at last turn Parliament into the mirror of society it was supposed to be and square the circle of admitting "large masses of the Working Classes" without "swamping" the rest of society.[141] Cole's institutions were the ones by which the body of MPs would finally come to "reflect and represent the opinions of their fellow countrymen."[142]

A final point ought to be made about the relationship between the designers of class-specific districts and the selective lowerers analyzed earlier. I have called the former more "radical" than the latter, and indeed they were in the sense that their preferred electoral arrangements departed more widely from the arrangements in place at the time. And yet it would be wrong to equate the greater radicalism of their institutional designs with a greater radicalism of social or party-political sympathies. As we have begun to glimpse, Victorian political thought is resistant to being broken down along a unitary left–right spectrum, and this is especially true on the subject of representation. Just as adherence to the variety-of-suffrages framework came to cut across partisan affiliation, so particular variations on the variety-of-suffrages theme did not correspond neatly to any rank-ordering of the general ideological predilections of the authors. Given that it seemed an open question to Victorians whether the reforms advocated by Bagehot, whose rhetoric was staunchly hostile to democracy, were not in fact more empowering of the working class than those of the "advanced Liberal" Mill, it should not surprise us to observe an even greater measure of confusion reigning within the various variety-of-suffrages camps.

This point about the indistinctness with which the institutional content of a given scheme mapped onto wider social-political sensibilities is well illustrated by a feature of Cole's essay on which we have not yet touched. Despite his unfrightened stance toward working-class political attitudes, his endorsement of class-specific constituencies, and his comparatively high allotment of sixty-nine seats for the urban working class, he saw

[140] Ibid., 64.
[141] Ibid., 1; also 21, 67. One of the most curious details of Cole's essay is the explanation he gives of the term "swamping," which was ubiquitous among mid-Victorians, to signal the classist character of universal suffrage: "The use of this expressive word, as applied to the franchise, has received the sanction of a great thinker of the age, Ralph Waldo Emerson. As a citizen of the United States, he has had personal experience of the lamentable fact that the Middle Classes in that country abstain, in despair, from taking any part in politics, because they feel themselves 'hopelessly swamped'"; ibid., 1. Apparently in Cole's mind the Transcendentalism of New England was a cousin of the variegated-suffrage school of old England. Cole was not far off the mark: there was an antidemocratic streak in Emerson; Anthony Hillbruner, "Emerson: Democratic Egalitarian?," *Communication Studies*, 10 (1959): 25–30.
[142] Cole, *Middle Classes*, 21. Cole was here turning a quote from John Bright against Bright himself.

himself as the champion of the (very affluently defined, in his sociology) "Middle Classes." To Cole, the reformed Parliament, rightly understood, was anything but the middle-class triumph which its Whig patrons advertised it as being: "the necessity of recognising the more important members of [the Middle Classes] as a definite political body or class, and of assigning to them a distinct political existence, continues to be disregarded by our leading Statesmen."[143] It was in order to remedy this state of neglect toward the country's most important class that Cole felt compelled to develop a "scientific" assessment for a "new distribution of political power" that would avoid either maintaining the unsatisfactory status quo or bringing about "the political extinction of the Middle Classes" which he predicted, in Tocquevillian–Bagehotian fashion, would ultimately follow any further uniform reduction in the property qualification.[144] His purpose was not, he stressed, to forge "such predominance of the Middle Classes over any other as to render class legislation possible." Rather, through the strategy of cordoning off a "first division" for them in the major cities, he sought to ensure to the "intelligent Middle Classes," a substantial band of MPs who "would represent their opinions, protect their interests, and give to them a direct and practical influence in the legislation of the country." Although it guaranteed a solid swathe of working-class MPs – outstripping the proportion of representatives from this class in the legislatures of many democracies today – the true target of this parliamentary affirmative action was not the lower orders but their betters, who rightly demanded a security that they "would not be swamped." For Cole, the class-specific constituency was an instrument not so much for empowering the working class as for insulating the middle class, for protecting those above from those below. It also had the advantage, he added, of being "open and direct" in its "methods."[145] Class-exclusivity was an instrument for delivering the good of meaningful middle-class representation in as fair and transparent a manner as possible.[146]

---

[143] Cole, *Middle Classes*, 7. To drive home this message about Whig shortcomings with respect to the political position of the middle class, Cole chose a quote from Macaulay on "that brave, honest, and sound-hearted class" as his epigraph; ibid., title page.

[144] Ibid., 19, 22, 72–3. He quoted *Democracy in America* to the effect that "when a nation begins to meddle with the electoral qualification, it may easily be foreseen that, sooner or later, it will happen that that qualification will be *entirely abolished.*"

[145] Ibid., 67, 55–6, 28. Importantly for our analysis later, Cole's foil for the openness and directness of his program was the "complicated puzzling method propounded by Mr. Hare" – that is, proportional representation.

[146] Cole's vision of class-specific constituencies as a prophylactic for upper-class influence is provocative in light of the recent zeal for class-based institutions in "populist" political theory; e.g. John McCormick, *Machiavellian Democracy* (Cambridge, 2011).

Comparing Cole's self-understanding as a promoter of a more robust and independent middle-class parliamentary presence with two figures from the previous subsection – Greg and Eardley-Wilmot – is further confirmation of the intractability of variety-of-suffragist schemes to neat left–right classification. Cole shared with Greg a strong conviction of the social preeminence and, hence, rightful political leadership of the middle class. Yet this shared conviction produced disparate institutional preferences, since Greg believed that the Reform Act had succeeded in establishing the deserved parliamentary hegemony of the middle classes, while Cole thought that 1832 had fallen short of "a fitting recognition of their real political importance."[147] Though each conceived of himself as an advocate of the same social group, Greg's contentment with the current structure led him to put forth little more than minor tweaks to the status quo in his reform writings, whereas Cole's discontent caused him to accept fundamental alterations to the traditional British electoral system.

In comparing Cole and Greg, then, we find institutional misalignment where we would have expected, from their common allegiance to the middle-class cause, to find alignment. However, in comparing Cole with another Tory, Eardley-Wilmot, we find a different sort of mismatch. Eardley-Wilmot, as noted earlier, took his project to be a vindication of working-class claims, a vindication meant to reflect the greater weight which working-class interests and opinions now objectively bore after decades of progress. Cole, on the other hand, was staunch in characterizing his plan as a pro-middle-class intervention. And yet there was a strong argument that of the two proposals Cole's was the more supportive of the working class. Recall that Bagehot thought the proper standard for measuring the degree to which a scheme improved the standing of the working classes was the number of *seats* rather than the number of *voters* it created – on its own the vote was a "useless" mirage "unless you give them some members [of the Commons] also."[148] According to Bagehot's rubric, Cole's plan would likely have been more parliamentarily empowering of the lower classes than Eardley-Wilmot's less concentrated, more "uniform Enfranchisement" program.[149] (It is hard to say for sure since Eardley-Wilmot, unlike most of his fellows, provided no estimate of the number of seats he meant to put "absolutely at their disposal."[150] Yet it is probable that on his plan the number of working-class seats would register below Cole's figure, since he boasted that on his scheme not only were the counties

---

[147] Cole, *Middle Classes*, 11.   [148] Bagehot, "Present Aspects," 257.
[149] Eardley-Wilmot, *Constitutional Plan*, 32.   [150] Bagehot, "'True Liberalism' and Reform," 358.

intended to "represent[] the element of property," but "property" would retain "its just and legitimate influence" even in all the boroughs.[151]) It is typical of the open and unsettled character of mid-Victorian political thought that a writer such as Cole, who ceaselessly lamented the political maltreatment of the "men who give the City its real importance,"[152] wound up a solider friend of the working class than those whose rhetoric more vigorously trumpeted the parliamentary claims of labor.

c   Radical Revisionism

The selective lowering of Bagehot and the targeted class specificity of Cole did not exhaust the efforts in favor of electoral variegation. A final camp was even bolder and more creative in departing from the status quo anchored in a set of territorially bounded counties and boroughs. These thinkers were as committed to the principle of the variegated suffrage as any of the foregoing figures, and often as invested in showing the compatibility of their schemes with the venerable lineage in English politics of the non-uniform franchise. And yet they applied this principle in radical and revisionist ways.

This subsection discusses four such radical revisionists. Unsurprisingly, given the foregoing analysis, the combination of fidelity to the principles of the variety of suffrages with openness to profoundly remodeling the electoral-parliamentary framework was not limited to any one corner of the ideological field. As a result, the quartet examined here includes two establishment spokesmen, a conventional Whig and conventional Tory; a working-class radical; and an unclassifiable eccentric. We begin with the latter.

i   George Harris and Universal but Unequal Enfranchisement

In 1857 George Harris, a lawyer and legal reformer, collector and cataloger of old manuscripts, and writer on all manner of subjects, published an essay with the grand title *The True Theory of Representation in a State*.[153] Though Harris was a protégé of the great Whig statesman and Lord Chancellor

---

[151] Eardley-Wilmot, *Constitutional Plan*, 12, 8.   [152] Cole, *Middle Classes*, 39.

[153] Harris, *The True Theory of Representation in a State* (London, 1857). He had earlier published a very different pamphlet under the same name (London, 1852). All references to *The True Theory* will be to the 1857 edition, the subtitle of which epitomizes the Victorian descriptive theory and the pluralistic sociological outlook that undergirded it: *or, The Leading Interests of the Nation, Not the Mere Predominance of Numbers, Proved to Be Its Basis*. On Harris personally, see E. I. Carlyle, "Harris, George (1809–1890)," rev. Catherine Pease-Watkin, *ODNB*.

Henry Brougham, he identified with the Tories throughout his life.[154] Yet the *True Theory* was hardly a text typical of either of England's great parties, even if Harris was confident that it could speak to the leading men of both.[155] Harris's essay is a strange document for its time. It is full of scholastic jargon and elaborate corporeal metaphors for the polity reminiscent of an earlier age, and its prose is difficult even for a philosophical treatise that promised to go to the "first principles of political government, and of parliamentary representation."[156]

Harris's tract was atypical not just stylistically, but substantively as well. In contrast to the general philosophical tenor of the period, which was resoundingly (if not very rigorously) consequentialist,[157] Harris operated in an explicitly combinatory framework, attempting to marry claims of "natural right" – of "an undoubted and inalienable right" to vote – with the utilitarian modes of thought dominant in these decades.[158] Harris was one of the rare authors (another was John Stuart Mill[159]) before the rise of the democratic Idealist tradition who would have agreed that "the enfranchisement of the people was an end in itself."[160] Harris stood outside the mainstream political culture in taking the vote to be a natural entitlement of (male) citizens.

Yet for Harris as for Mill these ideas contained only part of the truth. Where Mill went on to clarify that from an equal right to vote it did not

---

[154] Harris, *The Autobiography of George Harris, LL.D., F.S.A.* (London, 1888).

[155] Harris, *True Theory*, vi–vii.

[156] Ibid., viii. The historian W. L. Burn called it – uncharitably, but understandably – a "pseudo-philosophical and far from lucid work"; Burn, "The Fancy Franchises," *PA*, 8 (1954), 243.

[157] E.g. the observation of the era's greatest Catholic critic of liberalism that the "deep thinkers of the day" had rejected the thought that there were "certain Rights of man"; John Henry Newman, *A Letter Addressed to His Grace the Duke of Norfolk, on Occasion of Mr. Gladstone's Recent Expostulation* (London, 1875), 75–6. Stuart Warner's description of James Fitzjames Stephen's basic normative outlook can be applied to the default Victorian philosophical ambience: "Stephen's utilitarianism was not the technical, philosophical doctrine that one finds represented in Bentham or presented in Henry Sidgwick's *The Methods of Ethics*. Rather, it was a certain disposition of mind that expressed itself by privileging observation and facts over abstract reason"; Warner, "Foreword," to J. F. Stephen, *Liberty, Equality, Fraternity*, ed. Warner (Indianapolis, 1993), x.

[158] Harris, *True Theory*, 58, 20.

[159] Mill likewise declared, contra the views of Bagehot and others, that it was "a personal injustice to withhold from anyone … the ordinary privilege of having his voice reckoned in the disposal of affairs"; Mill, *Considerations*, 469.

[160] T. H. Green, "Parliamentary Reform," Speech of 25 February 1868, in *The Collected Works of T. H. Green*, ed. Peter Nicholson, 5 vols. (Bristol, 1997), vol. 5, 234. Despite their common association with natural rights discourse, there has always been a strain of interpretation – which read Chartists as valuing political rights purely as instrumental to economic ends – according to which not even Chartism would have fit the bill of conceiving electoral participation as *une fin en soi*; see e.g. Élie Halévy, *Histoire du socialisme européen* (Paris, 2006), 58–9.

follow that there was a right to an equal number of votes, and that therefore plural voting violated no fundamental norms of political equality,[161] Harris accompanied his egalitarian proclamations with the clarification that a natural right to the suffrage did not entail that constituencies be constructed in a sociologically undifferentiated manner.[162] The half-truths of "the numerical or democratic theory" were, instead, to be subordinated to the exigencies of making "the representative body in a State" "an epitome or abridgment of whole civil body or community" that could "fairly reflect or shadow forth the form or outline of it." The parliamentary image which a democratic suffrage would produce would be distorted and partial, because the uniformity of its electoral regulations was out of sync with the diversity that characterized the "general and leading interests of the state." Consequently, the endeavor to design representative institutions was to be guided by principles which were distinct from and which superseded the egalitarian implications of a freestanding subscription to natural rights. These principles which were to regulate institutional design came in the form of "four distinct axioms":

> 1. That all the essential and real interests of the State ought to be represented in its legislative assembly. 2. That they ought all to be directly represented there. 3. That each ought to be represented in due proportion to its relative importance. 4. That they ought so to be represented that, as much as possible, they may all harmonise together.[163]

Thus, for all of his rhetorical and philosophical heterodoxy, at the end of the day the core Whig tenets of descriptive representation won out in Harris's vision of Parliament. It is a testament to the gravitational pull of the theory in this era that even a quasi-scholastic, half-natural-rights theorist would nevertheless give a quite orthodox list of mirroring standards for the construction of national assemblies.

The a priorist egalitarian strand of Harris's thought was not, as we will see later in this section, mere hollow verbiage. But it was not on the terrain of natural rights that the action of his book took place. For the natural-rights strain dictated simply that as many people be enfranchised as possible. But how was this mass enfranchisement to be accomplished in

---

[161] Mill, *Considerations*, ch. 8.

[162] Modern democratic theory remains split on this question of whether sociological undifferentiation is demanded by the value of political equality. For a negative answer, see Charles Beitz, *Political Equality: An Essay in Democratic Theory* (Princeton, 1989), chs. 6–7; for an affirmative one, see Jonathan Still, "Political Equality and Election Systems," *Ethics*, 91 (1981): 375–94.

[163] Harris, *True Theory*, 18, 23–4, 9, 21.

such a way that distortion and partiality were prevented from afflicting the image of society created in the assembly?

Harris's answer was simple: by undoing 1832. In contradistinction to several of the other variety-of-suffragists who pushed for another measure of reform on the grounds that the uniformizing tendency of the First Reform Act was harmful *and* that recent developments in society had caused its sociological accuracy to deteriorate, Harris was completely uninterested in the latter of these reasons. In another interesting departure from the norms of his period, no narratives of historical progress enter into his thinking. The evils of 1832 did not require a subtle grasp of recent social history to be understood.

On Harris's evaluation, the Reform Act was such a bad piece of legislation that it pulled off the difficult feat of possessing seemingly contradictory deficiencies. On the one hand, by diminishing the extent of differentiation in the franchise, it had proceeded implicitly on the principle that "numbers" alone were to be "taken into consideration in the establishment of this system."[164] And yet, because the government that passed Reform had lacked the courage of its democratic convictions, the Act imposed censitary requirements that left vital components of British life out of the system altogether: "freemen, and those who were distinguished by the uneuphonious title of 'pot-wallopers,' and as 'scot-and-lot' voters, were all engulphed together in the merciless abyss of this tremendous measure."[165] The entire "popular element" had been swept aside.[166]

Hence, the result of 1832 was a wholly "defective representation."[167] In the aftermath of this legislative folly, the task facing the architect of

---

[164] Ibid., 43.

[165] Ibid., 18. "Scot and lot" and "potwalloper" were varieties of franchise which had obtained in "democratic" districts; Porritt, *The Unreformed House of Commons*, 4.

[166] Ibid., 19. This is not to say that Harris thought property qualifications were simply oligarchic; he allowed that there was some sense to the older idea that a minimal property requirement could *enhance* popular representation. The argument for the populist interpretation of censitary thresholds went as follows: (a) meeting the property threshold was a sign of independence; (b) dependent citizens were corruptible; (c) corruption rendered the assembly unrepresentative of public opinion. Hence, it was possible to defend property restrictions "not from any jealousy of the people partaking too largely in the representation, but in order to prevent the legitimate influence of the people being unduly swayed by those who are possessed of wealth and power," although Harris himself dissented from this view; ibid., 20. Such arguments that extending the suffrage too far merely increased corruption and the rule of money were far from peculiar to Harris; e.g. Bagehot, "How to Amend the Reform Bill," 88–9. For this defense of property restrictions in the American context, see Alex Keyssar, *The Right to Vote: The Contested History of Democracy in the United States* (New York, 2000), 10, 22, 322.

[167] Ibid., 42. For Harris there was another reason, supplementing this sociological inaccuracy, to reject the censitary baseline for the suffrage. This was that it sent an overly materialist message about the nation's values; it promoted "the money-loving spirit of the age"; ibid., 18. The Christian Socialist

parliamentary reconstruction was to restore the principle of electoral variety to its former preeminence and to apply it such that the legislature would "correspond with ... the different interests of the State."[168] A more accurate mirror of society through finely targeted electoral diversity: this was the lesson of the *True Theory*.

For all his eccentricities, when Harris set out to provide this mirror he followed the method of institutional construction implicit in the variety-of-suffrages theory with a notable scrupulosity. As noted earlier, if the accurate reflection of interests and communities was the basis of a representative assembly's legitimacy, it followed that an account of what those groups were had to precede and guide any attempt at institutional design, even if this account was left unstated in a particular text. Harris obliged explicitly, carrying out an exercise in sociology before setting forth his own proposal. Interestingly, and contrasting with the bulk of his differentiated-suffrage comrades (although not with Bagehot), Harris confessed the challenging character of the sociological enterprise: the "definition and adjustment of these different ... interests," the inquiry "into the nature and relative importance of the different great interests of the State," was hardly self-evident – it was "a task of considerable difficulty, and may admit of very wide discussion."[169] His prose may have been opaque, but he practiced the mirror theory conscientiously and was transparent about its difficulties.

Harris's admission that answers to the sociological question were disputable may well have been in response to incredulity at his own notion of the makeup of the nation, for he offered a distinctive reading of the constitutive elements of British society. In keeping with his unusual indifference toward social-historical change, his sociology was a kind of deduction of the a priori necessary characteristics that inhered in the concept of a society; as he explained in the sociological portion of the book, he was striving to illuminate how "*every political body* is ... as extensively and as essentially influenced by different interests, as it is constituted of different individuals." From this murky deductive process Harris emerged with a sixfold classification of the interests for which

---

Frederick Denison Maurice lodged an identical critique against the reformed Parliament's property requirements for "mak[ing] money the standard of worth, the characteristic glory of the citizen"; Maurice, *The Workman and the Franchise* (London, 1866), ix. See also Holyoake's linkage of the Reform Act's property requirements with "that worship of materialism and property which is attaining a deplorable prevalence in England, so destructive of the finer qualities of man"; Holyoake, *The Workman and the Suffrage* (London, 1859), 8.

[168] Harris, *True Theory*, 59.   [169] Ibid., 22–5.

representation had to be secured: "I. Virtue. II. Intelligence. III. Order. IV. Property. V. Professional. VI. Popular."[170] Here, it is possible only to sketch the categories as presented in the *True Theory*, which contains in-depth explorations of each. By *virtue*, Harris meant those sectors of society and stations of life that were particularly associated with "religion and morality" and the "principle of rectitude," chief among which were the clergy, which Harris came close to envisioning as an estate of the realm in the manner of an *ancien régime*.[171] This "interest" was to a marginal degree already satisfied by "the presence of the bishops in the House of Lords," but since the upper house had ceased to play an important role in legislation it was imperative to find a point of entry for them into the Commons.[172] By *intelligence*, Harris hoped for the expansion of the university constituencies into a "distinct and independent separate representation" of "learned bodies" and groups of highly educated citizens. The third category, *order*, was the least readily comprehensible: in the abstract it comprehended all those social avenues through which the values of "law," "justice," and "allegiance" were realized, though in the concrete he seems mostly to have been concerned to maintain the large number of "lawyers" in the House. The final triumvirate of *property*, *professional*, and *popular* referred to more familiar demographic groups – with the latter, which he also titled "the people generally, more especially . . . the poor," constituting as "essential [a] branch of the community" as any other.[173] Such was the confusing medley of pieces which made up (British?) society on Harris's reckoning, and which it was the obligation of the designer of a representative system to convey accurately into the assembly.

Before outlining the institutions which he believed were dictated by this analysis, it is worth making a final observation about the sociological side of his theory. Counter to most of his variety-of-suffrages cohort, Harris distinguished between the mirroring required to create a satisfactory assembly and a complete mirror that would reflect every aspect of social reality. For Harris, the parliamentary mirror was a necessarily selective one.

---

[170] Ibid., 24–5 (my italics). It is worth noting the parallels between Harris's hypostasis of norms and attributes into real social entities such as to extend the realm of what it was possible to represent and the expansive view of representation which Pierre Rosanvallon supports and theorizes today; Rosanvallon, *La légitimité démocratique: Impartialité, réflexivité, proximité* (Paris, 2008).

[171] Harris, *True Theory*, 25, 27. Compare Harris's understanding of the clergy with that depicted in Robert Lord, "The Parliaments of the Middle Ages and the Early Modern Period," *Catholic Historical Review*, 16 (1930): 125–44.

[172] Harris, *True Theory*, 25, 27.

[173] Ibid., 28–31, 35–6. He employed, as was his wont, a corporeal metaphor for clarification: "the people are to a State what the body and the vital functions are to a man, the care of which . . . it is absolutely essential should obtain a due share of attention"; ibid., 36.

For one thing, a line had to be drawn between the "real and true interests [which] should be represented" and those "influences," such as "anarchy and corruption," which, however great their effect on society, were to be kept out due to their harmfulness.[174] He illustrated the point about the selectivity of descriptive representation with the example of "thieves and pickpockets" who, despite being "a very numerous, a most intelligent, and a particularly industrious body of men," had never been made the subject of a "formal complaint ... to Parliament that they are not adequately represented there" – even though, he continued cheekily, "if they were so represented, great ameliorations in our criminal code might through their aid be effected."[175]

The requisite discriminations for the composition of the representative body were not limited simply to guarding against the inclusion of obviously pernicious social factors. Within the class of "true and real" interests a division had to be made between those the nature of which was to participate in the representative system and those which "require no representatives"; he gave, as instances of the latter group, the "judicial, and naval, and military interests of the nation."[176] He did not, however, set forth criteria for separating these two groups of real interests – one might call them the *representation-necessitating* and *representation-excluding* interests[177] – assuming, it seems, that the matter would be obvious to readers.

Harris, to be clear, did not regard these selections as controversial; he was not granting that there existed a space of indeterminacy or reasonable disagreement about which aspects of society were deleterious or unworthy of inclusion in Parliament and which were positive and merited it. He thought he was merely making the commonsensical (though often elided) point that representative government did not entail the reproduction *simpliciter* of society; representativeness did not mean indiscriminateness or comprehensiveness in imaging society. But in conceding that the

---

[174] Ibid., 37. Jane Mansbridge similarly accepts the need for normative selectivity in descriptive representation today, and Melissa Williams emphasizes the need for "a set of defensible standards by which to distinguish those attributes of citizens which deserve representation from those which do not" (although she understands providing such standards as correcting or transcending descriptive representation rather than being a constituent feature of it). Williams, *Voice, Trust, and Memory: Marginalized Groups and the Failings of Liberal Representation* (Princeton, 1998), ch. 1; Mansbridge, "Should Blacks Represent Blacks and Women Represent Women? A Contingent 'Yes,'" *JP*, 61 (1999), 634.

[175] Harris, *True Theory*, 14.   [176] Ibid., 38.

[177] A similar set of discriminations were involved in the more "populist" version of descriptive representation championed by the American antifederalists; Bernard Manin, *The Principles of Representative Government* (Cambridge, 1997), 111–12.

sociological work entailed by the theory of the differentiated franchise inevitably involved a layer of judgment, a screening process about what and what not to include that was not reducible to simply reading off the collection of elements that in toto constituted the nation, Harris came closer than his fellow variety-of-suffragists to acknowledging that the sociological component of their projects was not a neutral accounting of social facts.

What was the institutional result of this process of sociological deduction, classification, and discrimination? By a path not easily retraced, he arrived at a fourfold division of types of seats: (1) "learned, professional, and commercial corporate bodies"; (2) "property voters"; (3) "professional voters"; (4) "personal voters." Each of these divisions was to receive 150 members, and each was to be voted for only by those in the relevant identity group. The composition of the second and third kinds of constituencies should be clear. The fourth consisted of all those (literate) men who were not enfranchised under one of the preceding headings; it corresponded to the "popular interest." Here, Harris's extremely expansive suffrage – "universal," in the parlance of the era, extending to all adult men contingent only on a demonstration of literacy without (as Mill stipulated) a further requirement not to receive public financial assistance – was a dramatic display that what many mirrorers objected to in the democratic formula of "uniform universal suffrage" was not so much the second adjective as the first. The affirmation of (something approaching) universal suffrage could be a component of variety-of-suffragist schemes so long as differentiation in voting regulations and construction of constituencies was preserved. The first and least clear category was a collection of bodies – ranging from universities to the Bank of England, from the East India Company to the London Stock Exchange, from mining companies to canal companies – to which anywhere from one to a half-dozen seats were granted and for which "membership, proprietorship, or annual subscription" conferred the vote.[178]

This plan was obviously a radical modification of the then-current arrangements. It incorporated class-specific constituencies[179] in a more far-reaching way even than the schemes examined in the previous subsection. Where the latter envisaged a twofold division in a subset of urban boroughs, Harris advocated a tripartite division (categories 2–4) for "every

---

[178] Ibid., 61–3.
[179] This term is appropriate to Harris only if we keep in mind the broad notion of class operative in Mackintosh; in keeping with the antiquated bent of Harris's mind, he did not really think in terms of the modern socioeconomic category of class.

town and county constituency." Further, he promoted a vast expansion of
nonterritorial membership-based constituencies which, as mentioned earlier, existed in the reformed system only in the form of seats for the
Universities of Cambridge, Oxford, and Dublin. Harris was striking out
far from the normal parliamentary path. And yet the inspiration for this
revisionism – the end to which all of these unconventional means were
directed – was perfectly orthodox: "that every class may be independently
represented, and that no one class may overwhelm the interests of the
others" and "virtually disfranchise" them.[180]

Several other features of Harris's plan deserve mention. First, it reduced
the size of the Commons from 658 to 600 members. Second, this reduction, as well as the carving out of seats for corporate bodies, was to be
effected at the expense of the small boroughs. As with Pochin in the
previous section, Harris did not lament the passing of the small boroughs,
for he attributed to them no special sociological value; "represent[ing] no
particular interest," they could be jettisoned without any harm.[181]

Third, the plan involved plural voting. Plural voting in the *True Theory*
did not take the more familiar form of weighted voting – that is, graduating
the number of votes that an elector possessed within a single constituency
according to the amount of property owned (as the future Tory Prime
Minister Lord Salisbury, then Lord Robert Cecil, was urging[182]) or the
degree of education attained (as in Mill's version of plural voting). Instead,
plural voting took place on Harris's scheme insofar as the citizen could
exercise *one* vote in *each* constituency for which he qualified for the
suffrage.[183] Importantly, a version of this nonweighted genre of plural
voting was already the law of the land in the Victorian era – owners of
property could vote in both their place of residence and the place in which
their property lay, and university alumni could vote both for their university seats and in the appropriate territorial constituencies.[184]

The most important observation to make about Harris's version of
plural voting is that it was *not* an exception to the sociological representativeness which oriented his theory. Consequently, when a wealthy
Edinburgh doctor who had bought land was permitted to vote for the

---

[180] Ibid., 57, 63.   [181] Ibid., 60.

[182] Salisbury, "The House of Commons," in *Lord Salisbury on Politics, A Selection of His Articles in the Quarterly Review, 1860–1883*, ed. Paul Smith (Cambridge, 1972), 185.

[183] Ibid., 60.

[184] Like the university vote, this latter form of plural voting – the so-called "business vote" in multiple constituencies – persisted in England until 1948. See e.g. Porritt, "Barriers Against Democracy in the British Electoral System," *PSQ*, 26 (1911): 1–31; Neal Blewett, "The Franchise in the United Kingdom: 1885–1918," *Past & Present*, no. 32 (1965): 27–56.

seats belonging to his university, the college of surgeons in the city, and the professional and property constituencies in his borough, while the Manchester working man was enfranchised only for the popular constituency in which he lived, this discrepancy was not meant to register the former's moral-intellectual superiority or even his greater economic "stake" in the body politic. Rather, the Edinburgh doctor's greater number of votes was meant to reflect the greater multifariousness of his social participation; since the more variegated person, so to speak, partook of a broader swathe of the manifold interests that constituted society, a mirroring suffrage could not but enfranchise him many times over.[185] Plural voting was therefore an ineluctable byproduct of the consistent implementation of the electoral mechanisms of mirroring. Such, at least, was Harris's interpretation of what he was doing: every provision of his plan was dedicated to producing an assembly "not only more fair for the various great interests of the State, but ... more liberal" and better able "to secure an efficient representation of the mass of the people, than any which has been either devised or demanded."[186]

The sociological-descriptive valence of Harris's program of plural voting as the multiplicity of single votes across several constituencies can be clarified by taking a short detour to consider two contending contemporaneous endorsements of plural voting: those of John Stuart Mill and James Lorimer. For Mill, plural voting was not a downstream result of fidelity to the goal of representativeness; a "graduated suffrage" based on education was, rather, a good in itself, an expression of fundamental values which it would it be "in principle wrong" for the representative system to ignore. Weighted electoral power was a matter of respecting the truth "that every one is entitled to some influence, but the better and wiser to more than others"; not to graduate the suffrage was to countenance the "false creed" that "any one man ... is as good as any other."[187] To Mill, the normative source of plural voting issued was quite other than that of representativeness and descriptive accuracy; it came from a moral elitism that was distinct from the mapping of interests which Harris thought relevant to the design of representative institutions.[188] Mill's educated citizen was not granted extra weight in respect of his participation in multiple interests or

---

[185] One can envision this practice as the political equivalent of the college professor with appointments in multiple faculties of the university and voting rights in each.

[186] Harris, *True Theory*, 64.   [187] Mill, *Considerations*, 478–9.

[188] Mill's rationale for plural voting, while not guided by it, did admit sociological-Whiggish content as a limiting condition. The distribution of the weights of votes "must on no account be carried so far, that those who are privileged by it, or the class (if any) to which they mainly belong, shall

communities, but because of his greater worthiness. For Harris, but not for Mill, social realities, and not elitist lessons, were the only subject matter of the representative system.

A different conception of plural voting appeared in the remarkable program elaborated by James Lorimer in a series of works from 1857–65. The Scotsman Lorimer was a jurist, who in the 1870s–80s became one of Europe's leading theorists of a natural-law approach to international law.[189] But in the earlier period relevant here he was keenly enough involved in the debates about parliamentary reform to be connected with our other two theorists of plural voting: a correspondent and admirer of Mill, he was also happy to acknowledge an affinity with Harris's *True Theory*.[190] Laid out in works with such expressive titles as *Political Progress Not Necessarily Democratic* and *Constitutionalism of the Future, or Parliament the Mirror of the Nation*, Lorimer's theory of plural voting was poised between Harris's and Mill's: in its means it resembled Mill's, although in its meaning or ends it was closer to Harris's.

Lorimer's proposal shared two features with Mill's. First, the mode of plurality was a single weighted suffrage, rather than – as with Harris and the existent electoral regime – the possession of a multiplicity of individual votes across several constituencies.[191] Secondly, his theory was explicitly elitist in its intent and in its underlying judgments about different categories of citizens; Lorimer spoke the language of "capacity" and of personal "inequality" which was more central to the *Considerations on Representative Government* than to the *True Theory*.[192] Like both Mill and Harris, he

---

outweigh by means of it all the rest of the community"; ibid., 476. It is therefore a bit misleading to identify the protection of pluralism and avoidance of majority tyranny as the motivation for plural voting; Mill makes clear that it is proportional representation that serves these ends, whereas plural voting's primary purpose is to impress a lesson of respect for greater knowledge and intellect. Compare Urbinati, *Mill on Democracy* (Chicago, 2002), 77–8 and Thompson, *John Stuart Mill and Representative Government* (Princeton, 1976), 100.

[189] John Cairns, "Lorimer, James (1818–1890)," *ODNB*.

[190] Lorimer, a Conservative himself, went so far as to identify Mill as a "philosophical Conservative," and he dedicated *Constitutional of the Future* to him: Lorimer, "Mr. Mill on Representative Government," *NBR*, 35 (1861): 534, 544; *Constitutionalism of the Future, or Parliament the Mirror of the Nation* (Edinburgh, 1865), v. For his appreciation of Harris, see Lorimer, *Political Progress Not Necessarily Democratic: or Relative Equality the True Foundation of Liberty* (Edinburgh, 1857), 253.

[191] Lorimer, *Constitutionalism*, ch. 7; *Political Progress*, chs. 14–16.

[192] He aimed to achieve "recognition of the principle of inequality within the franchise," to calibrate the suffrage according to "other influences, powers, and capacities, besides mere numbers"; *Constitutionalism*, 100–1, 69. Unlike Mill, the devout Lorimer understood inequality as fundamentally an ordination of providence.

accepted the "radical" insight that exclusion from the franchise except on grounds of disqualifying conduct was ipso facto an injustice,[193] and he wished to extend the suffrage to all men while avoiding the fate of despotism by the "numerical majority."[194] Despite these points shared with Mill, though, Lorimer united with Harris against Mill in tracing the ultimate normative basis for plural voting back to *mirroring social diversity*. Where Mill rejected gradation of the suffrage derived from any criterion but education on the grounds that any other basis for the calibration of electoral weight was morally unjustifiable,[195] Lorimer held that *all* forms of "social power" had to be attributed proper weight in structuring the suffrage lest Parliament fail in its sole task, which was "simply to *represent* society as it exists."[196] The aim of a system of representation, he held, was not to isolate good from bad forms of difference among citizens so that justice, conceived as a sort of Aristotelian proportional equality, might be achieved by rewarding just superiorities with public power. It was simply to translate accurately the manifold divisions, inequalities, and diversities among the citizenry into the Commons: "a perfect representative system would be one which, so to speak, photographed society – the function of the suffrage corresponding to that of the camera."[197] Accordingly, Lorimer laid out a plan in which many different characteristics and affiliations of citizens would correspond to different degrees of voting strength.[198]

To Lorimer, then, Mill had made a kind of category mistake. Rather than recognizing that education was merely "*a* ground of political power" among the many of which an "organic" electoral system would have to take account, Mill had actually abandoned the terrain of representation altogether.[199] Because Mill recommended greater voting weight solely for those differences between citizens which he himself judged normatively salient and which suited his moral sympathies, "in

---

[193] Ibid., 105

[194] Lorimer, "Mill on Representative Government," 546, 551; *Constitutionalism*, 119. As with Mackintosh and others, Lorimer rejected reforms which would "convert the constitution into an oligarchy, which would be very far from representing our existing society"; *Constitutionalism*, 144.

[195] Mill, *Considerations*, 473–5.   [196] Lorimer, "Mill on Representative Government," 557.

[197] Ibid., 122–3. The advances in photography over the course of the Victorian era are worth bearing in mind in considering the metaphors about representation quoted throughout this volume; Jennifer Tucker. *Nature Exposed: Photography as Eyewitness in Victorian Science* (Baltimore, 2005).

[198] "Not intelligence only, but property, and many positions in society, are unquestionable elements of social weight"; *Constitutionalism*, 123, also 155, 164–73. He listed citizenship, age, political experience, property, education, and profession as other factors which had to be factored into electoral regulation.

[199] Lorimer, *Constitutionalism*, 129, 164.

place of devising a scheme to represent, he has devised one to reconstruct society."[200] In contrast, Lorimer saw himself as upholding the "strictly representative character of the suffrage" against the likes of "Mr. Mill" who attempted to exploit the regulation of the franchise to advance their own theory of the good (what Lorimer called a "standard of rectitude"), instead of accepting that it was inappropriate to build into a representative system discriminations between "the good and the evil" in society.[201]

To sum up our detour: Mill did not adopt the plural vote as a mechanism for mirroring;[202] instead, he endorsed proportional representation to fulfill this desideratum. He embraced plural voting as a way of inculcating lessons about the *correct* grounds for discriminating between the political worth of different persons. Notwithstanding the differences in their schemes, neither Lorimer nor Harris took up plural voting for this Millian reason. For them both, plural voting followed from the lone "function" of parliamentary reform: to "give expression to the powers of the community *as they exist*," to "express the whole influences of the community."[203]

The primacy of mirroring in Harris's electoral architecture related to a final crucial feature of his theory – namely, that of all the interests into which Harris dissected society it was the "poor" or "popular" element which he believed was most benefited by his scheme. Under the unrepresentative structures of the Reform Act no group was "suffer[ing] more than the one comprehended in Class VI"; a principal motivation of Harris's intervention was to bring about a reversal of their fortunes. From no voice at all in Parliament, he wished to lift them to occupancy of a quarter of the seats – an "influence" which was sufficiently "extensive" to reflect their sociological significance, and which would give them "fair sway" in the House. He was so confident in the robustness of the popular component of his plan that he predicted that it would put an end to democratic agitation: "all sincere radicals, all the advocates for universal suffrage and for the general extension of the franchise" would be satisfied by such a large and "fair" transfer of power to the lower class. (It would, naturally, also satisfy the "Conservative Party" since it would "ensure the fair representation of intelligence, and property, and the higher influences of the State." The *True Theory* was, hence, the path to national reconciliation.) Harris

---

[200] Lorimer, "Mill on Representative Government," 560–1.
[201] *Constitutionalism*, 114, 109–10. Here, though, Lorimer appears less intellectually frank than Harris, who had confessed to an element of selectivity in his theory: after all, Lorimer made no attempt to give extra weight to pickpockets' votes either.
[202] Mill, "Recent Writers on Reform," 356–7.   [203] Lorimer, *Constitutionalism*, 109, 119.

thought his program was one of popular liberation – not liberation, of course, for Class VI to become a "despot" or to usurp "the only influence" in Parliament, for no class was entitled to such standing.[204] But liberated, nevertheless, in what was to him the only sense that accorded with *representative* government – that is, enabled as a community to participate independently and with due weight in the forum of national legislation.

ii   Other Radical Recommendations

Harris perceived a kinship between his proposal and an earlier essay by one Augustus Stapleton. In fact, for reasons which we will discuss in Chapter 2, the connection between their ideas was imperfect, and Stapleton fits a little uneasily with the other authors in this chapter. Harris, however, welcomed Stapleton's work which, even if it did not fully conform to proper "first principles," helped to reinforce "practical" convictions in favor of his kind of descriptivist scheme.[205]

Stapleton's *Suggestions for a Conservative and Popular Reform* exceeded the self-declared "conservative" entries in the variegated-suffrage catalog which we have examined so far in the vociferousness with which it announced its allegiance to the Tory party. In his youth Stapleton had served as private secretary to Tory Prime Minister George Canning, and he was devoted to propagating the Tory cause.[206] On the subject of reform, his rhetorical strategy hung largely on outflanking the Whigs and revealing them as betrayers of their own values of variety and representativeness. With the opposition discredited, political space would open for the Tories to step in with their own sociologically rich project of reform. The *Suggestions* thus advanced in two stages: 1) an assault on the Whigs; 2) the exposition of a suitable Tory alternative.

Stapleton's attack centered on the 1832 Reform Act, of which he had an even lower opinion than Harris. He condemned the Reform Act for the diminution of Parliament's representativeness through the elimination of "the direct representation of the poor." For Stapleton, 1832 was an exercise in Whig hypocrisy: he contrasted the Whig philosophy that the Commons should mirror the nation with the impairment of the representation of the "various classes and different interests which make up this entire nation" caused by the standardizing law which they had passed.[207] As with Harris,

---

[204] Harris, *True Theory*, 42, 37–8, 97, 54.   [205] Ibid., viii.

[206] W. P. Courtney, "Stapleton, Augustus Granville (1800/01–1880)," rev. John Wolffe, *ODNB*.

[207] Augustus Granville Stapleton, *Suggestions for a Conservative and Popular Reform* (London, 1850), 46, 35–6. He presented the Whig, pro-diversity point of view through a series of quotations from Russell.

Stapleton traced the uniformization effected by Reform to the tacit "demo-cratick" acceptance that the "numerical majority" was the sole foundation for parliamentary legitimacy, and he explained the imposition of the censitary requirement as a failure of courage on the part of the Reformers. The reality of the Reform Act was that only property over a certain value had a voice in government; its principle, on the other hand, was that only the "mere will" of the majority, rather than the full extent of the nation's diversity, had a claim to be present in the assembly.[208] And these two adverse notions, which only a law as flawed as the Reform Act could manage to combine, were equally far from the truth about Parliament.

After having dispatched the legacy of 1832, Stapleton delivered his own prescriptions for reform. Two are of significance here. First, under the rather capacious heading of "the learning and education of the country," he assigned fifty-eight seats directly to a series of corporate bodies (many of which would reappear in Harris's more creative list) ranging from the Inns of Court to retired military servicemen to the clergy of both established and dissenting churches.[209] These seats were to be made available through the consolidation of small boroughs which, in contrast to these bodies, could make no claims to possessing particular knowledge or interests. Stapleton was thereby executing a transfer of seats away from territorial constituencies – territory, again, was being downgraded in favor of another method of sorting, and providing seats for, relevant groups.

Second, Stapleton made provision for the re-entry of "the poor man" within the pale of the constitution. In order that "the poor should have some persons chosen by themselves to explain their sentiments and state their grievances to the legislature," he suggested that twenty-six seats be regulated on the inclusive "Scot and Lot" franchise, with one seat being allocated to each of twenty-six geographical divisions based on the dioceses of the Anglican Church.[210] This was a smaller number than Harris granted his "popular element," and it was even lower than the more modest totals of the plans which sought working-class enfranchisement within major urban boroughs alone. But, despite the smaller sum, Stapleton shared with Harris the aspiration to achieve a truly *national* representation of the poor, as opposed to the liberal projects that sought the enfranchisement of the "advanced," urban segments of the working class alone.

Though less empowering of them in terms of its effect on the House's membership, Stapleton's plan was more *inclusive* of the whole of the

---

[208] Ibid., 37.   [209] Ibid., 41–6.   [210] Ibid., 47.

working classes than most of the selective-tailoring or urban class-specific schemes surveyed earlier. Hence, within the variety-of-suffrages literature we encounter a version of the paradox noted above whereby the First Reform Act widened the electorate while also increasing its exclusiveness: Stapleton's proposal bestowed the vote on many more individual citizens from these classes than a figure like Bagehot's more targeted selection, but it gave fewer seats to the lower classes than his competitors'.

Almost the diametric political opposite of Stapleton was a third radical revisionist: Henry George Grey, the Third Earl Grey. While Stapleton was a Tory spokesman, Grey was a leader of mid-century Whiggery, one of the party's most prominent politicians and most prolific publicists.[211] Befitting his paternity – he was the son of the prime minister who had passed the Reform Act – Grey's reformism was not tinged with sourness toward 1832. He stepped onto the terrain of parliamentary reform not to repudiate 1832 but to carry on its "wisdom."[212]

Continuing in the spirit of 1832 did not mean leaving its measures uncriticized. Remarkably, given the identity of his father, Grey voiced the dissatisfaction with the homogenizing aspects of the Reform Act so common in this generation. It was

> an error in the Reform Act . . . that it gave the whole Representation of the country to constituencies which were everywhere so much of the same character. The former distinction, with respect to the nature of the Franchise between Counties and Boroughs, was indeed kept up, but the great diversity which had prevailed in the right of voting in different Boroughs was almost entirely done away with; and in spite of some reservation of vested rights, the £10 householders were made everywhere the masters of the town representation. It has been argued, and I think with justice, that though there were obvious and decisive objections to the capricious manner in which the Franchise varied in different Boroughs under the old constitution of the House of Commons, this arrangement, with all its faults, had yet the advantage of giving a better representation to some classes of society than they now enjoy.

Like Greg, Grey saw the Reform Act as fundamentally a work of electoral compression. By its provisions the political influence of both the poor and

---

[211] He was one of the "three most prominent contemporary writers" on representation in the buildup to the Second Reform Act; K. Theodore Hoppen, *The Mid-Victorian Generation* (Oxford, 1998), 238. According to Hoppen, the other two were Mill and Thomas Hare.

[212] Grey, *Parliamentary Government, Considered with Reference to Reform*, second edition (London, 1864), 97.

"the higher class of the town population" had been reduced.[213] But where Greg celebrated this diminution of the representation of the socioeconomic extremes, judging it to stem from a just recognition of the preeminence of the middle class above the other segments of British society, Grey lamented that this compression had gone too far. As a result the country was now perilously close to being ruled by one class alone:

> Under the Reform Act, the £10 householders are everywhere masters of the Borough elections, and thus the middle class to which they belong is invested not with a preponderance (which it is admitted it ought to have), but with a monopoly of political power, to the injury of the working class on the one side, and of the highest class of the town population on the other.[214]

The light of subsequent experience had made clear that, accompanying its great successes (such as counteracting corruption), the Reform Act had damaged the Commons qua mirror of society. The second act of the reform movement would therefore need to incorporate variegation into the electoral structure in order to repair its machinery for descriptiveness and inclusiveness.

The difficulty was that, in Grey's eyes, there was no possibility of reviving the variety of suffrages in anything resembling its old form. The haphazard character of the unreformed assortment of borough suffrages had been acceptable when it was revered as an organic growth, a heritage passed down through centuries of success in constitutional government. But to *impose*, through parliamentary legislation, distinctions without differences – to pass new laws granting the vote, as Bagehot and others were advocating, to the "artisan in Manchester" while withholding it from the identical "artisan in Macclesfield" – would not be tolerated in mid-century Britain.[215] In short, Bagehot and those like him were correct in *retrospectively* placing a high value on the unreformed variegated franchise, but they were wrong in *prospectively* recommending it as the next

---

[213] Ibid., 117–18. *Pace* Greg, for whom the traditional landed aristocracy was the group at the top that had been most diminished politically, Grey did not express much consternation about the reduction of its influence. The object of Grey's concern in this passage seems more likely to have coincided with what Mill meant by the "most intellectual persons of the kingdom" who lived in these cities.

[214] Ibid., 118. Also 206: "The changes made by the Reform Act, and especially the abolition of the various rights of voting formerly to be found in different towns, and the establishment of one uniform Franchise in all the English boroughs ... tended somewhat to impair the character of the House" with regard to "representing most of the different classes of society, and of the various and conflicting opinions and interests to be found in the Nation."

[215] Bagehot, "Parliamentary Reform," 223.

stage of reform.[216] What was needed in this more modern, more rationalized political environment was a way for the diverse elements of society to gain access to Parliament without instituting a new set of *locally* varied suffrages.

How was one to achieve a sociologically satisfactory inclusion of the salient divisions in society without recourse to a mode of suffrage that had become an anachronism? Grey articulated more the intimations of a plan than an actionable scheme.[217] Yet the general thrust was clear: the local constituency needed to be supplemented with other units of representation. "The present facilities of communication," he urged, could be utilized to enable "men united together not by living in one place, but by engaging in some common pursuit" to vote for "a common Representative."[218] This transcendence of territoriality as the grounding for the distribution of seats would allow for representatives elected exclusively by specific "classes" and "industries."[219] Grey did not go into detail regarding the allocation of seats to particular classes, professions, and sectors of the economy, but three aspects of his sketch stand out.[220] First, much like Harris, he emphasized that the most important beneficiary of these quotas would be "working men."[221] Second, there was an openness to his call for profession-based representation that even the zeal of Harris to catalogue and integrate existing corporate bodies did not rival: Grey seems to have envisioned that even professions which had not already developed civil society associations should be organized for the purpose of sending a member to

---

[216] "The fact that the former variety in the rights of voting did, at least to a certain degree, answer the purpose described, cannot be denied, but it would scarcely be practicable in the present state of society to return to the system of allowing such arbitrary differences to exist between different places"; Grey, *Parliamentary Government*, 214. Grey was here applying to the topic of the suffrage the familiar idea in nineteenth-century political thought that variety, however salutary, was extremely fragile when confronted with the standardizing tendencies of modern reformism. Constant gave a characteristic statement of it: although "the freest country in our world, Great Britain, is governed by very diversified laws," it was unfortunately true that "this variety could hardly serve as a model" for theorizing or designing institutions from scratch; Benjamin Constant, *Principles of Politics Applicable to All Representative Governments*, in *Political Writings*, ed. Biancamaria Fontana (Cambridge, 1988), 155.

[217] James Winter, "The Cave of Adullam and Parliamentary Reform," *EHR*, 81 (1966), 50.

[218] Grey, *Parliamentary Government*, 214. The idea that "modern technologies of communication and locomotion" should be understood as having eliminated "physical proximity" as a proper basis for constituency construction is still heard by radical reformers today; e.g. Thomas Pogge, "Self-Constituting Constituencies to Enhance Freedom, Equality, and Participation in Democratic Procedures," *Theoria*, no. 99 (2002), 43.

[219] Grey, *Parliamentary Government*, 213–14.

[220] In addition to the three highlighted here, he also favored the more conventional proposition of expanding university representation; ibid., 209–13.

[221] Ibid., 213.

Parliament.[222] Third, in contrast to the other authors discussed so far, he empowered the Commons to hold internal elections. These intra-Commons elections were for two groups of members: (a) twelve to fifteen life-tenured members of special eminence or expertise;[223] and (b) a supplement of a "limited number of Members" that would enable the party in government to hold a more stable majority.[224]

Summing up Grey's place in this tradition is not a straightforward task.[225] On the one hand, he is almost an emblem of the theory of the differentiated suffrage. His endorsement of it as a leader of mid-Victorian Whiggery and the son of the second Earl testifies to its main-stream appeal in the period, and his willingness to embrace creative innovations of the electoral fabric evinces the resources for creativity in institutional thinking inherent in the theory. For Grey, the variety of suffrages was as eternal a first principle as it was adaptable in its applica-tions to particular political contexts. On the other hand, he endorsed reforms that accorded uneasily with the tradition: the third of the proposals considered in the previous paragraph, as will emerge in Chapter 2, stood in tension with core normative values of the theory. Additionally, he flirted with a form of minority representation, the cumulative vote, which (as Chapter 4 will show) took him into terrain foreign to that of the differentiated suffrage.

The ambiguous philosophical position underlying Grey's relationship to the variety-of-suffrages school did not trouble G. J. Holyoake. Socially and temperamentally, Holyoake was about as far from Grey as was possi-ble: he was an atheist who had been jailed for blasphemy;[226] a working-class socialist of the cooperative stripe who began his activist life as

---

[222] "I am not aware of any reason why those who have worked in certain trades for a given time should not be registered and formed into a corporate body with the right of electing Members of the House of Commons"; ibid., 213. Grey's work in particular reveals the continuity between the more radical version of the English mirror theory and the continental tradition of corporatist representation; see Anthony Black, *Guild and State: European Political Thought from the Twelfth Century to the Present* (New Brunswick, 2003), part 3.

[223] Ibid., 217–19.

[224] Grey, *Parliamentary Government*, 217–19, 229–35. Similar measures – known as the "Majority Bonus System" – have been used in Italy, among other countries; Roberto D'Alimonte, "The New Italian Electoral System: Majority-Assuring but Minority-Friendly," *Contemporary Italian Politics*, 7 (2015): 286–92.

[225] E.g. Gavin Coull's oscillation between treating Grey's reform plans as indicating his partisan impartiality or as fundamentally an exercise in Whiggery; Coull, "The Third Earl Grey, the Coming of Democracy, and Parliamentary Reform, 1865–67," *Durham University Journal*, 87 (1995): 11, 15, 192.

[226] E.g. Holyoake, *The Last Trial for Atheism in England: A Fragment of Autobiography*, fourth edition (London, 1871).

a heterodox disciple of Robert Owen;[227] and, most strikingly of all, a former Chartist campaigner.[228] Despite a biography antipodal to that of a Whig aristocrat, Holyoake cited Grey as an exemplary writer on reform.[229] The alignment of Holyoake and Grey illustrates pointedly the diffusion of this vision of representation, corroborating the complaint of the young jurist and democratic sympathizer Albert Venn Dicey that "this view is entertained by persons who disagree in everything else."[230]

Holyoake was more rhetorically and conceptually eclectic than the orthodox Whig. For example, Holyoake followed Mill, whom he lionized as a champion of working-class presence in the Commons, in his occasional willingness to invoke the language of democracy.[231] And like Harris, Holyoake was comfortable appealing to notions of abstract right; in keeping with his Chartist background, he decried the withholding of the franchise as the violation of "a moral right" and equated the condition of the "non-elector" with that of "the slave."[232] Also in step with Harris, however, was the fact that his heterodox pronouncements did not issue in substantive dissent about the foundations and composition of Parliament. Quite the contrary; he agreed with the likes of Bagehot in condemning simple electoral democracy as that old "Radical rut." While Holyoake did not himself predict any great ills from the working-class hegemony that would come from immediately lowering the suffrage, he felt that an "absolute guarantee" had to be given against the newly enfranchised groups "swamping" the other elements in society. He was adamant that it was no moral gain at all to effect a mere swap of class power, to put "the educated and wealthy classes" into the "position" of "sufferance" which had traditionally belonged to those below them in the social hierarchy. On the contrary, the only just mode of settling the reform question was a suitable system of "qualified franchise." As a model, Holyoake enthusiastically held up "Earl Grey's

---

[227] A conviction that culminated in his landmark *History of Co-operation in England: Its Literature and Its Advocates*, 2 vols. (London, 1875–79).

[228] Malcolm Chase, *Chartism: A New History* (Manchester, 2007), 91.

[229] Holyoake, *The Liberal Situation* (London, 1865), *passim*.

[230] Dicey, "The Balance of Classes," 67. Holyoake himself noted the oddity that he would speak in support of "an Earl," yet the latter was "the chief politician who has seriously proposed to obviate the difficulty and discredit of partial representation"; *Liberal Situation*, 7. Holyoake's enthusiasm for Grey's writing was part of a growing post-Chartist skepticism about democracy within the working classes, in part as a result of the cautionary tale of Louis Napoleon in France; e.g. Biagini, *Liberty, Retrenchment, and Reform*, ch. 4.

[231] E.g. Holyoake, *Working-Class Representation: Its Conditions and Consequences* (Birmingham and London, 1868), 2.

[232] Holyoake, *The Workman and the Suffrage*, 10; *Liberal Situation*, 5.

scheme, so far as relates to the establishment of Guilds" as a mechanism to "enable Labour to be heard in its own name in the House of Commons" and to give "some representation to their own feelings, interests, and ideas" that did not risk an "absolute transfer of power" that would wrongfully put all other groups at the mercy of the laboring element. Thus, on the "franchise question" there was little daylight between the radicalism of the activist for working-class emancipation and the radicalism of the Whig patrician.[233]

Harris, Stapleton, Grey, Holyoake – thinkers of conflicting temperaments and allegiances all drawn to a traditional theory, counterintuitively, for the sake of the radical potential intrinsic to it for reimagining the sites and scope of representation. Fulfilling the promise of a mirroring Commons and maintaining fidelity to the precept of differentiation in the suffrage did not mean timidity in confronting the nation's greatest institutional question.

3   The Decline of the Variety of Suffrages

For all its vibrancy in its mid-Victorian heyday, by the end of the century the variegated-suffrage vision appeared to be a practical failure. Its active political force deteriorated in the face of the diversity-reducing and "democratizing" Second and especially Third Reform Acts, the latter of which established a uniform and expansive (though not quite universal) suffrage and equal electoral districts;[234] its philosophical cogency diminished as the egalitarian-democratic Idealist school made incursions against the more utilitarian and experiential outlook to which the variety of suffrages had been largely yoked;[235] and it gradually lost the theoretical and activist steam behind "mirroring" to the PR movement.

Yet the theory did not suddenly evaporate; amidst a slew of uncompelling appearances[236] it would receive a vigorous *fin-de-siècle* statement. This came from the Anglo-Irish historian and philosopher W. E. H. Lecky. In his magisterial *Democracy and Liberty* Lecky expressed the Mackintoshian outlook with about as much fidelity as is imaginable after the passage of eight transformative decades. It is a testament to the tenacious appeal of this theory that it could be defended a few short years shy of the twentieth

---

[233] Holyoake, *Liberal Situation*, 32, 1–3, 7, 11.
[234] E.g. Chris Cook, *The Routledge Companion to Britain in the Nineteenth Century, 1815–1914* (London, 2005), 56–64.
[235] David Boucher, "Introduction," to *The British Idealists*, ed. Boucher (Cambridge, 1997).
[236] E.g. Andrew Jones, *The Politics of Reform, 1884* (Cambridge, 1972), 3, 27, 110–1.

century by a sitting Liberal-Unionist MP (as Lecky was) as the best possible institutionalization of liberal values.

Lecky's political thought was more nuanced than the reactionary paternalism traditionally attributed to him.[237] He was, for instance, an advocate of the referendum, a firm critic of "plutocracy," and a sympathizer with many aspects of trade-unionism.[238] But these "modern" sympathies did not dampen his disaffection with one prominent feature of turn-of-the-century politics: the uniform democratic suffrage. In its place, he advocated a modified version of the "old system of representation" whereby, through "a diversity in the system of election," it was possible to "represent, and to represent in their due proportions, the various forms and tendencies existing in the nation."[239] The advent of electoral democracy had accustomed Britain to a condition "much less truly representative" than under the older arrangements, which instantiated the recognition that the true purpose of legislative assemblies was "to represent with the same completeness and proportion the various and often conflicting class interests, so that the wants of each class might be attended to and the grievances of each class might be heard and redressed."[240]

Not only did Lecky bring history to bear in support of his preferred vision of representation; he also set up as a predictor of future trends: he prognosticated a return to the old model once Britons had come to realize that "democracy destroys the balance of opinions, interests, and classes on which constitutional liberty mainly depends."[241] As a timeless truth, the mirror theory, thought Lecky, would outlive electoral democracy, which was neither the endpoint of political history nor the last word on the theory of representative institutions. Were he to observe our ongoing "crisis of democratic representation,"[242] he would feel at home in the thought that it remains unclear what institutions await liberal societies in the coming decades. Indeed, Lecky's warnings raise the

---

[237] E.g. B. E. Lippincott, *Victorian Critics of Democracy* (Minneapolis, 1938), ch. 7.

[238] Lecky, *Democracy and Liberty*, 2 vols. (London, 1896), vol. 1, 288–9, 393–6; vol. 2, 468.

[239] Ibid., vol. 1, 12, 2. The "old system," he noted, rightly stressed that the element of "property" needed to be "specially and strongly represented."

[240] Lecky, *Introduction to Democracy and Liberty* (London, 1899), vii; *Democracy and Liberty*, vol. 1, 12. Rather than "reflect[ing] faithfully in its variety and due proportion the opinions, the interests, and the intelligence of the community," democracy "impaired the representative character of Parliament, by submerging or swamping the varieties of genuine opinion by great uniform masses of ignorant and influenced voters"; *Democracy and Liberty*, vol. 1, 25, 21.

[241] Lecky, *Democracy and Liberty*, vol. 1, 256–7, also 264, 276.

[242] E.g. *The Crisis of Representation in Europe*, ed. Jack Hayward (London, 1996); Pierre Rosanvallon, *Counter-Democracy: Politics in an Age of Distrust* (Cambridge, 2008).

question of whether the strong push in recent years for mechanisms of more robust representation of the diversity of social groups is best understood as an effort to deepen democracy, or rather as an attempt to rehabilitate and adapt ideas and techniques of representation other than democratic ones.

CHAPTER 2

Diversity without Democracy: The Theory of the Variety of Suffrages

Part Two: Values and Criticisms

Having examined the sociological and institutional dimensions of the variety-of-suffrages paradigm, this chapter inquires more deeply into the values which underpinned it. Why did the diverse, inclusive, mirroring Commons strike so many mid-Victorians as a cardinal political good?

First, a preliminary observation about the relationship between this chapter and the previous one is in order. The level of values was less divided than the level of schemes. While institutional plans varied widely, a relatively stable set of values underpinned endorsement of the variety of suffrages. Although there was a great deal of consistency in the articulation of these values across the spectrum of our authors, certain authors gave greater weight to some values over others – and some authors' presentations of the normative side of their schemes exposed strains and fissures in the connections between these values. In the course of presenting the ends and ideals which coalesced in the theory of the variety of suffrages, I will also explore these tensions and the criticisms to which they gave rise.

Four values formed the normative core of support for the variegated franchise: justice, the rule of public opinion, deliberation, and stability. Each of these will be examined in turn.

I Justice

The first of these values, justice, was the least clearly articulated of the four. Appeals to it were made, but usually in an undertheorized manner; it seldom received a fully fledged argument demonstrating its connection to their preferred electoral system. This peculiarity of the variety-of-suffragists' treatment of justice seems to have derived from trepidations about the relationship between claims of justice and the consequentialism (relatively loose and undogmatic as it was) that dominated the public-intellectual landscape of the time. The allergy to natural-rights argumentation that marked the bulk of these authors extended to the discourse of justice, which likewise seemed to push in the direction of an individualistic egalitarianism that, if accepted, would ultimately usher in a democratic franchise.[1] With only a few exceptions, the authors in this chapter were not philosophers, and they lacked the philosophical interest or acumen that led Mill to demonstrate that, despite the ordinary-language distinction between justice and expediency, justice could feature coherently in moral-political discourse without positing its "existence in Nature as something absolute."[2] As a result, their propensity was to speak of the mirroring Commons more as a source of benefits than as a site of justice.

Nevertheless, an implicit conception of justice – and occasionally even explicit invocations[3] – underlay the imperativeness characteristic of the variety-of-suffragists' advocacy. In particular, the moral gravity with which they imbued their frequent pronouncements that carrying an accurate image of the nation into the Commons *just was* what made the British government representative bespeaks a conviction that representativeness as they understood it was not simply one among a number of commensurate political goods which, in the complicated conditions of modern politics, had to be traded off against one another. By and large, proponents of the differentiated suffrage sought, without officially questioning a basic con-sequentialist framework, to lift their mirroring, differentiated suffrage above the process of "weighing and balancing" multifarious "considera-tions" and instead to treat it as an absolute good in itself.[4] This belief in the lexical priority of representativeness vis-à-vis other qualities of the Commons shines through *inter alia loca* in Bagehot's claim that, even if the course of policy being pursued were excellent, "the House of Commons will be defective" so long as "the single, unbending franchise introduced in 1832" persisted in excluding the urban working class.[5]

[1] The heart of the "the democratic theory" was "its supposed conformity with the abstract rights of man"; Bagehot, "Parliamentary Reform," 202. On Whigs' utilitarianism and aversion to abstract principle more generally, see Biancamaria Fontana, *Rethinking the Politics of Commercial Society: The Edinburgh Review 1802–1832* (Cambridge, 1985), 43. Of the figures discussed in this chapter, Lecky alone articulated a conceptually serious dissent from philosophical consequentialism; Lecky, *The History of European Morals from Augustus to Charlemagne*, 2 vols. (London, 1876), vol. 1, 34–54.

[2] Mill, *Utilitarianism*, in *CW*, vol. 10, 240. Witness, for example, the ham-handedness with which even one of the most philosophically acute members of the school, Bagehot, strove to demonstrate the unfoundedness of "the sense of unfairness" engendered in some readers by his project of enfranchis-ing a laborer in one location but not in another. He could do little more than assert feebly that "there is no injustice in allowing expediency to adjust the claims of persons similarly entitled" – which was the very issue under debate. "Parliamentary Reform," 224.

[3] As when Cole portrayed his scheme, in contrast to the "sham" that was the "present system," as "founded on reason and justice"; *Middle Classes*, 40.

[4] George Herbert, "Liberty and Socialism," reprinted in *Herbert Spencer and the Limits of the State*, ed. Michael Taylor (Bristol, 1996), 107.

[5] Bagehot, *English Constitution*, 315.

Whether we consider their reflections as having contained a theory of justice proper or not, the critical point is that adherents to the tradition of electoral variety ascribed an independent normative weight to the inclusion of the full range of important classes, views, and segments of society, a weight not clearly reducible to any utility calculus. Unlike an orthodox Benthamite such as James Fitzjames Stephen, who would launch a blistering attack on Mill for distinguishing between the categories of "wrong in itself" on the one hand and "hindrances to human improvement" on the other,[6] even such an unsteady subscriber to the mirror theory as W. R. Greg could describe the parliamentary marginalization of the working class as not only a "defect" but an "injustice."[7] This was not justice in the democratic sense of electoral equality, but it was what we might term "justice as inclusivity." An inclusive constitution ("the fair participation of *all* classes in the representation and the government") was of the very essence of representative government – it was what separated it, as we have encountered time and again, from democracy (the rule "of numbers") and oligarchy (the rule "of property").[8] These rival regimes were less just because they did not carve out space in the state's representative bodies for the several groups which constituted the nation. While the vast majority of the authors surveyed here disagreed that it was (as Mill put it) "a personal injustice" to be denied the vote, this disagreement was not equivalent to a denial that the misdistribution of the suffrage could constitute an injustice. But the locus of the injustice shifted between the Millian and the variety-of-suffragist mind: from the nonpossession of the suffrage to the lack of a spokesman with whose social-ideological position one could identify. Citizens had no claim of justice to possess an equal vote, but they did have a claim of justice to be ruled by an assembly of the right sort – that is, a mirroring assembly.[9]

---

[6] J. F. Stephen, *Liberty, Equality, Fraternity*, 129.   [7] Greg, "Parliamentary Purification," 567.

[8] Greg, "Representative Reform [2]," 257; "Parliamentary Purification," 567.

[9] E.g. the way in which John Stuart Mill, just shy of his twentieth birthday and still every inch the Benthamite radical, expressed the Mackintoshian theory against which he was arguing: "It is alleged, then, first, that if the right men get into the House of Commons, it is of very little consequence how they come there ... The second [argument] is, that to form a representative assembly, it is not necessary that the representatives should be chosen upon any uniform plan: it is sufficient if every interest has its representatives in the house ... and it is added that there is not a shade of opinion, not a variety of political sentiment, which does not find advocates in the House of Commons, which is quite sufficient for the ends of good government" (Speech on the British Constitution [1], May 1826, in *CW*, vol. 26, 363). A similar genre of argument to that made by variety-of-suffragist thinkers that concern for the descriptive and deliberative features of the Commons trumped "individualist" claims about equal enfranchisement occurs today in defenses of judicial review against "democratic" attacks. In each case, the right to live under a government of a certain kind or quality takes precedence over the claims of individuals to any particular kind of (electoral) participation or exercise of power.

The significance of this freestanding normative investment in socio-logical inclusivity can be grasped more clearly when contrasted with another prominent nineteenth-century theory of representative govern-ment, one in which elitist notions of political capacity triumphed over descriptive aspirations. In the decades leading up to the climax of the variety of suffrages in Britain, across the Channel the historian-statesman François Guizot and his *doctrinaire* school combated the idea that the representative system properly conceived had anything to do with imaging or reflecting the underlying society.[10] The *doctrinaire* notion of "political capacity" was opposite to variety-of-suffragist descriptiveness: it was designed to screen all but men of "reason, truth, and justice" out of the electoral process.[11] As prime minister in the latter days of the July Monarchy, Guizot adamantly rejected any extension of the limited fran-chise of that regime – a franchise so restricted that, although Guizot consecrated his political career to the cause of middle-class government, the censitary requirement was actually too high for most of the bourgeoisie to participate.[12] Guizot maintained that, even in an era in which "the representative form of government" was the centerpiece of "the political institutions of Europe," the electoral domain belonged uniquely to the elite of the capable.[13]

Compare variety-of-suffragism with Ronald Dworkin, *Freedom's Law* (Oxford, 1996), 30: "there is no necessary connection between a citizen's political impact or influence and the ethical benefit he secures through participating in public discussion or deliberation. The quality of the discussion might be better, and his own contribution more genuinely deliberative and public spirited, in a general public debate preceding or following a judicial decision than in a political battle culminating in a legislative vote or even a referendum."

[10] This point has been made by Pierre Rosanvallon: "there is nothing to 'represent,' in the etymological meaning of the term, for Guizot"; *Le Moment Guizot* (Paris, 1985), 93–4. The judgment that Guizot had emptied representation of any meaning substantially corresponded with Tocqueville's blistering contemporaneous critique of the July Monarchy as a system in which only a narrow slice of the bourgeoisie had any voice; Tocqueville, *Souvenirs* (Paris, 1999), 13–14.

[11] François Guizot, *The History of the Origins of Representative Government in Europe*, trans. Andrew R. Scoble (Indianapolis, 2002), 295, 334. On this Guizotian doctrine and its relationship to his principle of "the sovereignty of reason," see Aurelian Craiutu, "Guizot's Elitist Theory of Representative Government," *Critical Review*, 15 (2003): 261–84.

[12] Only roughly 200,000 Frenchmen, out of a total population of 35,000,000, could meet the property requirement for the franchise; Alistair Cole and Peter Campbell, *French Electoral Systems and Elections since 1789* (Aldershot, 1989), ch. 3.

[13] Guizot, *History of Representative Government*, 12. Guizot's original conception of capacity had been more capacious, comprising a series of what in the English reform context would be known as "fancy franchises" in order to include those "capacities" in the plural which were not necessarily linked to property, although this equation of capacity with property was too dominant in French liberalism for such a view of "*capacités variables*" to have gained traction practically, and Guizot wound up settling for a strictly property-based signification of capacity without compunction; Rosanvallon, "Guizot et la question du suffrage universel au XIXe siècle," in *François Guizot et la culture politique*

Guizot was not a popular figure with this group of British authors. His unpopularity was overdetermined; other reasons for their disfavor will be discussed in Section 4. But it was anchored primarily in the contrast between the kinds of opinions for which the *doctrinaires* and the variety-of-suffragists believed there ought to be spokesmen in the assembly. Whereas Guizot wanted only objectively wise and reasonable ones to be entertained in the Chamber of Deputies, to British descriptivists nonjudg-mentalism about the "truth" or "reasonableness" of views held in the electorate was dictated by the commitment to representativeness.[14] As Cole put it, in a striking display of the anti-Guizotian sensibility manifested by variety-of-suffragists, "the Working Classes and the little shopkeepers connected with them, should have members of their own in Parliament, to represent and explain their wishes and opinions, and make their dumb voice articulate" whether "their grievances [were] real or imaginary."[15] Similarly for Bernard Cracroft, the grounds for "introduc-[ing] a distinct working class element into the House, in order to represent working class thought and feeling *there*," were unrelated to the character of their beliefs but hinged solely on their being "the third great interest in the country" alongside "land and commerce."[16] Unlike its British counterpart, the "Chamber of Deputies," as the maverick Whig politician Lord Brougham had written during the July Monarchy, was not a "real organ of the opinions of the country. The qualification for voters . . . deprives the mass of the people of any share in the choice of the national representatives . . . . The Chamber, at present, is not representative of the nation. It is not in harmony with great masses of the people. Its members are emphatically delegates of the *Bourgeoisie*" alone.[17]

This disagreement with the *doctrinaires* emerges with particular clarity in Bagehot's writings. Bagehot demanded that "all opinions," regardless of their content, which were "extensively entertained" and "widely diffused" find entry into Parliament. Electoral systems were not meant as techniques for confining the political process solely to correct views – ones that could

---

de son temps, ed. Marina Valensie (Paris, 1991): 129–46; Kahan, *Liberalism in Nineteenth-Century Europe*, 35–45. Guizot's more pluralistic approach to institutionalizing capacity shared a certain family resemblance to the variety-of-suffragists whose sociologies were more heavily inflected by idioms of capacity, such as Stapleton and Greg, though most were uncomfortable with too close a link with "fancy franchise" proposals; see e.g. Cole, *Middle Classes*, 33.

[14] Bagehot, "The Withdrawal of the Reform Bill," 333: "the views and the feelings – if you like the errors and the prejudices – of the working classes should be heard in Parliament."

[15] Cole, *Middle Classes*, 23. [16] Cracroft, "The Reform Session of 1866," 47–8.

[17] Brougham, "France," *The British and Foreign Review*, 1 (1835): 503–4. And see Roger Soltau, *French Political Thought in the Nineteenth Century* (New Haven, 1931), 61.

in Guizotian fashion be recognized from some higher perspective as reasonable and true.[18] The legislature, Bagehot underscored, had to contain "the sentiments, the interests, the opinions, the *prejudices*, the wants, of all classes of the nation."[19] Bagehot's elevation of the value of inclusiveness stemmed in turn from a foundational feature of his political theory, which was that the proper arbiter of the performance of a "parliamentary government" could only be the public opinion of the nation:

> Who is to judge [whether parliament is doing well]? Is it to be some panel of philosophers, some fancied posterity, or some other outside authority? I answer, no philosophy, no posterity, no external authority, but the English nation here and now.
>
> Free government is self-government – a government of the people by the people.[20]

Although few of his fellow variety-of-suffragists traced their institutional preferences back to the foundations of political epistemology in this way, they were united in holding that concern for the fortunes of a favored agenda or the desire to secure the field for correct tenets could not be allowed to trump the representative dimension of political life.

(Unsurprisingly, these authors did not always live up to their theory. In particular, they could blanch in the face of socialism, and the fear of some of these writers that a politically empowered "people" were sure to embark on a program of expropriation kept them from complete consistency in their descriptivist commitments.[21] Nevertheless, while most variety-of-suffragists adhered to some version of classical-liberal political economy, the terror at impending socialism was for many of them constrained in comparison to those political writers most resistant to mirroring

---

[18] Lorimer agreed wholeheartedly. He identified "the error ... which pervades ... the whole of M. Guizot's eloquent book on the history of representative government" as being his incorrect notion of the suffrage as a means for "testing the absolute justice of claims, or estimating their value" instead of as a "device ... simply for giving a true and accurate political expression to them as they exist." In other words, Guizot mistook representation for an "ought" system rather than an "is" one; *Political Progress*, 222.

[19] Bagehot, "Parliamentary Reform," 195 (my italics).

[20] Bagehot, *English Constitution*, 306. Bagehot, of course, did not have a democratic interpretation of the meaning of that last phrase; in fact, he thought that the "American form of government" was "in every true sense less popular" than the English; "The Present Crisis in America," in *CW*, vol. 6, 175. Holyoake, similarly, contrasted a regime of "Qualified Suffrage" as an institutionalization of the value of self-government with the sort of "paternal theory" of aristocratic domination held by Victorian patricians; Holyoake, *Liberal Situation*, 31–3.

[21] E.g. Greg, "Representative Reform [1]," 466; Eardley-Wilmot, *Safe Plan*, 8; Donald Winch, "The Cause of Good Government," in Stefan Collini, Donald Winch, and John Burrow, *That Noble Science of Politics* (Cambridge, 1983), 103 (on Macaulay).

values, such as Lord Salisbury, John Austin, Robert Lowe, and Henry Maine.[22] Especially in the 1850s–60s, liberal antidemocrats could commonly be found denying that their opposition to democracy was grounded in fears of its inherently socialist propensities. During these years, the bitter opposition to the "Red Menace" of socialism that underpinned Napoleon III's overwhelming popularity among the French lower classes made difficult any attempt to link democracy and socialism too tightly. France was the only European country, after all, to have equal manhood suffrage at this time. Instead, figures such as Bagehot claimed that what they feared most from a democratic suffrage was the entrenchment of plutocracy and the rule of money.[23])

The rejection by Bagehot and company of the *doctrinaires'* strictly capacitarian conception of electoral politics was, it should be said, partly epistemic in its motivation – as will be shown in Section 3, subscribers to the differentiated franchise were not only *descriptivists* but also *deliberativists*, and as such they ascribed a central role in the process of answering political questions to the national discussion that culminated in the "deliberative House of Commons."[24] Yet it was equally a difference at the level of justice, of what was owed under representative government to the different segments of the community. To hold to a rigid censitary cutoff – to maintain, as Guizot had done, that the "scattered elements of reason" which the Chamber had to "collect and concentrate" were all effectively located within a single rung of the socioeconomic ladder[25] – was to evacuate representative government of any meaning and instead to institute simple class rule.[26] It was to supplant the vision that politics should

---

[22] E.g. Salisbury, *Lord Salisbury on Politics,* e.g. 33, 144, 186, 210; Austin, *A Plea for the Constitution,* second edition (London, 1859), 19–21; Lowe, "Reform Essays," *QR,* 123 (1867): 244–77; Maine, *Popular Government: Four Essays* (London, 1885), 36–7.

[23] E.g. Bagehot, *English Constitution,* 406; "The Lessons of the Plebiscite," and "The Liberals and the Emperor," in *CW,* vol. 4, 143–50.

[24] Bagehot, "Conservative Criticism on Liberal Politics," in *CW,* vol. 6, 321.

[25] Guizot, *History of Representative Government,* 345.

[26] This argument about the betrayal of representative principles involved in excluding a group from the vote out of consideration of its intellectual character or the content of its views was taken up by the women's movement in response to Liberal politicians who cited women's conservatism as a reason to continue their disfranchisement: "Surely representative institutions require that all differences of opinion should have their due and proportionate weight in the legislature. No class of persons ought to be excluded on account of their political opinions ... A representative system which excludes half the community from representation surely is a farce. The question ought not to be 'How will women vote if they have the franchise?' but, 'Is representative government the best form of government that can be devised?' If the answer is in the affirmative, the exclusion of women from electoral rights can in no way be justified"; Millicent Garret Fawcett, "The Electoral Disabilities of Women," in *The Subjection of Women: Contemporary Responses to John Stuart Mill,* ed. Andrew Pyle (Bristol, 1995), 232–3. The essay originally appeared in *FR,* 1870. To put Fawcett's

have a connection to society in its integrity with the a priori selection of a part that should rule over the whole.

The distance between their outlook on representation and the Guizotian-*doctrinaire* one entailed, as these mirroring theorists were willing to admit, giving up on any dream of the Commons as a congress of the nation's wisest individuals. Indeed, they not only allowed that the descriptive enterprise would in practice produce a membership that would deviate from what a process that selected only for wisdom or correctness would yield; they also understood themselves to be abandoning the latter as a theoretical ideal. The variety-of-suffragist school could not agree with the young Salisbury that "the very Utopia of representation" would be simply to jam all the wisest heads into the Commons.[27] To be sure, it is worth reiterating that variety-of-suffragists were far from untouched by elitist presuppositions or concepts of capacity.[28] Yet they generally perceived that the maximization of intellect or right-thinking and the achievement of representativeness stood in tension; in contrast to the PR supporters inspired by Thomas Hare discussed in Chapter 5, they believed that priority had to be given to one over the other. While one does not encounter in this tradition statements equivalent to accepting (what are often given as *reductios* of projects of descriptive representation) that "morons should be represented by morons,"[29] mid-century mirror authors were not afraid to acknowledge that their search for representativeness involved some intellectual sacrifices.[30] Hence, the outcome Bagehot desired from his proposed measures of working-class representation was not "simply to find representatives in the best of the working classes" or to find seats for "the most thrifty and careful of the working classes ... the best judging of their class." Quite the contrary: "we are not now seeking legislators who will exercise a correct judgment, but rather

---

thought here in the vocabulary that has guided this chapter, she saw the gender restriction as instituting *male class rule*, as opposed to representative government. On the uptake of and resistance to the deployment of class-exclusion-based claims by feminists, see Ben Griffin, "Women's Suffrage," in *Languages of Politics in Nineteenth-Century Britain*, ed. David Craig and James Thompson (Houndmills, Basingstoke, 2013): 168–90.

[27] Salisbury (then Lord Cecil), "Theories of Parliamentary Reform," in *Oxford Essays, Contributed by Members of the University* (London, 1858), 56.

[28] E.g. Bagehot, "Parliamentary Reform," 203–4. Even Bagehot was not always clear about the relationship between mirroring and wisdom-maximizing principles for the composition of the Commons, although he was generally forthright about the priority of the former; "Mr. Mill's Address to the Electors of Westminster," in *CW*, vol. 3, 546.

[29] J. Roland Pennock, *Democratic Political Theory* (Princeton, 1979), 314. Also A. Philips Griffiths and Richard Wollheim, "How Can One Person Represent Another?," *Aristotelian Society*, 34 (1960), 190.

[30] E.g. Mackintosh's frank statement that "the best choice" was "not the sole object of representation"; "Universal Suffrage," 191–2.

spokesmen who will express popular sentiments."[31] With a refreshing frankness, Bagehot and company admitted that no institution could guarantee both a desired quotient of diversity and the selection of only the wisest or most deserving members.[32] To advocate the mirroring Commons was to dispense with classical exhortations that "Government should be in the hands of the wisest" in favor of accepting more modest intellectual expectations for Parliament: instead, "all which we ought to desire" was that the Commons should "contain true and adequate exponents of all class interests [and] should coincide in opinion with the fair intelligence of the country."[33] In consequence it is not surprising to find these authors offering the consoling thought that great knowledge and sagacity were not needed to be an MP; one of the central themes in Bagehot's studies of contemporary politics was that English government got on fine even though MPs were merely "excellent specimens of the average Englishman."[34] In making representativeness the first virtue of the just legislature, the variety-of-suffragists were moving away from the purely meritocratic notion of the electoral system as a means of filtering out a chosen body of the wisest citizens, and accepting that the individuals composing it might fall well short of what one would envision as "natural aristocrats."[35]

Viewed in isolation from other values and assumptions, however, the analysis of their notion of justice alone has only so much illumination to offer; the goal of justice, as interpreted here, certainly does not demand the acceptance of the specific institutions which upholders of electoral differentiation promulgated. One question, in particular, has likely occurred to the reader. If inclusivity was important on the grounds of justice, how could the exclusions which existed in some of these schemes – typically that of the rural laborer – be defended?

---

[31] Bagehot, "Parliamentary Reform," 218–9.

[32] Greg articulated the tension with striking clearness: "Parliament may be viewed in two lights . . . It may be conceived either to comprise the *collective wisdom* of the nation, or to represent the *collective opinions and feelings* of the nation." Note well the kicker: "Whichever of these be the true theory – or whether the genuine conception be not a modification of the two – the democratic proposals are equally wide of carrying it out"; "Expected Reform Bill," 248.

[33] Salisbury, "Theories of Reform," 54; Bagehot, "Parliamentary Reform," 200–1.

[34] Bagehot, "The Unseen Work of Parliament," in *CW*, vol. 6, 47; John Burrow, "Sense and Circumstances: Bagehot and the Nature of Political Understanding," in Collini et al., *That Noble Science of Politics*, 178–9.

[35] E.g. *The Federalist*, nos. 10 and 57. On the classically elitist side of elections, see Olivier Christin, *Vox Populi: Une histoire du vote avant le suffrage universel* (Paris, 2014); Manin, *Principles of Representative Government*, passim.

To answer this question, and to begin filling out a normative picture that is left underspecified by justice alone, we need to turn to a second plank of the mirror theory: the rule of public opinion.

2   The Rule of Public Opinion

Attestations of the rightful reign of public opinion abounded in the mid- and late-Victorian periods. A young John Morley, the Liberal writer and future parliamentarian, satirized his countrymen for treating the phrase with a talismanic reverence,[36] but even when writers took issue with the slogan, as did the economist William Stanley Jevons, they frequently wound up acknowledging that nothing could dislodge public opinion from its perch as "the ultimate court of appeal" in British politics.[37] Both the normative investment in the idea that the primary force in politics ought to be public opinion and the impression that public opinion did in fact determine the direction of public affairs were at all-time highs.[38] How did this omnipresent refrain – one incanted as well by those who were anything but diversity-appreciating descriptivists about representation[39] – operate among the variety-of-suffragists?

a   Exclusion and the Opinion-Holding Principle

First, for advocates of the exclusion of certain groups from the suffrage, invocation of the rule of public opinion served to justify those exclusions. This issue brings us face-to-face with a fundamental divide within the camp of electoral diversity: those who believed that the population of rural laborers ought not to possess the suffrage, and those who sought to include them as one among the several basic elements of British society. The omission of rural workers from the reform proposals of the former stemmed, as has been glimpsed heretofore, from the conviction that they lacked substantive opinions about politics. In contrast to the artisans in

---

[36] Morley mocked "the ceaseless panegyrics upon the majesty of public opinion"; Morley, "The Weakness of Public Opinion," in *Modern Characteristics* (London, 1865), 239–40.

[37] Jevons, *The State in Relation to Labour* (London, 1882), 20. Other important testaments of the centrality of public opinion in the Victorian political psyche include Leslie Stephen, "Our Rulers – Public Opinion," *CM*, 21 (1870): 288–98; Dicey, *Lectures on the Relation between Law and Public Opinion in England during the Nineteenth Century* (London, 1905), ch. 1.

[38] Saunders, *Democracy and the Vote*, 7–8, 23, 134.

[39] E.g. the use which Richard Congreve, a leading English apostle of Auguste Comte who had little time for paeans to diversity, made of the concept; Congreve, *Essays Political, Social, and Religious* (London, 1874).

urban centers whom Bagehot sought to include in order that the distinctive sentiments on politics which had developed among them could gain a parliamentary hearing, in the rural and underdeveloped semi-urban areas (as his brother-in-law put it) the "lower classes had no political principles and no social strength or independence"; they displayed an "utter inability to form any political opinion."[40] In light of the opinion-lessness which characterized all of the lower classes except the advanced artisans, democracy in mid-Victorian Britain could only be the rule of those with no opinions over those with opinions. It would effect the transfer of electoral power from "sincere" citizens acting on behalf of genuine "views and feelings" about matters of public concern to "men who have no political convictions and scarcely any personal predilections"; the man "who has no political opinions at all" would now be the most numerous participant in elections.[41] Given that Victorian morality placed great weight on sincerity and earnestness in acting on one's opinions and on a thorough, impartial acquaintance with evidence in forming them, the enactment of a democratic suffrage in conditions of a dearth of lower-class belief would mean a decline in the moral caliber of politics as judged from the perspective of the "ethics of belief."[42]

Even more fundamentally, such an electoral situation impaired the task of representation. This impairment stemmed from the fact that, if the rural working classes were without opinions, then they necessarily did not contribute to that public opinion into alignment with which these reformers sought to bring the Commons. Being without opinions, they ought to be without the vote, because those who "had no opinion on matters of legislation and administration" by definition could not "send to Parliament members" who would represent their views. If the criterion for the possession of "political power" was some kind of "political capacity," this capacity was defined by variety-of-suffragists largely in terms of being "intellectual enough to form opinions."[43] If the limits of the

---

[40] Greg, "The Achievements and the Moral of 1867," *NBR*, 47 (Sept. 1867), 219, 212. And recall the analysis in Chapter 1.

[41] Greg, "Achievements of 1867," 232; "Parliamentary Purification," 577, 583.

[42] Walter Houghton, *The Victorian Frame of Mind* (New Haven, 1957), chs. 10, 14. The ethics of belief was a widespread Victorian concept even before its hallmark appearance in an 1877 essay by the scientist-mathematician W. K. Clifford; Clifford, "The Ethics of Belief," in *The Ethics of Belief and Other Essays*, ed. Timothy Madigan (Amherst, 1999): 70–96.

[43] Bagehot, "History of the Unreformed Parliament," 285, 304. Other versions of the principle of opinion-holding as the baseline for enfranchisement occur at: "The State of Parties," 168; "How to Amend the Reform Bill," 87–8; *English Constitution*, 403. Note the differences from a Guizotian notion of *capacité*.

franchise did not respect this threshold, the result was that elections would introduce distortions of public opinion into the very process of composing a Commons. Public opinion, therefore, would not reign. By lifting a large but opinionless class into a majority in all districts, democratization involved almost by definition a kind of usurpation: instead of public opinion ruling, the composition of parliament would be swayed by votes which had no opinion-content – no truly "political state of mind" – behind them.[44]

For many Mackintoshian mirrorers, however, the case was even more dire than the analysis so far has made out, for this necessary falsification of public opinion by democracy could be exacerbated by one (or a combination) of two deleterious processes.

The first was that money would crowd all other considerations out of politics. With no convictions of their own determining their vote for a certain person or party, Bagehot believed that such opinionless persons were "almost sure to be corrupt" and would give their vote to whichever side offered the largest bribe.[45] Without the stake in politics that the possession of beliefs and principles furnished, there was no reason for them to "abstain from selling their vote," and thus it was illusory to pursue democracy when democracy would only "mean the rule of money."[46] In all probability, a democratic suffrage would yield a corrupt, cynical plutocracy, thereby sacrificing, for the sake of greater formal inclusiveness in the political system, the influence of genuine public opinion on the course of government.[47]

[44] Bagehot, "The Contest in Ireland," in *CW*, vol. 8, 124.
[45] Bagehot, "History of the Unreformed Parliament," 305. Or, in the words of his brother-in-law, "it seems probable that some of our democratic moves may produce effects the very reverse of democratic, opening wider and wider the doors of political life to rank and wealth, especially to hereditary wealth, and closing them more and more to real talent when unsupported by these adventitious aids"; "democracies, just like aristocracies – perhaps more than aristocracies – *have a perpetual, nearly irresistible, tendency to degenerate into oligarchies*"; Greg, *Rocks Ahead, or, The Warnings of Cassandra* (London, 1874), 34. This equation of democracy and the rule of money is connected with the descriptivist case for excluding the poor on corruption grounds mentioned in Chapter 1, and drew on a long lineage of distrust of democracy for its corrupt and plutocratic tendencies; see e.g. Paul Langford, *A Polite and Commercial People* (Oxford, 1992), 154, 718.
[46] Bagehot, *English Constitution*, 403, 406. Three decades later Sidgwick was still following Bagehot exactly on this point; Sidgwick, *Elements of Politics*, second edition (London, 1897), 382–3.
[47] The equation of democracy plus corruption yielding plutocracy was a frequent one; e.g. Harris, *True Theory*, 20; Stapleton, *Suggestions*, 27; Salisbury, "The House of Commons," 174. Mill himself was not immune to such worries; e.g. Speech of 4 April 1864 on Corruption at Elections, in *CW*, vol. 28, 10–11. These "plutocratic" forms of corruption were indeed on the increase until at least the late 1880s; K. Theodore Hoppen, "Roads to Democracy: Electioneering and Corruption in Nineteenth-Century England and Ireland," *History*, 81 (1996): 553–71. There is an interesting resemblance here between the prediction that formal democracy would lead to practical plutocracy and Hobbes's famous denial that in practice a democracy could be anything other than an

If nothing else, though, the thesis of working-class lack of belief would seem to have spared authors such as Bagehot and Greg the prospect of "swamping" which typically frightened the defender of electoral variegation. For in the absence of beliefs, how could the enfranchised masses stand in sufficient unison to expel less populous groups from the representation? A second doleful eventuality squared this circle. Bagehot's prediction, for instance, was that, although the un-advanced working classes lacked any definite ideas or principles to guide their political conduct, they would nevertheless feel themselves "supreme in the country." This feeling of class supremacy would lead them to form a "permanent combination" in order to ensure that the only candidates returned came either from their own class or from that subset of middle- and upper-class politicians who were willing to ape the manners of the working man.[48] On this second scenario, Bagehot was presaging a kind of "identity politics" *avant la lettre*, where the clear perception of interests and the discussion of policy and principle would take a backseat to questions of personality and group membership. The working class, unguided by anything that could properly be called "political sentiments" but spurred on by "demagogues" and exultant at being liberated from having to "acknowledge their superiors," would fill Westminster only with their "single class."[49] On this second prognosis of democratized politics, public opinion would be betrayed not by the outright reign of money, but by the replacement of the idea-possessing, public-opinion-shaping, politically experienced upper and middle classes with the blind majority of the working class. There is a sense, then, in which this second prognosis presented the bleakest depiction of working-class swamping; instead of one set of ideas and convictions crowding out all others, on this forecast a set of feelings and instincts unworthy even of the name of ideas and convictions would displace *all* true ideas and convictions – a bleak potentiality of democracy the realization of which they believed they were witnessing in the rule of the "Crowned Democrat of Europe," Napoleon III, in France's plebiscitary Second Empire.[50] And hence an ideal which united otherwise disparate threads of mainstream nineteenth-century

"aristocracy of orators"; perhaps we could say that the former was the nineteenth-century version of the latter. Thomas Hobbes, *Elements of Law*, ed. J. C. A. Gaskin (Oxford, 1994), II.xxi.5.

[48] Bagehot, *English Constitution*, 174.

[49] Bagehot, "Parliamentary Reform," 205; and "The Defeat of the Ministry and the Prospects of Reform," 307.

[50] E.g. Bagehot, "The Emperor of the French," in *CW*, vol. 4, 105–9. For Napoleonic Caesarism's self-understanding as democratic, see e.g. Adolphe Granier de Cassagnac, *L'empereur et la démocratie moderne* (Paris, 1860).

British political thought – that not will but reasons be the currency of parliamentary government[51] – would suffer a decisive demise.

Thus, the first way in which the value of the rule of public opinion entered into mid-century mirror theory was to justify exclusion of the non-opinion-holding segments of the nation. Within the more exclusionary strand of the mirror theory, then, the valorization of public opinion, filtered through sociological perceptions of the distribution of ideas and combined with what we might call the *opinion-holding principle* for qualification for enfranchisement, served to define the boundaries of the suffrage.

The opinion-holding principle could possess this justificatory power by virtue of the special link between the variety-of-suffragist vision of accurate representation and *opinion* – the conjuncture of the rule of public opinion and the mirror theory of representation installed opinion as an important item on which the machinery of descriptive representation was to operate. For this reason I employed earlier the ungainly term *cognitivism* to describe a facet of their theoretical orientation; by this I mean simply that in the long list of objects of representation which appears in these texts – classes, interests, groups, elements, stations, parts, opinions, ideas, sentiments, convictions, views – the latter half of the list, the cognates for belief, had a particular salience. The various attempts to divvy up the "objective" social space captured by the former half of the list, as we will see more clearly in analyzing their notion of deliberation, were ultimately valued because they tended to correspond to differences of opinion or outlook. It was this correspondence which, they believed, saved their schemes from the charge of arbitrariness which would have ensued if they had proposed (to adapt Locke's famous examples of civically irrelevant categories) to carve out special constituencies for those with "black Hair or gray Eyes."[52]

---

[51] The principle received innumerable formulations: that the "House yields" only to "reason" and "argument," that "the arms of reason" and not "mere will" be the tools of the Commons, that "not the mere will of the majority ... govern a Nation, but justice and reason"; Inglis, *Parliamentary Reform*, 49; Grey, *Parliamentary Government*, 181; Bruce Baum, "Freedom, Power, and Public Opinion: J. S. Mill on the Public Sphere," *HPT*, 22 (2001): 501–24.

[52] "Suppose this Business of Religion were let alone, and that there were some other Distinction made between men and men, upon account of their different Complexions, Shapes, and Features; so that those who have black Hair (for example) or gray Eyes, should not enjoy the same Privileges as other [56] Citizens ... "; John Locke, *A Letter Concerning Toleration*, ed. Mark Goldie (Indianapolis, 2010), 55. As will be seen in Chapter 3, supporters of equal manhood suffrage were unconvinced by variety-of-suffragist arguments on this point, and could express themselves in language quite similar to Locke's; e.g. the former Chartist and influential union organizer George Howell's attack on the distinction between boroughs and counties: "Why not disfranchise people because they have black hair or blue eyes?," quoted in Biagini, *Liberty, Retrenchment, and Reform*, 280.

The mirror theory – even when it was given the names of class or interest representation – was a mechanism for ensuring that the "grounds . . . of full debate," the array of "arguments" and "differences of opinion" were positioned in the house in a manner that accorded with their felt strength in the nation at large.[53] To take measures to guarantee the parliamentary presence of a group which one could reasonably expect *not* to have any distinctive political vision to advance (say, constituencies based on the first letter of one's surname) was to violate the spirit of the theory by drawing distinctions without differences.[54] From this perspective, to enfranchise those who not only had no distinctive vision, but rather *no vision at all*, was to court political risks which were not worth running. Even though the making of philosophically precise distinctions between categories such as class or interest, on the one hand, and opinion or perspective, on the other, occupied little of the variety-of-suffragists' attention, this privileging of the latter was intrinsic to the logic of their position.[55] To state the point differently: the Anglophilic French liberal-republican Eugène Pelletan was contemporaneously devising a theory of electoral politics which might be summed up by the phrase "we vote because we think."[56] By amending this phrase we can arrive at something like a formula under-lying the Victorian implementation of sociologically accurate representa-tion: "a group has seats in the Commons because it *thinks differently* in some relevant way." Contributions to public opinion which could not be expected to come from another source were what furnished an "interest" with a claim for the assurance of seats on its behalf.[57]

[53] Pochin, *Plan*, 18; Cole, *Middle Classes*, 67.

[54] This theme is echoed in contemporary descriptive representation literature which invokes a salience or relevancy criterion; e.g. Mansbridge, "Should Blacks Represent Blacks?," 634. Opponents of descriptive representation reject such a criterion as a means of covertly introducing normative notions into a discussion which presents itself as empirical; see Andrew Rehfeld, *The Concept of the Constituency: Political Representation, Democratic Legitimacy, and Institutional Design* (Cambridge, 2005), 149.

[55] Bagehot's terminology in his description of the "expressive function" of the Commons confirms this undertheorized privileging of opinion. For while one might defend or stand for an interest or class, it is hard to see how one can express them; instead one expresses opinions. E.g. "Parliamentary Reform," 195; *English Constitution*, 289–90.

[56] "The political life of a people consists at once of thinking and of voting; by thought, it forms an opinion; by the vote, it records the opinion; if a people never thought, it would not have need of the vote; it is obvious that it votes only on the basis of a good or bad idea, but an idea all the same. At bottom it is thought alone which constitutes the political life of a nation"; Pelletan, *Les droits de l'homme* (Paris, 1858), 127–8.

[57] The line of thought articulated by Pelletan could be pushed far enough to deny that units such as interest or class should factor at all into the representative process; Mill, dissenting from much of the thought of the time, advanced such a view when he dismissed interest representation, though it had some "plausibility," on the summary grounds that "what is wanted is a representation, not of

Yet, if in excluding a wide swathe of the working classes, variety-of-suffragists were simply following the logic of descriptive representation in an age obsessed with public opinion, why did a large number of our authors depart from Bagehot and make provisions for the parliamentary participation of rural workers? There were two reasons for this discrepancy, though they were not always spelled out by the authors themselves. The first was a disagreement on the empirical front. These figures, it appears, would have denied that there was actually any deficit of political ideas among the rural lower class; that they did have such ideas seems to have been the assumption on which proposals such as Creasy's and Stapleton's to divide the whole nation into a number of equally sized districts reserved for the working class proceeded.

More difficult, however, is a case like Harris. Given Harris's avowal of an abstract right to vote, his enfranchisement of the entire working class did not need to involve any dispute over the facts of opinion-holding in different demographics. Thus, his heterodox adherence to natural rights dictated that "the people" not be left out while the professional, learned, landed, clerical, and commercial elements were afforded a voice. But his unconcern about any reputed deficiency of opinions among those workers not comprehended in the "town artisan" category also bespeaks his resistance to the just-described cognitivist bent of his variety-of-suffrage comrades – a resistance that fit with his being out-of-sync with the intellectual tenor of the time more generally. While Harris worshipped at the Victorian altar of public opinion, he did not link this value with an injunction to investigate the intellectual condition of the country at the present moment. On the contrary, the deductive bent of his sociology pushed him to classify the several interests according to his sense of the essential *functional* parts of a society – a proceeding that accords less well with his own mid-century environment than with either a "premodern" notion of society's natural orders[58] or the pluralist-corporatist standpoints which would take on such prominence early in the next century.[59] Just as older images of the estates of the realm gave ideological diversity no place in its system of social differentiation but instead grounded this differentiation in the estates' "natural"

men's differences of interest, but of the differences in their intellectual points of view"; *Considerations*, 358. The more dominant variety-of-suffragist position in which interests and opinions were treated as linked is a sort of antecedent of the more appreciative attitude toward "interests" espoused by some modern theorists of deliberation such as Jane Mansbridge in "A Deliberative Theory of Interest Representation," in *The Politics of Interest: Interest Groups Transformed*, ed. Mark Petracca (Boulder, 1992): 32–57.

[58] Antonio Marongiu, *Medieval Parliaments: A Comparative Study*, trans. S. J. Woolf (London, 1968).

[59] Cécile Laborde, Pluralist Thought and the State in Britain and France, 1900–25 (London, 2000).

differences of role and purpose, Harris does not seem to have thought that opinions might have any special status in the project of mapping the social world.[60] Due to his mix of faith in natural rights with indifference to the intuition that it was in the last analysis something like opinion which provided the representation-relevant basis for distinguishing social groups, Harris did not wind up with the Bagehot–Greg stance of excluding the portions of the lower classes altogether on the grounds of their opinionlessness.

Before moving on to consider other characteristics of the variety-of-suffragist conception of the rule of public opinion, a final feature of the opinion-holding baseline for enfranchisement should be noted: its indeterminacy. Like any attempt to apply a notion of the capacity requisite for political participation, this criterion was pliable with respect both to the figures who would wield it and to the groups against which it could be applied.[61] Beyond the confines of Bagehotian liberal descriptivism, many later Victorian intellectuals of a range of political stripes warned of the dangers of ushering mass opinionlessness into electoral politics and, depending on the sociological vision and ideological premises of the author, any number of groups could be singled out as lacking the possession of proper political opinions. For instance, two of the "university liberals" who had been very sympathetic to the democratic cause in their youth came to regard the absence of genuine ideas among parts of the demos as a great peril.[62] The scholar and Liberal politician James Bryce would attribute a deterioration in the governance of large US cities to the Americans' wrongheaded enfranchisement of recently arrived immigrants, a group that "can hardly be said to possess" "political opinions . . . for they have not had time to learn – to know the institutions of their new country."[63] Similarly, the essayist and historian Leslie Stephen came to

---

[60] Though I think that he presses this point with too much absoluteness (how, for instance, can one reduce the notion of "function," which has played such a large role in modern corporatist and pluralist theories of representation, to "opinion"?) seeing how out-of-step Harris was with his contemporaries does highlight the kernel of truth in Pierre Rosanvallon's argument that "opinions" have replaced "social estates" as the basic units of representation in the modern world; Rosanvallon, *Le peuple introuvable* (Paris, 1998), 141–3.

[61] For an excellent contemporaneous analysis on this point, see the liberal politician and intellectual Prosper Duvergier de Hauranne's analysis: "La démocratie et le droit de suffrage," *Revue des deux mondes*, 74 (1868): 617–28, 790–1. Duvergier de Hauranne was well-informed about English philosophy and institutions and developed his thought in dialogue with thinkers such as Mill, James Lorimer, Grey, Hare, and others.

[62] Paolo Pombeni, "Starting in Reason, Ending in Passion: Bryce, Lowell, Ostrogorski, and the Problem of Democracy," *HJ*, 37 (1994): 319–41.

[63] Bryce, *The American Commonwealth*, second edition, 2 vols. (London, 1889), vol. 2, 260.

bemoan the impact of "newly emancipated masses without developed political convictions," whom he feared were vulnerable to manipulation by superstitious priests, especially in Ireland; in Victorian terminology, he worried that enfranchising the masses would lead to the supplanting of "public opinion" by "clerical opinion."[64] As Stephen's anxieties about Ireland indicate, the opinion-holding criterion was susceptible to utilization in global and imperial contexts.[65] Finally, a common target for exclusion via this principle was women, who, in keeping with Victorian notions of domesticity and privacy, were frequently judged not to possess ideas about public matters. Early female suffrage leaders recognized the force of this charge as a justification for the disfranchisement of women – hence the emphasis which Lydia Becker placed on the fact that "women have opinions of their own on political and kindred matters."[66] In an age obsessed with notions of public opinion and the morality of belief, the logic behind the opinion-holding threshold was powerful, pervasive, and deployable beyond the confines in which the mainstream of antidemocratic descriptivism most often applied it.

b   Aspects of Public Opinion

Now that we have seen how the value of the rule of public opinion could serve to vindicate a seeming incongruity between the ideals of inclusivity and representativeness and the endorsement of certain exclusions, it is worth taking note of a few of the more salient dimensions of the

---

[64] Stephen, "Are We Christians?," in Stephen, *Essays on Freethinking and Plainspeaking* (London, 1873): 126–76; Jeffrey Paul von Arx, *Progress and Pessimism: Religion, Politics, and History in Late-Nineteenth-Century Britain* (Cambridge, MA, 1985), 32. Even self-proclaimed "democrats" acknowledged that the question of whether "a large number of the inhabitants of these islands [were] capable of forming an opinion on the conduct of public affairs" lingered over much contemporary political contemplation; Leonard Courtney, "Political Machinery and Political Life," *FR*, 20 (1876), 74; Mill, Speech of 2 November 1868 on the Westminster Election, in *CW*, vol. 28, 339; Rodney Barker and Xenia Howard-Johnston, "The Politics and Political Ideas of Moisei Ostrogorski," *PS*, 23 (1975): 415–29.

[65] E.g. the way in which concern about the lack of opinion-holding informed Bagehot's analyses of Ireland and France; "The Contest in Ireland," 121–4; "The Ultimate Evil of French Politics," in *CW*, vol. 8, 217–21. Something close to an opinion-holding requirement also entered into Mill's famous justification of imperialism: "When nobody, or only some small fraction, feels the degree of interest in the general affairs of the State necessary to the formation of a public opinion, the electors will seldom make any use of the right of suffrage but to serve their private interest, or the interest of their locality, or of some one with whom they are connected as adherents or dependents"; *Considerations*, 414.

[66] Lydia Becker, "Female Suffrage," *CR*, 1 (1867): 308–9. Also Peter Nicholson, "The Reception and Early Reputation of Mill's Political Thought," in *The Cambridge Companion to Mill*, ed. John Skorupski (Cambridge, 1998): 464–96, at 472.

conception of public opinion shared by virtually all subscribers to the mirror theory. How did they conceive of the public opinion to which they devoted so much attention, and how did their conceptualization of it compare with other contending visions? Let us look at four features of public opinion as they envisioned it.

First, for the proponents of electoral diversity, "public opinion" came with a condition of durability. The concept for them had a necessarily temporal dimension; an intellectual snapshot of the nation at a given moment – in modern politics, the results of a single "public opinion poll" – did not necessarily reveal anything deserving of the name. For they distinguished caprice, or the reaction of the people in an "excitable" moment – what Lecky called "mere fashion"[67] – from public opinion properly so-called. It was through its staying power that an idea proved its place as a "genuine conviction"; the country had to show itself to be "determined" or "in earnest" on a question, and a view had to ratify itself as belonging to the "free and deliberate opinion of the nation" before it attained the normative status at which it demanded translation into law.[68]

This accent on durability had an elitist skew to it; it incorporated into the very definition of public opinion the condition that the "influential and educated portion of the numbers of the community" should have weighed in and been heard by the populace over the din of mere "demagogues" who preyed on the passions.[69] Yet the slant of the concept toward the "superiors [who] understand these matters"[70] was attenuated in comparison to other currents of nineteenth-century thought.[71] Moreover, although the influence of the "educated classes" was in their eyes necessary for the formation of a proper public opinion, their vision of public opinion was unspecified with regard to content. As mentioned earlier, members of

[67] Lecky, *Democracy and Liberty*, vol. 2, 406.
[68] Lecky, *Democracy and Liberty*, vol. 2, 406; Bagehot, *English Constitution*, 268; Harris, *True Theory*, 98. For the mid-Victorian generation of writers, the paradigm instance of such a rightful conversion into policy of durable public sentiment even when it had economically and socially revolutionary implications was the repeal of the Corn Laws in 1846; e.g. Greg "Representative Reform [2]," 271.
[69] Greg, "Expected Reform Bill," 214; Cole, *Middle Classes*, 80.
[70] Greg, *Enigmas of Life* (London, 1872), 48. This notion was itself the persistence into the mid-Victorian era of a view of public opinion inflected by the notion of the guidance of "natural superiors" from earlier in the nineteenth-century; J. G. A. Pocock, *Virtue, Commerce, and History* (Cambridge, 1985), 307.
[71] James Thompson's observation about the relative inclusivity of Bagehot's notion of public opinion – "he was careful not to impose overly stringent intellectual requirements on membership" in the domain of public opinion – applies to the variety-of-suffrages cohort more generally; James Thompson, *British Political Culture and Idea of Public Opinion, 1867–1914* (Cambridge, 2013), 56.

the variety-of-suffrages camp occasionally blanched at the implications of their theory when confronted with socialism. Yet on the whole they resisted the temptation to build into the concept of public opinion a set of "correct" substantive beliefs about politics. This forbearance from determining the content of the public opinion which they exalted stood in sharp contrast with earlier theorizations of public opinion, such as the liberal Tory W. A. Mackinnon's inclusion of "proper religious feeling" as a defining element of public opinion in his 1828 treatise *On the Rise of Public Opinion*.[72] Variety-of-suffragists were concerned to differentiate "settled opinion" or "real public opinion" from the "passing clamour" stirred up by "loud agitators,"[73] and to do this they invested the durability or persistence of beliefs with normative significance. But they refrained from restricting the category of public opinion to particular convictions or points of view, and they accepted that the ultimate arbiter of political disputes was "public opinion [when it] has been finally made up."[74]

If public opinion was characterized by durability, this was a consideration that applied to the short- or medium-term. In the long-term, however, theorists of electoral diversity envisaged public opinion as dynamic and shifting: "You can no more expect different generations to have exactly the same political opinions, to obey exactly the same laws, to love exactly the same institutions, than you can expect them to wear identical clothes, own identical furniture, or have identical manners."[75] To affirm the rule of public opinion was to commit to a kind of political open-endedness.[76] It was to eschew finality, not only in norms and values but also in institutions – including electoral institutions. In contrast to the aim of achieving a final settlement of the franchise question often attributed to the makers of the First Reform Act,[77] at its mid-century height the school of electoral diversity mostly disavowed any intention to erect permanent rules for the suffrage. As the social-intellectual shape of the nation changed, electoral arrangements would need updating in order to track these changes. "Finality is a delusion"; in order to keep the parliamentary system in sync with the rise of new classes, interests, and opinions,

---

[72] Mackinnon, *On the Rise, Progress, and Present State of Public Opinion, in Great Britain and Other Parts of the World* (London, 1828), 1–8.

[73] Grey, *Parliamentary Government*, 238; Bagehot, "Mr. Gladstone," in *CW*, vol. 3, 438–9.

[74] Grey, *Parliamentary Government*, 64.

[75] Bagehot, "The Chances for a Long Conservative Regime in England," in *CW*, vol. 7, 229.

[76] G. M. Young, *Today and Yesterday* (London, 1948), 243.

[77] Michael Brock, *The Great Reform Act* (London, 1973), passim. For dissenting scholarship on the significance of finality as an end for the Whigs of 1832, see e.g. John Milton-Smith, "Earl Grey's Cabinet and the Objects of Parliamentary Reform," *HJ*, 15 (1972): 55–74.

future generations would have to carry on in "the good old track of Constitutional progress by means of Constitutional Reform."[78] The social, economic, and intellectual progress which had rendered previous systems inadequate could be expected to continue, and thus allowance for "safe and timely extension . . . at some future time" was a vital part of any reasonable outlook on reform.[79] The variety-of-suffrages conception of the authority of public opinion thus contained in its own way more than a small dose of the old Benthamite search for a politics in which "the dead [do not] chain down the living."[80]

A third feature will likely come as no surprise at this point: the vision of public opinion with which the mirror theory operated was not an individualistic or aggregative one. Instead – like much political thought of the time, and against the cliché of the Victorian age as straightforwardly individualist[81] – it was communitarian or corporatist. Just as the units to be represented through their institutions were not *persons* but *groups*, so the public opinion which was integral to their understanding of free government or national self-determination rejected individualistic-aggregative modes of characterization. For this band of writers, to believe that the sociologically indiscriminate counting of heads produced government by public opinion was simply to mistake what public opinion *was*.[82] Here, for instance, is Greg forcefully stating his dissent from individualistic premises:

> For what is a *Nation*, in a highly advanced and complicated state of civilisation like ours? Not a mere aggregation of millions; not a homogeneous mass of units; but a congress of ranks and classes . . . having, it is true, one common real ultimate interest, but varying in their characters, occupations, and immediate aims; called to special duties, discharging separate functions, guided by peculiar tastes and desires, representing

---

[78] Creasy, *Text-Book*, 63.   [79] Pochin, *Plan*, 17.

[80] Bentham, "Anarchical Fallacies," in *The Works of Jeremy Bentham*, 11 vols., ed. John Bowring (Edinburgh, 1838–43), vol. 2, 494. In Bagehot's words, using a term the import of which will resonate throughout this study in different registers, one sought to avoid those "forms of government [which] *stereotype* society" – "The Working of Trades Unions," in *CW*, vol. 8, 22.

[81] Eugenio Biagini, "Introduction: Citizenship, Liberty, and Community," in *Citizenship and Community: Liberals, Radicals, and Collective Identities in the British Isles, 1865–1931* (Cambridge, 1996): 1–17.

[82] A similar conception of public opinion persists today in, for example, John Dryzek's "discourse" model of deliberative democracy and his proposal of a "Chamber of Discourses"; Dryzek, "Legitimacy and Economy in Deliberative Democracy," *PT*, 29 (2001): 651–69, and Dryzek and Simon Niemeyer, "Representation," in Dryzek, *Foundations and Frontiers of Deliberative Governance* (Oxford, 2010), ch. 3. See also the idea that "issues" and not just "persons" should be objects of democratic representation; Nadia Urbinati and Mark Warren, "The Concept of Representation in Contemporary Democratic Theory," *ARPS*, 11 (2008): 387–412.

different phases of intellect and opinion, and considering questions of government and social policy from widely divergent points of view.[83]

What it meant that the nation ruled itself was, quite simply, analytically unrelated to the results of a process that would tabulate the views "at the top of the head" of an assortment of individuals.[84] The constituent parts of the "public opinion" which it was the duty and even the definition of representative governments to render into law were, rather, ranks, classes, characters, phases of intellect – that is, social-ideological facts the existence of which transcended what one would extricate from a procedure of random sampling or sociologically unspecified suffrage.[85] As Lecky stated later: "Every one who will look facts honestly in the face can convince himself that the public opinion of a nation is something quite different from the votes that can be extracted from all the individuals who compose it." Instead, public opinion was a term that denoted a kind of intellectual geography. To discern it was akin not to the mathematical task of adding up individual expressions of belief but to the work of the cartographer; the political scientist had to map "the area of public opinion," the surface of which was made of "the various interests and opinions of a great nation."[86] Given that public opinion was an entity of a different order than doing sums of individual preferences, the electoral system which would realize its sway over Parliament placed no intrinsic value on – and could only incidentally approach – one which sought to translate into the assembly the personal desires of the citizenry considered in an undifferentiated manner.[87]

This anti-aggregative picture of public opinion was hardly unique to the descriptive tradition that has occupied us here. A range of schools of

---

[83] Greg, "Expected Reform Bill," 250.

[84] John Zaller, *The Nature and Origins of Mass Opinion* (Cambridge, 1992). A similar skepticism about how informative such surveys are – how genuinely the findings gleaned really constitute anything deserving of the name *opinion* – pervades much American political science.

[85] Greg, "Expected Reform Bill," 214.

[86] Lecky, *Democracy and Liberty*, vol. I, 21. On the cartographic imagery, see also Kahan, *Liberalism in Nineteenth-Century Europe*, 33. In Lorimer's heavy phrasing: the "national will as a whole" was to rule, which meant that "the whole nation [was to be governed] by the whole nation, not numerically indeed, but dynamically considered . . . by applying the whole forces which make up the national life to the whole work which the nation has to perform," making room for all "the intelligence, the interests, the wishes, the feelings, and idiosyncrasies of the nation"; Lorimer, *Constitutionalism of the Future*, 51–2, 81; "Mr. Mill on Representative Government," 546.

[87] Jacques Barzun, "Bagehot as Historian," introduction to *CW*, vol. 3, 27. The greatest French antidemocratic mirrorer had put the point trenchantly (and with a strong elitist tinge): "le voeu national" was not only different from "le suffrage universel," but the later had on many occasions "étouffé l'opinion publique"; Sismondi, *Études sur les constitutions*, 52–62. Also his earlier *Examen de la constitution française* (Paris, 1815), 54–5.

thought with diverging political orientations espoused a version of it – including majoritarian democrats who often conceived of the local geographical constituency as an integral community of opinion,[88] and even some proponents of the "individualistic" method of the single transferable vote (STV), both of which will be covered in the following chapters. For example, one can find in Victorian positivism – that exotic attempt to plant Auguste Comte's philosophy in inhospitable English soil[89] – disavowals of individualistic ideas of public opinion that exceeded in forcefulness any expressions in Mackintosh's or Lecky's corpus.[90]

What distinguished variety-of-suffragism from other "communitarian" approaches to public opinion was a fourth important feature: diversity. To positivists such as the indefatigable journalist and critic Frederic Harrison, the "controlling power of opinion – the corner-stone, that is to be, of all rational government," was comprised of two parts: the moral energy of the working class to set the ends of politics, and the leadership of strong and expert executive authority to devise and enforce the means. The latter element was not an equal partner. It was a concession to the complexity of social problems – since the working class were "not capable as a body of efficient administration of affairs," they were in practice restrained "not to rule but to supply the motive to rule." But when it came to the "choice" of leaders and the determination of "results" to be pursued, Harrison granted this solely to the working class, because, in a manner similar to Marx, "the working class is the only class which (to use a paradox) is not a class. It is the nation. They represent, so to speak, the body politic as a whole."[91] Like the *doctrinaire* equation of the French nation with the bourgeoisie or an aristocratic *ancien régime* social imaginary in which the class of gentleman stood as the only "true class,"[92] the

---

[88] Colin Tyler, *Idealist Political Philosophy: Pluralism and Conflict in the Absolute Idealist Tradition* (London, 2006), 70.

[89] E.g. T. R. Wright, *The Religion of Humanity: The Impact of Comtean Positivism on Victorian Britain* (Cambridge, 1986).

[90] In the words of Frederic Harrison: "public opinion abhors this fatal mathematical equality, this absurd multiplication of ciphers"; "The Revival of Authority," *FR*, 13 (1873), 18. See also his distinction between "the *independent* opinion of individual voters" and "the *organic* opinion of masses"; *Order and Progress* (London, 1875), 98.

[91] Harrison, *Order and Progress*, 147–52, 230–2. While this tenet of Harrison's positivism appealed to the rising ranks of English socialists, we should avoid the assumption that it characterized the full socialist spectrum. Ramsay MacDonald, for instance, saw the relationship between representation and diversity in a way that was continuous with much of the variety-of-suffrages tradition, as did many elements of the labour movement in the last third of the century. See MacDonald, *Socialism and Government*, 2 vols. (London, 1909), esp. vol. 1, ch. 2; A. W. Humphrey, *A History of Labour Representation* (London, 1912), passim.

[92] Clark, *English Society*, ch. 2.

positivist manner of subsuming society as a whole into a single class
was opposed to the embrace of sociological complexity which marked
the proponent of electoral variety. Given that the society which they
strove to represent was a complex, multipart organism, the opinion
that arose to guide its politics would necessarily include several
streams of thought; if, in the words of their Christian Socialist
contemporary Frederick Denison Maurice, the "sign of what this age
is" was above all a profound appreciation of the "medley of parties
and influences" and an "evident consciousness" in "contending parties
that its own conclusions and position are not entirely satisfactory,"[93]
then the variety-of-suffragists had as strong a claim as any political
movement to be exemplary of their epoch. Public opinion was in their
eyes a diverse, composite phenomenon: "it is natural" that men "will
habitually differ; [that] great national questions will divide the nation;
[that] great parties will be formed."[94] The consensus (or more precisely, series of consensuses) which emerged to claim the mantle of
public opinion was not a monolithic ideal or interest – this was, the
variety-of-suffragists agreed with Mill, the mark of stagnant or Asiatic
societies[95] – but an assemblage of partial truths.[96]

Distilled from this diversity was what was variously called
a "determination of public opinion" or a "resolution of the national
mind," and it was these determinations and resolutions which were ultimately to set the direction of national policy if Britain was to consider itself
free. But was there good reason to believe that from this forge of diversity
came good policy?

This question was answered by a third value: deliberation. Deliberation
was at the heart of variety-of-suffragism – and it was the locus of much
critical reaction from their contemporaries.

---

[93] Maurice, *The Workman and the Franchise*, 187.

[94] Bagehot, "History of the Unreformed Parliament," 273.

[95] On Bagehot, Mill, and the fear of "the awful, rock-like immobility of most of human society," see
Burrow, *Whigs and Liberals*, 108–10.

[96] The emphasis on public opinion as a split, polyphonic agglomeration of different strands competing
and coalescing can be contrasted not only with the Comtean position but also with an older view of
public opinion. This view, characteristic of the eighteenth century, took public opinion to be a kind
of monolithic constraint on the freedom of action of potentially maleficent rulers; see e.g.
Joseph Priestley, "The Stability of Governments," in *Priestley's Writings on Philosophy, Science,
and Politics*, ed. John Passmore (New York, 1965), 189: "The sense of the people, as we call it, though
no nominal part of the constitution, is often felt to be a real check upon public measures by
whomsoever they are conducted; and though it is only expressed by talking, writing, and petition-
ing, yet tumults and insurrections so often arise when the voice of the people is loud, that the most
arbitrary governments dread the effects of them."

3 **Deliberation**

This value and the foregoing one were linked by the fact that public opinion played a dual role in their theory. On the one hand, public opinion was the object of representation: its accurate reflection was the *end* or outcome of the electoral machinery which they sought to implement. On the other hand, however, it was the *means* – the material cause, in Aristotelian terms – of another aspect of the legislative process: the deliberation which took place in the Commons, what one Anglophilic French moderate-liberal lauded as "the practical, serious, and free discussion of general interests" on which "parliamentary government" was founded.[97] Public opinion in its polyphony was, to variety-of-suffragist eyes, the subject-matter of parliamentary deliberation. It was the stuff of which "government by discussion," to use a ubiquitous Victorian phrase, was made.[98]

a *Diversity and Progress*

As a result of its dual position, the misrepresentation of public opinion caused a twofold wrong. First, misrepresentation meant that certain strands of public opinion were marginalized or excluded, which was a miscarriage of justice to the groups involved. Their conceptualization of this wrong was the subject of Section 1. If this was the wrong as seen from the strictly descriptivist standpoint, it took on a different dimension when seen in the deliberativist light. From this perspective, the mistranslation of public opinion rendered deliberation partial and therefore rendered it a less reliable bearer of the benefits expected from it. To employ a favored term of this discourse, this partiality created a "class Parliament" in one direction or another;[99] hence, the repeated condemnations of class rule expressed not only a defect of representativeness, but a defect of deliberativeness as well. To allege that an assembly had succumbed to the dominance of a class was to call it both unrepresentative and undeliberative.

This was not, to mid-century champions of electoral diversity, a simply conceptual point about what followed logically from the dual place which

---

[97] Lucien-Anatole Prévost-Paradol, "De la monarchie de Juillet," in *Nouveaux Essais de politique et de littérature* (Paris, 1862): 11–22, at 20. Prévost-Paradol would wind up taking up the post of ambassador to the United States upon the promise of the Empire's liberalization, only to commit suicide in Washington upon the outbreak of the Franco-Prussian War at only forty.

[98] C. H. Driver, "Walter Bagehot and the Social Psychologists," in *The Social & Political Ideas of Some Representative Thinkers of the Victorian Age*, ed. F. J. C. Hearnshaw (London, 1933), 194–221.

[99] Maurice Cowling, *1867: Disraeli, Gladstone, and Revolution* (Cambridge, 1967), 40.

they assigned to public opinion. Instead, they worked tirelessly to craft a theory that would explain *in concreto* why the inclusion of the full scope of public opinion enhanced the assembly's deliberations. What they meant by the problem of the partial Commons was tantamount to an earlier, broader version of what is now known as the "diversity trumps ability theorem."[100] For our purposes, we might call it the "diversity trumps character" postulate, to better reflect the moralistic tenor of the period and the blend of intellectual capacities and moral dispositions on which Victorians focused in describing their exemplary legislator.[101]

Bagehot, for example, made the "moderate" MP a central character in the success story that was English parliamentary history. Only if "the overwhelming majority of representatives are men essentially moderate" was it possible to maintain parliamentary government; "intrinsically moderate, careful, and almost shrinking men" were the best suited for legislative positions.[102] Bagehot was thus anything but agnostic about the kind of temperament desired in assemblymen. And yet, despite his profound interest in the character traits appropriate to MPs, he was clear that even the prevalence of this moral disposition was insufficient for the creation of an epistemically robust legislature.

No mechanism of appointing legislators solely on the bases of their personal characteristics could compensate for the lack of a mirroring electoral system that brought within it all relevant perspectives. For Bagehot, moderation without the diversity that came with descriptive representativeness would mean that, despite the best intentions of MPs, it would be impossible for them to govern with the wisdom that could only come from including the full range of relevant groups; they would lack the "materials" for "a judgment" that could embrace public opinion in its many facets. The "diffused multitude of moderate men" were "just as likely to be tyrannical towards what they do not realise, inapprehensive of what is not argued out, thoughtless of what is not brought before them, as any

---

[100] E.g. Scott Page, *The Difference: How the Power of Diversity Creates Better Groups, Firms, Schools, and Societies* (Princeton, 2007).

[101] On Victorian notions of morality and character, see e.g. Richard Bellamy, "T. H. Green and the Morality of Victorian Liberalism," in *Victorian Liberalism: Nineteenth-Century Political Thought and Practice*, ed. Bellamy (London, 1990): 131–51.

[102] Bagehot, *English Constitution*, 299, 297. It was the lack of this quality that had caused the French – an "overexcitable population" addicted to "grand principle[s]" and thus unable to respond pragmatically to social problems as they arose – to prove so inept at operating parliamentary institutions and to repeatedly succumb to authoritarianism; Bagehot, "Letters on the French Coup d'État of 1851," in *CW*, vol. 4, 60–1. Also Georgios Varouxakis, *Victorian Political Thought on France and the French* (Houndmills, Basingstoke, 2002), 84–90.

other class can be," and consequently it was "of the utmost importance that there should be in the House of Commons some persons able to speak . . . the wants, sentiments, and opinions of every section of the community." In other words, a moderate assembly could still be a "stubbornly stupid" one if it was rendered unable to respond to public opinion due to the absence of a suitable diversity among its members.[103] There was no substitute at the level of individual MPs' personal attributes for the realization of multifaceted public opinion at the level of the composition of the collective.

The theme of "diversity trumping character" was echoed in various ways by authors sympathetic to the project of differentiated franchises. Pochin stated it in unadorned fashion with respect to the gains he saw from earmarking seats for the urban working-class: "the information thus obtained would be of great service to the country, both as affording an opportunity for conviction by argument . . . and also as affording reliable data for future legislation."[104] Without working-class input in the Commons, decisions made by even the most enlightened and best-intentioned membership would suffer, for they would lack the attitudes and attributes which only the working class could provide. Therefore, their nonindividualistic, class-based version of *quod omnes tangit* was not only a principle of justice but also a precondition of epistemic success.[105] To this school of thought there was no substitute for the expression of group preferences and perspectives by those who belonged to the group; these figures flatly denied the possibility of the Millian ideal of a person so open-minded that he would be able to understand the position of his opponents even better than they could themselves.[106] Even those who had a "profound and almost passionate" concern for the welfare of another class were likely to prove "inaccessible" to its "points of view" due to the

---

[103] Bagehot, "Parliamentary Reform," 195. And see the similar sentiment expressed by the Liberal MP Edward Buxton in his essay "The Liberal Dilemma," quoted in Saunders, *Democracy and the Vote*, 168.

[104] Pochin, *Plan*, 18.

[105] For their understanding of *quod omnes tangit*, see e.g. William Edward Hearn, *The Government of England: Its Structure and Its Development*, second edition (London, 1866), 425. Also Daniel Stasavage, "Representation and Consent: Why They Arose in Europe and Not Elsewhere," *ARPS*, 19 (2016): 145–62.

[106] "The hardiest assertor, therefore, of the freedom of private judgment – the keenest detector of the errors of his predecessors, and of the inaccuracies of current modes of thought – is the very person who most needs to fortify the weak side of his own intellect, by study of the opinions of mankind in all ages and nations, and of the speculations of philosophers of the modes of thought most opposite to his own . . . A man of clear ideas errs grievously if he imagines that whatever is seen confusedly does not exist: it belongs to him, when he meets with such a thing, to dispel the mist, and fix the outlines of the vague form which is looming through it"; Mill, "Bentham," in *CW*, vol. 10, 91.

limits of our "moral and intellectual sympathy."[107] Consequently, even the most "patriotic" and "noble race of men," if in full possession of the assembly, would produce "class legislation," the only true antidote for which was to allot to all fundamental interests a "sufficient force to carry weight and authority into deliberation." Not the character of the politicians, but the presence of "representatives of [each] class" gave security against Parliament's instigation of "class evils."[108] Only if a parliamentary inlet for the "beliefs" of the "organic portion of the working classes" were found, wrote the Christian Socialist leader Maurice, could the nature of social and political problems be "thoroughly and satisfactorily expressed": "A whole set of questions which are now most imperfectly handled in the House of Commons – handled by men looking at them from a distance – seeing them from their own points of view – unable to sympathize with labourers if they wish it ever so much – would then be submitted to fair and reasonable discussion."[109]

As one would expect given their classification of democracy as a form of class rule, variety-of-suffragists believed that legislatures suffered deliberative deficits not only when the lower classes went without sufficient weight and authority to make their wants and reasons heard, but when higher and more powerful classes were unduly marginalized as well; the perception that this marginalization was occurring with regard to the commercial ranks of the great cities was, as we glimpsed in Chapter 1, the source of Cole's dissatisfaction with the status quo.[110] The philosopher Henry Sidgwick, who sympathized with the variety-of-suffrages model but (as Chapter 3 shows) ultimately held it to be untenable, gave a cogent *fin-de-siècle* recapitulation of this line of thought. Unless the "various elements of the community" were directly represented through an "adequate selection of persons who ... combine special experience in different departments of social life," the "assembly" would be liable to lack both a "keen *concern* for the interests" of all parts of society and a wide enough "knowledge" for "dealing in a statesmanlike manner with all the problems presented to

---

[107] R. H. Hutton, "William Rathbone Greg," in *Criticisms on Contemporary Thought and Thinkers*, 2 vols. (London, 1894), vol. 2, 137.

[108] Cracroft, "The Reform Session of 1866," 27–8. On the dangers of "class legislation," see e.g. Herbert Spencer, "Parliamentary Reform: The Dangers, and the Safeguards," *WR*, 17 (1860): 486–507.

[109] Maurice, *The Workman and the Franchise*, 233.

[110] Citizens of "great commercial importance, wealth, and tax contributions," "bankers, merchants, professional men and traders" lacked suitable representation for their "political views, feelings, and opinions"; there was a dearth of MPs "who can speak authoritatively the opinions of the important classes"; Cole, *Middle Classes*, 39.

a modern legislative body." Given "men as they are," it was not possible for
an assembly to approximate wisdom – to "possess such knowledge as is
obtainable of the general tendencies of social development and the effects
of different social causes" – other than through a measure of variety in
membership.[111]

In this sensitivity about the harm threatened to legislation by the
absence or minimization of important strands of interest and opinion
were blended two separable worries. The first is the more humdrum one
encapsulated by the adage "out of sight, out of mind": that the welfare of
those classes who were without parliamentary sway would be neglected;
this was what Holyoake had in mind when he castigated the reformed
Commons as a "Rich Man's Club" that paid attention to little but the
"views and comforts of the 'upper ten thousand.'"[112] (It is crucial to recall in
connection with such aspersions that they were occurring in the context of
a nonstipendiary Commons; payment of members did not begin until 1911.
This was a persistent, although far from unanimous,[113] source of complaint
by democratic and working-class movements from Chartism onwards.[114])
Yet this was the less fundamental strain of their criticism. For it was liable
to the simple counter that, however it may look to those who wished for
different policies to be pursued, the current members were concerned with
and looking after the well-being of all classes.[115] Instead, the foundation of
their picture of the policymaking costs incurred by unrepresentativeness
was that unrepresentativeness *could not but* impoverish the discussion by
which measures were enacted and majorities were formed, and therefore
could not but have a general tendency to yield worse lawmaking.[116]

---

[111] Sidgwick, *Elements of Politics*, 371.   [112] Holyoake, *Liberal Situation*, 17.

[113] To take just one famous example: Mill, a hero of the movement for greater labour representation, opposed payment of members; J. S. Schapiro, "John Stuart Mill, Pioneer of Democratic Liberalism in England," *JHI*, 4 (1943): 127–60.

[114] E.g. Joseph King, *Electoral Reform: An Inquiry into Our System of Parliamentary Representation* (London, 1908), ch. 16. Mark Bevir, "Republicanism, Socialism, and Democracy in Britain: The Origins of the Radical Left," *Journal of Social History*, 34 (2000): 351–68.

[115] E.g. the Tory poet William Edmonstoune Aytoun's "Reform Measures of 1852," *BM*, 71 (1852): 369–86; Austin, *Plea for the Constitution*, 10.

[116] The poet and critic Matthew Arnold expressed this sense of necessity with particular crispness: "if experience has established any one thing in this world, it has established this: that it is well for any great class and description of men in society to be able to say for itself what it wants, and not to have other classes, the so-called educated and intelligent classes, acting for it as its proctors, and supposed to understand its wants and to provide for them. They do not really understand its wants, they do not really provide for them. A class of men may often itself not either fully understand its own wants, or adequately express them; but it has a nearer interest and a more sure diligence in the matter than any of its proctors, and therefore a better chance of success." Significantly, unlike so many in the 1850s–60s and even after, in the early 1880s he was applying this lesson in favor of the

If Parliament were to be dominated by only one or a few social types, then the truths conveyed by the excluded groups would not bear on the legislative agenda.

The essence of the variety-of-suffrages rendition of "diversity trumps character" amounted, then, to the warning that there were no workarounds for the harms resulting from partial deliberation, that the deliberative deficit resulting from inadequate representative machinery could not be made up for by maximizing the enlightenment or moderation of the personnel. This warning was, in turn, of a piece with the observations about the one-sidedness, partiality, and fallibility of the human mind which figured so largely in Victorian theories of intellectual liberty and the tolerant society; it was the lesson of (in one liberal Anglican theologian's words) "the one-sided imperfectness" and "limited ... perception" of the individual transposed to the parliamentary plane.[117] This was *On Liberty* for legislatures. Mill himself recognized this congruence. The best way of "persuading possessors of power to give up a part of it," he said, was

> not by telling them that they make a bad use of their power – which, if it were true, they could not be expected to be aware of – but by reminding them of what they are aware of – their own fallibility. Sir, we all of us know that we hold many erroneous opinions, but we do not know which of our opinions these are, for if we did, they would not be our opinions. Therefore, reflecting men take precautions beforehand against their own errors, without waiting till they and all other people are agreed about the particular instances; and if there are things which, from their mental habits or their position in life, are in danger of escaping their notice, they are glad to associate themselves with others of different habits and positions which very fact peculiarly qualifies them to see the precise things which they themselves do not see. Believing the House to be composed of reasonable men, this is what we ask them to do. Every class knows some things not so well known to other people, and every class has interests more or less special to itself, and for which no protection is so effectual as its own ... Is there, I wonder, a single member of this House who thoroughly knows the working men's views of trades unions, or of strikes, and could bring these subjects before the House in a manner satisfactory to working men? ... What is asked is a sufficient representation to ensure that their opinions are fairly placed before the House, and are met by real arguments, addressed to their own reason, by people who can enter into their way of looking at the subjects in

"agricultural labourer"; Arnold, "The Future of Liberalism," in *Irish Essays and Others* (London, 1882), 146–7.
[117] S. R. Bosanquet, *Eirenicon* (London, 1867), 50, 17.

which they are concerned . . . [At present, if MPs] condescend to argue [with laborers], it is from premises which hardly any working man would admit; they expect that the things which appear self-evident to them will appear self-evident to the working classes; their arguments never reach the mark, never come near what a working man has in his mind, because they do not know what is in his mind. Consequently, when the questions which are near the hearts of the working men are talked about in this House – there is no want of good will to them, I cheerfully admit – but all that it is most necessary to prove to them is taken for granted.[118]

This drawing of the link between the fallibility of the human mind and the urgency of institutions which would secure to each class its own representatives occurred, it should be said, in a speech in favor of an un-variety-of-suffrage-like 1866 reform proposal, and Mill's idea of a proper system of representation was PR and not a plan for revived electoral variegation. But as far as rooting the need for every class to possess its own parliamentary spokesman in a psychology of limitation and one-sidedness, and of thereby charting the route from the partiality of the Commons to the deterioration of its policy, there was hardly any daylight between Mill and this chapter's reformers. This psychology of opinion, and the aspiration to overcome it through the norms and institutions of a deliberative society, were not peculiar to Mill, so we should not be shocked to see its lessons carried out at the level of Parliament by a slate of reformers who likewise dwelt much on these themes of fallibility and the consequent necessity of diversity in their political thinking.

Lecky, for one, still sounded much like Mill in describing the epistemic impairment of a democratically class-ruled assembly in terms of the monopoly of lower "class interests and animosities" with no opening for "conditions of thought and life widely different from their own."[119] Similarly, Bagehot's notion that "true Liberalism" upheld "the true ideal of Parliament [which] is to have the largest number of really organic interests and ideas meeting together in the representative assembly, *to try each other's strengths and weaknesses*" could easily be mistaken for a passage from the *Considerations on Representative Government*.[120] Just as it was a hallmark of "genuine Liberalism" in the public sphere to recognize "that a willingness to hear every side of every question is the condition . . . of vigorous faith,"[121] so it was a hallmark of liberalism in the parliamentary sphere that

[118] Mill, Speech on the Representation of the People [2], 13 Apr. 1866, in *CW*, vol. 28, 64–5.
[119] Lecky, *Democracy and Liberty*, vol. 1, 369.
[120] Bagehot, "'True Liberalism' and Reform," 360 (my italics).
[121] Leslie Stephen, "Social Macadamisation," *FM*, 6 (1872), 165.

"discussion at least among all possible views and interests *before [legislative] decision* be ... part of the system."[122] If toleration and a free press were prerequisites for the individual to have justified confidence in his beliefs,[123] by parallel reasoning there could be no justified confidence in the quality of legislation if important perspectives could not be "heard at all" within the assembly.[124] Public opinion was more expansive, more incorporative of the array of "consolidated feelings and matured opinions" in which inhered those partial truths of which good legislation had to take account,[125] than the mind of any one kind of person or the prepossessions of any one class could be. The reflection of public opinion was, accordingly, the bedrock of a truly deliberative Commons.

Once the dictate to realize public opinion in full was met, then the logic of the epistemic defense of toleration – famous in this period from *On Liberty* but elaborated in a slew of other less canonical texts as well[126] – kicked in with respect to the Commons's direction of policy; as Cole put it, "differences of opinion" in the Commons were to be cheered, not feared: "when discussion is free, the best arguments will prevail in the end, and the country at large derive advantage."[127] As an anonymous mirror theorist had written in defense of the unreformed Parliament: in a "fair field of debate" for the "free expression" of all relevant sentiments, such as was provided by an assembly in which the member from one class or interest had to "be content to take his seat by the side of" members from other groups, the "truth" could not but "command [the House's] assent."[128] If Victorian liberals regarded modern societies as arenas for the playing out of a kind of practical theodicy with respect to the evolution of beliefs,[129] their assemblies were not exceptions to this optimism but settings in which it was borne out.

But were not the dynamics in Parliament different from those in society at large? Even if "the truth will, in the long run, pierce all the mists raised by

---

[122] Bagehot, "'True Liberalism' and Reform," 360.

[123] What David Edwards, discussing Mill, has described as the idea that "toleration is the social condition of certainty" held for Victorian liberals more widely; Edwards, "Toleration and Mill's Liberty of Thought and Discussion," in *John Stuart Mill's Social and Political Thought, Critical Assessments*, ed. G. W. Smith, 4 vols., (London, 1998), vol. 2, 346.

[124] Bagehot, "'True Liberalism' and Reform," 360.   [125] Greg, "Expected Reform Bill," 233.

[126] As Frederic Harrison observed, *On Liberty*'s epistemic dimension is to be understood less as an "original" argument than a "masterpiece" of recapitulation, "condens[ing] ... all the best" of the common fund of Victorian wisdom on the topic; Harrison, *Tennyson, Ruskin, Mill, and Other Literary Estimates* (London, 1899), 293.

[127] Pochin, *Middle Classes*, 67.   [128] *Observations on the British Constitution*, 39, 42.

[129] Gregory Conti, "James Fitzjames Stephen, John Stuart Mill, and the Victorian Theory of Toleration," *HEI*, 42 (2016): 364–98.

the intrigues of the jobber, or the violence of the partisan,"[130] it was not clear how the conquering power of truth applied to decisions on specific bills by members who might be devoted to the advancement of particular interests and ideologies. Were there not passions and pathologies peculiar to assemblies, incentives of party loyalty, personal advantage, etc., among members which clouded the consideration of arguments on their own terms? Did the variety-of-suffrages crew simply skirt these questions by stipulating that whatever legislation a properly constituted assembly approved was by definition the optimal one?[131] Why was the legislature not the exception to this progressive rule?

Before delving into the specifics of their answers to these questions, it ought to be reiterated that the rosy picture painted of the epistemic properties of a diverse Commons applied *only* when their properly representative Commons was realized, or at least approximated. If corruption – whether of the "plutocratic" genre sketched earlier or an older kind of monarchical patronage with which eighteenth- and early-nineteenth-century Whigs were preoccupied[132] – were prevalent, then parliamentary deliberation would be hollow, since members would be responding not to public reasons but to private interests. And, of course, if the electoral regulations invested one class with such an overwhelming preponderance that their will could be imposed without needing to answer to reasons not their own, lawmaking would tend to be hasty and sectarian rather than public and enlightened. All their optimistic assurances about the quality of policy were predicated on avoiding these fates.

Yet overcoming these barriers still left the more mundane problem of personal selfishness or class-interestedness on the part of MPs. What about such facts as that members sitting for the agricultural interest were unlikely to examine disinterestedly and in conformity to a proper "ethics of belief" a bill on the indemnification of diseased cattle?[133]

---

[130] Brougham, "French Parties and Politics," *ER*, 61 (1835), 216.

[131] Another way of framing the question is to ask whether their paeans to parliamentary wisdom were committing the kind of "survival" fallacy that Frederick Schauer has associated with certain facile epistemic arguments for freedom of speech in which the truth is simply identified with whatever view is left standing at the end of a discussion. See Schauer, *Free Speech: A Philosophical Enquiry* (Cambridge, 1982), 20–2.

[132] On the former, e.g. Bagehot, "John Stuart Mill upon the Increase of Corruption," in *CW*, vol. 6, 347–50. On the latter, e.g. Brougham, "Parliamentary Reform," in *Contributions to the Edinburgh Review by Henry Lord Brougham*, 2 vols., (London, 1856), vol. 2, 347–83; J. A. W. Gunn, "Influence, Parties and the Constitution: Changing Attitudes, 1783–1832," *HJ*, 17 (1974): 301–28.

[133] This was an issue which particularly exercised Mill. His first two speeches in the Commons were devoted to opposing "The Cattle Diseases Bill"; see *CW*, vol. 28, 46–52.

It is indisputable that certain grand, quasi-metaphysical assumptions about the emergence of truth and the march of mind inflected even their more "scientific" attempts at analysis of parliamentary deliberation.[134] Without doubt, mirror theorists imported the broader convictions of their milieu that "one error counteracts or neutralizes another" and that the "variety of our beliefs" was generative of epistemic advance from other domains of thought into the Commons without a full argument spelling out why these wider conclusions applied here.[135] Nonetheless, they were far from uninterested in the empirics of deliberation in the legislative forum, and they crafted models of how the Commons could deliver on its promise as a deliberative space that did not depend on a naïve view of all MPs as impartial deliberators motivated solely by the demands of reason.[136]

For one thing, theirs was not an image of legislative deliberation as foolproof. Despite their general progressivism, Bagehot and his ilk admitted that there was "no sort of infallibility about the court" of public discourse,[137] and they allowed an even greater margin of error to the court of MPs, operating under the host of pressures and constraints that attended the politician's life. But they remained confident that assemblies constructed along the lines they laid out would make good policy more reliably than would any alternative. This confidence derived from the belief that if the manifold of classes and ideologies were present in the assembly, then in most debates a set of MPs would be present whose selfish interests or bedrock ideological commitments did not have a clear bearing on the question. This crop, supplemented by those members whose natural love of the common good outweighed the tug of personal or class gains, would have no reason to be unreceptive to argument or to decide the question on grounds other than the respective strength of the cases presented. Given the existence of this undetermined clutch of members, even the biases of self-interested or prejudiced members could work to good effect insofar as these interests and prejudices motivated them to state the case for their positions in the strongest possible terms, to leave no stone unturned in

---

[134] Progress was not only the grand idea of radicalism, "advanced liberalism," and the century's many utopian philosophies, but also of orthodox Whigs such as Russell; A. Wyatt Tilby, *Lord John Russell: A Study in Civil and Religious Liberty* (New York, 1931).

[135] Edward Adolphus Seymour, Duke of Somerset, *Christian Theology and Modern Skepticism* (London, 1872), 163.

[136] Deliberative democrats are making an effort to start giving a similarly "systematic" account of the whole economy of deliberation in public life; e.g. the essays in *Deliberative Systems: Deliberative Democracy, at the Large Scale*, ed. John Parkinson and Jane Mansbridge (Cambridge, 2012).

[137] Bagehot, "The Metaphysical Basis of Toleration," in *CW*, vol. 14, 61.

their support.[138] Adamancy or heatedness in error could therefore serve the end of sound legislation.[139] The presence of fervent champions on all sides of an issue, including the incorrect ones, was essential to the process of crafting policy that would serve the public good, since it meant that no trenchant objection or salutary amendment would be overlooked[140] – and since, contra Guizot, the variety-of-suffragist held that one learned which opinions partook of justice and reason only after evaluating how they fared in the trial of government by discussion. If their requirements for the composition of the Commons were satisfied, then what was true of the general "struggle to discover truth" – namely, that "if a man plays his part manfully and honourably in such a struggle, he deserves our gratitude, even if he takes the wrong side," for "our antagonists" were doubling, from a higher point of view, as "our co-operators"[141] – would hold true as well of the pursuit of good legislation.

In short, without having ideal deliberators, something approximating an "ideal legislative speech situation"[142] with respect to the quality of deliberation and the goodness of policy was, the variety-of-suffragists believed, nevertheless practicable. Of course, there could be no guarantee that this disinterested, reason-guided core would always be in a position to tip the scales. But given the multifaceted character of society and public opinion

---

[138] This is a parliamentary version of familiar thoughts about the "necessity of error"; e.g. C. L. Ten, "The Liberal Theory of the Open Society," in *The Open Society in Theory and Practice*, ed. Dante Germino and Klaus von Beyme (The Hague, 1974), 144.

[139] The French liberal Catholic politician Charles Forbes René de Montalembert highlighted the deliberative emptiness of France's legislative life in an age of electoral domination from Emperor Napoleon's official candidates by contrasting his country's condition with the better fortunes of England. In this vein he hailed England as having already reached the comprehensiveness in deliberation that the variety-of-suffragist reformers were hoping could be attained by their schemes. The English Parliament was "the great council of a great people, where all the passions and all the prejudices have a right to sit and to vote, but where their inevitable danger encounters as counterweights and remedies all the forces, all the enlightenment, and all the independence that this virile and prudent race contains within it. Even now all real needs have found a free manifestation there; all serious interests have been sagely pondered there. No other form of government has given to man more chances to encounter the just and the reasonable, more facilities for avoiding and repairing error"; *L'avenir politique de l'Angleterre*, fifth edition (Paris, 1857), 134–5.

[140] Thus, "the affairs of the country are best transacted by making the House of Commons a great mart of political business; a great clearing-house of political ideas" and "opposite opinions," including those "we do not share"; George Cornewall Lewis, "Marshall on the Representation of Minorities," *ER*, 100 (1854), 230. Duvergier de Hauranne was not exaggerating when he identified the link between "la composition variée de la chambre des communes" and its "sagesse" as the leading idea of English parliamentarianism; "La démocratie et le droit de suffrage," 632.

[141] Leslie Stephen, "The Morality of Competition," in *Social Rights and Duties*, 2 vols. (London, 1896), vol. I, 161.

[142] This phrase is adapted from Habermas, *On the Pragmatics of Social Interaction*, trans. Barbara Fultner (Cambridge, MA, 2001).

which they sought to represent, they believed that with some regularity it would be; when this regularity was not being obtained, that was a sign that the electoral system was failing in its representative dimension and that a further installment of reform was needed. Put differently, the Commons could fulfill its function as a "mediator" among the "wide variety of social 'interests'" only if it contained a group of persuadable members, and the school of electoral diversity believed its programs were effective means to keep such a group there.[143]

b Epistemic Divisions of Labor

This explanation of why improved mirroring would counter the "many errors in legislation" traceable to "defective representation" received an assortment of expressions from different authors.[144] What united them was their attempt to portray the healthy representative assembly as a space in which a kind of epistemic division of labor was operative. In the economy of giving reasons relevant to legislation, MPs of different kinds would do different jobs: attacking, defending, moderating, combining different insights, and settling the final decision. This image of the intra-Commons differentiation of deliberative tasks was not only essential to nineteenth-century parliamentarianism, but also supplied a font from which conceptions of the progress of thought in "open societies" such as their own could be drawn. Toward the end of his life, Bagehot depicted "the process by which truth wins in discussion" among the English public on the model of "quasi-judges" who distilled a sober synthesis out of the maelstrom of ardent arguments put forth by "a sort of advocates."[145] Such a figuration of the salutary division of epistemic functions in the nation at large was suggested to Bagehot by his lifelong attentiveness to parliamentary affairs. More than the legislative success of the Commons being grasped as a microcosmic version of the larger processes that allowed truth to emerge in society, the intellectual fruitfulness of the public sphere was understood through analogy to a diverse, representative Commons.

---

[143] Angus Hawkins, "'Parliamentary Government' and Victorian Political Parties," 650.

[144] Harris, True Theory, 41–2.

[145] Bagehot, "Metaphysical Basis," 223. In this Bagehot was giving in to what has proven to be a very strong temptation to political theory across the ages, namely, the temptation to cast public deliberation of all sorts in a judicial mold. More speculatively, there is an interesting resemblance between Bagehot's account of Parliament and of conscience; he approved of Bishop Butler's understanding of the latter as a "judicial" faculty that, so to speak, fielded the claims from competing impulses and then passed a judgment on what was good; "Bishop Butler," in CW, vol. I, 240. For Bagehot, then, Parliament operated in a real way like the conscience of the nation.

Bagehot thought that his proposed reforms would enable an appropriate distribution of seats between "class advocates," unyielding "delegates" of the major "wants, sentiments, and opinions of every section of the community," and "unbiassed judges" who were not predetermined by "class prejudice or class interest."[146] This latter group served as the "critical and impartial audience" which could evaluate the solidness of the claims advanced by "every class and every class interest."[147] "Argument in the legislature" was enlightening because "those representatives" who on a given issue assumed "the character of advocates" for "particular opinions and interests" and "singular wants and notions" were incomparable from the perspective of generating reasons, expressing wishes, proffering amendments, or posing objections; while the "neutral and judicial" members were fit to evaluate with dispassion the merits of all these ideas, they were competent to "weigh their arguments, estimate their often conflicting assertions, and in the last resort decide."[148] Once "due voice" was given to the heap of "special type[s] of thought" from the "shipowner" and the "manufacturer" to the "landlord" and the "clergy," once every "eccentric idiosyncrasy," "characteristic creed," and class bias had made itself heard, a verdict emerged which was both "purged of class prejudices" and which encapsulated the best that "ordinary intelligence" could make of the matter.[149] This quasi-"judicial" model of deliberation in representative assemblies – in which "various members [who] ought to represent the various special interests, special opinions, special prejudices, to be found in the community" served as "commissioned advocate[s]" bringing cases, and a "neutral body of no sect" approximating the "general average intelligence" of the country passed judgments as the "judge"[150] – was the soundest possible engine for accumulating the full span of views in society and turning this sum into reasonable, impartial decisions about policy[151] –

[146] Bagehot, "Note of 18 Feb, 1859, to 'Parliamentary Reform'," 176; "Parliamentary Reform," 195.

[147] Bagehot, "Present Aspects," 252.

[148] Bagehot, "Parliamentary Reform, 195; "Oxford and Mr. Gladstone," in *CW*, vol. 3, 442.

[149] Bagehot, "Present Aspects," 252.

[150] Bagehot, *English Constitution*, 219–20; "Oxford and Mr. Gladstone," 442.

[151] To use a term from Melissa Williams's categorization of different notions of impartiality, the proponents of a variegated suffrage conceived of impartiality as "inclusiveness of issues"; Melissa Williams, "The Uneasy Alliance of Group Representation and Deliberative Democracy," in *Citizenship in Diverse Societies*, ed. Will Kymlicka and Wayne Norman (Oxford, 2000): 124–52. Other categories of hers – "impartiality as absence of bias: participants" and "impartiality as inclusiveness: persons" – would have been rejected by this school. For further discussions in political theory today about inclusive group representation as a condition of impartial outcomes, see e.g. Roberto Gargarella, "Full Representation, Deliberation, and Impartiality," in *Deliberative Democracy*, ed. Jon Elster (Cambridge, 1998): 260–80; Iris Marion Young, "Justice, Inclusion and Deliberative Democracy," in *Deliberative Politics: Essays on Democracy and Disagreement*, ed.

an urgent task for an era which gave great attention to the aspiration for an impartial state.[152] As one Liberal MP summed up pithily, in a statement in which one could glimpse both the point about diversity in membership ensuring comprehensiveness in deliberation and the point about different members occupying different roles with regard to the setting of policy: "This is the use of a Parliament. We educate each other. All knowledge is brought to account ... Even prejudice has a certain use in checking excess in another direction. The decision is taken in the main by a number of shrewd and silent judges, whose ears are ever open and minds are ever at work."[153] Because of this division of epistemic labor, properly representative assemblies could be expected to perform to a high standard, to obtain the best policy that "ordinary intelligence *minus* class prejudices" could offer.[154]

The confidence in the division of epistemic labor among MPs was articulated in different ways by different authors. As one would expect from a group which comprehended such variation in sociological analysis, they were not in perfect accord about how to describe the roles fulfilled by different sorts of MPs in this economy of parliamentary deliberation. For Bagehot, for example, while members of the several groups would find themselves occupying the roles of advocate and judge on different occasions, to a large extent the neutral, judgment-passing "average intelligence" would be supplied by members from the "small boroughs," who on the whole possessed "less definite character" and "characteristic prejudice" than members hailing from constituencies more closely marked by class or by the "special dialect of any bit of England."[155] The combination of these small-borough members, the more open-minded and public-spirited of the "advocates" of particular interests, would form, he hoped, a "preponderance" capable of crafting a centrist consensus which would stand for the judgment of "the nation itself" amidst its diversity.[156] This differed from the proportion of "advocates" to "judges" which Greg seems to have envisioned, at least in his more agonistic moments – his idea of

Stephen Macedo (Oxford, 1999): 151–8; Michael Rabinder James, *Deliberative Democracy and the Plural Polity* (Lawrence, 2004), esp. ch. 5. There is significant overlap with Victorian descriptivism in these analyses.

[152] Philip Harling, "The State," in A Companion to Nineteenth-Century Britain, ed. Williams 110–23.

[153] Sir John Salusbury Salusbury-Trelawny, quoted in T. A. Jenkins, *Parliament, Party, and Politics in Victorian Britain* (Manchester, 1996), 18.

[154] Bagehot, "Present Aspects," 252.

[155] Bagehot, "Present Aspects," 252; "Oxford and Mr. Gladstone," 443. This had been Russell's reasoning, during the debates on the Reform Bill in 1831, in favor of leaving so many smaller boroughs intact; Russell, HC Deb 24 June 1831, *Hansard*, Third Series, vol. 4, 338.

[156] Bagehot, *English Constitution*, 220; "Present Aspects," 252.

"middle-class government" did not involve a tepid, consensual politics.[157] Stapleton assigned the task of "impartial umpires, between contending interests" to those members who sat for "learning and education," while everyone else would, it appears, be an advocate of some interest.[158] Mackintosh's seminal early statement partook of a more traditionally hierarchical differentiation of epistemic tasks: "judgment" was best rendered by the "landed proprietors" among MPs, who as a class tended to be more "neutral" and "impartial on more subjects than any other class of men."[159] These members of "leisure, large property, [and] temperate character" were to sit in judgment on the claims brought forth by spokesmen of other classes less inclined to contentment with the status quo, in particular those proposals of innovation and reform originated by the distinctive representatives of "the lower classes."[160] The latter's "character was an important element in its composition," but it had "to be checked and restrained by others of a different character" – although of course the same could be said "of any other of those bodies which make useful parts of a mixed and various assembly."[161]

Underneath this multiplicity of depictions of the epistemic division of labor was a common belief in the positive relationship between social and ideological diversity and the quality of political decisions. "The great variety ... of different elements entering into its composition," remarked Grey, was the cause of the historic excellence of the Commons and (with appropriate reform) would continue as its cause in future.[162] "The most dangerous of experiments," Greg wrote, would be a "change" which "would throw the representation" into just one

---

[157] "The conservative sentiments of the sturdy drags" and "keen and impatient energy"; "the refined and philosophic" and "the contentious and extreme"; "those who cherish pastoral delusions" and those suffering "the hallucinations of bare utilitarianism"; "those who love peace" and "those who love progress" – Greg wanted all of these "permanent elements of the nation" to face off in the Commons; "Expected Reform Bill," 252.

[158] Stapleton, *Suggestions*, 40.   [159] Mackintosh, "Universal Suffrage," 176.

[160] These were "men of popular talents, principles, and feelings; quick in suspecting oppression; bold in resisting it; not thinking favourably of the powerful; listening, almost with credulity, to the complaints of the humble and the feeble; and impelled by ambition, where they are not prompted by generosity, to be the champions of the defenceless"; ibid., 176–7. Mackintosh's thought here would find echoes in the postmortems for the July Monarchy. For instance, the moderate liberal Prévost-Paradol thought it a defect of the July Monarchy that the Chamber was reserved for "only citizens arrived at a certain fortune, a solidly settled fortune, who were in consequence mostly content with their fates, which is a bad disposition of mind for recognizing in a timely way the need for change and progress by which modern societies are always more or less agitated"; *La France Nouvelle*, second edition (Paris, 1868), 324–5.

[161] Mackintosh, "Universal Suffrage," 177.   [162] Grey, *Parliamentary Government*, 71.

of the several hands which now played different instruments in the
symphony of deliberation.[163]

A related picture of how "conviction by argument" could direct the
legislature even if the morality and intellect of most MPs were far from
perfect found its way into the *Considerations on Representative Government*:

> if the representative system could be made ideally perfect, and if it were possible
> to maintain it in that state, its organization must be such, that these two classes,
> manual labourers and their affinities on one side, employers of labour and their
> affinities on the other, should be, in the arrangement of the representative
> system, equally balanced, each influencing about an equal number of votes in
> Parliament: since, assuming that the majority of each class, in any difference
> between them, would be mainly governed by their class interests, there would be
> a minority of each in whom that consideration would be subordinate to reason,
> justice, and the good of the whole; and this minority of either, joining with the
> whole of the other, would turn the scale against any demands of their own
> majority which were not such as ought to prevail. The reason why, in any
> tolerably constituted society, justice and the general interest mostly in the end
> carry their point, is that the separate and selfish interests of mankind are almost
> always divided; some are interested in what is wrong, but some, also, have their
> private interest on the side of what is right: and those who are governed by higher
> considerations, though too few and weak to prevail against the whole of the
> others, usually after sufficient discussion and agitation become strong enough to
> turn the balance in favour of the body of private interests which is on the same
> side with them. The representative system ought to be so constituted as to
> maintain this state of things: it ought not to allow any of the various sectional
> interests to be so powerful as to be capable of prevailing against truth and justice
> and the other sectional interests combined.[164]

Some scholars have been dismayed to find Mill pinning such hopes on this
(what strikes them as flimsy) view of the ground of "reason's" steady
influence over lawmaking.[165] In light of the Victorian *Weltbild* about
these matters, however, it would have been surprising *not* to have found
such a passage in the Millian oeuvre. Read in context, what is surprising is
not that Mill should have assented to this thought about how a realizable
"deliberative body" would work, but that his version of the theme should
have been so neutered – amounting basically to hoping for a 50–50 split of
seats between labor and capital and invoking a moralistic notion of the few

[163] Greg, "Expected Reform Bill," 253. He had in mind here the ills caused by the monopoly of
representation by "the energetic, and the pushing – the men to whom repose is torture – the men to
whom the past is all contemptible, the present all sombre, the future all golden."
[164] Mill, *Considerations*, 447.
[165] Pitkin, *Concept of Representation*, 203; Graeme Duncan, "John Stuart Mill and Democracy," in *John Stuart Mill's Social and Political Thought*, vol. 3, 79.

truly deliberative individuals who turned the tide – relative to the more pluralistic and fluid social imaginaries at work in other figures.[166] In contrast to competing contemporary visions and to other aspects of his own writing about deliberation and representation, Mill's portrait of the intersection of these two themes in the Commons was rather stilted.

Supplementing the more proximate, policy-relevant benefits of the deliberative Commons were a wider, longer-term set of educative effects. For many scholars, the idea of an educational impact deriving from politics in the nineteenth century conjures up Tocqueville on the sense of empowerment and industriousness which democracy spread through civil society, or John Stuart Mill on the improving power of the franchise.[167] But to mid-Victorians, neither of these was the most common way in which politics was supposed to operate educatively. Instead, the chief educational contribution of politics was the rich debate in the Commons. The contestation in the Commons *focused* the national mind – it gave the public a site in which it could evaluate the different positions taken; since all facets of society ideally were present there, following its debates gave the citizen an occasion to transcend the limited domains of his region, religion, or occupation and to encounter the nation as a whole in what we might call its reason-giving dimension.[168] Thus, parliamentary deliberation was a preeminent "means of enlightening the minds of the People, and dispelling prevailing errors." Government could act as a spur for "intellectual activity and moral improvement" insofar as it made "those contests for power which are inevitable amongst men, take the form of debates upon questions of policy, and upon the measures affecting the interests of the Nation which are brought before Parliament. These debates are thus rendered a valuable

---

[166] Mill, *Considerations*, 424.

[167] E.g. Jon Elster, "The Market and the Forum," in *The Foundations of Social Choice Theory*, ed. Elster and Aanund Hylland (Cambridge, 1986), 103–32.

[168] Of course, Parliament was not the sole site which Victorians understood as possessing deliberative properties: local government, certain imperial bodies, the legal system, and even more informal domestic settings could all be invested with deliberative value. (The essays collected in Jose Harris, *Civil Society in British History: Ideas, Identities, Institutions* [Oxford, 2003] offer a jumping-off point for consideration of some of these other venues.) However, in keeping with the era's reputation as the "classical age of parliaments," a parliamentary model of deliberation was primary in the period: it was believed that Britain's broader deliberative culture was sustained by the presence of a potent deliberative institution at the apex of the state which could make the value of deliberation visible before the eyes of the public. It was this sense of the indispensability of a deliberative legislature which undergirded the great prestige of parliamentarianism in the mid-nineteenth century and which led figures such as Bagehot to reject not only French Caesarism and other "authoritarian" regimes, but also American presidentialism, which was considered a nondiscussive form of government; e.g. *English Constitution*, 216–18. Befitting the mid-Victorian reverence for Parliament, voluntary associations often modeled and marketed themselves after Westminster; Lawrence Goldman, "The Social Science Association, 1857–1886: A Context for Mid-Victorian Liberalism," *EHR*, 101 (1986): 95–134.

instrument for enlightening the public mind."[169] Bagehot called this the "teaching function" of the Commons – a function which, on his taxonomy, was parasitic on the fulfillment of another "office," the "expressive" one, for its debates could only be educative on the condition that they fully "express[ed] the mind of the English people on all matters which come before it."[170] The assembly's deliberations enhanced wisdom in a very broad sense: they enabled wiser decisions on legislation, and they helped the citizenry itself to become wiser.

But there was certainly a paradox, or at least what looks like one from a twenty-first-century democratic standpoint, about this latter benefit. What made the legislature such an indispensable intellectual institution was that it was "only by parliament, the great national institution in which every one takes some interest" that an "efficient discussion in practice" of an issue could draw the attention of all "the very miscellaneous multitude" that was "the public."[171] Yet this discussion was edifying only if it encompassed the diversity and descriptive accuracy to qualify as genuine deliberation – and this qualification was capable of fulfillment (depending on the author) only if either some citizens were excluded from the franchise or if the suffrage, although universal, proceeded on a basis of sociological differentiation which rendered the electoral impact of voters unequal. Thus, in order for the Commons to discharge its duty of providing enlightenment for all, it was necessary that not all participate equally in the electoral system.[172] For Parliament to improve all minds, it could not simply be the product of the undifferentiated aggregation of all votes. To be edifying the Commons had to be deliberative, but to be deliberative it had to avoid democracy – this was really the cornerstone of mid-Victorian antidemocratic but inclusive parliamentarianism.

c   Realism and Utopianism

It is important to bear in mind two points when considering this exalted picture of the assembly's salutary division of epistemic labor and the positive "effect on the country" that the "respect for Parliamentary discussion" had.[173] First, to reiterate: with the exception of the status quo

---

[169] Grey, *Parliamentary Government*, 71, 13.
[170] Bagehot, *English Constitution*, 289–90. The two were so closely linked that he distinguished them only as "a sort of technicality."
[171] Bagehot, "The Non-Legislative Functions of Parliament," in *CW*, vol. 6, 44.
[172] Democracy entailed that there be "only one sort of vote and only one size of constituency all over England, and then the reign of monotony will be complete"; Bagehot, "Lord Althorp and the Reform Act," 225.
[173] Russell, *History of the English Constitution*, fourth edition, 184.

defenders, this model of deliberation was seen as, at best, only incompletely actualized, and they aimed to ameliorate its deliberative character through greater descriptive inclusivity. And yet, second, there were sufficient glimpses of true legislative deliberation to make their deliberative ideal seem realizable with the right reforms. The conditions of the era's politics were such that deliberation even on their demanding conceptualizations of it seemed that it could be the lifeblood of the modern legislature – this is part of what is meant in the frequent references to this as the "classical age" of parliamentarism.[174] These authors came of age in and developed their conceptions of politics at a time of "genuine parliamentary government," those "few brief decades in English history, [when] what was said in the Commons actually swayed the outcome of legislation."[175] As has been mentioned, party discipline was weak in this period – too weak for some, such as the greatest of all Victorian statesman, William Gladstone.[176] While the bulk of our authors attributed a positive role to parties in helping to secure working majorities for the passage of legislation and facilitating the appointment of a functioning cabinet, the parties they lauded were mild and club-like in comparison to modern party machines.[177] Centralized parties which could enforce unanimous adherence to a platform were anathema to this kind of deliberativism; party hegemony would prevent members from responding to the full array of reasons in an epistemically valuable way, constraining them and effectively transferring the locus of power from parliamentary debate to the "wire-pullers" behind the scenes who directed the parties' movements. This period of the "heyday of the private member" – when party considerations were present but not determinative, and parliamentary oratory could appear a real means of changing hearts and minds – was a rich backdrop against which to theorize

---

[174] E.g. D. C. Somervell, *English Thought in the Nineteenth Century* (London, 1929), 73; R. H. S. Crossman, "Introduction," to *The English Constitution*, ed. Crossman (London, 1963), 17, 35; Walter Arnstein, *The Bradlaugh Case: A Study in Late Victorian Opinion and Politics* (Oxford, 1965), 3.

[175] Boyd Hilton, *A Mad, Bad, & Dangerous People, England 1783–1846* (Oxford, 2006), 209.

[176] Gladstone, "The Declining Efficiency of Parliament," *QR*, 99 (1856): 521–70. On the nadir of party discipline in the middle decades of the nineteenth century, see e.g. Derek Beales, *The Political Parties of Nineteenth-Century Britain* (London, 1971); Randall McGowen and Walter Arnstein, "The Mid-Victorians and the Two-Party System," *Albion*, 11 (1979): 242–58.

[177] Norman Gash, *Politics in the Age of Peel* (New York, 1971), 31–2; Grey, *Parliamentary Government*, passim. Hawkins depicts an absolute break in the nature of British parties after the Second Reform Bill, although other scholars have described a more gradual process of centralization and consolidation; e.g. Hawkins, "'Parliamentary Government' and Victorian Political Parties," 667; Gary Cox, "The Development of a Party-Orientated Legislature in England, 1832–1918," *BJPS*, 16 (1986): 187–216.

a politics in which deliberation was central.[178] Moreover, this apogee of the Commons's deliberativeness corresponded with the height of interest in its debates: the House was in its most "majestic" historical moment and served as the focal point of the intellectual attention of virtually the whole literate strata of the British population.[179] Because for Victorians it was a truism that the House's debates percolated through society as a whole, influencing the intellectual tone and political convictions of the nation, it was urgent to raise parliamentary discourse to the highest possible level. The epistemic and educative properties ascribed to the assembly's deliberation did not come from nowhere; they were rooted in the experience of the age. To employ a phrase from another sphere of political theory, for these authors deliberative representative government looked to be a "realistic utopia."[180]

If the previous paragraph fleshed out the *realistic* portion of the above phrase, it is worth putting the accent on the latter word as well for a moment. It is well known that Mill proclaimed "the ideally best form of government" to be "representative government."[181] He was, it ought to be evident by now, not alone in such sentiments: a wide swathe of mid-Victorian thinkers was in accord that a reformed version of English parliamentarianism was the best conceivable political system. This attitude amounted to a kind of utopianism. But what kind? There are variations of utopianism, encompassing milder and more extreme species. When these authors held deliberative representative government to be the best form of government, they did not mean that it was the first among good options, that it was merely preferable by degree to less representative, less deliberative, more authoritarian forms. For them, the consequence of lacking their desired institutions was not simply less effective policy, less sagacious lawmaking. It was worse; the fate of societies without such governments was that most formidable of nineteenth-century bugbears: stagnation.[182]

---

[178] H. J. Hanham, *The Nineteenth-Century Constitution, Documents and Commentary*, ed. Hanham (Cambridge, 1969), 256–8.

[179] J. P. Parry, *The Rise and Fall of Liberal Government in Victorian Britain* (New Haven, 1993), 7–14; Stefan Collini, *Public Moralists: Political Thought and Intellectual Life in Britain, 1850–1930* (Oxford, 1993), 34, 122. Collini tries to give the modern reader a sense of the magnitude of this interest with an analogy: debates were "followed by the educated classes with the avidity and familiarity now more commonly reserved for the major televised sports."

[180] The term comes from John Rawls, e.g. *The Law of Peoples* (Cambridge, MA, 2001).

[181] Mill, *Considerations*, 399.

[182] On Victorian notions of stagnation, e.g. Harold Laski, *Authority in the Modern State* (New Haven, 1919), 187–8; Stefan Collini, "The Idea of 'Character' in Victorian Political Thought," *TRHS*, 35 (1985): 29–50.

In short, they not only held up their preferred form of government as the best possible; they also had a dystopian image of those forms that fell short of it.

The reason for their dystopianism about nondeliberative regimes was that "government by discussion" was not just the capstone of societies characterized by discourse and debate as opposed to arbitrary power – it was their precondition, as well. Victorians believed that most societies (even in Europe) were stagnant. This meant (depending on the approach and phrasing of the author) that one class, one character type, one set of ideas and values dominated the social–mental landscape in such a way that innovation and novelty could not arise.[183] This was the primitive state of society, and most peoples had never emerged from it.

But the situation was even bleaker than the foregoing would indicate. Not only was it difficult to exit the primitive condition, escaping it was not a once-and-for-all achievement. The progressiveness that came with entering the "age of discussion" was fragile, for relapse was always possible. The main avenue by which a progressive society could be undermined was that the legislature would cease to operate deliberatively. What was the connection between the degree of deliberativeness in the legislative forum and broader societal-intellectual regression? Once again, it was Bagehot who expounded the logic in most depth.

For Bagehot, government by discussion was the soul of modern, civilized societies (read: England), without which they would return to the condition of premodern ones such as India;[184] it alone could durably keep at bay the forces hostile to diversity and new ideas which were inherent in human nature. On this perspective, the deliberative Commons caused and preserved world-historical intellectual gains. In the absence of the stimulus provided by this form of government and the exemplars of the deliberative virtues that it supplied, progress would cease, for the primitive instincts of man which encouraged imitation, submission to custom, and hatred of

---

[183] "The great danger which threatens nations [is] that they may crystallise, like the Chinese, into inflexible habits of thought and feeling that shut them out from progress"; Hutton, "Clifford's 'Lectures and Essays,'" in *Criticisms on Contemporary Thought*, vol. 1, 260.

[184] Bagehot, *Physics and Politics; or, Thoughts on the Application of the Principles of 'Natural Selection' and 'Inheritance' to Political Society* in *CW*, vol. 7, chs. 1–2. Bagehot's equation of premodernity with the unfitness for and nonexistence of discussion not only crystallized a longstanding discourse on the interrelations of progress, evolution, diversity, and deliberation (he was especially influenced by the great Victorian jurist, legal historian, and Indian imperial administrator Henry Maine); it also remained an orthodoxy of English political discourse for decades to come, with important implications for the theory of imperialism. For similar ideas across this span, see Frederic Harrison, "The Religion of Inhumanity," *FR*, 13 (1873), 690; D. G. Ritchie, "Social Evolution," *International Journal of Ethics*, 6 (1896): 165–81; William Graham, *English Political Philosophy from Hobbes to Maine* (London, 1907), 348–415 (on Maine and his impact).

minority views would bring an end to intellectual inquiry.[185] As soon as the Commons, on which so much of the nation's attention was trained, substituted "unimpeded command" as modeled by the world's "*best finished democracy*"[186] for "reasoned arguments" in "regular representative assemblies," "the mass" of the country would cease to be amenable to "important thought."[187] If political power proved to be inaccessible to "the impact of argument and the play of mind upon mind," then a major impetus to intellectual inquiry and a source of courage in maintaining and arguing for presently unpopular opinions would dry up.[188] Only government that "lives by discussion" could provide the public with the resources and the motivation for "continual learning" by which it could "grow and learn" and "come[] to know great principles and understand great questions."[189] But for the fact that deliberative assemblies provided daily testimony of their importance to the "*business*" of public affairs, "argument and dissertation" would seem meaningless to the average man.[190] Without government by discussion to "quicken[] and enliven[] thought all through society," stultification would overcome all aspects of life, even those, like the natural sciences, that appeared furthest from politics.[191] As Bagehot immodestly concluded, the reason why Darwin and Newton had appeared in England and not elsewhere was because England was the nation in which government by discussion had operated longest.[192]

Because of the close continuity between the political reasoning – and the mental life more broadly – of Parliament and of the public, getting reform wrong entailed enormous danger. Bad representative institutions threatened to turn Britain from a "progressive" to a "retrograde" society.[193] Paralleling the judgment passed by defenders of intellectual and expressive

---

[185] Bagehot, *Physics and Politics*, 110.
[186] He was referring here to the Second French Empire under Napoleon III. On the antidemocratic lessons which many Britons drew from the Empire, see J. P. Parry, "The Impact of Napoleon III on British Politics, 1851–1880," *TRHS*, 51 (2001): 147–75.
[187] Bagehot, "Caesarism as It Now Exists," in *CW*, vol. 4, 112–3; "The Collapse of Caesarism," in *CW*, vol. 4, 156.
[188] Bagehot, "The Present Crisis in America," 173. Similarly for Greg, it was in Parliament that the meaning of "individual independence" and "moral courage" – which he gave the lovely name "*pluck*" – was brought "within the reach of ordinary minds"; "French Judgments of England," *ER*, 103 (1856), 583.
[189] Bagehot, "France or England," in *CW*, vol. 4, 91.   [190] Bagehot, *English Constitution*, 217.
[191] He wrote further: "Nothing promotes intellect like intellectual discussion, and nothing promotes intellectual discussion so much as government by discussion"; Bagehot, *Physics and Politics*, 130–2.
[192] Bagehot, *Physics and Politics*, 132–3. This conviction of the "degradation of public life" that attended nondiscussive modes of government was central to Bagehot's attack on the American constitution; "The Federal Constitution Responsible for Federal Apathy," in *CW*, vol. 6, 168–71; "The Present Crisis in America," 172–5.
[193] Bagehot, "France or England," 91–2.

freedom that apathy and absence of inquiry were worse than any error could be,[194] the replacement of genuine deliberative government by intolerant class rule or an arbitrary "overweening dictator" was far more deleterious than any particular policy mistake could be.[195] It would mean the end of what Mill's French translator Charles Dupont-White, in a coinage that distilled much about the Victorian scene he knew so well, called the *société discuteuse*.[196]

The conception of deliberation with which the variety-of-suffragists were at work was, in sum, a mixture of detailed consideration of its practical operation and almost utopian expectations.[197] The complex character of the commitment to deliberation among this strand of parliamentary reform belies the gap that is sometimes imagined to have existed between Mill – the "saint of rationalism" and speculative thinker on politics par excellence[198] – and the practical, realist, businesslike political culture of the mid-Victorian era.[199] Compare Mill, for example, to Bagehot. While Bagehot himself contributed to the stereotype of Mill as

---

[194] H. T. Buckle, "Mill on Liberty," *FM*, 59 (1859), 531: "On any subject, universal acquiescence always engenders universal apathy. By a parity of reasoning, the greater the acquiescence the greater the apathy ... Give us paradox, give us error, give us what you will, so that you save us from stagnation."

[195] Bagehot, "Average Government," in *CW*, vol. 6, 87. The tight connection posited by these authors between the deliberative legislature and the broader deliberative society complicates Saunders's thought that nondemocratic reformers had simply made a conceptual mistake when citing Tocqueville on the intellectual decay of democracies. To Saunders, these men had simply failed to note that Tocqueville was remarking on "democratic *societies*" rather than on the "democratic *franchise*"; Saunders, *Democracy and the Vote*, 147. But since writers such as Greg, Grey, and Bagehot denied the practical possibility of a gap between government and society on this score, they were in fact quite right by their lights to have invoked *Democracy in America* on the lack of "true liberty of discussion" in democracies, as Grey did when he mounted his "grave objection" against democratic government, namely, that it suppressed "discussion of conflicting opinions"; *Parliamentary Government*, 173–5.

[196] "Note well that progress takes place only where there is discussion, which is to say in the West; and that among western societies, the most rapid progress belongs to the most discussive (*la plus discuteuse*)"; Dupont-White, *Le Rôle et la liberté de la presse* (Paris, 1866), 28. Dupont-White was one of the most interesting and idiosyncratic French thinkers of the Second-Imperial era, and a close follower of the English philosophical and parliamentary scene. He was also a friend, translator, and insightful analyst of Mill. See Sudhir Hazareesingh, *Intellectual Founders of the Republic: Five Studies in Nineteenth-Century French Republican Political Thought* (Oxford, 2001), ch. 2.

[197] This is a combinatory space that modern deliberative democracy tries to occupy today; witness the frequent desire for a more "institutional" deliberative democratic theory, as in Graham Smith and Corinne Wales, "Citizens' Juries and Deliberative Democracy," *PS*, 48 (2000): 51–65.

[198] This was Gladstone's moniker for Mill; e.g. Georgios Varouxakis and Paul Kelly, "John Stuart Mill's Thought and Legacy: A Timely Reappraisal," in *John Stuart Mill – Thought and Influence: The Saint of Rationalism* (New York, 2010): 1–18.

[199] E.g. Émile Boutmy's classic contrast between the businesslike and un-idealist English and impractical and moralistic French; Boutmy, *Essai d'une Psychologie politique du Peuple anglais au XIXᵉ siècle* (Paris, 1902), esp. 205–21.

a more speculative thinker than righter-minded compatriots like himself,[200] Bagehot was, every bit as much as Mill, an eager evangelist of discussion and deliberation, of the "salutary effect" of the "collision of opinions" (Mill's words), of the "action and reaction of many kinds of minds" and the contestation between "men of various occupations, various tendencies, and various sympathies" (Bagehot's).[201] Mill may, as he claims, have derived his ideal of "many-sidedness" and his hymns to diversity from foreign sources such as Humboldt and Tocqueville,[202] but the British public had been prepared to receive his lessons through a venerable domestic tradition: the tradition of the representative–deliberative Commons.

In sum, Bagehot and the bulk of his colleagues in representative but nondemocratic reform maintained, with a fidelity equal to Mill's, the vision that what was permanently valuable in politics was the interplay of diverse opinions and ideas. "The whole fabric of English society is based upon discussion," Bagehot wrote – a claim which not even Mill could outdo.[203] When Carl Schmitt was looking for worshippers of the parliamentary idols of "discussion and openness," he might just as easily have selected Bagehot as Mill.[204] After all, it was Bagehot who used the pages of *The Economist* to give this forceful response to malcontents who decried parliamentary government as "mere talk": "those who so think have simply no conception of the nature of popular government. In such a government it is not too much to say that 'speech is action.'"[205] Deliberation was the essence of what a nation did in its political capacity. It was society's central task qua body politic, and it was also the wellspring of the wider set of goods which marked it as a free and progressive society.

This fundamental fact about Bagehot's theory has proven difficult for even the most sensitive of his readers to appreciate. His admiring biographer, for instance, complained that Bagehot had "confuse[d] means with ends" and failed to specify "what all this discussion should be about," had failed to construct a "vision of society" to stand as the outcome of his deliberative parliamentarianism.[206] While one may wish to reject the political theory of Bagehot and the variety-of-suffragists for any number of reasons, it would be wrong to attribute to them this particular confusion

[200] See Bagehot's two review articles on Mill's *Considerations on Representative Government*, in *CW*, vol. 6, 336–46, esp. 341–2.
[201] Mill, *On Liberty*, in *CW*, vol. 18, 257; Bagehot, "Parliamentary Reform," 193.
[202] Mill, *Autobiography*, in *CW*, vol. 1, 200, 260–1; *On Liberty*, 215, 261.
[203] Bagehot, "Average Government," 87.
[204] Schmitt, *The Crisis of Parliamentary Democracy*, trans. Ellen Kennedy (Cambridge, MA, 1988), 2.
[205] Bagehot, "The Non-Legislative Functions of Parliament," 43.
[206] Buchan, *Spare Chancellor*, 210.

in their conception of the value of deliberation. The variety-of-suffragists were aware that their conceptions of public opinion and deliberation committed them to a kind of open-endedness and provisionality in the substantive prescriptions which they offered.[207] The conversation – "the giving of reasons ... discussion, explanation, controversy" – was greater, they thought, than any of the particular conclusions to which it led.[208]

d   Criticisms

Deliberation was a watchword of mid-Victorian parliamentarianism. There was widespread assent that the country received great blessings from having "an assembly which so much takes to itself the character of a deliberative council."[209] Given its prominence, we ought not to be surprised that the view of it elaborated here was not the only picture of legislative deliberation current in this milieu, and that there was contestation and uncertainty about what exactly a deliberative legislature involved.

The remainder of this section is devoted to examining three anxieties provoked by the variety-of-suffragist treatment of this theme. The subjects dealt with are an interesting blend of criticisms overtly made at the time and tensions that the theorist today can draw out of their thought, even if the extent to which they were themselves aware of them is difficult to ascertain. We might name these three sources of concern about the version of deliberation presented in this chapter the *technocratic rebuttal; Greg's problem*, after the heterodox religious thinker and defender of the 1832 settlement W. R. Greg; and *Grey's problem*, after the Third Earl from the great Whig family.

i   The Technocratic Rebuttal

The technocratic rebuttal is the easiest to understand of this trio, in part because it remains with us in a form similar to that which it had then; the fight today between epistemic democrats and the defenders of the rule of experts and intellectual elites closely echoes this particular Victorian clash. This rejoinder involved a straightforward denial of the mirror theory's conception of deliberation. While these objectors retained the language of deliberation and could imagine no better way of exalting the Commons than by calling it the greatest "deliberative Assembly that ever existed," in

---

[207] As a young Frederick Pollock, the jurist and historian, wrote characteristically: "at no given time and place can a final and complete answer be given to any of the problems of society and government"; "Liberty, Equality, Fraternity," *FM*, 8 (1873), 86.

[208] Bagehot, "Average Government," 87.

[209] Henry Hallam, *Constitutional History of England*, sixth edition, 2 vols. (London, 1850), vol. 2, 400.

their minds deliberation had no special relationship to the kind of diversity which obsessed the mirrorers.[210] Instead, it was an activity which the wise few who possessed the "science of government" performed on behalf of the rest of society.[211]

For our purposes the most interesting articulation of this point of view was that of Robert Lowe. Lowe's opposition to the enfranchisement of the working class proved extremely controversial, both for the inflammatory terms in which he spoke of the lower classes and for his instrumental role in defeating Gladstone's Reform Bill of 1866 (and ending his government) even though he was a Liberal MP.[212] Lowe was a liberal both in respect of party and of his own broader ideological self-conception, and he could even occasionally be heard to sing a paean to a "House [that was] a faithful reflection of the opinion of the country" when it seemed most germane to the antidemocratic message. But his defense of the settlement of 1832 did not rest on any of the arguments about the representativeness of the status quo described earlier. Instead, he upheld the Reformed Commons as an assemblage of the most competent men in the kingdom, as a body possessed of the technical knowledge, broad culture, and phronesis required for directing a "complicated and artificial society." To Lowe, the sole vector of evaluation of an assembly was whether its membership was possessed of these knowledges and competencies; any additional question of correspondence between this membership and an image of the society outside the House was irrelevant. Indeed, Lowe was completely nonplussed by the epithet of "class government," and he cited Macaulay (with only partial accuracy, on my view) to prove the Whig credentials for his indifference to descriptive accuracy.[213]

For Lowe, the proof of this legislative wisdom was in the pudding. He explicitly rejected the proposition that working-class input could have improved policy even in those areas which most intimately affected them; he believed that their interests were better looked after by the

---

[210] Robert Lowe, *Speeches and Letters on Reform* (London, 1867), 86, 36. [211] Ibid., 34.

[212] On Lowe's fascinating life, see Arthur Patchett Martin, *Life and Letters of the Right Honourable Robert Lowe, Viscount Sherbrooke*, 2 vols. (London, 1893). The bluntness of Lowe's animadversions on the working class were an embarrassment to MPs with similar substantive views, but Lowe was a radical on many other issues, and provided an important voice in favor of trade unions in the debates over their legal status in the mid-1870s; Jonathan Spain, "Trade Unionists, Gladstonian Liberals, and the Labour Law Reforms of 1875," in *Currents of Radicalism: Popular Radicalism, Organised Labour, and Party Politics in Britain, 1850–1914*, ed. Eugenio Biagini and Alastair Reid (Cambridge, 1991): 109–33.

[213] Lowe, *Speeches and Letters*, 175, 10, 164–5. Alongside its descriptive tradition, there was a Whig tradition of more unqualified capacitarianism and "rule of the wise" on which Lowe could draw; Ellis Wasson, "The Great Whigs and Parliamentary Reform, 1809–1830," *JBS*, 24 (1985): 434–64.

Reformed Commons than they would have been by an assembly more responsive to their voices. It was to him a definitive rebuttal to Gladstone's and other reform proposals that "no one has ... shown a single practical grievance under which the working classes are suffering which could be remedied by the proposed alteration."[214] Here we spot a crucial difference between the Lowean technocratic vision of the Commons and the mirroring representative one: whereas someone such as Pochin supported reform even as he acknowledged having a high opinion of the current membership's character and performance,[215] for Lowe such a stance was not even conceivable – one of the main thrusts of his apologetics for the current arrangements was precisely to foreclose the possibility of evaluating the membership of the Commons as a concern distinct from its performance.[216]

This difference was noticed in the moment. Critics of Lowe were aghast that he should have continued to speak of representative government when his arguments consisted of nothing but "indirect ridicule of the representative principle"; they were "perhaps the first time in our history that the theory of a paternal oligarchy has been so nakedly stated; or that the House of Commons has stood forth in the new part of the Benevolent Autocrat."[217] Whatever continuities of vocabulary were preserved,[218] Lowe had, it was believed, substituted a strictly capacitarian for a descriptive politics – he wanted English parliamentarianism to instantiate *outre-Manche* the July Monarchy – and consequently it was natural for resistance to his views to call upon the values of justice and the rule of public opinion reconstructed above. But the dispute with the theory of technocratic paternalism that Lowe incarnated took place as well on the terrain of this third value of deliberation. His opponents were not satisfied just to point out that the MP for Kidderminster had fallen afoul of widespread norms of representativeness. More ambitiously, as we have learned,

---

[214] Lowe, *Speeches and Letters.*, 43. Needless to say, most of his opponents thought that they had amply pointed out such grievances.

[215] Pochin, *Plan*, 4.   [216] Lowe, "Reform Essays," 247–58.

[217] Cracroft, *Essays*, vol. 1, 161; Harrison, *Order and Progress*, 132. Such critiques of Lowe resemble the aforementioned attacks on Guizot and the *doctrinaires* for having emptied the word "representation" of any meaning. Kahan has observed a resemblance between Lowe and Guizot as well; *Liberalism in Nineteenth-Century Europe*, 48.

[218] In one area there was a meaningful terminological discrepancy: instead of the Bagehotian jumble of units of representation which, as we analyzed, ultimately privileged "opinions," Lowe spoke in terms of "interests." Since, rightly understood, all interests were aligned ("Reform Essays," 266–7), there was no reason to aim to reflect society's divisions but merely to engineer that the most accurate discerners of the true interest filled the assembly. This vision of interest, as was recognized at the time, was foundational to Lowe's "paternalism": Lowe, "Reform Essays," 247; Brodrick, "The Utilitarian Argument against Reform, as Stated by Mr. Lowe" in *Essays on Reform*, 7–9.

they hoped to have their cake and eat it too – to use their conception of diversity as an epistemic trump to prove that the wise legislation which proponents of a Commons of experts desired could only be the result of the mirroring which he rejected.

Once Lowe's pole of the debate has been brought into the picture it becomes easier to observe fissures and gradations within the school of electoral variegation. While, as we have seen, one could justify earmarking a number of seats for the "intelligent classes" from within the sociological or descriptive framework either on the basis of their greater contributions to public opinion and national prosperity or, as Harris did, by building "intelligence" and "virtue" ontologically into one's account of society's functional parts, one could of course also straightforwardly recommend measures to increase the intellectual caliber of the membership without worrying about any descriptive or communitarian roots for them. Stapleton, for one, switched between a descriptive idiom (as when he wrote of seeking that "*learning* and *education* would obtain their due weight in the legislative scale"), and something more like Lowe's language of capacity or fitness (as when he prized constituencies that would return "men of an elevated morality" "best fitted for discharging legislative duties" and not "the puny ranks of democratick politicians.")[219] Likewise, Greg did not bother to square the suggestions he made to enhance the "ability" and "high-mindedness" of the membership or to give greater security for the parliamentary voice of the most capable citizens with his more basic aim of mirroring the diversity of classes and communities.[220] There was a comparable ambiguity in Grey, whose defense of his proposal of internally elected life members seems to have been driven partially by the diversity-promoting motivation of providing space for "unpopular opinions" and partially by the competence-promoting one of guaranteeing the "ablest men" seats.[221] If no amount of intellect or virtue could save the assembly from the harms that followed a lack of diversity, they were hopeful that diversity might be accompanied by these excellences rather than by stupidity or immorality, even if they accepted that the value of representativeness was inconsistent with any project for maximizing merit. And they were not always exemplars of philosophic clarity in precisely specifying when they veered from the path of mirroring or descriptiveness in order to target intelligence and wisdom.

---

[219] Stapleton, *Suggestions*, 46, 38. Similar ambiguities ran through the broader argumentation on behalf of "fancy franchises," on which see Eric Evans, *Parliamentary Reform in Britain, c. 1770–1918* (Abingdon, Oxon, 2013), ch. 3.

[220] E.g. *Rocks Ahead*, 29–31; "Parliamentary Purification," 619–20. And see ch. 1, note 85.

[221] Grey, *Parliamentary Government*, 71, 218.

ii   Greg's Problem

The technocratic rebuttal thus exposed a certain tension in the variegated-suffrage theory of deliberation. But it was a tension of a relatively mild sort, for there was no logical inconsistency in affirming diversity to be indispensable to legislative deliberation while also according an important role to the personal attributes of the members. This was what Bagehot did coherently in describing an ideal Commons as one that joined moderation in its members' character with representativeness of "really organic interests and opinions." A more acute tension emerges in what I referred to as *Greg's problem*. Greg's problem, which could travel with the kinds of concerns that motivated the technocratic rebuttal but was analytically distinct from them, was the challenge of whether the Commons could be both deliberative and representative at once. Stated differently, it was the question of whether the values of deliberation and the rule of public opinion were consistent with one another. I give the dilemma this name not because it was an issue peculiar to his writing (it was not), but in recognition of the fact that Greg made an effort to respond theoretically to the issue. This was a problem which went to the heart of mirroring parliamentarianism, but which was largely ignored by our authors, in contrast to the directness with which some of them addressed the trade-offs between descriptivity and meritocracy. At the least, it is certain that none of them *solved* the tension.

Before entering into the project of reconstructing the problem as they saw it, it is worth stating that I do not regard their lack of a clear-cut resolution as a failure. Much as Dennis Thompson reads John Stuart Mill's political theory as a dialectic between the principles of competence and participation without considering it a failure that Mill never resolved one into the other,[222] much of what makes the wider orbit of nineteenth-century British political thought so rich is the interaction between the principles of deliberation and representation. Moreover, it is not simply that in this time and place the tension between these two ideals was more creative than destructive. On the contrary, *Greg's problem* points to a kind of perennial antinomy that any comprehensive theory of modern politics will have to take up.[223] The cause for disappointment with the variety-of-suffragist treatment of the matter lies in their having so seldom openly broached the conceptual disjunction between the aspirations to deliberative and to representative government.

---

[222] Thompson, *John Stuart Mill and Representative Government*.

[223] This issue qualifies as one of what Rosanvallon calls "contestations and tensions always being reborn"; *La démocratie inachevée*, (Paris, 2000), 405.

Greg's problem arose when skeptics about this optimistic account of how descriptive representation and deliberation worked in tandem drove a wedge between the two concepts. For these critics, deliberativeness and descriptive representativeness were not complementary dimensions of an assembly, but rather conflicted with one another.

What did they mean by saying that these two values stood in tension? They meant, first and foremost, that mirror theory deliberativism was flawed because it only looked at public opinion in one light; it saw public opinion solely as the resources or materials for deliberation, rather than as a *constraint* on deliberation (which was, to the critics, its more salient feature). Public opinion was a set of pressures external to the House which distorted the deliberation within it. If the Commons was to arrive at its decisions in a deliberative manner, then the dictates of public opinion as such must be of no significance. A particularly vigorous statement of this perspective had come from the Tory Robert Inglis in the early 1830s. Although he defended the variegated franchise as part of his effort to kill Whig attempts to remodel the historic Constitution, Inglis harshly criticized the reverence for public opinion that was – and would become even more so at mid-century – an unquestioned tenet of most mirrorers. "The mere multiplication of numbers," he asserted with regard to the reform agitation, "asking for what they have not, can never, without reference to the reasons which they urge, be an argument to which a deliberative body can be justified in yielding." Public opinion, considered as the distribution of views and preferences in the country, was, to a thinker of Inglis's persuasion, simply of no relevance whatsoever to the conduct of the Commons: "we are not sent here day by day to represent the opinions of our constituents . . . their general interests we are bound to consult at all times; but not their will, unless it shall coincide with our own deliberate sense of right." If the fact that the public "*demanded*" a policy were reason for its enactment, it followed that the Commons would not be a deliberative assembly at all, but more like the American Electoral College as it has come to operate; it would be simply a kind of grand and unnecessarily numerous notary of the popular will. Indeed, if this public demand were interpreted to contain a threat of civil disturbance unless a given law were passed, then it "will entirely annihilate our deliberative character, and will reduce us to the mere function of speaking the will of others."[224]

---

[224] Inglis, *Parliamentary Reform*, 13, 4–5. On this "Tory" line of thought in the context of the debate over the Reform Act, see Joseph Hamburger, *James Mill and the Art of Revolution* (New Haven, 1963), 44.

From this standpoint, it was not only when the importunities of the populace threatened revolt that true deliberative government was contravened. Rather, the standing of the House was compromised as soon as MPs even took notice of "the wishes and wants of the people." Somewhat implausibly, Inglis seems to have believed that the debates of the House required MPs to draw a veil of ignorance over the happenings beyond the Palace of Westminster's walls. The "myriads of [the public's] petitions . . . the millions of their hands" belonged to a different category of thing than genuine reasons. Instead, what constituted a body as deliberative was that it was determined *solely* by the quality of arguments – and not at all by pressures or clamors or simple numbers: "This House yields, when it yields at all, to the reason and the arguments by which those wishes and those wants are enforced."[225] In other words, a truly deliberative assembly never, properly speaking, gave public opinion as such any weight: "I am sent here to legislate, not for their will, but for their interests."[226]

For Inglis and like-minded writers, then, the state of public opinion revealed only what the country wanted but not whether those wants were justified or rational or in their interest – the latter questions were what the deliberation in the House was to decide.[227] On the standard variety-of-suffragist picture, public opinion was a composite entity which by its diversity enriched the conversation that could be had in the Commons. In contrast, these figures perceived public opinion as a force attention to which was more likely to harm than to refine consideration of the legislative matters at hand by distracting MPs from sounding the true merits of the question.[228] Consequently, they thought, public opinion and the

---

[225] Inglis, *Parliamentary Reform*, 49. Also Paul Smith, "Introduction," to *Lord Salisbury on Politics*, 41. Inglis's hostility to an understanding of public opinion as in any way normative or directive for MPs was founded on much of the eighteenth-century understanding (common to Britain and America) of "the representative as a quasi-magistrate to whose commands constituents owed presumptive obedience"; Richard Buel, Jr., "Democracy and the American Revolution: A Frame of Reference," *William & Mary Quarterly*, 21 (1964): 165–90.

[226] Inglis, *Parliamentary Reform*, 58.

[227] The greatest Victorian politician with this attitude was Peel, who saw public opinion as "only an irrational frictional element"; Peter Ghosh, "Gladstone and Peel," in *Politics and Culture in Victorian Britain: Essays in Memory of Colin Matthew*, ed. Ghosh and Lawrence Goldman (Oxford, 2006): 45–73. He dissented from the mainstream of variety-of-suffrages parliamentarianism as well in being a strong believer in executive rule over the assembly.

[228] To such skeptics about public opinion, the sense of its antideliberative character was tied to the threat of revolt and violence which extra-parliamentary movements that claimed to represent the public were often willing to brandish (as, most famously, with "physical force chartism"), as well as to the mood of fragility and fear that European upheavals cast throughout the first two-thirds of the century; Paul Pickering, "Peaceably If We Can, Forcibly If We Must: Political Violence and Insurrection in Early-Victorian Britain," in *Terror: From Tyrannicide to Terrorism*, ed. Brett Bowden and Michael Davis (St. Lucia, Queensland, 2008): 113–33.

outcomes of the Commons's deliberative process would coincide only casually and sporadically – namely, when public opinion happened to be right. Any more intimate connection between public opinion and the course of legislation, such as that envisioned by mid-century descriptivists, was without place in their thoroughgoing deliberative assembly.

It was remarked in Chapter 1 that Augustus Stapleton fit more uneasily than the other authors into the mold of mid-Victorian descriptivism. The reason for this qualification can now be made apparent: like his fellow Tory Inglis, he detached public opinion from deliberation in a manner distinctly unlike figures such as Bagehot. Stapleton regarded public opinion with the jealous eye of someone whose top priority was to guard the independence of the "deliberative assembly." Despite the many aspects of his tract which overlapped with the mirrorers, he was at odds with them in his contempt for public opinion. "The present House of Commons," he lamented, "is easily swayed on one side or the other by the breath of public opinion." The important question, he went on, was not whether the Commons "'responded quickly and readily to publick opinion.' But the reall important question is, has this responsiveness resulted in an increase of publick happiness and prosperity?"[229] To Stapleton the latter query was simply rhetorical; he was quite certain that it had not, and he listed many policies which to his mind had been foolhardy.[230] But underlying these criticisms of particular policies was the deeper message that there was a disjuncture between a statesmanlike approach to public affairs and a subservient one in which the politician sought to descry the movement of public opinion and follow its trail.[231] The first, from his standpoint, corresponded to a deliberative assembly; the second, to an assembly that was merely representative.

This desire for freedom from public opinion in the evaluation and formation of policy had its bounds, even for Inglis–Stapleton Toryism. These bounds were elections.[232] But even these limits they wanted drawn

---

[229] Stapleton, *Suggestions*, 8–11. The internal quotation was from Russell.   [230] Ibid., 14–26.

[231] As a protectionist, he naturally chose the 1846 repeal of the Corn Laws as an instance of the latter: "Now the permanent *status* of the country could not have so completely changed in so short a time, as to render *that* advisable in 1840, which was not advisable in 1846. But the sentiments of the people were either changed, or were supposed to have changed, and *that* was what Lord John deemed sufficient reason for changing upon a question, which ought to have been viewed with a Statesman's eye, to have been decided by considerations of the general *permanent* good; but above all, which ought not to have been definitely settled on the ground of popular *will*"; ibid., 25–6.

[232] "If in our conduct there be error, our constituents have their remedy at a dissolution. At that time we surrender our stewardship to those by whom it was committed to us; and receive it again, or not, according to their will, and their estimate of our conduct"; Inglis, *Parliamentary Reform*, 14.

loosely. For one thing, election was seen by them as (prospectively) a means of entrusting one person with the power to act in their constituents' name, and (retrospectively) a mechanism of accountability interpreted in the sense of punishing misdeeds, not of enforcing a specific legislative program favored by constituents. The idea that the import of elections was that the MP had a duty of fidelity to the views of his constituents was anathema to them.[233] Indeed, they were happy that competitive elections did not return all the members of the Commons; they defended the array of "close" or "rotten boroughs," those which were "owned" by a "proprietor" who could nominate whom he wished for the seat, in large part for being what we would call in today's parlance the ultimate "safe seats" – seats in which the member by virtue of the security of his tenure could afford to focus entirely on the quality of arguments for and against proposed legislation.[234]

Now, it was open to the more orthodox mirror who held that his plan reconciled the just claims of public opinion and parliamentary deliberation to respond that by "public opinion" he did not mean mere "shifting currents of popular will" but rather a conviction that emerged from extended discussion in which all the standpoints and opinions had been weighed. This was true: in seeking a politics of public opinion rightly understood they did not believe that they were doing anything that would inhibit "due consideration of objections to measures for which there is a popular cry" or impair the process of "testing by discussion the soundness or fallacy of conflicting arguments."[235] And yet this response did not address the heart of the objection, but only postponed the question. For even if public opinion were rational and durable rather than passionate, minatory, and contrived by demagogues, there still arose a conflict between the identification of the Commons's duty as being to craft laws that would realize or conform to the public mind and the identification of its duty as being to engage in free deliberation about the public good. Even if the

---

[233] This minimalist interpretation of electoral accountability was an attempt to justify and preserve (or, in the case of mid-century writers such as Stapleton, to restore) unreformed parliamentary practice; compare these writings with Hegel's examination of the weakness of the elective principle in his 1831 treatment of English parliamentarianism; "On the English Reform Bill," in G. W. F. Hegel, *Political Writings*, ed. Laurence Dickey and H. B. Nisbet (Cambridge, 1999), 258.

[234] Although the "close-borough system ... doubtless was grossly abused by some of those who had controul over those boroughs," it was nevertheless true that "the close-borough representatives were, in reality, the ballast of the unreformed House of Commons ... they were destroyed, and thus was the ballast of the unreformed House of Commons got rid of, and none other was shipped in its room to steady the vessel in its renovated state. Every constituency was changed; hardly one was left to return a member, who might be free from the predominating controul of a fickle popular opinion"; Stapleton, *Suggestions*, 10.

[235] Grey, *Parliamentary Government*, 238, 82.

idealized "Whig" view of public opinion were correct, it remained the case that some independence from public opinion was required for the Commons to qualify as a deliberative body, and not as a mere notarizing or ratificatory one.[236] Just as someone carrying out instructions from a manual is not a deliberator even if these instructions were themselves written by a committee after deliberation, so parliamentary government – that is, government by legislative discussion – was not actualized even if the parties or constituencies which dictated to the House exemplified deliberativeness in their own domains.

The recognition that there was a tension between deliberation and representation in the sense of accordance with the wider distribution of views was not solely an insight of outsiders to this school of thought. Hints of such recognition found their way into even the most orthodox theories of deliberative, descriptively-representative government. For instance, during the first of his articles on parliamentary reform, Greg urged that it could be opportune for the House to take up a question when there was "general silence and indifference" on the issue in the country, since such a "quiet time" furnished an excellent occasion for the House's "wide and profound consideration" of the "merits alone" of the various "measures to be proposed." We can spot in this passage an awareness of how the claims of deliberation and representing public opinion could pull apart. Greg's message here was not just the familiar one that the fires of "popular passion" and "impatient excitement" were not ideal for reasoned "deliberation," though it was in part that.[237] At a deeper theoretical level, his point was that deliberation did not need to wait on representation; he was opposing the idea that what we might call the *spokesman* function comprised the whole of the MP's purpose, for this idea would imply that, in the absence of views in the constituencies for which the MP could advocate, he could not participate in parliamentary discussion of a particular matter.[238]

---

[236] Hence Macaulay's enigmatic attempt, in one of his most "aristocratical" moods, to thread the needle between too ready responsiveness to and too much independence from public opinion: for the Commons to qualify as the "great council of state," it had to be "influenced by the opinion of the people, and influenced powerfully, but slowly and circuitously"; Macaulay, "Hallam's Constitutional History," in *Critical and Historical Essays*, fifth edition, 2 vols (London, 1848), vol. 1, 214.

[237] Greg, "Expected Reform Bill," 235–6.

[238] His best elaboration of the point occurs at ibid., 235. Nadia Urbinati resists the label "descriptive representation" in part because she wants to avoid the implication that she is denigrating the constructive role of the MP; Urbinati, "Representation as Advocacy," 760. As the mid-Victorian example shows, however, these ideas need not be mutually exclusive.

More commonly, however, moments of clarity about the distinction between deliberation and representation came not from considering the status quo or reflecting on their own proposed systems, but emerged in a second strand of their critique of democracy. In addition to the central objection to democracy as an unrepresentative and class-based regime, several figures launched a further attack. When Sidgwick, writing in amazement at "the nature and extent of the influence of parties on representative government" near the turn of the century, stressed how little this phenomenon was foreseen by earlier generations of writers, he in fact was underestimating his forebears.[239] Many antidemocrats, including variety-of-suffragists such as Bagehot, had predicted that the need to mobilize large numbers of voters that would arise with a democratized electorate would transfer effective political power from a deliberative assembly to centralized parties directed by unelected "wire-pullers" whose art was not practical reasoning or deliberation but "electioneering."[240] Legislative deliberation would dwindle, for members would have no leeway to change their minds and therefore would not be susceptible to being convinced by an exchange of ideas in the House. Bagehot referred to such a state of affairs – which he predicted both from first-past-the-post democracy and from PR, regardless of the degree of enfranchisement – as "constituency government," which he deemed a direct contravention of "parliamentary government." The mild parties and measure of independence for the individual MP which were essentials for a "deliberative assembly" would vanish in a democracy because democracy meant the dominance of party.[241]

The upcoming chapters on proportional representation will examine a critique of strong parties for being unrepresentative. But it is important to note that what alarmed Bagehot and his ilk here was not that parties diminished representativeness per se, but that they stripped the assembly of its capacity for deliberation. "Party bands and fetters," after all, could be seen as augmenting the representativeness of members insofar as they put forth a "doctrinal creed in politics" to which voters could clearly assent. But even if such a creed was the epitome of "goodness," the MP in thrall to the disciplined party and its motivated base was still "hopelessly enslaved,"

---

[239] Sidgwick, *Elements of Politics*, 590.
[240] Bagehot, *English Constitution*, 297–9. Also e.g. Greg, *Rocks Ahead*, 31–2, 162–5; Aytoun, "Reform Measures," 370; J. F. Stephen, *Liberty, Equality, Fraternity*, 155; W. Fraser Rae, "Political Clubs and Party Organization," *NC*, 3 (1878): 924–7; Moisei Ostrogorski, "Les Origines des associations politiques et des organisations de parti en Angleterre," *Revue Historique*, 52 (1893): 259–97.
[241] Bagehot, *English Constitution*, 298, 304.

a "mouth-piece" and not a true deliberator. There was, Bagehot believed, a basic trade-off between the MP being "free" and the constituency or party to which he answered being "in earnest."[242] Where the latter state of affairs was in existence, the MP may well have been more likely and able to bring sentiments and ideas truly held by a portion of the public to bear on parliamentary debate. But a Commons made up of such MPs was deliberatively weakened, for the House's deliberation was better served by electorates which on the whole were characterized by only "vague preferences" at the level of "particular doctrines."[243]

So far we have envisioned Greg's problem as a tension about how to divide up the political terrain between the public opinion that was supposed to be represented and the deliberation that was supposed to occur in the assembly. But another way to conceive of it is as a tension from within the perspective of the individual MP. The MP appeared to be under dueling obligations: a "representative" obligation of faithful advocacy of the views of his electors, but a "deliberative" obligation of openness to evidence and a willingness to modify his views if proven inconsistent with the common good. To uphold deliberative representative government was to deny that there was a *single* duty encompassing the MP's position.[244]

In addition to its intrinsic interest, examining the challenge faced by electoral-diversity-based reformers of conceptualizing the relationship between deliberation and representation also deepens our understanding of a more famous controversy: the eighteenth- and nineteenth-century debate about delegate versus trustee conceptions of the representative.[245] Contrary to what is often thought, this was not a simple contest between an "aristocratic" notion of the intelligence and virtue of the MP and a "democratic" desire for accountability and control. While variety-of-suffragists' resistance to delegation contained an "elitist" dimension – they agreed with Mill's analogy of the legislator to the physician who worked for

---

[242] Bagehot, *English Constitution*, 304–5. Bagehot provocatively analogized the status of an MP in this situation to "the case of a dissenting minister" who was "ruled by his congregation."

[243] Ibid., 304. Sidgwick was one of many thinkers who would continue through the end of the century to follow Bagehot's line on the drawbacks for representative government of electors having very strongly held views, even going so far as to say that it was important to "keep alive in the mass" of citizens the sense that they ought not to have "fixed political dogmas"; *Elements of Politics*, 557–8.

[244] In this way they overlap with contemporary political theory's aspirations to give a more complex or plural conceptualization of representation; e.g. Andrew Rehfeld, "The Concepts of Representation," in *APSR*, 105 (2011): 631–41.

[245] An excellent overview is A. H. Birch, *Representative and Responsible Government: An Essay on the Constitution* (London, 1964).

the patient's health without following the patient's orders[246] – this resistance was not reducible to elitist premises about the intellectual demands of statesmanship. Indeed, the hostility to voter mandates rested more fundamentally on the seriousness with which they took the ideal of the Commons as a deliberative body.

The variety-of-suffragists and their ideological neighbors opposed delegation as a comprehensive statement of the representative's function (as, for example, in some philosophic-radical literature).[247] Yet they did not adopt the stock Burkean position either.[248] Too strident a denial of delegation looked like it might hollow out their notion of representation altogether; the Burkean belief that the MP owed his electors nothing but his "unbiassed opinion, his mature judgment, his enlightened conscience" risked bringing their picture of the Commons too close to the Lowean technocratic one.[249] The position they wished to occupy was a middle ground – a position close to Mill's mature stance, although they were even less interested than Mill in entering into any exact casuistry about the circumstances in which binding or leaving the member at liberty was appropriate.[250] Representatives were charged with maintaining a connection with the views of their constituents; they were not to discuss and make policy as if indifferent to the latter. But qua deliberator on the public good they could not be locked into specific positions by voters (or by parties). In the words of Brougham, who wound up preferring a more democratic electoral system but whose thought on the MP–constituency relationship remained orthodox to traditional Whiggery, all that the "soundest views of representative legislation" could stipulate was that there ought to be a "*general* coincidence between the conduct of the delegate and the sentiments of the electors."[251] Here, they seem to have felt, they ran up against the limits of what political theory could say.

---

[246] Mill, "Pledges [1]," article in the *Examiner* from 1 July 1832, in *CW*, vol. 23, 491; "Appendix to *Dissertations and Discussions*," in *CW*, vol. 19, 651. Also Greg, "Expected Reform Bill," 219–21; Bagehot, "Lord Althorp and the Reform Act," 229–30.

[247] Grey, *Parliamentary Government*, ix; George Cornewall Lewis, *An Essay on the Influence of Authority in Matters of Opinion*, second edition (London, 1875), 184–7.

[248] It was no coincidence that Lecky described this uncompromising hostility to delegation as part and parcel of a "tone of political feeling" that had disappeared with the eighteenth century; Lecky, *Democracy and Liberty*, vol. 1, 6–7.

[249] Burke, "Speech to the Electors of Bristol," in Burke, *Miscellaneous Writings*, ed. Francis Canavan (Indianapolis, 1999), 11.

[250] Mill, *Considerations*, ch. 12.

[251] Brougham, "Speech on Parliamentary Reform," Oct. 7, 1831, in *Works of Henry Lord Brougham*, 11 vols. (Edinburgh, 1873), vol. 10, 371.

Given the deeply contextual nature of the balance of considerations that would determine when it was proper to act as the committed spokesman versus the unencumbered deliberator,[252] it is not particularly surprising that they developed few elaborate treatments of the delegate–trustee question specifically. But it is surprising that they made so few attempts at a more general theory of the relationship between constituency and representative that would capture the tightrope which they wanted to walk between values. In part this was because the perfect union of deliberation and representation as it regarded the level of the individual MP and his constituents was not their primary locus of concern; they were concerned with the Commons as an institution and (as we investigated in Subsection 3b) at that level the medley of defects on the individual plane could redound to the benefit of the whole.[253] So long as a healthy distribution of "special advocates" and "impartial judges" obtained, it was not very important if the former had been reduced to mere mouthpieces by parties with prefabricated platforms, or if the impartiality of the latter in fact stemmed from their paying less scrupulous attention to the views of their constituents than perfect fulfillment of their role-obligations would dictate. The Victorian theory of parliamentary deliberation was not centered on providing an ethics for MPs, but on depicting a functional economy of reasons and arguments.[254]

Nevertheless, Greg did come close to delineating a theory of the ideal relationship between voter and MP. Fittingly, given his renown for importing German Biblical Criticism into England, he named it in his favorite tongue: *stand-punct* representation. Greg gave this concept an openly traditionalist and hierarchical inflection.[255] His target was the

---

[252] For a similar modern view of the "indeterminacy" of theory on these questions, see Jane Mansbridge, "Rethinking Representation," *APSR*, 97 (2003): 528.

[253] Perhaps surprisingly given the moralistic tenor of Victorian culture, the variety-of-suffragist preoccupation with, and faith in, the well-functioning of a suitably diverse *system* made their theory less prescriptive about the character and behavior of representatives than much democratic theory today (such as Suzanne Dovi, *The Good Representative* [Oxford, 2007]). As Chapter 5 will show, the theory of representation of the time which was most ethically demanding on individual representatives was PR.

[254] Although it was not theorized in the modern analytic manner, Victorian parliamentarians were operating with something like Mark Warren's distinction (developed in the context of citizen representation) between the accountability of individual representatives to stand for certain specific interests and values of their constituents, and the accountability of the institution as a whole to the public for a satisfactory deliberative and decision-making performance; Warren, "Citizen Representatives," in *Designing Deliberative Democracy*, ed. Warren and Hilary Pearse (Cambridge, 2008): 50–69.

[255] For instance, it appeared alongside a defense of the power of the Lords that was much stronger than that provided by Bagehot. In general, the variety-of-suffragists of this period believed in the

expansion of delegation: he wanted to prevent electors who wished to "decree what shall be done themselves" from encroaching on the province of the MP in a way that threatened to bring back "the old Athenian plan of direct government by the people, practised before the principle of representation was discovered." The electorate had to be kept from "deciding on measures instead of selecting men." But despite his attachment to the idiom of "men not measures" as the voter's domain, Greg did not limit the voter to considering solely the personal fitness of the candidate; had he done so, he would have contradicted many of his other pronouncements on the subject of representation. Instead, the elector was to alight on someone who shared his perspective; he was to choose, and grant some deliberative wiggle room to, a qualified candidate, but he was to do so within the camp of people *like him* in the relevant ways. "The function, theoretical and actual, of the electors, was that of choosing men qualified, by knowledge of their interests and participation in their point of view (identity of *stand-punct*, as the Germans would express it) . . . to represent them."[256] This manner of demarcating what was being described or reflected by descriptive representation has echoes today in theories of "perspective" or "experience" as the object of primary concern in evaluating descriptive inclusion in political assemblies, and this modern literature often presumes that there is something distinctly democratic about such a conception.[257] For Greg, however, this attachment to "point-of-view" as both the basic unit of representation and the proper link between voter and representative was simply a faithful updating of the "original[]" assumptions underlying the development of a "great council of the *tiers-état*," which was that lords did not share a standpoint with commoners and therefore that the latter needed their own space of representation.[258] *Stand-punctism* was just an extension of a venerable tradition of English thought.

Many variety-of-suffragists would have dissented from this manner of carving up the spheres of deliberation and representation. They usually expressed no quarrel with voters fixing on true believers in their particular

de facto entire supremacy of the Commons and thought the Lords a mostly practically defunct or symbolic institution; they did not foresee the resurgence via an assertive Tory veto against Liberal measures which the Lords would make from the end of the century until finally being crushed by the Parliament Act of 1911; Corinne Weston, *The House of Lords and Ideological Politics: Lord Salisbury's Referendal Theory and the Conservative Party, 1846–1922* (Philadelphia, 1995).

[256] Greg, "Representative Reform [1]," 469–70.

[257] E.g. Anne Phillips, "Democracy and Representation: or, Why Should It Matter Who Our Representatives Are?" in *Feminism and Politics*, ed. Phillips (Oxford, 1998): 224–40.

[258] Greg, "Representative Reform [1]," 469.

sentiments and ideas; indeed, their system was intended to facilitate this and turn it to best political effect.[259] Yet some set of thoughts with the rough shape of these passages in Greg would seem to have been required of them. Why, then, did more adherents to deliberative representative government not attempt to construct analogs to Greg's *stand-punct* conception, imperfect as it was, of the place of the representative in the broader economy of opinion-holding and reason-giving? There seem to have been two reasons for this dearth of explicit theorizing about a middle road that could do justice to both the deliberative and representative functions. First, they appear to have assumed that it was obvious that they were trying to achieve just such a balancing act. For instance, even if the topic did not receive sustained attention, it seems that Grey held one accomplishment of his *Parliamentary Government* to be the charting of a third way in which the Commons would be "alive to public opinion" and yet keep its members free from the yoke of "popular caprice."[260] Deliberative representative government existed in the sweet spot between (on the one hand) a harmful insulation from public opinion and (on the other) complete dictation of representatives' views and conduct by nonparliamentary actors. Insofar as proponents of electoral diversity implicitly endorsed such a middle ground, their political commentary was not overly hampered by the absence of a more widely shared and explicit concept of *stand-punctism*, although from a theoretical perspective this absence makes for a disappointing lacuna.

The second reason why so many variety-of-suffragists neglected to offer their own equivalent of a *stand-punct* theory on how to reconcile representativeness with deliberation was that they lacked the motivation to consistently hold these two functions separate in their minds. This conflation was in part due to the manner in which their faith in the epistemic power of conversation among diverse points-of-view connected the two in their eyes. But it also owed much to the fact that these authors saw the mid-century Commons as both imperfectly deliberative and imperfectly in tune with public opinion, and as far as the actual Commons of their time was concerned they traced the former imperfection largely to the latter. In their eagerness to cast their plans as corrective of all that troubled the country's parliamentary regime, they overlooked the distinctness of the deliberative

---

[259] Even the Tory Stapleton drew the line in a way more empowering of the elector, who was to seek out exponents of his "principles" although preferably not of his "*specifick*" measures"; *Suggestions*, 8.
[260] Grey, *Parliamentary Government*, 218.

and representative deficiencies.[261] They ran together two discrete deficits because they thought they were suffering from both.[262]

The flip side of this perception of a simultaneous deficit of deliberativeness and representativeness was a confidence that by their desired reforms improvements would occur on both fronts. Their conviction that the fuller realization of public opinion in the Commons was also the condition of improved legislative deliberation prevented them from treating the two values with the distinctness and clarity which would have been necessary for them to possess a truly complete theory of a politics at once representative and deliberative. Because they believed that the present arrangements were neither sufficiently attuned to public opinion nor sufficiently deliberative, it was easy for them to assume that representativeness and deliberation always traveled together.

iii Grey's Problem

A more significant theoretical inadequacy, however, was what I term *Grey's problem*. Greg's problem denoted a sin of omission, a missing piece which kept this body of literature from attaining the heights it might have reached; it was not inconsistency at a fundamental level. Yet this latter is what one finds in Grey's influential tract.

Grey's trouble arose from this: in this chapter we have encountered two accounts of the source of legitimacy for the Commons. One, exemplified by Inglis and by Lowe, staked the normative credentials of the assembly on the quality of its deliberation and the wisdom of its policy. The other, the mainstream mirroring view, identified the normative grounding of the Commons with its representativeness and treated deliberation, as crucial as this was, as the product of its achievement. While there were certainly moments of ambiguity, it is reasonably clear that these thinkers' last word was that Britain was a *representative government* and that this meant that resemblance to

---

[261] They were liable to the kind of attack that the great Victorian economist F. Y. Edgeworth lodged against Benthamism for having unwittingly yoked together the separate principles of equality and utility. Edgeworth complained of Bentham's formula "the greatest happiness of the greatest number": "is this more intelligible than the 'greatest illumination with the greatest number of lamps?'"; Edgeworth, *Mathematical Psychics* (London, 1881), 117.

[262] Modern deliberative democracy is more sensitive to these tensions; see e.g. John Dryzek, "Difference Democracy: The Consciousness-Raising Group Against the Gentlemen's Club," in *Democratizing Deliberation: A Political Theory Anthology*, ed. Derek Barker, Noëlle McAfee, and David McIvor (Dayton, 2012): 57–82; Judith Squires, "Group Representation, Deliberation, and the Displacement of Antinomies," in *Democratic Innovation: Deliberation, Representation, and Association*, ed. Michael Saward (London, 2000): 93–105.

the salient realities of their society was what ultimately legitimated the dominant chamber.

Despite being such a prominent voice for the "qualified suffrage" and supporting many reforms that fit clearly within the variety-of-suffragist framework, with Grey the matter was not so neat. On the one hand, Grey was certain of the indispensability of diversity for a satisfactorily deliberative Commons – both for the epistemic advantages in crafting legislation and for the wider educative effects. The presence of "able men holding unpopular opinions, as well as of Members expressing the conflicting views of the various classes of society, and of the many different interests which exist in the Nation" was the hallmark of an excellent Commons; at its best, "the House of Commons is also very unlike all the other Representative Bodies of which I have ever seen a description. It is distinguished from them mainly by the variety of the elements which enter into its composition."[263] The opportunity of "making their arguments heard in Parliament," distributed among all the possible wellsprings of enlightenment which existed in society, was the goal of the composition of the Commons.[264]

This rhapsodizing about the blessings of a diverse assembly fit comfortably within the standard mid-Victorian mirroring vision of the Commons – as did his frequent statements that descriptive representation was the bedrock of the House. But at times the Third Earl appeared not so sure of his footing, for he equivocated on the relationship between the intra-Commons diversity which he so lauded and the principle of representation. "The notion commonly entertained of a perfect Representation of the People" was, he said, not beloved of the Greys – it had not motivated his father in making the Reform Act, nor was it guiding his own suggestions. "What is called a perfectly pure system of Representation" bore no relation to proper reform, for "some of the most faulty parts of our present system of Representation incidentally serve useful purposes."[265]

Why did Grey occasionally switch into this representation-deflating idiom? For two related reasons. First, he was unable to hold his ground as steadfastly as his variety-of-suffragist fellows against the advance of

---

[263] Grey, *Parliamentary Government*, 71, 65. "It would be desirable," he went on, in a show of amity toward Hare and Mill, that "men of almost every variety of opinion" should find their way into the House; ibid., 205. He agreed with the inclusivity- and descriptiveness-based rationales for PR, but ultimately rejected it in anticipation of certain problems with its practical operation. Interestingly, and tellingly for later themes in the book, Grey here demonstrates that he saw PR as largely continuous, in its ends if not its means, with the variety-of-suffrages tradition.

[264] Ibid., 216.   [265] Ibid., 66–7, 134.

a quite different idea of representation: a democratic view in which representation was not a technique for creating an image of the nation but was instead a mechanism for delivering consent or authorization – consent which had to come from each individual equally. In the face of these "Chartist" or "French" or "abstract democratical" notions, the thoroughgoing mirrorer was simply unmoved: he denied that such "complete suffragists" were in possession of a theory of "representation" at all; branded them campaigners for "exclusive or overwhelming" class rule; and flatly asserted their incorrectness in light of "our whole Parliamentary theory."[266] Grey, however, was less solid in his resistance to this alternative. Much like Charles I two centuries prior conceding to his antimonarchical opponents the usage of the symbolically important term "Republique,"[267] Grey could not keep himself from the sporadic concession that "representation" hinged on everyone voting in some approximation to equal electoral power. Hence, true representative government sometimes appeared in his eyes to be "the strict principle of popular Representation," and thus the excellence of the British Commons had to be considered a deviation from representation strictly speaking, a balancing of representation against other goods.[268] Whereas a Mackintosh or Harris consistently distanced democracy from representation conceptually, for Grey the boundary was more permeable.[269]

Second, if Grey could rhapsodize about diversity within the Commons as well as anyone, he sang fewer hymns to diversity outside its walls. This was unusual: for Bagehot, for instance, prescriptions for a diverse Commons were continuous with a profoundly pluralistic social imaginary. Where the editor of *The Economist* envisaged public opinion as multifaceted, heterogeneous, and (therefore) the carrier of much wisdom, it appears that the Earl pictured it as a kind of cross between an older conception of a monolithic onrush of popular feeling[270] and a species of Tocquevillian groupthink squeezing out minority opinions.[271] In lieu of Bagehot-style reminiscences on the composite and dynamic character of

---

[266] Greg, "Expected Reform Bill," 251.

[267] Charles I, *His Majesties Answer to the XIX Propositions of Both Houses of Parliament* (London, 1642), 9. My thanks to Eric Nelson for impressing upon me the importance of this moment.

[268] Grey, *Parliamentary Government*, 67.

[269] A similar equivocation, perhaps more understandable in a Britain close to universal suffrage and accepted by many as "democratic," crept into Lecky, *Democracy and Liberty*, vol. 1, ch. 1.

[270] E.g. Joseph Priestley's notion of "the spirit of the time"; *An Essay on the First Principles of Government*, in Priestley, *Political Writings*, ed. Peter Miller (Cambridge, 1993), 33.

[271] E.g. Claude Lefort, "From Equality to Freedom: Fragments of an Interpretation of *Democracy in America*," in *Democracy and Political Theory*, trans. David Macey (Cambridge, 1988), 203.

the national mind, Grey lamented the force exerted by "the feelings and passions of the numerical majority of the population," and warned in alarmed tones of "popular caprice," "the sudden variations to which [the "people's"] opinions and feelings are liable," the "prejudices of a popular Constituency." "Popular opinion, or clamour (for they are not always easily distinguished)" was potent enough that "wise" thoughts often went unstated "from a fear of offending the prejudices of the day." Under such a yoke, it was urgent to gain for some members, especially those of great talent and prudence, insulation from "the prevailing opinion of the day."[272] In conjunction with his weakness for a "democratic" definition of representation, his recurrence to a vision of public opinion as the howl of the people and an oppressive constraint on debate led to an image of a Commons that looked more detached from the nation than in the more intimate relationship between legislature and society depicted by someone like Bagehot.

The gap that emerged at times in Grey's writing between a polyphonic, contestatory Commons and a univocal, flattened society[273] raised fundamental questions about interaction between deliberation and representation in his theory. Was he engineering deliberative diversity, or representing real societal diversity?[274] If the former, then what were descriptive representatives in Bagehot's or Harris's theory – that is, figures whose legitimacy and purpose was tied to their standing for a class, interest, or other group – were something different in Grey's theory. They were, rather, more like devil's advocates or machines for the enunciation of certain kinds of arguments needed for the House to legislate wisely. Was the Commons reflecting diversity, as in the traditional construction, or was it, in a reversal of the equation, generating diversity for its own epistemic needs? It is unlikely that even Grey himself knew.

These ambiguities about the exact extent to which Grey's Commons was underwritten by the principle of representativeness come out in his interpretation of *close boroughs*. The number of these boroughs, staples of "old corruption" in which the borough "proprietor" had the power to name whom he wished to the seat, was reduced by the Reform Act.[275]

---

[272] Grey, *Parliamentary Government*, 75, 82, 216–17.

[273] These passages of *Parliamentary Government* resonate with the more hierarchical liberalism of postrevolutionary France; Annelien de Dijn, "Aristocratic Liberalism in Post-Revolutionary France," *HJ*, 48 (2005): 661–81.

[274] Similar ambiguities and tensions arise in deliberative democracy; e.g. Jon Elster, "Introduction," to *Deliberative Democracy*, 13.

[275] E.g. Gash, *Politics in the Age of Peel*, chs. 7–9.

In the mid-century, there was a notable strand of nostalgia for these boroughs – although typically qualified with the admission that they could not be revived in light of current notions about corruption. The most common strain of this nostalgia focused on close boroughs as an avenue for introducing talent into the House and a safe haven for eminent statesmen whose support of unpopular causes had lost them seats in larger, more competitive constituencies. In Inglis's words, close boroughs were the means by which "many of those who . . . have constituted the chief ornaments of this House in the past and present age, have entered Parliament; many of whom, if this way had been closed, would never have entered these walls"; and it was often noted that such great parliamentarians as Pitt, Walpole, and Burke had all sat for such boroughs.[276] Another supposed merit of the close boroughs was that they had aided in the stability and quality of the ministry by allowing a seat for those appointed to a cabinet position. Grey subscribed to both of these positive valuations.[277] Notably, neither of these commonly cited virtues had a representative dimension. But Grey also added an appreciation of the close boroughs that hinged on their representative contribution: to wit, that they had served as guarantees of the presence of "minority" opinions in the House.[278] Grey's reading of the positive place which close boroughs had once occupied in the ecology of the Commons thus hung midway between (a) yearning for a time in which representation counted for less, in which the parliamentary system was more openly geared to the production of nonrepresentative political goods such as the insulation of wisdom and enlightenment from popular vagaries, and (b) celebrating a set of constituencies which, however anomalous they may have appeared to the sensibilities of modern rationalizers, in reality had enhanced the Houses's ability to represent the diversity of society. To use nineteenth-century terms, we might say that Grey could not make up his mind with regard to whether the close-borough MPs

---

[276] Inglis, *Parliamentary Reform*, 34.   [277] Ibid., 120–1.

[278] He stressed that this presence was demanded for the minority "even if it were clear that they were in the wrong"; Grey, *Parliamentary Government*, e.g. 215–16. Two other routes were available by which to justify the close borough in terms of representativeness. First, close boroughs could be lauded as having been venues for the representation of the real social entities which were the nation's intelligence and learning. Second (as mentioned earlier in the case of Alison), close boroughs' representative character could be linked to the fact that they were frequently purchased by those who had risen to wealth or prominence at various posts throughout the Empire and thus offered to colonial and imperial interests an "unobtrusive but spacious channel which admitted their representatives to the British Parliament." E.g. Harris, *True Theory*, 46–7; Stapleton, *Suggestions*, 46; Alison, "The Reform Bill," 15–16, 26–7.

constituted a kind of Coleridgean "clerisy" dropped into an otherwise representative body,[279] or whether they stood for elements of the social-intellectual fabric of the country in a way not fundamentally different from their counterparts of less "corrupt" constituencies.

The ambivalence of Grey's commendations of the close boroughs, and of his account of the relations between the representative and deliberative aspects of the Commons more generally, returns us to an important lesson: that political theory is characterized by an indeterminacy and multiplicity of routes between, on the one hand, first principles and fundamental commitments, and, on the other, institutions and practical recommendations. Grey did not have to make a clear decision about the normative foundations of his reforms because several paths could take him to his institutional destination. *Grey's problem* further reminds us that in investigating the thought of even highly reflective politicians, one rarely finds clarity of principles at the bottom.

The mirroring vision of deliberation and its treatment of the interaction between deliberation and other desiderata for the Commons was at once its most intricate, most sprawling, and most problematic aspect. A more straightforwardly depicted value rounded out the normative side of their theory.

4   Stability

Proponents of the variegated franchise attributed a fourth advantage to their model: stability.

As with their account of the epistemic benefits of intraparliamentary diversity, the case they made for the stabilizing benefits of their system closely resembled arguments that were being made in the domains of toleration and freedom of discussion.[280] A primary instance of this overlap

---

[279] Coleridge had influentially argued for using the institutions and resources of the Anglican Church to provide a permanently endowed class of educated minds, a kind of cultural-intellectual establishment devoted to "producing and re-producing ... preserving ... continuing, and perfecting, the necessary sources and conditions of national civilization." See Coleridge, *On the Constitution of Church and State* (London, 1830), 64; Ben Knights, *The Idea of the Clerisy in the Nineteenth Century* (Cambridge, 1978).

[280] Promoters of the variety of suffrages overwhelmingly cheered the consolidation of the freedom of the press and religious toleration that marked their century. The Tory opponent of the First Reform Act, Archibald Alison, was the most borderline case. Although he stopped short of advocating repressive measures, writing in the early 1830s he was deeply suspicious of a democratic–populist bias distorting the publishing market and advocated significant state subsidies to the conservative press to offset this structural disadvantage; Alison, "The Influence of the Press," *BM*, 36 (1834): 373–91.

was that variety-of-suffragists anchored the capacity of their programs to ensure domestic tranquility in an optimistic moral psychology that also underpinned much nineteenth-century advocacy for toleration and the liberalization of the press.[281] In this regard, the variety of suffrages was continuous with a contemporaneous pacific theory of free speech built around the psychology of "fair play"[282] – a continuity which should not be surprising in light of the common Whig provenance of these ideas.[283]

One of the most cogent articulations of the bearing of this "fair play" psychology on the representative sphere came from W. R. Greg. "There is a wide and indestructible difference," he wrote, "between being not successful and being not heard – between being outvoted and being excluded – between being defeated after full deliberation in a legislative assembly and being denied a hearing and a seat in the assembly." This difference was, Greg continued, not merely a normative principle on which philosophers dwelt for the sake of, say, determining whether a given government was legitimate. It was also an empirical law about the temperament of citizens under parliamentary regimes. In most cases, discontented citizens' "ground of complaint is, not that their candidates are outvoted in Parliament, but that they are not allowed to go there, – that their opinions are rejected, not *after*, but *before*, discussion"; the basic demand of ideological and interest groups was not to impose their wishes on society, but rather the reasonable one that they be participants in the deliberation, that they be not "altogether overpowered, suppressed, and virtually non-existent because non-apparent."[284] Given that the desire for inclusion in

---

[281] "For several generations," Lecky wrote in the 1890s, it had been a "deep-seated conviction of English political life" that opinions are only "dangerous" when "their free expression is suppressed"; *Democracy and Liberty*, vol. 2, 402. For statements of this view from earlier decades, when the struggle to liberalize the press was most acute, see e.g. Robert Hall, *An Apology for the Freedom of the Press, and for General Liberty*, seventh edition (London, 1822), 21; Brougham, *Inaugural Discourse of Henry Brougham, Esq., MP: On Being Installed Lord Rector of the University of Glasgow* (Glasgow, 1825), 47.

[282] E.g. Greg, "Difficulties of Republican France," *ER*, 92 (1850), 513; Lecky, *The History of European Morals*, 145–6; J. F. Stephen, "Journalism," *CM*, 6 (1862): 52–63, 57. After his active variety-of-suffragist days, Holyoake would go on, in characteristic Victorian fashion, to identify fair play as simply the *definition* of toleration; Holyoake, *Hostile & Generous Toleration: A New Theory of Toleration* (London, 1886), 11. As its importance to Holyoake indicates, the notion of "fair play" had deep roots in working-class culture: see e.g. Rohan McWilliam, "Radicalism and Popular Culture: the Tichborne Case and the Politics of 'Fair Play,' 1867–1886," in *Currents of Radicalism*, ed. Biagini and Reid: 44–64. Advocates of PR and minority representation schemes were eager to appropriate the concept for their cause, as well: Anon., *The Franchise: What Shall We Do to It?* (London, 1858), 19–20; Mill, Speech on Personal Representation, 30 May 1867, in *CW*, vol. 28, 177.

[283] Joseph Hamburger, "The Whig Conscience," in *The Conscience of the Victorian State*, ed. Peter Marsh (Syracuse, 1979): 19–38.

[284] Greg, "Parliamentary Purification," 622.

the arena of deliberation was more basic and powerful than the need to see one's views triumph, a representative system that truthfully reflected underlying social realities could be relied on to keep the peace in the diverse and conflictual societies of the modern world.

Greg was hardly alone in his certainty that being heard – the satisfaction with what we might term the receipt of deliberative consideration – trumped the desire for one's group to capture political power or for policy to be dictated by one's own priorities. Professions of faith in the pacific properties of representative (as opposed, in their lexicon, not to direct, but to class) government abound in the variety-of-suffrages literature. Bagehot wrote that the "uniformity set in 1832" had made the task of preserving "calm" in times of "popular excitement" more difficult by shutting off from the lower classes any means of "adequate expression" in the Commons.[285] Creasy believed that "men who, while unfranchised, are the noisy opponents of all establishments, will, when they receive the franchise, often become their steadiest and most zealous supporters"; accordingly, a "prudent mind" would not risk letting any group grow "alienated" and "sullen" by its electoral exclusion.[286] Where "an equal chance" was afforded to "both sides" of a dispute, Pochin held, then the decision arrived at was strengthened; "all ground of refusal to abide by" it vanished when the losing side evidently had nothing to blame for its loss but its failure to "convince" others of the "justice" of its cause.[287] This "reasonable" temperament obtained even among the working classes who, despite having been unjustly excluded from parliament, did "not ask for the whole" of the electoral power but only for a "share" consistent with keeping their views from going "unrepresented."[288] With a proper "settlement of the question of Reform" "every class and interest in the Country would be represented, and would combine and be equally interested in upholding the Constitution, because from the land-owner to the working man all would have a voice in the Councils of the nation."[289]

---

[285] Bagehot, "Lord Althorp and the Reform Act of 1832," 224.   [286] Creasy, *Text-Book*, 55, 61.

[287] Pochin, *Plan*, 18–9. Pochin added a further stabilizing credential to his plan's list of virtues, namely, that incorporating the urban working class into the Commons would end the unrest caused by demagoguery. Demagogues, on Pochin's telling, were able to stir up the people only by virtue of the latter's being kept out of the political process: as soon as the lower classes possessed "a definite and tangible guarantee, that in all matters of legislation their interests shall not be overlooked, or their own view of disputed cases inadequately stated," then the "floating suspicions mostly in the nebulous state lurking in the minds of some of them" which were "extremely useful to demagogues" would dissipate; ibid., 8. Macaulay had shared this belief that inclusivity in representation was a key to ending demagoguery; Joseph Hamburger, *Macaulay and the Whig Tradition* (Chicago, 1972), 38.

[288] Pochin, *Plan*, 7–8.   [289] "Reformer," *View*, 20.

This dimension of the variety-of-suffrages framework drew upon the progressive hopefulness of the period, its vision of political society as an open and cooperative enterprise. It was not an age prone to dwell in Hobbesian fashion on the dynamics of vainglory or unsociability. Instead, the variety-of-suffragists built upon the contemporary sense that inclusion and the opportunity for expression were more basic human needs than dominion or supremacy. A "liberalism of fear" this strand of liberalism decidedly was not.[290] For these authors, hallmarks of liberal government such as toleration and mirroring parliamentarianism were what exempted the nation from fearfulness about its politics.

Securing the country against the discontent caused by being excluded from the Commons meant ruling out both oligarchic and democratic suffrages. The perils of the former were graphically illustrated by the downfall of the July Monarchy of France under Guizot in 1848. Although the Monarchy was a parliamentary regime that on many fronts pursued policies approved of by mainstream British liberals, to the variety-of-suffragist its highly restricted franchise founded on a uniform censitary requirement made the regime a kind of ticking time-bomb. Bagehot, for example, decried Guizot's fidelity to this "bourgeois" franchise as "a great misfortune" that invited a revolutionary backlash from those excluded.[291] In parallel, democracy could be cast as a form of government that was unstable because it was exclusive. While the democratic electorate was not formally exclusive – this is, of course, what made it democratic – the forecast that "the views of all other classes" would "inevitably be swamped" due to the vast numbers of the working class conveyed a kind of practical exclusion as the result of uniform universal suffrage.[292] These "swamped" groups would be every bit as restless and unsatisfied with their condition as the classes formally disenfranchised by the oligarchic state. "Democracy," as Alison wrote, lacked stability due to "the fatal principle of *uniformity in representation*":

> uniformity necessarily excludes a great proportion of the nation from the legislature. The electors, composed – or, what is the same thing, for the most part composed – of a certain class in society, cannot sympathise with other

[290] Judith Shklar, "The Liberalism of Fear," in *Liberalism and the Moral Life*, ed. Nancy Rosenblum (Cambridge, MA, 1989), ch. 1.

[291] Bagehot, "M. Guizot," in *CW*, vol. 4, 443. Guizot's intransigence in favor of the censitary suffrage remains widely credited with bringing about the February Revolution that ended the July Monarchy: François Furet, *Revolutionary France, 1770–1880* (Oxford, 1992), ch. 7; Pasquale Pasquino, "Sur la théorie constitutionnelle de la monarchie de Juillet," in *Guizot et la culture politique*, 111–28.

[292] Pochin, *Plan*, 19.

bodies; they are careless as to their complaints, indifferent to their welfare, swayed probably by an adverse interest; and the inevitable consequence is, that the ejected classes become discontented, and public dissatisfaction goes on accumulating, till it terminates in a convulsion.[293]

Democracy shared with oligarchy the fault of lacking surety against the neglect of integral components of society.

The differentiated suffrage was thus conceived as stabilizing for the same reason that it was thought to be just and deliberative: it realized a kind of equal opportunity for the different "classes, interests, and opinions" of which modern Britain was constituted. The effort to explain stability in this way led to some interesting and questionable *façons de penser*. For one, variegated-suffrage supporters had a tendency to personify the opinions, ideas, interests, and classes with which they were so preoccupied. In a manner that parallels the objection today to affirmative action programs or quota systems that they essentialize the groups intended to benefit from them,[294] the Victorian theory of descriptive representation could seem to critics to efface actual citizens from the representative domain and replace them with a hypostasized assemblage of impersonal categories. The political order risked upheaval if certain *ideas* were not given a parliamentary space of appearance; revolution would be courted if certain *interests* were not accorded the respect which they merited. At the end of the 1860s, Charles Renouvier, a leading French Kantian, methodological and normative individualist, and devoted republican, divided theories of representation into those which (wrongly) accorded ideas and other social "entities" their own ontological status over and above individual people, and those which (rightly) operated on the view that systems of representation had no other objects than persons.[295] Needless to say, several strands of the variety of suffrages fell on the wrong side of Renouvier's classification.

A second, less ontological but still questionable presupposition was that there existed a potent connection on the citizen's part with the "representatives like him," the representatives who stood for or belonged to his group. To the Victorian descriptivist about representation, it was enough to ensure stability that all the relevant social-ideological groups be

---

[293] Alison, "The Reform Bill," 15–6. Also Russell, *History of the English Constitution*, fourth edition, 180–1.

[294] E.g. Tzvetan Todorov, "Du culte de la différence à la sacralisation de la victime," *Esprit*, 6 (1995): 90–102.

[295] "The right of being represented (*se faire représenter*) belongs, as do all possible rights, to men, and not to ideas, and every idea which does not have the force to cross the channel of the representation of persons ... cannot aspire to a social role. Let it content itself then with the ordinary ways of propagating ideas"; Renouvier, *Science de la morale*, 2 vols. (Paris, 1869), vol. 2, 248.

represented because every citizen could feel consulted and included in the legislative process through the strong tie that bound him to the represen- tatives of the shared group-identity.[296] This felt commonness of identity between the artisan and working-class representatives, or the dissenter and dissenting MPs, facilitated the acceptance by the nation of the policies that passed the Commons; even those segments of the population who had resisted a given law accepted it with grace once passed because they had been consulted (virtually) in the process by which the law was made. Although parliamentary government was not a magic elixir that could guarantee that all the citizens of a diverse society would be satisfied with the *results* of legislation, it did provide a *process* that satisfied everyone. Because of the close "confidence" which "might undoubtedly be pre- sumed" to bind the "class of members" "within the walls of the House of Commons" with the corresponding group of citizens in society at large, a genuinely mirroring Commons "enhance[d] the value and authority" of the decisions made "to an incalculable extent."[297] Accuracy in reflecting society, in conjunction with the power of the bond felt by the citizen toward the members sharing the identity(ies) salient to him, guaranteed a kind of procedural satisfaction that could outweigh the moments of disappointment when one's preferred policies lost. Being "virtually" pre- sent in the legislature through the members associated with one's commu- nity, mirror theorists posited, was more important to citizens than substantively getting their way, even on bitter contests of principle.[298]

To put this much of the burden of social stability on the shoulders of descriptive representation was a leap of faith all the more remarkable given

---

[296] A similar thought appears in the comeback that "virtual representation" is making today, as conceived by some deliberative democrats. In multiple articles Jane Mansbridge has stated that "advocates of particular political views who lose in one district . . . can hope to be represented by advocates of those views elected in another district"; e.g. Mansbridge, "What Does a Representative Do? Descriptive Representation in Communicative Settings of Distrust, Uncrystallized Interests, and Historically Denigrated Status," in Citizenship in Diverse Societies: 99–123, at 113. She prefers the term "surrogate representation" and denies that she endorses virtual representation, but compare her language with that of the Gladstonian defense of virtual representation in the 1860s as presented by Floyd Parsons, "Ignis Fatuus vs. Pons Asinorum: William Gladstone and Proportional Representation, 1867–1885," *PH*, 21 (2002): 374–85. Andrew Rehfeld similarly reads Mansbridge as returning to a traditional notion of virtual representation; Rehfeld, "Representation Rethought: On Trustees, Delegates, and Gyroscopes in the Study of Political Representation and Democracy," *APSR*, 103 (2009): 214–30.

[297] Pochin, *Plan*, 18.

[298] Stapleton, *Suggestions*, 47. Also Russell, *History of the English Constitution*, fourth edition, 180. On the basis of this moral psychology, variety-of-suffragists were confident in denying that their arrangements violated any rule against "invidious comparisons." Cf. Estlund, *Democratic Authority*, 36, 168.

that it was rather out-of-step with the intellectual tenor of the time. The nineteenth century is typically credited with the realization of the limits of politics, with the discovery of "society," "the economy," or "culture" as coequal or greater forces than the political system in shaping the course of human events.[299] As Sidgwick wrote, summing up generations of thought before him: it was an "allusion [sic] that any form of government can ever give a complete security against civil war," for this security "must rest on a moral rather than a political basis."[300] The variety-of-suffrages school, at least in its more enthusiastic moments, demurred from this analysis; getting political institutions right, which fundamentally collapsed into the problem of crafting a truly representative reform, was sufficient to keep away the specter of revolution.[301]

Despite its weaknesses, the attempt by the variety-of-suffragists to theorize the pacific advantages of their representative system is a testament to their continuing relevance. What they hoped and believed was, fundamentally, that the formula of *diversity plus justice* could outperform the older ideal of a homogeneous or unanimous society *even on the issue of stability*. Do we not still hope that this is so, and are we not still searching for explanations as to how this could be the case?

Although the claims of the differentiated franchise to enhance stability received wide assent, they were subjected to several lines of critical interrogation. One of these is of special concern to us, and can serve as a kind of bridge into the broader democratic response to this school of representation covered in Chapter 3.

The bitterest objectors to the stability component of the variety-of-suffrages outlook were not authoritarians alleging that the ship of state could be steered safely only by strong hands.[302] Instead, they were democrats. To these latter, the plans we have been surveying reified harmful class divisions and delivered the Commons over to a sectarian mindset that

---

[299] E.g. Karuna Mantena, *Alibis of Empire: Henry Maine and the Ends of Liberal Imperialism* (Princeton, 2010), ch. 2.

[300] Sidgwick, *Elements of Politics*, 648.

[301] E.g. Mackintosh's essentially electoral-parliamentary account of why England had not been susceptible to revolutionary turmoil: "Our ancient policy did not trust the preservation of order and liberty to those general principles of morality which, in all countries, influence the conduct of good citizens; it bound all classes, by ties of pride and attachment, to a system which bestowed important privileges on all. As every new class arose, it was fastened to the Government by these constitutional links. This policy left no class politically powerful, who did not visibly draw their power from the Constitution"; Mackintosh, "Parliamentary Reform," 481.

[302] Such authoritarians were, after all, relatively a rare breed in the period; A. L. LeQuesne, "Carlyle," in LeQuesne, George Landow, Stefan Collini, and Peter Stansky, *Victorian Thinkers* (Oxford, 1993), esp. 80–7.

would exacerbate existing social tensions. Albert Venn Dicey, whom we will soon see was primarily exercised by fundamental philosophical problems with the variety of suffrages, nonetheless painted a lamentable picture of the fracturing impact which schemes for class- and interest-representation had in practice. "Incalculable evils," he wrote, followed from the "tendency to intensify differences" inherent in these plans.[303] Instead of "members" who aimed at and deliberated upon the common good, those who felt themselves to be "special representatives of a class" were disposed to believe that there was "something sacred" in defending at all costs their own "classes," "orders," and "interests."[304] Plans of differentiated suffrage would encourage MPs to see their mission as fidelity to the group for which they stood rather than to the nation for which they made laws; "from their very position" they would feel it their duty to "display and intensify class feeling," and consequently "the most fanatical, the most narrow" minds would be drawn to parliamentary politics.[305] In the mid-1830s Mill had similarly bemoaned that, on theories of the Mackintosh sort, representatives were reduced to "mere attorneys of certain small knots and confederacies of men" who would treat the legislature as a battlefield of "private interests."[306] This was hardly a recipe for stability. Instead of a deliberative idyll in which the various sectors of society congregated to settle on a commonly acceptable course of action, the Commons would be something more like disputed terrain on which hostile, implacable adversaries fought. The rosy psychological premises to which these thinkers appealed may well have been true as a general matter, but the deleterious effects of their schemes rendered them inapplicable in the sphere of representation.

---

[303] Dicey, "The Balance of Classes," *Essays on Reform*, 81. This yearning for a sense of national unity that would transcend the estrangement of classes was characteristic of the essays in this volume taken as a whole. For Gladstone's similar turn away from "class representation" in this period, see Saunders, *Democracy and the Vote*, 181–2; Cowling, *1867*, 29.

[304] Dicey, "The Balance of Classes," 79, 81. As a democratic pamphleteer put it, there ought not to be "representation of a class" but only "representation of the 'people' – that is to say all classes blended and, as it were, welded together"; " Political Euclid," *The Reform Problem: Its True Solution* (London, 1866), 27–8.

[305] Dicey, "The Balance of Classes," 80.

[306] Mill, "The Rationale of Representation," in *CW*, vol. 18, 44. Distaste and distrust for the aim of "interest" or "class"-based allotments of seats has a special standing in Mill's political thought, for unlike so many of its other aspects this remained constant from his "radical"-democratic youth through his "modified"-democratic maturity. Compare his teenage debating-speech mocking the doctrine of the "representation of classes" as "the tigrish interest should be represented, the wolfish interest should be represented, all the other interests should be represented, and the great body of the beasts should be represented" with his attack on the "sophistical doctrine of a representation of interests" four decades later; Mill, Speech on the British Constitution [2], 376; *Considerations*, 358.

Fears that the variegated electorate would in fact result not in national harmony but in more adversarial social relations could occasionally spill over into the ranks of variety-of-suffragists themselves. Greg, for instance, opposed projects for "assigning to the working classes a certain number of *special* representatives, to be chosen by them exclusively" because of the "unseemly and perilous antagonism" it would create when questions with a strong class-valence came up for debate.[307] The sectarianism of class-specific constituencies and the too-close identification of MPs with particular classes would "perniciously aggravate, that disseverance and hostility of classes, that separation of society *into horizontal layers* ... which, of all the features and tendencies of the condition of England, is, perhaps, the most uncomfortable and menacing."[308] In Greg's anxiety about the corrosive impact that integrating more class-based elements into the electoral system might have, we encounter again the convergence of opposite ends of the ideological spectrum. Of the authors we have considered, Greg had among the most thoroughly elitist sensibilities. And yet, in turning against all institutionalizations of the mirroring thesis more radical than his own, he made use of an argument dear to the Idealist branches of democratic thought that were just beginning to gain around the Second Reform Act: namely, that the health and stability of society depended on a shared moral purpose that transcended class affiliation.[309]

The champions of electoral variety did not have a satisfactory response to these criticisms; for the most part, this aspect of their clash with the democratic camp consisted of a kind of "we say, they say" exchange. Cole's answer to the "objection" that his plan would "provoke" an "invidious" "contest of classes" was simply "a denial of the fact that any such consequences would ensue."[310] Neither side could convince the other; indeed, it was far from clear what would count as decisive evidence that the pacific gains attributed to the feeling of being included and deliberatively considered would or would not be offset by the destabilizing risks associated with heightened group-identification. Insofar as the contest between the mirror theory and its democratic critics revolved around the question of stability, it generated more heat than light.

---

[307] Greg, "Representative Reform [1]," 474–5. Modern opposition to quotas often takes this form; e.g. Enid Lakeman, *How Democracies Vote*, third edition (London, 1970), 135–6; Rehfeld, *The Concept of Constituency*, 230, 236.

[308] Greg, "Representative Reform [1]," 476.

[309] Melvin Richter, *The Politics of Conscience: T. H. Green and His Age* (Cambridge, MA, 1964).

[310] Cole, *Middle Classes*, 66.

CHAPTER 3

Democracy, Diversity, and Contestability:
Democracy against the Variety of Suffrages

Knowledge of the variety-of-suffrages tradition is important for political theory in its own right: it was a sophisticated attempt to realize an ideal of descriptive representation under conditions of diversity and to provide a theoretical and institutional base for a "liberal" government that would avoid class rule. But recovering this theory is also significant instrumentally, for it enables us to come to a fuller understanding of the history of democratic theory itself. Without recognizing how pervasive and potent the theory of electoral diversity was, we are liable to overlook crucial arguments for manhood (or at least widely extended) suffrage in this formative period for modern democratic theory. For it was incumbent on mid- and late-Victorian advocates of a more democratic franchise to address this powerful alternative on its own terms, and this they tended to do in one of two ways. This chapter will examine these strands of democratic argumentation.

Before beginning our analysis, an important difference between this chapter and the others should be acknowledged. This chapter is more limited in its scope and goals than either the two-chapter sequence preceding it or the two chapters following it. Whereas those aim to capture entire institutional-normative paradigms of representation, the present chapter looks solely at a specific segment of the democratic thought of the time. The universe of Victorian "democratic" thought, at least if we use that term broadly, was vast. A great deal of it centered on beliefs that, while sometimes commingling with the ideas covered in this volume, were largely orthogonal to our main concerns; for instance, arguments for the extension of the suffrage grounded in the improvements in character which the lower classes had demonstrated, while they could be made to dovetail with arguments about the reflection of public opinion, often proceeded on the independent logic that proven worth or fitness ipso facto generated individual entitlements to the vote.[1] This and other lines of democratic advocacy have for the most part to be left untreated here.

Most importantly, it follows from the narrower compass of this chapter that a discussion of Chartism is mostly left out. There are both historical/chronological and substantive/theoretical reasons for this omission. Although Chartism was the largest democratic movement in nineteenth-century British history, its expiration was complete by the end of the 1840s,[2] and hence it could not have responded to the revival of the variety-of-suffragism in the 1850s–60s on which Chapters 1 and 2 concentrated. The democratic thinking taken up in this chapter belongs to a period subsequent to Chartism: the so-called mid-Victorian age of tranquility and equipoise.[3]

The historical distance between Chartism and the figures examined in the following pages was, if anything, smaller than the substantive gap separating them. While Chartism contained heterogeneous groups and agendas,[4] across these variations there was an understanding of what grounded a democratic franchise that simply bypassed mirroring or class-based views: namely, that equal suffrage was a lexically primary *individual right* the denial of which constituted oppression or even a kind of enslavement.[5] This right could be treated historically as the restoration of the true inheritance of all Englishmen derived from a democratic "ancient constitution" which had been perverted, or it could be treated philosophically as an a priori natural right of all men.[6] Either way such premises were quite outside the bounds of descriptivism, and did not give rise to a critique that approached the mirrorers' logic with much seriousness. Moreover, Chartism's hope for the class's united action against its enemies, and the countenancing of "physical force" by parts of the movement,[7] were far

---

[1] E.g. John Garrard, "Democratization in Britain," in *European Democratization since 1800*, ed. Garrard, Vera Tolz, and Ralph White (Houndmills, Basingstoke, 2000): 27–49.

[2] E.g. Gregory Claeys, "General Introduction. The Chartist Movement: A Brief History," in *The Chartist Movement in Britain, 1838–1850*, 6 vols, ed. Claeys (London, 2001), vol. 1: xix–xxxviii.

[3] On these periodizations, e.g. G. D. H. Cole, *Chartist Portraits* (London, 1965), introductory story; Asa Briggs, *The Age of Improvement, 1783–1867*, second edition (London, 2000).

[4] Asa Briggs, "The Local Background of Chartism" and "National Bearings," in *Chartist Studies*, ed. Briggs (London, 1962): 1–28, 288–303.

[5] Betty Fladeland, "'Our Cause Being One and the Same," in *Slavery and British Society, 1776–1846*, ed. James Walvin (London, 1982): 69–99.

[6] E.g. F. C. Mather, "Introduction," to *Chartism and Society*, ed. Mather (London, 1980): 9–46; Gareth Stedman Jones, "Rethinking Chartism," in *Languages of Class: Studies in English Working Class History, 1832–1982* (Cambridge, 1983): 90–178. These fundamental commitments owed much to the late-eighteenth-century radicalism of Thomas Paine and John Cartwright; John Cannon, *Parliamentary Reform, 1640–1832* (Cambridge, 1973), esp. chs. 6–7.

[7] E.g. Trygve Tholfsen, *Working Class Radicalism in Mid-Victorian England* (London, 1976), 85–101; Chase, *Chartism*, passim.

removed from the kind of deliberative democracy for which many of the mid-Victorians considered here longed. Finally, it ought to be noted that Chartists were more uncompromisingly democratic, more consistent in their demands for the universality of the suffrage,[8] than some of the authors in this chapter, who tended to couple a strong theoretical endorsement of democracy with a fuzziness about the exact measure of extension of the suffrage which they desired.[9] In other words, while they supported a large expansion of the suffrage on terms of uniformity and equality and lacked older liberals' fretfulness about "mass politics,"[10] they could be vague about whether parliamentary reform had to go so far as "complete suffrage."[11] On the other hand, we should avoid imagining that some kind of iron curtain separated Chartists from the exponents of democratic thought depicted here. Christian Socialism, for instance, offered a point of contact between the latter and late Chartism. And after Chartism's demise many of its adherents found their way into later, more moderate and "liberal" campaigns for extending the suffrage, such as Edmond Beales's Reform League, with which the authors discussed in this chapter were involved.[12]

With these qualifications in mind, we can now ask: what responses did mid-Victorian proponents of an expansive uniform franchise offer to the variety-of-suffragism of the century's middle decades?

1 Diverse Democracy

In an age as obsessed with the theme of diversity as the Victorian era was – and as convinced of its epistemic benefits and its indispensability to societal progress – democrats had to show that parliamentary democracy was not inconsistent with diversity. This was quite a tall order; an animating thesis of the theory of electoral differentiation was that democracy would stifle

---

[8] Chartism was "ultra-democratic," an appellation which few other movements or thinkers until the end of the century could earn; Christopher Harvie and H. C. G. Matthew, *Nineteenth-Century Britain: A Very Short Introduction* (Oxford, 2000), 38. Also John Walton, *Chartism* (London, 1999).

[9] Christopher Harvie, "Ideology and Home Rule: James Bryce, A. V. Dicey, and Ireland, 1880–1887," *EHR*, 91 (1976): 298–314.

[10] Their favorable experience and understanding of the United States had much to do with this absence of worry; Hugh Tulloch, *James Bryce's American Commonwealth: The Anglo-American Background* (Woodbridge, 1988), 25–33.

[11] On the "complete suffrage" campaign led by the Chartist Joseph Sturge, see Alexander Wilson, "The Suffrage Movement," *Pressure from without in early Victorian England*, ed. Patricia Hollis (London, 1974): 80–104.

[12] On "university liberals" and the Reform League, see Christopher Harvie, *The Lights of Liberalism: The University Liberals and the Challenge of Democracy* (London, 1976), 135, 182. On the broader trajectory of post-Chartists into mid-Victorian Liberalism, see Brian Harrison and Patricia Hollis, "Chartism, Liberalism, and the Life of Robert Lowery," *EHR*, 82 (1967): 503–35.

diversity, that, by transferring electoral power entirely to "one class of the community" and erecting the rule of "mere numbers," it would prevent the translation of Britain's social and ideological diversity into the House of Commons and thus lead to the atrophy of the national discussion that was responsible for the country's greatness.[13]

Advocacy of the variety of suffrages rested on two sets of claims: the first concerning the positive worth of a mirroring parliament and the deliberative-epistemic significance of diversity, and the second concerning the inconsistency of a democratic suffrage with the realization of the foregoing ideas. One important strain of Victorian democratic theory consisted of accepting the first while rejecting the second. The nexus of representative–deliberative–epistemic values that inspired the programs analyzed in Chapter 1 were endorsed by these democrats as the correct *ends* for the designers of electoral-legislative structures. Their contribution to the democratic cause lay in upholding a widely extended, uniform suffrage as an appropriate *means* for the achievement of these ends. They envisioned democracy, among its other qualities, as an electoral system which was *welcoming and inclusive of* new ideas, which gave space to the full range of different social agendas and ideologies. Democracy, therefore, was compatible with the deliberative political culture which was responsible for England's enlightenment, progressiveness, and political success.[14] After the hardships of the Hungry Forties, with the confidence that came with the simultaneous belief in England's exceptionalism in avoiding the Continental alternations between anarchy and authoritarianism and in its preeminence and beneficence on the international stage,[15] it is not surprising that much of the democratic thought of the 1850s–60s should have been keen to emphasize the continuity between democracy and a system that many saw as historically successful.

To recast democracy in this mold meant dispelling the fear that a further extension of the suffrage would give Parliament over to a monolithic clique of members who sprang from or appealed exclusively to the working classes and who would thereby crowd out the spokesmen of all but one set of ideas

---

[13] James Fitzjames Stephen, "Liberalism," *CM*, 5 (1862), 71.

[14] The Radical-Liberal intellectual-cum-statesman John Morley, who would be one of the most important disciples of Mill in the last third of the century but who rejected Mill's beloved PR in favor of a wide suffrage under plurality rule, defined the sources of progress with which democracy would have to prove consistent in eloquent terms: "the birth and diffusion of a constant succession of new and even startling ideas are an essential condition of any society which is to escape stagnation"; Morley, "New Ideas," in *Modern Characteristics*, 135.

[15] On the limits to these common generalizations about the period, which included such tumultuous episodes as the Crimean War and Indian Mutiny of 1857–8, see *An Age of Equipoise? Reassessing Mid-Victorian Britain*, ed. Martin Hewitt (London, 2017).

and interests. Such a state of affairs in the legislature would create a politics that was both tyrannical and undeliberative – or, rather, that was the former because it was the latter: where parliamentary discussion was nonexistent due to the exclusion of contending viewpoints, policies could be nothing other, Grey deplored, than the imposition of "a mere will."[16] Deliberation meant a politics of reasons and not of will; it required opposition, debate, and difference, all of which were eschewed by despotic exercises of will, whether those of a single Napoleonic figure or of an unchecked multitude that monopolized seats in the legislature.[17]

In light of the powerful hold exercised by this condemnatory picture of democracy, democrats had to make the case that a fundamental premise of the antidemocratic argument from the value of diversity was false: namely, the premise that the working classes thought and acted as a unified body. Without this unity, the fact of the "overwhelming preponderance" of its "numbers" would be far less threatening to liberal ideals;[18] it was because they constituted, or could most often be expected to constitute, a consolidated ideological-political "bloc" that their entrance into the electoral arena would block the other streams of interests and opinion from the Commons and cause parliamentary politics to become unrepresentative.[19] Any hope of reconciling to the democratic cause the influential liberal circles which adhered to programs of variegated suffrage would depend upon defeating this view of a crushing working-class homogeneity. Notwithstanding the exception of the alarm at the advance of socialistic ideas noted in Chapter 2, the debate over the ideological unity or dividedness of the working classes proceeded in a characteristically Victorian way in that it was at least as interested in the *distribution* of working-class beliefs as in their content. If it were true that, as an influential writer on the freedom of discussion in the early- and mid-Victorian

---

[16] Grey, *Parliamentary Government*, 181. Interestingly, despite their differences on the suffrage and the desiderata of parliamentary representation, Grey explicitly derived this foundational conceptual distinction between reason and will from Guizot.

[17] Of the manifold statements of how the French Second Empire proved the inconsistency of democracy with deliberative representative government, perhaps the most philosophically trenchant came from Lorimer. Perceiving what was "scarcely remember[ed]" by his contemporaries, that "equal" and "universal suffrage" was at the basis of Hobbes's system of "voluntary acceptance of despotism," he dubbed Napoleon III "the living embodiment of the *Leviathan* of Hobbes. Ostensibly founded on a plebiscite, his despotism continues to rest securely on the principle of equality"; Lorimer, *Constitutionalism*, 35.

[18] Alison, "The Reform Bill," 15.

[19] David Moore, *The Politics of Deference: A Study of the Mid-Nineteenth-Century English Political System* (Hassocks, 1976), 388. See also Leslie Stephen's discussion of Mill and Henry Fawcett on the "probability of a union of opinion amongst working-men"; Stephen, *Life of Henry Fawcett*, third edition (New York, 1886), 215–16.

period put it, "in any given state of knowledge or ignorance, it is much better that the error and ignorance should be of a multiform than a uniform character,"[20] then it was especially critical to establish that intellectual variety existed among the class on whom a lowered suffrage would accord hegemony.

The argument that the beliefs of the working classes reached this necessary threshold of mulitformity took two basic forms. The first was a simple empirical claim about the present distribution of working-class opinions. Democratic reformers were insistent that the image of the working classes as a monolithic mass that thought and moved in concert (often at the behest of demagogues) was merely a nightmare induced by fear of the unknown, a nightmare belied by the reality that the working classes were riven by disagreements on political topics. As the historian and Liberal-party publicist George C. Brodrick wrote: "We speak of the working class for the sake of convenience, but in reality the working class is not a class at all in any political sense, but an unstratified and incoherent aggregate ... [who] are perfectly incapable of being rallied under one banner."[21] For Brodrick, the "working class" was a sensible term only when used to pick out a socioeconomic condition; to treat it as denominating a single political or ideological integer was to indulge in empirically unfounded hypostatization.

The lesson that it was "idle to talk of unity among the working classes" featured even more prominently in the work of another author closely linked to Brodrick: John Boyd Kinnear.[22] Kinnear was a radical figure – an uncompromising individualist, supporter of women's suffrage, and virulent critic of "privilege" – and he had a brief moment in Parliament before being unseated by the future Liberal Prime Minister H. H. Asquith.[23] He was also, in contrast to much of mid-Victorian liberalism, distressed by the decline of concern for the "abstract rights of men in politics," and he wished to re-inspire his compatriots with a notion of "the extension of the franchise" as a matter "of infinite value in itself alone." These high phrases notwithstanding, Kinnear devoted more of the treatment of the suffrage in his 1865 political treatise to the heterogeneity of working-class belief than to anything resembling a proof of a natural right to the vote. "All our fear" and "half the folly that is uttered on this topic" of working-class

---

[20] Samuel Bailey, *Essays on the Pursuit of Truth and the Progress of Knowledge*, second edition (London, 1844), 242.

[21] Brodrick, "Household Suffrage and Parliamentary Government," in *Political Studies* (London, 1879), 282.

[22] John Boyd Kinnear, *Principles of Reform: Political and Legal* (London, 1865), 19.

[23] Gordon F. Millar, "Kinnear, John Boyd (1828–1920)," *ODNB*.

enfranchisement would dissipate, he assured his readers, if they acknowledged that "there is not a single question on which they are united and form 'a class.'" Like Brodrick, he preferred to pluralize the name of the group he wanted added to the register: "it is not a 'working class' that is to be admitted: it is 'the working classes'"; "there is no object or motive that can be suggested," he went on, "which we shall not see at a glance would affect them all differently."[24] Kinnear put the point with particular forcefulness, but the core idea of these passages attained the status of a sort of refrain in reform camps. Even the Liberal MP John Bright, the archetype of the crusader for urban manufacturing interests against the traditional landed elite rather than the sort of liberal moved by the discourses of diversity and deliberation, emphasized that "opinions differ just as much among [the working classes] as among the people above them."[25]

As the quotation from Bright indicates, reformers attempted to draw on the political experience of the already enfranchised portions of the population to make their point that the "horizons and planes of thought and sentiment" that characterized a particular class included a range of "differences" in "feelings, opinions, and traditions."[26] Democrats hoped that even upper-class conservatives could be brought to acknowledge that the normal condition of economic classes was ideological heterogeneity, since a basic fact of parliamentary life was that it engaged members of the upper classes in policy debates and political conflicts with fellow members of their ranks. If this multiformity of belief and allegiance obtained in the classes already enfranchised, then surely, democrats judged, it was reasonable to attribute the same variations and disagreements to the working classes, even if these variations were less apparent among the lower orders due to their current marginalization in the political process: "on any question of the day, we shall find them holding as great a diversity of sentiment as their superiors in station"; "nothing is more certain than that they have no intrinsic element of coherence, and will on every question be moved by the same infinite variety of motive and reason which influence the minds of those whom we call the 'upper' or the 'middle' classes"[27]

---

[24] Kinnear, *Principles of Reform*, 10–11, 16, 19.

[25] Quoted in Saunders, *Democracy and the Vote*, 124. See also P. F. Clarke, "Electoral Sociology of Modern Britain," *History*, 57 (1972): 31–55.

[26] Cracroft, "The Analysis of the House of Commons, or Indirect Representation," in *Essays on Reform*, 169.

[27] Kinnear, *Principles of Reform*, 16, 18. He continued, "There are Whigs among them and Tories; there are Federals and Confederates; there are Churchmen and Dissenters; there are some for, and some against, compulsory education; there are supporters and opponents of the Permissive Bill; there are approvers and disapprovers of foreign intervention; there are peace-at-any-price men, and there

Applying to the currently excluded portion of his countrymen the familiar postulate of the naturalness of diversity, Kinnear argued that one must expect diversity among them

> simply and necessarily because the working classes are composed of men, not of electric clocks, all worked by a central battery, and because each man among them thinks as much for himself as the average of those above them do, while they contain a full proportion of those who follow their own judgment in each separate question of the day with as positive confidence that their own particular reason is better than their neighbours', as does the most independent or obstructive member of the House of Commons … [We must] try to remember that we really have not to deal with any huge vague image of some unknown and awful power, but only with a certain number of individuals who act and think under the same rules as ourselves.[28]

To presume unanimity among the lower orders was nothing less than to conflate a difference of socioeconomic status with a difference in human nature.

To this breed of reformer, the existence of diverse opinions within the working class meant that the arrival of electoral democracy was wrongly conceived as the unleashing of the sort of unstoppable "moral and political force" which was believed to have been divined by Tocqueville.[29] An extended and uniform suffrage was, instead, simply a mechanism for making the system of representation more "adequate" by including a "true representation of labour."[30] As Dicey wrote in an important turn-of-the-century reflection on the debates about reform of decades earlier: the "dread" of the "tyranny of the majority" had been misguided; it was "fallacious" to impute to democracy the dominance of "any one kind of legislative opinion" maintained by the unified will of the lower class

---

are *Cives Romani*; there are adherents of Mr. Bright and admirers of Lord Palmerston." According to Woodward and Biagini, among other historians, this was an accurate depiction of working-class ideas; see Woodward, *The Age of Reform*, 161; Biagini, *Liberty, Retrenchment, and Reform*, 290. Notably, even Bagehot, seven years after the Second Reform Act which he bitterly opposed and near the end of his life, conceded that his opponents in the reform debates might have been correct on this point: "It *was* apprehended that the working classes would take all the decisions to themselves – would combine as a class and legislate for their own class interests, or what they thought such. But as yet we see nothing of the sort"; Bagehot, "Not a Middle Party but a Middle Government," in *CW*, vol. 7, 201.

[28] Kinnear, *Principles of Reform*, 16–17.
[29] Seymour Drescher, *Tocqueville and England* (Cambridge, MA, 1964), 220. Among modern writers, Jeremy Waldron has leveled a similar argument against fears of majority tyranny; Waldron, "The Core of the Case against Judicial Review," *Yale Law Journal*, 115 (2006), 1398.
[30] Cracroft, "The Reform Session of 1867," in *Essays, Political and Miscellaneous*, vol. 1, 175.

holding an iron grip on political power.[31] In Kinnear's words, the upshot of this truth about workingmen's opinions was that "the fear that there is a class ... which would be supreme, and 'swamp,' as the phrase is, all the rest" was groundless.[32]

The important role which the postulate of the multifariousness of working-class opinion played in dissolving the apparent tension between the values enshrined in the mirroring-sociological theory and a downwardly expanded suffrage is well illustrated by the Christian Socialist Frederick Denison Maurice. Among the central missions of his formidable activism were the education of working men in preparation for their enfranchisement and the promotion of working-class involvement in politics.[33] But he also retained a strong attachment to the deliberative ethos that inspired so much of the variety-of-suffrages theorizing. He decried, in a way reminiscent of Grey, the elevation of the "will of the majority" above any "standard of truth," and he expressed fear at what he thought were the potentially deleterious moral consequences of "the slavish reverence for numbers" and the "talk about the 'will of the majority'" which he heard being trumpeted by some segments of the democratic movement. Nevertheless, even while laborers still suffered, in his eyes, from a very imperfect state of education, he scoffed at the dreadful forebodings of a "general suffrage" turning the Commons into a monolithic, despotic arm of the working class, and he did so in no small part due to his conviction that the diversity within the working class would prevent it from "swamp[ing] all the other classes in the country." How did he know that this salutary division prevailed in the working class? Because, if the most numerous class really were so tightly bound ideologically as to have one will, it would not need to wait to be "admit-[ted] to vote" before imposing it. No set of political arrangements could guarantee society against the dangers of a "mere multitude" united by a single political mission, and it was consequently a waste of political ingenuity to continue engineering dikes for a flood which, if it came,

---

[31] Albert Venn Dicey, *Lectures on the Relation between Law and Public Opinion in the Nineteenth Century*, 425, 218. What makes this particular set of comments extraordinary was that Dicey was making them in the midst of his disenchantment with the "socialist" and "collectivist" direction of contemporary English politics, but he refused to blame this waywardness on any natural unity of the working class.

[32] Kinnear, *Principles of Reform*, 15.

[33] Despite these arguments, Maurice was an unreliable democrat and mixed moments of acceptance of suffrage-extension with a broader conservatism about political reform; Paul Jones, "Jesus Christ and the Transformation of English Society: The 'Subversive Conservatism' of Frederick Denison Maurice," *Harvard Theological Review*, 96 (2003): 205–28.

could not be held back.[34] Happily, due to the country's deliberative, tolerant ethos, this misfortune was unlikely to befall England, and the probability of its occurrence was not increased by widening the suffrage.

For conservative opponents of a reduction in the property qualifications for the franchise, this particular talking-point was an especially tiresome element of their adversaries' propaganda; they voiced annoyance at how "much stress" was placed "on the fact that all the working class do not agree in politics."[35] Lord Salisbury (at the time Viscount Cranborne) railed against this refrain as nothing more than "unsupported assertions": "the first thing which the friends of this Bill tell us is, that the working class will not act politically *en masse*," and therefore that worries about a permanent working-class "preponderance" were not justifiable grounds on which to limit the suffrage. This issue was, Salisbury concurred, "the root of the matter," but he dissented wholeheartedly from what he took to be the reformers' naïve optimism on the matter; however "divided in opinion" the working class was on some ancillary questions, on "matters upon which their pecuniary interests are concerned" they exhibited "perfect party discipline" under the "exacting and despotic rule" of trades-union leaders.[36] With the exception of a small band of socialists, supporters of a more democratic franchise denied, in contrast, that there was greater uniformity (let alone a "rigorous obedience" to communistic dictates[37]) in the working class on economic questions than on any others. Brougham replied caustically to this prediction that the working classes would

---

[34] Maurice, *The Workman and the Franchise*, 224, 211, 217.

[35] George Robert Gleig, "The Reform Bill," *BM*, 99 (1866), 666. He was quoting a speech by the conservative Lord Stanley, who was complaining of the belaboring of this point by Gladstone.

[36] Salisbury, "The Reform Bill," in *Lord Salisbury on Politics*, 210. The status of unions in this arena of reform debate was a vexed one. There were, of course, spokesmen of industrial capitalism and adherents of laissez-faire political economy who regarded unions with simple horror as portents of expropriation or socialism. Figures like Salisbury added another layer of trepidation: seeing unions as sites in which the workers submitted in lockstep to a coercive leadership cabal, they viewed the spread of unions as proof that democracy was irreconcilable with the preservation of diversity and deliberation. Nonetheless, in two ways that appealed to different vantage points on reform, the mid-century growth of unionism could be treated as evidence in favor of lowering the suffrage. First, their organization and management could be interpreted as demonstrations of the heightened *capacity* of the working class, and hence as justifying their inclusion in a capacitarian framework; similarly, in providing an institutional setting through which laborers could express themselves socially and politically, their appearance could be seen as strengthening claims that the working classes comprised distinct *interests* for which a descriptive system would have to find a place. See Herbert Spencer, "Parliamentary Reform," 493, 505; Nassau Senior, "Lewis on Authority in Matters of Opinion," *ER*, 91 (1850), 555–6; Erskine May, *Democracy in Europe: A History*, 2 vols. (London, 1877), vol. 2, 492–3; J. S. Mill, "Thornton on Labour and Its Claims," in *CW* 5, 667; Bagehot, "Trade Unions and Reform," in *CW*, vol. 8, 15–19.

[37] Salisbury, "The Reform Bill," 212. Cf. Kinnear, *Principles of Reform*, 18–19.

leverage their numerical advantage under a wider suffrage to expropriate the upper classes: this forecast

> assumes that there is to be a union of the working classes all over the country in order to return this majority. Then, if they are likely to combine for the purpose of indirectly effecting the confiscation of property, why do they not now combine for the purpose of seizing upon it directly? For assuredly they possess this power in every country, and yet in none is there any more alarm felt respecting such a measure, than there is an apprehension of the horses in the country combining to kick, or the oxen to gore men to death.[38]

Much like Maurice in the quotations from a few pages ago, Brougham thought it perfectly adequate to defuse alarm at wide extensions of the suffrage to remark that the lower classes could do as much damage without the vote as with it, and to infer from their present state of disunity, peaceableness, and respect for property that they would continue to exhibit these characteristics in a more democratic England.

An appreciation of the centrality of the question of the extent of lower-class ideological diversity to debates about democratization enables us to notice a generally overlooked dimension of the persistent Victorian inquiry into the deference, or lack thereof, among the lower orders.[39] The thesis of the English populace as a "deferential" one is normally, and correctly, thought of as part of the debate over whether democratic rights could be harmonized with proper authority, whether it was "safe" to extend the franchise in the sense that the leadership of the country would not be seized by an unfit rabble.[40] Yet, the reality which the concept of "deference" was intended to capture in this era was not a simple acquiescence to a time-honored caste of wise rulers. The early- and mid-Victorians are famous for their self-stylings as inhabitants of "an age of transition" in which intellectual and social leadership was splintered and contested,[41] and this notion of their zeitgeist accorded well with the thought that in their present the authorities who received this deference were not themselves unified in outlook. Unlike in the ages of what the great radical critic William Hazlitt had called

---

[38] Brougham, *The British Constitution* (London and Glasgow, 1861), 95–6. The young J. S. Mill had conveyed the same message in polemics in favor of reform in the 1820s: "He asserts that the people are desirous of destroying property. I shall not enter into this question for I consider it to be irrelevant, but I cannot refrain from saying if the people desire to destroy property why do they not destroy it now? Have they not the physical power that they must always have?'" Mill, Speech on the British Constitution [2], 19 May 1826, in *CW*, vol. 26, 380.

[39] Geoffrey Best, *Mid-Victorian Britain, 1851–1875* (London, 1971), ch. 4.

[40] E.g. Cowling, *1867*, 58–9; David Moore, *The Politics of Deference*, passim.

[41] Mill's "Spirit of the Age" (in *CW*, vol. 22, interspersed from 227–316) articles set the tone for much of this discourse even into the final third of the century.

the "feudal lord and sovereign king" before "public opinion,"[42] deference to the Victorians meant not the veneration of unquestioned powers but the continuation down into the lower socioeconomic ranks of a heterogeneous pattern of thought and interest each stripe of which had its own tenets and luminaries. It was in this light that the Whig politician George Cornewall Lewis could see political *parties* in the plural as channels through which intellectual excellence could attain a directing influence on government and public opinion, and that Brougham could have confidence that a basically democratic suffrage would operate consistently with accurate representation of the greater sociological importance of the upper classes.[43] Because at least a critical mass of lower-class electors could be trusted to follow traditional political leaders, and because these leaders were divided among themselves, there was no threat, these reformers thought, of deliberation among contesting viewpoints being displaced by an unvarying slate of delegates from a unanimous class.[44]

Taken too far, though, this defense of the democratization of the suffrage based on the multitude's susceptibility to the "moral prestige" of "intelligence" or the legitimate "influence of property" had some rather perverse consequences for the theory of democracy.[45] If it showed that a regime more inclusive of the working class was "safe," it also risked making its achievement seem less urgent. For it eliminated one of the most powerful reasons for bringing the working classes into the electoral fold in the first place – namely, that they had their own distinctive "sentiments on public affairs," that there were peculiar "notions, right and wrong, which are fermenting in the minds of the working classes" the exclusion of which from the formal channels of politics would impoverish parliamentary discourse and undermine the assembly's claim to representativeness.[46] There remained, as mentioned earlier, plenty of

---

[42] Hazlitt, "The French Revolution," in *Selected Writings* (Oxford, 1981), 86–7.

[43] Lewis, *Influence of Authority in Matters of Opinion*, 149–50, 181; Brougham, *British Constitution*, 82, 74. Of the Whig architects of the First Reform Act, Brougham came closest to endorsing a simple democratic franchise; ibid. 73, 95–6.

[44] Kinnear was representative as usual in his thinking on this front. He wrote that, since the working classes were divided into patterns of belief similar to those in the already enfranchised strata, they would "when admitted to power, merely add to or turn the majority in each locality according to its particular circumstances, leaving us still governed by the prevailing sentiment in all classes, and distinguished into parties much the same as at present"; *Principles of Reform*, 16.

[45] Leslie Stephen, "The Value of Political Machinery," *FR*, 18 (1875), 846, and "Reform," *MM*, 15 (1867). Ideas about "legitimate influence" of this sort remained quite stable from early on in the reform agitation: see Francis Jeffrey and Henry Brougham, "Parliamentary Reform," *ER*, 17 (1811), 264; Alan Heesom, "'Legitimate' *versus* 'Illegitimate' Influences: Aristocratic Engineering in Mid-Victorian Britain," *PH*, 7 (1988): 282–305.

[46] Bagehot, "Parliamentary Reform," 196.

reasons to endorse an augmentation of working-class electoral power without this one: the gains to stability of making the political process more inclusive; the moral and educational benefits of citizenship; the recognition of the deserving character of working-class citizens, among others. But, in comparison with the argument for working-class inclusion based on their distinctive thoughts and perspectives, these other rationales were lacking in one respect: they had little to say about what the groups that were to be enfranchised *contributed to* politics. The arguments from recognition of desert or from the educational advantages of political participation concerned the benefits reaped *by* the working classes from their inclusion, and the argument from stability, if inflected with a strong note of deference, could look like nothing more than the implementation of the cynical credo of the archduke of antidemocracy, the young Salisbury, that "the best form of Government ... is one where the masses have little power, and seem to have a great deal."[47]

The question of whether the right way to understand the incorporation of a hitherto-excluded group was as conferring a benefit upon that group, or as improving the political life of the nation more broadly through that group's unique contributions, was reprised in another reform movement: that for women's suffrage. There was a split within the rationales given for female enfranchisement between, on the one hand, the family of views that saw this measure as done for the sake of women – either because it was a natural right that was simply owed to women, or because possessing the vote would yield boons to women's welfare – and, on the other, those which conceived of it principally as an enhancement of the epistemic capacities of the political system through the addition of the distinctive perspectives and ideas that derived from women's *difference* from men.[48] "With regard to the differences between men and women, those who advocate the enfranchisement of women have no wish to disregard them ... On the contrary, we base our claim to representation to a large extent on them. If men and women were exactly alike," the political thinker and leader of the women's suffrage movement, Millicent Garrett Fawcett, summed up characteristically, "the representation of men would represent us; but not being alike, that wherein we

---

[47] Salisbury (then Lord Cecil), "Theories of Parliamentary Reform," 66.

[48] On the relative standing of these different kinds of arguments, see Barbara Caine, *Victorian Feminists* (Oxford, 1992); Martin Pugh, *The March of the Women: A Revisionist Analysis of the Campaign for Women's Suffrage, 1866–1914* (Oxford, 2000). Despite his official utilitarianism, Mill occupied an equivocal position on this matter, poised between an abstract-right-based view about what was owed to women as a matter of justice and a justification based on the advantages to society as a whole that women's enfranchisement would produce, as in the ambiguous declaration that "the legal subordination of one sex to the other – is wrong in itself, and now one of the chief hindrances to human improvement"; *The Subjection of Women*, in *CW*, vol. 21, 261.

differ is unrepresented under the present system."[49] This latter standpoint, which had always formed part of the movement's argumentative arsenal,[50] remained prominent up to the First World War.[51]

The democrat of deference, then, presents something of a conundrum, akin to that presented by a certain Whiggish or skeptical line on religious toleration, associated with figures such as Macaulay in nineteenth-century England and Bayle or Voltaire during the Enlightenment. A democracy in which the working classes had nothing distinctive to say was like a toleration of infidels on the grounds that the ways in which they differed from the orthodox were of no practical significance.[52] In the same way that

---

[49] M. G. Fawcett, *Home and Politics*, third edition (London, 1894), 3. It was in particular the "maternal" and "domestic" aspects of "womanhood" that made its inclusion especially salient from the point of view of political representation. See also David Rubinstein, "Millicent Garrett Fawcett and the Meaning of Women's Emancipation, 1886–99," *VS*, 34 (1991): 365–80. While not embedded in a Victorian social theory of gender roles, the idea that descriptive representation of women is justified on the grounds of fundamental differences between the sexes has remained a potent argument; for instance, passage of the French "parity" law affirmed quotas for women on the grounds of reflecting the natural, ineradicable dualism of humankind. Joan Wallach Scott, "Parité," in *The French Republic: History, Values, Debates*, ed. Edward Berenson, Vincent Duclert, and Christophe Prochasson (Ithaca, 2011): 182–8.

[50] Perhaps the sharpest statements from the early phase of the women's suffrage movement came from Lydia Becker: "If the opinions and interests of women are identical with those of men of a similar social grade, there could be no possible harm in giving them the same means of expressing them as are given to men. On the other hand it is said that women are morally and intellectually distinct from men ... and consequently the ideas which they may form on questions of national polity will be of a different character, or based on different principles, from those entertained by men. On this view, however ... the recognition of the right of women to vote seems absolutely necessary in order to secure that fair representation of all classes of the community"; Becker, "The Political Disabilities of Women," in *Before the Vote Was Won: Arguments for and against Women's Suffrage 1864–1896*, ed. Jane Lewis (London, 1987): 118–40.

[51] E.g. the liberal sociologist L. T. Hobhouse's declaration that "the larger wrong done by the repression of women is not the loss to women themselves ... but the impoverishment of the community as a whole, the loss of all the elements in the common stock which the free play of woman's mind would contribute"; Hobhouse, *Liberalism*, in *Liberalism and Other Writings*, ed. James Meadowcroft (Cambridge, 1994), 54. Ramsay MacDonald stated unequivocally that if "there is a case for the enfranchisement of women, it should consist in a proof that women's experience is different from men's"; MacDonald, *Socialism and Government*, vol. 1, 67–76.

[52] Ursula Henriques usefully dubs this the argument for toleration from the "mere irrelevance" of the beliefs in question; Henriques, *Religious Toleration in England, 1787–1833* (Toronto, 1961), 201. Of the major Victorian writers, Macaulay was the classic exponent of the irrelevance argument for toleration: e.g. "Civil Disabilities of the Jews," in *Critical and Historical Essays*, vol. 1, 296–7: "We hear of essentially Protestant governments and essentially Christian governments, words which mean just as much as essentially Protestant cookery, or essentially Christian horsemanship ... The points of difference between Christianity and Judaism have ... no more to do with his fitness to be a magistrate, a legislator, or a minister of finance, than with his fitness to be a cobbler .... Any man would rather have his shoes mended by a heretical cobbler than by a person who had subscribed all the thirty-nine articles, but had never handled an awl. Men act thus, not because they are indifferent to religion, but because they do not see what religion has to do with the mending of their shoes. Yet religion has as much to do with the mending of shoes as with the budget and the army estimates."

a dissenter or a Catholic might have accepted the policy of toleration while balking at the dismissive spirit in which it was granted, to the modern liberal democrat the attitude of the democrat of deference toward those whom he would enfranchise may sound objectionable. Relative to this kind of democrat, the twenty-first-century reader may have more sympathy with those authors in the previous chapters who, seeing the working classes as quite able and likely to dissent from the conclusions of their social superiors, paid them the tribute of trying to limit their power. After all, Bagehot's motivation for seeking seats for urban artisans was precisely that they had "peculiar sentiments" to "express," that there existed such a discrete social-intellectual entity as the "views of the working classes."[53] The democrat of deference counted the absence of distinctive working-class views as a point in favor of uniform universal suffrage;[54] the Whiggish, variety-of-suffrages sociologist perceived the singularity and originality of their thought as a reason both for including the working classes and for restraining their numerical predominance over other classes, for discovering the means whereby "the lower classes are to be admitted to a share of political power without absorbing the whole power."[55] At the risk of sounding overly provocative, we might say that the insistence on the extent of ideological division among the working class, when bound up too tightly with the assertion of continuity with the status quo distribution of beliefs among the already enfranchised strata of society,[56] amounted to a liberal-pluralist version of the organic-hierarchical social philosophy of the Tory democrats.

To return to the main thread: the argument about the current extent of heterogeneity among working-class beliefs and policy preferences was a crucial element in the democratic response to the theory of the variegated suffrage, deflating the anxiety about the demographic advantage of the working classes leading to distortions of the Commons's sociological accuracy and its inclusiveness of all the major streams of interest and opinion. This was not, however, the only form in which the thesis of the sufficient diversity of opinion among the working classes appeared. Unlike the preceding contention, this second form was not an empirical assertion

---

[53] Bagehot, "Parliamentary Reform," 207, 201.
[54] Such deference-based arguments for enlarging the franchise included not only Disraelian advocates of "Tory democracy" but also, and more controversially, moderate Whigs and middle-class radicals of the James Mill mold; e.g. Russell, *English Government and Constitution*, fourth edition, 236 and James Mill, "Government," in Mill, *Political Writings*, 41–2.
[55] Bagehot, "Mr. Gladstone," 438.
[56] "Few bodies of working men pull wholly together, but are as much subject to diversity of opinion as other classes, and as likely to return Conservative as Liberal members"; "A Reformer," *A View of Parliamentary Reform*, 9–10.

about the present, but a predictive claim about the future distribution of opinions under a democratic franchise. This prediction was central to what is arguably the most important document of democratic theory from the mid-Victorian period, although it is neglected in political theory today: the *Essays on Reform* of 1867, a collection of articles from a group of young scholars and professionals known as the "university liberals" which "not only favoured the extension of the franchise but expressed sympathy with the ideal of democratic government."[57] Among the contributors were Leslie Stephen, James Bryce, and A. V. Dicey before the days of their fame, as well as other authors – Kinnear, Brodrick, and Cracroft – who have already appeared in this chapter. It was, for the wing of the Liberal party most friendly to democracy, something of a showcase of rising stars.

This second, academic-liberal argument for the harmony of democracy with the priorities of the mirror theorists punted on the foregoing question of whether the working classes currently contained one or multiple viewpoints and agendas. Instead, it offered a forecast about the distribution of opinions among them *once they were granted the suffrage*. Dire prognoses of deliberative politics succumbing to a united lower-class ideology or of the multitude's blind submissiveness to demagogues were irrelevant, ran this line of argument, because one could not generalize from the condition of mass opinion under an exclusive franchise to its condition under a democratic one. Even if lower-class beliefs in the 1860s were homogeneous or (as some imagined) nonexistent, political participation could be trusted to produce the optimally diverse allocation of opinions.

This prediction was the offspring of the combination of two quintessential tenets of Victorian political thought, both of which have appeared already in this study. The first was the idea that widespread ideological diversity was natural to modern, "civilized" societies like the England of their day; the second was the deep faith in the educative power of political life. If the engagement with public affairs that followed receipt of the public trust of the vote could be expected to call into play latent intellectual and moral faculties, to draw attention to an array of complex problems, to involve the mind in new and various modes of thought, it could accordingly be expected to increase diversity. Whatever unanimity existed among the working class up to the present time was thus best understood as an artifact of the intellectual dormancy which naturally attended political exclusion. Consequently it was wrong, as Leslie Stephen wrote in his installment for the *Essays*, to fear that democracy would unleash workingmen simply to impose their desires, for once they had the vote and sent their own members to Parliament "they would have to discuss these questions before the whole nation, instead of fighting in the dark; the whole intelligence of the country would be brought to bear upon their claims and detect their unsoundness: the mere putting them into shape and discussing them would infallibly bring out the differences among the workmen themselves."[58] The conservative-turned-popular reformer Lord Houghton was likewise confident that the same kinds of thoughtful divisions of political allegiance and principle that characterized the then-current political classes would come to exist among the working class: "diversities of thought" would emerge among working men once they were brought within the pale of parliamentary discussion – "in proportion as [the newly enfranchised citizens] are taught to argue" and "have learned to think on such subjects," Houghton averred, "their inductions will be various, and their conclusions contradictory."[59] "Great differences of opinion," wrote R. H. Hutton, a close friend of Bagehot who nonetheless opposed him on the franchise question, were sure to be an important part of working-class politics.[60] Or, as Gladstone bluntly stated it, when leading the charge for an expansion of the suffrage in 1866, "there is no proof whatever that the working classes, if enfranchised, would act together as a class."[61] In short, division, diversity, fragmentation, contestation – these phenomena were intrinsic to politics itself, rather than peculiar to any particular governmental forms or electoral arrangements. The deliberative political culture so valued by the exponents of the variegated suffrage was in no danger from democracy, for the nondemocratic electoral arrangements they lauded had never in fact been the cause of the enlightening interplay of different views which, they concurred with their opponents, had rescued England from the "monotony" and "uniformity" perceived to afflict the rest of the world.[62]

---

[58] Leslie Stephen, "On the Choice of Representatives by Popular Constituencies," in *Essays on Reform*, 122.

[59] Richard Monckton Milnes, 1st Baron Houghton, "On the Admission of the Working Classes as Part of Our Social System; and Their Recognition for All Purposes as Part of the Nation," in *Essays on Reform*, 64.

[60] Hutton, "The Political Character of the Working Classes," in *Essays on Reform*, 43.

[61] Gladstone, "Speech on Moving the Second Reading of the Bill for the Extension of the Suffrage, April 12," in *Speeches on Parliamentary Reform in 1866*, 109. As evidence for this prediction, he cited the behavior of the working classes in municipal elections, where the franchise was at that time wider.

[62] As in Macaulay, "History," in *The Miscellaneous Writings of Lord Macaulay*, 2 vols. (London, 1860), vol. 1, 268–9.

The dynamic, future-oriented nature of this argument for diverse democracy flipped the script on the way of conceiving of the relationship between enfranchisement and the holding of opinions described in Chapter 2. Whereas Bagehot, Greg, and authors of their ilk set the possession of opinions (and sometimes even of *distinctive* opinions) as the baseline for being granted the suffrage, the academic liberals behind the *Essays* believed that enfranchisement was itself a mechanism for creating opinions – and diverse ones at that. The former wanted the suffrage to reflect and react to the contours of public opinion; the latter viewed the suffrage as a generator of opinions and an engine for their fragmentation. Notably, a similar thought carried beyond the ranks of these moderate democrats themselves. In portraying electoral politics as itself productive of the opinions necessary to participate in political life they would quickly be followed by promoters of female suffrage, who saw it as a way of countering the application of the opinion-holding threshold against women.[63]

Separable from but complementary to these arguments about the current and future distribution of beliefs in the working class was a depiction of the intellectual character of the working class which often appeared alongside the former arguments. In diametric opposition to traditionally bleak views of lower-class benightedness, closed-mindedness, and intolerance, democrats portrayed the working classes as open-minded and tolerant. Frederic Harrison, the leading Victorian positivist, thought the working classes were unique in "being without class prejudice" and being "open to conviction" by the best ideas, from whatever quarter they may have emerged.[64] Morley praised them for being "less hindered by fixed ideas than other classes," and Hutton assured his readers that "no class is so tolerant of differences of opinion as they are."[65] From this perspective, the important issue was less the distribution of opinions that prevailed or was going to prevail than the kind of people that workingmen were; even if a seemingly unquestioning unanimity endured for a time, this was not to be taken as indicative of stagnation or majority tyranny. When new breakthroughs and dilemmas occurred and new information was brought to

---

[63] "Granted that women are ignorant of politics, so are many male ten-pound householders ... No mass of human beings will or can undertake the task of forming opinions on matters over which they have no control, and on which they have no practical decisions to make ... When women have votes ... they will become interested in a wider circle of ideas, and where they now think and feel somewhat vaguely, they will form definite and decided opinions"; Barbara Bodichon, *Reasons For and Against the Enfranchisement of Women* (London, 1869), 12–13.

[64] Harrison, *Order and Progress*, 147, also 173–4.

[65] Morley, *Fortnightly Review*, 1868, quoted in D. A. Hamer, *John Morley: Liberal Intellectual in Politics* (Oxford, 1968), 84; Hutton, "The Political Character of the Working Classes," 42.

light, argued these democratic reformers, the appropriate fissures and
contestations would arise and the full range of perspectives be canvassed,
because these consequences followed from the character of the British
demos.[66] Contra the likes of Lowe and Bagehot, a political system in
which the working class was the numerically predominant element
would be no more (and probably less) inhospitable to new ideas or diverse
views than any preceding system.

Because these encouraging truths about the working class gave the lie to
the image of democracy as a system of class rule or majority tyranny,[67]
these democrats of diversity could lay claim to all of the pacific and
stabilizing benefits that the variety-of-suffrages school ascribed to its version of inclusivity and representativeness. The dire ruminations of conservatives such as Alison on the social-political collapse that democracy
would bring were utterly misleading. Since all citizens could truly conceive
of themselves as participating in and represented by a democratic government, since "the feelings and wishes" of the whole population would find
adequate reflection in a democratic political structure, democracy would
typify "not only stability" but "strength."[68] A more democratic suffrage
would shore up the political foundations of England, for "political representation is the soul of political safety."[69] Houghton gave an eloquent
articulation of the thesis of democratic stability. No political innovation
could serve better as "a security for the common support of the Law and
Public Order" than the democratization of the franchise, which brought all
"passions working in the popular mind" into "the free atmosphere of

---

[66] As the historian and politician Lord Acton would put it in 1868, celebrating the Liberal victory in the
first election held after the Second Reform Act: the "real working class is more receptive to ideas and
principles" than other classes; quoted in Roland Hill, *Lord Acton*, (New Haven, 2000), 96. See also
Gertrude Himmelfarb, "Introduction," to Acton, *Essays on Freedom and Power*, ed. Himmelfarb
(Boston, 1948), lix–lx.

[67] It is important to avoid the impression that opposition to democracy on the ground that there were
moral-intellectual defects peculiar to the lower classes vanished upon the passage of the Second
Reform Act and the appearance of these democratic arguments. Defenses of democracy and
proposals for further franchise expansion continued to be met with arguments about the dangers
that democracy posed to diversity, tolerance, and progress throughout the century, arguably
reaching their crescendo in the anguished response of one of the most influential Victorian
minds, the jurist and historian Henry Maine, to the Third Reform Act's mass enfranchisement.
Contrary to another longstanding criticism of democracies as fickle and unstable in their policy,
Maine attacked democracy as the regime par excellence of intolerance. This was based in his idea
that the average uneducated mind was deeply closed to all novelty and conflict; tolerance and
openness to disagreement and new ideas could only ever be the purview of a relatively small upper
stratum of the population. Therefore, democracy meant an end to freedom of mind and
a suppression of nonconformity – in everything from scientific inquiry to seeming trivialities of
manners and fashion. See Maine, *Popular Government*, passim.

[68] Bryce, *American Commonwealth*, vol. 2, 275.   [69] Cracroft, "The Reform Session of 1866," 78.

political debate"; democracy was unrivaled as "a security against the sudden and violent ebullitions of social discontent," for it "afforded a legitimate safety-valve of political discussion [that] can hardly be overlooked."[70] "Democratic institutions" gave everyone a "share" of the representation, making it possible that all citizens could "give their wishes a legitimate expression through [the Constitution's] ancient organs."[71] Democracy's credentials for inclusivity and representativeness were match-less, and it was therefore the best bet for achieving a stable and peaceful future for Britain.[72]

On every front, then, democracy was a better instrument for realizing the ideals of deliberative representative government than the electoral engineering efforts of the variety-of-suffrages school. To these adherents of what we might call *diverse democracy*, to subscribe to descriptiveness and mirroring entailed committing to democratic institutions, for the facts about the demos's congeniality to diversity and deliberation rendered groundless the long tradition of anxieties about its classist and unrepre-sentative nature.[73]

Before leaving this section, a word on the afterlife of this cluster of diversity-friendly democratic arguments is in order. The last two decades of the century witnessed the onset of the bifurcation of British politics around class[74] and the fading of the schemes of variegated suffrage into the past,

---

[70] Houghton, "Admission of the Working Classes," 51, 54, 52.

[71] Bryce, "The Historical Aspect of Democracy," in *Essays on Reform*, 273.

[72] This thought about democratic stability would become a staple of turn-of-the-century Idealism, where it would often be recast in an evolutionary idiom; see e.g. D. G. Ritchie, "Evolution and Democracy," in *Ethical Democracy: Essays in Social Dynamics*, ed. Stanton Coit (London, 1900): 1–29, esp. 17.

[73] This school of thought finds a modern analogue in a perhaps unlikely place: the theory of "epistemic democracy." As epistemic democrats seek to justify democracy before an independent criterion of correctness, so our first group of Victorian democrats sought to vindicate the practical operation of democratic institutions in light of norms of deliberation and representativeness that possessed a venerable nondemocratic lineage. E.g. Hélène Landemore, *Democratic Reason: Politics, Collective Intelligence, and the Rule of the Many* (Princeton, 2013); Melissa Schwartzberg, "Epistemic Democracy and Its Challenges," *ARPS*, 18 (2015): 187–203.

If there is an important similarity in the basic structure of epistemic democracy and this brand of Victorian democracy, there is an equally revealing distance between the latter and today's "delib-erative democrats." While some of its practitioners have taken a more "institutional turn" of late, the dominant approach within deliberative democracy still appears to be to treat deliberation as a value that inheres analytically in the concept of democracy. (E.g. Joshua Cohen's essays, "Deliberation and Democratic Legitimacy" and "Procedure and Substance in Deliberative Democracy," in *Deliberative Democracy: Essays in Reason and Politics*, ed. James Bonham and William Rehg [Cambridge, MA, 1997]). Such an approach would have been anathema to this brand of Victorian democrat, for they wanted to support democracy only if it could be shown that demo-cratic institutions would perform in accord with a deliberative ideal which they held independently.

[74] Hawkins, *Victorian Political Culture*, 340.

and with these trends the stress on pluralism and disagreement within the working class subsided. Yet the legacy of this particular piece of democratic doctrine lasted beyond its mid-Victorian heyday and demonstrated a surprising tenacity. Take, for instance, the work of the Scottish Hegelian, socialist, and Idealist D. G. Ritchie.[75] Ritchie's thinking about democracy was extremely rich across the philosophical, historical, and institutional levels; more will be said about it later (see Chapter 5) in connection with his denunciations of PR. Briefly, he believed that the nature of the political sphere was to be an arena in which different individuals and groups advanced different visions of and programs for their society, and that a democratic political sphere would not fail in this regard – rather, it would be superior, for it was the only completely inclusive regime, the only one which made space for every possible dissenting voice, which was open to every movement that might arise. Ritchie was one of the first British theorists to attempt to derive the freedoms of the press and public discussion from the ideal of democracy itself; unsurprisingly, he did not expend so much theoretical energy for liberties which he expected to do no more than sit sterilely on the books. So long as "the right of freedom of speech and freedom of association" was respected, then "it is the very chief advantage of democracy over oligarchy that, while it establishes the power of the majority, it puts that majority potentially in the hands of those who have ideas and are able to make them spread."[76] For Ritchie, then, democracy, properly understood, was the *open* system.[77] Here he was following directly in the footsteps of a positivist such as Harrison, who envisioned democracy as the sole regime in which confidence was warranted that all new projects and ideas, which by definition originated with "minorities," had a fair chance to "convert" the rest of

---

[75] On Ritchie's life and work, see David Boucher, "Introduction" and "David George Ritchie," in *The Scottish Idealists, Selected Philosophical Writings*, ed. Boucher (Exeter, 2004): 1–22, 159–61.

[76] Ritchie, *Principles of State Interference: Four Essays on the Political Philosophy of Mr. Herbert Spencer, J. S. Mill, and T. H. Green* (London, 1891), 73.

[77] The rise of Idealism in the work of T. H. Green and his followers such as Bernard Bosanquet is often seen as marking a stark break with the utilitarian and Whiggish-liberal traditions ascendant in the mid-century. One such area of their thought that has been supposed to mark out their distinctiveness was their relative insouciance about the possibility of majority tyranny. However, as the example of Ritchie hints, and as we will see further in the Idealist skepticism about PR in Chapter 5, their unconcern about majority tyranny is evidence of continuity as much as of discontinuity with previous strands of political thought – it can be understood in part as the translation into Hegel-inspired jargon of the efforts of mid-Victorian democrats to portray the working class as a segment of society tolerant of diversity and pluralism. On the Idealists on majority tyranny and pluralism, see e.g. Richter, *Politics of Conscience*, 203, 256; Peter Nicholson, *Political Philosophy of the British Idealists* (Cambridge, 1990), 214–18; Tyler, *Idealist Political Philosophy*, 70–1.

society to "a reasoned concurrence" and to contend for the "real preponderance of the social force."[78]

This connection of a diverse demos with the possibility of inclusive democratic representation retained considerable power over later democratic thought, as we can observe in a perhaps unlikely place: the socialist theory of Ramsay MacDonald, the future first Labour Prime Minster. For MacDonald, as for all socialists, democracy was wrongly conceived in an "individualist" mode as an aggregation of personal preferences. Surprisingly, however, he also claimed that it was equally misunderstood as the government of *a class*, for "no class, however enlightened, can then represent the whole community." Democracy was, instead, founded on the fact that at a "particular stage of [a society's] evolution" it became impossible to attain an "accurate representation of the State personality," a "complete representation of experience in the State," without relying upon universal suffrage.[79] In contrast to the well-known fear of Victorian "classical liberals" that socialism would prove a system of totalizing domination inimical to dissent and diversity,[80] what recommended democracy in the socialist form in which MacDonald imagined it was that, in an epoch of complexity, differentiation, and multifacetedness in social relations, only democracy could deliver the inclusiveness and descriptive accuracy in representation that could make the Commons an epistemically robust "deliberative assembly":

> [I]t is not the idea of equality which I see underlying the democratic franchise, but the recognition of the value to the State of the experience of the individual, or perhaps, to speak more accurately, of the section of the community to which an individual belongs. For it is not individuals but classes and descriptions of individuals that are admitted from time to time to the franchise.[81]

Democracy was, in short, the appropriate political response to the modern sociology of diverse opinion; it was, in contradiction to the theory of the variety of suffrages, the latter's true institutional corollary. For the greatest socialist politician of the early twentieth century, the democratic suffrage was the fulfillment in the modern era of the traditional British promise of a pluralistic, mirroring Commons.[82]

---

[78] Harrison, *Order and Progress*, 100.   [79] MacDonald, *Socialism and Government*, 91, 46–7, 61.

[80] John Roach, "Liberalism and the Victorian Intelligentsia," *Cambridge Historical Journal*, 13 (1957): 58–81.

[81] MacDonald, *Socialism and Government*, vol. 1, 110, 50.

[82] In this respect there is underrated continuity between MacDonald's theorization of early Labour politics and the pluralistic underpinnings of social-democratic regimes of the third quarter of the

2   **Radical or Undescriptive Democracy**

Running alongside this strand of diverse or deliberative democracy was another pro-democratic line of argument in which the theme of diversity figured prominently. This line was a more radical departure from the sociological-descriptive framework than the foregoing. The clash between the proponents of the democratic arguments surveyed in the preceding section and the champions of the variety of suffrages such as Bagehot, Grey, and Cole was a kind of family squabble. Hence, the former might be considered a Whiggish school of democrats: they shared many ideals with their opponents, but disputed the assessment that a democratic suffrage could not operate in accordance with them. In this sense the difference between a Houghton and a Cole was one of species more than of genus; "diverse democrats" existed on the far end of a continuum that reached, at its other end, to the likes of Greg or Macaulay, who combined subscription to the ideals of diversity and sociological accuracy within the assembly with a belief that fidelity to these ideals meant a suffrage that privileged the middle-class. Figures such as Houghton were, at bottom, the democratic wing of a deliberative-mirroring tradition that had undergone varied institutional permutations and theoretical articulations over the course of its distinguished history.

One democratic response to the theory of the variegated suffrage was, then, to show that the values that animated the theory would be best served by abandoning the electoral-parliamentary institutions usually thought to instantiate them. Yet another, to which we turn now, was to dismiss the sociological claims that underlay this way of thinking as inappropriate to modern politics. This response was not always clearly distinguished by democratic publicists from the former, and could sometimes be found alongside the previous one – indeed, this appears dramatically in the *Essays on Reform*, where the article by Houghton just discussed was followed immediately by a distinct case for democracy from Albert Venn Dicey.[83]

---

twentieth century; Alain Bergounioux and Bernard Manin, *Le régime social-démocrate* (Paris, 1989), ch. 2.

[83] In *Essays on Reform*, Houghton's essay was the third chapter, and Dicey's "The Balance of Classes" was the fourth. It should be noted that Dicey himself assented *en passant* to the picture of a working class that contained a range of political viewpoints, though this assessment of the ideological dividedness of the lower classes was not central to his essay: "But if it be alleged that tyranny is specially to be feared where numbers are supreme, there seems to be little proof for the allegation. In all countries the majority must be a fluctuating, unknown, indefinite body, which has neither the will nor the power to act with systematic tyranny . . . it is highly improbable that the whole of the poor (and it is only when acting as a whole that they could in any case be supreme) would act together as one man in opposition to the wishes of all those who are not technically working men.

While these two positions came together in their practical recommendation of a democratic franchise, the reasons for their dissatisfaction with the
alternative offered by theorists of the variety of suffrages differed
fundamentally.

Dicey would wind up as eminent a Victorian as any who would be
subjected to Lytton Strachey's scorn, and would spend the latter decades of
his life in disillusionment with the functioning of his country's much-
democratized parliamentary system (especially in its economic, Imperial,
and Irish dimensions).[84] He would achieve fame as England's greatest
constitutional scholar, and his *Law and Public Opinion in the Nineteenth
Century* continues to exercise great influence on the historiography of the
period. But in the mid-1860s all that remained in the future, and Dicey was
still a relatively green lawyer-journalist and a zealous democrat, even in
comparison to the crop of fellow reform-minded young intellectuals who
contributed to the *Essays*.[85]

One important prong of Dicey's offensive against the mirror view, and
the one which concerns us here, was in effect an internal critique. Dicey
wanted to show that, even should one accept the accurate reflection of
classes, interests, and opinions as the correct parliamentary *ideal*, assent to
this ideal could not produce a satisfactory institutional settlement.
The crux of his objection to the mirroring ideal was that, however compelling one found it as a general statement of the desirable composition of the
legislature, this vision of parliamentary representation fell short of the
standards of *mutual acceptability* and *action-guidance*. To argue this, he
insistently pressed the point that we saw even the occasional promoter of
electoral differentiation, such as Bagehot and Harris, concede: namely, that
the resolution of the sociological question – of what the condition of
society and public opinion was in "the English nation here and now," as
Bagehot wrote[86] – was hardly a straightforward one.[87] Answering this
question was, explicitly or not, the first order of business for theorists of
electoral variegation. After all, the variety of suffrages was not meant to be

For the so-called working class is, like all others, notoriously broken into divisions"; "Balance of
Classes," 74.

[84] Richard Cosgrove, *The Rule of Law: Albert Venn Dicey, Victorian Jurist* (London, 1980).
[85] Morley called Dicey's essay "the most unflinchingly democratic" of the collection; quoted in
K. J. M. Smith, *James Fitzjames Stephen: Portrait of a Victorian Rationalist* (Cambridge, 1989), 108.
[86] Bagehot, *English Constitution*, 306.
[87] As Lorimer confessed, in a moment of startling frankness, even among those who accepted his
inegalitarian-mirroring "principle," "the proportions in which power may be claimed, by the
various classes into which every civilized community divides itself . . . will still remain a very grave
and difficult question;" *Constitutionalism*, 37.

instituted at random, with, say, different voting rules and qualifications allocated by lottery across constituencies. Such a method of random allocation was unacceptable because there was no reason to imagine that a haphazard distribution of voting privileges would produce an electoral result faithful to public opinion. Therefore, it was necessary that some definitive account of the makeup of public opinion – of which regions, which classes, which ideas contributed with what significance to the makeup of the national mind – precede the assignment of the various suffrages to the different constituencies. And yet any such sociology would itself be contestable; given that the society which they were seeking to represent was heterogeneous and multifaceted, consensus on how to translate this sociology into Parliament was not to be expected. Hence, any particular variety-of-suffrages plan was liable to a charge of arbitrariness – that is, of imposing on the nation's politics one contestable vision of society which was not acceptable to all parties. As we have seen, even two thinkers such as Bagehot and Greg – who not only bore a family resemblance in their political thought, but who actually belonged by marriage to the same family – disagreed about the relative importance of the various classes in England and the adequacy with which they were being represented. In light of the very fact about the British social order with which Bagehot and so many of his like-minded contemporaries were preoccupied – that the public opinion which, by general consent, was the supreme authority of modern British politics was itself a split and multifaceted entity, an amalgam of many different streams of thought and interest – the thought of arriving at such a conclusive account was a rather fanciful conceit. And the attempt to base electoral regulation on any such views constituted an unfair skewing of the political process in favor of certain substantive outcomes.[88]

This was the core of Dicey's objection to the so-called "principle of the English constitution, that Parliament should be a mirror."[89] Much as the designer of a variety-of-suffrage scheme might be confident that his proposal had more "reality" in it than either the "sham" that was the "present system" or any contending scheme, much as he might be certain that his

---

[88] The liability to challenge on the score of arbitrariness and lack of mutual acceptability remains for theories of descriptive representation today: e.g. Andrew Rehfeld, "On Quotas and Qualifications for Office," in *Political Representation*, 236–68, Bernard Grofman, "Should Representatives Be Typical of Their Constituents?" in *Representation and Redistricting Issues*, ed. Grofman, Arend Lijphart, and Robert McKay (Lexington, 1982), 97–9.

[89] Dicey, "The Balance of Classes," 67. Dicey was quoting here from a speech by the Conservative politician Hugh Cairns.

plan alone was "founded on reason and justice,"[90] the fact remained that quite other notions of what the composition of the Commons would have to be in order to qualify as a "reasonable and just" mirror were prevalent. Dicey had no patience for the idea that the exercise of "political reason" alone could produce such a mirror,[91] and he directed at such pretensions his most withering prose:

> Advocates of class representation have expended immense ingenuity in devising schemes for effecting an hypothetical balance of power, and the complexity of these devices has given an appearance of philosophic profundity to the theory which makes such devices necessary; for it is difficult for any one to believe that an object which needs thought and ingenuity for its attainment may, after all, not be worth attaining. But calm observers, though willing to give all due weight to the objections which may be urged against the representation of numbers, may yet be inclined to suspect that thinkers who advocate the establishment of a balance of power, entertain views open to greater difficulties than are the theories which these thinkers assail.

However confident those of Cole's mold may have been that the picture of society which undergirded their prescriptions for reform was the right one, their schemes were nonetheless "open to a primary charge of utter impracticability" resulting from the absence of consensus about the "weight and importance" of the discrete elements of society. Dicey dwelt at length on this theme:

> Their object is to give "due" weight to each interest, but no standard exists by which the "due" weight may be measured. Mr. Disraeli is honestly convinced that the landed interest has not its due share of power. Most other persons would think a diminution of the influence of the country gentlemen essential to the establishment of a fair constitutional balance; but there exists no test by which to decide between the correctness of Mr. Disraeli's views and the views of his opponents, unless principles be introduced which are fatal to the theory of the balance of power [of the various classes and interests].[92]

---

[90] Cole, *The Middle Classes and the Borough Franchise*, 40.   [91] Holyoake, *Liberal Situation*, 14.

[92] Dicey, "Balance of Classes," 75–6, 65. The logical structure of Dicey's attack on a fair balance of interests is brought out by juxtaposition with Marx's formally similar critique, eight years later, of those schools of socialism which invoked the principle of a "fair distribution of the proceeds of labour": "What is a 'fair distribution'? Do not the bourgeois assert that the present-day distribution is 'fair'? . . . Have not also the socialist sectarians the most varied notions about 'fair' distribution?"; Marx, *Critique of the Gotha Program*, in Marx, *Selected Writings*, ed. Lawrence Simon (Indianapolis, 1994), 318–19.

Dicey, who, like almost all liberals of his age, was bullish about the burgeoning social sciences, did not mean to suggest that there was no fact of the matter about the relative contributions of different "orders" of society to the nation's social, intellectual, and economic life. His point, part-political, part-epistemological, was that there was no uncontroversial criterion by which "persons of opposite views, such as Mr. Mill and Mr. Disraeli, could be brought to agree on the exact proportion of influence which ought to be retained by the landed, commercial, and working classes."[93] In the face of these disagreements, Dicey believed, any plan of reform which depended on its acceptance as *the* means of reflecting the truth about modern English society in all its diversity must be unsatisfactory.

Dicey had no affection for the "mirror" principle, and did not contemplate with regret the imminent passing which he expected for it. But even in his essay one gets a sense of a sort of romantic tragedy about the theory which he was assailing. While he lamented that the "principles" of his antagonists "tend in practice ... to the establishment of a Plutocracy," he did not think that the mirror theory was a cynical cloak for upper-class power-hunger, and he was in any case uninterested in such ad hominem arguments. Instead, even this theory contained (to use the lingo of the era) a "partial truth." This was the respect for diversity and the conviction that including it within Parliament was advantageous: "An argument of real force ... is that the introduction into the legislative body of members belonging to different orders of the community would tend greatly to improve the character of the legislature. No candid critic can deny that there is some truth in this allegation."[94] Proponents of the variety-of-suffrages/mirroring position observed, valued, and attended to the diversity in their societies; they developed a serious theory of the epistemic and policymaking benefits which diversity produced; they were guided by a desire to do justice to the various elements of the polity. But they never squarely faced the objection that wide swathes of their countrymen might dispute their assessment of the shape of the "public." Though they celebrated and sought to give expression to the true state of society and public opinion in all its diversity, they did not recognize the diversity of opinions that existed with respect to this state itself, and the theory to which they subscribed lacked the resources to address the contentions arising from this second-order diversity.

[93] Dicey, "Balance of Classes," 77–8.   [94] Ibid., 78, 72.

This was the deep difficulty, and the tragic aspect, of the variety-of-suffrages theory. That it was responsive to the conditions of modern diversity gave it great appeal and normative power in an age absorbed with these themes, but this diversity to which it was so attentive would always render its prescriptions contestable and unsatisfying. Only a society that was divided and diverse would need such careful planning to do justice to all parties. But a divided society was precisely the kind of society in which it was least likely that agreement on the exact contours of these structures would be found. Whiggish theorists of representation assumed that unanimity could be found at this second-order level – at the level at which each theorist was painting his own picture of society – while first-order diversity persisted. The essence of Dicey's critique was to cast this assumption as implausible. In this regard Dicey was closer to a defender of the variety of suffrages such as Bagehot than he was to a moderate sociologist of diverse working-class opinion such as Houghton. For both Dicey and Bagehot, democracy and the descriptively-representative, deliberative legislature were irreconcilable – but where Bagehot chose representativeness and deliberation, Dicey chose democracy.

Dicey added a further dimension to his critique: the temporal. In a manner that reminds the modern reader of Nozick's argument that the exercise of liberty over time inevitably disrupts patterned theories of distributive justice,[95] Dicey allowed, *arguendo*, that somehow a consensus that bridged the social and ideological divides in Britain could be reached. A consensus of this sort, could, however, only be fleeting and was therefore of little permanent benefit: "such an agreement would be as worthless as it would be illusory; for in politics nothing is more certain than that it is impossible to predict how political and social forces will adjust themselves under a new Constitution." This mode of theorizing, which relied on imprinting a "stereotype" of the social-intellectual order of society on the legislature, was utterly unbefitting of political thinkers who rejected static notions of society in favor of a (in Dicey's eyes, true) developmental, evolutionary perspective.[96] This was a powerful, persuasive maneuver, since many champions of the variegated suffrage were committed to

---

[95] Robert Nozick, *Anarchy, State, and Utopia* (New York, 1974), 160–4.

[96] Dicey, "Balance of Classes," 77. In Victorian debates on representation the worry about "essentialism" which appears in modern discussions of descriptive representation was absent, although the resistance to "stereotyping the social" expressed here does come close: see e.g. Jane Mansbridge, "Quota Problems: Combating the Dangers of Essentialism," *Politics & Gender*, 1 (2005): 622–38; Michael Rabinder James, "The Priority of Racial Constituency over Descriptive Representation," *JP*, 73 (2011): 899–914. Robert Paul Wolff's argument that postwar American pluralism imprinted a "frozen" picture of society on political discourse can be seen as an expansion of Dicey's concern

a deeply progressive social thought. Dicey delivered the *coup de grâce* with the claim that, had Whigs genuinely adhered to their mirror theory, their greatest legislative achievement, the First Reform Act, would have died on the vine: "Had it been deemed requisite to ascertain beforehand what would be the exact amount of weight given by the Reform Act to each section of society, Gatton and Old Sarum might still be sending up Members to Parliament."[97] It was a fanciful piece of self-flattery on the part of Whigs to ascribe their success in 1832 to the country's approval of the law as an instrument for creating a prospectively accurate image of society; rather, the country had embraced the Reform Act for more pedestrian reasons, because, in a time of crisis, it promised to expunge great and obvious evils. In short, Dicey was not only convinced that in modern, diverse, progressive nations, consensus on the image of society that was to be transplanted into the legislature was improbable; he was also convinced that even if one could suspend disbelief and conceive of this improbability being momentarily overcome, the consensus reached would shortly become outdated and, hence, an unfit basis for representative government.

A temporal aspect entered into Dicey's argument in another way. In keeping with the historicist bent of Victorian political inquiry, Dicey could not refrain from injecting a remark on the broad sweep of British history. If the sociological premises on which mirroring schemes depended were, as a theoretical matter, always contestable, they reached a heightened pitch of implausibility in modern social conditions:

> In a society such as that of the Middle Ages, where marked orders existed, representation by orders, with all its disadvantages, arose, as it were naturally, from the surrounding condition of civilization. In a society like that of modern England it is difficult to find the orders on which laboriously to build a scheme of class representation. Take, for example, a class frequently mentioned in political discussions, that of the £10 householders. What, after all, is the real community of view or interest, which binds the members of the class together? They are of different politics; they pursue different professions; they belong, in many cases, to different religious bodies. Looked at in one point of view, they may be called a class; looked at in another, they are a disconnected mass of different small classes ... Who can say where the upper class ends, or where the middle class begins?

beyond the electoral-parliamentary sphere; Wolff, "Beyond Tolerance," in Wolff, Barrington Moore, and Herbert Marcuse, *A Critique of Pure Tolerance* (Boston, 1965), 41–7.

[97] Dicey, "Balance of Classes," 77. Gatton and Old Sarum had been two of the most notorious rotten boroughs of the unreformed Parliament.

The simple fact was that in the modern world, marked by the decline of the old structures of differently privileged "estates" or "orders" and now defined by the expansion of individual liberty and the freedom and diversity of opinion, "classes were intermingled" and "it had become absolutely impossible to draw a clearly marked line between the different divisions of the nation."[98]

Dicey's essay was the most pointed articulation of the thought that the prevailing theory of representation was doomed by the very diversity which it sought to represent accurately. But he was not alone in making this critique, even in the *Essays*.[99] His fellow *Essay*ist George C. Brodrick made the same accusation in his own reform writings. "The relative importance of these mysterious aggregates ["classes" and "interests"] is ordinarily measured, not by reference to any independent standard, such as numbers, wealth, or intelligence, but by the weight which the individual writer may be disposed to attribute to each, having regard to what he considers should be the predominant influence in Parliament," Brodrick had written in an 1859 essay.[100] He restated the charge in the first chapter of *Essays on Reform*, there invoking as well the temporal dimension stressed by Dicey:

> To know what is a just balance of classes, we must have determined before-hand what degree of weight each ought to possess in the State, and have solved most of the problems which it is the special function of a reformed Parliament to investigate. Not long ago, it was considered a fair distribution of legislative power that a few hundred noblemen should not only compose one estate of the realm co-ordinate with the Commons, but should also exercise, through relations and nominees, a preponderating influence in the popular branch of the Legislature ... What appears to a landlord or employer "a just balance of classes," may appear the very reverse to an impartial critic, as well as to a tenant or artizan, especially if it has been

---

[98] Ibid., 81–2, 74. Also Julia Stapleton, "Introduction," to *Liberalism, Democracy, and the State in Britain: Five Essays, 1862–1891*, ed. Stapleton (Bristol, 1991): 7–40. Dicey's historicized thought here bears an unlikely affinity to the late-twentieth-century revival of liberal theory in France; the difficulties for group representation caused by the end of a society of orders have been remarked upon by Claude Lefort, Marcel Gauchet, and Pierre Rosanvallon. See Gregory Conti and William Selinger, "The Other Side of Representation: The History and Theory of Representative Government in Pierre Rosanvallon," *Constellations*, 23 (2016): 548–62.

[99] Not all of the fellow contributors to the *Essays*, though, were comfortable with Dicey's critical line on the mirror theory. As was noted in Chapter 2, Bernard Cracroft was a believer in the traditional mirror theory even as he supported Gladstone's bill to reduce the suffrage in both counties and boroughs. Consequently, in writing about the lessons of the *Essays* as a whole he felt compelled to downplay the severity of Dicey's attack in a way which dramatically distorted the latter's message; Cracroft, "The Reform Session of 1867," 162.

[100] Brodrick, "The Principles of Parliamentary Reform," in *Political Studies*, 146.

adjusted on the monstrous supposition that the more numerous a class is, the more jealously should it be excluded from the franchise.[101]

To radical democrats, the proper response to these problems was to drop all mirroring aspirations and accept that the only fair way of organizing Britain's public, collective life was to enact a conception of democracy as equal voting power for all citizens.

Brodrick was much readier than Dicey to expose "the self-interest" which, according to him, lay beneath espousal of this theory of representation,[102] but like his co-contributor he recognized that the more fundamental theoretical problem was the inability to travel from the ideal of a truthful reflection of society to an incontrovertible sociology that could serve as a template for electoral regulations. All reform proposals that purported to "give to each [of the various elements of which the nation is composed] its proportionate weight and influence" and in consequence to actualize "that equipoise of conflicting forces which has come to be regarded as the capital problem of political dynamics" were guilty of "*petitio principii.*"[103] Writing after the passage of two general elections under the Second Reform Act's expanded franchise, this message was echoed forcefully by a scholar who would become England's leading legal historian. "A consideration of the complexity of interests," wrote a young Frederic Maitland, demonstrated that plans for a "representation of interests" or "classes," as opposed to a "representation of numbers," could not but rest on the pernicious drawing of "arbitrary lines."[104]

Nearer the end of the century and in an England much closer to electoral democracy, Maitland's objections would be articulated more fully by his former teacher at Cambridge, the great philosopher Henry Sidgwick. In the 1890s Sidgwick was certainly among the target audience for the dwindling contingent of writers who had retained hopes for a return to the

---

[101] Brodrick, "Utilitarian Argument against Reform," 7–8.   [102] Ibid., 7.

[103] Brodrick, "The Principles of Parliamentary Reform," 145, 147.

[104] Maitland, *A Historical Sketch of Liberty and Equality: As Ideals of English Political Philosophy from the Time of Hobbes to the Time of Coleridge* (Indianapolis, 2000), 162–4. This precociously learned text was composed for a Trinity College fellowship in 1875. Maitland expounded further on the difficulties as he saw them: "Human interests are not so simple … Men do not want to vote only in their economic character, they want to vote as Churchmen, as Dissenters, as Total Abstainers, as friends of Peace at any price. The line dividing the realty from the personalty does not even roughly coincide with some of the most important distinctions. The consequence would be that in Coleridge's scheme some men, e.g. merchants, would be refused votes because if they had them their class would be over represented. A merchant will say that he does not want to vote quâ merchant but quâ Ritualist, and he will feel his exclusion as arbitrary. Some merchants must be left out; but why should it not be his Evangelical neighbours? … It might be different could we label men as belonging to different "interests," but this becomes more and more difficult every day."

kind of group- and interest-representation characteristic of the variety of suffrages. Not only was he utterly resistant to admitting "any supposed 'natural right'" to the vote,[105] he also valued the epistemic advantages of diversity and retained the Millian fear of parliamentary tyranny of the majority under a democratic suffrage.[106] Nevertheless, he found the objection from contestability, indeterminacy, and second-order diversity insurmountable. Indeed, he generalized the Dicey-Brodrick critique, in a way that they had not themselves done, to include all other forms of "electoral inequality," such as plural voting.[107] Any political theory built upon the principle of "due" representation – of giving "due weight" in the legislature to each class or group, or to attributes such as wealth or intelligence – suffered from its inexact and ineluctably controversial character:

> [H]owever fully we admit the general considerations above stated, any scheme for applying them must necessarily be to a great extent arbitrary: we have no means of determining, with any pretence to exactness, how much additional electoral power is due to wealth on account of the implication of social with private interests, or how much properly corresponds to any available evidence of probable superiority in political judgment.

Such theories were doomed by what Sidgwick did not hesitate to call the "impossibility of a satisfactory criterion" for making the kinds of finely tailored adjustments and gradations of the suffrage required for their realization.[108] This lack of a criterion, this internal indeterminacy, had practical consequences. For instance, Sidgwick thought that schemes of representation based on such theories were liable, from the necessarily disputable and arbitrary-seeming quality of their prescriptions, to have a destabilizing impact: "any particular plan of electoral inequality will always present plausible grounds for agitation to modify the standards applied: while

---

[105] Sidgwick, *Elements of Politics*, 377.

[106] "Good legislation is a result more likely to be attained in a representative assembly in which such class interests are fairly balanced, as each class is more open to sound reason and impartial consideration of the common good where the interests of others are concerned. For this reason, as we have seen, a widely-extended suffrage involves a danger ... that the ultimate interests of the whole community may be sacrificed to the real or apparent class-interests of the numerical majority of the electors, either through ignorance or through selfishness and limitation of sympathy"; ibid., 389.

[107] Ibid., 391. Similar charges of arbitrariness and indeterminacy were brought against plural voting by others. E.g. Leslie Stephen, "Reform," 529: "Of course it is totally impossible to find any proportion whatever" by which to regulate assigning "to the wealthy, and exalted, and intellectual people votes to correspond to the force which they ought to have ... What Rule of Three will answer this question: – If John Smith has one vote, how many should Mr. Mill have?"

[108] Sidgwick, *Elements of Politics*, 391–2.

the interests of classes and parties will always supply strong motives for such agitation." But it was also a theoretical defect; in current philosophical parlance, we might say that Sidgwick criticized such theories for not being *action-guiding*. The injunction to produce a mirror of society or a just balance of classes was valueless because it did not provide rules for selecting among the diverse lights in which these phenomena could be reasonably regarded. "In considering balance of interests, it must be borne in mind that it is impossible to divide society into classes which remain identical and equally distinct for all legislative purposes": hence, it was eminently disputable whether the central "conflict of interests" around which the composition of the Commons needed to be oriented was that between the "'agricultural' [as] opposed to the 'manufacturing' interests," or that "between manual labourers generally and their employers," or perhaps that between "persons to whom fixed money-payments are due and the rest of the community." As "we pass from one proposed law to another," Sidgwick observed, "the important lines of division are continually changing," and one of the lessons he drew from this fluidity and many-sidedness of political subjects was the foolhardiness of any aspiration to devise in advance a set of electoral-parliamentary structures that would reflect the true state of society.[109] A mirroring Commons was, to Sidgwick, at base not much more than a myth. The normative foundation of parliamentary authority had to lie elsewhere than in its descriptive accuracy.

These authors articulated a powerful critique of the mirror-sociological theory of representation. Nor were similar ideas the sole property of a small band of democratically-inclined academic liberals; as Chapter 4 shows, these concerns were arguably pressed further and with more absoluteness by the movement for proportional representation, which the authors featured in this chapter opposed. It should be noted, however, that in comparison to this critical project their own defenses of the normative superiority of democracy can look scanty and suggestive. Indeed, much as this trio shared the perception of a theoretical inadequacy underlying the variety-of-suffrages position, it cannot be said that they shared a theory of democracy. There are several reasons for this. Sidgwick, for one, can only with a great deal of contortion be classified as a democratic theorist, for he believed that unqualified adherence to any specific form of government was incompatible with the "utilitarian point-of-view."[110] The most that could be asserted was that while "the general arguments for a representative legislature lead *prima facie* to the inclusion of all sane adults," in practice

---

[109] Ibid., 391–2.   [110] Ibid., 379.

these reasons were defeasible by a host of factors.[111] This did not mean that there was not much to be said for democracy.[112] It did accord with the values of fairness and nonarbitrariness, and thus was not liable to provoke "a sense of injustice" in those groups who were excluded or whose impact was deliberately constrained; democratic electorates, for all their faults, did a "tolerably satisfactory" job of electing competent officials; and nondemo- cratic schemes were riddled with theoretical dilemmas, the reasoning behind them consistently "less plausible" for a "modern state." Yet he was alarmed by many features of his country's nascent democracy, such as the tightening grip of party, and he was "perfectly happy to have his political-theoretical efforts understood as an attempt to marry the virtues of democracy with those of aristocracy."[113] Sidgwick's impression that nondemocratic applications of the descriptive ideal would be on the losing end when faced with democratic objections did not translate into any great keenness for the gains of democracy in his lifetime.

With Dicey and Brodrick the case is different. It is beyond the scope of this chapter to reconstruct their complete thought about democracy. But it does behoove us to consider one piece of their thought – or, rather, one lacuna in their thought. This is that, unlike Sidgwick, they made an immediate and essentially unargued leap from the rejection of descriptive representation to the acceptance of democracy. Why did they assume that the demonstration of the difficulties of contestability and arbitrariness that afflicted schemes developed on the traditional mirroring ideal amounted to an argument for democracy?[114] After all, in purely theoretical terms a plan for appointing a monarch or an assembly via lottery would have been just as immune to the objections that they lodged against the programs of variegated suffrage.

It is difficult to give a sure explanation for the absence of an argument, but a few informed speculations can be offered. First, in equating the rejection of the variety-of-suffrages framework with the embrace of democ- racy, Brodrick and Dicey were in effect taking up the debate where their opponents left off. Greg framed the reform issue as a choice between sociological schemes and the "universal suffrage, which all deprecate,"

---

[111] Sidgwick, *Elements of Politics*, 378.

[112] He even allowed, in his Cambridge lectures on the ancients, that democracy had a special "naturalness"; Sidgwick, *The Development of European Polity* (London, 1903), 100–1.

[113] Sidgwick, *Elements of Politics*, 374, 378–9, 589–603. For an analysis of Sidgwick's complex views on democracy that resonates with many of my conclusions, see Bart Schultz, *Henry Sidgwick: Eye of the Universe* (Cambridge, 2004) ch. 7.

[114] Brodrick would end his life disillusioned with the march of British democracy, mostly due to the movement for Irish home rule; Harvie, *Lights of Liberalism*, ch. 9.

and Cole confronted England with the choice between a plan such as his own and "the condition of universal suffrage."[115] If the terms of public debate were already that democracy or a system of variegated suffrage were the only options available,[116] then democrats did not need to take on the extra work of showing the correctness of this binary.

But there are two other, more substantive reasons for this feature of their thought. The first is that they seem to have sided with the social contract tradition rather than with Burke on the question of the primordial character of majority rule.[117] One can glimpse in Brodrick and (especially) Dicey the thought that democracy was simply the default mode of politics, and that rather than continue on with what they took to be an "utterly impracticable" series of attempts to bring the country into agreement on a "fair constitutional balance," it was preferable to have recourse to the default option.[118]

A second, and more important, reason for their treating it as self-evident that refutation of the descriptive ideal meant the triumph of democracy was that their attack on the variety-of-suffrages school was, in their minds, more than just a contest of one institutional vision against another. It was also something like a defense of the political sphere against encroachments on its terrain: "To divide citizens, therefore, into classes, and to marshal them according to their comparative claims to power, simple as it seems, is to undertake the responsibility of deciding beforehand in what proportions the great political jury is to be packed, and thereby virtually to anticipate their verdict."[119]

Inherent in the accusation of arbitrariness was the worry that implementing one of these mirroring schemes would prevent decisions about the nation's trajectory from being made in a truly collective manner. However

---

[115] Greg, "Representative Reform [i]," 507; Cole, *The Middle Classes and the Borough Franchise*, 73.

[116] This sense of the limited alternatives available drew in part from a contemporary climate of opinion preoccupied with the "inevitability" of democracy; James Colaiaco, *James Fitzjames Stephen and the Crisis of Victorian Thought* (New York, 1983), ch. 1.

[117] For Burke's famous argument about the conventionality and unnaturalness of majority rule, see *An Appeal from the New to the Old Whigs*, in Burke, *Further Reflections on the Revolution in France*, ed. Daniel Ritchie (Indianapolis, 1992), 164. For the contractarians on the foundational character of majority rule, see Hobbes, *On the Citizen*, ed. Richard Tuck (Cambridge, 1998), ch. 7, §5; Locke, *Two Treatises of Government*, ed. Peter Laslett (Cambridge, 1960), II §95–6.

[118] It is worth stating explicitly that Dicey and Brodrick were operating with a minimalist notion of democracy common in their context. For Dicey, democracy consisted of the acceptance of two simple premises: first, that the equal treatment of "persons," rather than a weighing of classes, ought to be the building block of political representation; second, that, if "supremacy" has to reside somewhere for political life to exist, the least objectionable and least controversial place to locate it was in the "majority."

[119] Brodrick, "Principles of Parliamentary Reform," 146.

"captivated" many of his contemporaries were "by the idea of Parliament being a mirror of the nation," that theory rested on the unacceptably apolitical "assumption that theorists can sketch out the future of the nation."[120] Perhaps the best (though a somewhat anachronistic) way to put it is that, for Dicey and Brodrick, democracy was envisioned as a way of moving the scene of the action from the *sociological* to the *political*. The representative system was no longer to be thought of as an arena for addressing the questions "What does society look like? How do we weigh its various elements? What is the shape of public opinion?," but rather as a set of structures that enabled citizens to come to an authoritative collective decision about what they as a nation wanted, about the direction in which the country should head. In championing democracy, they believed that they were championing a true political process against the deformations of politics that had prevailed in the recent history of Britain.

Before concluding this section, a final word ought to be said about this line of Victorian democratic theory. In the critiques of the mirror theory of representation by Dicey, Brodrick, and Sidgwick, there is observable a phenomenon familiar in the history of political thought: if extremes did not quite meet here, they certainly approached one another. For both these democrats and the Tories who had opposed the First Reform Act shared a strong sense of the arbitrariness of projects to "reform" Parliament without inaugurating "democracy."[121] But while for democrats of the second half of the century this arbitrariness was a philosophical defect, a proof of the inadequacy of the underlying theory to provide a normative foundation for representative government, for Tories of the first half this arbitrariness had been not so much a philosophical problem as a practical one. The former group claimed that the incoherence and indeterminacy of the sociological ideal proved a democratic suffrage to be the only theoretically sound basis on which a modern parliament could rest; the latter group had predicted that, if the suffrage were treated not as a near-infallible and undesigned product of national history and tradition but as an object of policy which could be revised to suit discrepant political agendas and social viewpoints, then this change of political outlook would lead inevitably to democracy. A crucial plank of the antireform Tory platform of the early 1830s had been that "the Whigs were opening a door that could not be shut," that "the least modicum of reform" would bring "ultimate democratic

---

[120] Dicey, "Balance of Classes," 84.
[121] For more on the rhetoric of these plans, see Saunders, "Democracy," in *Languages of Politics in Nineteenth-Century Britain*, 142–67.

consequences" and "open the floodgates to democracy."[122] Whigs had denied any such unavoidably democratic telos implicit in their policy of reform, and they had done so, as we have seen, for a compelling reason: namely, because they disavowed any necessary connection, practical or conceptual, between representative government rightly understood as anchored in descriptive representativeness and the democratic franchise.

This was one of the central axes of the Tory–Whig struggle leading up to 1832. Whigs argued that in amending the traditional electoral map to bring the Commons into accord with the recent preeminence of the middle class, they were engaged in an improvement of the representative dimension of the British Constitution in response to objective social facts about the discord between Parliament and the public at large. Tories replied that piercing the armor of the organic perfection of the Constitution would leave any nondemocratic electoral arrangements constantly exposed to the charge of arbitrariness regarding the limits of the suffrage they erected, whatever they might be.[123] In 1831 the prolific Tory Archibald Alison pronounced it fantastical of Reform Whigs to imagine that they could articulate "grounds of justice," acceptable to those who would be left unenfranchised, for the boundaries of the suffrage which they intended to draw.[124] The conservative poet-philosopher and proponent of class representation Samuel Taylor Coleridge agreed, putting his opposition to the Whig Reform proposals in typically hectic and colorful language: "no man can trace a line of separation" through the "blending and interfusion" of persons and property that made up society "except such a confessedly unmeaning and unjustifiable line of political empiricism as £10

---

[122] J. R. Pole, *Political Representation in England and the Origins of the American Republic* (Berkeley, 1966), 498; Donald Southgate, *The Passing of the Whigs, 1832–1886* (London, 1962), 16. Classic statements of this view are Peel's speeches of 3 Mar. 1831, cited in Chapter 1, and of 6 July 1831 (*Hansard*, HC Deb, Third Series, vol. 4, 890), where he spoke of not "open[ing] a door which I saw no prospect of being able to close"). See also Norman Gash, *Sir Robert Peel: The Life of Sir Robert Peel after 1830*, second edition (London, 1988), 20. Tocqueville saw the issue in the same light: that tampering with suffrage rights would inevitably lead to electoral democracy was "one of the most invariable" of the "rules that govern societies"; *Democracy in America*, trans. Arthur Goldhammer, 2 vols. (New York, 2004), vol. 1, 64.

[123] As an historian of the First Reform period wrote picturesquely one century ago of Peel, the Duke of Wellington, and their Tory resistance to the Reform push of 1830: "The gentlemen politicians felt in their bones that there could be no finality in reform till their ark was pulled to pieces. Slowly, at the distance of a century, their instinct is being justified"; Brown, *The French Revolution in English History*, 174. Peel had famously argued that, once one admitted the principle that the historically inherited franchises could be altered, no answer was possible to those who would ask "Why confine the privilege of voting to those who rent a House rated at £10-a-year?"; Peel, Speech of 3 March 1831, 30.

[124] Alison, "The Reform Bill," 43.

householders," and the attempt to do so would not "stop short of universal suffrage."[125] To the Tory mind, the resistance to reform measures guided by a descriptive ideal was not so much that they *were*, in the theoretical sense, arbitrary, but that they could not help but *look* arbitrary and thereby serve as "a stimulus to further agitation" that would put Britain "on the highway to universal suffrage."[126] From this perspective, the later critiques of Dicey, Brodrick, and Sidgwick would have seemed the inevitable theoretical expressions of the psychology of discontent with the electoral system which Tories predicted would prevail, and prevail *with good reason*, in the aftermath of 1832. Hence, the unreformed Tory was the ideological neighbor of a certain style of Victorian democrat, for they both resisted the endeavor to remake the Commons in the hope of perfecting its sociological reflectiveness.

From the 1860s onward, defending democracy as these authors understood it involved defeating not only the traditional descriptivism of the variety-of-suffragists, but also a newer entrant into the fray over parliamentary reform. This was the theory of *personal* or *proportional representation*. This theory shared much of the value-system and vocabulary of the variety of suffrages, but was crucially different in several regards, and accordingly had to be rebutted on distinct grounds – as we will see was done by the likes of Kinnear and Dicey, who articulated quite different grounds of concern about the program of Thomas Hare and John Stuart Mill than they had about the views of the likes of Bagehot and Greg. Likewise, although several variety-of-suffragists would express respect and sympathy for PR in light of the important areas of overlap between their theories, Bagehot, Greg, and others rejected PR with every bit as much ardor as the Diceyans rejected them, if for different reasons.

What was this third approach to mirroring representation, and why did its appearance in the parliamentary-reform landscape generate such an extraordinary range of responses, from cheering it as the perfection or salvation of deliberative representative government to condemning it as a potentially fatal blow to parliamentarianism? Chapter 4 takes up these questions.

---

[125] Coleridge, "The Great Reform Bill: 1832," entry of 24 April 1832, selections from *Table Talk*, in Coleridge, *The Political Thought of Samuel Taylor Coleridge*, ed. R. J. White (London, 1938), 229–31. To impress just how disastrous it would be to start down the Reform Act's slippery slope to democracy, he added that women were likely to wind up enfranchised as well.

[126] Aytoun, "Reform Measures," 373.

CHAPTER 4

Diversity with Democracy? Proportional Representation
Part One: Concepts and Techniques[*]

In 1914, nearly a half-century after his fight for a democratized suffrage led him to attack the hallowed tenet of a mirroring Commons, Dicey, now England's most venerable authority on the Constitution, wrote in unflattering terms of the condition of political thought in his lifetime:

> In no part of English history is the tardy development of new constitutional ideas more noteworthy or more paradoxical than during the whole Victorian era (1837 to 1901). It was an age full of intellectual activity and achievement ... but it was an age which added little to the world's scanty store of political or constitutional ideas.[1]

This appraisal was tendentious, to say the least, and stemmed more from the disillusionment with parliamentary politics and the Irish question that dominated the last three decades of his life than from a disinterested survey of the history of ideas.[2] There might, however, appear some truth to his claim, for neither the variety-of-suffrages vision (which was anchored in the historical legacy of the British electoral system), nor the idea of a widely extended suffrage *tout court* (already long in place in America and France[3]), could easily meet Dicey's curmudgeonly baseline of "original" ideas.

---

[*] A word on terminology is needed at the outset of this chapter. In political science, a contrast is typically drawn between PR and "first-past-the-post" (FPP) systems. However, this latter term is not strictly apposite to the British case before the Third Reform Act of 1884, which established single-member districts as the rule (more on this later). For the most part what had historically obtained might be better called a "first-and-second-past-the-post" system, since most constituencies had dual membership. These were also not, strictly speaking, "majoritarian" electoral arrangements, since the candidates did not need to reach a 50 percent vote threshold to be elected. The best term to designate the British system in contrast to the proportionalist alternatives discussed here is therefore the most generic one: "plurality rule." I will primarily use this term, although for linguistic diversity and literary convenience others may slip in here. For a brief survey of the UK's exotic electoral arrangements, Daniele Caramani, "United Kingdom," in *Elections in Western Europe since 1815: Electoral Results by Constituencies* (New York, 2000), part 2, ch. 18.

[1] Dicey, *Introduction to the Study of the Law of the Constitution*, eighth edition (London, 1915), lix.

[2] Ian Christopher Fletcher, "'This Zeal for Lawlessness': A. V. Dicey, *The Law of the Constitution*, and the Challenge of Popular Politics," *PH*, 16 (1997): 309–29.

[3] Depending on one's view of the "ancient constitution," it could be seen as having British antecedents as well; for an archetypal statement of the democratic view of the ancient

But there was a constitutional program whose originality even Dicey had grudgingly to admit.[4] This was the theory of *personal* or *proportional representation* developed by Thomas Hare and instantly christened "*the great discovery in representative government*" by the most influential mind of the age, John Stuart Mill.[5] Like the schools of electoral variegation and democracy hitherto examined, it was oriented around notions of diversity, deliberation, descriptive representation, and inclusiveness. And it was in support of and reaction against Hare's innovation that the most sophisticated set of reflections on representation in the final third of the nineteenth century emerged. To Dicey, however, PR barely registered as a serious proposal, and its appearance on the scene was not sufficient to alter his sense of the poverty of constitutional thinking in his epoch.

Dicey's downplaying of the significance of PR was motivated in large part by his "grave objections" to it.[6] Yet his failure to grant proper recognition to the place of PR in British political thought is indicative of larger trends that have continued to this day. In Anglo-centric scholarship, the history of PR has, oddly, been a victim both of its success and its failure. On the first front, the implementation of PR systems throughout Europe and beyond (a process already well underway in Dicey's lifetime[7]) has made historians and political scientists less attuned to its *British* pedigree. On the second front, the failure of the movement for PR in Britain inclines us to downplay the mark it left on British political theory.[8] The truth is that PR was a major theme of Victorian and Edwardian political-intellectual life, and an understanding of the development of ideas of representation, democracy, and parliamentary government demands that the Victorian controversy over PR be taken seriously.

My inquiry here will be limited in various ways. Most importantly, although I will highlight some significant dates and attend to major intellectual shifts, this is not a narrative history of the PR movement but a conceptual analysis that treats the Victorian theory of PR as a relatively

Constitution, see Edward Freeman, *The Growth of the English Constitution from the Earliest Times* (London, 1872).

[4] Dicey, *Law of the Constitution*, lix.

[5] Mill, Letter to Thomas Hare, 19 Dec. 1859, in *CW*, vol. 15, 653, italics in original.

[6] Dicey, *Law of the Constitution*, lxxiii.

[7] "By 1920 Britain was the only democratic country in Western Europe not to have adopted some form of PR"; Peter Hain, *Proportional Misrepresentation* (Hants, 1986), 4. In the UK, PR has been adopted in the contexts of devolution and elections to the European Parliament; Richard Wyn Jones and Robert Scully, "Devolution and Electoral Politics in Scotland and Wales," *Publius*, 36 (2006): 115–34. On the history of the adoption of PR in Europe, e.g. Thomas Mackie and Richard Rose, *The International Almanac of Electoral History*, second edition (London, 1982).

[8] Even accounts of mid- and late-Victorian politics that draw heavily on the history of political thought often neglect PR entirely; e.g. R. C. K. Ensor, *England 1870–1914* (Oxford, 1936) or, more recently, Angus Hawkins's *Victorian Political Culture*.

coherent body of thought. On this point, it is worth noting that this chapter gives greater consideration to early-twentieth-century texts than the previous chapters have done.[9] With regard to PR, the Victorian era extends into the second decade of the twentieth century; a fairly cohesive set of references and arguments ran from Hare's major works until the First World War.[10]

This chapter considers the conceptual and institutional core of the Victorian theory of PR in light of the schools of thought on representation examined so far. It shows that Victorian PR cannot be understood as simply a variant of the longstanding descriptivist theory of electoral variegation, nor as a subset of either of the democratic outlooks just examined. Instead, Victorian PR is best seen as constituting its own integral tradition. PR proponents, it is true, laid claim to the widely shared descriptivist values of diversity, inclusivity, and deliberation. But they sought to achieve these ends through an unprecedented recipe of individualistic aggregation procedures and uniformity of suffrage. In doing so, they radically diverged from the conceptual landscape of the variety-of-suffrages, overturning its cardinal tenet that electoral rules ought to be direct reflections of a group-based sociological imaginary and replacing it with a new idea of mirroring representation as the product of a procedure which granted electors perfect liberty from all restraints on the disposal of their votes. Victorian PR had a similarly divided relationship to democracy. It contained several features that imparted to it a certain democratic ideological momentum, and its argumentation overlapped in some important ways with the democratic theories just examined. But it was also distinctly elitist in its early days, and was only haltingly reconciled to democracy over the course of our period. In sum, Victorian PR comprised a distinctive set of concepts and techniques oriented around the promise of *mirroring-through-freedom* that both included and reshaped ideas from contending schools of thought. Chapter 5 then picks up on this reconstruction to analyze the debate surrounding the moral impact and practical consequences of PR.

Before investigating the nuts-and-bolts of PR, though, it will be useful to familiarize ourselves with a few developments that laid the groundwork for the debate on PR proper.

---

[9] The period around World War One was the high tide for PR's chances in the United Kingdom. In 1914 the Home Rule Bill included STV for the Irish Senate and for some seats in the Irish Commons, though implementation of the law was suspended due to the outbreak of the war; upon gaining its independence, however, Ireland instituted STV. And in 1917 the Speaker's Conference on Electoral Reform recommended STV for around a third of the Commons, but the Representation of the People Act 1918, which established universal male suffrage and a measure of woman's suffrage, established it only for the university seats. See Hart, *Proportional Representation*, chs. 8–9.

[10] This periodization corresponds roughly to what Pippa Norris has called the "first wave" of PR-based reform; Norris, "The Politics of Electoral Reform in Britain," *IPSR*, 16 (1995): 65–78.

1   The Prehistory of PR in Britain

For John Stuart Mill, 1859 was a landmark year. It was, for one, the year of *On Liberty*'s appearance. It was also the year he read the first edition of Thomas Hare's *Treatise on the Election of Representatives*[11] – and, consequently, the year in which one of the final "modifications" of his "practical political creed," the solution to the problem of representation, fell into place.[12] Mill instantly became an ardent proselytizer of Hare's system,[13] and he and Hare struck up a friendship which, while rooted in their devotion to the proportionalist cause, encompassed as well a more general sympathy of political outlook and intellectual interests.[14]

With Hare's book – and, even more, Mill's advocacy – the debate on PR in Britain begins in earnest and takes on many of the characteristic features that it retains up to the present, such as the focus on the single transferable vote (STV).[15] Proportional representation, however, did not commence in the late 1850s; it had both an American and a Continental history anterior to Hare.[16] Indeed, not even STV was original to Hare, although Hare was unaware of his antecedent at the time of formulating his scheme.[17] While we must largely leave the international dimension of PR's evolution aside,

[11] Hare, *A Treatise on the Election of Representatives, Parliamentary and Municipal* (London, 1859). Unless otherwise noted, references to the *Election of Representatives* will be to the third edition (Hare, *The Election of Representatives, Parliamentary and Municipal: A Treatise*, third edition [London, 1865]); it is the clearest and best-written of the four editions, and there is not much substantive change between it and the final edition. Parsons charts the modifications the text received over its several iterations in his monograph. The *Treatise* was not his first elaboration of his scheme; two years earlier he had released two editions of a short tract, *The Machinery of Representation* (both London, 1857), which garnered little public attention.

[12] Mill, *Autobiography*, 201.

[13] Among the numerous instances of Mill's praise, he declared himself Hare's "zealous apostle," and he ranked PR, along with the emancipation of women, as one of the "two greatest improvements which remain to be made in representative government"; Mill, Letter to Thomas Hare, 3 March 1859, in *CW*, vol. 15, 599; *Autobiography*, 284.

[14] Like Mill and many other figures in this book, Hare had a long experience in civil service and the professions. He trained at the Inns of Court, practiced as an equity lawyer, and beginning in the 1850s had a long career in the administration and reform of endowed charities. From a young age he had been an evangelist of free trade, and he would go on to membership in many of the great "liberal" social-intellectual institutions of the era (the Athenaeum and Political Economy Clubs, the Social Science Association). See Parsons, *Thomas Hare and Political Representation*, ch. 1; W. P. Courtney, "Hare, Thomas (1806–1891)," rev. Matthew Lee, *ODNB*. On Mill's and Hare's personal relationship, see Richard Reeves, *John Stuart Mill: Victorian Firebrand* (London, 2007), ch. 12.

[15] STV has been called the "'Anglo-Saxon' method of securing proportional representation"; Vernon Bogdanor, *What Is Proportional Representation?* (Oxford, 1984), 76.

[16] The French socialist Victor Considerant and the American lawyer Thomas Gilpin had both devised early versions of the list system in the mid-1840s; Alva Edward Garey, *Proportional Representation* (MA Thesis, University of Wisconsin, 1920).

[17] Earlier in the decade, the Danish Finance Minister Carl Christopher Georg Andrae had conceived a system of STV which was actually (though only briefly) used for elections to the Danish Upper

there was also a prehistory of PR in Britain. This was grounded in two plans for *minority representation*, and some awareness of it is needed for historiographical and conceptual purposes.

To understand what was so innovative about these projects of minority representation, we must note that variety-of-suffragists and diverse democrats were united by a particular vision of the relationship between the composition of the assembly and the electoral constituency. While these authors were remarkably imaginative about how constituencies could be constructed and differed in the specifics of their schemes, they all remained tied to British constitutional tradition in an important respect. This was that the accurate translation of social diversity which they sought was to emerge entirely from the interplay between constituencies. Diversity would be transferred into the assembly because constituencies were meant to be unalike in relevant ways.[18] Thus, while what were minority groups relative to the population of the whole kingdom were able to place their spokesman in the Commons – say, the shipping interest via the borough of Whitby and the Catholic community via Arundel,[19] or, on Stapleton's proposal, the clergy through constituencies specific to their vocation – no minorities as such were represented.[20] Instead, minorities at the national level entered the assembly by virtue of constituting the majority at some point(s) on the electoral map; the variegated suffrage was therefore an exemplification of the practice of majority-minority districting elevated to a high degree of sociological nuance and sophistication. What these traditions lacked was an attempt to give representation to minorities as they existed within a single constituency. Put another way, to these writers the accurate reflection of society arose out of an assortment of discrete constituencies treated integrally; the diversity that obtained internal to the constituency was not a direct object of parliamentary inclusion.

This notion of the representative order as a concatenation of constituencies that were integral wholes was related to an important fact about the

House; Salem Dutcher, *Minority or Proportional Representation: Its Nature, Aims, History, Processes, and Practical Operation* (New York, 1872), 111–14.

[18] "The great irregularity of the civil divisions of the country" defied a "uniform system of franchise," and so "the size, wealth, [and] population of the places" sending members differed greatly; Homersham Cox, *The British Commonwealth: or a Commentary on the Institutions and Principles of British Government* (London, 1854), 161. Interestingly, Cox's depiction of the realities and justification of the existent electoral system did not prevent him from dissenting strongly from the creed of "class representation" and from "the utter confusion" of the franchise even after 1832.

[19] Hawkins, *Victorian Political Culture*, 92; Parsons, *"Ignis Fatuus* vs. *Pons Asinorum,"* 376. Arundel remained a proprietary borough of the Duke of Norfolk, head of the most powerful British Roman Catholic family, even after the First Reform Act.

[20] As we will see in what follows, due to the multimember nature of constituencies the situation was actually somewhat more complicated.

English electoral system, one which has been mentioned but not explored in depth: namely, that the English constituency had historically been a multimember one, with two-member constituencies obtaining almost universally before 1832, at which point they were accompanied by a growth in three-member constituencies that held during the classical age of mid-century parliamentarism. These constituencies had always been regulated on what is now known as the "block vote" – that is, each voter possessed as many votes as there were seats to be filled in his constituency (two in two-membered, three in three-membered, and so on).[21] The block vote has come to be regarded as the electoral system with the greatest potential for "distortion" from the modern perspective on proportionality as each party receiving a percentage of seats in the assembly identical to its percentage of the overall vote.[22] This distortionary quality was increasingly recognized as the century wore on. Typically for the English, this recognition owed much to their perception of the practical failures of this system on the Continent (especially in Belgium, Switzerland, and naturally France).[23] It owed something as well to a clearer consciousness of the electoral-theoretical explanations of why the block vote, if detached from a system of a multiplicity of different districts distributed to capture "the varied interests, opinions, and feelings of the entire community," could yield outcomes that were strikingly unrepresentative by just about any measure.[24] Yet, for most of the century, these worries were treated as irrelevant, and the block vote in two-member districts was seen as no impediment to a mirroring Commons as conventionally understood.

Taking minorities in a strictly electoral sense, then, there was nothing intrinsically minority-friendly about the traditional British electoral

---

[21] Michael Steed, "The Evolution of the British Electoral System," in *Adversary Politics and Electoral Reform*, ed. S. E. Finer (London, 1975): 35–54. This predominance of dual membership had descended from the call of King Edward in 1295 for counties to return two knights of the shire and boroughs to return two burgesses (even earlier, four had been summoned; Courtenay Ilbert, *Parliament: Its History, Constitution, and Practice* [London, 1911], ch. 1). The block vote is also commonly referred to as *scrutin de liste*, though this latter term was inconsistently applied by Victorians. Before the Second Reform Act, all three-member constituencies were counties.

[22] John Carey and Andrew Reynolds, "The Impact of Electoral Systems," Journal of Democracy, 22 (2011): 36–47.

[23] E.g. Senior, "Lewis on Authority in Matters of Opinion," 545; Albert Grey, "Proportional versus Majority Representation," *NC*, 16 (1884): 935–64, at 943–6. Also Andrew Carstairs, *A Short History of Electoral Systems in Western Europe* (London, 1980), 12, 50–2, 138–40. It was in reaction to the perceived distortive, monopolistic character of the block vote that the United States banned multimember districts for congressional elections in 1842; Joseph Colomer, "On the Origins of Electoral Systems and Political Parties: The Role of Elections in Multi-Member Districts," *Electoral Studies*, 26 (2007): 262–73.

[24] E.g. Lewis, "Marshall on Minorities," 227.

system. Yet the multimember character of these districts had the unin-
tended effect of stimulating experimental thinking about the possibility of
transmitting divisions *internal to the constituency* into the Commons. Two
proposals made this momentous move of turning inside the constituency,
as it were, in order to represent minorities within electoral districts.

One of these was the cumulative vote. Laid out a half-decade before
Hare's scheme by James Garth Marshall, a former Liberal MP, the cumulative vote was "a system of voting where each elector in a constituency
having as many votes as there are representatives to be elected in his county
or borough, and distributing his votes as he pleases, may at his option give
one vote to each candidate, or accumulate the whole number of his votes in
favour of one candidate."[25] Marshall desired (mostly) three-member
constituencies;[26] on his plan, the voter in these tri-cornered constituencies
could give his three votes in any (whole-number) allotments which he
wished, rather than being bound to give no more than one vote per
candidate. The cumulative vote was centrally, therefore, a proposal to
increase flexibility in the distribution of the several votes traditionally at
the electors' disposal; its mirroring aims, which were central to Marshall's
project,[27] were achieved by the removal of a formal constraint on the
elector.[28] With this greater freedom came another benefit, one which
Marshall highlighted as a "practical advantage" of his plan over rival
reforms – namely, that it enabled the elector to express in a clear way the
intensity and not merely the fact of his preference for a candidate.[29]

---

[25] Marshall, *Minorities and Majorities: Their Relative Rights* (London, 1853), 13–4.

[26] In deference to the four members which the City of London then possessed, he allowed for the
application of his plan to four-member constituencies. Ibid., 22, 29–36.

[27] Ibid., 5–8.

[28] It should be noted that the bare fact of possessing two votes *but not being compelled to use them both*
already granted a greater measure of freedom to the elector than exists in single-member constituencies; the British elector had always been free to "plump" (that is, use only one of his two votes) for
a candidate to whom he wanted to show a special degree of support; e.g. Hawkins, *Victorian Political
Culture*, 212.

[29] Marshall, *Minorities and Majorities*, 13–14. This expressive, intensity-conveying value only obtains if
voters display a wide range of behavior in distributing their votes; if, however, it becomes the norm
for voters to give all of their votes to their first-choice candidate, then this characteristic of the
scheme vanishes and it becomes basically identical to the single nontransferable vote (SNTV). It was
on this ground that Charles Lutwidge Dodgson (better known as "Lewis Carroll") rejected the
cumulative vote: "The method of 'cumulative voting' will usually have no other effect than to
increase the 'specific gravity' – so to speak – of a vote. Let each Elector have 4 votes, with permission
to 'lump' them if he chooses, and in the end you will find most of the votes given in lumps of 4, and
the result much the same as if each Elector had had *one* vote only. The conclusion is that *the* important point is to let each Elector give *one* vote only"; Dodgson, *The Principles of Parliamentary
Representation*, in *The Pamphlets of Lewis Carroll, Volume Three: The Political Pamphlets and Letters
of Charles Lutwidge Dodgson* (New York, 2001), 27.

The cumulative vote was not without prominent supporters, including the Third Earl Grey and (for a short time) John Stuart Mill, and it was implemented in several places, including in Illinois and in South Africa.[30] It was not, however, an impactful player at the level of parliamentary reform.

The second, more influential proposal was the limited vote, by which the elector in a multimember district was restricted to fewer votes than the number of representatives to be returned. In the British context, this meant assigning two votes per elector in three-cornered constituencies, or occasionally three in four-member constituencies. The limited vote appears to have first been mooted by the Tory poet and MP W. M. Praed during the debate on the First Reform Act, although without gaining traction. But it became an important player in mid-Victorian parliamentarianism when Lord John Russell pushed for its application to forty-six districts in his failed 1854 reform bill, and ultimately the Second Reform Act implemented it in twelve three-cornered constituencies and the four-member City of London.[31] This legislation was a landmark in British history, both because it was the first time in which an electoral law had contradicted the premise of the corporate unity of the constituency, and also because of the practical and ideological significance it would have in the following decades. This legislation was credited with spurring the growth of modern party discipline, for the creation of the Liberal Association or "caucus" by the Liberals of Birmingham was a direct response to the limited vote. The Liberal party in Birmingham strove for tighter organization and greater direction of supporters' votes in order not to lose the city's third seat to a Tory, which would lessen the city's strength as a bastion of advanced Liberalism.[32] In consequence, the limited vote left an indelible mark on Victorian political culture, contributing to the rise of new party conditions and leaving the impression that "minority representation" necessarily entailed "the practical despotism of the new political associations [that is, the party organizations]."[33]

---

[30] Grey, *Parliamentary Government*, 206–7; Coull, "The Third Earl Grey and Parliamentary Reform," 14; John H. Humphreys, *Proportional Representation: A Study in Methods of Election* (London, 1911), 69. Lecky favored the cumulative vote as a method by which hereditary peers would select representative peers as part of his plan to reform the Lords; Lecky, *Democracy and Liberty*, vol. 1, 461. It was also used for school board elections between 1870 and 1902 in England.

[31] Nicolas Saripolos, *La Démocratie et l'élection proportionnelle: étude historique, juridique, et politique*, 2 vols. (Paris, 1899), vol. 1, 30–1.

[32] E.g. Joseph Chamberlain, *The Radical Programme*, ed. D. A. Hamer (Brighton, 1971), 6; John Walton, *The Second Reform Act* (London, 1996), 46. For a dissenting interpretation that minimizes the role of hostility to the limited vote in the origins of the Birmingham caucus, see Trygve Tholfsen, "The Origins of the Birmingham Caucus," *HJ*, 2 (1959): 161–84.

[33] Charles Seymour, *Electoral Reform in England and Wales: The Development and Operation of the Parliamentary Franchise: 1832–1885* (New Haven, 1915), 501. Similar charges of perniciously

The limited vote had, then, a notable practical impact, and its conceptual significance as an attempt to think about representation as concerning not only the relations *between* but also *within* constituencies is hard to overstate. And yet, in another respect the theoretical ambitions behind limited-vote advocacy were limited. For the limited vote was not articulated as an independent theory of representation; even in the most robust proposals for its use, such as Lord John Russell's in 1854, it was applied as the exception rather than the rule. It was meant to operate as an adjunct to the variety-of-suffrages vision of mirroring, a corrective to deal with the advent of larger districts for which more than the traditional two members were considered requisite. Since these districts were more heterogeneous than traditional constituencies which, in the history of British electoral theory, were closely identified with *a* specific interest or group rather than with multiple groups,[34] the limited vote was meant as merely remedial, inserted for a particular set of difficult cases to preserve the overall working of the variety-of-suffrages method of descriptive representation.[35] As much as a faltering step toward proportionality in the modern sense of awarding seats to parties or coalitions according to their vote-share, the push for the limited vote is to be understood in context as an effort to refine the accuracy of the representation of "interest communities" in a way that better suited the newer, more cumbersome circumstances of large heterogeneous districts.[36] It was the variety-of-suffrages school pushed just to the point where it doubted the universality of its methods. It was not intended as a stepping-stone to a "one-man, one-vote" conception of the equality of the worth of each elector's franchise.[37]

In keeping with this view of the limited vote as a refinement on the machinery of electoral differentiation in the service of more finely targeted group representation, proponents of these minority-representation reforms stressed the continuity between their recommendations and the time-honored practices of British parliamentarianism.[38] And yet, it was hard

---

enhancing the control of party cadres would be leveled against the cumulative vote, although they loomed less large in the English debates; e.g. Raoul de la Grasserie, *De la représentation proportion-nelle de la majorité et des minorités* (Paris, 1889), 32–3.

[34] Although he does not directly connect this up with the endorsement of the limited vote, David Moore provides an analysis of Russell's shift later in his career toward greater favorability toward heterogeneous districts; Moore, *Politics of Deference*, 325–6, 381–2.

[35] Russell, *English Government and Constitution*, 240.

[36] Biagini and Alastair Reid, "Currents of Radicalism, 1850–1914," in *Currents of Radicalism*, 1–19.

[37] Although Marshall inched closer to this idea than most; *Minorities and Majorities*, 14, 21.

[38] E.g. Marshall on such values as stability, the right of groups to be heard in the assembly, and the epistemic advantages of diversity; *Minorities and Majorities*, 8–9, 11, 17. Marshall cited Burke, Russell, Grey, and other Whig authorities on the constitution. And he repeatedly played down

to overlook that these programs contained new ways of thinking about the nature of the constituency as an electoral unit, the relationship that obtained between groups of citizens within the same constituency, and the relationship between these groups and parliamentary representatives. Not even as sanctimonious an admirer of the British constitution as Russell could pretend that minority-representation techniques were straightforward extensions of previous constitutional practice.[39] Before leaving these schemes behind, it behooves us to ask where exactly their novelty with respect to variety-of-suffragism lay.

Three related areas of discontinuity are noteworthy. Together, they indicate the conceptual paths along which "pure PR" would travel even farther.[40]

First, in disrupting the integrality of the constituency, it upended conventional notions that through elections something like a single "voice" of the community was heard. As Gladstone said during his first premiership, when the limited vote which he had opposed was in operation, minority representation violated

> the principle of Parliamentary representation [which] is, that we should recognize each constituency as being in itself an integer – as being in itself a community – and what we want in this House is to have the prevailing sense of the community. We do not want to have represented in miniature particular shades of opinion that may at the moment prevail in it, but the sense of the majority, which represents the whole community.[41]

Both the limited and the cumulative vote were premised on the rejection of any such univocal "sense" of the fixed electoral community.

The theory of electoral differentiation as instantiated by Mackintosh or Bagehot was reliant on the idea that one could be represented without having voted for any sitting MP, even without possessing the franchise at all. What mattered instead was the presence of members standing for the

---

the extent to which he was innovating: his "simple change in the method of voting" was not among the innovations which would be "opposed to our established habits and customs"; and so on. Marshall, *Minorities and Majorities*, 1, 4, 6, 13, 24.

[39] "If there were to be any deviation from our customary habits and rooted ideas on the subject of representation, I should like to see such a change as I once proposed, in order to obtain representatives of the minority in large and populous counties and towns"; Russell, *English Government and Constitution*, 240.

[40] Modern political science classifies the limited vote as "semi-proportional"; David Farrell, *Comparing Electoral Systems* (Houndmills, Basingstoke, 1997), 38. On STV as "pure PR," see e.g. Matt Cole, "Party Policy and Electoral Reform: A Survey of Developments, Motives, and Prospects," *British Elections & Parties Review*, 9 (1999): 72–86.

[41] Gladstone, HC Debate, 15 June 1870, 147.

interest or community with which the citizen identified; so long as these were present in the assembly, he was suitably represented. The second divergence marked by the advent of minority representation comes in the decline of faith in this kind of *virtual* representation that minority-representation plans signaled. This decline could take on two valences. One was more modest and practical, and was tied to the point above about the remedial aspirations of endorsers of the limited vote. From this stand-point, minority-representation schemes simply compensated for the failure of proposals like Bagehot's to include a particular group of electors who were so important to the overall sociological satisfactoriness of the Commons that it had to be able to place members in the assembly of its own choosing: namely, the affluent, educated class in the major cities.[42] This demographic was too special to have their chances of direct inclusion in the Commons left to the uncertain outcome of electoral contestation with the petty bourgeoisie (the "£10 householders") – and, if the franchise were extended further in the boroughs, with the even more numerous working classes. Minority-representation advocates denied that the absence of members directly selected by the urban upper crust was ade-quately compensated by the representation of "wealth" or "property" in the counties or smaller boroughs, where a more restricted suffrage would continue to obtain; for these persons in particular, no meaningful equiva-lents could be found elsewhere in the nation, and thus if they did not elect an MP themselves the representativeness of the Commons would be impaired.[43]

In addition to this practical or remedial concern, the rationales advanced for minority representation contained the seeds of a more far-reaching objection to virtual representation. For it was in the presentation of these schemes that the fruitful concept of the "wasted vote" entered the picture.[44] At their most basic level, minority-representation schemes were mechanisms for getting more votes to count toward the placement

---

[42] Russell, *English Government and Constitution*, 237–40.

[43] In other words, minority-representation advocates were on the side (sometimes a few years *en avance*) of Mill in his dispute with Bagehot about whether instituting universal suffrage in the major urban boroughs, with its threat of swamping the "intellectual persons" in those places, was an acceptable sacrifice to make to achieve the representation of urban labour.

[44] On "wasted votes" under first-past-the-post systems, see e.g. R. J. Johnston, "Seats, Votes, Redistricting, and the Allocation of Power in Electoral Systems," in *Choosing an Electoral System: Issues and Alternatives*, ed. Arend Lijphart and Bernard Grofman (New York, 1984): 59–69. Even that erstwhile defender of the status quo, W. R. Greg, showed support for the cumulative vote on the grounds of preventing such "waste"; "Parliamentary Purification," 622–3; Hart, *Proportional Representation*, 17.

of candidates in office, because now not only would the votes of the majority contribute to the election of an MP, but the votes of the largest minority in the constituency would contribute to the return of a member as well, rather than being simply "lost." The implication of this notion was that a citizen was only represented if he had voted for a winning candidate – an implication that was in fatal contradiction to the idea of virtual representation.

Two points about this contravention of virtual representation were especially fecund for subsequent developments. First, it is worth noting precisely where the gravity of this notion lay. What was crucial about the "wasted vote" was not so much the conceptual identification it made between the individual's status of being represented and recording one's vote for a successful candidate as the *moral charge* that this identification was now supposed to carry. As examined in Chapter 1, even Bagehot had allowed that the sort of durable intraconstituency minority status that he expected for upper-class citizens in the boroughs to which he would grant universal suffrage was akin to "disfranchisement." He simply viewed this result as nothing to lament, since the rungs of affluence and education would continue to gain entry to the House via other constituencies which had higher property requirements. What separated the supporter of virtual representation from the champion of minority representation was therefore less a conceptual dispute than a normative judgment. For the former, the question of the adequacy of a system of representation was to be resolved entirely by the overall economy of descriptiveness and deliberativeness in the representative system; the electoral fortunes of any particular cluster of individuals as such was a matter of moral indifference. This indifference was challenged by minority-representation schemes.

Second, the desire for fewer votes to be "wasted" was not reducible merely to aspirations for descriptive representation. After all, one can imagine an electoral system which, through judicious apportionment of constituencies and franchises, would achieve a high degree of descriptiveness while within each district the winning candidates were returned only by very small pluralities, thus wasting lots of votes.[45] Instead, the concern about wasted votes seemed to hint at a view that for an assembly to be legitimate it was required that each elector have authorized with his vote a sitting member.[46] In the end, though, these tantalizing hints in the direction of something like

---

[45] The *reductio* is instructive: some theorists favor lottery on descriptive grounds, and yet in a lottery there are of necessity zero "effective votes." Cf. Ben Saunders, "Estlund's Flight from Fairness," *Representation*, 46 (2010): 5–17.

[46] Marshall, *Minorities and Majorities*, 8–9.

a morally urgent personal right to authorize a representative in the legislature were left dormant in these texts. For most supporters of these schemes in the 1850–60s, an interest in the cumulative or limited vote was not felt to trouble the deeper commitment that "classes and not numbers are what we seek to represent," and the dominant perception remained that a minority-representation plan was simply a patch for the one hole in an otherwise satisfactory system: the lack of "security to property and education" in the great boroughs.[47]

The final area of divergence between conventional notions of descriptive representation and Marshall's and Praed's style of reform was a shift toward a recognition of *opinions* as the sole objects of representational concern.[48] Chapter 2 showed that, while variety-of-suffragists engineered their schemes to track classes, interests, groups, etc., with a few exceptions writers of Grey's and Bagehot's ilk assumed that these categories corresponded to politically relevant cleavages in opinions or perspectives. However, this importance of opinion remained latent in the orthodox adherents to electoral variegation, and they never considered the prospect of reflecting the opinions of the electorate in a manner that was divorced from these sociological markers – hence Bagehot's fondness for indiscriminate jumbles of terms such as "sentiments, wants, desires, needs, classes, interests, opinions, regions." Yet with the limited and cumulative vote the case was different – opinion explicitly became the privileged element in political representation. This was due to the fact that electoral majorities and minorities are patently *not* sociological facts which have any standing outside the electoral process. After all, a district in which everyone votes the same way does not contain *electoral* majorities and minorities, no matter how variegated its population might be along socioeconomic, religious, ethnic, or other lines. Rather, electoral majorities and minorities exist only through the disagreement among citizens, expressed in their voting behavior, over whom they wish to win office, and therefore they cannot be understood except as phenomena of opinion.

Minority representation's magnification of the status of opinion comes out as well in an enhanced attention paid to *party*. In order to justify the radical move of dissolving the corporate unity of the constituency, promulgators of these plans pointed to the plight of electors who supported a party that had little chance of winning majority support in their local district. It was in the difference of partisan support that the importance of

---

[47] Greg, "Representative Reform [2]," 269; "Achievements," 222.
[48] On this point Rosanvallon is trenchant; *Le peuple introuvable*, ch. 4.

the gap between minority and majority voters within a constituency, and the "unfairness" of identifying the voice of the constituency solely with the majority, were revealed.[49] But to aim in this way for a closer correspondence between the strength of parties in the electorate and in the House was to accept that it was in the last accounting the *opinions* of the citizenry to which a parliamentary assembly was meant to be faithful, since parties are constituted solely by the allegiance of individual electors.[50] The stress on opinions and parties also and importantly entailed a measure of *individualization* and *voluntarism* in thinking about representation. For while electoral majorities and minorities, and the party affiliations which go along with them, are collective, they depend on the individual opting in, rather than on attributes of group-belonging that are independent of the person's will or preferences.

It is easy to underestimate the significance of these changes, especially because the older sociological language of classes and interests persisted alongside the newer concentration on opinions. But the momentousness of this shift is evident from the following: while the "working class" might be thought to exist independent of their members' sense of belonging to it, a "working-class party" could not. Consider the difference between the way in which Bagehot, through reflection on the state of society and public opinion, determined that in certain regions of the country "labour" had come to have distinct political sensibilities meriting inclusion in the Commons and went about engineering electoral structures to incorporate this group, and the way that "minority representation" advocates would later think about electoral justice as mandating that the Labour party's share in the House correspond to its share of the national vote.[51] Thus, despite the modest, remedial ambitions of most of their mid-Victorian exponents, defenses of the cumulative and limited vote cut against the grain of descriptivism inherited from

---

[49] Via such schemes "we might have a *Liberal* country gentleman sitting for Buckinghamshire, and a *Conservative* manufacturer for Manchester"; Russell, *English Government and Constitution*, fourth edition, 240 (my italics).

[50] E.g. Marshall's preference for the compound "parties and opinions" to describe what it was his system would represent: "the fair and proportionate representation of the various political parties or opinions"; "the mechanism of the elective process should be such as to allow all parties and opinions to be fairly represented in the House of Commons"; "any party or opinion" should be enabled to secure "proportionate representation"; *Minorities and Majorities*, 5, 8, 12. More generally, while "interest and opinion" appear coupled together in Marshall's text in a rather standard manner, "class" is seldom invoked. That he recognized opinion as the grounding element of his system also shines through in several places: "a justly proportioned weight to the *opinions* both of minorities and of majorities"; provision had to be made for including "sufficient diversity of *opinion*"; *Minorities and Majorities*, 13, 19 (my italics).

[51] E.g. the speech of the Labour statesmen Philip Snowden reproduced in *Representation*, 6 (1913): 103–5.

Paley and Mackintosh in a number of ways – opening up *individualistic* or even *democratic* ways of thinking about representation in their rejection of the corporate unity of the constituency, their criticisms of virtual representation, and their elevation of opinion and party allegiance against the traditional sociological modes of conceiving of the objects of representation.[52]

These two minority-representation plans hardly vanished upon the appearance of Hare's proposals in the late 1850s; as noted earlier, the greatest legislative success of these pre-PR systems occurred with the inclusion of the limited vote as part of the Second Reform Act in 1867. But with the arrival of STV, the standing of these schemes in public debate altered. There were thinkers who continued to believe in the cumulative or limited vote as a first-best option, and some politicians sympathetic to proportionalist ideas clung to them as alternatives that were more likely to garner public support than Hare's exotic system.[53] Nonetheless, after Hare most theoretically attuned commentators abandoned these "insignificant makeshift[s]" for the "perfection" that was "Mr. Hare's system of personal representation."[54]

2   The Institutional and Conceptual Core of Victorian PR

With the background of minority representation in place, we are ready to tackle the conceptual and institutional foundations of Victorian PR. As noted at the outset of the chapter, Victorian PR meant the system of STV put forth by Thomas Hare. There are innumerable permutations of PR,[55] and the proliferation of schemes of PR had a detrimental impact on the fortunes of proportionalist reform in Britain.[56] Yet Hare's program stood out as "that which has obtained more support in this country and the British Dominions than any of its rivals"; it set the terms of debate in

---

[52] In this they resemble both the radical democrats of the previous chapter and a later, mostly Continental school of radical democracy which embraced PR and which insisted on its antisociological character as a core dimension of democracy; e.g. Hans Kelsen, *General Theory of Law and State* (New Brunswick, 2006), 298.

[53] Russell characteristically described it as out of "conformity with good old English notions of representation"; *English Government and Constitution*, 239.

[54] Mill, Speech on the Reform Bill [8], 5 July 1867, in *CW*, vol. 28, 207; Speech on Personal Representation, 185.

[55] Bogdanor, *What Is Proportional Representation?*, 46; Reeve and Ware, *Electoral Systems*, 4, 6.

[56] Hence the complaint of a leading proportionalist a half-century after Hare's debut: "There are said to be some 300 systems in existence, and the ingenuity of inventors shows no sign of exhaustion. The unkindest thing that a proportionalist can do is to invent a system; unfortunately the joys of paternity often outweigh the call of an ascetic devotion"; J. Fischer Williams, *Proportional Representation and British Politics* (London, 1914), 30.

Britain by virtue of being both the first to take the field and being perceived as a native growth.[57] Other schemes of PR, consequently, never managed to dislodge the primacy of Hare's scheme. This continuing priority was also due to the fact that the most active pressure group for PR, the Proportional Representation Society, sponsored Hare's plan.[58] While Hare was amenable to changes in certain technical features of the scheme, such as the manner of calculating the quota, and while he could contemplate bending on some matters for the sake of political expediency,[59] its core elements remained stable.

Despite his centrality to the debate, Hare's own presentation in *The Election of Representatives* was far from limpid, and this contributed to a widespread impression that PR was confused and overcomplicated.[60] *The Election of Representatives* was a daunting tract. It was at once a professional legislative document – it contained a bill in thirty-three clauses of painstaking legalese – and a lengthy exposition of the normative ideals of representative government. Furthermore, the institutional essentials of the proposal were interspersed with a stunning array of claims about the benefits that would flow from its enactment, and so the intrinsic difficulty of understanding his novel arrangements was compounded by the fact that the institutional components tended to get lost within a vast armature of broader moral and political argument. These facts about the forbidding way Hare presented his ideas point to an important truth: that Hare believed himself to be elaborating not merely a plan of electoral reform, but an intricate and integral theory of politics.

In consequence of the almost unapproachable manner in which his book was composed, there developed a subgenre within Victorian political literature: "the clarification of Hare" pamphlet. To grasp the key pieces of Harean STV, let us use take one of these, composed by the Liberal MP,

---

[57] Williams, *Proportional Representation and British Politics*, 30.

[58] In the British context other PR visions – such as the SNTV, the party-list system, and the method of "clubbing" in which the candidate disposes of his surplus as he sees fit – all had to be advanced self-consciously as alternatives to the hegemonic STV ; see, respectively, Percy Greg, "Redistribution: Right and Wrong Directions," *NR*, 2 (Feb. 1884): 807–23, at 818–23; James Meredith, *Proportional Representation in Ireland* (Dublin, 1918), xiii–xiv; Dodgson, "Parliamentary Elections," in *Political Pamphlets of Lewis Carroll*, 158–9.

[59] E.g. the alterations made for the fourth edition to adjust the scheme to the Ballot Act of 1872 (London, 1874), 124–6. Like Mill, Hare had been opposed to the introduction of the ballot; *Election of Representatives*, third edition, 139–45.

[60] E.g. the verdict of a writer sympathetic to Hare's scheme as the "most logical and satisfactory method": "the principles of his scheme appear in so highly elaborated a form in his own writings, that his system is vaguely regarded by most people as a theory of incomprehensible complexity"; J. Parker Smith, *University Representation* (London, 1883), 30–1.

economist, and ardent Hare supporter Henry Fawcett.[61] Fawcett broke Hare's scheme down into seventeen propositions, those of greatest concern to us being the following:

[4] Each elector votes by a voting-paper. He arranges any number of *the names of the candidates* who have presented themselves *for any constituencies, in the order he is desirous they should be returned . . .*

[8] The Registrar-General divides the number of voting-papers so returned to him by the whole number of members composing the House, and the quotient so obtained, called the "quota," represents the number of electors entitled to have one representative.[62]

[9] The Registrar-General forms a list of all candidates whose names stand first on a number of voting-papers equal to or exceeding the "quota" . . .

[10] The candidates on such list are returned to Parliament.

[11] No candidate shall require for his return more than the "quota" of votes . . .

[12] If a candidate's name appears first in more than the "quota" of voting-papers which must be appropriated to his return shall be selected from those papers which respectively contain the fewest names . . .

[14] If the House is not completed by members returned under the preceding clauses, the Registrar-General makes a list of the candidates whose names appear either first or second in the remaining voting papers a number of times equal to or exceeding the "quota," and the names appearing in the list are returned as members . . .

[16] If the number of members is still not made up, the Registrar-General proceeds in a similar way to make a similar list of those candidates whose names appear either first, second, third, &c. the

---

[61] *The Blind Victorian: Henry Fawcett and British Liberalism,* ed. Lawrence Goldman (Cambridge, 2003).

[62] This formula for the quota (the "Hare quota," or v/s) was typically abandoned in favor of the "Droop quota" ($v/s+1$) once it was devised in the late 1860s. (Here, v = *total votes, s* = *number of seats to be filled.*) The preference for the Droop over the Hare quota persists in modern systems of STV, but there remains controversy over the best formula for calculating the quota, as there is over many other technical details. I do not consider these technical debates here, nor accusations that STV suffers from technical glitches such as nonmonotonicity. For discussion of these matters, see e.g. Michael Gallagher, "Comparing Proportional Representation Electoral Systems: Quotas, Thresholds, Paradoxes, and Majorities," *BJPS,* 22 (1992): 469–96; Kenneth Benoit, "Which Electoral Formula Is the Most Proportional? A New Look with New Evidence," *Political Analysis,* 8 (2000): 381–8; David Austen-Smith and Jeffrey Banks, "Monotonicity in Electoral Systems," *APSR,* 85 (1991): 531–7.

requisite number of times in the remaining voting-papers, and the process is repeated until the House is completed.[63]

This was the institutional skeleton of Hare's program. Unlike on the block vote, the elector would cast only one vote. However, he could list not only his top choice, but also rank as many candidates (*not* parties – the vote was to be cast for individuals) as he wished. Instead of being bound to vote only for those candidates who stand in his local constituency, he could vote for any candidate from across the Kingdom. Rather than (as under plurality rule) those candidates being returned who had won the most votes in the contest within their constituency, those candidates would be elected who gained a "quota" of votes calculated from the total number of votes cast which determines how many votes a candidate must receive to earn a seat. Then the "surplus votes of elected candidates are transferred to other candidates favored by those who voted for the elected candidates; candidates are eliminated sequentially and their votes transferred to other candidates, with the candidate eliminated at each stage generally being the one with the fewest current votes."[64] The process of transferring votes continues until all of the seats are filled. Through this procedure the "waste of votes" would end, for all electors (except a small remainder) would see their vote (either via their first or a later preference) count toward a quota. Thus, every elector would have personally authorized a sitting MP. Furthermore, each MP would represent an equal number of voters; and the possibility of earning a seat would be made available to all viewpoints held by a quota's worth of voters from across the country as a whole.

Today, Hare's name is associated either with STV and proportional representation generally or, more technically, with his formula for calculating the quota. But, as this summation makes clear, his plan was comprised of *several* institutional components which could be revised or reconfigured to produce something different from the whole which he envisioned. And these institutional components were embedded in a wider set of ideas and assumptions which shaped his understanding of the kind of electoral system he had devised. Thus, to understand Victorian PR, we need to examine with some care several different aspects of the complex package that Hare christened his "perfect system of personal representation."[65]

[63] Henry Fawcett, *Mr. Hare's Reform Bill Simplified and Explained* (Westminster, 1860), 6–8 (my italics).

[64] Nicolaus Tideman, "The Single Transferable Vote," *The Journal of Economic Perspectives*, 9 (1995): 27–38.

[65] Hare, *Election of Representatives*, xxxvi.

Five dimensions of Hare's program warrant particular consideration: (a) its relationship to the suffrage; (b) the nature of its electoral constituencies; (c) its opposition to territoriality in districting; (d) the sociological imaginaries which underlay and inspired it; and (e) the mechanism for transferring votes to candidates lower on the elector's preference ranking. The remainder of this chapter takes up each of these features in turn.

a   STV, the Suffrage, and the Value of the Vote

At different moments in his campaign for Hare's system, Mill could be found depicting it in seemingly opposed ways. This was especially true with regard to its relationship with the concept of democracy. Take for instance this pair of assessments:

> No real democracy, nothing but a false show of democracy, is possible without [Mr. Hare's plan].
> [Personal representation] is neither democratic nor aristocratic.[66]

Mill was speaking in different registers and contexts in the two cases above. Nevertheless, the juxtaposition of these statements is revealing of a larger truth about the reception of PR in the Victorian era: to wit, that while Britons were convinced that PR had something essential to do with democracy, the nature of this connection was unclear and was interpreted in multiple ways. This difficulty was enhanced by the fact that – apart from Mill, whose own record was equivocal – the earliest adopters of PR were disinclined to accept that theirs was any sort of *democratic* project. Indeed, "personal representation" as inaugurated by Hare was nondemocratic in the most straightforward sense: it did not include equal universal suffrage.[67]

Importantly, there were two sides to the absence of universal suffrage as a part of Hare's program. These dimensions correspond to the distinction between STV as a method for translating votes into electoral outcomes and "personal representation" as a complete theory of representative politics, and even Hare himself struggled to keep them apart. First, sometimes universal suffrage appeared not to be included in Hare's reform because *no recommendation on the suffrage* was: "the suffrage is a matter so distinct from electoral organisation, that the legislature should deal with the two things in separate Acts. Blending them together tends to confuse and

---

[66] Mill, *Considerations*, 452; Speech on Personal Representation, 177.
[67] Hare, *Election of Representatives*, 267, 289.

embarrass the discussion of both"; "the system of representation in this work" did not bear on "the subject of the suffrage."[68] As Henry Fawcett put it: "it will be perceived that this scheme has no particular connection with any opinion respecting a democratic extension or an aristocratic limitation of the suffrage . . . The plan is adaptable to every extent of the franchise."[69] In these moments "the scheme" was treated as coextensive with the STV mechanism, and from this vantage point the question of its preferability to the method of "local majorities" was simply orthogonal to the "question of the suffrage."[70]

These judgments of the independence of STV from the regulation of the suffrage were basically accurate. Yet the matter was complicated by the fact, mentioned earlier, that Hare – and his followers – went beyond the preference for STV over plurality rule. As a theorist of representation and not simply an innovator in vote-aggregation procedures, Hare had views about the proper limits of the franchise. He left the specifics fuzzy, bearing out his verdict that the enfranchisement issue was "of far less [importance] than that of organization" of the voting mechanism.[71] But underneath this fuzziness about the nature of a "wisely-regulated franchise" there lay a clear disfavor toward an expansive suffrage.[72] "The pecuniary standard adopted by the Reform Act seems to afford no unreasonable criterion," Hare wrote, comfortable with the restrictive mid-Victorian electoral status quo.[73] Similarly, to take just one more example, Fawcett, considered one of the most famous "friends of Democracy" within the PR ranks, was not averse to property qualifications at the time that he took up PR.[74]

Beyond this conservative strain, two aspects of Hare on the suffrage must be emphasized, for they both marked decisive divergences from the

---

[68] Ibid., 281, 258.

[69] Fawcett, *Mr. Hare's Reform Bill*, 8. He went on to stress that this agnosticism applied not only to the level of enfranchisement but also to the weighting of voting power: "It would be entirely foreign to Mr. Hare's scheme to express any opinion upon the question, whether or not intelligence and wealth should obtain a plurality of votes. Were this principle adopted, the scheme would be as well adapted to it as to any other"; ibid., 16.

[70] Hare, *Election of Representatives*, 167; "Representation in Theory and Practice," *FM*, 61 (1860): 188–204, at 201.

[71] Hare, "Representation in Theory and Practice," 201.

[72] Hare, *Election of Representatives*, xxxviii.

[73] Ibid., xxxviii, 267. Also Carstairs, *Short History of Electoral Systems*, 194. In Denmark Andrae had likewise been content with restrictive censitary requirements; Clarence Hoag and George Hallett, *Proportional Representation* (New York, 1926), 172.

[74] Fawcett, *The Leading Clauses of a New Reform Bill* (Cambridge, 1860), 4. His requirements were somewhat more generous than Hare's. For Fawcett as belonging to the "democratic" ranks, e.g. George Shaw-Lefevre, "The Representation of Minorities," *CR*, 45 (1884): 714–33, at 715.

variety-of-suffrages paradigm. First, his deepest commitment on the suffrage issue was to its *uniformity*. In direct opposition to the variety-of-suffragists, Hare saw the steps toward standardization in suffrage rules taken in 1832 as a trend to be completed rather than a course to be reversed; he looked on the continuing differentiation of borough and county franchises as a preposterous anachronism.[75] In addressing the suffrage, what mattered to Hare was to speak "on behalf, – not of any particular qualification, – but of an equality of qualification."[76] From the perspective of personal representation, variations in electoral requirements were not inheritances of the longstanding wisdom of British constitutionalism, but bare "anomalies" to be expurgated.[77]

If uniformity or "equality" in the franchise was to be pursued, what next needed to be asked was on what basis this uniform standard was to be fixed. On this front too, the divergence from the variety-of-suffragists was noteworthy. For Hare and Fawcett, the basis was solely and straightforwardly *capacitarian*. Deciding on a baseline which would admit only the capable was a tricky task,[78] but they nevertheless believed it was a political duty to limit the franchise to those with "fitness,"[79] and their desire to standardize the suffrage at the level of the Reform Act's £10 borough householder was grounded in the belief that this threshold aligned with the demarcation between fitness and unfitness.

Hare denied that a capacitarian threshold for the franchise would turn politics into the domain of a caste – he disavowed the desire for a "perpetual exclusion" of certain "classes and conditions," "employment[s] or situation-[s]" – and he was open to the establishment of "educational tests" as avenues to enfranchisement in addition to meeting the property qualifications.[80] But, as wide as he might wish to cast his notion of capacity,[81] Hare's mode of delimiting the suffrage was opposed to the variety-of-suffragist mode – and this difference amounted, from the variety-of-suffragist point of view, to a decline in inclusivity. In their lingo, personal representation bordered on

[75] "It may be hoped, however, that when the subject is examined in all its bearings, every party will agree on the abolition of distinctions, which are unworthy of the age in which we live, and carry us back to the times of the Norman villeins or the Saxon thralls"; Hare, *Election of Representatives*, 258–9.

[76] Ibid., 260. Also Fawcett, *Leading Clauses*, 4, 13.   [77] Hare, *Election of Representatives*, 259.

[78] It was "the business of our legislators to select . . . that which is the test or qualification best suited to our country, our age, and our social condition"; ibid., 265.

[79] Hare, *Election of Representatives*, 263–6; Fawcett, *Leading Clauses*, 1, 11–15.

[80] Hare, *Election of Representatives*, 266–7.

[81] "Ordinary industry and skill in his calling, and ordinary prudence and self-denial in his conduct" were to put the subject within the pale of the suffrage; ibid., 266.

class rule; to follow Hare's prescriptions on the suffrage would be perilously close to accepting what Grey had described as the monopoly of £10 householders. Hare and company claimed that his system would avoid this fate because it would permit the full range of diversity that existed within the uniformly-defined enfranchised stratum to make its way into the assembly. But a crucial point of difference remained. At least the more philosophical advocates of electoral variegation had a justification for leaving portions of the population unfranchised that was descriptive in nature – namely, that they did not contribute to public opinion and that endowing them with voting power would therefore have a distortive effect on the representation. Hare's criterion for enfranchisement, in contrast, hinged not on a cartography of diverse social groups, but on a single substantive notion of worthiness and ability. For Hare, the objective in setting the boundaries of the suffrage was not to map the contours of sociological reality, but simply to select the fit among the citizenry.

The gap between the variety-of-suffragist use of suffrage regulations as descriptivist tools and this purely capacity-grounded notion of the limitation of the franchise is highlighted by Hare's affection for Guizot. Despite the mid-Victorian period having been a low ebb for his reputation, Guizot is cited with astonishing frequency in *The Election of Representatives*, including in direct support of the thesis of individual capacity as the sole ground of electoral participation.[82] Though proponents of Hare's invention would make much of its ability to do justice to diversity, Hare's affection for Guizot points us to the important fact that the diversity to which PR in its original formulations sought to give a more accurate parliamentary reflection was different from that which a Bagehot or Mackintosh conceived of their schemes as capturing. To the latter, what the assembly needed to contain were the salient divisions in society; to the former, the differences existent within the ranks of the capable. Rather than the variety-of-suffragist enterprise of mapping the array of social groups onto Parliament, Hare was engaged in developing a technique for improving the quality of electoral participation for "les capables."[83] While

---

[82] "Le gouvernement représentatif . . . examine quelle est la capacité nécessaire pour cet acte; il appelle ensuite les individus qui sont présumés posséder cette capacité, tons ceux-la, et ceux-la seuls"; ibid., 205 (at Guizot, *History of Representative Government*, 62). See also Hare's Guizotian clarification that, though he pursued "equality" (re: uniformity) in the franchise, he disowned the doctrine of "an equality of every man with every other, which the common sense of mankind has in all ages repelled"; Hare, *Election of Representatives*, 260.

[83] Ibid., 205, quoting here from Guizot.

Guizot was too uniformly oligarchical and capacitarian for much of British liberalism, he proved a guiding light for the founder of a system now seen by many as the last word in representative democracy.

In addition to his endorsement of a uniform capacitarian threshold for the suffrage, Hare's theory possessed another striking inegalitarian feature. While in liberal democracies today, the fact that PR secures *equality for each vote* (that is, it gives "to every vote an equal value" in the sense that each vote represents the same fraction of a member because the quotas returning members are of equal size[84]) is equivalent to securing *equality for each voter*, these two were not identical at PR's founding. Indeed, while the former was trumpeted as a great breakthrough of the scheme,[85] the latter was no part of it – as was made spectacularly clear by Mill's coupling of STV with plural voting based on education.[86]

The question of plural voting divided the PR community.[87] Hare's own version of personal representation was inconsistent with the then-current operation of a plurality of votes in parliamentary elections through the property owner's or university affiliate's belonging to multiple constituencies, but this incompatibility was due not to normative but to *technical* factors.[88] On the many STV plans which did not adopt Hare's single national constituency, it would have been perfectly possible for "the same individual" to possess "more than one vote" in the sociological manner of the "present franchise" by casting a vote in several districts.[89] Indeed, this would almost certainly have been the default had PR ever been passed; a separate measure of legislation would have been required to repeal this kind of plural voting. Moreover, forms of PR are easily conjoined with

---

[84] Albert Grey, "Proportional versus Majority Representation," 936.

[85] Hare, *Election of Representatives*, 205, 67, 108.

[86] J. Joseph Miller, "J. S. Mill on Plural Voting, Competence, and Participation," *HPT*, 24 (2003): 647–66. See Hare's approving remarks of such a possibility; *Election of Representatives*, 123.

[87] Early on there was considerable support, although after Mill's days this dwindled greatly. For strong statements contra, see e.g. Henry Vere Hobart, "Parliamentary Reform," *MM*, 13 (1866): 259–72, at 271–2; Dodgson, *Principles of Parliamentary Representation*, 195. Dodgson's antagonism to plural voting gave occasion to a typically brilliant literary flourish: "This arrangement would no doubt be unwelcome to certain 'pluralists' who are now able to vote in several different Districts ... But even if no remedy were found, the justice of allowing one Elector to vote as if he were, 'like Cerberus, three gentlemen at once,' seems so doubtful that the objection hardly deserves serious consideration." Dodgson, who had been intended for the priesthood, was punning here on the ecclesiastical meaning of pluralism, the infamous practice of bishops holding multiple benefices.

[88] Because he wanted the entire United Kingdom to form a single constituency, his own version of PR was by necessity incompatible with this more "descriptive" form of plural voting; Hare, *Election of Representatives*, 123.

[89] Ibid., 123.

the graduation of voting power, as Mill recommended and as would be enacted in turn-of-the-century Belgium.[90]

It was noted in Chapter 1 that Bagehot accused Mill's reform plans of inadequately empowering the working class. Regardless of whether Bagehot's appraisal was correct, it should now be apparent that Bagehot was driving at a surprising feature of Victorian personal representation: namely, that for its most famous defenders the suffrage and the vote-aggregation mechanism did *not* derive from a single, integrated normative framework.[91] The latter had a diversity-inclusive, freedom-enhancing rationale; the former depended, for several of its most prominent champions, on judgments of "quality and of worth."[92]

The nondemocratic character of this approach to the suffrage complicates what might otherwise have been a straightforward story about the progress of democracy or the rise of consent as a value in British political theory. The narrative would run as follows: the longstanding, Whiggish consensus about representation examined in Chapters 1 and 2 did not see elections as devices for delivering consent; they were, rather, means for producing a desired composition of the assembly and a set of attendant benefits. However, over the course of the century advocates and theorists of democracy began to dissent from the consequentialist ethos that had long predominated. Against this, they held up the consent of every citizen to the government which rules him as a precondition for political legitimacy. This demanding vision of legitimacy required not only universal suffrage, but also the opportunity to cast an effective vote such that each citizen would authorize a representative in the assembly, in order to compensate for the impossibility of his participating directly in the making of the laws. PR, on this account, was valued for respecting, insofar as was feasible, the right of the individual to live under laws to whose formation he had contributed.

Something of this view would gain traction, particularly from the mid-1880s onward.[93] But this is not how Hare and most of his disciples saw the

---

[90] Léon Dupriez, *L'organisation du suffrage universel en Belgique. Vote plural, vote obligatoire et représentation proportionnelle* (Paris, 1901). Beyond his support for Mill's suggestions, further evidence that Hare approved of graduated voting *in principle* comes in his endorsement that graduation based on rates of taxation be preserved in municipal governance; *Election of Representatives*, 288–90; " Ideal of a Local Government for the Metropolis," *MM*, 7 (1863): 441–7.

[91] This characteristic is brought out dramatically by the very first words of the "Advertisement to the Second Edition" of the *Machinery of Representation*: "The design of these pages is – without discussing in what hands the parliamentary suffrage should be placed . . . "

[92] Hare, *Election of Representatives*, 271.

[93] E.g. Albert Grey, "Proportional versus Majority Representation," 953; Herman Finer, *Fabian Tract No. 211: The Case Against Proportional Representation* (Westminster, 1924), 34.

matter. In its approach to the suffrage, Victorian PR – especially for its earliest but also for some later supporters – did not include an egalitarian notion of consent, and it cannot be considered an episode in an inexorable march toward democracy.

Not only was PR not proposed as an avenue toward democracy's realization: because it embraced *uniformity* but not *universality* in the franchise, it could also be regarded as among the *most exclusive* representative arrangements on offer. Compare two texts from the late 1850s: Hare's *Election of Representatives* and George Harris's *True Theory*. The latter, we may recall, eschewed democracy understood as uniform universal suffrage, advocating instead a variety of mechanisms to apportion the franchise in a manner that respected social diversity; but it did recognize a "democratic" imperative of a sort – namely, the inherent right of every individual to have a say in the government – and therefore it extended the suffrage to all male citizens, although of course differentially and unequally. The official position of the former on the suffrage, by contrast, contained no elements that, within the Victorian framework at least, could really be denominated *democratic*; Hare simply did not want the franchise extended any further.

Yet despite the preferences of Hare and much of his following for a limited capacitarian suffrage, his movement's relationship to democracy was never one of entire hostility. From its first appearance – and even more after the Second Reform Act – the attractiveness of Hare's scheme had much to do with the prospect of democracy.[94] Mid-Victorian PR occupied the strange position of having been desired in light of the likelihood that democracy was on the horizon more than because those who embraced it were themselves committed democrats.[95] While there were self-described democrats who latched onto PR in its early years from a feeling of fidelity to their democratic affiliation, it was more common for those fearful or skeptical of democracy to turn to Hare as providing a way to make democracy more palatable if it had to arrive.[96] Precisely because STV is a procedure for distributing votes to candidates whatever the size and shape of the

---

[94] In this respect the mobilization for PR was exemplary of Victorian liberalism's penchant for "overmuch dwelling on the democratic vista"; Vincent, *Formation of the Liberal Party*, 2, 153.

[95] Hare promised that "amendment of the electoral method" will save the "mistake [of democracy], if it be one" from bringing about as "gloomy" a future as it threatened to do; "On the Suggestions Afforded by the Application of the Cumulative Vote and by the Other Incidents of the School Board Elections," *Sessional Proceedings of the National Association for the Promotion of Social Science*, 4 (1871), 225–6.

[96] As usual, Dicey was perspicuous in identifying a shift in outlook: "[PR] was once considered a check upon democracy; it is now supported as the best method for giving effect to the true will of the democracy"; Dicey, *Law of the Constitution*, lxxiii.

electorate may be, it was always available to be promoted in the event that universal suffrage was passed. As a result, even if PR accompanied by Hare's preferred limits on the franchise was less empowering of the working class than the variety-of-suffrages alternatives, Hare's outlook was less hostile to democracy than they were. This apparent paradox followed from the simple fact that that the variety of suffrages was in its essence an attack on uniform suffrage, whereas Hare's innovation was incorporable into any suffrage arrangement. From the beginning, therefore, STV was marketed to the *reluctant democrat*: "it is not only consistent with the most democratic suffrage, but, by greatly mitigating its dangers, would probably reconcile to it many who are now among its most strenuous opponents."[97] In a Tocquevillian spirit, Hare admonished those whose "fear of democratic progress" led them to ignore solutions which could cohere with the "principles" of "every democrat."[98] To Victorian eyes, STV had the odd property that, while not by nature democratic any more than it was by nature oligarchic, it nevertheless had the power of making democracy less bad.

The reasons for this judgment about PR's ameliorating effect on democracy will be dealt with in due course. For now, we must address the accuracy of Hare's and Fawcett's impression that, while STV would be of special value in a democracy, support for it did not determine a favorable attitude toward universal suffrage. True, the founders of STV were wary of democracy, and they accurately perceived that the contest between STV and plurality rule was analytically separate from the question about how far voting rights should be extended. Nonetheless, it might still be true that democratic implications of a sort were embedded in the Harean framework, that there existed an elective affinity or ideological kinship between STV as a vote-aggregation mechanism and uniform universal suffrage as a mode of franchise regulation.

To see how this could be so, recall Hare's basic tenet, flagged in the name *personal representation* itself – that not groups but individual voters were at the basis of his system. As was noted in discussing the earlier minority-representation plans, to see "wasted votes" as a problem demanded that one adopt other criteria for judging representation than the kind of sociological accuracy which a Mackintosh or a Bagehot prized; it drew from the intuition (however inchoate) that the individual elector

---

[97] Fawcett, *Mr. Hare's Reform Bill*, 29–30.
[98] Hare, *Machinery of Representation*, 51–2. And Mill, Speech on Personal Representation, 186: "Those who are anxious for safeguards against the evils they expect from democracy should not neglect the safeguard which is to be found in the principles of democracy itself."

had a right to have a representative whom he had chosen actually sit in the assembly.[99] Hare and his followers pushed this effort much further; instead of merely trying to get *more* votes to count by giving a representative to large minorities in a territorial district who banded together behind a candidate, they sought to get *every* vote to count. In seeking to render each vote "successful,"[100] PR campaigners called upon a notion of what was owed to the elector, rather than upon a picture of the desirable composition of the assembly.[101] Hareans articulated this notion of individual right in terms of realizing representation.[102] To be given a vote and yet not to contribute to installing a member of one's choosing was to be given a kind of sham-right; meaningful political participation, in the context of representative government, entailed effective exercise of the vote. STV, Hare claimed, marked an advance insofar as it more reliably delivered a good to the individual, namely, that of "enabl[ing] every elector . . . to participate in the choice of some representative."[103]

The important point for now is that this "personalistic" rather than "sociological" orientation could not only be said to deliver *better* or *truer* democracy if universal suffrage were adopted,[104] but could actually incline one to accept universal suffrage from its very logic. In particular, four aspects of the personalism of Hare's vision pushed in this direction. First, in keeping with the turn away from the group-based sociological discriminations of variety-of-suffragism, PR supporters offered a set of criticisms targeted at *arbitrariness* – criticisms which not only resembled, but occurred at an even more fundamental level, than those which would be lodged by Dicey and Brodrick. For Hareans included as objectionably

---

[99] To vote for a losing candidate, or to not bother to vote from the certainty that one's preferred candidate would lose, was to be "blotted out"; Mill, *Speech on Personal Representation*, 178.

[100] Contemporary STV campaigners have come to call this "the right to cast an effective vote"; Kathleen Barber, *A Right to Representation: Proportional Election Systems for the Twenty-First Century* (Columbus, 2000).

[101] E.g. John Lubbock, "Proportional Representation," *NC*, 15 (1884): 713, on the "right not merely of recording a vote, but of doing so in such a manner as to give it all just and reasonable effect."

[102] Hare spoke of "making representation a reality"; described the claim that someone was represented by a member for whom he had not voted as "an untruth"; and asked his readers "whether we are to proceed towards a system of representation, or towards something else – not representation, but a substitute for it"; Hare, *Election of Representatives*, xxxiv–xxxv, 128; "Representation of Every Locality and Intelligence," *FM*, 61 (1860): 532.

[103] Hare, *Machinery of Representation*, 16.

[104] Despite supporting plural voting and certain suffrage restrictions, it was Mill who popularized "true democracy" as a motto for the PR campaign – although given the antidemocratic commitments of its early supporters, the use of this language did not really pick up until after his death; e.g. Mill, *Considerations*, ch. 7; Speech in the Westminster Election of 1865 [4], 8 July 1865, in *CW*, vol. 28. Also Acton, "Sir Erskine May's Democracy in Europe," in *The History of Freedom and Other Essays* (London, 1907), 97–8; this essay was originally published in *QR*, 1878.

arbitrary even *territorial* divisions. While for Dicey an electoral system was suitably nonarbitrary if it distributed the vote equally and uniformly across geographical districts, for Hare all systems of representation except his own depended on the drawing of "arbitrary line[s]" and the making of "arbitrary selections."[105] They all relied on sorting electors in a way that could be judged inconsistent with the "fair share" of some group based on an opposed perspective.[106]

The trouble for an admirer of Guizot such as Hare, however, was that if the current "geographical division[s]" and "the parade of distinct interests and distinct objects in the country and the town" that justified them were "arbitrary,"[107] the signs of "capacity" seemed no less so. Indeed, in the political history of the last two centuries, the idea of shaping the electorate after judgments of intelligence or fitness has provoked far more discontent than the idea of dividing electors territorially. Worse still, evaluations of capacity had no clearer basis for expectation of widespread assent from a divided public than attempts to ground the electoral system in other kinds of sociological discriminations.[108] To "select for admission to the franchise only the best of the unrepresented classes" was as contestable a mission as to secure "due balance of interests" in the assembly; no less disputable "criterion" was available to "ascertain ... intellect" than to pursue traditional mirroring aspirations.[109] As the influential political scientist Goldsworthy Lowes-Dickinson wrote in his summation of a century's worth of change in theories and institutions of representation: the "limit of competence" proved as "shifting" and indeterminable

---

[105] Hare, *Machinery of Representation*, 26; "Mr. Hare's System: A Grouping of Parliamentary Electors that Combines a Just and Equal Distribution of Seats and the Free Expression both of Individual and Public Opinion with the Smallest Degree of Disturbance from Corrupt Influences," in *Transactions of the National Association for the Promotion of Social Science, Manchester Meeting, 1866*, ed. George Hastings (London, 1866), 207–8. Also Hobart, "Parliamentary Reform," 267; Williams, *The Reform of Political Representation* (London, 1918), 4.

[106] Hare, "Just and Equal Distribution," 207.

[107] Hare, *Election of Representatives*, 60, 65. For similar censures of fixed constituencies in the modern literature, see e.g. Robert Sugden, "Free Association and the Theory of Proportional Representation," *APSR*, 78 (1984): 31–43; Arend Lijphart, *Electoral Systems and Party Systems: A Study of Twenty-Seven Democracies, 1945–1990* (Oxford, 1994), 140.

[108] E.g. Ramsay MacDonald, *Socialism and Government*, vol. 1, 56–62; Kinnear, *Principles of Reform*, 2–3. Interestingly, Dupont-White attacked the *doctrinaires* on precisely these grounds; the translator for Hare's greatest supporter was, thus, attacking one of Hare's foremost inspirations. Dupont-White, "Introduction" to J. S. Mill, *Le Gouvernement représentatif*, trans. Dupont-White, third edition (Paris, 1877), xlii.

[109] J. Holland Rose, *The Rise of Democracy*, second edition (London, 1904), 172–3; Salisbury (then Lord Cecil), "Theories of Parliamentary Reform," 54.

a guideline as the "adequate representation of varied interests."[110] Given their hostility to basing the representative system on judgments about even the geographical districts to which electors ought to belong, it was not clear why this same hostility did not apply to the wish to restrict access to the vote to those alone who were judged "able" to exercise it well. Put differently: if it violated principles of fairness and nonarbitrariness to dictate to the "people themselves who are affected" the boundaries of the constituencies in which their votes were to count, it violated these same principles to set an "incapable" portion of the population outside the boundaries of the electorate altogether, even if Hare and other early PR adherents resisted drawing this conclusion themselves.[111]

A second democratic implication stemmed from the promise to waste the fewest possible votes and to secure for every voter an authorized representative in the assembly. For Hare, as has been noted, the "realization" of representation for each voter was a freestanding normative good, a kind of first principle. Other writers, however, seem to have been less comfortable with treating electoral personalism as an original postulate, and instead sought to derive it from a prior principle or image of politics. This was supplied, for some authors, by direct democracy. On this view, representation was not a sociologically grounded method of producing a ruling assembly, but a concession to the fact that assemblies of the whole people were no longer possible. As the mathematician Henry Richmond Droop put it in 1869 (when England's institutions remained quite far from instantiating one-man, one-vote):

> In a modern state the recognised mode of ascertaining the opinions of the people is to convene a representative assembly. This representative assembly has superseded the general assembly of all the citizens which we read of in classical and medieval republics ... Instead of the various questions of legislation and government being brought directly before the whole body of citizens to discuss and vote upon, a certain number of persons, fixed upon by some process of election, are deputed to represent the people, and the decisions of this representative assembly are accepted as equivalent to decisions of the whole body of electors.[112]

---

[110] Lowes-Dickinson, *The Development of Parliament during the Nineteenth Century* (London, 1895), 58–60. Lowes-Dickinson was, among other things, an intellectual architect of the League of Nations.

[111] Hare, *Election of Representatives*, 49.

[112] Henry Richmond Droop, *On the Political and Social Effects of Different Methods of Electing Representatives* (LSE Selected Pamphlets, 1869), 1. See also the slightly later imploration that for the "government of the whole people by the whole people" to be achieved, institutions needed to approach as closely as possible to "a true democracy, [in which] the whole people assemble for

It was in light of this view that the Commons was to be seen as the functional equivalent of an assembly of the nation in toto that Droop would endorse STV.[113] (Recall that the variety-of-suffrages school, by contrast, simply rejected any such equivalency as undesirable; the decisions of a deliberative, representative assembly were not expected to reproduce what an assembly of the whole people, which was necessarily ruled by "mere numbers," would have preferred.) If representation was a contrivance to allow for "self-government" in an age in which citizens no longer all gathered in the square, then it was required that, if each citizen was not able to perform their functions in person, each could be shown to have authorized a member to act on their behalf.[114] Thus, the relationship between (a) the ambition to deliver a representative to each elector and (b) the commitment to democracy was a two-way street. It was not only, as is usually imagined, that some of those who were already wedded to democratic principles came to value PR as a fuller realization of them. Influence ran equally in the opposite direction: Hare desired to realize representation for only a limited set of capable citizens, but his theorizing seemed to call upon a direct-democratic imaginary about what was due to citizens.[115]

A third democratic ramification of Hare's "personalism" about representation was its elevation of the principle of majority rule. This can sound paradoxical given the lineage of PR in "minority representation" schemes, and indeed the nomenclature surrounding PR remained complicated; despite persistent efforts by proponents, in Victorian England PR never succeeded in shedding the "minority representation" label.[116] The question

legislation, [and] the majority and the minority are equitably represented"; John Heywood, *The Representation of Minorities: A Practical Plan* (Bristol Selected Pamphlets, 1884), 1.

[113] On the link drawn to direct democracy, see John Chamberlin and Paul Courant, "Representative Deliberations and Representative Decisions: Proportional Representation and the Borda Rule," *APSR*, 77 (1983): 718–33.

[114] "Self-government" became a rallying cry of the PR side; e.g. Hare, "The Reform Bill of the Future," *FR*, 23 (1878), 75–84, at 84; Leonard Courtney, "The Representation of Minorities," *NC*, 6 (1879), 143.

[115] Similarly with Mill: although he did not advocate universal or equal suffrage, his support for PR was linked with his own interest in Athenian history as evidence of the consistency of direct democracy with justice to minorities and the leadership of a rightful elite; Biagini, "Liberalism and Direct Democracy: John Stuart Mill and the Model of Athens," in *Citizenship and Community*: 21–44.

[116] Shaw-Lefevre, for one, mocked the turn toward "proportional representation" over "minority representation" as a pitiful attempt at rebranding; see "Representation of Minorities," 721. The perception that PR was antimajoritarian was quite durable, despite the best efforts of many of its proponents to dispel it, even among some of the more sophisticated commentators on the topic: e.g. Kinnear, "Practical Considerations on the Representation of Minorities," *FR*, 4 (1866), 55; Fawcett, "Proportional representation, from the last speech of the Right Hon. Henry Fawcett,

of whether this label was appropriate will be answered in the next subsection. But regardless of the answer we give regarding its status as minority representation, from Hare forward it was a major boast that PR alone could guarantee majority rule; indeed, the distinction between representation and rule or decision was a fundamental piece of the PR architectonic.[117] An assembly that was returned by a concatenation of local pluralities could very well contradict the principle that "the majority of those who vote at each election shall rule" and result instead in "minority control of [the] assembly."[118] Only if every elector's vote had contributed to authorizing a member could one be certain that 51 percent of the membership of the assembly translated into 51 percent of voter support; on the other hand, a majority of members who themselves had been elected by pluralities within their constituencies would often stand for only "a minority of the whole" instead of a "numerical majority" of the electorate at large.[119] Without PR, there was no security against the government of false majorities.[120]

Because this lesson about the "truth" of legislative majorities under PR is standard within the modern study of electoral systems, it is important to stress just how striking a departure it was from other visions of representation. The variety-of-suffragist was of course utterly unimpressed by any appeals to majorities outside the House; what was of significance to him was *sociological* rather than *numerical* fairness and accuracy. But even the conventional democrat was not especially concerned with the problem of majoritarianism as the PR champion understood it – that is, as a matter of assuring *correspondence* between degrees of support for a policy inside and outside the assembly. Instead, from the Chartists to Dicey, democrats were

MP, delivered to his constituents at Hackney, October 13, 1884" (Earl Grey Pamphlets Collection, 1884), 1.

[117] E.g. Hare, *Election of Representatives*, xxx–xxxi; Albert Grey, "Proportional versus Majority Representation," 936. In this context, it is notable that Hare was loathe to speak of his scheme as a solution to majority tyranny. The phrase was absent from Hare's major works and he was more likely to decry the "tyranny of minorities"; Hare, "A Note on Representative Government," *FR*, 18 (1875), 102–7, at 102.

[118] Edmond Beales, W. R. Cremer, G. J. Holyoake, Walter Morrison, R. A. Cooper, George Odger, James Acland, Thomas Hare, and George Howell, *Representative Reform: Report of the Committee Appointed by the Conference of Members of the Reform League, and Others, on Mr. Hare's scheme of representation, held 28th February, & 7th & 21st March, 1868* (London, 1868), 4; Henry Richmond Droop, "On Methods of Electing Representatives," *Journal of the Statistical Society of London*, 44 (1881): 141–202.

[119] Mill, *Considerations*, 304.

[120] As was discussed in Section 1 with respect to the cumulative and limited vote, the majoritarian element in PR was also related to its asociological character; when "interests" or "communities" are not ingrained in the system, only the aggregation of individual votes (and thus the units of majority and minority) can be invoked to justify a decision.

principally concerned with equality in access to a right (the franchise), rather than with the accuracy of Parliament in registering the distribution of political preferences or conveying exact demographic quotients of consent to particular policies. What they desired was just that the members of the House be elected on a "one-man, one-vote" basis; that "intra-house" majorities be identical to "extra-house" ones was no substantive worry of theirs. Approval of electoral democracy was detachable from the deepening of commitment to majoritarianism that was intrinsic to PR's interpretation of the goal that "the whole nation [be] fairly represented in Parliament." To rest the legitimacy of parliamentary decisions not on the equal extension of voting rights but on the assurance that a majority vote in the Commons conveyed majority consent "in the country" was the peculiar province of PR.[121]

This expansion of what majority rule required imparted a democratic momentum to the theory of personal representation that outran the suffrage conservatism of its founding figures. If nothing but "the predominance of majorities" understood in this demanding fashion could confer legitimacy on the decisions of the Commons,[122] it was far from obvious on what legs the restriction of the franchise to the capable could stand. Hare, as noted, supplied no clear answer; it just was a bedrock principle for him that legislative decisions needed to carry the authorization of what one might call a *true majority of the capable*, the capable being coextensive with the electorate.[123] But this was hardly satisfactory. If it were troubling that a majority in the Commons should not correspond to a majority out-of-doors, even though members of the Commons were presumed to be more informed and intelligent than the latter,[124] it was not clear why the regress needed to stop here: why should not the majority of those with *capacité* be made to align in some way with the majority of the whole citizenry?[125] Hare

---

[121] Millicent Garrett Fawcett, "Proportional Representation," *MM*, 22 (1870), 382.

[122] Courtney, "Political Machinery," 89.

[123] Characteristically, he quoted Guizot: "representative government ... seeks the majority from amongst those who are capable" [*cherche ensuite la majorité parmi les capables*]. For Guizot, unlike for Hare, limiting participation in representative government to *les capables* was not simply an isolated argument but stemmed from his cardinal theoretical commitment, the principle of the "sovereignty of reason." Despite the epistemic emphasis of much of Hare's thought, he cannot really be said to have been in command of any such theory. Compare Hare with Guizot as presented in Aurelian Craiutu, *Liberalism under Siege: The Political Thought of the French Doctrinaires* (Lanham, 2003), ch. 5.

[124] Hare, *Election of Representatives*, fourth edition, 367.

[125] A similar thought drove one of the traditional arguments against the ballot – namely, that where a limited suffrage prevailed, the publicity of the vote helped to ensure some correspondence between the wishes of electors and nonelectors by allowing the latter to "influence" the former: Southgate, *Passing of the Whigs*, 92; Clarke, "Electoral Sociology of Modern Britain," 40.

does not seem to have been especially bothered by the apparent capriciousness of halting the momentum of his majoritarianism where he did. But there is no doubt that personal representation's message that "not only an arithmetical misstatement, but also a great political injustice, takes place" when "true" majorities were not secured led, in many minds, to the embrace of an ideal of "government of the whole by the whole."[126] To value electoral majorities so dearly could seem inseparable from support for democratic suffrage.

The fourth and final way in which the aspirations inherent in STV pointed toward a democratized suffrage came in the argumentation against virtual representation. The rejection of virtual representation was implied in our earlier discussion of how PR exponents conceived of the aim of *realizing* representation. But the character of their explicit attacks on the claim that electors could be virtually represented merits a short examination in its own right.

As Section 1 showed, defenses of the limited and the cumulative vote already contained an implicit critique of virtual representation. This critique, however, was most often practical in nature; it expressed an anxiety that certain identifiable groups in identifiable constituencies were underserved by the status quo and that this threatened the functioning of an otherwise healthy system. Thus, one departed from the rule in order to preserve it; minority representation as instantiated in the limited or cumulative vote remedied a defect in a system of which virtual representation remained a major element. With Hare and company, though, the critique went deeper. To proponents of PR, virtual representation was entirely inadmissible as an aspect of representative government.

Frequently, the way in which the PR community articulated its opposition to virtual representation was to speak of it as a "lie"; it was akin to telling someone that he was virtually rich because another person to whom some sort of relationship with him could be drawn was wealthy.[127] "Virtual representation" was "false in fact"; to speak of "virtual" as against "actual" representation was simply to confess that "we have not had representation"

---

[126] Robert Lytton, "Report by Mr. Lytton, Her Majesty's Secretary of Legation, on the Election of Representatives for the Rigsraad," printed in *Personal Representation, Speech of John Stuart Mill, Esq., MP, Delivered in the House of Commons May 29, 1867, with an Appendix*, second edition (London, 1867), 19.

[127] Demonstrating the continuing impact of Bentham on Victorian political culture, the label used to express the denigration of virtual representation was frequently "fiction": Hare, "Representation in Theory and Practice," 199–200; Election of Representatives, xxxv, 8, 90. See Bentham, *Bentham's Theory of Fictions*, ed. C. K. Ogden (New York, 1932).

at all.[128] To illustrate why it ought to have been conceived as a falsehood instead of as simply an alternate manner of being represented, Hareans often invoked arguments that were essentially descriptive – that is, they made claims about the fallaciousness of virtual representation that turned on mistakes in the sociology of opinion. The literature on PR abounds with demonstrations of the untruth of the contention that the adherents of an interest or party that lost in one district were represented just as well by victories won by this interest or party in other districts:

> To tell the Liberals of Kent and Surrey that they are represented by the Liberal members for Scotland and Wales [is misleading] ... Perhaps the one question about which Kentish farmers care most is the subject of extra-ordinary tithes ... But the farmers of Kent cannot expect the Liberal members from Scotland to help them as regards extraordinary tithes. It is possible that they do not even know what extraordinary tithes are.[129]
>
> The idea of the minority in one place being represented by the majority in another is certainly ingenious, but it overlooks the fact of there being any differences between members of the same political party. There are Liberals and Liberals, and it was probably no source of consolation to Mr. Mill's supporters in Westminster that in Marylebone Mr. Harvey Lewis had been returned ... It may perhaps be replied that the English Catholics [who returned no members] had no reason to be dissatisfied [since many Irish Catholics were turned] ... but it is extremely unlikely that Catholics in Ireland exactly coincide, even in questions bearing on their faith, with the opinions of Irish Catholics.[130]

Testimonials such as these served to drive home that it was a "false assumption" that losing citizens in one districts could be "adequately compensated" by other electoral results and thus to prove the inconsistency of virtual representation with parliament's standing as "a mirror of the nation."[131]

On this logic, then, what undermined "the old and exploded" contention about being "virtually represented" was that it would inevitably involve drawing false equivalences between different sets of beliefs.[132] Compared to the remedial concerns of the minority-representation advocates, this critique was more thoroughgoing and principled insofar as it alleged that it was intrinsic to programs of virtual representation to wrongly conflate unlike sets of ideas and preferences. Nevertheless, this

[128] Percy Greg, "Redistribution," 810; Hare, *Election of Representatives*, 128.
[129] John Lubbock, *Representation* (London, 1885), 18–19.
[130] Fawcett, "Proportional Representation," 377, 379.
[131] Meredith, *Proportional Representation in Ireland*, 11; Lubbock, *Representation*, 64.
[132] Lubbock, *Representation*, 18.

critique was still firmly lodged within the domain of the sociology of opinion – and this led it into theoretical difficulties regarding the degree of correspondence between the beliefs of constituents and MPs reminiscent of those addressed earlier under the heading of *Greg's problem.*

The trouble was this: implicit in this hard critique of virtual representation was the identification of the status of being represented with a complete agreement of opinion between the citizen and his representative. Short of this unanimity, difficulties about how to draw the line between sufficient and insufficient agreement between voters and their MPs would open the door for virtual-representational claims about the satisfactoriness of current arrangements to re-enter: who could say that the overlap between Liberals from Kent and Scotland, or between Catholics from England and Ireland, was not enough to make the "compensation" of one by the other defensible?[133] And yet PR theorists were not prepared to guarantee this unanimity, as is clear from their rejection of delegation.[134] This rejection was premised on the grounds both of the superiority in intellect and expertise of the MP and the incompatibility of deliberation with dictation from the constituency, but in either case it contradicted the full identity of views that was necessary for a rebuttal of virtual representation based wholly on the mirroring of the electorate's opinions. Furthermore, because this line of attack on virtual representation was premised on claims about the condition of opinion in the country, it had to fit the facts, which were disputable. On the one hand, if there were not a great deal of ideological diversity, if the country was rather naturally divided into two blocks of partisan allegiance, then PR looked less urgent and perhaps hardly an improvement at all upon the present system.[135] But, on the other hand, there could not be too much diversity, lest even the members returned by PR seem no more than the products of ill-fitting coalitions that lacked a clear identity of views.[136] An immutable match between the sociology of opinion and PR in any of the versions in which it

---

[133] Hare, *Election of Representatives*, 10.

[134] The PR movement was at one in rejecting delegation: e.g. Mill, *Considerations*, 510–12; Moisei Ostrogorski, *Democracy and the Organization of Political Parties*, trans. Frederick Clarke, two vols. (London, 1902), vol. 1, 606–7; Wordsworth Donisthorpe, *Individualism: A System of Politics* (London, 1889), 52.

[135] Gladstone, "Declining Efficiency," 560, 567; Parsons, "*Ignis Fatuus* vs. *Pons Asinorum*," 376–9; Finer, *The Case Against PR*, 13; Shaw-Lefevre, "Representation of Minorities," passim.

[136] If "all great subjects" really were so "many sided" that, as on a standard caricature of *On Liberty*, there were as many shades of political opinion as there were citizens, the notion that even PR could be truly descriptive would collapse; see Hare, *Machinery of Representation*, 42. This difficulty would be made more acute when Hare's original plan of entirely doing away with territorial divisions was amended to include multimember geographical districts. This alteration is covered in Subsection c.

was promulgated was a thin reed on which to hang proportionalist advocacy. There was, in short, no airtight case for replacing virtual representation with PR on mirroring grounds alone.

As a result, we find that yet another aspect of Harean argumentation ultimately rested on extremely strong premises about electoral authorization: to wit, that "political justice" in the domain of "the greatest moral object that society is called upon to undertake – the formation of a legislative assembly" was not achieved unless every elector had authorized a member thereof, and that authorization entailed that one's vote contributed to the set of votes which secured that member's election.[137] The nonnegotiable, justice-demanding character of personal representation was a matter of ending the fiction which covered for the "disfranchisement" inherent in plurality rule, and establishing once-and-for-all the only kind of representation worthy of the name.[138]

This analysis of the nature of their objection to virtual representation thus returns us to the basic Harean conundrum: if it was an injustice to "disfranchise" by rendering a vote inefficacious through its having been cast for a failed candidate, it was hard to see why it was not a greater injustice to leave large swathes of the population altogether without the vote. Indeed, precisely because the advent of STV promised to erase all traces of virtual representation within the electorate, it made nonpossession of the suffrage stand out as a more glaring deprivation. On the old virtual-representation model, there was a continuum of groups who were marginalized from the perspective of electoral efficacy – American colonists, residents of cities such as Manchester before 1832, minorities within a specific constituency – but who were nevertheless said to be adequately spoken for from the point of view of the system of representation as a whole.[139] But given that their theory dismissed all of this, the limitations on the franchise which Hare and company endorsed gave their system a forbidding air of exclusivity. The opponents of democracy covered in Chapters 1 and 2, after all, defended their restrictions on the grounds that these *improved* the descriptiveness and inclusivity of the assembly. Hare's proposal, however, was premised on denying that it was legitimate to pursue the goal of inclusivity by this means. Since inclusivity was a widely shared value of British parliamentarism, there was strong ideological pressure on Victorian thinkers who were attracted to PR to make their system more

---

[137] Hare, *Election of Representatives*, 61, 65.
[138] E.g. Mill, "Recent Writers on Reform," 357, 359, 364; *Considerations*, 448, 453.
[139] H.T. Dickinson, "The Representation of the People in Eighteenth-Century Britain," in *Realities of Representation: State Building in Early Modern Europe and European America*, ed. Maija Jansson (Houndmills, Basingstoke, 2007): 19–44.

compatible with the ideal of the inclusive constitution in the only way available to them: by extending the franchise to all.[140] If Hare's attack on virtual representation contained the judgment that "a government is not good which, as to numbers of its people ... allows them no voice in the choice of their legislators,"[141] then it is no surprise that, as decades passed and the electorate was widened, many of its adherents would ultimately reframe their support for PR as part of a larger democratic project, even if with some misgivings and qualifications.[142]

Personal representation's hostility to virtual representation was so stark that it supplied a democratic impulse to the movement in spite of the reservations of its major early figures. But how was this transcendence of virtual representation to come about?

b The Voluntary Constituency

As we have begun to see, many issues are involved in the debate between PR and plurality-rule systems, and STV as presented by Hare claimed to deliver improvements along several dimensions: to equalize the value of each vote; to eliminate the waste of votes; to make each elector the authorizer of a member of the assembly; to create a Commons that "registered [public opinion] with an accuracy resembling that of a thermometer."[143] But what was to make all of these goods possible was the transformation of the constituency. The minority-representation plans examined above had accepted that electors voted as members of fixed constituencies – Birmingham or Westminster or Oxford University – but they had attacked the longstanding premise that the constituency was a corporate unity represented by the majority and had sought to give MPs to both majority and minority sections of voters within it. Hare went further and jettisoned the fixed constituency altogether.

The simplest way to characterize the revolution in the constituency wrought by Harean PR was that it changed constituencies from the settings in which discrete, prearranged blocks of citizens voted to groupings of voters fabricated by the distribution of votes itself.[144] One way of

---

[140] For this reason it is not coincidental that many of the great figures in British PR – Mill, Hare, the Fawcetts, among others – were also strong supporters of women's suffrage.

[141] Hare, *Election of Representatives*, xxi.   [142] E.g. Lubbock, *Representation*, 2.

[143] Hare, *Election of Representatives*, 239.

[144] For a critical discussion of the distinction between voluntary and involuntary constituencies in modern literature, see Michael Rabinder James, "Two Concepts of Constituency," *JP*, 77 (2015): 381–93.

construing the difference between Hare's proposal and the status quo was temporal: from being settled before the election, constituencies were now to be constructed through the election itself by the action of the elector qua elector. Another way of articulating the change made by PR was in terms of identity and affiliation. On the traditional models of representation, the prearrangement of constituencies imparted to the elector an affiliation additional to the object of his vote. Beyond voting for candidate so-and-so, the elector was also a member of such-and-such geographical (or professional or class) constituency. Under personal representation, the elector was identifiable with nothing beyond his chosen candidate; there was no intermediary level of association between the voter and the candidate. With the erasure of established constituencies, Harean STV left only the voters themselves as the material of the electoral system, and this step of taking the individual electors as the be-all and end-all of political representation was truly unprecedented.

This abolition of fixed constituencies was the technical feature that lay behind the prevalent, usually pejorative depiction of PR as "individualistic."[145] The debate about PR's individualism was multi-layered, with three separate issues subsumed under this label: (a) the technical issue of how voters were to be grouped; (b) the objects to which in practice PR sought to give representation; and (c) the broader sociopolitical consequences of implementing the system. The third issue, which might more properly be described as the question of whether PR was *individualizing* or *atomizing* in its effects, is taken up in the Chapter 5; the second is treated in Subsection d. As for the first, on this score it undoubtedly warranted the label. Hare's method of personal representation was individualistic in a strict sense; with the prearranged constituency abolished, its machinery made use of no "corporate" elements.[146] MPs would be returned not by winning the most votes in districts carved up in advance of the election, but solely by "quotas" of autonomous electors whose only link was their common will to have him serve in the Commons.[147]

---

[145] The perception and critique of PR's individualism is covered extensively in Chapter 5.

[146] As a quartet of the leading writers on PR of the 1880s phrased it: "The only corporate opinion of which proportional representationists recognise the claim in principle is that of the nation"; John Lubbock, Leonard Courtney, Albert Grey, and John Westlake, "Proportional Representation: Objections and Answers," *NC*, 17 (1885): 312–20, at 312.

[147] The Cambridge-trained Australian lawyer and historian William Jethro Brown, who had firsthand experience of STV as a professor in Tasmania, which had implemented it a few years prior for elections to the federal assembly, offered one of the most interesting *fin-de-siècle* interpretations of

The "voluntary constituency" was Hare's name for this radical innovation whereby the only groupings of electors were those constructed through the preferences expressed by individuals.[148] That he considered this voluntariness to be the bedrock of his plan was clear from his definition of the "opposite" of his system as one founded on "involuntariness" in drawing constituencies through "geographical, local, and corporate divisions of electors."[149] The substitution of voluntary for involuntary constituencies involved a further change, namely that constituencies would be *unanimous* rather than divided: hence, "voluntary unanimity" worked as a succinct slogan of the great change he proposed. Unanimity was cherished because it was only via "unanimous constituencies" that the waste of votes could be avoided and the status of being "really" and not merely "fictitiously" represented be secured for all electors. The "principle of unanimity" and the "voluntary constituency" were alternate ways of expressing the same fundamental fact: that Hare thought the only tolerable electoral groupings were those fabricated by the shared wills of electors to be represented by the same candidate.[150]

How did Hare and Victorian PR conceptualize their voluntarism about constituencies? Most generally, they conceived it as a system of individual liberty. Freedom was as foundational to the normative architecture of Victorian PR as mirroring.[151] Moreover, proportionalists' emphasis on this value was unique, distinguishing them alike from variety-of-suffragists, Chartists, Chapter 3's diverse and radical democrats, and outright technocrats or aristocrats.[152] Hare was especially emphatic about his program's

---

PR. Brown rightly perceived that the voluntary constituency was the keystone of the Harean arch, but, fascinatingly, he went on to characterize this innovation as an instantiation of one of the classic "individualistic" Victorian theses, Henry Maine's distinction between ancient law (based on one's fixed status in traditional groups based on kinship and hierarchy) and modern law (based on autonomous individuals' freedom of contract): "The tie by local contiguity is to be superseded by the bond of kinship – kinship not of blood but of ideas! The great law of progress, defined by Maine as *from status to contract,* already abundantly illustrated in the sphere of private law, is to find a new illustration in the domain of *jus publicum*" (*The New Democracy: A Political Study* [London, 1899], 34).

[148] Hare, *Election of Representatives*, ch. 2.

[149] Ibid., xl, 40–1. The Danish inventor of STV, C. C. G. Andrae, saw it in the same light; Poul Andrae, *Andrae and His Invention: The Proportional Representation Method, A Memorial Work,* trans. Vaughn Meisling (Copenhagen, 1926), 14.

[150] Hare, *Election of Representatives*, vii, 24, 28, 195.

[151] For this reason, PR has tended to attract those thinkers who wish to prioritize freedom over equality as the primary value of democracy; see e.g. Hans Kelsen, *The Essence and Value of Democracy,* trans. Brian Graf (Lanham, 2013),72, 97; Urbinati, *Mill on Democracy*, 78. Urbinati is wrong to proclaim Mill's uniqueness in highlighting liberty as the great advantage of PR; it was common among proportionalists to seize on the value of liberty in their propaganda.

[152] Historically, the value of electoral freedom had not played a role in British practices of representation either; Michael J. Turner, "Political Leadership and Political Parties, 1800–46," in *A Companion to Nineteenth-Century Britain*: 125–39.

libertarian credentials. "The system here proposed," he wrote, would best be denominated "the system of individual independence" since its chief impact was to accomplish "liberation" and "freedom of action in representative institutions"; its "basis" and "condition" was "individual independence."[153] It was the "free electoral system" built upon the "free action of electors" as channeled into "free constituencies."[154] His "cardinal idea," he proclaimed, had been to "give to every voter this freedom": "at the root of all real reform [lies] the question of the measure of individual power and liberty of action which shall be afforded to the electors."[155] Later generations of Victorian proportionalists agreed: their goal was to inaugurate the era of the "free and independent elector," to establish a "*régime* of liberty."[156]

The freedom associated with STV centered on the conditions of choice. To this there were two dimensions. Unfortunately, the terminology used to describe these different aspects was rather unstable. Here are a couple of Hare's attempts to categorize the two lines along which his scheme would improve the choice situation. It would: (1) (a) "relieve every elector wholly from any extraneous control" and (b) "give him an unrestricted choice from among all his countrymen"; his plan could secure two desiderata, both (2) (a) "*freedom* of choice" and (b) "*extent* of choice." What these two formulations make clear is that Hare had a maximalist vision of liberty according to which one was freer the wider one's field of choice was; he denied that an unimpeded "Hobson's choice" could be called free.[157] Further, both of these phrasings highlight the dual nature of the freedom-enhancing project intrinsic to the voluntary constituency as he understood it. STV was meant both (a) to reduce the dependence of the efficacy of one's vote on the electoral conduct of others and (b) to widen the range of candidates from whom electors could pick.

[153] Hare, *Election of Representatives*, vii, xxxvi, 140–2, 216–18, 169, 256. Also Hare, "John Stuart Mill," *WR*, 45 (1874): 122–59, at 150: "Its fundamental principle is, in fact, a corollary of that of Individuality. It puts forward in a practical shape the necessity of freedom for individual action."

[154] Ibid., 108, 114–15. Similarly, Andrae offered the system of "free election" as the best name for his scheme, since it resulted in "making election a free act"; Andrae, *Andrae and His Invention*, 34.

[155] Hare, "Individual Responsibility in Representative Government," 4 (1886): 350–8, at 352; "Reform Bill of the Future," 76.

[156] Grey, "Proportional versus Majority Representation," 954; Courtney, "Political Machinery," 85. This rhetoric made its way across the channel; *la liberté électorale* was a key slogan for French proportionalists. See e.g. Émile de Girardin, "Suffrage Universel et Centralisation," in *Force ou Richesse: Questions de l'année 1864* (Paris, 1865), 21.

[157] Hare, *Machinery of Representation*, 34; *Election of Representatives*, 140; Beales et al., *Representative Reform Report*, 17.

To take the first dimension first: the primary work of an institution of electoral liberty was to secure noninterference. STV's "first" object was "that the conduct of others, whatever it be, may in no respect interfere with [the elector's] free exercise of his own political functions, and that he may be enabled to select the candidate in whom he has the most confidence, without regard to the sinister or other influences by which any portion of the constituency may be actuated."[158] STV claimed to effect this reduction of interference by lifting constraints which existed solely as a function of plurality-rule elections in fixed constituencies. These constraints arose because under the current system the success of a candidate was a matter not of his earning a certain proportion of the overall national vote (the quota), but of his having *beaten* other candidates who had stood for the same fixed constituency. Making the return of a candidate contingent on his beating other contenders caused two linked kinds of dependence.

First, in the eyes of Hare and his disciples, the dominance of parties and the power of their "wire-pullers" over the nomination of candidates was tied to the plurality-rule territorial system. Once party machines settled on a candidate for a district, they could pressure all other sympathetic citizens not to stand lest the worse option put up by another party slip in on a divided vote.[159] And if a figure subordinate to party dictates had the fortitude to present himself anyway, voters in agreement with him would have to weigh their desire to cast their vote for the person they sincerely endorsed against the likelihood that doing so would redound to the benefit of those politicians who were farthest from him ideologically. Thus, the voter was not free in the sense that if he were to desire that his vote be efficacious, he could not simply vote his sincere preferences, but would have to take into account strategic considerations such as electability.[160] "Tactical" or "strategic" voting, as it has come to be known,[161] was in this literature ipso facto a mark of unfreedom. A second point – which was to a degree implicit in the problem of having to vote based on electability – was that an aspiring MP's fate was determined not just by the amount of support he inspired, but also by the amount of dislike which he elicited. Under the current arrangements an incumbent could have the same

---

[158] Hare, "A Note on Representative Government," 105.

[159] Hare, *Election of Representatives*, 85–6.

[160] It was characteristic of PR supporters to deplore strategic voting as both immoral in its own right and a distortion of the representative aims of an electoral system; e.g. Dodgson, *A Method of Taking Votes on More Than Two Issues*, in *Political Pamphlets of Lewis Carroll*, 46–58, at 56–7.

[161] On strategic voting in relation to STV and other systems, see Michael Dummet, *Voting Procedures* (Oxford, 1984).

number of supporters as in a previous election, but could lose a re-election campaign because a small knot of residents (who perhaps had not even voted previously) had joined the ranks of an opponent solely to block him – and, it was typically thought, had done so only at the instigation of party wire-pullers.[162] In such conditions, voters were dependent in the sense that the return of their preferred candidate was put at the mercy of the sentiments and actions of others who did not endorse him.[163]

Calling this a system of "individual independence" or "personal liberty" was, strictly speaking, inaccurate; in a collective project such as electing representatives, the individual could never in fact attain "a perfect freedom of action in choosing representatives," which had to remain more of a regulative ideal. For all its individualism, "the liberation of individual electors from a compulsory union with others" (that is, the *voluntary* constituency) could not achieve the complete emancipation of the individual, even if the cruder kinds of dependence in local plurality-rule arrangements had been eliminated. Instead, it promised to guarantee the independence of all "particular groups of voters" equal to the quota in size.[164] Every "quota of voters" could now be secure in placing their candidate regardless of any "manoeuvres" elsewhere in the electorate, since quotas were insulated from the shifts in preferences and tactics of voters who supported other candidates.[165] No set of voters could pool their combined strength to keep out a candidate who would have attracted a quota's worth of support from across the entire national electorate.

In sum, the unit whose independence was guaranteed was the quota, not the individual. But since a representative body made up of a series of quota-earners did loosen constraints placed on voters under first-past-the-post

---

[162] E.g. Williams, *Proportional Representation and British Politics*, 62; Edward Hugessen Knatchbull-Hugessen, "Redistribution of Political Power," *MM*, 27 (1872), 73.

[163] Intriguingly, this genre of dependence was also given the label "swamping"; Max Kyllman, "Mr. Hare's System of Personal Representation," *LSE Selected Pamphlets* (reprinted from the *Examiner and Times*, 2 Oct. 1866), 1.

[164] Hare, *Election of Representatives*, 113, xiii. This difference is made apparent by a comparison of *On Liberty* with the *Considerations*. Whereas in the former Mill asserted that an injustice was committed if a "contrary opinion" held by "only one person" were silenced, in the latter it was "the influence of every mode of thinking *which is shared by numbers*" which he declared "ought to be felt in the legislature"; *On Liberty*, 229; *Considerations*, 507. The public sphere can be open to everyone, but even the freest legislature can only be open to every *group*. The legislature, by nature, cannot be as individualistic as the public sphere more generally. It was in recognition of this "limitation of individual influence which is the inevitable consequence of the collective nature of representation" that the influential Swiss theorist Ernest Naville called the "principle of the equality of electoral groups" the foundation of PR; Naville, *On the Theory and Practice of Representative Elections* (London, 1872), 10.

[165] Williams, *Proportional Representation and British Politics*, 73.

systems by giving each voter a greater margin for efficacious action, the individualistic-libertarian tone in which personal representation was often presented did capture an important element of the change which it sought to effect. The most precise formula for the pledge to emancipate the voter from susceptibility to the control of other electoral forces was accordingly something like this: the independence of each aggregate of electors equivalent to the size of a quota in the sense that the return of its MP could not be defeated by how other voters acted,[166] combined with the removal of impediments to the elector's power to "unite himself with [any] number of his fellow-countrymen" with whom he happened most to agree.[167]

This impatience with the "embarrassing restrictions" obstructing the free disposal of the vote according to the voter's genuine preferences was linked to the second side of the freedom promoted by Harean PR: the expansion of the range of choice.[168] Under plurality rule, one could choose from only those politicians who stood for one's district; with PR, one was enabled to rank candidates from across the entire country (or a much larger multimember constituency, in the modified versions). This greater expanse of choice was not just a boon, but was treated as a constituent element of electoral freedom by Hare; any structure that "prevents the electors of the kingdom from choosing any man whom they may consider the most fit to represent them" had to be rejected as "antagonistic to and subversive of their rights." Moreover, Hare believed that the field of candidates itself would expand as a result of the destruction of territorial districts, since candidates who were unlikely to triumph in any specific plurality-rule election might now present themselves in the hopes of attaining a quota by collecting votes from what were then several separate constituencies.[169] Because parties would no longer have to worry about splitting their vote,

---

[166] "The representation of any section of political opinion" should depend solely on "the number of its supporters" and not on "the attitude taken toward it by other parties"; Humphreys, *Proportional Representation*, 86; also Williams, *Proportional Representation and British Politics*, 27. Humphreys had in mind here the evils of the "second ballot" system even more than of straightforward plurality-rule elections; as two-round or "ballotage" arrangements gained ground on the Continent, British PR reformers came to denigrate them as a step backward even from single-member plurality-rule districts.

[167] Hare, *Election of Representatives*, 21.

[168] Ibid., xxxvi. Also 140: "The system of individual independence offers him a freedom of choice, not only of two or three, but probably of two or three thousand candidates."

[169] Hare, *Election of Representatives*, 100, 132–3. And see "Representation of Every Locality and Intelligence," 529: "Our system thus gives to a few persons [i.e. party "wire-pullers"] ... the power of practically limiting the competition to one or two candidates of each party ... The obstacles which thus confer a monopoly upon two or three candidates, to the exclusion, in effect, of all the rest of their countrymen, are coupled with the electoral arrangement which confines every candidate to the votes of one particular constituency."

pressure to limit the number of candidates wearing their colors would vanish, and consequently a wider array of options not only outside the main parties but also within them could emerge.[170] In sum, the "artificial restraints" that stemmed from the vote being split up into numerous districts and the parties holding a stranglehold on the selection of candidates were to give way to a "magnificent field of choice."[171] Hence, the voluntary constituency was conceived as enabling an expansion of liberty which comprised (a) a measure of insularity from the attitudes and strategies of other electors (through the guarantee of a seat for every candidate whose support reached the quota), (b) the unencumbered ability of the voter to enter into a union with any other set of voters in favor of any candidate in the kingdom, and (c) the broadening of the set of candidates.

The conception of liberty embedded in the voluntary constituency was not understood as an isolated construction for its peculiar sphere. Instead, it was seen as an overdue extension to the electoral arena of the liberty that existed in other areas of life.[172] Two *façons de penser* about liberty from other domains were particularly potent for Victorian PR.

The first was economic: electoral liberty was the political equivalent of free trade. While PR had support from economic "centrists," interventionists, and socialists of various kinds, it is significant that many of the leading publicists for PR were free traders and that they took these two issues to be part of a common moral-political package.[173] Hare was not only adamant in his support for free trade[174] but eloquent about the connections which he saw between it and his design for representative reform:

> An age which has achieved the freedom of commercial intercourse in spite of the pretensions of local protection and monopoly, may not unreasonably hope to find advocates for the free interchange and communication, as well of political action as of political thought, against the far less plausible and more insolent claims of dominant inhabitants of arbitrarily selected and privileged boroughs and districts to a monopoly of the great right of national representation.

---

[170] Walter Baily, *Proportional Representation in Large Constituencies* (London, 1872), 19–20; Smith, *University Representation*, 35–7.

[171] Hare, *Election of Representatives*, 45, 133.

[172] Hence it was requisite for "men who profess to be advocates of general freedom" to subscribe to PR; Hare, "Representation of Every Locality and Intelligence," 535.

[173] Ted Bromund, "Uniting the Whole People: Proportional Representation in Great Britain, 1884–5, Reconsidered," *HR*, 74 (2001): 77–94.

[174] His first excursion into political debate had caught the eye of the influential champion of economic liberalism William Huskisson; Parsons, *Thomas Hare and Political Representation*, 10–17.

The purpose of this work is to show how practically small in form is the change that would suffice to liberate the elector from the bonds that now tie him to the other voters of the borough in which he happens to dwell, whereby his action is absolutely fettered to theirs.[175]

Similarly, PR proponents drew on the language of the free trader concerning the "natural laws" of the market in casting PR as a "return to nature and freedom."[176] The "so-called doctrine of free-trade," Hare's most famous apostle had said, went hand-in-hand with the truth that "all restraint, *qua* restraint, is an evil."[177] In parallel, PR was meant to eliminate the evil of restraint from the world of elections.

There was another "economic" aspect to Hare's theory of representation – one that was tied to his affection for the *doctrinaires*. Guizot had characterized political representation as an extension of the economic division of labor. In choosing his representative the citizen "only did what is done virtually every day" in entrusting a portion of his affairs to another person "capable of efficiently conducting them."[178] Hare agreed that voting was not generically different from selecting a plumber or a bank. In "an advanced state of civilization" representation "is a matter of daily occurrence, and common necessity. It is the vicarious performance of duties which cannot be personally executed. It intervenes in commerce, in jurisprudence, in education, and in a thousand other forms."[179] What is so interesting about Hare, however, is the argumentative end to which he put the identification of political representation and the division of labor. To French authors, as well as to the English thinkers who took it up,[180] the import of this identification was not to supply an argument for one electoral system over others; rather, it was used to justify representation *tout court* as better suited to modern societies than more direct-democratic

---

[175] Hare, *Election of Representatives*, 21–2.

[176] Courtney, "Representation of Minorities," 152. Also Marshall, *Minorities and Majorities*, 23: As "Free Trade" was "founded on just natural laws – so in the case of the Cumulative Vote, the adoption of it will, I believe, be simply an advance to a natural and equitable mode of taking votes . . . we shall find that the natural laws which determine whether parties at any given time shall be large or small, extreme or moderate, will act at least as well, and there is every reason to think will act better and more freely"; Marshall, *Minorities and Majorities*, 23.

[177] Mill, *On Liberty*, 293.

[178] Guizot, *History of Representative Government*, 287. The thought went back to Sieyès. On the Abbé and his "economic" vision of representation, see Pasquale Pasquino, "Emmanuel Sieyès, Benjamin Constant et le 'Gouvernement des Modernes'," *Revue française de science politique*, 37 (1987): 214–28; Richard Tuck, *The Sleeping Sovereign* (Cambridge, 2016), 172.

[179] Hare, *Election of Representatives*, xxxv–xxxvi.

[180] E.g. Brougham, *The British Constitution*, 62; Sidgwick, *Elements of Politics*, 373–4.

visions.[181] But for Hare, the observation of the contiguity between "the choice of parliamentary representatives" and the "select[ion of] persons to fill other fiduciary or vicarious offices" was not meant to ward off direct democracy[182] – the prestige of the mid-Victorian Parliament was too great to take such alternatives seriously. Rather, its purpose was to justify the principal "novelty of [his] proposal": the "very much larger field from which to choose."[183] If "the exercise of individual judgment and delibera-tion suffice[d]" for the enormous array of "circumstances [in which] people are compelled to place themselves and their interests in the hands of others," then it should not stop at the selection of MPs.[184] Both of the economic inflections of his theory of representation had, then, the same end: to show that with PR the economic and political spheres would constitute a sort of seamless fabric of freedom.

A second influence on British PR's libertarian self-conception also had economic dimensions, although it was broader in scope and thus better described as *social*.[185] This was the thought that voluntary associations were the lifeblood of a free society. No less than Tocqueville famously had been, many Britons were struck by the vibrancy of associational life in the Anglophone world,[186] and Hare seized on the respect for voluntary asso-ciations as both consequence and guarantor of liberty to depict what voting was like under personal representation. His aim was for the electoral arena also to give "full scope" to the "voluntary and natural disposition to associate," to "bring the disposition for voluntary association to the busi-ness of political life." "The power of voluntary association," the faculty of "free action" to enter into a "society or partnership," were now to be extended to elections.[187] The electoral sphere should resemble civil society in the latitude of liberty it provided, and it was this resemblance, PR devotees believed, which the mechanism of the voluntary constituency provided. If it achieved this similarity, the colorful mosaic of associations and cooperative groups that characterized modern civil society would extend into politics.[188] This is an important point: given the formal

---

[181] Michael Sonenscher, "Introduction," to Sieyès, *Political Writings*, ed. Sonenscher (Indianapolis, 2003): xxix–xxxi.

[182] Hare, *Election of Representatives*, xxxvi.   [183] Hare, "Just and Equal Distribution of Seats," 204.

[184] Hare, *Election of Representatives*, xxxvi.   [185] Courtney, "Representation of Minorities," 152.

[186] E.g. the Liberal statesman Édouard René de Laboulaye looking longingly at how in England and the United States "l'association suffit à tout"; *L'État et ses limites*, fifth edition (Paris, 1871), 85. To understand their admiration, it must be remembered how pertinacious Revolutionary restric-tions on rights of association were in nineteenth-century French law.

[187] Beales et al., *Representative Reform Report*, 6; Hare, *Election of Representatives*, 47, 33, 23.

[188] Courtney, "Political Machinery," 85, 91.

individualism and antisociological, anticorporatist method of the scheme, there was nothing else to represent but what emerged during the electoral process itself via voters "associat[ing] themselves voluntarily."[189] Since "the vesting in every elector of a power to act . . . without any trammel created by the particular section of voters to which he is nominally annexed, is the keystone of parliamentary reform," the only entities within the system were sets of "wills" unanimously agreed to join together for the purpose of being represented by the same candidate.[190] The voluntary association of electors was what was left standing after Hare's purge of all "corporate" elements of the representative system.

A final point should be made regarding the system of free election conceived as voluntarism in constituency construction. This point has been implicit in the foregoing, but it is important enough in marking the contrast with the variety-of-suffrages school to merit explicit treatment. This is that a complete system of voluntary constituencies cut out all forms of mediation between the total aggregate of voters and the collection of MPs. There were no intermediary levels of sorting – all of these were denounced as fetters on the voter. It followed from this unmediated, unstructured character that PR was irreconcilable with all kinds of quotas, understanding this term very broadly. The quota was, in a manner of speaking, the instrument par excellence of the traditional descriptivist, and it is a factor in any electoral system that retains even a territorial component.[191] For Paley or Mackintosh or Bagehot, the electoral system was truly an elaborate set of quotas. What Hare and his most uncompromising successors envisioned was the antithesis of this: the most thoroughgoing antiquota scheme possible. In this regard Hare's program distinguished itself even from other forms of PR, such as the party-list, where quotas can be reinserted at the level of the party.[192] While a party-list system preserves the voluntariness of constituencies, they introduce an element of indirectness – since the vote is for the party rather than the candidate, the party can be made the site for inscribing sociological determinations back onto the assembly. Harean STV, however, had no layer at

---

[189] Hare, "The Coming Steps in Representation," *FR*, 37 (1885), 221.

[190] Hare, *Election of Representatives*, 38.

[191] For example, the US electoral system's guarantee to each state of two senators and a number of congressmen proportioned to its population can be interpreted as quotas, paralleling how an affirmative action program might mandate that certain portions of the student body be reserved for specific demographic categories.

[192] As has been done frequently lately with regard to quotas for women; e.g. Aili Mari Tripp and Alice Kang, "The Global Impact of Quotas: On the Fast Track to Increased Female Legislative Representation," *Comparative Political Studies*, 41 (2008): 338–61.

which such criteria could be imposed; the composition of the assembly that comes out of it is an unmediated product of the electors' will. Victorian PR and the variety-of-suffrages were, consequently, at opposite ends of the spectrum when judged from this perspective: in the former, everything was constructed from the tally of votes given in conditions of maximal freedom; in the latter, the electors' task was to choose the specific people who would fill the various slots preappointed to different segments of society.

Out of this analysis of the voluntary constituency two questions arise concerning the genre of representation to which Victorian STV should be said to belong.

First, we are now in a position to answer the question of whether STV constituted a form of *minority representation*. "Minority representation" was a common label for Hare's plan for at least the first two decades after its arrival, although "proportional representation" had mostly won out by the end of the nineteenth century. While many STV proponents would ultimately reject the name "minority representation" as "misleading,"[193] others remained content with it. This satisfaction was sensible enough. Like the original minority-representation schemes, STV was opposed to the principle of "majority representation" by which only "local majorities" could gain representation and "due weight to the minority" within districts was denied; all its supporters acknowledged that they wished to end a system that "deprive[d] the minority ... of any share of representation."[194] The genius of STV was that it could give representation to what were minorities according to block-voting or single-member-district arrangements, and the older nomenclature captured this facet well.

Nevertheless, there were a number of reasons for Hareans to repudiate the name,[195] the most important of which being that it was not technically accurate. Unlike the schemes in Section 1, STV represented no minorities as such. This was due to the fact that in "convert[ing] what are now only majorities into unanimous constituencies," STV necessarily put an end of the status of "minorities" as a matter of electoral accounting.[196] On Hare's plan there were neither minorities nor majorities, but instead a *collection of equal unanimities*; in dissolving the fixed district and allowing, through the transfer, every elector to contribute to an equal quota for the election of

---

[193] Lubbock, *Representation*, 4.
[194] Hare, *Election of Representatives*, 30, 3; Courtney, "The Seats Bill," *FR*, 37 (1885), 31.
[195] Including the strategic one that it fed into the widespread democratic-radical mistrust of PR as antimajoritarian, noted earlier.
[196] Hare, *Election of Representatives*, vii.

a member, no elector was left in the position of minority within his constituency. Thus, Hare and others were perfectly justified in asserting that his "method has no affinity with any which has been suggested for the mere representation of minorities."[197]

Second, there is the matter of PR's *descriptiveness*. The question of whether Victorian PR was democratic has received some scholarly attention,[198] and we have already addressed it in the previous subsection. Less well considered are its descriptive credentials, perhaps because PR has been seen as a textbook example of descriptive representation.[199] Our reconstruction of the broader spectrum of nineteenth-century thought on representation, however, makes this interpretation look less straightforward.

That "Parliament should be the mirror of the nation" was announced as a central goal of PR,[200] and, as will be seen going forward, this goal was attended by a conviction about the extent of diversity in their society that occasionally exceeded that of the variety-of-suffragist. But delivering an assembly of "genuinely representative character,"[201] as the sociologist L. T. Hobhouse put it in summation of a half-century's worth of "liberal" arguments for PR, was a fundamentally different enterprise for Hare and his followers than for the more longstanding currents of descriptivism.

For one thing, compared with the variety-of-suffrages approach, mirroring was an *indirect* outcome of STV. On the former, the regulation of the electorate was directly guided by sociological premises; it achieved mirroring in that the scheme itself was based on an ex ante correct picture of the nation. On the latter, on the other hand, mirroring resulted indirectly from freedom; it was because free action was not impeded that personal representation would yield a "perfect representation" and constitute a kind of "political thermometer, indicating sensitively the national pulse."[202] With PR, inclusiveness and respect for diversity – "the

---

[197] Hare, "Individual Responsibility," 350. His Danish counterpart Andrae was also firmly opposed to this term; Andrae, *Andrae and His Invention*, 27, 111.

[198] This is especially true with regard to the literature on Mill, where it is contested whether Mill's support of PR reveals his commitment to or fear of democracy. For the "antidemocratic" interpretation, see Alan Kahan, *Aristocratic Liberalism: The Social and Political Thought of Jacob Burckhardt, John Stuart Mill, and Alexis de Tocqueville* (Oxford, 1992), 71–4; Paul Kern, "Universal Suffrage without Democracy: Thomas Hare and John Stuart Mill," *Review of Politics*, 34 (1972): 306–22. For the democratic interpretation, see Urbinati, *Mill on Democracy*, ch. 3.

[199] E.g. Hanna Pitkin, *Concept of Representation*, 62–3.

[200] M. G. Fawcett, "Proportional Representation," 378. Also Hare, *Election of Representatives*, xxxiv, 12, 134; Albert Grey, "Proportional versus Majority Representation," 937–40; Lubbock, *Representation*, 2, 50.

[201] Hobhouse, *Liberalism*, 117.   [202] Hare, "Individual Responsibility," 353.

representation of all minorities, and subsections of opinion"[203] – was downstream of the counting of each vote equally and the guarantee of each vote's "effectiveness" under conditions of liberty and expansive choice; these virtues had become completely detached from the possession of a correct understanding of society and its salient fissures.

Another way of stating the difference is that Hare's innovation was a *purely procedural mechanism of vote aggregation*; it dispensed altogether with the sociological phase of the mirror theory as practiced by someone like Bagehot or Harris. While Hare's PR program may yield outcomes of greater diversity and inclusiveness, welcoming into the assembly "varieties of opinion and feeling," "diversities of thought and sentiment," which would otherwise have been left unspoken for,[204] it denied the possibility of actually mirroring some objective truth about the nature of society – it folded all the action into the electoral procedure. Claims about social-ideological conditions against which the assembly could be compared had no place. The independent criterion which had existed for Britain's original descriptivism was gone under proportional representation.

The differences between PR and the descriptive ideal as it had been traditionally known in England raise the question of whether PR ought to be considered a form of descriptive representation at all. At the least, the recovery of the fact that Britain had a robust tradition of genuine descriptive representation which was well entrenched at the time of the advent of PR can, I think, help explain the puzzle that, despite being the cradle of pluralism,[205] Britain is one of the few European nations never to have adopted PR at the national level.

The mainstream mirrorer, it will be recalled, was convinced that one could know the "objective" truth about the state of the nation. In light of this conviction, there was no reason to turn the composition of the assembly over to a supposedly "neutral" and nonarbitrary mechanism that left everything to the free judgment of all voters treated equally. Harris revealed the conflict between variety-of-suffragist and proportionalist reasoning when he denied, against "some very enlightened and philosophical reformers," that any concern about the wasted votes of minorities within fixed districts was appropriate, since his use of a variety of mechanisms to apportion the franchise in a manner that respected sociological

---

[203] Henry Fawcett, "Mr. Mill's Treatise on Representative Government," *MM*, 4 (1861), 101.
[204] Hare, *Election of Representatives*, 16.
[205] E.g. Julia Stapleton, "English Pluralism as Cultural Definition: The Social and Political Thought of George Unwin," *JHI*, 52 (1991): 665–84.

differentiation guaranteed that "the legitimate influence of the opinions and interests entertained by such minority will, where those are of real value and deserving of representation, have been already provided for in the State."[206] To Victorians who were already attached to the descriptive ideal and who saw it as a national heritage, it was far from self-evident that PR marked an advance in descriptiveness, or that it qualified as a descriptive system at all. We saw earlier, for instance, that Bagehot tossed aside Mill's support for PR with a broader suffrage supplemented by plural voting as insufficiently representative to the working class. Similarly, anyone who felt that the £10 household franchise in boroughs was exclusive of the working class would not find Hare's wish to go to STV while settling on this line as a uniform basis for enfranchisement to be a satisfactory solution to the crisis of representation.

What's more, in the event that equal universal suffrage arrived, PR did little to make democracy more palatable to the traditional mirror. For in that case PR would still give the working class electoral power in proportion to its numbers. But this was a fate which the Victorian descriptivist was attempting to avoid, since he was certain that, though the working classes made up by far the largest percentage of the population, they were but one part of the nation properly understood in its diversity; to put a great preponderance of legislative seats under working-class control, as PR combined with an equal universal franchise promised to do, would thus vastly exceed the "due share" of the "lower orders."[207] The "conservative" view that under uniform universal suffrage PR was the only route available to ensure some seats for the upper classes – that is, the embrace of PR to avoid an even more lopsided form of lower-class hegemony if democracy were to come – should not be confused with the positive acceptance of democratic PR as furnishing a genuinely accurate mirror.[208] To take up this latter stance one would have had to sign on to an individualist,

---

[206] Harris, *True Theory*, 39. Harris was writing too early to have encountered Hare's scheme and hence had only the minority-representation plans in mind, but his thought here would have applied equally to the arguments of STV supporters.

[207] Greg, "Expected Reform Bill," 251; "Representative Reform [1]," 476. Or, as he phrased it elsewhere, "they [the labouring classes] comprise nine-tenths of the *numbers*, but only a fraction and segment of the *nation*"; Greg, "Representative Reform [1]," 466. Also Stephen, "The Value of Political Machinery," 851–2. And Bromund, "Uniting the Whole People," 92, for Salisbury's agreement on this point.

[208] This is where Lorimer, the elitist exponent of mirroring plural voting, came down. He accepted that under universal suffrage PR would be preferable to plurality rule. But in the end the improvement, he thought, would be negligible, since the descriptively "false" individualist-aggregative "machinery" of PR was inadequate to the task of mirroring and did not obviate the "dilemma" of having the "whole political power in the State thrown into the hands of a class." Lorimer, *Constitutionalism*, 177–8; "Mill on Representative Government," 550.

aggregative understanding of society and public opinion which was fore-sworn by many thinkers across the ideological spectrum.[209] And one would have had to give up on the thought that the composition of the assembly was ultimately answerable to any external, nonelectoral standard.

In conclusion, PR had some claim to having squared the circle of reconciling diversity with democracy: it could preserve a measure of inclusivity and deliberativeness under a uniform, even democratic, suffrage while skirting the kinds of sociological judgments that would lead to charges of arbitrariness. But the cost of doing so was that it narrowed the vision of what mirroring representation amounted to and what it could be said to achieve.

If the descriptive credentials of Hare's program could be cast in doubt, another aspect that has been stressed here – its nonarbitrary and freedom-enhancing character – had a firmer basis. But this relied not only on those facets of his project already covered, but also on one that has remained in the background, even if has been implicit in the discussion of the abolition of involuntary constituencies: the abandonment of territoriality.

c   The Transcendence of Territoriality

As we have seen, Hare undertook to grant a maximum of freedom to the voter and thereby to produce a legislature that was "a true epitome of the political opinions of society" and not merely of a few "stereotyped expression[s] of political sentiment."[210] To achieve this, he judged that it would be necessary to do away with territorial divisions, because such divisions limited the elector to solely those candidates who presented themselves for his local district. And he did not flinch from following these judgments through to their logical conclusion. Hare's desire was the complete replacement of "rigid territorial districts" with "personal districts."[211] Each MP would represent an identical number of voters without any compulsory geographical element entering the equation.[212]

---

[209] From the "far left," so to speak, e.g. Harrison, *Order and Progress*, passim. Furthermore, however certain communist parties may have felt about their chances under PR at specific political junctures, as the most thoroughly anticorporatist, proceduralist, and preference-based system Hare's sort of PR is the electoral system most directly antipodal to a communist understanding of representing society. Cf. Rosanvallon, *Le bon gouvernement* (Paris, 2015), 316.

[210] Hare, *Election of Representatives*, 309, 39.

[211] Albert Grey, "Proportional versus Majority Representation," 954.

[212] This was shared with Andrae: "the two systems have further in common the principle of giving voters full liberty to unite over the entire territory as in one electorate"; *Andrae and His Invention*, 35. The Netherlands and Israel today both have nationwide districts in this way, although they use list systems. Denmark, Sweden, and Norway also have nationwide districts at one level of a two-

As part and parcel of the abolition of involuntary groupings of voters, the chief source of this grouping, the territorial, had to go.

Fittingly for a Victorian, Hare's proposal of a single, kingdom-wide constituency had a historicist dimension. "All is now different," he proclaimed in 1860, from the days in which limitations on communication and transportation had bound people to act in tightly circumscribed localities; one only needed to observe the successful operation of "the Post-Office, that vast contrivance" to know that the "present facilities of communication" were capable of uniting Britain in one great constituency.[213] The advances that had made personal representation possible were, on Hare's estimate, quite recent: the nineteenth century was the first one fit for electoral freedom. Therefore, Hare's judgment was not so much that English governments of the past were blameworthy for having had unfree institutions, but that it was wrong to continue with the inherited system in light of the potential for freedom in modern times.[214]

Hare impressed this historicizing lesson through the aforementioned analogy to free trade. He joined many of his contemporaries in seeing free trade less as an eternal verity than a principle suited for their advanced epoch. For example, he decried majority representation in one- and two-member districts as a "protection [that] has not any of the excuses which were sometimes urged for the prohibitions of trade."[215] Regulation of trade may have looked sensible in earlier eras, but that did not derogate from the fact that freedom of trade had now become an article of justice. Likewise, however well this electoral patchwork had operated in the past, Victorian Britain was fit for freedom in the sense of dropping a territorial basis to its representation that could now be no more than a set of "artificial bands."[216]

Hare was bolder than many of his successors, however. Doubts about the practicability of his scheme often focused on his recommendation of

---

tiered list system. Lijphart, *Patterns of Democracy, Government Forms and Performance in Thirty-Six Countries*, second edition (New Haven, 2012), 139–40.

[213] Hare, "Representation in Practice and in Theory," 199; *Election of Representatives*, 27; *Machinery of Representation*, 16. Compare with Grey's remarks in Chapter 1, Section 2c.

[214] "The change proposed" was "nothing more than an application, in the business of electing our representatives, of the readier and more perfect means of action which the conditions of our times afford in almost all the operations of life"; Hare, "Reform Bill of the Future," 79.

[215] Hare, "Representation of Every Locality and Intelligence," 529.

[216] Hare, *Election of Representatives*, 148. His most remarkable passage on this parallel ran as follows: "We know the history of the struggle [for free trade] which, within the last few years, has succeeded in emancipating the trade of the kingdom from these trammels. It is the progress of development overcoming the doctrine of repression ... To say that [PR] is not necessary now, because in earlier times communication was difficult or impossible, would be as reasonable as to say that as free trade was not needed in the infancy of society, when each community depended on its own productions, it is therefore unnecessary now"; "Just and Equal Distribution of Seats," 204–5.

a single constituency for the whole kingdom, and therefore this was, for its practical chances, one of the most harmful pieces of his program.[217] In response, PR supporters developed plans to carve Britain into several large, multimember districts without provoking too many *cris de coeur*,[218] and in the late 1860s even Hare, with great reluctance, relented to pressure to offer a version of his scheme which would avoid this fount of objections, although he continued to insist on the practicability and preferability of the single nationwide constituency.[219]

Importantly, though, this reinsertion of territoriality was not a mere return to the status quo.[220] Instead, the role of territoriality in PR was altogether different than in previous systems: territorial divisions were a practical necessity and not themselves a positive component of the descriptive principle, as they were for those who treated local communities as the carriers of "interests." This difference is made clearer by investigating the Third Reform Act of the mid-1880s.

The package of bills passed in 1884–5 commonly known as the Third Reform Act altered the electoral system in three important ways.[221] First, it expanded the suffrage, so that roughly 60 percent of adult males were now eligible to vote. Second, it standardized the suffrage between boroughs and counties and moved toward equalizing the population of districts, establishing the principle of uniformity of electoral regulation throughout

---

[217] Judging the situation a half-century on, a campaigner for PR lamented this chapter in its history: "This suggestion [that the whole kingdom should form a single constituency] raised a barrier of prejudice against all proposals for proportional representation, which only to-day is being broken down"; Humphreys, *Proportional Representation*, 110.

[218] For instance, Droop settled on eight- to ten-member districts; Dodgson wanted six-member districts; Courtney thought five-members a good norm (although he denied ever having given up on the feasibility of implementing "Hare's system in its entirety"). Droop, "On Methods of Electing Representatives," 184–7; Dodgson, *Principles of Parliamentary Representation*, 180; Courtney, "Seats Bill," 35.

[219] Norris, "Politics of Electoral Reform," 70.

[220] Importantly, even if the reintroduction of geographical districts derived from fears about impracticability, once reintroduced they did present some problems of contestability. This was because most PR plans did not recommend dividing the country into a number of equal districts, but rather sought to follow the "familiar divisions of the country," assigning to each however many members accorded with the population of the designated area with a minimum of three members per constituency. So, for example, a large city might constitute a fifteen-member constituency, while a sparsely populated rural area might be made a three-member district, with all manner of gradations in between. The difficulty, though, was that the project of "enlarging our electoral areas" without violating the natural divisions in the nation was not immune to the charge of being executed in an "arbitrary manner," even if proportionalists were confident that they could meet this objection. See Humphreys, *Proportional Representation*, 110; Fawcett, *Leading Clauses*, 26, 32.

[221] For a précis of its complicated details, see Mary Chadwick, "The Role of Redistribution in the Making of the Third Reform Act," *HJ*, 19 (1976): 665–83.

Britain.[222] Third, it converted almost all constituencies into single-member districts. The PR campaign reacted differently to different pieces of this package. They were divided on whether to extend the suffrage, although by this date most of the leading figures seem to have favored or at least reconciled themselves to this "democratizing" measure; and they were happy to accept uniformity in principle, for reasons discussed in Section a of this chapter. But they wholly opposed the switch to single-member districts, which were antipodal to the multimember constituencies necessary for STV to operate.[223]

This clash between STV and first-past-the-post single-member districts brought some intriguing conceptual points to the fore. The first was constitutionality. Just as university seats provided a foothold within Britain's political heritage for the definition of constituencies on nonterritorial grounds that could then be exploited by imaginative theorists of electoral variegation, the fact that multiple membership had historically been far more entrenched than single membership gave, to the eyes of some observers, the proportionalists' desire for districts of 6–10 MPs the patina of greater constitutionality than the move to single membership.[224] It was not obvious that even Hare's proposal of a single very numerous multimember district, let alone the modestly sized districts in other STV plans, were a greater departure in principle from Britain's customary electoral-representative practices than the course that would be followed in the Third Reform Act.[225]

Second, and more significant theoretically, were arguments that occurred under the rubric of "community" versus "personal" representation. As has been observed, to many thinkers of different partisan hues territory was less a freestanding principle than the means to realizing the accurate representation of communities. In antiproportionalist discourse there was an equivocal character to the notion of community – on the one

---

[222] On the amount of variegation that remained in practice, see e.g. Henry Pelling, *Social Geography of British Elections, 1885–1910* (London, 1967).

[223] Courtney, for one, resigned from Gladstone's cabinet in protest; H. C. G. Matthew, "Courtney, Leonard Henry, Baron Courtney of Penwith (1832–1918), *ODNB*.

[224] Although it seems strange from the perspective of today, when we have a tendency to center narratives of "democratization" around expansions of the suffrage, it was common at the time for the transition to single-member districts, rather than the extension of the franchise, to be regarded as the most revolutionary feature of the Third Reform Act. See Philip Norton, *The Constitution in Flux* (Oxford, 1982), 228; H. J. Hanham, *Elections and Party Management: Politics in the Time of Disraeli and Gladstone* (London, 1959), xvi–xvii.

[225] To this end it is noteworthy that Hare cited Burke frequently as part of a general strategy of establishing his scheme's consistency with constitutional practice; *Election of Representatives*, 1, 6, 18, 48–9.

hand, it sometimes simply referred to the locality which was supposed to be coextensive with the territorial district; on the other, as in the variegated-suffrage framework, it defined any group with a common interest or opinion, whether geographically linked or not, to which the territorial constituency could stand in a "virtual" relationship or for which nonterritorial constituencies might be devised.[226] What is of most relevance now is the former, locality-based electoral communitarianism.

From this standpoint, localities were organic communities whose cohesiveness and integrity would be broken by large multimember districts or the single national constituency. This communitarian counter to PR comprehended a set of predictive claims about the negative consequences that would attend the end of electoral localism, which are addressed in Chapter 5. What matters at present is that the widespread Victorian attack on PR as antilocal[227] focused not just on the method of PR but also on its substantive effects on the composition of the Commons. Critics were arguing not only that it operated on a nonlocal basis – PR supporters were, after all, more than happy to admit this obvious truth – but that, as a result of this methodological alteration, localities would no longer be represented, that among the constellation of things for which MPs would "stand" local groups would cease to be among them. Was this attack accurate?

Yes and no. PR's transcendence of territoriality would have been of little consequence if it left the play of political forces unaffected. In this vein, it was imagined that PR would weed out certain evils that attended local representation, such as a "parochial" spirit that encouraged candidates to appeal to "petty local jealousies and prejudices" rather than to issues affecting "general interests" and appropriate to the "wider relations of national life."[228] It thereby promised emancipation from the worst effects of binding local constituencies. Moreover, much like the class-specific and

[226] It is important to recognize that support for single-member districts did not have to involve conceding diversity to the STV crowd. Instead, it could be argued that "variety of representation will be sufficiently arrived at, and the minority of the whole fairly represented, without any artificial attempt to secure it"; Shaw-Lefevre, "The Representation of Minorities," 732. Likewise Lord Salisbury, who clinched the move to single-member districts via his deal with Gladstone over the redistribution of seats, held up at the same time the "object" of a "perfect representation of the interests, the opinions, and the divisions of the nation; of minorities as well as majorities; of interests which are weak, as well as of those which are strong"; " The Value of Redistribution: A Note on Electoral Statistics," *NR*, 4 (1884): 145–62.

[227] Hare cited "that it is too complicated to be practical" and "that it is hostile to our local system" as the two most common complaints about his proposal; *Election of Representatives*, vii.

[228] Hare, *Election of Representatives*, 73; Knatchbull-Hugessen, "Redistribution of Political Power," 73–5; Rose, *Rise of Democracy*, 163.

corporatist reformers analyzed earlier, it was essential to PR reformers' brand of pluralism that mirroring the nation involved finding space for views and interests that were not easily "localizable."

And yet PR reformers denied that their system's large districts and its transfer to "personal" from "territorial" constituencies were equivalent to the eradication of local concerns from parliamentary life. Perhaps surprisingly, they bitterly contested the claim that their intention was to "delocalize" the Commons. This criticism, they argued, was based on a mistaken conflation of the elimination of the binding quality of territoriality with the foreclosure of local factors from entering into the assembly; as Hare put it, all that his system did was to make "geographical limits" no longer "the *sole* basis of political action and association." Harean PR was formally neutral with respect to local ties, as it was to all communal ties – this is what made it *personal* representation. This neutrality in no way prevented "contiguity of place" from "assert[ing] its influence."[229] In a way that recalls the well-known plea for toleration that if a religion were true then it ought not to have to rely on the coercion of the magistrate to flourish,[230] supporters of PR argued that if local influences really were important then they should fare well under a liberty-enhancing system that gave "free play" to all "forces" in society.[231] Precisely because PR was an open system, it was open to local influences as well.[232]

Hare, and especially his disciples who were most active during the debates over the Third Reform Act, did not stop here, however. Some promoters of STV claimed that their scheme was actually *more* hospitable to genuine local attachments than the territorially based alternatives, especially single-member districts. The system of voluntariness, as Hare put it, was best at empowering the "wholesome influences of locality," which would be "destroy[ed]" on any other arrangement.[233] This superiority was connected to the more general difficulty of trying to provide a mapping of the social world in a progressive society. Whether one had

---

[229] Hare, *Election of Representatives*, xii, 73.
[230] E.g. William Godwin, *Enquiry Concerning Political Justice*, 2 vols. (London, 1793), vol. 2, 589–91; Samuel Bailey, *Questions in Political Economy, Politics, Morals, Metaphysics, Polite Literature, and Other Branches of Knowledge* (London, 1828), 156–8.
[231] Courtney, "Seats Bill," 33.
[232] "If people are so animated with a local feeling that they must vote for one man in their own neighbourhood, they would have perfect liberty to do so. You give them power to join with those who are allied with them in feeling and thought, instead of those who live next door; but you don't force them to go afield, and wherever local wants demanded local representation they would be sure to secure it"; Courtney, "Representation of Minorities," 153.
[233] Hare, *Election of Representatives*, xii.

a "democratic" theory in which equal numerical districts were the rule or a nonaggregative, group-based mirroring vision in which constituencies were meant to track common interests, if the electoral system had "a reliance on localities" it would "continually involve" redrawing boundaries to track social and demographic "changes."[234] This constant tinkering[235] – which was associated pejoratively with American and French democracy[236] – could not but result in splitting up communities which were developing organically. Without a "self-acting process" that adapted itself to "the changes necessarily incidental to the progress of time," the integrity and individuality of distinct local communities would be ever under assault.[237] Hare contrasted "a system of arbitrary divisions, constructed entirely for electoral purposes" and for which "there will not be wanting reasons for its reconstruction to-morrow" with true respect for locality. This latter principle he defined (invoking Burke's authority) as the avoidance of interference with "these political incorporations which grow out of the constantly operating causes by which all human associations, like material things, are dissolved and reorganized, [and] are found to have the deepest roots."[238]

According to proportionalists, this harmful slicing up of the nation into artificial segments reached its apogee in the Third Reform Act's move to single-member districts, which "involves the arbitrary division of natural communities" and in consequence "weaken[s] local life."[239] "The first and most obvious evil" of that installment of reform "would be the utter extinction of that local representation which is so valuable an element of Parliamentary thought and of national life." The "living creature" that is a "communal existence," an "organic constitutional being with ideas, traditions, interests of its own, with a collective thought and will," a "real

---

[234] Hare, *Machinery of Representation*, 25.
[235] "Any electoral division founded solely on a geographical or territorial basis . . . has constantly to be reconstructed"; Hare, *Election of Representatives*, 61. His finest articulation of this point was present from the first edition, a full quarter-century before the switch to single-member districts which galvanized much of this discussion: "In the mobile and susceptible condition of population and society at this day, it is impossible not to observe the purely speculative character of all conclusions founded upon what the permanent interests of the inhabitants of a particular district may be, – upon what they will themselves consider them to be, or upon what their majority may resolve. In a revision of our electoral system, all those who would found the Parliamentary strength of interests or classes upon the basis of constituencies formed for their support, should consider with what degree of safety they can rely upon a body of electors within any certain area remaining permanently faithful to the principles by which they may be at present guided"; ibid., xxvii.
[236] Seymour, *Electoral Reform*, 496; Percy Greg, "Redistribution," 815.
[237] Hobart, "Parliamentary Reform," 264, 272.
[238] Hare, *Election of Representatives*, 41–2. Also Fawcett, *Leading Clauses*, 26–7.
[239] Lubbock, *Representation*, 8.

local existence and community" imbricated in "local institutions, corporations, municipal existence and government" – all were going to be "chopped" up into "inanimate machinery" by the "complete rupture" of 1884–5.[240] The defenders of the new organization of districts were not insensible to such worries, and when it came time to draw the new districts the bureaucrats in charge of doing so were instructed to respect the different "pursuits of the people" and to "take note of variety [of interests] and in a rough manner keep like with like."[241] But these instructions immediately raised problems of how to decide what counted as a "pursuit" and how to weigh certain kinds of interests against others[242] – and, moreover, even if these questions could be settled satisfactorily in one instance this would do nothing to address the damage anticipated from subjecting districts to frequent reconstruction. In trying to base the whole system of representation on a finely drawn set of geographical limits, single-member districts in fact undercut the organically developing localisms for which a parliamentary presence was rightfully due. Locality instead had to be represented by the free assent of voters to its importance – indeed, only under conditions where compulsion had been ended and the "widest scope and inducement for local combination," as for combination for any ends, been afforded could it be said that genuine local representation obtained at all.[243]

The PR reformer's insistence on the continuing place of locality within his post-territorial representative system raises two further issues. First, what it meant practically that "a real living society" like "Manchester"

---

[240] Percy Greg, "Redistribution," 814–15. And see John Heywood, a SNTV supporter, on how single-member districts would paradoxically destroy true spokesman of "important" local interests by "parochializ[ing] the representation" too much; Heywood, *The Representation of Minorities*, 3.

[241] *Report of the Boundary Commissioners for England and Wales, 1885. Part One: Counties* [C.-4287] (London, 1885), 7; Jones, *The Politics of Reform, 1884*, 9.

[242] Matthew Roberts, "Resisting Arithmocracy: Parliament, Community, and the Third Reform Act," *JBS*, 50 (2011): 381–409.

[243] *Election of Representatives*, xii. Intriguingly, a similar argument about the inefficacy of involuntary constituencies to further a specific set of interests or attachments would be deployed by Weber as part of his bitter attack against "electoral corporations" based on "*organic*' structures" in society and the economy. These "misconceived projects" would fall prey to "the autonomous operation of political interests": "when herded together in such electoral corporations, the supposed bearers of 'professional solidarity' would be set at one another's throats by denunciations and boycotts" and an "attempt to compel them to unite . . . would be a purely mechanical compulsion which would put an end to their inner life." The best way for interests, occupations, or classes to play a role in representative politics was, Weber concluded, to leave them to fight for adherents by "*free* recruitment," "free, independent initiative." Weber, "Suffrage and Democracy in Germany," in *Political Writings*, ed. Peter Lassman and Ronald Speirs (Cambridge, 1994), 80–129; Peter Baehr, *Caesarism, Charisma, and Fate: Historical Sources and Modern Resonances in the Work of Max Weber* (New Brunswick, 2008), 109.

would continue to figure in the Commons was that candidates who devoted themselves to these local interests or who expounded ideas native to the place would be returned;[244] unlike in list systems, where parties with centralized platforms were the objects of the vote, in STV one voted for candidates who retained every power to prioritize local questions over other issues. Second, as we have stressed repeatedly, MPs were to be returned by constituencies which were constructed by otherwise unaffiliated individuals opting to support the same candidate; STV was, therefore, formally agnostic about sociology, including no referents to groups within it. But this formal agnosticism and individualism did not restrain Hare and his ilk from invoking substantive sociological premises in explaining how their proposals would work. "Locality" was, after all, as much a corporate category as the "classes, interests, and opinions" compound that featured in variety-of-suffrages literature. Their confidence that "wholesome" localism would endure in a PR-chosen Commons, then, poses the question of the relationship between their individualistic electoral method and their own understandings of their society. How were these voluntary constituencies supposed to relate to social realities beyond the hustings? What sociological premises and assumptions guided Victorian PR?

d　Social Imaginaries and the Objects of Representation

Although Hare's innovation of voluntary constituencies was formally asociological, his and his followers' enthusiasm for it was attached to their understandings of the nature of their society and of the features of it which were relevant to a system of political representation. Strikingly, the sociological underpinnings of Victorian PR consisted of two quite different strands.

The first sociology was grounded in what Floyd Parsons has called Hare's "premise of pluralism."[245] The paragraph which best lays this out deserves quotation in full:

> A perfect *representation* is plainly inconsistent with the exclusion of minorities; but the subject of representation would be very inadequately conceived, if it were regarded as a mere question between majorities and minorities. The formation of electoral majorities and minorities is no more the natural means of arriving at political representation than it

---

[244] Percy Greg, "Redistribution," 814.
[245] Parsons, *Thomas Hare and Political Representation*, 142.

would be a natural result of any other association that it should be divided into two parties, one perpetually labouring to counteract the wishes of the other. The order and the occupations of mankind, – the distribution of population, and the supply of its necessities, are all provided for by physical and moral laws operating on the diversities of nature and of character which are found amongst men. These differences preserve the harmony and the vitality of social life. In political sentiment there is not less variety than in the other motives of human conduct, and abstractedly it would be no more likely that the political opinions of the electors of a borough should fall into two or three antagonistic divisions, than that they should be composed of twenty, fifty, or a hundred distinct views or conceptions. The dissimilarity would be much more probable than the similarity. Opinion and action in politics would be as various as opinion and action in other sciences, if there were not causes that enter into political bodies, and create a disturbed and unhealthy movement, provoking antagonistic divisions.

In keeping with the general bent of his thought, this observation about the wide extent of political diversity was a historicized one: "the extension of knowledge and the progress of civilization open the door of inquiry, prompt activity of thought, encourage diversities of opinion, and thus lead the way to social improvement."[246] The greater diversity in opinion in the contemporary world was a byproduct of the fact that there were simply more opinion-holders than ever before: "The progress of education and knowledge, the habit of reading, and of free and broad discussion, have vastly increased the number of the people who are capable of forming opinions for themselves."[247] Modern Britain, in short, had arrived at such a point in the march of progress that ideological diversity was now the norm.[248]

A few points should be stressed about this first strand of Hare's sociology. First, it was concerned with *opinion*; it was above all a sociology of political ideas. PR was preferable because it was respectful of "the natural and unrestricted operation of the variety of *opinions* and *sentiments* existing among a free people"; it was in view of "the varieties of *opinion* and *feeling*"

---

[246] Hare, *Election of Representatives*, xxix–xxx, 10. In giving diversity of opinion this modern accent Hare resembled, among others, Wilhelm von Humboldt, the Prussian philosopher and educationalist from whose manifesto of individual liberty and the limited state Mill would draw the epigraph for *On Liberty*. Humboldt had judged that "an infinitely richer and more satisfying moral and intellectual variety" distinguished modern Europe from antiquity or the Middle Ages; Humboldt, *The Sphere and Duties of Government*, trans. Joseph Coulthard (London, 1844), 17.

[247] Hare, "Just and Equal Distribution of Seats," 203.

[248] As in the treatment of territoriality, this was thus another respect in which Hare was happy to affirm that "the traditional method of filling the House of Commons" was "suitable . . . in earlier times" but not now; *Election of Representatives*, 75.

that his reform plan was required.[249] And the modern magnitude of ideological diversity was not just a sort of freestanding social fact, but was itself an
expression of the deep epistemological truth that "many sided all great
subjects are"[250] – a view which, notably, he had espoused even before
On Liberty's appearance and the commencement of his friendship with Mill.

Second, this notion of the diversity of opinion marked a divergence
from the theory of electoral variegation. As noted in Chapter 2, opinion did
have a kind of primacy on the variety-of-suffrages outlook, but Hare – at
least this side of Hare – differed from the adherents to this school in his
breathless awe at the extent of pluralism.[251] This perception of the sheer
vastness of the diversity of beliefs was a crucial reason why freedom was
such an important value in PR but not in the variety of suffrages. Both
schools believed that "Parliament should be a deliberative assembly" and
thus that all relevant points-of-view should be included.[252] For the variety-
of-suffragist, though, this category of relevant points-of-view was roughly
coextensive with and bounded by significant social cleavages, while for
Hare they were potentially inexhaustible and therefore any constraint in
the electoral system was likely to be prejudicial to some number among the
great "diversities of thought and sentiment."[253] In a truly free and open
system electors would "look into and consider the reasons" behind the
"various appeals" which they heard, and the "real representation" thereby
produced in the assembly would constitute a mosaic of the "varieties of
expression that have in modern times been called into existence."[254]

The third important point about this sociology of opinion was that, in
its emphasis on the great scope of ideological fragmentation, it seemed to
take a stand on the recurring question of the connection between class and
opinion: namely, running counter to much of the variety-of-suffrages
corpus, classes appeared here to be heterogeneous in opinion.
An "endless variety of thought and intelligence" was inconsistent with
the assumption that common class affiliation implied ideological
agreement.[255] This postulate of the ideological polyvalence of classes fit

---

[249] Hare, "Individual Responsibility," 358; *Election of Representatives*, 16 (my italics).

[250] Hare, *The Machinery of Representation*, 42.

[251] "Infinite variety of character and temperament" was observable even among "opinions which
approve themselves, and sympathies which are common to any considerable number of minds";
ibid., 26–7.

[252] Lubbock, *Representation*, 64.   [253] Hare, *Election of Representatives*, 16.

[254] Hare, "Reform Bill of the Future," 84; *Election of Representatives*, 128.

[255] Hare, "Representation of Every Locality and Intelligence," 528. He went on to quote Ruskin's
Modern Education: "Among all men, whether of the higher or lower orders, the differences are
eternal and irreconcilable between one individual and another."

awkwardly with a program of class representation,[256] and PR proponents could sound like the diverse democrats of the previous chapter in their espousals that "working men were as much divided in opinion as other classes."[257]

Indeed, the anthem of the naturalness of diversity of opinion could be sung so loudly as to sound in disharmony with one of the justifications for preferring PR to simple territorial democracy. This was for the reason that, if no "swamping" from the lower class could be anticipated because of the infinite array of differences in society, then it also looked unlikely that there could be any majorities or large pluralities which could claim enough victories in separate districts to monopolize seats or otherwise render the Commons gravely less inclusive.[258] It might look, then, as if Harean PR was a solution without a real problem to solve. The reason this was not so was that, for this strand of PR sociology, the locus of the problem of unrepresentativeness had been displaced from where it was situated by the variety-of-suffragist. Here, the brute numbers of a majority social group – the working class, or Irish Catholics – were not the primary cause of alarm. Instead, parties were. Since on this view a great class could not be the enemy of the accurate translation of opinions due to the fact that classes were not conceived as corresponding to ideology, parties took their place as the main enemies of this branch of proportionalists.[259] They – and their tendency to duopoly in plurality-rule arrangements[260] – were what created the defects of both descriptiveness and deliberativeness, compressing the domains of thought and sentiment that could make their way into an assembly that ought to have contained the full spectrum of shades of opinion in society. To Hare's disciples, those who accepted the two-party dominance of first-past-the-post were committing a similar sort of error to that which James Mackintosh had attributed to Benthamites – that

---

[256] It was, for instance, a major reason why the French inventor of PR, the mathematician Joseph Diaz Gergonne, had found more conventional plans for class representation, based on the fixed allotment of seats to specific groups, inadequate; compare Gergonne, "Arithmétique Politique. Sur les élections et le système représentatif," *Annales de Mathématiques*, 10 (1820), 281–8, with the class-representation treatise which he was criticizing, Pierre-François Flaugergues's *De la représentation nationale et principes sur la matière des élections* (Paris, 1820).

[257] Leslie Stephen, *Life of Fawcett*, 215. Stephen was paraphrasing Fawcett here, not speaking in his own voice.

[258] Ibid., 215.   [259] E.g. Hare, "Reform Bill," 77.

[260] E.g. Droop, *Political and Social Effects*, passim; Goldwin Smith, "The Political Crisis in England," in *Essays on Questions of the Day, Political and Social*, second edition (London, 1897), 103, 110–11. The first-mentioned essay here has been called a landmark in electoral theory for containing the first articulation of Duverger's Law; William Riker, "The Two-Party System and Duverger's Law: An Essay on the History of Political Science," *APSR*, 76 (1982): 753–66. Hare and other proportionalists, however, had already been operating with this idea in mind.

is, that they had a wrong notion of the electoral procedures that would yield a representative regime because they underappreciated the extent of diversity in their society.[261]

In addition to being a driver of the antiparty orientation of Victorian PR, one other aspect of this first sociological strand warrants attention. This is an ambiguity concerning the kind of existence which ideological diversity had. Hare and other PR theorists insisted on the naturalness of extensive diversity, but it was less certain whether it was natural in the sense that (a) in a proper electoral system it would arise or that (b) it was already there in the modern world. In other words, was PR going to (a) generate or promote the diversity of opinions, or (b) would it merely translate it into the Commons? This was, quietly and probably not very visibly to Victorians themselves, a fissure separating different camps within PR advocacy on the question of how electoral politics related to the intellectual life of the nation more broadly. For the most part, Hare came down on the side of (b). He treated the great array of political beliefs as a straightforward empirical reality, akin to the diversity in aesthetic tastes and life-projects which he considered characteristic of modern societies. Insofar as the sociology of opinion was concerned, PR's task was important but modest: to bring this diversity into the parliamentary arena.

It is arguable that side (a) – the more intellectually–sociologically ambitious side – also crept into Hare, for some passages read as if PR would *act on* the distribution of opinions and not simply reflect it better.[262] Yet on balance it seems safest to say that Hare meant to stay on the more modest terrain. Other writers, on the other hand, were willing to make weightier claims about the stakes of PR, such as the political economist and anti-imperialist Liberal Leonard Courtney. Courtney saw the implementation of PR as a matter of ensuring the possibility that a variety of opinions could exist at all; it promoted ideological pluralism by providing the atmosphere in which less popular opinions were viable, so to speak:

> And what is the effect to be apprehended [from single-member districts with a two-party system], not only on the representation of the people in Parliament, but on the condition of political life among the people themselves? Those who are not ready with the shibboleth of party must stand aside. Reduced to inactivity, their sterile existence ends in death. The springs of vitality are staunched. Removed from the sphere of political

---

[261] E.g. Droop's allegation that one of the greatest obstacles to PR's implementation was the "belief that our English division into two parties . . . is not due to artificial causes" but to nature; Droop, *Political and Social Effects*, 25.

[262] E.g. Hare, *Machinery of Representation*, 42.

energy they suffer, but the life of the country suffers with them . . . Variety of representation is wanted, not only that Parliament shall exhibit the competitive opinions of the nation, but also that opinion shall have everywhere the freedom and play of life.[263]

PR protected the realm of public opinion(s) from constriction and "death." It could accomplish this promotion of ideological diversity in virtue of a kind of cascading effect from the electoral-parliamentary arena to other realms of thought; the "emancipation of political thought" would trigger a "move onwards" toward greater "liberty" in "literature," "conversation," and even "silent speculation." Such a "great thing" would it be for PR to "set the nation free, to liberate the action of each political function, to give the opportunity of vitality and power to every new birth of political thought" that Courtney was able to contemplate unafraid the further expansion of the suffrage; democracy with PR was not a frightening prospect for the champion of liberty and diversity.[264] Courtney had a grandiose vision by which PR would turn Britain into a utopia of unshackled thought and expression, and in consequence he was comfortable disregarding dire predictions about how democracy would crush new ideas under the weight of majority tyranny and popular conformity.

Courtney's celebration of PR's potential to shape the emergence and distribution of opinions in society complicated further the fraught issue of the mirroring status of PR. Typically, he said his aim was a "representative chamber [that] would be a trustworthy mirror of the mind of the nation."[265] But in modern parlance we might say that he ran into an "endogeneity" problem here: by his own admission, the electoral system was not independent of the "mind of the nation" that it mirrored.[266] In truth, then, Courtney was posing the question of the desirability of PR not in the form "ought the electoral system to be an accurate mirror of the national mind?," but rather in the form "what kind of national mind ought we to want to be mirroring?" What Courtney desired was, at its most foundational level, a free and pluralistic national discourse – the intellectual-sociological *impact* of PR was to him its most treasured attribute.

---

[263] Courtney, "Seats Bill," 31.   [264] Courtney, "Political Machinery," 89–90.   [265] Ibid., 89.

[266] While they did not use the modern terminology, Victorian thought therefore did contain the insight into the endogeneity of opinion to the electoral system that Maurice Duverger would later make foundational for modern political science; Duverger, *Political Parties: Their Organization and Activity in the Modern State*, trans. Barbara and Robert North (New York, 1963), 380–2. As we will see in the final chapter, Victorian critics of PR were especially preoccupied by the fact that the electoral system did not merely reflect, but conditioned and molded, public opinion.

The appreciation of the natural diversity of opinions and the endeavor to represent (and perhaps even generate) multifarious streams of thought transcending the constraints of party was only one way in which Victorian proportionalists related their scheme to an image of society. The second sociological outlook contained a more traditional descriptivist preoccupation with classes and interests. "The sole and simple principle of personal representation," when inserted into this familiar matrix of sociological reasoning, seemed to differ from variety-of-suffrages schemes only in technique.[267] Rather than an exaltation of diversity and freedom of opinion in themselves or a move toward the subjectivization of politics,[268] its animating insights looked kindred to those of someone like Bagehot.[269] Indeed, this kinship could appear within the work of a single author: Lecky, who seems to have always regarded the variety-of-suffrages form of class representation as the best, nonetheless applauded "Hare's system" in the 1890s on the grounds that "under no other system would the representative chamber reflect so truly ... the various *classes, interests*, and *opinions* of the nation."[270] Even Wordsworth Donisthorpe, an ardent philosophical and political individualist,[271] praised PR's transcendence of territorial districts for making possible an improved representation of "important interests."[272]

These more traditional characterizations of the objects of representation were authorized by the way in which Hare himself had written of the units of representation. The inclusion of "interests" and "classes" still functioned in the Hare lexicon as a metric for determining the justness of the representative system.[273] In this light it should not be surprising that Mill himself flitted back-and-forth between (a) the position depicted first of preoccupation with the great diversity of opinions[274] and (b) this second,

---

[267] Hare, *Election of Representatives*, xxviii.   [268] Rosanvallon, *Peuple introuvable*, 130–47.

[269] Hence, despite his vigorous opposition to PR, Bagehot confessed to "a feeling of romance" about Hare's work before launching into harsh criticisms; *English Constitution*, 299–300.

[270] Lecky, *Democracy and Liberty*, vol. 1, 269 (my italics).

[271] Donisthorpe was one of the truly amazing Victorian polymaths. A self-proclaimed "philosophical anarchist," he wrote voluminously to apply Spencerian evolutionary-libertarian principles to many legal-political subjects. On his remarkable achievements across a range of fields including chess and film technology, see M. W. Taylor, "Donisthorpe, Wordsworth (1847–1914)," *ODNB*.

[272] Donisthorpe, *Individualism*, 53.

[273] His system "permitt[ed] every *class* to associate as the views of its members may dictate, without restraint of any boundary or district, and free therefore from the assaults of any adverse bodies who may invade their territories, or seek to undermine or usurp their franchise"; Hare, *Machinery of Representation*, 35 (my italics). Also *Election of Representatives*, 6, 233; Lytton, "Report on the Election of Representatives for the Rigsraad," 19

[274] It was in this mode that he spoke of "every mode of thinking which is shared by numbers" as "entitled" to a legislative presence; Mill, *Considerations*, 507.

more conventional mirroring stance according to which the "variegated character" of the assembly connoted the presence of "advocates" for all "interests" and "classes" and the prevention of the "most numerous class" from "swamp[ing] and politically annihilat[ing] all other members of the community."[275] For Mill as for Hare, PR served as both the parliamentary machinery for the intellectually, discursively freewheeling society of *On Liberty* in which even the most unpopular views received a hearing,[276] and an electoral plan that respected and carried on "the good points of class representation."[277]

These two sociologies were not logically incompatible, but there was a certain tension between them. This was due to the fact that endorsing class representation depended on the conviction that each class needed its own MPs, that due to the limits of "intelligence and imagination" only those belonging to the class in question could "understand" its "wants": a good Commons must "take account of[] the dispositions and circumstances of every class in the population. If any one class is dumb, the result is that Government is to that extent uninformed"; "a representative assembly of the Commons, without this element [of 'persons able to view all questions from *their* side'] is grossly defective."[278] For MPs to be identified with particular interests or classes, however, there had to be a group coherence behind these labels, a perspective proper to "advanced artisans" or "agricultural laborers" or "educated professionals." But this group coherence sat ill with the pronouncements of a kaleidoscopic welter of opinions which seemed to imply that socioeconomic position and other kinds of group-markers did not correlate with determinate political stances.

Recognizing the pervasiveness of this classical sociological strand in PR discourse is significant because, if the underlying sociology resembled that of the variety of suffrages, then the advent of PR marked more a technical than a substantive-normative change in representation. And this is precisely how Albert Grey, the nephew and heir of the Whig statesman examined earlier, understood it.[279] The younger Grey conceived of PR as

---

[275] *Considerations*, 465; "Recent Writers on Reform," 363. Mill dubbed this latter line of thought "conservative" in an attempt to woo Tory support (*Speech on Personal Representation*, 183).

[276] E.g. Mill, *On Liberty*, 229; Hare, *Election of Representatives*, 233.

[277] Mill, *Considerations*, 465.

[278] Courtney, "Representation of Minorities," 144–5; Hobhouse, *Liberalism*, 113; Hare, *Election of Representatives*, 37; Fawcett, "Mill's Treatise," 100.

[279] Albert Grey would become the Fourth Earl Grey upon his uncle's death in 1894, and would also serve as Governor-General of Canada in the early twentieth century; Carman Miller, "Grey, Albert Henry George, fourth Earl Grey (1851–1917)," *ODNB*.

the latest installment of the representative tradition to which his uncle had subscribed: "so long as there was a wide difference between the borough and county franchise, and a great variety in the size of the constituencies, the principle of community representation, as opposed to the individual, secured to us the variety in the representation which the different interests of the country demanded." The trouble was that "as soon as we establish in every constituency the same uniform electorate, the representation of localities no longer supplies us with any security for variety of representation ... We have hitherto secured this by the plan of variety of franchise and local representation." In 1884, though, with uniformity and an extensive suffrage about to be enacted, a different technique had to be adopted to pursue the same goal: "It by no means follows that because a particular method of election secured us a fairly representative House when we had a variety of franchise that it will do the same when we have a uniformity of franchise." In these circumstances of "uniform franchise over the whole kingdom," a "good House of Commons approximately reflecting the different interests of the country" could only be secured by abandoning territorial, communitarian methods in favor of "individual" methods.[280] But it was still by the justice it did to "interests," conceived much as his father and grandfather had done, that the machinery of representation was to be evaluated. Tethered to the traditional sociology of Britain in this fashion, mainstays of the movement such as Mill, Hare, Albert Grey, Sir John Lubbock,[281] and others could argue that they were presenting the next step in a continuous evolution of the British electoral system, the phase suited for a period when "anomalies in the representation" were being "swept away."[282]

If PR were just the latest stage in the representation of classes, interests, localities, and other such groups, then its formal individualism did not need to be thought of as violating or distorting a true "organic" representation of society and public opinion grounded in cohesive communities of

---

[280] Albert Grey, "Proportional versus Majority Representation," 937. For a slightly earlier statement of this logic of continuity, which ascribes this view to Mill as well, see *Mr. Albert Grey, MP, and the Redistribution of Seats* (Earl Grey Pamphlets, 1880), 9–16.

[281] Like the others listed here, Lubbock had a varied and interesting career. In addition to being a leading light of the PR cause from the 1880s onward and a prominent Liberal (then Liberal-Unionist) politician, he was a notable Darwinian natural scientist and anthropologist; Timothy Alborn, "Lubbock, John, first Baron Avebury (1834–1913)," *ODNB*.

[282] Hare, *Machinery of Representation*, 51. Also Bruce Kinzer, Ann Robson, and John Robson, *A Moralist In and Out of Parliament: John Stuart Mill at Westminster 1865–1868* (Toronto, 1992), 105–7, as well as the appendices to Lubbock, *Representation*, 67–75.

interest and sentiment.[283] Thus, as much as its "individualism" was cause for praise insofar as every other system set the individual voter in a "degrading subjection," this unshackling of the individual was not tantamount to a positive assertion of an atomistic view of public opinion.[284] The inherently communal nature of public opinion was indeed a presupposition of Hare's thought. This comes through, for instance, in a bizarre passage in which he contrasted his theory with the idea of the state of nature. Conceding that his individualistic system might look as if it instantiated an "anarchic" principle which would reduce the country "to a state of natural society," he then reassured readers that, on the contrary, the principle of PR was respect for "the natural tendency of association" and the "innumerable knots" which "linked and tied ... men to their fellows."[285] "The system of individual independence," Hare insisted, need not be grounded on an individualistic or atomistic social ontology.[286]

Before turning to the final piece of Hare's theory, the transfer mechanism, an additional point needs to be made about the proportionalists' sociological vision. First, noting the great importance that traditional communitarian categories retained in the thought of Hare and others helps to clarify a confused area of the secondary literature. The Victorian PR movement has often been described as "elitist."[287] There is truth in the description, but applied in a general manner it is too blunt to be helpful. Three components of Harean reform might warrant this label. One is the capacitarian cutoff for the suffrage, discussed in Section a of this chapter. A second will be examined in Chapter 5: the prediction that through the wider range of choice and the reduction of dictation by parties the personnel of the Commons would be improved.

A third "elitist" facet, however, pertained directly to the classical sociology of classes and interests on which we have been dwelling. Hare and his

---

[283] Hearn, *The Government of England*, 470.

[284] Hare, "Note," 105. On the territorial front Hare put it this way: "by enabling every unanimous quotient of actual voters to elect a member in the national representation, we not only avoid any disfranchisement, and preserve the corporate action of all counties, cities, and boroughs, but permit any number of additional boroughs to be created and enfranchised, provoking amongst them all a generous rivalry in the manifestation of public spirit"; "Reform Bill of the Future," 84. Or as he put it more succinctly: "individual independence [is] consistent with local and territorial interests, but not *è converso*"; *Election of Representatives*, xliii. Also Mill, "Recent Writers on Reform," 366.

[285] Hare, *Election of Representatives*, 80–2. And see Williams's assertion that the *fin-de-siècle* spread of "collectivism" was consistent with support for PR; *Reform*, 5.

[286] "Mr. Hare sought to introduce an organic element into our system of representation ... under the semblance of innovation [there is] the reality of an ancient practice"; Brown, *New Democracy*, 64.

[287] E.g. Parsons, *Thomas Hare and Proportional Representation*, 3, 187; Paul Smart, "'Some Will Be More Equal than Others': J.S. Mill on Democracy, Freedom and Meritocracy," *Archiv für Rechts- und Sozialphilosophie*, 76 (1990): 308–23.

followers identified the educated upper classes, especially in the great urban districts, as the most important of the groups or classes which STV would prevent from being swamped. Given the powerful trend toward an expansive uniform electorate, it appeared to many proportionalists that only "accidental circumstances which appear to be passing away" had previously provided for the inclusion of any members "but those who are chosen by the lower classes of electors, and those who concur with or conform to them"; the major thing to be warded off was "the danger of excluding from their just share in representation the more educated and intelligent classes."[288] Of the "many classes" whose "alienation ... from political life" looked to be on the horizon, it was the groups that made up "the wealthier and more instructed part of the nation," those "highly educated and public-spirited persons ... of the large towns," whose expulsion from the Commons Hare and company were most determined to prevent.[289]

The boast that STV would protect the urban professional, educated, and monied ranks was often attended with expressions of doubt about the preparedness of the working classes for political life,[290] and consequently a distrustful impression of PR as classist and countermajoritarian developed on the part of radicals and working-class reformers. The most telling thing about this third "elitist" factor, though, was how ordinary it was, how in keeping it was with the broad sweep of all sociologically concerned theories of representation in the period. For note that in order for this fear of working-class swamping under plurality rule to have traction, some version of a belief in working-class ideological homogeneity or identity politics à la Bagehot was required. Against the first, extreme-pluralist sociology, on this more traditional sociological outlook it was class that was again determining politics, at least in the lower rungs of society. Viewed from this angle, PR schemes differed from variety-of-suffrages ones only as these latter did

---

[288] Hare, *Machinery of Representation*, 2; *Election of Representatives*, xxxiv.

[289] Courtney, "Political Machinery," 84; Hobart, "Parliamentary Reform," 269. And Mill, Letter to Lord Overstone, 25 Mar. 1860, in *CW*, vol. 15, 690: "Mr Hare has discovered, what the best political thinkers have rather lamented the want of, than hoped to find – an effectual and practicable mode of preventing numbers, in a popular constitution, from swamping and extinguishing the influence of education and knowledge."

[290] E.g. Hare, *Machinery of Representation*, 44–5; C. L. Ten, "Democracy, Socialism, and the Working Classes," in *Cambridge Companion to Mill*, 372–95. Interestingly, despite his own conservatism on the suffrage Hare denied that "because, from the present state of popular education, the majority is especially liable to error ... it ought not to be entrusted with the franchise"; *Machinery of Representation*, 46. The under-education of the working class was an argument against its monopoly of the representation but not against its representation. It is not clear that this more inclusive attitude vis-à-vis the working class was consistent with his quite exclusive capacitarianism; certainly his guide on the suffrage question, Guizot, felt that the latter precluded the former.

among one another – that is, in the number of seats they were expected to put at the disposal of the various classes and interests.

Two sets of sociological premises, then, ran through the Victorian theorization of PR, with one prioritized by some authors, the other by different authors, and sometimes with both commingling uneasily in a single text. Was it urgent to adopt PR because modern nations such as Britain, having passed beyond the old class unities and hierarchies of traditional societies,[291] harbored a polyphonic welter of cross-cutting intellectual and cultural energies which ceaselessly produced ideological novelties of the most varied sort? Or did the appeal of PR rest on its promise to preserve much of the older nondemocratic liberalism – to conserve a space for each of a relatively small and discrete set of groups and classes whose presence in the assembly was threatened by the move toward a voting regime based on principles of equality and uniformity? Where the balance of proportionalists' theoretical investment lay between the two is tough to parse with precision, but ultimately the latter, more traditional side seemed to prevail. Thus, while PR introduced a new understanding of what it meant for the citizen to be represented and a new set of electoral techniques based around individual freedom, it could draw support even from thinkers whose hearts remained with the longer-standing mirroring school.[292] The most faithful adherents to Hare's system, of course, accepted his stringent claims about the individual right to authorize an MP, and regarded the implementation of PR as a matter of justice. But due to the persistence in their theories of so much of the social imaginary that had guiding mirroring reform from Mackintosh to Bagehot, they were able to appeal for a more circumstantial and pragmatic kind of support from contemporaries who simply sought a new technique for representing the old kinds of social diversity.

e The Transfer

If the previous subsection ended on a note of continuity, we now turn to what was indisputably a major and striking departure: the transferable

---

[291] E.g. Ostrogorski, *Democracy and Political Parties*, vol. I, 110.
[292] This is well illustrated by the way an enthusiast for Hare opened his pamphlet: with a recitation of all the great historical "authorities" upon "the true principles of parliamentary reform" from Burke on, the message being that they would of course have accepted PR as the modern functional equivalent for their own views in light of the changes to the representative system that had transpired; Frederick Calvert, *The Representation of Minorities* (London, 1881). See also the use which Sir John Lubbock made of the Third Earl Grey and Bagehot as authorities in his work; Lubbock, *Representation*, i, 71.

vote. There was no precedent in the British constitution for allowing the elector to list multiple preferences and then allocating his vote to the highest-ranked candidate to whose quotient it could contribute.[293]

The transferable vote was as controversial as any part of Hare's plan, but most of the controversy that it provoked occurred on the "moral" front of the following chapter: the most pointed parts of the disagreement about the transfer concerned opposed evaluations of its political and intellectual ramifications. The questions which complete this chapter's analysis of the conceptual apparatus of Victorian PR are somewhat different. They are: What was the *mirroring* value of the transfer? Was it primarily a mirroring device, or did it serve other purposes and stem from other grounds? The answers are not straightforward.

The cardinal way in which the transfer could be said to function as a mirroring device was in its encouragement of electors to vote their true preferences. This was in keeping with what has emerged as a core Harean principle, that of *mirroring-through-freedom*. Just as the transcendence of territoriality provided a more accurate gauge of opinion than did local districts by expanding the field of choice and reducing parties' stranglehold over the selection of candidates, the transfer increased electoral freedom by making it possible for citizens to cast their votes for their favored candidates even if their return was uncertain without fear that the votes would be wasted.[294] STV rendered it unnecessary to vote for the least-bad option out of concern for electability, and it therefore liberated the citizen to rank-order candidates in the way that best expressed his own beliefs, to "act upon his conclusions in all earnestness and sincerity."[295] As a result, a Harean parliament would be marked by the inclusiveness of a wider range of beliefs and a diminishment of the "stereotyping" of belief that party-dominance encouraged.[296] The transfer was a tool of emancipation, and this was emancipation in service of the revelation of the truth about the state of beliefs and preferences in society.

In contributing to the augmentation of electoral liberty, then, the transfer had a strong claim to mirroring credentials. On the other hand, a commitment to mirroring – even mirroring as understood in a strictly

---

[293] The first Englishman to think of a transfer mechanism was the schoolmaster Thomas Wright Hill. But he did not publish his researches and they were unknown in his home country until after Hare; Hart, *Proportional Representation*, 6–8; Thompson Cooper, "Hill, Thomas Wright (1763–1851)," rev. C. A. Creffield, *ODNB*.

[294] Hare, *Election of Representatives*, vii–viii, 121–2.   [295] Ibid., 144.

[296] Hare, "Just Expression" 203 and "Reform Bill of the Future" 77; Humphreys, *Proportional Representation*, 45, 55, 210–13.

proportionalist framework and not along the variety-of-suffragist lines of allotting "due weight" to preappointed sociological categories – did not demand that one support Hare's transferable vote. For two linked sets of reasons, the norm of mirroring, even in the wholly procedural sense of accurately translating the aggregate of individual voter preferences into legislative seats, hardly required the transfer mechanism. There were both (1) mirroring-based objections to the transfer and (2) programmatic alternatives that seemed to satisfy this version of mirroring equally well.

To begin with (1): recall that the transfer counts lower-ranked preferences equally with higher-ranked ones. Later preferences are only turned to if the above-listed candidate(s) have already attained the quota. But if brought into play, the tenth-listed choice is worth a full vote just as much as the top-listed one. This aspect of Hare's transfer provoked hostility for being distortionary or antidescriptive. Following the critique of the influential political scientist Graham Wallas, we might call this the "intellectual misconceptions" attack on STV.[297] According to this line of objection, STV was founded on an error of social psychology or political epistemology: namely, that it ignored the truth that the great bulk of citizens had a quite limited stock of genuine beliefs and opinions. To ask them to do more than choose their most preferred candidate, argued the Irish critic of STV James Creed Meredith, was to introduce votes that, because they were "late preferences," had no "value" as bearers of opinion.[298] To ask the elector to "arrange in order more names than there is time during the election to turn for him into real persons" was to introduce noise into the representative system, for the "ordinary citizen" lacked the capacity "to acquire a really clear conception of the personality" of very many candidates or of the "causes which they all advocate."[299] Nor was the problem simply that the late preferences called upon by STV did not correspond to real convictions worthy of impacting the national representation.[300] It was also that, even if the voter really did have an

---

[297] Graham Wallas, *Human Nature in Politics*, ed. Sugwon Kang (New Brunswick, 1981), 232.

[298] Meredith, *Proportional Representation in Ireland*, 70, 19. Meredith was a jurist, playwright, translator of Kant, and, despite his Protestantism, an Irish nationalist. He would go on to serve on the Supreme Courts of both the revolutionary Irish Republic and, later, of the Irish Free State; James Casey, "Republican Courts in Ireland, 1919–1922," *Irish Jurist*, 5 (1970): 321–42. Unlike the other opponents of STV covered in this book, Meredith attacked not out of allegiance to plurality rule but to list PR. There is some irony that the most intellectually serious champion of the party-list in these debates came from Ireland, one of the few nations which retains STV in the present day.

[299] Wallas, *Human Nature in Politics*, 238 and "The American Analogy," *Independent Review*, 1 (1901), 505–16, at 512.

[300] E.g. Dodgson, "Parliamentary Elections," 159.

ample supply of genuine opinions about the relative preferability of a long slate of politicians, he simply could not approach the later rankings on his voting-paper in the same spirit as he approached the first, since the odds of their actually serving as an effective vote were smaller.[301] It was simply untrue that, in the real world, a late preference was worth as much as a first preference, and yet STV depended on the pretense that they were "equal."[302] In consequence, it delivered a legislature that was not a true likeness of public opinion.

This intellectualist-fallacy critique was, surprisingly, continuous with an element of the variety-of-suffragist outlook: namely, it reinjected an element of "objectivity" in evaluating the condition of society and public opinion back into the theory of representation. For the likes of Wallas and Meredith, the rejection of STV was based on the belief that it did not accord with the relevant facts out there, and this was the kind of reasoning on which variety-of-suffragists founded the support for their schemes. This objection operated on a similar logic to that of the argument by which a Bagehot or Greg had excluded certain groups from the franchise altogether; it was the *opinion-holding criterion* of the more exclusive practitioners of the variety of suffrages transplanted from the sociological to the psychological/epistemological domain. The likes of Wallas and Meredith upheld the idea that only genuine opinions should participate in the electoral system, but they used it to discriminate between the various preferences of the individual rather than between the various segments of society.

Even if one was untroubled by this line of objection, though, it was still not obvious that the transfer was an appropriate instrument for advancing the legislature's mirroring capacity. Consider two alternatives to the transfer by the voter which were not liable to these criticisms of Meredith and Wallas, but which were consistent with the other dimensions of Hare's plan covered so far. Neither has been widely implemented, but tellingly both were listed as "proportional systems" in Clarence Hoag and George Hallet's *Proportional Representation* of 1926, which doubled as both one of

---

[301] Meredith offered a couple different formulations of the point: "Under the single transferable vote system he has only one vote, and for which candidate that vote may count is a matter of speculation on contingencies which it is difficult to estimate. As the contingency becomes more and more remote, the elector becomes more and more reckless"; "Under the single transferable vote system there is every inducement to vote for a crank, and he generally manages to amass a considerable number of late preferences. For most of us are cranks when probed as deep as a ninth or tenth preference"; *Proportional Representation in Ireland*, 65, 71.

[302] Ibid., 70.

the great early textbooks on electoral systems and a work of advocacy for STV.[303]

The first, which Hoag and Hallett named the "schedule system," replaced the voter-designated transfer with a *candidate*-designated one.[304] It was sometimes stipulated that before the election the candidate would publish a list of the other candidates to which his surplus of votes would be given, but this was not an essential provision; some proponents were happy simply to leave the transfer to the candidate without any binding declaration of how he would use it. For this reason I prefer to call it the *candidate-chosen* transfer, to highlight the real point of opposition with STV – that what Hare and company wanted done by the voter was now to be done by the politician who received the votes. Although it has been neglected in the historiography of political thought, this plan was actually endorsed by a few prominent Victorian writers on representation, including Oxford mathematician and literary genius Charles Lutwidge Dodgson (a.k.a. Lewis Carroll, author of *Alice in Wonderland*), the English barrister Walter Baily, and the Irish barrister Archibald Dobbs.[305]

The second was what Hoag and Hallett dubbed the "proxy system."[306] On this plan there is no transfer whatsoever; instead, a threshold of votes is established for election to the assembly, and then the voting power of each member is weighted according to the number of votes received beyond the threshold. Thus, in deciding on a bill the vote of a Gladstone might be worth, say, fifty times more than the vote of an obscure backbencher and twice as much as a respected Cabinet-level statesman. This proposal was rarer than the preceding, but it was eloquently advocated by the Christian Socialist John Malcolm Ludlow, who remarkably devised it a decade before Hare's innovations.[307] It shares a certain affinity with the countercurrent in early-/mid-Victorian English political culture, often associated with the

---

[303] Although both were American academics, Hoag and Hallett were very well-versed in English theory and institutions, and the Victorian context was central to their text.

[304] Hoag and Hallett, *Proportional Representation*, 53–6.

[305] Dodgson called this the "clubbing method," which he took to be the "chief novelty" of his "'Proportional Representation' scheme." He was wrong to think it novel, however, since both Baily and Dobbs had beaten him to it: Francine Abeles, "Introduction to 'Proportional Representation'," in *Political Pamphlets of Lewis Carroll*, 116, 119; Dodgson, *Principles of Parliamentary Representation*, 192–4; Baily, *A Scheme for Proportional Representation* (London, 1869); Dobbs, *General Representation, On a Complete Readjustment and Modification of Mr. Hare's Plan* (London, 1871). See also Ernest Naville's short summary of the first wave of thinking about this device in *La pratique de la représentation proportionnelle* (Earl Grey Pamphlets, 1882), 14–16.

[306] Hoag and Hallett, *Proportional Representation*, 57–9.

[307] Ludlow has claims to be the founder of Christian Socialism as well as the most explicitly democratic of its leading minds. He was both a critic of and sympathizer with Chartism, a major voice of the

influence of Thomas Carlyle,[308] which wanted to unshackle strong leaders in a way that parliamentarism historically had not, as well as with justifications of the gradual process of centralization of power in the cabinet against the assembly as a whole, although Ludlow himself did not justify it in those terms. In light of its potential to greatly empower a few very popular politicians, we might call this the *Caesarist assembly*.

Even this quick peek at these two alternatives is enough to suggest the crucial point: that Hare's version of the transfer was not self-evidently the device to employ if mirroring alone (or even mirroring plus the minimization of wasted votes) were the goal of reform. It is unclear why the weighting of voting power according to the share of first-preferences received, or why transferring at the candidate's discretion rather than the voter's, suffered any deficit of *mirroring* in comparison to the employment of the medley of higher and lesser preferences demanded by the transfer to secure equal quotas. Evaluating the Harean transfer-mechanism on the baseline of its ability to accurately reflect individual preferences could only be indeterminate, for it was, at the least, arguable that the Caesarist or candidate-chosen assembly was more faithful to the salient facts of parliamentary life and to the way in which opinions were actually held by electors than STV was. Dobbs, for instance, was emphatic that the switch to candidate-designated transfers was not just a remedy for the "practical difficulty" associated with voter-designated transfers, but was also an improvement in the assembly's representativeness:

> Each candidate can have only one seat in the House, and one vote in divisions of the House, but even now votes in the division list are of very different weight in the public estimation, though of equal voting power. A statesman of high character, by whatever constituency he may be elected, though it were the smallest and least important, has necessarily more weight and influence in the great council of the nation than an insignificant person, though he should sit for the largest borough or county in the realm ... The plan, as modified, herein, makes evident the general popularity of each statesman, and enables him to gauge it for himself at each election, just as

cooperative movement, and an important defender of the legal claims of working-class associations. Although representative institutions were not one of his primary topics, he was an interesting thinker on that score beyond his advocacy of the proxy system, including advocating an imperial parliament with colonial representation: Edward Norman, *The Victorian Christian Socialists* (Cambridge, 1987), ch. 4.

[308] E.g. Carlyle, *On Heroes, Hero-Worship, and The Heroic in History* (London, 1841).

the changing height of the mercury in a barometer shows the varying weight and ebb and flow of the atmosphere, or as the fluctuating quotations on the Stock Exchange are a sure indication of the rising or falling credit of States or Companies, and the shifting to and fro of investments.[309]

More remarkable still was Ludlow's articulation, as early as 1848, in the rush of Chartist agitation and Continental revolutions, of how only the proxy system could achieve the values which would later be espoused so ardently by Hare. By his plan alone would England "acquire at once the basis of a system of Equal Representation, capable of being enlarged to Universal Representation":

> Surely it is a partial disfranchisement of a constituency, when instead of a public man whom they know and trust in, they are obliged to put up with a mere voting automaton, thrust upon them as a sort of party stopgap. The electoral body is not fully represented, so long as its choice is fettered by the rule which forbids members from sitting for more than one constituency, and gives no more weight to the vote of a leading statesman than to that of the veriest cipher in his or the opposite party.
>
> The remedy for this ... consists in giving every member as many votes as he may find constituencies to elect him; just as in a joint stock company, shareholders are entitled to a number of votes proportional to their share in the capital. For government too, in constitutional countries, may be likened to a joint-stock company, the capital of which is public confidence.[310]

---

[309] Dobbs, *General Representation*, I, 16–17. Dodgson maintained in a complementary spirit that the "clubbing" or "candidate-chosen" technique accorded better with what it was actually like to want someone to represent you: "somebody shall decide how to use the surplus votes. But who? ... Surely the Electors would not have so much confidence [in anyone] as in *the man himself* [for whom he voted]. And to *him* I would refer the question, who is to have the surplus-votes. The Elector should be made to understand that, in giving his vote to A, he gives it him as an absolute property to treat as he will – either by using it to secure his own return, or to help another candidate of whom he approves, or (if there be none such in the field) by leaving it unused. If he cannot trust the man, for whom he votes, so far as to believe that he will use the vote for the best, how comes it that he can trust him so far as to wish to return him as Member?"; Dodgson, "Parliamentary Elections," 158–9.

[310] Ludlow, "Electoral Districts and the Representation of Minorities," in Ludlow, F. D. Maurice, and Charles Kingsley, *Politics for the People* (London, 1848), 211–13. See also in the same volume his "Universal Suffrage Not Universal Representation," at 13–14. Notably, Ludlow's support for the proxy system did not diminish after encountering STV, for he maintained against Hare that "if ten, twenty constituencies should desire to be represented by Mr. Gladstone or Mr. Disraeli, why should not Mr. Gladstone or Mr. Disraeli ... be entitled to ten, twenty votes in the House of Commons? Why should anyone be debarred from being represented by the member of his choice, simply because too many others of his countrymen are of the same mind with him"; Ludlow, "Mr. Hare's Scheme of Parliamentary Representation," *CR*, 9 (1868): 80–97.

As Ludlow saw it, to force public opinion to be represented via so many tiny, equal channels was to distort it; it was, he thought, untrue that Gladstone, Peel, or Palmerston *just* stood for a single constituency in the same way as some unknown backbencher.[311]

If the superiority of STV could not be proven by appeal to the value of mirroring alone, it had to be preferred, ultimately, on another ground. And this was the conviction that these alternatives would undercut the possibility of the kind of assembly that Hare, STV advocates, and indeed a broad consensus among thinkers about representation wanted. Such an assembly had to be numerous to include many shades of opinion and interest such that a working division of epistemic labor might form; it had to avoid being given over to a monopoly of any social group or all-powerful figure such that "will" might silence reason; it had to possess a margin of independence from party dictates and from temporary shifts in desire at the local level; it had to empower candidates to follow their consciences and to debate in good faith. What Hare's version of the transfer could do better than these other "proportionalist" arrangements, he and his followers believed, was deliver a true "deliberative body," make the Commons a "place where every interest and shade of opinion in the country can have its cause even passionately pleaded, in the face of the government and of all other interests and opinions, can compel them to listen, and either comply, or state clearly why they do not."[312] Even in the 1910s, when the luster of the deliberative Commons had waned due to the rise of mass parties, the growth of the administrative state, and the executive's increasing dominance over the legislature,[313] it was still a core element of the STV creed that "duties of discussion" were preeminent in Parliament and that the "common will" which its legislation was meant to embody required that every section of "the opinion of the community" be given "consideration" within it.[314]

---

[311] Even the young Bagehot had defended the Imperial practice of Louis Napoleon specifying his candidates before elections to the National Assembly with arguments that could justify Ludlow's scheme: "Nor do I concur with those who censure the President for 'recommending' avowedly the candidates he approves. It is a part of the great question, How is universal suffrage to be worked successfully in such a country as France? The peasant proprietors have but one political idea, that they wish the Prince to govern them; – they wish to vote for the candidate most acceptable to him, and they wish nothing else. Why is he wrong in telling them which candidate that is?"; Bagehot, "Letters on the French Coup d'État of 1851," 81.

[312] Mill, "Recent Writers on Reform," 358; *Considerations*, 424, 433.

[313] E.g. Harold Laski, "The Problem of Administrative Areas," in *The Foundations of Sovereignty and Other Essays* (New York, 1921), 36–7.

[314] Williams, *Proportional Representation and British Politics*, 19.

As with the variety-of-suffragist or the diverse democrat, the Victorian proportionalist was guided not by an isolated ideal of representativeness, but by this ideal as it was shaped by a theory of deliberation and a commitment to a certain image of the Commons.

And it was because they conflicted with this broader image, and not because they failed the test of mirroring per se, that mainstream PR supporters rejected these other proportionalisms. To them, let alone to conventional plurality rulers, the proposals of Ludlow, Dobbs, and Dodgson seemed to have gone through the looking glass. The candidate-chosen transfer was liable to the objection that it would further tighten the grip of parties, thus compromising the prospects for true deliberation in the assembly; it appeared like a less straightforward version of the dreaded party-list system,[315] which Victorian reformers, in their desire to temper or even transcend disciplined parties, regarded with horror.[316] The proxy system was even worse: in taking the unprecedented step of abandoning the "very old tradition" of "the equality of members in a representative body,"[317] it threatened to implant something resembling plebiscitary or presidential government within liberal representative structures. These lesser-known schemes laid claim to robust mirroring credentials, and with reason: they could not be said to translate the preferences of the electorate into the composition of the assembly incorrectly in any obvious

---

[315] E.g. John Chapman, "Politics, Sociology, Voyages, and Travels," *WR*, 41 (1872), 525. The fact that Meredith, who trumpeted list over STV, judged Dobbs's scheme a "considerable improvement" over Hare's further supports the impression that it seemed to be more on the list side of the PR spectrum; Meredith, *Proportional Representation in Ireland*, 45.

[316] It is importantly not an anachronism to say that even early figures such as Hare preferred candidates over parties as the object of the vote: he and all conscientious Victorian reformers were aware of the progress of list systems elsewhere; e.g. Hare, "Minority Representation in Europe," *Journal of Social Science*, 3 (1871), 185–91. Their distaste for this alternative was expressed characteristically and bitingly by Mill: "Is representation of parties all we have a right to demand from our representative system? If that were so, we might as well put up three flags inscribed with the words, Tory, Whig, and Radical, and let the electors make their choice among the flags, and when they have voted, let the leaders of the winning party select the particular persons who are to represent it ... Why is it, then, that such a system of representation would be intolerable to us? Sir, it is because we look beyond parties; because we care for something besides parties; because we know that the constitution does not exist for the benefit of parties, but of citizens; and we do not choose that all the opinions, feelings, and interests of all the members of the community should be merged in the single consideration of which party shall predominate. We require a House of Commons which shall be a fitting representative of all the feelings of the people, and not merely of their party feelings. We want all the sincere opinions and public purposes which are shared by a reasonable number of electors to be fairly represented here; and not only their opinions, but that they should be able to give effect by their vote to their confidence in particular men"; Mill, *Speech on Personal Representation*, 182.

[317] Hoag and Hallet, *Proportional Representation*, 58; Hearn, *Government of England*, 509.

way.[318] Nonetheless, they were anathema to Victorian PR – so much so that its champions did not even deign to argue against the proxy system, but simply ignored it. STV was, then, far from a neutral "report" of what was "out there," even if it avoided what it saw as forms of arbitrariness in other systems. Like the variety-of-suffragist, albeit to a different degree, Hare and company were engineering the machinery of representation not just to mirror society, but to ensure the existence of a certain sort of assembly.

Rather unexpectedly, then, this subsection closes on a note similar to the previous one. The most exotic aspect of Hare's reinvention of representation – the transfer – in fact manifested the depth of his fidelity to the historic parliamentary model. Above all else, Hare was a devotee of something close to the "Whig" ideal of a Commons at once educative, enlightened, diverse, and deliberative. His aim was to permit the assembly to continue to meet these criteria even after the utility of "the traditional method of filling the House of Commons" had ceased; he pursued traditional ends by the only means he thought adequate to them – namely, nontraditional ones.[319]

This conclusion fits the basic arc of nineteenth-century political thought. PR was essentially a product of a transitional age in the perception of representative government. The mid-century was the zenith of prestige for parliamentarism, but as the decades rolled on it became increasingly common to depict a crisis of parliamentary government, with the "mother of Parliaments" suffering from "declining respect."[320] As with his anxieties about the tightening grip of centralized partisanship, which anticipated by a decade or so the main chorus of complaints about party government replacing parliamentary government, Hare was among the earlier voices to

---

[318] "*Contemplating only the nature of an election* . . . it undoubtedly appears that electors numbering three, five, or ten times the electoral quota are entitled to choose the same proxy and to entrust him with three, five, or ten votes, and that to prevent several electoral groups from entrusting their proxies to the same representative, is a limitation of their liberty which is not necessitated by the nature of things. But the object of the election is to secure the investigation of subjects by means of parliamentary debates. If the accumulation of votes on the same deputy were allowed, it might happen that an electoral body divided into two camps, concentrated its votes on two men, one of whom would have more votes than the other and would be able to decide everything by himself. Discussion would thus be suppressed by the election of a *legislative dictatorship*"; Naville, *Theory and Practice of Representative Elections*, 11 (my italics). It is illuminating to compare such a passage with Schmitt; *Crisis of Parliamentary Democracy*, 34–5.

[319] Hare, *Election of Representatives*, 75.

[320] Lubbock, "Proportional Representation," reprinted in *Political Pamphlets of Lewis Carroll*, 140–4, at 144 (originally published in the *Daily News*, 15 May 1884); Lecky, *Introduction to Democracy and Liberty*, vii.

fret about the "diminution of that respect with which the House of Commons is now regarded."[321] When many of his peers still believed that the electoral-parliamentary system was functioning healthily if not perfectly, he was already viewing his mission as restorative.[322] Consequently, in its early decades PR came under fire for being based in an alarmist, inaccurate diagnosis of the status quo: critics charged that Hare was offering a cure worse than the disease, that in trying to fix Parliament he was jeopardizing something that was not broken in the first place. Later, as the century drew to a close, with faith in parliamentary government crumbling, PR proponents stood out for their unshaken devotion to the old ideal.[323] Instead of contending that the PR camp was unduly critical, opponents now argued that their fidelity to the classical model of the Commons was quixotic; PR, they thought, was ill-equipped to stem as strong a tide as "the almost universal decline in the reverence felt for elected assemblies."[324] Throughout the political and intellectual shifts of a half-century, Hareans remained devoted to a familiar interpretation of what parliamentary politics involved. It is to the distinctive spin which they put on the norms and ends of parliamentarianism, and the equally distinctive avenues of thought which appeared in response, that we now turn.

---

[321] Hare, *Election of Representatives*, 102.

[322] In this regard Hare was in a position parallel to that of his friend Mill on the liberty of thought: the bleakness of Hare's assessment of then-current parliamentary politics struck many of his contemporaries as exaggerated in the same way that Mill's cries against his society's despotic conformity did. See e.g. R. W. Church, "Mill on Liberty," in *Liberty: Contemporary Responses to John Stuart Mill*, ed. Pyle (South Bend, 1994): 210–54.

[323] The goal of restoring public faith in the Commons remains powerful in STV advocacy; see e.g. S. A. Walkland, "Parliamentary Reform, Party Realignment, and Electoral Reform," in *The Politics of Parliamentary Reform*, ed. David Judge (Guildford and King's Lynn, 1984): 37–53.

[324] Dicey, "The Political Situation: 'On the Brink of an Abyss'," *NC*, 67 (1910), 784.

CHAPTER 5

Diversity with Democracy? Proportional Representation

Part Two: The Debate on PR's Moral and Political Effects

There is not an airtight separation between the subject matter of this chapter and that of Chapter 4. In analyzing the conceptual foundations and technical machinery of Victorian PR, we were inevitably led to consider some of the values – for example, electoral liberty – which it was intended to realize. The Victorians, obsessed as they were with the "*spirit* of the institutions of a country,"[1] would not have minded such trespassing, for they were keenly aware that considerations of the technical aspects of an electoral system were ultimately undetachable from moral judgments.[2] Nevertheless, there is a shift between the two chapters, parallel to that between Chapters 1 and 2. The preceding chapter focused on the question "what kind of institution was Victorian PR?" This one, on the other hand, takes up the question "what were the 'moral' effects which PR was supposed to have?"[3] In addition, this chapter features more centrally the opposition between proponents and critics of PR, reflecting the fact that controversy over the adoption of an institution tends to take place much more on the terrain of weighing values and predicting effects than at a technical–conceptual level.[4] Appropriate to the Victorian era's "moralistic" political climate, gauging the effects of PR on the character of public life occurred on hotly contested turf.

This chapter reconstructs the "moral" cases for and against PR. Though detailed, it does not aim at comprehensiveness. The ameliorative impact

---

[1] Mill, *Considerations*, 478.

[2] E.g. Duncan Black, *A Mathematical Approach to Proportional Representation: Duncan Black on Lewis Carroll*, ed. Iain McLean, Alistair McMillan, and Burt Monroe (New York, 1996), 14.

[3] To adapt a distinction from Christian List: from a focus on its *mechanical* dimensions, we now attend primarily to PR's *behavioral* effects; List, "The Discursive Dilemma and Public Reason," *Ethics*, 116 (2006): 362–402. The adjective "moral" is throughout construed broadly in the Victorian fashion to include political, cultural, ethical, and intellectual factors, as in their use of the phrase "moral science" to designate the whole gamut of what we would now call the social sciences; Theodore Porter and Dorothy Ross, "Introduction," to *The Cambridge History of Science, Vol. 7: The Modern Social Sciences*, ed. Roy Porter, Theodore Porter, and Dorothy Ross (Cambridge, 2003), 1–10.

[4] André Blais, "Introduction," to *To Keep or to Change First Past the Post? The Politics of Electoral Reform*, ed. Blais (Oxford, 2008): 1–6.

that Hare's school awaited from its reform was as "many-sided" as their social epistemology believed truth itself to be; as one American disciple wrote, PR would be "a specific against almost all the ills of government."[5] Consequently, I will not canvass the whole assortment of advantages to the "life of the nation" that were supposed to follow – nor, conversely, will I survey the entire range of counterclaims from PR's opponents.[6] Two areas, in particular, will take second rank in my investigation. First are topics common in the modern political science literature, such as the comparative efficiency of FPP versus PR governments. Second, as this study has hopefully made clear, PR was part of a family of discourses and institutional designs oriented toward a mirroring Commons. Fittingly, its moral and practical justifications were a mix of those peculiar to its adherents and those shared with the longstanding English descriptive tradition. At the limit, supporters who saw PR as merely an updated mechanism for "admit[ting] *all the interests* of the community," "contain[ing] in itself no novelty in point of principle,"[7] could simply appropriate the arguments of the variety-of-suffragists. Yet, befitting such a technically innovative proposal, complete continuity of moral argumentation was rare. Hare and his followers articulated a singular set of benefits in the promulgation of their reform even as they drew on arguments developed for other institutional settings. This study prioritizes those lines of thought that were most distinctive to PR; where they did not offer at least a new spin on an old song, PR champions' views will not enter here.

The chapter proceeds as follows: Section 1 depicts the cardinal benefits that were distinctively associated with PR. These were chiefly concentrated in two domains. First was the improvement of the caliber of individual MPs such that the legislative personnel would consist of a true elite. Notably, however, PR champions believed that their reform would not only improve the makeup of the legislature, but would also spark a moral and intellectual advance in the citizenry. These two benefits were linked by a libertarian hopefulness which saw the individualistic innovations discussed in Chapter 4 as sufficient to unleash a wholescale revolution in the

---

[5] Simon Sterne, *On Representative Government and Personal Representation* (Philadelphia, 1871), 15. He claimed here to be citing Mill, though it was actually a slight misquote. The presentation of STV as a panacea for a whole host of societal maladies continues in modern British PR advocacy; David Judge, "Introduction," to *The Politics of Parliamentary Reform*: 1–8.

[6] Courtney, "Representation of Minorities," 151; Robert Collier, *The Representation of Minorities* (London, 1868), 14.

[7] Calvert, *The Representation of Minorities*, 6; Ludlow, "Mr. Hare's Scheme of Parliamentary Representation," 80.

character of public life, including the breaking of (what they considered) the intolerant and oligopolistic control of the political process exercised by parties. Bolstered further by an original series of reflections on the sources of stability in representative government, the optimistic expectations of PR advocates constituted an expansive and ambitious moral project.

Sections 2 and 3 then take in turn two major streams of criticism from PR's opponents. Section 2 depicts a "Millian" set of rebuttals based on the conviction that PR's individualistic methods would undermine the dynamism and antagonism of British political culture and inaugurate a period of stagnation. It also examines criticisms that Hare and his disciples operated with an excessively intellectualized picture of how citizens navigated political life. Section 3 discusses objections that PR was grounded in an improper understanding of parties. On this front, Hare's system was attacked from opposite sides: on the one hand, for perniciously strengthening the control of party apparatuses; on the other, for failing to appreciate the indispensable positive functions that parties had to play in an increasingly democratic nation. Through these lines of debate, the question of PR provided an important forum in which Victorian thinkers grappled with the rise of the extra-parliamentary domains of public life and the concomitant decline of the parliamentary assembly from its unchallenged perch atop the deliberative polity.

1   The Moral Benefits of PR

Because such an expanse of "possible results" was attributed to PR by its champions, it can be tough to get a handle on the moral side of PR.[8] Some clarity can be gained, however, by dividing up the terrain into two channels of improvement. While the border between them was porous, it is helpful to approach Victorian PR as positing advantages arising from two basic causes: the freedom and efficacy of the vote, and the inclusiveness of the assembly. We begin with the former, for, as the more peculiar property of its electoral machinery, it was the generator of a greater number of claims original to the PR school.

a   Freedom and Efficacy

What sort of improvements would follow from the elimination of constraints on the disposal of the vote and the related augmentation of the

---

[8] Hare, *Election of Representatives*, 169.

efficacy of the vote (the likelihood that it would make up part of a quota to select a candidate rather than be "wasted")? Electoral liberty was expected to work a positive change in British public life through three main avenues.

i Cleaning up Corruption

A first area can be addressed with relative brevity, for it has been touched on already and was not unique to PR.[9] This was the problem of corruption. Nonetheless, if concerns about corruption were common, supporters of "Mr. Hare's arrangements" had a unique understanding of how "bribery and intimidation" could be diminished.[10]

The ultimate, long-term fix for this problem was the moral elevation of the citizenry which PR promised to foster.[11] But there were also reasons to think Hare's plan could have an immediate effect on countering these ills.[12] Two mechanisms for diminishing the extent of "bribery and intimidation and other forms of corruption and undue influence" were especially salient.[13]

First, in plurality-rule territorial contests, bribery flourished because, where the outcome was at all uncertain, candidates felt compelled to buy off the "margin of electors" that were "neutral or indifferent" in order to gain the narrow edge that might decide the election.[14] This system drove up election expenses, which were extremely high in these decades.[15] The exorbitant cost of campaigning worked to the advantage of two small cadres: (a) "the wealthy," who could shoulder the financial burden; and (b) the "wire-pullers" and "electioneers" in major parties, who knew how to direct funds to the most corruptible portion of the electorate and who were practiced in the arts of coordinating the purchase or intimidation

---

[9] On electoral-parliamentary corruption, see Cornelius O'Leary, *The Elimination of Corrupt Practices in British Elections, 1868–1911* (Oxford, 1962). Hare was typical in seeing corruption both as "more extensive, systematic, and effectual" than it had been in previous generations and as liable to grow even greater if one "extend[ed] the suffrage under the present system"; Hare, *Election of Representatives*, 87–8; "Representation in Practice and Theory," 193–5.

[10] James Thornton Hoskins, *A Modification of Mr. Hare's Scheme for the Election of Representatives*, second edition (London, 1860), 12.

[11] E.g. Maurice's brief comments on PR: "To utter the phrase, 'The suffrage is not a privilege so much as an obligation' is easy; to awaken the sense of obligation in our own minds or in the minds of working men is the difficulty. Mr. Hare's scheme would remove one chief hindrance to the efforts of those who try to awaken it. It would give the suffrage another than a market value"; Frederick Denison Maurice, "The Suffrage, Considered in Reference to the Working Class, and to the Professional Class," *MM*, 2 (1860), 97.

[12] PR would confine corruption "within such natural and inevitable limits as to take from it nearly all its political and most of its personal evil"; Hare, *Election of Representatives*, vii.

[13] Droop, *Political and Social Effects*, 8.   [14] Ibid., 9.

[15] Hanham, *Elections and Party Management*, chs. 12–13.

of voters.[16] Hareans, then, aligned with other reformers in decrying the role of corruption in transforming the Commons into a plutocratic body,[17] although they tended to place greater emphasis than their contemporaries on the connection between the explosion of election costs and the tightening of the control of parties. In their minds, however, PR alone could counteract the upward spiral of electoral expenses due to the various forms of "treating" required to win over marginal voters. They reasoned that, where the goal was not to beat out one or two contenders for a local seat but instead to obtain a "quota" that could be collected from votes across the nation (or at least from a much larger constituency[18]), the "pecuniary value of every vote" would be "reduce[d] to its minimum."[19] By simple laws of supply and demand, PR's transcendence of local constituencies would render the baser forms of corruption less enticing.[20]

Second, the implementation of PR would, its advocates promised, limit corruption by quarantining it.[21] Because candidates who were resistant to bribing or intimidating voters could now abstain from such artifices if they could gather the support needed to reach the quota from across the nation, "upright and conscientious electors" needed not fear that their preferred candidate would be denied his place in Parliament because "the corrupt portion of the constituency" had been paid to "turn the scale of balanced parties."[22] While a particular plutocrat or social climber might still manage to bribe his way to a quota, his achievement of a place in the Commons, although corrupt, would no longer have been gained by "overpower[ing] in any particular borough the efforts of the upright electors." Further, the infamy that would fall upon MPs who might yet happen to gain their seats in such a manner would be greater, they predicted, than under the current

---

[16] Hare, *Election of Representatives*, 87; Fawcett, *Leading Clauses*, 11, 22, "Mill's Treatise," 102.

[17] For a classic mid-Victorian castigation of "plutocracy," see Mill, "Speech of 4 April 1864 on Corruption at Elections," in *CW*, vol. 28, 10–11. For a major statement from the end of our period, see Hilaire Belloc and Cecil Chesterton, *The Party System* (London, 1911).

[18] M. G. Fawcett, "Proportional Representation," 381.

[19] Hare, *Election of Representatives*, xxiii–xix.

[20] "Under a system which, as now, places two candidates in competition, and makes the local success of one involve the defeat of the other, it becomes of intense importance to gain the indifferent, the waverers, and all whom bribery will reach. Candidates, their supporters, even men of character and position, on both sides, now commonly vie with one another in resorting to every means of influencing enough voters to turn the scale. Votes thus rise in value, and acquire what economists call the scarcity price"; Hare "Individual Responsibility," 354.

[21] "The method of unanimous quotas encounters this moral disease in a manner analogous to that with which the physician deals with disease. If cholera or typhus be prevalent, he first endeavours to isolate it – to deal with existing cases in such a manner that it shall be prevented from spreading to those in health"; ibid., 354.

[22] Hare, "Reform Bill of the Future," 81–2.

system where recognition of the necessity of not allowing uncommitted voters to be bought off by one's opponent had diminished the "obloquy" that ought to have been attached to such tactics.[23]

Before turning to our next topic, it should be noted that the expectation that PR would counteract electoral corruption was important for one further reason: that it permitted supporters more easily to reject that more celebrated anticorruption device, the ballot[24] – a rejection which dovetailed closely with the sense of the elector's great moral responsibilities that coursed through the campaign for PR.[25]

ii   Improving the Legislative Personnel

In its approach to corruption, the PR movement differed comparatively little from the conventional wisdom of the age.[26] In contrast to their treatment of the "tendency and temptation to bribery," however, the endeavor to theorize how their system could attain another important good led them into territory more truly their own. This was the PR contingent's pledge to "prodigiously improve the *personnel* of the national representation."[27]

Victorian PR's evaluation of the quality of MPs diverged from much contemporary opinion. As has been stressed hitherto, dissatisfaction with the existing social-ideological composition of the Commons was common to all who sought a more inclusive Parliament. Yet, from Bagehot through early labour representation leaders,[28] this dissatisfaction with the descriptive or inclusive dimension of the Commons was surprisingly rarely accompanied by attacks on the ability of MPs as individuals. To the contrary, Victorian PR's negativity toward the "present system" derived

---

[23] Hare "Individual Responsibility," 354–5.

[24] "[Hare's] scheme will be a far more effectual check to bribery, and other sinister influences, than the ballot," Hoskins, *Modification*, 12.

[25] E.g., Hare, "Representation in Practice and Theory," 193; H. S. Jones, "John Stuart Mill as Moralist," *JHI*, 53 (1992): 287–308.

[26] The exception to this consensus was a set of figures who held on to the eighteenth-century attitude that corruption did not interfere with the nation being represented. A tenderness for this lenient view could creep into even some of the authors we have covered (including Greg and Grey); see Selinger, "Fighting Electoral Corruption in the Victorian era: An Overlooked Dimension of Mill's Political Thought," *EJPT* (forthcoming).

[27] Mill, "Recent Writers on Reform," 362.

[28] E.g. the remarks of the early working-class MP Thomas Burt in Humphrey, *History of Labour Representation*, 62. See also John Shepherd's reconstruction of the "Lib-Labs" and the working-class tradition they inherited, in which the desire for the inclusion of "a social class hitherto excluded" was largely detached from attacks on the ability of sitting parliamentarians; Shepherd, "Labour and Parliament: the Lib.-Labs. as the First Working-Class MPs, 1885–1906," in *Currents of Radicalism*: 187–213.

not only from its exclusion of the "great varieties of opinions and sympathies" but from the want of "personal standing, elevation of character, or integrity of purpose" that characterized the average legislator.[29] So vexing did Hare find the dearth of men of "a higher order of intelligence" among MPs that he turned to the rhetoric of divine retribution. An arrangement under which "the so-called representative" was likely not to "possess a single quality fitting him for the high trust committed to his care" demanded to be "cleansed"; it was urgent to achieve the "purification of the temple which has been thus defiled" by supplying the glaring "want of . . . wisdom and integrity" in the parliamentary personnel "lest we realise the other part of the Gospel parallel, and our last state be worse than our first."[30]

Hare's judgments on the caliber of sitting MPs were especially vehement. But the aspiration to renew a body overfull of "the local grandee . . . who neither has, nor deserves to have, the smallest influence anywhere" by the infusion of "m[e]n of talents and virtue" spanned the movement.[31] The claim that STV would turn this medley of mediocre characters into a house "containing the very *élite* of the country" would be a central theme of PR through the First World War.[32]

As we move through the multilayered logic behind its claims to produce a set of MPs more fit for their duties, it is important to bear in mind that the population of the assembly with "better men" was ultimately to be generated by *liberty* (with a helpful assist from the transfer device).[33] Emancipating the elector would, they predicted, suffice as a remedy for

---

[29] Hare, *Machinery of Representation*, I, 43, 4.

[30] Hare, *Election of Representatives*, 214, 105, 89–90.

[31] Mill, "Recent Writers on Reform," 362. As Millicent Garrett Fawcett put it, the objective of PR was to deliver the nation from rule by "promoter[s] of false and fraudulent companies," "religious bigot[s]," and "m[e]n who ha[ve] never read a book or had an idea"; "Proportional Representation," 380. The widespread Victorian belief in the low caliber of American politicians – inherited from Tocqueville and repeated ad infinitum – also lent itself readily to a pro-PR spin: "the absence of the first intellects in the country from the helm of public affairs," a fact which "has brought discredit upon free government ... in the United States," was due to FPP; Hobart, "Parliamentary Reform," 266.

[32] Mill, *Considerations*, 312. And compare, for example, Hare on how plurality-rule methods caused "the discouragement of the best men and the tempting of the worst men to aspire to the more elevated positions of the State" with H. G. Wells on how the "best men" would enter Parliament because the "difference in effect between Proportional Representation and the old method of voting must ultimately be to change the moral and intellectual quality of persons profoundly." Hare, "Representation in Theory and in Practice," 194; Wells, *In the Fourth Year* (London, 1918), 127–8.

[33] This phrase became a standard part of the lexicon of PR among American progressives; Kathleen Barber, *Proportional Representation and Electoral Reform in Ohio* (Columbus, 1995). Though Barber is attuned to the Victorian origins of the American debate on PR, she does not observe that this element of it was a direct importation from Britain.

the deficit of "personal merit" in the legislature.[34] This was because this deficit was the product of obstacles to the realization of the elector's true preferences which existed only because of *constraints* on his disposal of the vote.

These constraints were essentially three, although they tended not to be distinguished with much analytical rigor. The "method of local majorities" hindered conscientious and intelligent citizens from entering Parliament by forcing them to submit to the interlinked forces of: (a) local prejudices and demands; (b) local political kingpins; and (c) party machines.[35] Depicting these obstacles – often in lurid, hyperbolic terms – accounted for a great deal of the ink spilled by PR authors over these decades.

First, a system based on small geographic constituencies discouraged the man of integrity who held opinions out-of-step with those of the local population from standing for office at all, since to do so would require him to employ "time-serving arts" and make "sacrifices of his convictions to the local or class prejudices and interests of any given set of electors." With a single national constituency or a set of large constituencies, the holder of minority beliefs could take heart from the expectation that his "spirited resistance" to ascendant ideas would "attract some electors in almost every place in which it was heard of" whenever the "prejudice [which he contested] was not universal in the nation."[36] Under a series of local districts, however, "better and more intellectual men" did not deign to make the "sacrifices" required of them to win local "popularity."[37] Further aggravating the situation was that in districts where the party affiliations of voters were relatively evenly split, they thought, upright holders of even very mainstream opinions often abstained from standing for office out of an unwillingness to debase themselves to "coquetting" with the prejudices (or even corrupt demands) of the clusters of swing voters who held the balance of the election.[38] The deterrent power of these conditions was amplified by that bugbear of British PR: party control. For one thing, party organization

---

[34] Mill, "Recent Writers on Reform," 362; *Considerations*, 463.

[35] The allergy to winner/loser contests has a modern counterpart in the attempt by "consensus voting" and "preferendum" systems to remove for/against contests – those votes which produce "outright winners" and "outright losers" – altogether from the repertoire of democracy; P. J. Emerson, *The Politics of Consensus* (Belfast, 1994). Naturally, it also retains a strong hold across the various camps in today's PR literature; Leslie Sykes, *Proportional Representation: Which System?* (Leicester, 1990), 76.

[36] Mill, "Recent Writers on Reform," 362.

[37] Hare, "Representation in Practice and Theory." Note that the logic holds against not merely territorially organized districts, but against any fixed districts (by profession or class, say).

[38] E.g. Lubbock et al., "Objections and Answers," 314. The worry about the excessive power of swing voters motivated an early PR document from America (by Thomas Gilpin, 1844), of which Hare

made the threat of lower-class monopoly of the Commons greater by imposing electoral cohesiveness on this vast group and thus shutting out all learned and open-minded critics of this party-orchestrated "will of the majority."[39]

What tended to occupy Harean reformers even more, however, was the dominance of small power-holding cadres over candidatures – a major facet of what would come to be known as the "oligarchic" character of parties.[40] The mechanics of party control shifted over the period, although the terminology remained surprisingly constant: denunciations of "wire-pullers," "managers," and "machines" populate the discourse from Hare through the Edwardian author of lofty works on PR, John H. Humphreys, a half-century later.[41] In the early days of STV proselytization, what Hare and company were targeting was the power of local grandees to "dictate" who would run under the party banners to which they adhered.[42] Over time – beginning with the rise of the "caucus" after the Second Reform Act and accelerating heavily through the last two decades of the century – the "party" which they sought to resist meant something more like the professionally run, centralized party of modern democracy.[43] In each case, though, the problem was the same: it was thought that men of intellect and integrity balked at submitting themselves to this kind of outside control; and, conversely, that those in positions of party dominance had every incentive to restrict the number of candidates to a few hacks on the basis of their fidelity to the party line and their "eligibility" in particular districts, with no preference for "men of mark" over "men of no mark."[44]

Breaking these local- and party-based barriers to the entry into political life of the "best and ablest" men was fundamental to British PR. Furthermore, this aim was closely intertwined with its goal of furnishing a parliamentary image of the full range of opinions, of every "considerable party and section" of the nation.[45] For, given the postulate of the natural-ness of ideological diversity, a heterogeneity of beliefs and policy

---

appears to have been ignorant; Edmund James, "An Early Essay on Proportional Representation," *Proceedings of the American Philosophical Society*, 34 (1895): 468–71.

[39] "A Moderate Liberal," "Can Any Class Be Trusted?" *NR*, 2 (1884), 800.

[40] Robert Michels, *Political Parties*, trans. Eden and Ceder Paul (New York, 1962).

[41] E.g. Hare, "Coming Steps," 217; Humphreys, *Proportional Representation*, 128. Humphreys was the secretary of the pro-STV "Electoral Reform Society" for most of the first half of the twentieth century.

[42] Hare, *Machinery of Representation*, 5–6.

[43] E.g. Francis Herrick, "The Origins of the National Liberal Federation," *JMH*, 17 (1945): 116–29.

[44] Ware, *Machinery of Politics*; Albert Grey, "Proportional vs. Majority Representation," 954–5.

[45] Lubbock, *Representation*, 64.

preferences was expected to characterize the nation's "true" elite as much as any other stratum. Consequently, when party domination or local prejudice shut out many lines of thought from the House, it was certain that a "large proportion of the best moral and intellectual elements of society" was being "waste[d]."[46]

Permitting candidates of distinction to appeal to like-minded electors from across the country, or at least from larger multimember constituencies; reducing the power of local political chieftains; loosening the grip of parties over selection – these achievements would contribute to an increase of "superior men" in parliamentary life.[47] Even better, once these obstacles were removed, a sort of virtuous circle would commence: a set of secondary processes that reinforced the likelihood of the best men earning seats would kick in as well. Three warrant discussion. First, since PR was a kind of cartel-breaking device, it would inject more competition into the electoral system – a competition which, in keeping with PR advocates' aforementioned free-market optimism, was forecast to yield higher-quality members.[48] Second, the "corrupting taint[s], and degrading element[s]" that barred "the most enlightened and the purest minds" from offering themselves as candidates also made the exercise of the vote look worthless to many people.[49] In addition to the political disengagement of those groups who perceived themselves to constitute a permanent minority in their local constituency, the "more highly instructed and conscientious" citizens who felt an election in which the best men were usually not among the candidates to be a "bitter mockery" declined to participate under plurality rule.[50] Thanks to the prospect of voting for candidates whom they actually respected, the "enlightened intelligence of a community" would vote in their full numbers once again, delivering "better elements" into the Commons.[51] Third, the conjunction of (a) the wide field of choice with (b) the power afforded by the transfer to rank several candidates in a way that would call forth deep reflection from electors would convert

---

[46] Hare, *Election of Representatives*, 12.   [47] Hare, *Election of Representatives*, xlv, appendix L.

[48] E.g. Hare, *Election of Representatives*, 118: "interest and feeling will alike prompt [those of less popular beliefs] to select the most able and accomplished exponent of their opinions." Interestingly, the French socialist Louis Blanc strongly picked up on the justification of PR as the sole means of getting "les hommes supérieurs" into the chamber; however, he avoided the language of beneficent competition and the free-market analogies so popular in the British presentation of "le système de M. Hare"; Blanc, "De la Représentation proportionnelle des minorités," in *Questions d'aujourd'-hui et de demain*, vol. I, 239–56, at 248–9.

[49] Hare, *Election of Representatives*, xxv.

[50] Hare, "Representation in Practice and in Theory," 197.

[51] Hare, "School Board," 215. And Hobart, "Parliamentary Reform," 266–7.

elections into something like optimal information-pools (akin, perhaps, to modern betting markets[52]) which would respond sensitively to new data about the worthiness of public figures for the parliamentary trust. Thus would ensue a dynamic of refinement toward ever-better representatives over time.[53]

Hareans' aims did not stop with opening the gates of Parliament to "men of knowledge, experience, and independence of character"; they wished also to provide them a measure of security for their "independence of action" and freedom to judge "the true interests of the country" once they were in office.[54] In contrast to modern political science's findings on the strength of "incumbency advantage,"[55] Victorian PR was alarmed at the weakness of tenure for sitting MPs. Indeed, this alarm was really the origin-point of British PR: Hare wrote his first reform pamphlet in 1857 in anger that several prominent antiwar politicians had lost their seats in the groundswell of jingoism occasioned by the Crimean War.[56] Making matters worse, the insecurity of tenure for "every member of parliament" who showed "independence" was not limited to emotional moments of national crisis like war but was a systemic problem that stemmed from the MP having only "a narrow tribunal before which to tender an account of his stewardship."[57] Hare's solution to this threat to the quality of the membership was, in essence, the flipside of the expansion of the elector's field of choice: the MP, under his scheme, would have a larger audience to stand in judgment of his conduct, insulating him from "dependence on the caprice of any particular constituency." Instead of being subject to "knots of agitators," "little knots of persons who take an interest in some trumpery matter," who might be able to flip a local district against even a hallowed statesman who had fallen afoul of some "shibboleth" of his party or

---

[52] E.g. George Bragues, "Prediction Markets: The Practical and Normative Possibilities for the Social Production of Knowledge," *Episteme*, 6 (2009): 91–106.

[53] "A representative assembly, chosen under a system thus free and expansive, would be a reflex of the feeling and intelligence of the people. Gradually elevated in character by the constant operation of the process of comparison which is so powerful in every department of science, by the introduction of the most distinguished men, and by the elimination of the inferior, it would become [once again] ... the great model of constitutional government, and the envy or admiration of all civilised nations"; Hare, *Election of Representatives*, 133–4.

[54] Grey, "Proportional versus Majority Representation," 958.

[55] Gary Cox and Scott Morgenstern, "The Increasing Advantage of Incumbency in the United States," *Legislative Studies Quarterly*, 18 (1993): 495–514. Because the likelihood of having the "best men" turned out was a defect inextricably linked to the machinery of plurality rule, Victorian PR advocates were convinced that the feebleness of incumbency advantage held elsewhere, regularly citing the United States; e.g. Droop, *Political and Social Effects*, 13.

[56] Hart, *Proportional Representation*, 26.

[57] Hare, *Machinery of Representation*, 31; Albert Grey, "Proportional vs. Majority Representation," 958.

locality, MPs would now be able to attract support from wherever "a love of fairness and justice, and respect for a manly, upright, and inflexible bearing" were to be found.[58] "A member who had already served in Parliament with any distinction," Hare boasted, "would under this system be almost sure of his re-election."[59]

Beyond these lines of argument for how their favored electoral machinery would "gather[] to the national councils our wisest men, who if they be truly so, must include our best men,"[60] Victorian PR's aspiration to raise the moral-intellectual fiber of legislators involved some striking assumptions.

Most obviously: underlying Hare's hopes on this front was the assumption that good government required that the Commons possess the crème de la crème – an assumption that was not shared by all schools of reform. For instance, Bagehot's insouciance about the aptitude required to sit in the Commons, his contentment with the "average sense" and "practical discretion" of the modal MP, was foreign to the anxiousness about the insufficient ability of MPs that animated Hare.[61] Hare sought "an assembly, consisting of nearly seven hundred of those persons in whom the people 'may discern that predominant proportion of active virtue and wisdom, taken together and fitted to the charge, such as in the great and inevitable mixed mass of human imperfections and infirmities is to be found.'"[62] Such splendid personages were, of course, rare.[63] This problem of the natural fewness of persons suitable for the legislature was exacerbated by plurality-rule arrangements. The combination of these two causes – nature's stinginess and the poor mechanics of plurality rule – made for a frightening paucity of worthy MPs. Their convictions about the high degree of aptitude needed from public officials, moreover, made Harean PR amenable to those trends in political thought and practice, such as the

[58] Hare, *Machinery of Representation*, 31–3; "Note," 104; *Election of Representatives*, 85.
[59] Mill, "Recent Writers on Reform," 363. After 1868 Hare built his most famous supporter's re-election defeat into his argumentation: he wished to replace "an electoral system which enables the moiety of a fractional part of the population by its veto to exclude from Parliament public men of national fame. Thousands of voters throughout the country desired that Mr. Mill should be in a position to contribute to the expression of profound thought in the House of Commons, amidst its superficial and frivolous talk. Half the voters in Westminster were able to prevent it"; "Note," 104.
[60] Hare, "Representation of Every Locality and Intelligence," 527.
[61] Bagehot, "Mr. Cobden," in *CW*, vol. 3, 288–9.
[62] Hare, *Election of Representatives*, 99. He was here quoting from Burke's *Reflections on the Revolution*.
[63] This sentiment resonated with his more general Guizotianism. Throughout, Hare gives the impression that the fate of the modern state depended on reassembling in the legislature "la raison publique" that was "dispersée" across society; Rosanvallon, "Guizot et la Révolution française," in *François Guizot et la culture politique*, 65.

development of a meritocratic civil service, which were concentrated on a rationalization of public life and the empowerment of a true intelligentsia.[64]

A second notable aspect of the thesis about upgrading the legislative personnel was its libertarian optimism. Under conditions of freedom the electorate would have no difficulty recognizing those deserving of office: the trouble "is not that the people fail to appreciate public virtue," but that "their electoral machinery" was failing them.[65] Hence, as low as the quotient of wisdom and integrity in the Commons had sunk, all that was required to correct it was the liberation of the voter. In this optimistic political epistemology Harean PR looks more like the belated offspring of the high Enlightenment than a typically angsty mid-Victorian product.[66] Just as a Voltaire or Joseph Priestley had been convinced that once the wiles of "priestcraft" were vanquished the natural reasonableness of mankind would shine forth,[67] Hare had no doubt that the statesmen deserving of "reverence and respect" who would populate the legislature after the institution of PR would bear out his "faith in the integrity of man."[68] That liberty was the necessary and sufficient condition for proper social choices was a grounding principle for Hare and most of his followers, and it embedded in Victorian PR a hyperrationalist ethos that has faded from today's controversies about electoral systems.

This analysis generated some tricky tightropes for these theorists to walk. For one, they had to hold together their bleak assessment of the actual with their optimism about the possible.[69] This meant absolving the electorate of blame for the poor condition into which Parliament had fallen; the grip of party machines and power-brokers were not to be ascribed to any limits of intelligence, uprightness, or interest native to the average citizen, but had to be grasped as pure artifacts of deficient representative structures. Likewise, they had to trace a fine line with respect to the abilities of the electorate. It was inherent in their dedication to

---

[64] Lawrence Goldman, *Science, Reform, and Politics in Victorian Britain: The Social Science Association 1857–1886* (Cambridge, 2004), 17.

[65] Hare, *Machinery of Representation*, 4.

[66] Bernard Wishy, "Introduction" to Mill, *Prefaces to Liberty*, ed. Wishy (Boston, 1959), 16–17.

[67] E.g. Voltaire, "An Address to the Public concerning the Parricides imputed to the Calas and Sirven Families," in *Treatise on Tolerance and Other Writings*, ed. Simon Harvey (Cambridge, 2000), 117–36; Priestley, "Utopia," in *Priestley's Writings on Philosophy, Science, and Politics*, ed. Passmore: 251–8.

[68] Hare, "Note," 106; *Election of Representatives*, 147.

[69] For this reason it was a fitting object of Mill's affection, since it parallels Mill's oft-noted combination of ecstatic hopes with the most biting condemnations of the state of affairs he actually encountered; e.g. John MacCunn, *Six Radical Thinkers* (London, 1907), ch. 2.

assemble in the Commons a true elite that most citizens could not fill this role. And yet voters had to (or would have to, under proper arrangements) be competent enough to recognize this fitness when it appeared at the hustings. Finding this sweet spot was not a challenge unique to the PR movement: the need to explain how ordinary people can be at once unfit to decide policy and settle legislation but yet fit to choose their rulers confronts any adherent to representative government who does not view it as merely a practical substitute for direct democracy.[70] Yet two factors rendered this challenge more acute for these PR theorists: (a) their uniquely spectacular vision of the attributes of this elected elite, and (b) their need to prove that elections could only fulfill this "filtering" function if a particular set of electoral-aggregative rules were in place.[71]

The final point to be made about the Harean conception of the improvement of the membership concerns the manner in which it was historicized. Chapter 2 noted the nostalgia that Grey and others felt for the close boroughs in which the seat was in the gift of a patron; they saw these as avenues for talented and independent men, men who had services to render but likely could not gain a local majority, to enter the Commons. Hare had a similar nostalgia, and he thought of his scheme as restoring the level of talent, expertise, and probity that had existed prior to 1832, thanks to the close or rotten boroughs.[72] What in the *ancien régime* had been accomplished by constriction, proprietorship, and influence would now be even better achieved by permitting "every intelligent and vigorous-minded

---

[70] E.g. the words of "Democraticus" in George Cornewall Lewis's *Dialogue on the Best Form of Government* (London, 1863), 85: I do not "maintain that all men are equally competent to judge of public affairs. What I maintain is, that all men are sufficiently competent judges for the exercise of the electoral suffrage, and for choosing representatives." The theoretical problem remains the same today; see Geoffrey Brennan and Alan Hamlin, "On Political Representation," *BJPS*, 29 (1999): 101–27.

[71] Hare, "School Board," 215. The polemic of science fiction writer, socialist, and philosopher H. G. Wells, coming at the very end of our period, fittingly sums up this aspect of PR thought. Wells was totally uninterested in the diversity and descriptiveness rationales for his preferred system and therefore had to rest the entirety of his case on its replacement of "party hacks" with "better types of public men." (In his eyes "the idea of getting a fairer representation of minorities" was just the motive that had happened to prompt its genesis, while he cared only for its other property of "getting a better type of representative.") The failures of the British governing class in preparing for and conducting the Great War and the general blindness to the drastically altered economic and international situation facing the country after the war convinced him that radically "better statesmen" were required. And yet Wells was also led to defend the wisdom of the average citizen in his role as voter in the right electoral system; *In the Fourth Year*, chs. 9–10.

[72] "It has been a subject of great and just regret, that one consequence of the abolition of the close boroughs has been, in a great measure, to impede the access to parliament of a class of able men, who by their aid were enabled to devote themselves, and were gradually disciplined, to political labours"; *Election of Representatives*, 56. He did admit that the "patron of a borough" was far from infallible at identifying talent; ibid., 56–7.

elector" to associate freely for "the return of a wise and honourable man."[73] As a legal-educational commentator who became enthused with Hare's scheme wondered, "cannot some substitute be provided" for the power the old "close boroughs" had of introducing "promising talents" and ensuring the "continuity" that had once allowed "leading statesmen . . . to pursu[e] their career without interruption"?[74] For all the unreformed era's problems, it was likelier "before 1832" than after that "the most eminent men of the day" would occupy a parliamentary place, and the magic of Hare's innovation was to marshal "the elective power of minorities" to the effect of rendering the representative system once again welcoming to those of "great abilities."[75] This rhetoric of functional equivalence to a valuable but irrecoverable practice of the past accorded well with the tranche of PR discourse that stressed its continuity with constitutional history.[76]

The large claims of Hare and his followers about the improvement of parliamentary personnel naturally did not go unchallenged. Three lines of criticism were especially prominent.

First was a general statement that PR was inadequate to secure the "best statesmen in Parliament" because this promise, although its "most plausible recommendation," was incompatible with its major goal of mirroring.[77] This was a version of the enduring "morons representing morons" charge against descriptive representation, discussed in Chapter 2; as we will see in Section 2, in the context of the attack on PR this charge would eventually merge into a more sophisticated range of objections against what was perceived to be its exaggerated intellectualism. For now, Leslie Stephen's objection can stand in for this line of critique: "it is plain that Parliament cannot be at once an accurate mirror of public opinion and a collection of the wisest men." PR *either* was a means of translating opinion correctly, this line of objection ran, *or* it was a device which, by some kind of intellectual alchemy, turned the judgments of "fools" into those of "wise men;" to possess both mirroring and personnel-improving features was impossible.[78]

---

[73] Hare, "John Stuart Mill," 151.   [74] Calvert, *Representation of Minorities*, 31, 29.

[75] Hare, *Election of Representatives*, 87; Calvert, *Representation of Minorities*, 31–2.

[76] Hare, *Election of Representatives*, 56. On the whole, however, PR supporters were not as keen on the affinity to close boroughs as variety-of-suffragists were. Mill, notably, never longed for these lost "avenues for talent." His holding out against this trope was a heritage of his having been so actively involved on the radical side during the struggle for the First Reform Act.

[77] Leslie Stephen, "Order and Progress," *FR*, 17 (1875): 820–34, at 824. Also Harrison, *Order and Progress*, ch. 8, on which Stephen was drawing in these comments, and Parsons, *Thomas Hare and Political Representation*, 139–41.

[78] Stephen, "Order and Progress," 824.

Articulated at this level of generality, this was not an especially potent critique. For one thing, it verged on proving too much. If the fact that citizens were "mostly fools" and "utterly incompetent to form an opinion worth having upon most political problems" was an argument against PR, it seemed just as much an argument against any elections in which anyone beyond a circumscribed elite participated.[79] Indeed, the logic of the complaint seemed to push toward the kind of evacuation of the notion of representation *tout court* that we analyzed in the thought of the techno-cratic liberal Robert Lowe. Unless one were to uphold those features of plurality-rule elections precisely for the reason that they thwarted the popular will or distorted the desires of the electorate – which almost no Victorian was prepared openly to do – then the Leslie Stephen-style assault against PR seemed to strike all of representative government.[80] After all, any vaguely inclusive electoral theory – let alone a democratic one such as that to which Stephen, in the 1870s, retained his sympathies[81] – relies on the thought that voters can appreciate political intelligence in candidates even if they are not themselves capable of directly making policy or running the government. Hence, it was open to defenders of PR to employ their own version of what would become a standard weapon in the armature of advocacy for the referendum:[82] to attack PR on "morons representing morons" grounds, they claimed, was to attack the idea of representation altogether.[83]

Stephen and similar objectors could reply by recasting their criticisms as intended to deflate the belief that under PR voters would become so much more adept at conferring office on their political superiors that the Commons would suddenly transform into "a national Walhalla" housing the "pure ore of wisdom and virtue."[84] Thus watered-down, however, the

---

[79] Ibid., 824, 829; Stephen, "Value of Political Machinery," 845–6.

[80] As the PR skeptic Dicey would put it later, there was no way around the fact that "parliamentary legislatures represent the folly no less than the wisdom of their electors"; Dicey, "Will the Form of Parliamentary Government Be Permanent?" *Harvard Law Review*, 13 (1899): 67–79, at 75.

[81] Stephen allowed that "the general body of voters is sufficiently honest and intelligent to recognise the weight of opinions represented by its ablest men"; "Value of Political Machinery," 845–6.

[82] "The point of this objection [that the people may not be so wise as their representatives] to every method of appeal from parliament to the populace cannot be got rid of. It may, however, to a certain extent be blunted by the consideration that to attack the referendum is to attack democratic government"; Dicey, "Democracy in Switzerland," *ER*, 171 (1890): 113–45, at 139.

[83] Hare equated Leslie Stephen's objections to the proposition "that government by the suffrage, is inherently vicious"; Note, 107. And see Williams, *Proportional Representation and British Politics*, 72: "At bottom, this distrust of the results of proportional representation in producing an incompetent House of Commons is a distrust of democracy."

[84] Hare, *Election of Representatives*, 134, 132.

objection struck only the utopian leanings of some PR proponents.[85] More modest claims about the improvement in personnel their reform would offer – that its greater freedom of choice made it possible for "wisdom" or "learning" to snag some seats; or that by giving local minorities a reason to return to the polls, a few talented holders of minority opinions might supplant the hacks controlled by "the secret strings" of "some political club" – were not really touched by Stephen's criticisms.[86]

Stephen's line of criticism, even if it scored glancing blows against the more grandiose branches of PR theory, failed to land a knockout punch. Beyond the difficulties just noted, this weakness was also due to the fact that, even if skeptics were correct that PR would yield less of an improvement in the caliber of MPs than was hoped, this was only one of the advantages which its supporters ascribed to it; thus, even with one plank of the platform gone, there remained ample reason for them to continue to endorse it. For these objections to have much weight they would have to go further and make the case that under PR the quality of MPs would deteriorate. Some critics went this extra mile. Unconcerned with the abstractly-stated conflict of principle between mirroring and wisdom, these opponents specified mechanisms by which PR would lower the quality of parliamentary membership. These negative anticipations could take several forms. The diverse democrat of Chapter 3, John Boyd Kinnear, for instance, feared that, quite to the contrary of what Hare promised, PR would exacerbate the plutocratic character of Parliament by permitting the exorbitantly rich simply to buy a quota's worth of votes from across a large constituency or the whole country; by contrast, in head-to-head local contests, the utility of "bribery" and "the triumph of mere wealth" were more "doubtful."[87] Running along parallel tracks was the allegation, which became commonplace especially toward the close of our period,[88] that moving to larger constituencies would exacerbate the influence of money on politics, since it would make working the district more expensive – an increase in cost which would either preclude all but the wealthy from running, or intensify dependence on party organizations for the supply of

---

[85] E.g. Stephen, "The Value of Political Machinery," 852.

[86] E.g. Hare, *Machinery of Representation*, 5; "Note," 106–7. Stephen himself came close to conceding as much; see "Value of Political Machinery," 846–7; "Order and Progress," 824.

[87] Kinnear, "Practical Considerations," 53–4, 62. Similarly, Robert Collier wondered how it could be that "open[ing] the market" would "discourage traffic" and saw "local boundaries" as setting limits to corruption; *Representation of Minorities*, 22–3.

[88] MacDonald, *Socialism and Government*, vol. 1, 153; Julius West, *Fabian Tract No. 168: John Stuart Mill* (London, 1913), 12.

funding and resources. PR was thus far from a recipe for delivering England from what a later writer, distilling a half-century of this discourse, would call the reign of "plutocratic cranks" and "secret party funds."[89]

More common than Kinnear's forecast was another thesis about the detrimental impact that Harean PR would have on the fabric of the Commons. This was a set of linked arguments that it would lead to a "limelight system" of parliamentary candidatures.[90] According to this strand of criticism, STV's ideas about improving the caliber of MPs relied on two errors: (a) an exaggeration of the number of persons of talent and eminence who were waiting to be ushered into the Commons through accumulating a scattered quota[91]; and (b) an exaggeration of the ability of voters to keep track of a number of figures based on their true political merits.[92] Consequently, STV was a recipe for the introduction of celebrity idiots into the Commons, not for the elevation of the membership through the influence of citizens of public spirit and genuine attainments. With this counterargument, antiproportionalists were repurposing the traditional concern that democracy would lead to demagogy. It was not the existence of mass suffrage on its own, these figures argued, that led to demagoguery; but with the discipline of local ties broken and the elector faced with both

---

[89] E. S. P. Haynes, *The Decline of Liberty in England* (London, 1916), 43.

[90] Meredith, *Proportional Representation in Ireland*, 101.

[91] "The number of such men is not very great. The single transferable vote has gained an undue amount of adherence owing to the fact that one readily thinks of one or two able men that might find it very difficult to get elected under the present system, but who would be certain of election under the other. But if one or two such names have occurred to the reader, let him ask himself if they would not also be certain under a list system ... It is not really these few men who would be more helped by the single transferable vote than by the list system, but those of far less ability who in a small way have moved in a somewhat local 'limelight.' They form good compromise candidates for the last seat. They have a small band of admirers that would give them sufficient first preferences to enable them to keep their flags flying until late preferences were reached. They would then begin to accumulate the votes of electors of each party who prefer them to members of the opposite party"; Meredith, *Proportional Representation in Ireland*, 79. Or more simply: "As to the eminence argument, I do not think there are enough eminent persons to go round"; Clive Morrison-Bell, "Proportional Representation – What Is It?," *NC*, 73 (1913): 1122–30, at 1129.

[92] "Lastly, the difficulties of the imperfectly educated voter would be enormously increased. Instead of having to vote for one or two ... he would be required to select ten names out of a list of twenty, at least, and twenty-five, thirty, forty, or even more in other cases. Chance, notoriety for quite irrelevant reasons, and numerous other factors would come into play. Numbers of persons would be returned to parliament not to represent a definite political policy or a particular view held by a small section, but because they bore a well known name, or owned a Derby winner, or had a son who played in the county cricket eleven or the borough football club"; Henry Schloesser, *Fabian Tract No. 153: The Twentieth Century Reform Bill* (London, 1911); Hare, "A Note on Representative Government," 14. For Schloesser, the decline in MP quality was also related to the *uptick* in election expenses that he expected would follow from the need for very large districts under STV; ibid., 14. Morrison-Bell agreed, warning that STV would demand that "flying" succeed "motor cars" as a campaign necessity; Morrison-Bell, "Proportional Representation – What Is It?," 1130.

a limitless sea of candidates and the task of listing more names than he
could possibly know well, STV would in fact cause the rise of "shallow
dogmatists" who grabbed attention by "the habitual use of violent and
inflammatory language."[93] To expect that personnel would improve
thanks to such arrangements was a fantasy.[94]

Finally, a third critique of the claim to raise the level of the membership
was advanced. It was quite potent, but seldom made; yet one author who
did present it superlatively toward the end of our period was the Irish
exponent of the list system, James Meredith. Among Meredith's many
gripes about STV was that its claims about bettering the personnel of the
assembly were not even intelligible, and therefore were made in bad faith:

> The warmest advocates of the single transferable vote will generally be found
> to be those who look with strong disfavour on the system of party govern-
> ment, and who believe that this peculiar method of securing proportional
> representation would result in the return of what are called "the best men" to
> Parliament. That the return of such men is a thing in itself pre-eminently
> desirable is assumed as axiomatic. Underlying this view there seems to be the
> curious notion that an assembly of the best men could be chosen irrespective
> of political opinions, and that they could then come together and evolve the
> best policy as the resultant of their united excellence. In particular there is
> a prevalent notion that this would be the most suitable method to adopt in the
> selection of the first Irish Parliament. The single transferable vote is hailed
> with delight by many who suppose that it is an ideal system for carrying out an
> election on such a basis ... The view simply reflects the vagueness of thought
> of those who feel that their own minds will become bankrupt of political ideas
> once the present question [of the future of the Union] is settled. Their
> minds are a misty grey, and so they naturally desire to be represented by
> a misty grey Parliament. But those who have a clearer sense of the concrete
> issues that will emerge no less naturally desire a Parliament of more decided
> colour, and are anxious to see the flags hoisted as soon as possible.[95]

Meredith's charge here combined two allegations. The first was that there
was a conceptual error in aiming at a higher quality of member, since in
politics the character and intellect of a person simply could not be evaluated separately from his views. In a manner that recalls the long line of
critiques of "liberal neutrality" more generally,[96] Meredith contended that,

---

[93] Collier, *Representation of Minorities*, 19.

[94] The argument from the improvement of the membership of the Commons was only "valid in some
hitherto undiscovered Utopia"; Morrison-Bell, "Proportional Representation – What Is It?," 1129.

[95] Meredith, *Proportional Representation in Ireland*, 100–1.

[96] E.g. in the Victorian context, J. F. Stephen, *Liberty, Equality, Fraternity*; in the modern,
Ronald Beiner, *What's the Matter with Liberalism?* (Berkeley, 1992).

on inspection, all judgments about the fitness or goodness of the membership simply collapsed into evaluations of the degree to which the distribution of MPs suited one's own convictions.[97] He illustrated this point, fittingly, with the Irish case: neither side of the debate over repeal of the Union would agree to staff an assembly tasked with deciding this momentous question by means of a procedure that vowed just to return the "best members." From this case he drew the lesson that *no* neutral, non-question-begging evaluation of the quality of members was possible. Rather, whenever praise for the "best men" in isolation from ideological allegiance was invoked, what this really expressed was a political viewpoint, such as, for example, the viewpoint that no "concrete issue" was currently at stake, or that the right answer must involve some compromise to be culled from within a settled range of contending positions.[98] Hence, a second allegation was bound up with that of conceptual incoherence: that STV supporters' longing for "better men" concealed a bias toward a sort of fuzzy, de facto acceptance of the status quo. Meredith was, in sum, launching a cogent theoretical objection to a central plank of the classical Victorian PR platform – an objection that resonated polemically due to the fact that throughout the long nineteenth century crusaders for PR were not always reticent to mix their substantive policy positions with their arguments in favor of their preferred electoral system.[99]

iii   The Moral Elevation of the Electorate

The argument that STV would yield better parliamentary personnel thus proved contentious. That it became such a lightning rod was natural enough, given the emphasis Hare and company placed upon it.

---

[97] In this attack Meredith had an unexpected ally: the Danish progenitor of STV, C. C. G. Andrae. Unlike Hare and his compatriots, Andrae dismissed the defense of his system on the grounds of superiority of members returned: "I shall not at all venture . . . to say that the most just elections are those which secure the *best* representatives. Who can judge who make the best representatives? No single person has any right to assume the authority of a judge in that matter and say, 'Now, this man will make a good representative and I reject the others.' It is very possible, indeed, that proportional representation will sometimes elect bad representatives – from a certain point of view. Possibly it would be much better if one man or some single corporation were charged with appointing all the representatives. But one thing would be certain about such a scheme. It would not effect any *representation of the voters*"; Andrae, *Andrae and His Invention*, 115.

[98] "Those who take this view do not imagine that such a basis would be a sound one under existing circumstances, or so long as the present dominant issue remained undecided. With that issue in the balance the best man for a Nationalist must be a Nationalist and for a Unionist a Unionist"; Meredith, *Proportional Representation in Ireland*, 100–1.

[99] PR campaigners drew on the likelihood of certain positions – especially free trade and Liberal Unionism – benefiting from their proposed reform. But perhaps their most pervasive substantive predilection was the fuzzier one that "moderation" would augment its yield of seats; see e.g. Lubbock, *Representation*, 68; Albert Grey, "Proportional vs. Majority Representation," 957.

Nevertheless, within the broad ambit of "political, social, and moral reform" which they promised, it was another cluster of benefits that tended to rank first.[100] As Mill wrote, with characteristic ardor: nothing was "more unspeakably beneficial" about PR than its capacity to "rais[e] the tone of the whole political morality of the country" and "elevate the minds of the electors themselves."[101]

Electoral liberty was not only an end in itself and a tool for getting superior representatives; it was also a means for improving the voters themselves. In the preface to the third edition of the *Election of Representatives*, after quoting Tocqueville to the effect that statesmen should focus less on using men "to effect great things" and "try a little more to make great men," Hare revealed the heart of his work, the great gain that would come from ceasing to "compel[] voters" and instead "allow[ing] them to associate together freely":

> Every detail of this scheme converges to one central point, – that of making the exercise of the suffrage a step in the elevation of the individual character, whether it be found in a majority or a minority. I disclaim for it, therefore, the title of a representation of minorities.

Hare followed this confession of his ultimate purpose by boasting that under PR "the political school of the 'every-day Englishman' would surpass in value that of the citizen of Athens in its proudest time" and be an unparalleled instrument of "moral and intellectual development."[102] What was most valuable in Hare's plan was "the educational effect of the system on the great body of the people," his reform organization announced; no less modestly, Courtney proclaimed that what awaited England under PR was "something like a regeneration of political life" throughout the population.[103] As these quotations indicate, the "education" furnished by their system comprised both intellect and character; due to the closeness with which the head and heart were intertwined in Victorian moral thought,[104] the two sides of this improvement cannot be prized apart. Nevertheless, this subsection moves roughly from moral-ethical questions more narrowly construed (such as motivation and responsibility) toward matters with a more epistemic flavor.

[100] Naville, *Theory and Practice of Representative Elections*, 18.
[101] Mill, "Recent Writers on Reform," 366.   [102] *Election of Representatives*, xix–xxi.
[103] Beales et al., *Representative Reform Report*, 9; Courtney, "Political Machinery," 85.
[104] Hence the perception even at the time that the moral angst of the age was profoundly *intellectualized*; as Mill's disciple John Morley wrote, the explanation for Mill's appeal lay in his grappling after "this peculiar morality of intelligence"; Morley, "Mr. Mill's Autobiography," in Morley, *Nineteenth-Century Essays*, ed. Peter Stansky (Chicago, 1970), 139–63, at 146. This essay was originally published in *FR*, Jan. 1874.

An atmosphere of moral enthusiasm permeated Harean texts, to the point that the moral amelioration of the electorate could appear to be mystically immanent in the very concept of electoral liberty that they were espousing: "as electoral action is freed, most of the evils which now accompany it will disappear"; "two or three elections" under his system would suffice to undo all the ravages wreaked by "half a century of torpidity and indifference." These ecstatic pronouncements were nonetheless accompanied by careful reasoning about the ways in which their favored institutions would affect the public. The "effect of the free action of every member of an electoral division[] in elevating the motives and objects which govern the general choice" consisted of an assortment of stages of progress and discrete psychological and behavioral consequences;[105] terms such as *regeneration* or *remoralization* summed up a series of predicted changes from the humdrum to the sublime, not all of which were accepted by all proponents, nor rejected by all opponents. PR's reversal of the tide of "the deterioration of political character" was a complex package.[106]

For the preponderance of PR supporters, the first step in this regenerative enterprise was one which remains familiar today: to boost turnout. The PR literature was full of talk about comparative rates of abstention.[107] The mid-Victorian era was an age of faith that, where public life was free, politics would "stimulate the faculties of the most inert," and so there was much fretting when practice seemed not to be confirming their optimistic predictions.[108] Yet Hare and company distinguished themselves by the almost existential anxiety which they felt about political disengagement and torpor; their laments of the "electoral *inertia*" shown by "vast numbers of persons [who] take little or no praiseworthy interest in elections" would sound out of place in Bagehot's corpus.[109] In a period preoccupied with defining the contours of the suffrage, Victorian PR distinguished itself by being troubled by a deficit of participation and interest in elections among those already enfranchised.

Hareans' assessment of the state of electoral apathy did not stop with a bare recitation of numbers. There was also, predictably, a sociological

---

[105] Hare, *Election of Representatives*, xviii, 55; *Machinery of Representation*, 34.
[106] Lytton, "Report on the Rigsraad," 20.
[107] E.g. *Election of Representatives*, 137; Fawcett, *Mr. Hare's Reform Bill*, 20. Hare apologized for the "pedantic reference to statistics" on which he often relied; *Machinery of Representation*, 49.
[108] May, *Democracy in Europe*, vol. 1, liii.
[109] Hoskins, *Modification*, 12. The PR movement's consternation about apathy became more mainstream toward the latter end of our period; see, for example, the late Dicey's worries on this score: Dicey, "Memorandum on Party Government (1898)," in Dicey, *General Characteristics of English Constitutionalism: Six Unpublished Lectures*, ed. Peter Raina (Bern, 2009), 141–61, at 151–6.

dimension to it. PR supporters were convinced that it was especially the "more highly instructed and conscientious men," "the men of influence, of intellect, of wealth and position" who, feeling it a sham to participate in what they considered an unfree election, stayed away from the hustings.[110] This conviction contained an interesting temporal ambiguity, for the early champions of PR delivered their condemnation of the ejection of the upper-classes from electoral life without waiting for the arrival of an expanded suffrage. Writing under a still highly restricted franchise, it was ambiguous whether Hare viewed the withdrawal of upper-class, educated folks as an existent problem or as an evil that would arise under a possible future democratic suffrage against which precaution had to be taken.[111] Around and after the passage of the Third Reform Act, however, a transformation is notable, and upper-class withdrawal is cast more consistently as a present problem than merely a future foreboding.[112]

This ambition to increase turnout was in many ways the flipside of the project of electing better statesmen. The chance to assemble votes over a wider terrain would attract potential candidates who were unwilling to stoop to the degrading arts required by local fights or whose "shade of opinion" was blocked by "party interests," and the prospect of voting for this new set of dignified contenders would entice "the intelligent minority" back to the "organs" of representation.[113] In turn, this re-engagement of the "highly-cultivated members of the community" in the electoral process would call forth a further increase in worthy candidatures.[114] There was, thus, unmistakably an "elitist" aspect to the electoral sociology motivating their reform impulses. Nonetheless, it is important to remember that the solution that Harean PR offered to this marginalization of the enlightened elements of the electorate was not itself skewed toward "elites"; it did not build in or formalize any special advantages for elite electors. Instead, PR was formally agnostic about all distinctions within the electorate; it promised to remedy the problem of swamping by doing away with involuntary

---

[110] Hare, "Representation in Practice and in Theory," 197; Lubbock, *Representation*, 13 (quoting a speech from Lord Spencer). This contrasts with contemporary American political science's findings on the role of high income and education levels in increasing political involvement; see e.g. Sidney Verba, Kay Schlozman and Henry Brady, *Voice and Equality: Civic Voluntarism in American Politics* (Cambridge, MA, 1995).

[111] E.g. his revealing equivocation "under the present system, and especially if accompanied with an extensive increase of the electoral body . . . "; Hare, *Machinery of Representation*, 44. For a predictive, forward-looking version, see *Election of Representatives*, xxxiv.

[112] E.g. Lubbock, *Representation*, 13.

[113] Edward Russell, "The Electoral Future," *CR*, 47 (1885), 257–8. Russell here was stating the arguments of proportionalists, although he did not personally agree.

[114] Mill, *Considerations*, 457.

constituencies so that the best voters, like all voters who were likely to be a minority in any specific local district, might band together from across the nation in order to return MPs in proportion to their numbers.[115]

What the linked goals of countering apathy and improving the membership therefore amounted to at bottom was the promise that through electoral liberty "a living connection" to the electoral process could be extended to all "minorities," be they of interest, opinion, or something more ineffable like sensibility.[116] Just as the dearth of capable MPs could be cured by expanding freedom, so this simple medicine would be sufficient to bring back to the electoral scene those citizens who had retired from it:

> It has been truly observed that a vast multitude of the electors are at present absolutely indifferent to their votes, and see no utility in going to a distant polling place to effect nothing . . . But once relieve every elector wholly from any extraneous control, and give him an unrestricted choice from among all his countrymen, and there will be very few whom the opportunity will not rouse and animate.[117]

If Hare's "elitism" dictated an especial concern for the way in which the present system disheartened and estranged potential upper-class electors,[118] the fundamental tenet underlying his attempt to counter apathy and withdrawal was that the genuine "interest" of all classes, including "the working classes," would be better expressed and represented when the demoralizing constraints of party and locality were removed.[119] The challenge of stimulating higher rates of participation was, therefore, less about reintegrating one class than about combating the conformist,

---

[115] The accurate reporting of "numerical strength" was the foundation of the "system of voting devised by Mr. Hare," which was the "most complete solution" to the "problem of representation"; W. R. Ware, *The Machinery of Politics and Proportional Representation* (London, 1872), 6, 14. Ware was American, but his essay was seized on by the Representative Reform Association and imported for an English audience.

[116] Courtney, "Representation of Minorities," 151.　　[117] Hare, *Machinery of Representation*, 34.

[118] "The State cannot afford to reject the services of any class, especially of any highly instructed class, among its sons"; *Election of Representatives*, 99.

[119] Ibid., 36. Precisely because Hare began promulgating his scheme against the backdrop of the First Reform Act's restricted franchise, which permitted only thin slices of the working class to qualify for the suffrage and hence made the working class minorities in the territorial districts, there was an opening for him to argue that PR would be especially favorable to the working class (e.g. *Election of Representatives*, 37–8). The Second Reform Act did not change Hare's belief that PR would prove more empowering of the working class than the status quo; in a passage added to the fourth edition of *Election* he estimated that given the restrictions that remained even after two reform bills, the working-class would acquire greater influence by "a just system of proportional representation" than by "the reactionary efforts in favour of exclusive majority representation" (Hare, *Election of Representatives*, fourth edition, 15). Hart agreed with Hare: "there can be little doubt that during the years 1868 to 1900 working men's interests would have been better represented in parliament if the Hare scheme had been in operation" (Hart, *Proportional Representation*, appendix A).

debasing tendencies that kept the "best among the electors" from bothering to vote.[120] In keeping with the focus on character so prominent in Victorian liberalism,[121] PR reformers understood electoral abstention not, as modern political scientists do, as the result of a certain socioeconomic situation, but as a *moral* phenomenon, to be remedied by altering the manner in which "civil institutions" worked upon the hearts and minds of citizens so that they bore more "wholesome fruits."[122]

Faith that the removal of the restraints operative in plurality-rule territorial systems was all that was required for full electoral participation reverberated throughout the Harean legions: it was the "absence of freedom [that] engenders utter indifference as to politics" and thus thinned the ranks of voters; PR would end "the inducement to withdraw from political activity which is now felt by those voters who possess exceptional refinement, conscientiousness, or ability" because it would extend to them the opportunity for "electoral power."[123] Armed with the freedom to select, in his exact order of preference, candidates from across the nation without fear of wasting their vote, no decent person would continue in "that indifference to political action which prevails so extensively."[124] Thus, in addition to an optimistic moral epistemology in which proper choices occurred naturally in conditions of liberty, Victorian PR was inflected by an optimistic political psychology in which freedom on its own guaranteed that electoral rights would be exercised.[125] Since Hare and his comrades

---

In part thanks to these estimates that it would enhance working-class presence in the House, Mill was confident in 1868 that "the most active & intelligent leaders of the working classes, are now converted to Mr. Hare's system" (Letter of 5 July 1868 to G. K. Holden, in *CW*, vol. 16, 1420). Nevertheless, the impression of hostility to the working class persisted through the Edwardian period and damaged the cause, notwithstanding: Mill's reputation for devotion to the working classes and particularly to the representation of labor; the outreach of mid-Victorian titans like Fawcett; and the efforts to convince the Labour Party in its incipient stages that PR would be more favorable to their interests as a third-party. See, respectively, Vincent, *Formation of the Liberal Party*, 149–60; Biagini, *Liberty, Retrenchment, and Reform*, 315–7; Williams, *Proportional Representation and British Politics*, 24–5.

[120] Courtney, "Political Machinery," 83.

[121] James Thompson, "Modern Liberty Redefined," in *The Cambridge History of Nineteenth-Century Political Thought*, ed. Gareth Stedman Jones and Gregory Claeys (Cambridge, 2011): 720–47, section two.

[122] Hare, *Election of Representatives*, 101. And xxi: "Institutions are good which call them habitually to perform such public functions as tend to awaken a true conception of their real interests and duties."

[123] Albert Grey, "Proportional versus Majority Representation," 955; M. G. Fawcett, "Proportional Representation," 381.

[124] Hare, *Election of Representatives*, 137.

[125] But see Douglas Amy, "The Forgotten History of the Single Transferable Vote in the United States," *Representation*, 34 (1996), 13–20.

joined the Victorian mainstream in seeing the vote as a trust and a duty, on this score as well it turned out that morality simply followed liberty.[126]

Important as it was, decreasing abstention was just a first step. Raising the number of voters was valuable in itself, of course, but also because, unlike under the current regime, the exercise of the vote in Hare's system would prove a morally beneficial act in several interlocking ways.

The first advantage claimed was, unsurprisingly, deliberative. PR proponents matched any group of Victorians in their devotion to the ideal of the deliberative society. To Hare it was of inestimable importance that "the system I suggest invites deliberation, and provokes and calls for the exercise of thought on political subjects in all in whom it can be awakened."[127] As the presence of Mill in Chapter 2's examination of the topic indicated, there was substantial overlap between PR and other strands of liberalism on foundational components of the theory of deliberation such as the conduciveness of diversity to truth and the indispensability of classes having representatives of their own due to the limits of human sympathy and comprehension.[128] Nevertheless, PR proponents introduced a few distinctive wrinkles into their treatment of the deliberative and intellectual dimensions of parliamentary-electoral politics.

The most singular aspect of their approach to deliberation was the hostility to parties. To PR standard-bearers, it was not just that the bogeymen of the party system – "wirepullers," "bosses," "machines" – oligopolistically restricted the set of persons who could realistically gain access to the Commons. Also, and perhaps even worse, parties stymied deliberation. The PR movement drew upon a background of anxiety about the party-system on deliberative grounds: as the historian Goldwin Smith, among the

---

[126] Hare, *Election of Representatives*, 95; Mill, "Thoughts on Parliamentary Reform," 328. In this they disagreed with contemporaries who saw electoral apathy as a less tractable phenomenon. As one skeptic wrote against the "panacea" of "Mr. Hare and his supporters": "it is idle to blink plain facts. And one particularly plain fact is, that a very large proportion of the electors require a good deal of persuasion before they can be induced to vote at all, and as the number of voters increases so, ceteris paribus, will the apathy"; Alfred Frisby, "The Next Reform Bill," *FR*, 32 (1882): 241–54, at 241.

[127] Hare, "Just Expression," 203.

[128] E.g. Mill on the "collision of opinion among . . . members" as what produces the "lights" which can guide public policy (Speech of 17 June 1868 on the Municipal Corporations Bill [2], in *CW*, vol. 28, 262); and Hare, *Election of Representatives*, 37: "There is much that touches the condition of the poorer classes which persons in a different social sphere can hardly feel or know . . . ['the working population'] ought to have the power of placing in the House some persons in whom they have confidence, and who are able to view all such questions from *their* side, who have been brought up with them, and know experimentally where and how their condition needs ameliorations. A representative assembly of the Commons, without this element, is grossly defective." Hare made no effort to square this uncompromising descriptivist stance with his capacitarian understanding of the limited suffrage.

most important Victorian commentators on America, wrote, "on any party question a debate has hardly been more worthy of the name of a deliberation than the exchange of fire between two regiments in a battle"[129] – and such sentiments grew especially strong after the growth of the "caucus" in the late 1860s–70s.[130] Moreover, PR theory tapped into a widespread Liberal distrust of overly rigid party structures as impediments to the exercise of individual reason.[131] Nevertheless, the critique of the antideliberative effects of party issued by Hare and his followers tended to proceed according to its own pattern.

In contradistinction to both traditionalist and Jacobin attacks on parties as fomenters of division and partiality that obscured an evident common good,[132] the British PR tradition rejected parties as too constraining of pluralism. Beginning from premises about the naturalness of diversity investigated earlier, PR theorists adjudged the party system guilty of constricting the flow of ideas into (usually two) prefabricated channels,[133] hence preventing an understanding of the true nature of social problems and undercutting the epistemic properties inherent in truly unrestricted deliberation.[134] In conditions of electoral freedom the distribution of opinion would naturally be gradated and multidimensional, but plurality rule artificially ossified opinion into a few discrete blocks. That Hare's sensitivity to the power of party duopoly to squelch deliberation was present in his work from its inception in the late 1850s is rather remarkable, since this was widely considered a period of party fragmentation and weak discipline. Hare's bristling at the antideliberative impact of parties even in a moment where their force was widely felt to be at low ebb established a tone that would only be made harsher as parties and their "rigid

---

[129] Smith, "The Political Crisis in England," 113.

[130] Alan Beattie, "1867–1906, Introduction," in *English Party Politics*, ed. Beattie, 2 vols. (London, 1970), vol. 1, 143.

[131] E.g. Matthew, *Gladstone*, 361.

[132] E.g. Marcel Gauchet, "Tocqueville, l'Amérique, et nous," in *La condition politique* (Paris, 2005): 305–43, esp. 326–8.

[133] Those content with the current system "tacitly assume that there are only two sections of opinion in the country, and that each elector should be satisfied with the representative system if it practically realizes a due and proportionate utterance of the shibboleths of Whig and Tory politics"; Fawcett, *Leading Clauses*, 19.

[134] The "diversities of opinion" that arose in the stage of "civilization" to which England had arrived were stamped out by "a system of government formed on numerical majorities alone" which "absorb[ed] all differences into one issue – a contest for power . . . the benefit of this progress in the composition of a representative assembly is excluded when every variety of opinion and shadow of thought is expurgated – thrown aside as so much lumber, in order that both sides may come unencumbered to the trial of strength which is to determine the single issue – the possession of power"; Hare, *Election of Representatives*, 10–11.

machinery [which] paralyses public opinion" fell into lower esteem during the late-Victorian and Edwardian periods among many commentators.[135] Thus, while fears of "plac[ing] all political power in the hands of one class, the others being silenced or excluded" which were more continuous with the variety-of-suffrages outlook always remained a member of the PR family,[136] the intricacy of PR's antiparty reasoning added its own dimension to Victorian thought about the conditions of deliberation.

These harms of misdirection and exclusion of opinion were not the only ways in which parties were understood to damage the prospects for fruitful deliberation. Three others deserve notice. Importantly, these were all picked up by the pioneering political scientist Moisei Ostrogorski, who was deeply versed in the British PR cause and who transmitted these ideas internationally, to Weber and the "elite theorists" of democracy above all.[137] First, the party system not only congealed into settled and unreflective blocs a diverse range of ideas that could otherwise have interacted fertilely; it also generated rancor and hatred between adherents of the opposed platforms. "Party warfare" was declared to be inimical to true "representative government ... The purpose of such a government is not satisfied by dividing the nation into two parties, and converting the area of legislation into a battle-field."[138] As one Millian summed up: "misunderstandings, prejudices, misrepresentations, weapons of bitterness ... are apt to overwhelm the voice of reason."[139]

Another, related harm was caused by parties' reliance on rigid platforms. These necessitated yoking together positions on discrete issues and encouraged unthinking submission to an entire package of views, rather than cultivating scrutiny of and debate on different issues on their own merits.[140] Centralized parties therefore compromised the power of

---

[135] Edward Wilson, "The Caucus and Its Consequences," *NC*, 4 (1878), 698.

[136] Lubbock, "Proportional Representation," 703.

[137] Ostrogorski's knowledge of the PR movement was apparent well before his landmark *Democracy and Political Parties*; see his "Introduction of the Caucus into England," *PSQ*, 8 (1893), 287–316. While Weber endorsed much of Ostrogorski's analysis, he pointedly differed from him in his scathing opposition to PR; e.g. Weber, "Politics as a Vocation," in Weber, *The Vocation Lectures*, trans. Rodney Livingstone (Indianapolis, 2004): 32–94.

[138] Hare, *Election of Representatives*, 10.   [139] Calvert, *Representation of Minorities*, 17.

[140] E.g. Hare, "Reform Bill of the Future," 77, on parties "suppressing the action of independent thought among the members." The binding together of a package of positions was seen as a problem of special gravity for the Liberal party; it was a common refrain that "Conservatism is homogeneous" (since it meant merely upholding the status quo) while "Liberalism is not"; there were, instead many ways to be a Liberal, since Liberalism was the "party of Progress." Consequently, it was argued that Liberals ought especially to cherish STV for its power of quelling the dynamic toward constriction and over-disciplining of party under plurality rule and list

Parliament to serve as a forum for the enactment of "genuine public opinion" and transformed what should have been a deliberative arena into a mere venue for horse-trading and logrolling orchestrated by the "machines."[141] A last supposedly antideliberative feature of parties was tied to the frequency with which the local involuntary constituency placed the balance of power in the hands of "the narrow margin by which that party outnumbers the other."[142] This aspect of the local-majorities method betrayed the spirit of government based on the "test and scrutiny of discussion" by encouraging political actors to deliver themselves into the hands of the parties, who alone could master the endless game of "intrigue . . . in order to catch the votes" of these marginal electors.[143] Adding insult to injury, the undeliberative ethos that this vote-catching modus operandi created was exacerbated by the fact that these knots of swing voters tended to be the morally and intellectually least valuable segment of the citizenry: not bothering even to develop "distinctive political opinions," they were "the most timid, the most narrow-minded and prejudiced," the most attached to "exclusive class-interest."[144] Thus, political dialogue was cheapened and misshapen by the necessity under plurality rule for parties to appeal to the worst portions of the electorate.

Close cousins of the promise to save deliberation from the wreckage of parties were two further boons expected from PR. They do not properly fall under the category of deliberation since they did not concern the interchange of ideas, but they likewise impacted the intellectual side of representative government. First, a couple of advantages were tied to the period's conception of toleration and the "ethics of belief." Chapter 2 charted connections between these ideas and the theory of the differentiated suffrage. But proportionalists felt that they could go one better on this front. For their innovations of electoral liberty and the involuntary

---

systems. T. E. Kebbel, "The Spirit of Party," *NC*, 11 (1882): 378–88, at 386; G. R. Searle, *The Liberal Party: Triumph and Disintegration, 1886–1929* (Houndmills, Basingstoke, 1992), 3–4. And see the testimonials of several leading minds of PR, including Hare, in *Why I Am a Liberal: Being Definitions and Personal Confessions of Faith by the Best Minds of the Liberal Party*, ed. Andrew Reid (London, 1885).

[141] E.g. Lecky, *The Map of Life* (London, 1901), 140. This diagnosis of the linked harms of binding platforms and logrolling under modern party government would be fundamental to the late-century movement for the referendum, as well; Mads Qvortrup, "A. V. Dicey: The Referendum as the People's Veto," *HPT*, 20 (1999): 531–46.

[142] Mill, *Considerations*, 451.

[143] Hare, *Election of Representatives*, xvii; Lubbock et al., "Objections and Answers," 314.

[144] Lubbock et al., "Objections and Answers," 314; Mill, *Considerations*, 451.

constituency partook of the venerable Lockean tradition that saw coercion as both futile at promoting unity and morally damaging to the coerced:[145]

> The means by which the 751, the 1501, or the 2250 voters, who are not associated by any pervading harmony of mind or feeling, but are gathered together by the mere accident of living in the same district or town, are led or forced, on pain of political extinction, always to agree in the choice of their representatives, are inconsistent with the free exercise of individual will, guided by those diversities of thought and sentiment upon which men form their various estimates of character; and *their subjection to such compulsion tends to the mental and moral deterioration both of the electors and the elected.*
>
> *It is beyond the power of law to compel men to unite for a common purpose, and labour in it with energy of will, unless it be one in which their nature prompts them to agree.* An electoral body, composed of the most heterogeneous and antagonistic materials, bound together by law, and told that they must act together, and find one person who can reflect the most dissimilar things, can be compared to nothing better than the melancholy spectacle of subdued and torpid natures, which is sometimes exhibited by the animal showman, in a cage, in the streets.[146]

Instead of this morass of insincerity and reluctant half-support, thanks to the involuntary constituency, the MP would be sure of the enthusiastic confidence placed in him by his voters and of the accord between his principles and theirs. He would finally have what toleration promised to all citizens in the realm of religious practice: a foundation from which he could speak truthfully. Some of the imagery used on this issue is worth quoting at length as an exemplar of colorful Victorian political prose:

> [Under a system of local majorities] [e]ach deputy is a sort of miniature parliament in himself; a colourless, insipid, fasciculus of negations, without a definite program, or even a definite idea. To begin with, as we all know, the aim of a candidate is to say as little as he possibly can before the election, for fear of giving offence to one or other of the groups in his constituency.

---

[145] Mark Goldie, "Introduction," to Locke, *A Letter Concerning Toleration and Other Writings*, ed. Goldie (Indianapolis, 2010), xiv–xvi.

[146] Hare, *Election of Representatives*, 16, 39 (my italics). Hare's points here about the inefficacy of compulsion related to his aforementioned argument against territorial constituencies on the grounds that they undermined the *true* local ties that it was meant to represent in the first place: "the system which really destroys the wholesome influences of locality is that which has long been, and still seems to be, most in favour with popular reformers, – grouping some boroughs, disfranchising others, here severing cities and counties, and there adding a score of villages to some small borough. The component parts are rather repelled than attracted by such undesired combinations. It is proposed to amend this anomalous patchwork, and allow the country spontaneously and without any arbitrary rule, to recover its natural subdivisions"; *Election of Representatives*, xii.

If he says a word in favour of temperance, the licensed victuallers look askance at him; if he ventures to suggest that a poor man has as good a right to his Sunday pint as a rich man to his Sunday bottle of port, the teetotallers gather together and talk ominously about the sons of Belial. If he dares to say more about the State church than that the question has not yet come within the domain of practical politics, a thousand tongues are instantly set in motion about the godlessness of advanced politicians. That an enemy can do more harm than a friend can do good, is well known by all who are conversant with electioneering; and the consequence is that every candidate confines himself as much as possible to the merest generalities ... It is impossible to declare his opinions boldly and frankly.[147]

In its facilitation of sincerity and forthrightness and its rejection of compulsion, the move beyond involuntary districts brought parliamentary reform into sync with its sister cause of toleration.[148] Little wonder that PR proponents judged those who held tightly to the status quo "extremely intolerant and exclusive in politics."[149]

In addition to permitting frankness and eliminating compulsion, Hareans placed great hopes in the intellectual effects that the act of voting itself would have in their system. The drawing-up of a long, preferentially ranked list from among all candidates across the nation (or, on the humbler versions, a large district) was to work wonders for the mental life of the citizen. First, just casting the vote in this manner would be enough to counteract the biliousness of current electoral politics.[150] This anticipation was modest, however, in comparison with the core claims about the revolutionary impact of the electoral act under STV. "As the extensive capacity of expression, and the interesting nature of the act of voting, comes to be felt, increased attention will be directed to it," Hare foretold, and "there is every reason to expect that much time would be given to the details necessary for the preparation of the voting-paper." "Political education" would proceed with rapidity from "the very inquiries to be made in so wide a field." "The constitution would open to every voter a scope for

---

[147] Donisthorpe, *Individualism*, 52–3.

[148] On the link between the two issues in another tradition of the period, see Timothy Larsen, *Friends of Religious Equality: Nonconformist Politics in Mid-Victorian England* (Rochester, 1999), 98, 118.

[149] Russell, *Hansard*, Third Series, HL Deb 30 July 1867, 447.

[150] "The habit of scrutinizing with attention the conduct of public men, and of forming an estimate of their relative merits ... will naturally dispose the minds of men towards political moderation, and render them tolerant of differences, which they now regard as impassable objections. As our views widen, our sympathies increase and multiply; all things become more precious, and in all we find good ... It is party which begets party. When an elector addresses himself to the task of forming on his voting-paper a list sufficient to compose an entire representative assembly, he becomes a mediator, rather than a partisan. He becomes less narrow, and more catholic in his opinions and prepossessions"; Hare, *Election of Representatives*, 136–7.

thought and reflection as wide as his intellectual and moral horizon" if, as under STV, "it gave him a choice from among all who by their candidature show that they aspire to public distinction." By combining unlimited choice with the opportunity to put into effect a detailed comparative analysis of the great political ideas and personages of the time, "men will be encouraged to think independently, and not to be led by popular clamour." As "the capacity of selection, and the disposition to select from such materials, would be infinitely various ... like the bounteous lap of nature," all directions in which "intelligence" and "industry" in examining political questions might move would ultimately be reunited in the electoral system. Furthermore, Hare's scheme operationalized in the electoral context a fundamental lesson of the progress of modern knowledge: "the constant operation of the process of comparison which is so powerful in every department of science" could be made to "gradually elevat[e]" the "feeling and intelligence of the people" through the proper electoral procedure.[151] Naturally Mill, who believed that "the most important point of excellence which any form of government can possess is to promote the virtue and intelligence of the people themselves," praised the "elevating effect on the minds of the electors" which Hare's method would have.[152] The sum of this was nothing less than a *humanization* of elections – STV's refashioning of the electoral deed for the first time made mass electoral politics an activity fit for rational beings.[153]

Humanizing elections meant not only giving the elector his freedom, but also augmenting his "power."[154] The assurance that one's vote would contribute to the return of a candidate would effect a growth of responsibility and civic-spiritedness. The current system stamped out the sentiment of duty that would naturally arise if the vote were given in a free and effective manner.[155] By contrast, under his system

---

[151] Hare, *Election of Representatives*, xx, 132–4, 137; *Machinery of Representation*, 34.

[152] Mill, *Considerations*, 390; "Recent Writers on Reform," 367.

[153] "The process of local condensation to which the numerical majorities owe their success has done much to extinguish independent thought, *convert men into machines*, and thereby deteriorate the result of the votes by which the supposed representative assembly has been actually chosen"; *Election of Representatives*, 12 (my italics).

[154] Ibid., vii.

[155] "Under the existing system of majorities, every elector may throw upon others the blame of a contemptible choice. 'Thou canst not say I did it,' may be the answer to every remonstrance. But the case will be very different when every elector may personally acquire respect, or incur disgrace, by the selection which he makes"; "A system which first destroys individual freedom of action, and with it the higher inducements which connect action with duty, necessarily introduces and tolerates baser motives;" ibid., 201–2, 138.

the attraction presented to each elector by the power of giving effect in his vote to his especial and cherished opinions and feelings, will, when he comes to appreciate it, animate him with a new spirit of incalculable power. Considerations of duty will intervene with all their force. Every man will feel that he is personally responsible for his own error, or his own neglect. His understanding must teach him how to act, and his conscience guide him to the performance.

The object is to give to every individual elector the most complete freedom and power of exercising his best judgment . . . There is no aspiration, no germ of the higher feelings, to which the knowledge of the voter that he possesses such a discretion and such a power may not appeal.[156]

While not all of STV's backers reached Hare's pitch of expectation regarding the level to which responsibility, dutifulness, and public spirit would rise due to the voter's liberation and empowerment, the basic logic held throughout the period.[157] The hope of Hare and others was that the felt increase of power generated by the voluntary constituency and the efficacious vote would lead to greater moral seriousness and uprightness in citizens' approach to public affairs. As was typical given their tendency to view the electoral-parliamentary system as a single seamless fabric, PR supporters saw their responsibilizing and purifying of the vote as certain to reverberate within the assembly itself; because the new citizen of integrity would be immune to the "huckstering of votes," "miserable intrigues," and "contemptible tactics" to which politicians hitherto had resorted, the Commons would be transformed into what it ought to be: "the sanctuary of legislation."[158]

As the last phrase above suggests, Hare's theorizations of the improving effects of his system were informed by his religious faith. For the devout Hare,[159] this electoral remoralization amounted to a kind of *sacralization* of the vote. His reform was guided by a conviction of the "sacred nature of the act of voting," of the need to "render voting a solemn and sacred act."[160] He reiterated the point near the end of his life: "In all that I have suggested on representative institutions my object has been to bring all the better tendencies into action, and give to the business of election even a sacred character."[161]

The rhetoric of sacredness was not ornamental; it reflected the connection between the libertarian and personalist character of his scheme and his religious beliefs, which despite being High-Church were shot through with

---

[156] Hare, *Election of Representatives*, 137–8; "Reform Bill of the Future," 79–80.

[157] Hobart, "Parliamentary Reform," 266–7; Williams, *Proportional Representation and British Politics*, 6.

[158] Hare, *Machinery of Representation*, 51–3.

[159] On Hare's High-Church Anglicanism, see Parsons, *Thomas Hare and Political Representation*, 39–40.

[160] Hare, *Election of Representatives*, 149, 126.   [161] Hare, "Coming Steps in Representation," 216.

Protestant individualism. In a manner that paralleled evangelical free-traders' arguments that restrictions on trade were interferences with the divine will,[162] Hare argued that attempts to group electors nonvoluntarily constituted obstructions of the "master builder" and his "divine energy." Because (Protestant) Christianity was a religion that eschewed compulsion and anchored itself in the soul of each person, the electoral arrangements of a Christian nation had to reflect this vision of the emancipation and moral personality of the individual; in this light, the current system was a straightforward contravention of "the aim of Christianity," which "is personal, or it is nothing."[163] Suitably reformed, the act of voting could take its place among a range of practices from across history which "connect-[ed] religion" to "important events" of the state.[164] It was in this context of intense religiosity that Hare himself – if not all his followers – thought about rekindling the sense of responsibility proper to the electoral function. While it is not novel to note the influence of religion on the history of electoral theory, this awareness tends to stop at the Middle Ages.[165] STV, however, ought to be added to the list of electoral breakthroughs with Christian origins.

Hare's notion of the remoralization of the vote was informed not only by his religion, but also by a surprising interpretation of English electoral history. The nostalgia of Hare and the variety-of-suffragists for the "talents" that were able to find a foothold in the Commons through the close boroughs has been acknowledged already. Yet his affection for what radicals regarded as hallmarks of the "glaring injustice" of Old Corruption also included a degree of idealization that went beyond the thought of a Grey or Greg.[166] For Hare went further, articulating an unusual roman-ticization of these districts as bastions of dutifulness and seriousness. This did not mean that they should be reinstituted, since as a good historicist he accepted that their time had passed.[167] Nevertheless, the approach taken by the holders of power in the era of aristocratic dominance was, to Hare's

---

[162] Boyd Hilton, *The Age of Atonement: The Influence of Evangelicalism on Social and Economic Thought, 1785–1865* (Oxford, 1986).

[163] Hare, *Election of Representatives*, 148–9. He quoted here the popular Evangelical tract *Guesses at Truth* by theologians A. W. and J. C. Hare.

[164] Hare, *Election of Representatives*, 149–51.

[165] Leo Moulin, "Les origines religieuses des techniques électorales et délibératives modernes," *Politix*, 11 (1998): 117–62; George Szpiro, *Numbers Rule: The Vexing Mathematics of Democracy, from Plato to the Present* (Princeton, 2010), chs. 1–3.

[166] Bailey, *A Discussion of Parliamentary Reform* (London, 1831).

[167] Since their heyday "the state of society silently underwent a change. The system which produced these results had fulfilled its purpose. It could not be perpetuated, the middle classes which grew up were not prepared to yield unreasoning obedience to hereditary leaders and ancient names"; Hare, *Election of Representatives*, 79.

eyes, not without laudable elements. Take, for instance, these extraordinary passages on the perspective of the close-borough patron on the task of
selecting MPs:

> These leading men ... felt a personal responsibility in making the selection –
> a responsibility which increased with the importance of the office ... They
> were answerable for the judicious exercise of this, as of all other influences
> which they possessed ... Responsibility is not the less real, because its
> sanctions are conventional.
>
> Throughout the whole of [the eighteenth century], it must not be
> forgotten that all elections were governed by persons acting under a sense
> of the importance and responsibility of their work.
>
> The powerful patron ... could form no part of a system of personal
> representation. But with the indicating mind is gone all sense of responsi-
> bility for the choice which is made ... In this diffusion of forces which were
> heretofore concentrated, it becomes of paramount importance to purify the
> sources from whence they derive their energy.

Hare's eulogium was not untempered; he acknowledged that, as great a sense
of duty as borough proprietors and aristocratic directors of elections felt, this
dutifulness was often redirected from "public interests" to "party" ones.[168]
Nonetheless, the lesson they offered stood: because aristocratic borough-
proprietors had felt their character and judgment directly implicated in the
performance of the man whom they had chosen, they did not treat their task
with the flippancy and unconcern which characterized nineteenth-century
electors. In light of this historical vision, one promise of PR was that it might
revive as much of the old feeling of personal implication in parliamentary
representation as was possible in an era after oligarchic power-brokerage. PR
would generalize the ethos of responsibility qua selector that had existed
among a cadre of aristocrats under the unreformed Parliament to
a responsibility qua elector among the whole voting population.

b   Parliamentary Inclusivity

As we have just seen, a striking series of benefits was expected from the
most distinctive parts of the scheme: electoral liberty and the transfer
through a list of multiple preferences. But of course PR was also
a *mirroring* theory, involving (its own variation on) the classical descriptivist aim.[169] Since this aspiration shared much with the variety-of-

---

[168] Ibid., 77–80.
[169] It was "the only mode in which it is possible to obtain this complete reflection in the House of the
convictions and preferences existing in the constituent body – to make the House, what we are so

suffragists and deliberative democrats, there was less originality to their exposition of the advantages that stemmed from the "perfection of representation" in the assembly.[170] For example, their conception of how deliberation would operate within such a consummately representative assembly was very similar to that of someone such as Bagehot: "the object and end of the House," as Courtney described it, "is to bring together talk, to give it form and shape, to put opinion against opinion, and thus to produce an outcome of policy."[171] Relatedly, professions of faith that "the natural influence of truth and reason" would win out in representative systems so long as provisions for diversity were made differed little from the epistemic optimism of supporters of electoral variegation.[172]

In one area, however, proportionalist theorizing about the significance of parliamentary inclusivity took a more original course.

i Stability

Stability loomed as large for PR supporters as it did for variety-of-suffragists. Compared to their counterparts on the side of electoral differentiation, though, this aspect of British PR was very international. To be sure, reformers in the variety-of-suffrages mold were responsive to foreign events and ideas: for instance, they wanted to avoid the cycles of instability and revolution they perceived abroad, especially in France.[173] But their reaction to foreign considerations was to look inward ever more appreciatively: England's peculiar constitutional heritage, they concluded, had left it with a set of techniques and principles uniquely adept at maintaining civil peace. Conversely, despite the Anglophilia of some continental thinkers and some

---

often told that it ought to be, the express image of the nation"; Mill, *Speech on Personal Representation*, 182.

[170] Hare, *Election of Representatives*, 17.

[171] As far as parliamentary deliberation was concerned, the biggest difference between the PR and variety-of-suffragist frameworks was perhaps that the former had an even more "elitist" accent to it, at least in the work of its founding fathers. The likes of Mill and Hare were convinced that their proposals would remedy a deficit of talent and wisdom among legislators; the "very ablest men" whose influx their system would enable would, naturally, not sit inert once in the Commons. "The representatives of the majority, besides that they would themselves be improved in quality by the operation of the system, would no longer have the whole field to themselves ... When any difference arose, they would have to meet the arguments of the instructed few, by reasons, at least apparently, as cogent; and since they could not, as those do who are speaking to persons already unanimous, simply assume that they are in the right, it would occasionally happen to them to become convinced that they were in the wrong ... The champions of unpopular doctrines would not put forth their arguments merely in books and periodicals, read only by their own side; the opposing ranks would meet face to face and hand to hand, and there would be a fair comparison of their intellectual strength, in the presence of the country"; Mill, *Considerations*, 457–8.

[172] Mill, *Considerations*, 477.   [173] E.g. Grey, *Parliamentary Government*, 95.

broad generic similarities between continental schemes of class representation and English variety-of-suffrage philosophy,[174] the language and system
of Mackintosh and Bagehot did not sink deep roots elsewhere in Europe. By
contrast, PR was a genuinely international movement. British supporters
interacted with PR thinkers abroad and took close note of the spread of
various PR systems internationally.[175] This outward-looking valence was
particularly significant on the current issue, for stability was at the center
of continental PR theory. This concern was emblematized by the Genevan
Ernest Naville. Naville, a Protestant theologian occupied with the classic
problems of free will and theodicy, was a correspondent of Hare and Mill
and an indefatigable champion of "true representation" whose influence was
felt in England and across the Continent.[176] Navillle took up the cause in
response to violent unrest in Geneva, and he consistently placed stability at
the center of his writings. Driven by the "desire to reestablish peace by the
means of justice," he wished to put an end to an electoral system based on
"combat" in which "one part of the citizens remains deprived of representatives, exactly like a power crushed on a battlefield rests, deprived of all its
rights, at the mercy of the victor."[177] This accent on peace and stability
united the vast European literature on PR, including proponents of different
forms of list system and STV. Versions of the claim that PR would usher in
"an era of peace and tranquility" by replacing a "fight without mercy" with
"a less violent fight, each party having the hope of being represented without
having to annihilate its adversary," were common.[178] British authors vigorously made such arguments as well – sometimes lifting them directly from
figures such as Naville. In doing so, Victorian proportionalists diverged from
variety-of-suffragists in two main ways.

First, as the quotations from Naville indicate, from the PR point-of-
view the conjunction of partisan politics and plurality-rule arrangements
was intrinsically destabilizing. PR sympathizers anticipated, and then participated in, a broader disenchantment with parties, a major piece of which

---

[174] The Prussian scheme of class representation in use from 1850–1918 based on universal but unequal
suffrage bore some resemblance to Harris-style variety-of-suffragism, although there were crucial
differences; Kahan, *Liberalism in Nineteenth-Century Europe*, 67–78, 141–50.

[175] For an overview of PR's adoption, see André Blais, Agnieska Dobrzynska, and Indridi Indridason.
"To Adopt or not to Adopt Proportional Representation: The Politics of Institutional Choice,"
BJPS, 35 (2005): 182–90.

[176] On Naville's life and thought, see Dominique Wisler, "Ernest Naville ou l'invention de la
représentation proportionnelle," conference paper, 2008 [www.researchgate.net/publication/
280977838].

[177] Ernest Naville, *La Patrie et les Partis* (Geneva, 1865), 7, 20. See also Genevan Antoine Morin's *De la
question électorale dans le canton de Genève*, (Geneva, 1867), 4–5.

[178] François-Marie-Jules Christophle, *De la représentation proportionnelle* (Paris, 1887), 30–2.

was the suspicion that parties had an inherent bent toward intolerance which was exacerbated in the current intellectually and morally stunted political culture; this view would receive its archetypal expression in Ostrogorski's analysis of the party as the modern equivalent of the persecutory church.[179] These proclivities toward groupthink, rancorousness, and obedience to the "machine" were aggravated by partisans' fear that the vagaries of winner-take-all elections would restrict their party's access to the legislature to far below the levels which they considered their due. PR, on the other hand, was unique among electoral arrangements in that it "*cannot* be dangerous"; it alone possessed "all the elements of strength and safety." The prospect of extralegal violence against the exclusive legislatures that majoritarian voting rules could produce was the natural outcome of a system which "divide[d] the nation into two parties, and convert[ed] the area of legislation into a battle-field." Riots and revolts were the predictable fruits of arrangements that "absorb[ed] all differences into one issue – a contest for power." Local-majority methods, no matter how wide the accompanying franchise, would always be liable to desperate assaults from proponents of viewpoints marginalized in or excluded from the assembly: "if the House of Commons be not the actual . . . organ of public opinion, the nation is left open to the attacks and the enterprises of irresponsible persons, who are thereby encouraged to usurp its office." "If the nominal representative body do not truly represent the people, or if it represent only a majority of numbers," Hare cautioned, "imperfect and deceptive" claims to act on behalf of the true public will proliferate, and the state will be swallowed up in a "vortex."[180]

The analysis of how party acrimony was heightened by (a) the "warlike" confrontations of plurality-rule elections[181] and (b) the prospect of certain parties having their representation drastically depleted relative to their overall electoral presence[182] redounded throughout British PR. This

---

[179] Ostrogorski, *Democracy and Political Parties*, vol. 2, esp. 615–17.

[180] Hare, *Election of Representatives*, xxxviii, 10–11, 230, 240–3.

[181] E.g. Calvert, *Representation of Minorities*, 13, 24–5: "This defect in our system produces very sore feelings amongst electors . . . To be defeated in an election-contest is often a severe trial; but the defeated party is further embittered by the reflection, that all the influence of the entire constituency, including their own influence, is to be exercised by the candidate, against whom they have maintained vigorously but unsuccessfully an uncompromising opposition"; "Again, the number of contests will be greatly diminished. There are many towns, in which the bitterness of electioneering contests has begotten quarrels, which have been intolerable, and have actually destroyed the society of place."

[182] For instance, as early as 1848 Ludlow was blaming "the present system" for driving Chartism to extremes because of its diminishment of the Chartist parliamentary presence relative even to what it

framework could then be filled out and nuanced in different ways. Three deserve notice.

First, PR authors were worried that "violent fluctuations in the balance of political power" – sudden swings from very liberal to very conservative governments, for instance – were in themselves destabilizing.[183] Due to the decisive impact it gave to small clusters of voters in marginal districts, the first-past-the-post system created a situation in which tiny shifts in the aggregate vote could initiate huge reversals in policy.[184] This lack of continuity rendered political life volatile, especially in Britain where there remained no effective constitutional checks on legislative action.[185] The ever-present possibility of rapid alternation between diametrically opposed policies, even on fundamental issues, was seen a recipe for civic unrest.

Second, in contrast to modern "economic" models of democracy,[186] a contingent of PR authors saw the adversarial electoral environment as not merely leading partisans to regard their opposition in a hostile manner, but also as pushing them substantively farther apart. Plurality-rule systems, they charged, were biased against moderate figures, and thus left no political actors who could mediate between the vocal crowds of true believers who called for party purity. They split the country "into opposing and solid blocks of conflicting opinion" by "driv[ing] the representation into the hands of extreme men, and pronounc[ing] upon those on both sides who hold moderate views, and who may be a majority of the whole, the sentence of nullity and political extinction."[187] To this "centrist" mindset, PR would prevent polarization by allowing the gradation of positions between the centrifugal platforms of the two parties to earn their full parliamentary presence.[188] A large but heterogeneous sensible center would emerge under STV to thwart the entrenchment of extremism and ensure stability.[189]

---

ought to have been under the restricted franchise of the time. "Hence it happens, that what may be called growing parties remain far too long unrepresented in Parliament, and are often driven to factious measures for the enforcement of their opinions. Even now, the Chartist body is very insufficiently represented, in proportion to its total bulk"; Ludlow, "Electoral Districts and Representation of Minorities," 212.

[183] Lubbock, "Proportional Representation," 706.
[184] Lubbock et al., "Objections and Answers," 313; Humphreys, *Proportional Representation*, 42–3.
[185] On PR as of the same genre of institutional solutions as America's constitutional checks, see e.g. Greg, "Redistribution," 808.
[186] E.g. Anthony Downs, *An Economic Theory of Democracy* (New York, 1957), chs. 7–8.
[187] Grey, "Proportional vs. Majority Representation," 957.
[188] Lubbock, *Representation*, 75; Humphreys, *Proportional Representation*, 58, 202.
[189] E.g. Hare, "Note," 107. Unsurprisingly, an emphasis on the possible anti-extremist, center-reinforcing effects of PR was important in the context of the French Third Republic; H. S. Jones, "Political Uses of the Concept of 'Representation': How the French Debated Electoral Reform, c. 1880–1914," *Redescriptions*, 4 (2000): 15–36.

Third, some PR champions cast their system as finally realizing the conditions in which a longstanding argument for the pacific properties of democracy would hold true. Tocqueville's articulation can stand for this line of thought, both for its eloquence and because many of our authors encountered the argument in this form:

> But of all causes that help in the United States to moderate the violence of political association in the United States, the most powerful, perhaps, is universal suffrage. In countries where universal suffrage is allowed, the majority is never in doubt, because no party can reasonably portray itself as the representative of those who did not vote. Associations therefore know that they do not represent the majority, and everyone else knows it too . . .
>
> The moral force of the government that these associations attack is thereby greatly enhanced, while their own moral force is greatly diminished.[190]

This logic, which we might call the *majority-revelatory* logic of democratic peace, was accepted in principle by proportionalists. What they denied was the extent of its applicability. The pacific virtues of revealing the majority such that extra-parliamentary claims to represent the people were neutered obtained, they held, only with PR; after all, they believed that only their system guaranteed "the due preponderance of the majority."[191] Hence, Tocqueville was correct that "real democracy" was a supremely stable political form; but since he was wrong to consider universal suffrage *tout court* to be real democracy, he imputed to it virtues that belonged only to certain, proportionalist configurations of universal suffrage.[192]

Such were the main paths followed by proportionalists in theorizing how PR remedied the destabilizing features inherent in the status quo. Beyond plugging these holes in the vessel of first-past-the-post, its advocates ascribed to it the positive power of generating an ethos that bolstered the stability of representative government. Two languages were used to depict this ethos. The first, which is closely related to the way in which Hare and company sought to trade on the Victorian vogue for voluntary associations, was to extol the "cooperative spirit" it would imbue. Mill was deeply invested in the concept of cooperation throughout his career,[193] both in the philosophical-historical sense that the "power of co-operation" was the distinguishing mark of civilized societies and in the more specific

[190] Tocqueville, *Democracy in America*, vol. 1, 221–2.
[191] J. Parker Smith, "Parliamentary Reform: Minority Representation," *WR*, 121 (1884), 163–75.
[192] Courtney, "Representation of Minorities," 154.
[193] Gregory Claeys, "Justice, Independence, and Industrial Democracy: The Development of John Stuart Mill's Views on Socialism," *JP*, 49 (1987): 122–47.

economic-policy sense of supporting a reconciliation of laissez-faire and socialism through the growth of workers' cooperatives.[194] And he was far from alone in the PR ranks on this point.[195] In extending the "means of co-operation" available to electors, Hare's scheme would tap into the spirit which "exists in co-operation, in unions for trade purposes, and for the promotion of art, of science, and of literature."[196] In contrast to a contentious all-or-nothing atmosphere, with PR the "generous senti-ments" and "desire to further the ... welfare of large numbers of men" which characterized hopes for cooperation in the economy would spread into politics as well.[197] The second language was that of "harmony." While present ab initio,[198] it was especially prominent in later decades, outlasting the mid-Victorian enthusiasm for the cooperative movement and resonat-ing with New Liberal attempts to reconstruct liberalism around a "harmonic principle."[199] As the decades rolled on, this claim to being the indispensable electoral basis of a harmonious society shored up PR's self-understanding as the true *liberal* method of elections, while also putting it in accord with the inveterate liberal anxiety to fend off class-based politics.[200] Though undoubtedly the rise of the Labour party at home and revolutionary socialism abroad caused important shifts in Liberal thinking about class conflict between the mid-Victorian and Edwardian eras, PR was commended throughout as a tool for fostering a holistic and solidaristic politics against destabilizing class confrontation.[201] Representative reform as an instrument of cooperative-ness and harmony – this was the "consensual politics" of the long first wave of British PR advocacy.[202]

The argument for PR as the system of stability par excellence thus contained two prongs: a negative one, explaining how it corrected for dynamics in plurality-rule systems that threatened domestic tranquility;

---

[194] Respectively, Mill, "Civilization," in *CW*, vol. 18, 119–47; *The Principles of Political Economy*, in *CW*, vol. 3, book 4, ch. 7. Mill's enthusiasm for cooperation grew throughout the second half of his life; for instance, he went beyond the normal focus on industrial or consumer concerns, shifting from the endorsement of peasant proprietorship in 1848 to support for agricultural cooperatives in later decades as the proper method for applying the democratic principle to the rural economy.

[195] E.g. Hare's enthusiasm for the "co-operative movement"; *Election of Representatives*, 37.

[196] Hare, "Representation of Every Locality and Intelligence," 530; "Just Expression," 203.

[197] Hare, *Election of Representatives*, 33.   [198] Ibid., xxx, 195.

[199] C. M. Griffin, "L. T. Hobhouse and the Idea of Harmony," *JHI*, 35 (1974): 647–61.

[200] Michael Freeden, "The New Liberalism and Its Aftermath," in Victorian Liberalism, 175–92.

[201] Compare e.g. Hare, *Machinery*, 42, with the concerns about a false "cleavage" between classes coming to dominate politics in Hobhouse's *Liberalism* a half-century later.

[202] E.g. Kenneth McRae, "Contrasting Styles of Democratic Decision-Making: Adversarial versus Consensual Politics," *IPSR*, 18 (1997): 279–95.

and a positive one, explaining how the quest for "party triumphs" would be replaced by a new atmosphere of "com[ing] together" and seeking "common ground."[203] It proved an attractive vision to many, although it was not without difficulties. One related to how and whether this "consensual" vision fit with another normative framework that seemed, if anything, prior to it: that of "Antagonism," the "great social function" that alone could stave off "degeneracy and decay," "the only real security for continued progress."[204] How was consensus to accord with antagonistic pluralism? As one critic derisively put it, Hare's theory seemed full of blithe assertions that somehow "diversities can give unity."[205] Victorian PR is far from unique among traditions in the history of political thought in having struggled to reconcile the rightful claims of unity and plurality;[206] it almost certainly is a problem that resists any final theorization.[207] Nonetheless, the tension between contestation and cooperation, antagonism and harmony, was more acute for the PR school than for variety-of-suffragists such as Bagehot, since the former did not merely hope for a working division of epistemic labor that could produce good policy and ward off stagnation, but aimed to robustly reshape the distribution of beliefs and the moral-intellectual qualities of citizens.

A more basic shortcoming of their case was a naïveté about the existential character of certain conflicts. Many in the PR ranks attributed to their system an almost supernatural capacity to resolve divides that went to the core of national morality and identity – as seen most spectacularly in their avowals that the American Civil War would have been averted by PR.[208] It would be harsh to fault them for not having devised institutions that would unfailingly carry a country safely through a conflict in which "a really fundamental point is touched," in which a "primary instinct" is

---

[203] Hare, "School Board," 219.

[204] Mill, *Considerations*, 458, 397. Hare placed great weight on these famous passages; "John Stuart Mill," 147–50.

[205] Collier, *Representation of Minorities*, 15.

[206] Deliberative democratic theory today has similar fissures between consensus-oriented and more agonistic approaches; see e.g. James Bonham and William Rehg, "Introduction," to *Deliberative Democracy: Essays on Reason and Politics*, ed. Bonham and Rehg (Cambridge, MA, 1997), x.

[207] It is far from clear that, for example, a claim like Joshua Cohen's that we should "expect important elements of political consensus to emerge" even as "different, independent moral traditions" persist marks any advance on Hare; Cohen, "Democracy and Liberty," in *Deliberative Democracy*, 185–231.

[208] E.g. Albert Grey, "Proportional versus Majority Representation," 956–7. These authors were quick to point to American documents which supported this view, especially an 1869 Senate report to this effect. For this thought as expressed by American writers, see e.g. J. Francis Fisher, *The Degradation of our Representative System and Its Reform* (Philadelphia, 1863), 16–17; John Commons, *Proportional Representation* (New York, 1896), 179–80.

"seriously and continuously outraged."[209] But their proclamations about how "sanguinary disturbances," "political convulsions," and "risings of the Peoples ... in all their terrors" would disappear once plurality rule was abandoned fed into the impression of skeptics that Hare's school were unserious utopians.[210] In the end, British proportionalists largely fell back on the beliefs that: (a) a splintered panoply of opinions and parties could share the assembly peaceably and might even prove a safer distribution of opinion than a bifurcation between governing and opposition blocs;[211] and that (b) what we have called *fair play* and *deliberative consideration* – the faith that from the average citizen's perspective there was a "vast difference between a minority and a nullity" – kept those who were on the wrong end of policy decisions from succumbing to feelings of alienation.[212] Stated thus, PR theory did not mark much of an advance on the ideas of Mackintosh or Bagehot about the sources of stability, nor did it justify its extraordinary rhetoric.

In another respect, though, PR theorists did go beyond variety-of-suffragist suppositions about stability. Recall that even W. R. Greg had worried that the basic building blocks of mirroring representation as he understood it – the special provision of seats for different groups – could backfire if wrongly implemented. Specifically, he had feared that certain traditional mirroring configurations would foment hostilities between economic classes. Of course, Greg's anxieties were targeted at poor instantiations of the system; for his apprehensions to have been any more sweeping would have undercut his descriptive program altogether. The innovation of PR theory – especially that side of it which remained faithful to the single national constituency – was to generalize Greg's fears and turn them against *all* fixed constituencies.

For reasons already addressed, Harean STV renounced all involuntary districts, and the remainder of the PR community accepted large constituencies only as a practical necessity. An additional reason for this stance was their judgment that peace required it. Any break with formal sociological agnosticism in the electoral system, they believed, had destabilizing consequences. This was true, in the first place, of territorial modes of

---

[209] Lowes-Dickinson, *Development of Parliament*, 161.
[210] *The Franchise: What Shall We Do to It?*, 18–22.
[211] This is in direct opposition to a traditional objection to PR, which is that its facilitation of the proliferation of small parties leads to governmental weakness and, ultimately, political collapse. After 1933 the prime example for this argument was, of course, Germany; Karl Loewenstein, "Militant Democracy and Fundamental Rights [1]," *APSR*, 31 (1937): 417–32; Reinhold Aris, "Proportional Representation in Germany," *Politica*, 2 (1937): 433–45.
[212] *The Franchise: What Shall We Do to It?*, 20. Also Courtney, "Seats Bill," 31–3.

erecting constituencies, which nonproportionalist democrats regarded without alarm. Plurality-rule territorial divisions had a tendency to set regions of the state against one another by giving a false impression that inhabitants of different regions were strongly divided ideologically. They yielded an "exaggerated expression" of the extent of the chasm in beliefs between residents of different areas that generated "disintegrating effects" for the polity; under nonproportionalist arrangements, the "geographical differentiation of political views" came to seem so great that it increased the chances of violent conflict among regions.[213] Among other instances cited, this argument about the exacerbation of geographical tensions relied on two cases, the first being the above-noted US Civil War. It was standard among proportionalists to blame plurality rule for "their disastrous civil war," alleging that it had kept a sizable antislavery (or moderate proslavery, antisecessionist) minority in the South from being recognized at the federal level and therefore made it easier for the North and South to face each other as unanimous adversarial blocs. Especially as the question of Irish Home Rule intensified from the 1880s on, PR proponents sought to draw links between Ireland and the American tragedy. The most important lesson they took was that their system was necessary to prevent the Catholic majority from swamping the loyalist Protestant minority everywhere outside of Ulster, a fate which, beyond its intrinsic undesirability from the English perspective, would diminish the likelihood of compromise and increase the probability of revolutionary violence or a war of secession.[214] First-past-the-post systems had the undesirable property of giving regional differences the appearance of close alignment with other sorts of divisions – racial, linguistic, ideological, religious – and thus of making violence and disintegration more likely than would be the case if the representative system furnished a more accurate image of the nation as a composite of various identities and affiliations that crisscrossed over its whole surface. Hence, their plan to "substitute . . . a mental distribution" for the "rigid geographical partition of electoral power" was required not only by considerations of liberty, justice, and inclusion – it also represented the kingdom's best chance for peace and permanence.[215]

---

[213] Humphreys, *Proportional Representation*, 56; Lubbock, *Representation*, 19.

[214] George Shaw-Lefevre, a critic of PR, admitted that Ireland was a great argumentative coup for his opponents; Shaw-Lefevre "The Representation of Minorities," 727. References to the Irish conundrum were frequent throughout the last two decades of the nineteenth and into the twentieth century: e.g. Williams, *Proportional Representation and British Politics*, 51–2; Lubbock, *Representation*, 21–2; Hare, "Coming Steps in Representation," 221; Eugenio Biagini, *British Democracy and Irish Nationalism, 1876–1906* (Cambridge, 2007), 14.

[215] Hare, "Note," 107.

Quotas based on nonterritorial kinds of group membership – on class, occupation, religion, etc. – came in for even harsher attacks. The existence of these sorts of quotas, Hareans believed, reinforced the very divisions they were meant to assuage.[216] This argument is of course not unique to British proportionalists,[217] although they made it with particular potency because it was interwoven with the arguments about contestability that weighed so greatly with nonproportionalist democrats as well. While territorially based constituencies had unsettling knock-on effects for the integrity of the polity and were not immune to the charge of being based on "invidious distinctions" between inhabitants of different areas,[218] for the most part citizens accepted electoral groupings based on location as natural facts, an unremarkable matter of course. This, however, was not true of other bases for constituency formation. To divide the electorate according to other kinds of classifications was bound, Mill cautioned, to "be invidious, and could only escape from being offensive by being totally without influence."[219] (It is puzzling that Mill believed that "a separate organisation of the instructed classes" would court destabilization and resentment, but that a plurality of votes based on the same principle would not.[220]) As an Edwardian PR supporter put it, criticizing a proposal which was intended to keep the religious peace in a few Indian provinces, "its working, as the working of all arbitrary schemes must, has evoked criticism on the ground that it does not hold the scales even as between the two sections to be represented."[221] In other words, the conceptual-theoretical difficulties facing any kind of electoral corporatism[222] translated into urgent practical

---

[216] This was close to the democratic argument against the variety of suffrages on grounds of stability discussed at the end of Chapter 2.

[217] See, for instance, Olivier Christin's account of the resistance to practices of confessional parity in sixteenth-century France; *Vox Populi*, 44–52. For similar views in contemporary theory, see e.g. Julia Stapleton, "Introduction," to *Group Rights: Perspectives since 1900*, ed. Stapleton (Bristol, 1995), xxxix; Lani Guinier, "The Representation of Minority Interests: The Question of Single-Member Districts," *Cardozo Law Review*, 14 (1993): 1135–74.

[218] As Hare himself believed them to be; *Election of Representatives*, 65.

[219] Mill, *Considerations*, 459.

[220] J. H. Burns, "J. S. Mill and Democracy [II]," *PS*, 5 (1957): 281–94. For more of the giants of PR on "invidious comparisons," see Fawcett, *Leading Clauses*, 17; Hare, *Machinery of Representation*, 24. The desire to avoid "introducing any new class privileges, which might be more or less odious to those excluded" also animated the invention of the cumulative vote; Marshall, *Minorities and Majorities*, 24.

[221] Humphreys *Proportional Representation*, 78. The scheme in question was adopted by Morley during his time as Secretary for India. Despite his Millianism, Morley was an opponent of PR; Vernon Bogdanor, "The Liberal Party and the Constitution," *Journal of Liberal History*, 54 (2007): 46–52.

[222] "The idea of representing separately the parts of the body politic that perform separate functions – the more and the less skilled wage-earners – professional persons – commercial classes, and so on –

menaces to the viability of representative government. To the proportionalist mind, even the concern for inclusivity and descriptive accuracy
motivating variety-of-suffragism and cognate "corporatist" approaches
was counterproductive to the cause of stability. For diverse modern societies with representative systems, only inclusivity purged of involuntariness
could guarantee a healthy, durable state.

2 Millian Rebuttals: The Local Constituency and the Threat of Stagnation

The moral universe of Victorian PR was vast. It shared much with lines of
thought from neighboring traditions of deliberative representative government, and laid claim to distinctive social and intellectual benefits.
As evidenced by the objections already examined, such grand professions
did not pass unchallenged. The remainder of this chapter is devoted to the
core of the critical response to PR. It is common –in both the primary and
the secondary literature – to find Victorian–Edwardian opposition to PR
ascribed to "misapprehension."[223] To be sure, there was some incomprehension, as befits a system that, apologists' protestations to the contrary
notwithstanding, *just is* complicated.[224] Nevertheless, opponents of Hare
articulated counterarguments that struck at the heart of the normative
vision underlying his reform.

a The Idealist Case for First-Past-the-Post

Ramsay MacDonald's *Socialism and Government* was a landmark of early
Labour-party political thought, an energetic articulation of how his evolutionary, communitarian socialism was meant to apply to the central questions of state organization.[225] Beyond this general significance, it has
already been observed that this text carried into early-twentieth-century
Labour ideology themes dear to the Victorian descriptivist-deliberativist
tradition. The equation of social democracy with an inclusive, pluralistic

---

is probably impracticable. For it is not clear that it is possible thus to assume with certainty what is
a man's chief function, and classify him accordingly to the neglect of all other sides of his
personality. And it is certainly not easy to frame the boundaries of constituencies defined by
functions and to determine how many members they are to return"; Williams, *Reform of
Representation*, 4.

[223] E.g. Lubbock, "Proportional Representation," 708; Hart, *Proportional Representation*, 137.

[224] Michael Dummett, *Principles of Electoral Reform* (Oxford, 1997), 127–31.

[225] Geoffrey Foote, *The Labour Party's Political Thought: A History* (Houndmills, Basingstoke, 1997),
57–64.

state rather than a class-based one; the rejection of capacity-based demar-
cations as arbitrary; the understanding of the purpose of broadening the
franchise as the admission to political life of groups which have different
perspectives, in contrast to the "French" model of commonality as the
ground of political representation[226]; the denial of delegation; the upholding of the deliberative status of the Commons – these facets of
MacDonald's thought would seem to have been more than friendly to
PR. In fact, however, he was a determined opponent.

MacDonald gave many reasons for his disapproval, including the way
STV would diminish the efficiency of the legislature and hinder the
formation of strong governments. His core objection, however, was that
PR would sap the intellectual vitality of Britain's political culture.
The culprit was a brand of "elitism," though by this MacDonald meant
something different from the accusations canvased hitherto. What he had
in mind was a sensibility that, in the very way in which it valorized
diversity, robbed this diversity of its political and epistemic value. PR

> is a method of election for securing the representation of fragments of
> political thought and desire, and for inviting those fragments to coalesce
> after and not before elections ... Proportional Representation ... seeks to
> emphasise the irreconcilable dogmatic differences which the *élite* consider to
> be precious, and to prevent the intermingling of opinion on the margins of
> parties and sections of parties which is essential to ordered and organic social
> progress.

Instead of the dialectic of conflict and cooperation that occurred under
FPP – where citizens who disagreed on some matters submerged their
differences for the sake of a common cause and contested forthrightly with
opponents over central issues of national concern – PR encouraged "splitting up" and "sectionalism," the cultivation of "dogmatic and academic
differences in parties which have no value in actual life."[227] Far from "a
simple and unanswerable demand of elementary justice," PR's demand
that every shade of opinion receive its place in Parliament reflected an
ideological or aesthetic fetish for diversity that, in practice, fostered
a cliquish attitude among citizens whereby their pet projects were accorded
more significance than the give-and-take required to solve major public
problems.[228]

---

[226] E.g. Julian Wright and H. S. Jones, "A Pluralist History of France?," in *Pluralism and the Idea of the Republic in France*, ed. Wright and Jones (Houndmills, Basingstoke, 2012): 1–22.

[227] MacDonald, *Socialism and Government*, vol. 1, 164–5, 138.

[228] Ibid., 156, 165: "Every group ... regards its own nostrum without reference to greater national interests, and holds it up in the market-place as a quack does his pills."

To MacDonald, the Harean keystone of electoral liberty was a curse rather than a gift, for it allowed citizens to settle complacently for spokesmen of their own idiosyncratic or "individualistic" wants. This was, in effect, a Millian response to Mill's preferred program. If Mill had been correct that truth had to emerge "by the rough process of a struggle between combatants fighting under hostile banners," then why should those citizens who did not even "form active minorities" and who could not be bothered to brave the "struggles of the hustings" simply be awarded seats?[229] Far better to preserve the involuntary constituency of FPP, which forced different groups within the district to confront one another and ensured that truly agonistic campaigns would occur. Instead of the current lively contestation which alone had the capacity of "testing" ideas, PR would cause public life to stagnate: "The dead or stranded minorities have not earned the right to representation, and if it were granted to them, their representatives in Parliament would only exemplify the barenness and political incompatibility of their supporters outside Parliament. There are dead opinions as well as dead men." PR granted small agglomerations of opinion a foothold in the assembly as if opinions were somehow rights-bearing entities in themselves. The traditional system of local constituencies, by contrast, imposed a kind of salutary probationary period on "new ideas":

> A Parliament representative of the mind of the nation, does not require to contain men holding every odd-and-end view which may find acceptance by a thousand or two individual electors. Before an opinion, or body of opinion, has earned the right ... to Parliamentary representation, it ought to be compelled to go through a certain evolution. It should have to stand the test of public criticism and be so acceptable as to gain not only a following, but a following which considers it to be of sufficient importance to bring it into the arena of politics in one or other of the several ways in which this can be done. It should also have to win a place in that arena and establish itself in relation to other opinions there at the same time. This is necessary in order that legislative acts may reflect the General Will. And, finally, every opinion which claims Parliamentary recognition should be asked to prove its staying power, lest it may have been favoured by temporary circumstances into a gourd-like growth. When an opinion has weathered these tests successfully, it has either formed round it a respectable national organisation or has become suffused throughout Society ... Representation in the legislative organ of Society is the result of the success of the propaganda of an opinion, not a right that can be claimed for it simply because it exists.

By investing all beliefs with a sort of mystical sanctity, PR ignored the considerable virtues of the present political process and thus, despite its

---

[229] Mill, *On Liberty*, 254; Hare, *Machinery of Representation*, 1.

advocates' intentions, would consign Britain to an unprogressive, unevolutionary public sphere.[230] In other words, Mill's reform would bring about the very outcome which Mill had hoped it would prevent: stagnation.

Three points about MacDonald's Millian criticism of PR warrant specific consideration. First, he believed the strengths of FPP in terms of testing and maturing opinions and causes were illustrated by the case of his own Labour party. Instead of lamenting the hurdles that FPP posed to small parties, he believed that his "movement" had benefited from "finding some obstacles in the way of Parliamentary representation," because these obstacles ensured that Labour had arrived in Westminster only when the party and its ideas were ripe for the occasion.[231] Second, it followed from MacDonald's analysis that FPP could not be regarded as prejudicial to minorities, since a minority that was unable to win seats was by that very fact proven not to merit them.[232] This aspect of MacDonald's thought interestingly shared elements with both nonproportionalist *and* proportionalist traditions. As with the latter, the result of the election itself constituted the standard for judging the "legitimate influence" of "minorities that are politically active"; no external standard, no independent cartography of "classes, interests, and opinions," was invoked. On the other hand, in a manner reminiscent of the variety of suffrages, an evaluation purportedly grounded in objective facts about the condition of opinions was used to justify support for FPP; MacDonald valued first-past-the-post for separating the wheat from the chaff and admitting only that segment of opinion which had "that political quality which justifies its being represented in the representative assembly."[233]

---

[230] MacDonald, *Socialism and Government*, vol. 1, 138, 155, 129–32.

[231] "This has been good for the country and good for Socialism. Then, when the new opinions had been sufficiently tested, had been adjusted to actual affairs, and had won a following large enough to secure being represented in Parliament, they were in a position to use the present system of election with as much advantage as any other part"; MacDonald, *Socialism and Government*, vol. 1, 136–7.

[232] "The representation which alone counts is that of a body of political opinion of sufficient general importance to be organised for political purposes ... A test should be placed upon opinions asking for representation. Are they of such a nature as to rouse any general interest? Are they so important as to cause a movement in the social intelligence? Are they vital ... If they are, they are bound through one channel or other to find representation in every popularly governed country; and if they fail to do this, one may safely assume that they are of no social consequence"; ibid., 129–30. On the contrary, MacDonald worried that the present system was perhaps overly welcoming to certain minorities, namely, "special interests"; ibid., 130, 152. MacDonald's point here was similar to an argument William Riker made in the modern literature; Riker, "Electoral Systems and Constitutional Restraints," in *Choosing an Electoral System*, 103–110.

[233] MacDonald, *Socialism and Government*, vol. 1, 132, 135, 129.

Third and finally, as Chapter 4 showed, while *social* minorities figured hugely in the traditional variety-of-suffrages framework, *electoral* minorities as such played no role. By contrast, later antiproportionalist democrats, responding as they were to several decades of formidable Harean literature, needed an account of what was owed to electoral minorities. Their answer was that what representative democracies owed to electoral minorities was the chance to become majorities. Mill and Hare, it will be recalled, assured parliamentary representation to all bodies of opinion as a matter of justice.[234] MacDonald, however, was unimpressed: he denied that a "mechanical contrivance" or "special scheme" could grant minorities anything but an illusory share of power. This deflation of the pretensions of PR was no cause for alarm, though, because the contestatory politics of FPP already ensured that "active minorities" had the occasion to change "public opinion" in their favor; in MacDonald's language, their ideas had the opportunity to sit the "test" of debate in the local constituency. Being made to sit this test, he went on, posed no obstacle to the fairness of democratic government, since in a democracy the "majority acts not by force, but by persuasion." Because the local district provided a setting in which all groups could press their claims and have their support competed for by prospective MPs, fears of majority domination were unfounded; indeed, "'majority rule'" was not even "an accurate description of the governing force. Representative government ... is not the government of the majority, but the government of the whole people." PR, in sum, was a cure in search of a disease. In nations blessed with a deliberative political culture, PR would dampen the ardor of political contestation and intellectual exchange by fostering a cliquish attitude among the different segments of the electorate; in societies lacking such a culture, fiddling with electoral regulations would hardly prevent majority tyranny.[235]

The charge that PR misunderstood the true normative standing of electoral minorities as *potential majorities* had recently been articulated

---

[234] "Convictions, when they exist in a people, or in any appreciable portion of one, are entitled to influence in virtue of their mere existence, and not solely in that of the probability of their being grounded in truth"; "So large a body of voters as should amount to a quotient of electors, entertaining a conviction that a particular measure would promote the general welfare, are entitled, in a self-governed nation, to a representative of their views"; Mill, *Considerations*, 510; Beales et al., *Representative Reform Report*, 19. The belief that justice required that "all opinions, even the most absurd ones, the most monstrous ones" were owed "representatives in a number proportional to their strength in the electorate" had been the core principle for the progenitor of the list system, Victor Considerant, as well; F. A. Hermens, "Political Science and Proportional Representation," *Social Science*, 15 (1940): 5–19.

[235] MacDonald, *Socialism and Government*, vol. 1, 130–1, 109, 81. Also Leslie Stephen, "Walter Bagehot," in *Studies of a Biographer*, 4 vols. (London, 1902), vol. 3: 144–74, at 171–2.

with even greater rigor by the Idealist philosopher of evolutionary social democracy, D. G. Ritchie. To Ritchie, it was due to the "abstract and artificial" approach of "Mill and other advocates of 'proportional representation'" that they could not understand the robust position minorities necessarily occupied in the broader economy of any minimally functional democracy. For Ritchie, PR's contempt for the involuntary constituency and fetishism of *intra*-parliamentary diversity ignored the way that elections and representation under FPP were interwoven with a broader set of rights and deliberative practices. In a democratic polity

> any minority which has really got life and vigour in it can make itself felt. I do not think . . . it would be desirable to construct any political machinery for giving a prominent place to the opinions of minorities that will not take the trouble to assert and to spread these opinions. The all-important and essential right of minorities is the right to turn themselves into majority if they can; this means freedom of the press, freedom of association, freedom of public meeting . . . Minorities that grumble at the whole world round them and have no desire and no hope of convincing other people are not a valuable factor in political or social life.
>
> In a genuinely democratic government votes are nominally merely counted; in reality they are weighed . . . in the sense that the energy and contagious enthusiasm of a few, who represent some living and growing idea, far outweigh the indifference and apathy of great numbers. Great movements begin with small minorities; but these minorities must consist of persons who wish to make others share their convictions.

PR, Ritchie alleged, was based on a forgetfulness that conquering the majority was the *telos* of active democratic citizenship. Plurality-rule systems, on the other hand, impressed the "duties" that minorities had to meet their fellow citizens where they were and persuade them that their purposes conduced to the common good.[236] The postulate that "the most valuable right of a minority is the right to turn itself into a majority" was another way of saying that the meaning of representative government was not to parcel out to each fraction of opinion its due but to establish the

---

[236] Ritchie, "The Rights of Minorities," in *The British Idealists*, 142–55. Also *Principles of State Interference*, 73, where an advantage of recognizing "the right to turn itself into a majority if it can" as the "most important and valuable right of a minority" was that it stymied the tendency toward solipsism that led minority groups to seek a place for themselves "apart from the organic whole." See also, a decade earlier, Edward Russell's anti-Harean proclamation that "the business of a minority is to make itself into a majority." Revealingly, Russell, an ardent Liberal, cited Disraeli's authority on this point, hence establishing it as a national and not merely partisan credo; Edward Russell, *Minority Representation* (London, 1883), 3.

"'common will' ... by a process of discussion."[237] FPP – by setting the terms of the electoral task as being for voters, bound by the common tie of residence, to decide on a representative for them as a whole – better incarnated the spirit of democratic politics as a simultaneously collective and agonistic enterprise.[238] In more properly realizing this spirit, it also called forth the public-interestedness and intellectual energy of the electorate. As another Idealist, explaining his resistance to Mill's preferred "political contrivance," put it:

> men would judge quite differently, acting under such a scheme, from the way in which they judge when they act in their locality. Everything depends on the context to which one's views and action have to be adjusted. If you have to fight out a set of opinions in practice and in discussion among your neighbors, that is quite a different process from letting the returning office look out a few thousand people in Great Britain who happen to agree with you on a single point. In the one case your whole life is really an argument, both unconscious and conscious, with reference to the general working scheme of society. In the other case you simply pronounce a single casual reflective judgment. It appears to me an apt illustration of the general or organic will as contrasted with the will of all as a number of units.[239]

Of the many interesting features of this organicist or evolutionary antiproportionalism, two stand out. First, like other facets of the philosophy of representation in the period, this Idealist rejoinder to PR was connected to the question of the meaning of toleration and freedom of discussion. Specifically, the Idealists' attack on the Millian plan of representation mirrored their attack on what they considered the "Millian" school of toleration. While Idealists favored a large measure of intellectual-expressive freedom, their understanding of this value was derived from Mill's antagonist James Fitzjames Stephen.[240] Stephen and his Idealist followers believed that Mill had replaced a sober appreciation of liberty as the precondition for contest and struggle between (hostilely arrayed) groups with a sterilized, placid public sphere in which all opinions were entitled to a kind of right of succor. For them, PR participated in this elevation of a fetishized concern for protecting diversity over a true vision of intellectual-expressive liberty as the

---

[237] Ritchie, *Natural Rights: A Criticism of Some Ethical and Political Conceptions* (London, 1895), 208; A. H. Birch, *Representation* (London, 1971), 94.

[238] The arguments here resemble Schmitt's later attack on PR in the Weimar context as elevating "fractions" and "different voter groups" in a way that was irreconcilable with the properly political representation of the "entire people"; *Crisis of Parliamentary Democracy*, 19–20; *Constitutional Theory*, trans. Jeffrey Seitzer (Durham, 2008), 269.

[239] Bosanquet, "The Reality of the General Will," in *The British Idealists*, 140.

[240] Nicholson, *Political Philosophy of the British Idealists*, 294.

"precautions" for a "fair fight" between contenders.[241] Conversely, Idealists valued plurality rule for incarnating in electoral regulation the simultaneously holistic and contestatory civic-intellectual culture which they believed to be the engine behind Britain's greatness.

The link between opposition to PR and the perception that Millians were advocates of a kind of affirmative action for unconventional opinions in the broader public culture was tied to a fact about Mill's thought to which Victorians were more alert than recent scholars – namely, that Mill neither invoked the notion of the "marketplace of ideas" nor conceived of liberty of discussion along the lines of competitive political economy.[242] The "protectionist" undertones which Stephen and the Idealists detected in Millian toleration they also found in his reform scheme – indeed, it was a trope among critics that, far from being the electoral equivalent of the free market that Hare had christened it, PR was a form of "intellectual protectionism" that, like economic protectionism, inevitably brought about "stagnation."[243]

Second, critics of Ritchie's ilk alleged that their opponents overlooked the temporal dimension of democratic politics. Whereas they conceived of democracy as a dialogic process that evolved over time, PR's champions apprehended the task of representation as being to provide appropriate recognition to separate, settled blocs. This "static" outlook was, critics believed, revealed in the PR movement's fondness for photographic metaphors. A "'snapshot' theory of representation" such as PR ignored the "dynamic and spiritual factors" of plurality-rule democracy.[244] Once these factors were recognized, however, the majority's voice could be rightly appreciated as itself an artifact of the inputs of the whole citizenry:

> During the actual discussion, indeed, each may stick to his opinion: it might even be said that, unless people showed some obstinacy, a debate would always be a failure. For minds in a perfectly flabby condition discussion is impossible: it implies a certain amount of mutual resistance. But . . . it will be found that after any serious discussion both parties have probably modified their opinions, and out of the conflict of two opposing principles may spring a new one, victorious over both. It is by the conflict of ideas that intellectual progress is made.[245]

---

[241] J.F. Stephen, *Liberty, Equality, Fraternity*, 68.

[242] Keith Quincy, "Samuel Bailey and Mill's Defence of Freedom of Discussion," *The Mill Newsletter*, 21 (1986): 4–18.

[243] Christopher Kent, *Brains and Numbers* (Toronto, 1978), 45; Leslie Stephen, "Value of Political Machinery," 844–5.

[244] Finer, *Case Against PR*, 10.   [245] Ritchie, "The Rights of Minorities," 152.

Since discussion was the lifeblood of democratic politics, and discussion in the context of local elections possessed these interactive and dialectical qualities, there was no deficit of inclusion for PR to overcome. And since majorities were not freestanding social facts but emergent products of a continual competition between the spokesmen of different worldviews and agendas, there was no problem of domination or "tyranny" to be solved.[246]

b *Early Defenses of the Territorial District*

MacDonald and Ritchie were exemplars of a late-Victorian/Edwardian reaction against PR for its inorganic, anticommunal, stagnating character. Yet, the core of their approach did not need to wait on the currents of Idealism, New Liberalism, collectivist social ontology, and evolutionary theory that gained the ideological upper hand toward the end of our period.[247] Instead, Ritchie and MacDonald built on a fear that the demise of the involuntary local constituency would spell the downfall of Britain's robust civic culture which had been articulated as early as the 1860s. Canvassing a handful of the versions of this claim from the quarter-century after Hare's tracts first appeared provides a sense of just how deep and long-running the clash over the moral-political repercussions of his reform was.

While this earlier crop of antiproportionalists lacked the philosophical overlay of the Idealist objections, their analysis was often quite subtle. Indeed, they could occasionally grant that PR might deliver some of the benefits to which its enthusiasts laid claim. For instance, the Liberal politician Edward Hugessen Knatchbull-Hugessen, 1st Baron Brabourne, was sympathetic to several of Hare's goals, and he expressed an openness to the use of the cumulative vote in small multimember districts. Nonetheless, the "utter abolition" of local constituencies would "inflict" great "grievances" – indeed, nothing less than that "the political life of England would be deadened." Knatchbull-Hugessen foresaw "the people, or a large portion of them . . . ceas[ing] to take an interest in political matters" under a proportionalist regime. Without the structure provided by "local representation" and its contest between known rivals for the right

---

[246] The Idealist picture of discussion as itself securing all the properties of inclusivity requisite for democratic legitimacy would reach its apogee in A. D. Lindsay, *The Essentials of Democracy* (London, 1929). A similar view retains currency in the deliberative democratic literature: compare Lindsay or Ritchie with Bernard Manin, "On Legitimacy and Political Deliberation," trans. Elly Stein and Jane Mansbridge, *PT*, 15 (1987): 338–68.

[247] E.g. David Weinstein, *Utilitarianism and the New Liberalism* (Cambridge, 2007), ch. 1.

to represent a specific borough or county, the electoral process would appear opaque and distant, causing attention to public affairs to dampen.[248]

Other writers fleshed out anticipations of PR's deadening effect more fully. One such figure was Kinnear. Kinnear's anxieties about PR were manifold: as noted in Section 1a, he feared that it would drive up corruption and drive down the quality of MPs, and he seized on the "elitist" notes in PR advocacy to cast PR as a paternalist, antimajoritarian institution.[249] His profoundest worry, however, was that via PR "all the educative influences of the representative system" would "be destroyed." It was the "local connection" – the defined territory in which the MP entered into a back-and-forth of instruction, argument, and criticism with a relatively stable set of inhabitants in the context of trying to maintain ascendancy against contenders for the role of representing the community's will – that supplied the most valuable engine of "a moderate, temperate, tolerant, yet clear and definite public opinion." In particular, what caused Kinnear consternation was a prospect that exhilarated Hare: that the enlightened classes would band together to return MPs of their own, immune to the sentiments of a "majority" which by definition was "less instructed and less sagacious."[250] However much proportionalists wished to pooh-pooh the fear that "political feeling would be deadened for want of local contests" or write this off as a mere "sporting" urge which detracted from the dignity of public life,[251] for Kinnear the competition within the local district was the lone means by which the edificatory effect of the best minds upon the less elevated ones could be obtained. "Would it be wise," he asked with regard to Hare's desire that "a highly instructed and wealthy minority" be able to form their own constituency insulated from their neighbors,

> to abstract the personal relations of the best portion of each constituency from the rest of it? Is it not well that the superior minds in each neighbourhood should be subjected to the duty of trying to influence those around them? By their influence in this way ... Mr. Mill has just been returned for Westminster, Professor Fawcett for Brighton, Mr. Torrens for Finsbury. Do not far more beneficial results follow from the existence of a system

---

[248] Knatchbull-Hugessen, "Redistribution of Political Power," 73–5.

[249] Kinnear, "Practical Considerations," 55–6. This somewhat confused complaint was important in the French context; e.g. Vincent Guillin and Djamel Souafa, "La réception de Stuart Mill en France," La vie des idées (2010) [www.laviedesidees.fr/La-reception-de-Stuart-Mill-en.html].

[250] Kinnear, "Practical Considerations," 60–1.

[251] Lubbock et al., 314; Humphreys, Proportional Representation, 259. On the "sporting" attitude in parliamentary elections, see Vincent, Formation, xv; Christopher Dawson, "Democracy and the British Tradition," Dublin Review, 212 (1943): 97–103.

which can only secure such men by inducing the educated electors, who can really appreciate them, to go amongst the less educated and teach them the true eminence of the candidates, than would follow from a system which would lead the educated to segregate themselves into special quotas, and leave the illiterates to return their nobodies? . . . It would lead to the higher class of minds withdrawing and isolating themselves.

It was possible, Kinnear conceded, that a "certain number of leading men, averse to popular discussions," might eke out seats under STV but not under plurality rule. But since "the popular discussions which they dislike are invaluable instruments of mutual education" – since it was deliberation and persuasion among *all citizens*, rather than within a rarified set, that gave politics its educative qualities to begin with – it was not clear what purpose was served by making special provision for brahmins who lacked the mettle to enter the fray of public discussion.[252]

Kinnear accompanied this complaint with a prediction of further harm. This was, *en avance*, a version of the Idealist claim about the cliquish attitude that would arise among portions of the electorate if they were no longer electorally bound to the bulk of their fellows who were not already true believers in the cause. PR would "increase the tendency to make small questions, or crotchets, a predominant motive in the minds of electors." It would engender a focus on "pet hobbies" in lieu of a proper consideration of the "larger questions" that concerned the community as a whole; it would "encourage persons to hold strong opinions on small points, [and] to set these points above the general weal in other matters."[253]

Kinnear's preferred term for such monomaniacal concentration on a "special question" was "crotchet."[254] Kinnear was relatively early in employing this term, which would gain steam from the late 1860s on as a pejorative designation for what we would now call "single-issue" politics. It was characteristic of the age, wrote the historian Erskine May in the 1870s, that many people had "made their special causes superior to the great political principles which concern the general government of the State";[255] and laments that national affairs had been subordinated to the dominance of "crotchet-mongers" intensified in the context of party fragmentation over the Irish question and dismay at how practices of logrolling and obstruction allowed recalcitrant minority blocs to force their agendas on the Commons.[256] The anxiety about crotchets was especially acute for

---

[252] Kinnear, "Practical Considerations," 61, 63. [253] Ibid., 62, 54. [254] Ibid., 54.
[255] May, *Democracy in Europe*, vol. 2, 490.
[256] Hamer, "Introduction," to *The Radical Programme*: vii–xliv; Dicey, "Unionists and the House of Lords," *NR*, 24 (1895): 690–704.

Liberal politicians and commentators, who had to balance their beliefs that Liberalism favored independence of mind and that the pursuit of progress was multifaceted with their need to forge a common agenda for the purposes of campaigning and governing.[257]

If crotchets and single-issue fixations were already causing havoc under plurality rule, then the problem could only worsen with a reform that vowed to open Parliament to unparalleled levels of ideological variety. Two anxieties about "crotchets" stood out in particular. The first concerned intraparliamentary harms. As a result of PR allowing crotcheteers to band together to return devotees of their narrow cause, the assembly would deteriorate; instead of productive diversity among "really organic interests and opinions," a pathological version of variety would come about. Bagehot, as so often, gave cogent expression to the thought. "Upon this (in theory) voluntary plan, you would get together a set of members bound hard and fast with bands and fetters, infinitely tighter than any members now," because "a voluntary constituency will nearly always be a despotic constituency." Hence, under PR the Commons would cease to be "a deliberative assembly" and instead transform into a "compound of all sorts of violence," a useless assortment of mere "messenger[s]" sent by "missionary constituencies" and "violent" men which would tolerate no policy but that which accorded entirely with their dogmas.[258] "Under its operation," wrote another critic, "our members of Parliament would be chiefly men possessed by only one notion, such as anti-vaccinators, believers in the Claimant, and so on." "Men who consider their crotchet as of more importance than those matters in which the nation at large is interested" would gain a sizable foothold in the House.[259] A parliament generated by a method which granted this "undue facility to independent sections and cliques to return members" would be a congress of ideologues, both uninterested in discussion and incapable of transacting the business of government.[260]

Given the importance of parliamentary deliberation in Victorian theories of politics, this attack presented a serious challenge to the PR movement. A second fear concerned its effect on the citizenry. What distressed

---

[257] P. C. Griffiths, "The Caucus and the Liberal Party in 1886," *History*, 61 (1976): 183–197, and "Pressure Groups and Parties in Late-Victorian England," *Midland History*, 3 (1976): 191–205.

[258] Bagehot, *English Constitution*, 303–5, 399. Bagehot was still being quoted on this point in polemics against PR in the fraught context of 1930s Continental politics; F. A. Hermens, "L'erreur proportionnaliste et le régime parlementaire," *Revue politique et parlementaire*, no. 163 (1935): 429–57.

[259] Frisby, "Next Reform Bill," 242–3.

[260] Shaw-Lefevre, "The Crusade for Proportional Representation," *FR*, 37 (1885), 206.

critics most of all was the prospect that PR would cause citizens to approach the public sphere with a less properly public, and more narrowly ideological, disposition.[261] Plurality rule concentrated citizens' minds on the task of persuasion and corresponded to the lone mentality which could sustain functional politics in an "age of discussion" – a civic disposition that Bagehot called "animated moderation," the balance between earnest belief in one's views and a willingness to seek consensus and appreciate the value in difference.[262] By contrast, PR would encourage people to remain ensconced within bubbles of true believers and avoid the hard work of making their opinions properly "political factors."[263] Hare's opponents fretted that his scheme would upset the fragile alchemy of British public opinion, which was both diverse enough to provide the conditions for epistemic success and yet not splintered into a mere patchwork of unyield-ing groups.[264] This aspect of antiproportionalist fears about sectarianism allied them, paradoxically, with the more intellectually–sociologically ambitious version of PR advocacy, epitomized by Courtney in Chapter 4, which conceived of PR as a method not just for *translating* public opinion but for *acting on* and *shaping* it. But whereas Courtney hailed the ways that his scheme would refashion the views and dispositions of electors, defenders of plurality rule such as Kinnear and George Shaw-Lefevre feared the skewing of the public sphere toward "crotchets and immature opinions."[265]

Shaw-Lefevre, a Radical-Liberal whose long career as an author and politician would carry into the 1920s,[266] followed Kinnear and Bagehot in deploring both the intra- and extra-parliamentary consequences of "crotchetiness." A Gladstonian in his politics, he followed "the People's William" in attempting simply to write PR out of consideration as a kind of category error – its individualist basis made it ontologically inappropri-ate for Britain, whose principle of representation was the "community" as an "integer."[267] But Shaw-Lefevre did not stop at stipulating the

---

[261] There is a resemblance between these antiproportionalists and the attempt of modern deliberative democrats to articulate an attitude of "accommodation," "mutual respect," or "reciprocal positive regard" by which citizens attempt to convince their fellows while also remaining "open to the possibility of changing their minds or modifying their positions"; Amy Gutmann and Dennis Thompson, *Why Deliberative Democracy?* (Princeton, 2004), 79.

[262] Bagehot, *Physics and Politics*, 131.   [263] Edward Russell, "Electoral Future," 265.

[264] These predictions drew on a long-running tradition of thought which saw minorities as having an inherent propensity toward dogmatism and extremism; e.g. Hazlitt, "Sects and Parties," in *Fugitive Writings*, ed. A. R. Waller and Arnold Glover (London, 1904), 360–3.

[265] Shaw-Lefevre, "Representation of Minorities," 733.

[266] Allen Warren, "Lefevre, George John Shaw-, Baron Eversley (1831–1928)," *ODNB*.

[267] He quoted this famous passage from Gladstone in "Representation of Minorities," 718.

inconsistency of PR with England's parliamentary foundations; he reasoned along Kinnearean lines that without the local electoral contest "political life" would become "stagnant."[268] His treatment of this issue was especially eloquent:

> Hitherto in political contests one of the main objects has been, by appeals on the platform or personal persuasion, to urge individual and special cliques to subordinate their interests to those of the public, and to vote for the member or members who on the whole best represent the public interests ... The very essence of the new scheme proposed to us is the reverse; it invites and enables special interests and cliques to secure a separate representation.
>
> The system appears to consecrate the principle of sectarianism as opposed to nationalism. It invites people to combine together in groups for the purposes not of the public interest, but their own private interests, or their own special views. As religious differences are among the principal motives of combination it is probable, nay, almost certain, that all the religious sects would specially endeavour to return as many members as possible ... Many special industries, sections or interests would do the same. It is difficult to see where there could be found those who would combine only for national interests ... The House of Commons would become a collection of men representing cliques and petty interests, and without any common views as to the general policy of the country.
>
> ... it would in practice ... give undue weight and prominence to groups and cliques of opinion not yet ripe for dealing with in Parliament; it would result in the return of members specially representing in greater proportions than now crotchets and immature opinions, and the interests of classes without reference to national questions; it would therefore inculcate among electors the moral that the interests of classes are to preferred to those of the nation.[269]

As MacDonald would do later in laying out the philosophical underpinnings of Labour's stance on representative institutions, Shaw-Lefevre was here turning Millian precepts in favor of plurality rule. Far from guaranteeing "improvement" and ensuring against "decline," as the Saint of Rationalism foretold, it would "destroy[] the motive for political activity" and lead to "greater apathy and political stagnation";[270] rather than elevating the "faculties, moral intellectual, and active," it would lead to withdrawal into private interests and an uncompromising investment in faddish causes.[271]

[268] Shaw-Lefevre, "Crusade," 203.
[269] Shaw-Lefevre, "Crusade," 209; "Representation of Minorities," 716, 729.
[270] Shaw-Lefevre, "Crusade," 204; "Representation of Minorities," 719.
[271] Mill, *Considerations*, 459, 436.

The greatest pre-Idealist challenge to PR from Millian premises, though, came from the pen of Robert Collier. Along with Shaw-Lefevre, Collier served as a Liberal MP, including during Mill's term, and in that capacity spoke against alternatives to plurality rule[272]; he would go on to serve as Attorney-General and as a member of the judicial committee of the privy council.[273] More crisply than any other text, his 1868 pamphlet *The Representation of Minorities* captures how antiproportionalists believed that cardinal moral goods were connected with the technical matter of the formation of constituencies and with the seemingly classificatory question of what the proper unit to be represented was.

Typically, Collier began with a declaration of the incorrectness of the individualistic notions behind Hare's "personal" representation.[274] Yet it was not respect for constitutional heritage that determined his fidelity to the communitarian foundation of representative government; he assented to it because, given the long experience of the boons it produced, the "dictates of reason and common sense" reinforced the "authority of pre-scription." The satisfactoriness of the traditional system derived first of all from the fact that the local constituency constituted the natural context for political activity. Against the view of Hare, Grey, and others that advances in communication and transportation weakened the claim of localities to be the focal point of the representative system, Collier maintained that the "inconsisten[cy] with local representation" was enough on its own to disqualify "Mr. Hare's scheme":

> Every elector knows the advantages of returning a local member: politics are thus as it were brought home to each man's door: each voter is himself a member of *his own local parliament*: if in the majority he triumphs, if in the minority he may very often look forward to a triumph; in any case he forms part of a community which would lose much in being deprived of its representatives – in that community his political opinions are of some importance; he has an influence among his fellow-citizens, he is endued with power, and with a perceptible amount of responsibility, but once

---

[272] E.g. the speeches of Shaw-Lefevre and Collier, *Hansard*, Third Series, HC Deb 05 July 1867, 1068–82. And see the appendix on these debates in the work of the one-time American Senator Charles Buckalew's *Proportional Representation: Or, the Representation of Successive Majorities in Federal, State, Municipal, Corporate, and Primary Elections*, ed. John Freeze (Philadelphia, 1872), 273–87.

[273] David Pugsley, "Collier, Robert Porrett, first Baron Monkswell (1817–1886)," *ODNB*.

[274] "This would be to introduce a change unparalleled in the history of Parliamentary reform, a change never contemplated even by the most determined enemies of tradition till within the last few years; no reformer, however advanced and extravagant his opinions, having hitherto dreamt of suggesting any other basis than the one universally accepted – namely, the representation of communities"; Collier, *Representation of Minorities*, 8.

enlarge the circle and where is he? . . . Local interests and local grievances are very real and prominent facts, and it is the time-honoured duty of a member to act in such matters as mediator between Parliament and his constituency.[275]

In Collier's eyes, any plausible political sociology had to acknowledge these truths about the local community providing the appropriate setting and scale for voters to engage with politics in a morally respectable and epistemically credible manner.[276]

The mode of electoral activity natural to the local constituency – the direct clash between candidates offering rival claims to represent the whole – was likewise beneficial. It was epistemically good: it motivated citizens to seek to persuade their neighbors and, by forcing the search for common ground with potential supporters for the dramatic prize of sitting their candidate for the locality in the Commons, restrained the predilection of many average citizens toward unfocussed and bizarre speculations about public affairs.[277] It was also valuable for civic cohesion: although it might appear paradoxical at the level of abstract reasoning, in fact the well-regulated conflict within the locality contributed to a spirit of compromise and a sense of integration among all citizens.[278] Plurality rule enabled the responsible and intelligent exercise of the franchise, and it struck the

---

[275] Ibid., 6, 8–9 (my italics).

[276] One way of conceiving this front of the clash over PR is as a confrontation over Guizot's legacy. As noted, Guizot was an important figure for Hare, who seized on, among other things, the *doctrinaire*'s characterization of the legislature as the locus for collecting the fragments of reason scattered throughout society. The trouble for the Harean enlistment of Guizot, though, was that Guizot was a passionate admirer of the historical legacy of the English electoral system, in particular how it grew out of local communities and hence was imbricated with a longstanding municipal framework, a set of local rights, and a well-established deliberative context (*une longue délibération antérieure*). Without this anchoring in genuine local community, the vote became an "intermittent and passing crisis," an act "suspended in air"; Guizot, "Élections, ou de la formation et des operations des collèges électoraux," in *Discours Académiques* (Paris, 1861), 382–3, 396–7. Guizot's electoral localism would be carried into the Third Republic by the great literary critic and historian Hippolyte Taine; Taine, *Du suffrage universel et de la manière de voter* (Paris, 1872), esp. ch. 7.

[277] In a plurality-rule contest "there is something definite, to which each elector is sensibly a contributor; namely, the political character of the borough or district in which he lives; the conversion of a few neighbours may be sufficient to turn the scale – here is a result for him to work for." PR unleashed, rather than counteracted, men's "liab[ility] to entertain views which are not only worthless, but utterly mischievous," which was rooted in the "disposition towards rash dogmatism, and . . . how strongly private interests or the interests of a clique will affect the judgment even of an honest enquirer"; Collier, *Representation of Minorities*, 9, 17.

[278] Ibid., 14–16. There are modern parallels to the manner in which Collier thought on this point. Marcel Gauchet's argument that, counterintuitively, it was the institutionalization of the battle between left and right that made possible democratic stability bears similarities to Collier; Gauchet, "La Droite et la gauche," in *Les Lieux de Mémoire*, ed. Pierre Nora, 3 vols. (Paris, 1984–92), vol. 3, 395–467.

difficult balance between competition and consensus in political life. In the words of a major constitutional tract released a year before Collier's pamphlet, the English "system of representation" took as its unit "population organized" – that is, it "regard[ed] men not merely as men but as neighbours."[279] Collier agreed with this reading of English representational principle, and was happy to judge it by its fruits.

Next to plurality rule's proven track record, Harean theory was bloodless and unconvincing. Collier dismissed the ideal of "perfect, or complete, representation" on the grounds that it invalidated the legitimacy of political representation altogether. If respect for "what is just and true" required something close to an identity of "views and opinions" between MPs and constituents, did this not lead to the *reductio* that no one was ever represented?[280] After all, even in the case of highly informed people voting for J. S. Mill under STV, could it really be said that these voters would be in accord with Mill on all of the thorny issues that would confront him over a term?[281] In light of this logical unsoundness, Collier denied that the photograph-like reproduction of elector's opinions was required by justice.

Further, Collier accused PR proponents of simply assuming that the absence of a particular viewpoint from Parliament constituted ipso facto an injustice, without showing what real harms resulted. (He was unfair here; Hare and his followers, as we have seen, were zealous chroniclers of the practical ills they saw in the status quo.) The truth was that already under the present system "new tenets," if they were sound, would

> obtain their proper place, in the majority; represent as many crotchets as you please, the temper of the nation must decide the acceptance or rejection of a measure. Where is the magic talisman which shall give to the voice of the Parliamentary charmer an influence denied to written treatises the most convincing and masterly? ... An opinion ought surely to have assumed some force and solidity before it is dignified with a Parliamentary mouthpiece; to hear the echo of one's sentiments in Parliament should be no slight ambition, and should represent no inconsiderable success.[282]

---

[279] Hearn, *Government of England*, 470.
[280] Collier, *Representation of Minorities*, 15; Hare, *Election of Representatives*, xxxv.
[281] "No man can perfectly represent any one but himself, still less can a member represent the views of all those who sent him to Parliament on every question, or even every important question of the day – it is quite beyond our power to ensure the collection of a representative assembly, whose views shall be in complete harmony with those of the country at large"; Collier, *Representation of Minorities*, 12.
[282] Ibid., 24.

This passage contains a revealing equivocation: Collier began by downplaying the significance of Commons seats (what did parliamentary presence matter when one could push one's cause in the press and other
forums?) but ended by hallowing them (by letting in spokesmen of valueless views, PR constituted an assault on the stature of the institution). But
his underlying objection was clear: pinpointing a group or belief left out of
the Commons was not tantamount to proving an "evil" in FPP.[283]

Collier accompanied these lines of critique with a proto-Idealist skepticism about the tyranny of the majority. Proportionalists' fears on this front,
he argued, demonstrated their failure to recognize that under plurality rule
the British public sphere was already thoroughly deliberative, and that as
a result the viewpoints of minorities were deeply interwoven into the fabric
of political life:

> A local, in common with a Parliamentary minority, no doubt labours under
> the disadvantage of having to submit to the decision of an adverse faction,
> the one is denied the privilege of choosing its own mouthpiece, and the
> opinions of the other find no place in the statute book, still in both cases the
> vanquished party has an existence, an existence which cannot but be felt;
> defeat is one thing, annihilation another, a vote is a vote whether in
> Parliament or in a borough; opinions are not separated by a hard line of
> demarcation, they blend gradually, and by the exertions of an adverse and
> criticising body the doings of the majority will be controlled and
> modified ... Besides, popular feeling is not immutable, may not every one
> hope to see his side in the ascendant? ... Every considerable minority has the
> following elements of power. It exercises an influence over the decisions of
> the majority, it has a chance of superseding its opponents, its tenets are
> heard in Parliament [by members of similar views or party from other
> districts], and for purely local purposes the local member belongs just as
> much to them as to the majority.

Picking up on his depiction of the local community as a parliament in its
own right, Collier administered the coup de grace: "those who descant on
the inestimable blessing of an enlightened minority in Parliament, should
be the last to deny the influence of such a body elsewhere."[284] As we have
documented, Hare's camp, like the variety-of-suffragists, was not short of
reasons for prioritizing parliamentary deliberation. Reversing the typical
equation of parliamentarist thought, however, Collier chose the

---

[283] Collier, *Representation of Minorities*, 25.

[284] Ibid., 10–11. Jeremy Waldron makes a similar argumentative move when noting, in his defense of
majoritarian democracy against judicial review, that after all courts decide based on majority vote;
Waldron, "The Constitutional Conception of Democracy," in *Law and Disagreement* (Oxford,
1999), 306–7.

constituency over the Commons as the political arena par excellence. Writing just one year after the quasi-democratic "leap in the dark" of the Second Reform Act, Collier was early in seeing and embracing the displacement of Parliament as the center of public debate which mass democracy would effect.[285] FPP was more consonant, he concluded, with the nascent reality that the most important political arenas were the communities in which citizens lived, rather than the chamber at the summit.[286]

The poor arguments of PR would translate, Collier warned, into poor outcomes. Once electors were "extricated from the ties" of the territorial plurality-rule system,[287] the gamut of ills with which we have now become familiar would kick in. The salutary contest among views vying for the community's approval would be supplanted by the undeliberative extremism of crotcheteers.[288] Further, "absolv[ing]" the "higher and more educated classes" from "the necessity of taking the lower orders into their counsels" and granting them instead the "privilege of having themselves only to please" would undermine the edificatory character of political engagement.[289] Finally, the atmosphere of compromise that the locality

---

[285] Herman Finer believed that predictions such as Collier's had been confirmed by the second decade of the twentieth century, and that this development cut against the case for PR: "we realise nowadays, as it was impossible to realise a couple of generations ago, when PR was born, that the major issues of politics are not determined in the House of Commons so much as in the constituencies. The advocates of PR still live within the fold of John Stuart Mill's political synthesis – before the Reform Bill, even, of 1867, and before the creation of the great 'parliament outside parliament,' the tribunal of an active and enfranchised electorate" (Finer, *Case Against PR*, 13). Charles Beitz's deflationary analysis of PR in the modern mass-democratic context has a similar logic; *Political Equality*, 137–8.

[286] Importantly, Collier was writing just as the age of great *extra*-parliamentary speechmaking and political rallies was getting going, which would bring a notable decline in the importance of Westminster oratory relative to other kinds of political communication; H. C. G. Matthew, "Rhetoric and Politics in Great Britain, 1860–1950," in *Politics and Social Change in Modern Britain: Essays Presented to A. F. Thompson*, ed. P. J. Waller (Sussex, 1987): 34–58.

[287] Collier, *Representation of Minorities*, 15; Hare, *Election of Representatives*, 55.

[288] "A vastly increased importance given to individual eccentricity would draw the mind by degrees into its own little corner, away from the consideration of those great and essential matters on which it might otherwise have exercised itself for the public benefit ... political eccentricity is usually, of all others, the shallowest and most unreasoning. To foster and encourage to the utmost what in ninety-nine cases out of a hundred is a man's weak point; to bribe him, as it were, to regard the wrong-headed fraction of his brain as the one part of it worth cultivating ... does not certainly appear to be a method of proceeding dictated by the highest wisdom"; Collier, *Representation of Minorities*, 15.

[289] Ibid., 18. Dissenting from his master Mill, Sidgwick would echo this skepticism about PR: "There is a danger of losing a valuable protection against demagogy, if we remove the natural inducements which local divisions give for the more instructed part of the community to exercise their powers of persuasion on the less instructed. If the divisions are local, the wiser few, in each locality, in order to carry the candidate of their choice, have to convince their neighbours, and thus the natural sociability springing from neighbourhood tends to become a channel of political education: but

fostered would give way to fragmentation and division; a spirit of self-ishness and entitlement would replace an atmosphere of accommodation and persuasion.[290]

John Stuart Mill knew Collier, as he knew Kinnear and Shaw-Lefevre. While the texts from Shaw-Lefevre quoted here came after Mill's death, this was not so for those of the other two. (He would, in any case, have heard Shaw-Lefevre in the Commons on these issues.) Mill learned of PR in 1859, and he commented on it frequently both in public works and in his correspondence until his passing in 1873. But his thinking on the subject did not discernably deepen over the course of those fourteen years. In particular, he tended to speak of critics of Hare's innovation as if they came from a separate moral universe from his own. In keeping with his reputation as contemptuous of English culture,[291] Mill wrote about PR as if the task was to convince his compatriots who were ignorant of deliberation, antagonism, and inclusivity, or who were indifferent to the edifying potential of politics, that these were the proper values. Judged in context, the most disappointing feature of Mill's thought on representation was that he failed to take account of the possibility that opposition to PR could arise not merely from the rejection of these values but from an alternative interpretation of them and of their institutional correlates. Just as Fitzjames Stephen claimed to be the "disciple" of the true Mill even as he rejected much in Mill's later writings,[292] so Collier and Kinnear could adopt Millian premises without believing that this committed them to endorsing Mill's institutions. Mill had little to say to such objectors, and he certainly evinced no foresight about the sophisticated way in which the Idealist turn in political thought would theorize plurality rule as the indispensable institutional setting for a democracy at once dynamic,

---

if an instructed minority were allowed to combine with others on their own intellectual level elsewhere, this valuable educative influence would tend to be lost"; *Elements of Politics*, 395.

[290] "Mr. Hare's policy is a policy of no compromise; each man for himself, for his own clique, and his favourite statesman. Discordant elements are not to be forced into coalition of stern necessity; in plain English, nobody is to give up anything ... Compromise is the soul of politics. On the principle that 'a little leaven leaveneth the whole lump,' it would be a fatal error to separate the bad from the wholesome influence of the good, who act as a kind of police; and a very few considerations will be sufficient to show how peculiarly dangerous individual eccentricities are in politics"; Collier, *Representation of Minorities*, 15–16.

[291] Joseph Hamburger, "Individuality and Moral Reform: The Rhetoric of Liberty and the Reality of Restraint in Mill's On Liberty," in *Mill's Social and Political Thought*, vol. 2: 402–45; Julia Stapleton, "James Fitzjames Stephen: Liberalism, Patriotism, and English Liberty," *VS*, 41 (1998): 243–63.

[292] J.F. Stephen, *Liberty, Equality, Fraternity*, 4–5.

agonistic, educative, and facilitative of compromise and concern for the common good – for a democracy, that is, as Mill would have wished.

c Fellow Travelers: Frederic Harrison and Graham Wallas

Before concluding this section, it is worth noting two other critics of PR who are of broader significance to the history of political thought. Frederic Harrison, a leader of English positivism, and Graham Wallas, the Fabian socialist and foundational figure for modern social psychology, each built criticisms of PR into their major works. Their criticisms, while not identical to the Millian line of rebuttal which we have been examining, shared certain features with it. Both *Order and Progress* and *Human Nature in Politics* portray support for PR as illustrating naïve modes of thought about politics which had to give way to a "scientific" approach, and both used an attack on Hare's proposal as a prism through which to examine a deeper set of political and intellectual concerns.

For Harrison, PR exemplified a kind of airy individualism that, while it had "in *logic* a tremendous case," misunderstood the collective and dynamic nature of politics.[293] In the eyes of the great positivist, Hare and company mistook the practical end of an election – the casting and tallying up of votes – for its normative content or inner meaning. Of course, in the electoral act itself there was no way around the necessity that votes be given by individuals. Because Hareans were excessively focused on the moment of voting, they drew the lesson that the purpose of a representative system was to ensure the maximum liberty of individual electoral action. However, in pursuing that goal they deprived the votes cast of their very meaningfulness, since the only reason to value these votes was that they were the outcome of a process that embodied precisely the contestatory and communal principles at which PR supporters bristled. The teaching of "Positivism," Harrison wrote, in contrast to the Hare–Mill form of "Liberalism," was that it was "the election agitation and contest" that contributed permanently to the efficacy of deliberative representative government, while the moment and results of the vote itself were of comparative insignificance:

> The votes, in fact, of 10,000 persons, voting individually as units, will present an utterly different result to the votes of the same 10,000 persons voting organically, as a community in a contest ... If we silently ask

---

[293] Harrison, *Order and Progress*, 89. Drawing on *Gulliver's Travels*, he compared Hare to a "professor of Laputa."

10,000 persons for their views, and register their answers, we get a product which is perfectly useless, for it gives us no clue to know what those persons as a political body will in action desire, do, and suffer to be done. If we give them full scope for political movement, that is let them collectively fight out a particular question, and then take the votes as of an organic force, we may perhaps get a rough measure of their will, but we shall have got it for most practical purposes before the voting begins. It is the "turmoil of the election contest," not the election, which really indicates political forces.

In defiance of these truths, PR "eliminate[s] from the voting process and from the result of the vote, just that one feature, the agitation and contest in the collective body ... which gives to the voting process any reality at all." It was a distortive and stultifying arrangement; it "collects the scattered votes of units, who do not and cannot act together politically ... For these reasons they have no collective or organic energy, and consequently are not political forces."[294] At the diametric opposite of Rousseau's impulse to hive off the vote from communication among citizens,[295] Harrison saw the vote itself as almost a superfluity next to all the (hostile, aggressive) talk which preceded it. Hence, the disruption of the agonistic-collective rhythms natural to plurality rule would yield a "catalogue of opinions," without any "ponderable political energy," for it would lack "the one thing, the previous collective agitation, which can make votes instructive and correspond to realities."[296]

To a great degree, then, Harrison used criticism of PR as an occasion to attack what he considered a false political ontology, the "ruinous ... theory of individualism."[297] From this philosophical mistake practical harms would follow, above all the desiccation or emptying out of political will and the "triumph of confederacies or cliques."[298] It would have costs epistemically, too. Here his analysis diverged from that of the other figures whom we have examined, for while they certainly believed that PR

---

[294] Ibid., 74–5. He made a suggestive analogy to the arts: "It would be as wise to assure us that the only way for an orchestra to render true music is for the various players to perform separately their own favourite composition."

[295] Rousseau, *The Social Contract*, in *The Social Contract and Other Later Political Writings*, ed. Victor Gourevitch (Cambridge, 1997), 60.

[296] Harrison, *Order and Progress*, 75–6.

[297] Ibid., 158. He went on: "The life and soul of representation in practice is the contact of man with man, the thrill of social vibration, the ascendency of visible character. Personal representation, where constituencies are formed of scattered units, is but the corpse of representation."

[298] Ibid., 78. He continued: "If the representatives of a constituency are to represent, not the wills of political aggregates, but a heap of heterogeneous projects, if our aim is not to measure the force of the citizens, but to form a museum of crotchets, where the schemes of all the cliques, pedants, and fanatics in the community may be collected and preserved like a wax-work show – we may find what we seek in Personal Representation."

underperformed plurality rule epistemically, they did not express their objection in quite the manner that Harrison did, which was that PR's underlying premises were not just wrongly individualistic, but also over-intellectualized. "The fallacy of personal representation consists in the enormous assumption that electors think; that they know what they think; and that they know whom they would choose to represent their thoughts," he judged. "It is mere hallucination which supposes that masses of average citizens have a tabulated scheme of political views, and keep ready-made lists of the public characters who exactly reflect their minds."[299] The tragic irony of Hare's indulgence in what Harrison considered to be rationalist fantasies was that Hare's excessive confidence in the perfectibility of his fellows rendered it impossible for them to even approach competence, whereas institutions, like plurality rule, which reflected a soberer assessment of the faculties of the elector in fact delivered better results.[300]

Three decades later, Wallas sounded a similarly frustrated note about how "intellectualist misconceptions" were infecting the campaign for PR. To Wallas, who sought to place the study of politics on true empirical foundations, the passion for PR was a last gasp of moribund rationalism – "too intellectual and logical" – masquerading as social science.[301] It was in this light that he interpreted the libertarian strain among PR advocates, which he understood as a mixture of two invalid claims: (a) that the greatest possible range of choice for and diminishment of interference with the elector was more important than any other desiderata; and (b) a quasi-religious faith in the connection between liberty and other goods which did not correspond to the real world.[302] Like Harrison, he attributed these mistakes to a narrow focus on the moment of casting the vote, rather

---

[299] Ibid., 77. It was quite simply "the *reductio ad absurdum* of representation" to imagine, as he accused Hare of doing, that "each Member of Parliament expresses … the dogmatic convictions of his particular constituency"; ibid., 158.

[300] "If the average elector, after twenty public meetings, tavern discussions, and torrents of newspaper articles, can make up his mind honestly that he thinks A would make a better parliament-man than B, the average elector has done quite as much as we can expect. But in order to do this he will need, and he ought to have, the rivals A and B engaged in public contest under his eye, that he may watch how each of them deals with men in organic masses. This is political life; but writing on a paper names of persons whom you never saw, is more like voting for candidates at a club or a charity"; ibid., 77.

[301] Wallas, *Human Nature in Politics*, 231–2.

[302] "Those who aim primarily at 'freedom,' and those who aim primarily at 'rightness,' are likely … to form different views of practical problems. Take first the plan of Proportional Representation, either as Hare introduced it, or in the modified form approved by M. Ostrogorski. Undoubtedly it makes the citizen more 'free.' The Imperialist teetotaler, the High Church Land Nationaliser, has much more liberty of choice in a long or considerable list of candidates, than in a single-member

than a more holistic grasp of representation as involving a long stretch of campaigning, deliberation, mobilization, and contest which was properly set in the local district: the arguments for "dropping the fetters" of the current system "suffer from the fatal defect of dwelling solely on the process by which opinion is ascertained, and ignoring the process by which opinion is created."[303]

For Wallas, the "'intellectualist' assumptions" undergirding PR produced another unfortunate effect: the strengthening of parties. As we have seen, the tradition of British proportionalism was firmly wedded to STV. This fidelity derived largely from British PR's hostility to disciplined, centralized parties. But the outcome of their desired reform, Wallas predicted, would be the opposite of what they had hoped: it would reinforce the hegemony of the "party organization," and would in practice be indistinguishable from the dreaded list system. If "Lord Courtney's proposal" were adopted, "it is the 'ticket' system which ... will be generally used. Each voter will bring into the polling booth a printed copy of the ballot paper marked with the numbers 1, 2, 3 etc., according to the decision of his party association." "The essential fact," Wallas summed up, was that due to the intellectual limitations of most voters it was improbable that they would engage in a profound comparative survey of candidates from across the nation and arrive at a detailed rank-ordering that they would then transcribe with solemnity and civic pride on their ballots. Instead, the many names the voter would be called on to arrange would not be for him "real persons," and he would fall back more than ever on the heuristic of "party allegiance" and simply "arrange" his ballot to the needs of "party tactics" as instructed by party leaders.[304]

Wallas invoked his "Baconian" conception of "political reasoning" against the proportionalist movement's "method of a priori deduction from large and untried generalizations" to justify his worries about the hardening of parties under PR.[305] For Wallas, critiquing the PR campaign

---

constituency with two, or perhaps three, candidates. But is he more likely to be right?"; Wallas, "American Analogy," 512.

[303] Wallas, *Human Nature in Politics*, 233. Although she supports PR, Nadia Urbinati's understanding of votes as not "mere quantities. They mirror the complexity of opinions and political influence, neither of which are arithmetically computable entities" and her injunction not "to forget this complexity and to assume that votes reflect individual preferences rather than render opinions and beliefs" formed in an interactive social process over the *longue durée*" carries on much of the sensibility of the anti-Harean conception of democratic representation; Urbinati, *Representative Democracy: Principles and Genealogy* (Chicago: 2006), 30–5. Were Wallas to have encountered PR embedded within Urbinati's theory of representation, he would perhaps have thought somewhat differently about it.

[304] Ibid., 237–9.   [305] Wallas, *Human Nature in Politics*, 157; "American Analogy," 512.

was principally an occasion on which he could carry out his larger polemic against "rationalism" and in favor of a true political science. The broader notion of "science" in which his examination of PR was embedded set it apart from earlier Victorian analyses. The substance, however, of this side of his antiproportionalism was not new. Indeed, it flowed directly out of the second great family of "moral" criticisms of PR: those which centered on its relationship to parties.

3 The Problem of Parties

The issue of parties has entered into our discussion at various points already. It has been shown, for instance, how anticipations of the rigidification of parties under a democratic suffrage caused Victorian liberals to fret, and how antipartyism became a driving force behind the Victorian PR movement. This section will not recap that material. Nor will it survey the entirety of thought about parties over these decades. Instead, it homes in on two lines of critique of PR that revolved around party. Interestingly, these criticisms came from opposite directions: one fearful of parties, the other appreciative of them; one associating party strength with PR, the other conceiving of plurality rule as the condition for strong parties.

a PR and Party Hegemony

Chapter 2 demonstrated that the prospect of democracy frightened upholders of the classical conception of the deliberative Commons because they forecast that democracy would entail a tightening of the control exercised by party organizations. A certain looseness of party, an absence of strict dictation and centralization, was, they thought, necessary for the ideal of deliberative government to be realized. However, several thinkers, among which the most notable was Bagehot, expected this harmful consequence to follow not only from the "ultra-democratic theory" but also from the other most prominent adversary of the variety of suffrages, the "scheme of Mr. Hare."[306] A similar ratcheting-up of the vise-grip of parties was feared from the implementation of STV at whatever level of franchise it was enacted – and feared in an even more extreme measure from the possible conjunction of PR with universal suffrage.

---

[306] Bagehot, *English Constitution*, 298–9.

For what reasons would "Mr. Hare's hopes" be so "deceive[d]" by his own plan? Precisely those which Wallas would cite later. Given the intellectual limitations of citizens and the internal logic of mass organizations, Bagehot argued, STV could only reinforce the dominance of the great parties:

> As the working of the new system would be exceedingly complicated, and the electors themselves would not in any way be able to secure a parliamentary political influence by their vote if they drew out a their own lists of candidates – nay, since, as we know, the majority of all electors know exceedingly little about the bearing of political affairs ... the result would in all probability be that 'Liberal' tickets and 'Tory' tickets would be prepared at a central office in London ... directing the electors what list of names they should send in to secure the best chance of a triumph for their party ....[E]very elector would soon be taught that if he did not accept the 'ticket' of his party, but substituted one of his own, the value attaching to his own would in all probability be *nil*. With so wide and vague a scheme, centralisation and strict co-operation would be absolutely essential ... it would soon be so clear that no rational weight would attach to a vote at all unless the advice of those who were in correspondence with all the local centres of the party were strictly followed.[307]

For those who valued the deliberative character of Parliament and its incorporation of shades of opinion and interest beyond a narrow set of inflexible party platforms, STV's practical indistinguishability from the list system consigned it to the company of "other electoral machineries" which were incompatible with the true liberal tradition of representation.[308] Unsurprisingly, Bagehot was far from alone in imagining a Harean future as a dystopia of party domination.[309] Dicey, in particular, would go on to update Bagehot's analysis for an age of great disenchantment with Parliament and the party system, alleging that PR would exacerbate such pathologies of party as logrolling and the distortion of public opinion.[310]

---

[307] Bagehot, "Considerations on Representative Government [2]," 344–5. Not only defenders of plurality rule, but also supporters of other proportionalist methods, made the charge that in practice STV would degenerate into competition between rival lists and increase the strength and rigidity of parties; Dodgson, "Parliamentary Elections," 158. Dodgson thought his "clubbing" method a more honest way of capturing the importance of party organizations while also, perhaps counterintuitively, being more likely to temper their rigidity.

[308] Bagehot, *English Constitution*, 300.

[309] Grey, *Parliamentary Government*, 205–6; G. O. Trevelyan, "A Few Remarks on Mr. Hare's Scheme of Representation," *MM*, 5 (1862): 480–6, at 483. Knatchbull-Hugessen connected STV's reinforcement of party dominance neatly with the worries discussed in the previous section: because PR would increase political apathy, citizens would then be more than ever putty in the hands of "agents and wire-pullers"; "Redistribution of Political Power," 73, 75.

[310] Dicey, *Law of the Constitution*, lxix–lxxii

It was not always obvious how this prognosis fit with the prophecies about the proliferation of crotchets that PR would unleash. At first glance, at least, the two prognostications looked inconsistent: how could there be both splintering into faddish mini-publics and a hardening of caucuses and machines?[311] Some authors, portending only one of these outcomes, felt no need to offer any reconciliation between them, and even skeptics such as Leslie Stephen, who within a single page accused PR of buttressing "national party-organizations" and of calling forth "scattered cliques" and the "belief in crotchets," often felt no compulsion to show how the circle was squared.[312] Others, however, were more explicit about how these scenarios could be compatible. For Bagehot, the explosion of "special fanaticisms" was the best potential result; it was what would occur if the practice of PR at all "answered Mr. Hare's hopes." This was a recipe for stagnation and paralysis, and it threatened to deprive the Commons of its valuable fund of "moderation." With this outcome, troubling as it would be, the Commons could at least still make some claim to be reflective of a pluralistic public opinion. Since practice seldom conformed to theory, however, a second "danger" of hardening and centralizing parties was likely to come to pass. Yet Bagehot did not believe that these were simply alternative possibilities; most likely of all was that "the practical working of Mr. Hare's scheme would be a compound of these two dangers." The simultaneous occurrence of these separate harms was possible because they fed upon different shortcomings in the electorate. The "mass" of uninformed and indifferent voters, unable to reason their way through a long series of candidatures, would acquiesce to the dictation of party managers, while ideologically driven electors would hive themselves off according to the "special ties" of their "sectarian" affiliation. Hence, PR foreboded total dysfunction: parties would be transformed from open cross-cutting coalitions into uniform top-down command structures incapable of compromising with one another. Making matters worse, these military-style parties would also be unable to "direct the general policy of the country" with a sure hand because of the number of seats siphoned off by the spokesmen of "*specialités*."[313]

---

[311] Mill thought that "the suppositions on which" these two grounds of complaint rested were "entirely opposite"; Speech on Proportional Representation and Redistribution, 29 Feb. 1868, in *CW*, vol. 28, 239–42.

[312] Stephen, "Value of Political Machinery," 844.

[313] Bagehot, "Considerations on Representative Government [2]," 344–5. Also see e.g. Shaw-Lefevre, "Crusade," 206; Frisby, "Next Reform Bill," 243.

These predictions of (a) the practical equivalence of STV and list systems and (b) the compossiblity of an increase in both party rigidity and crotcheteering struck a blow against the PR movement, raising doubts about the antipartyism that was such a strong selling-point for many of its leading voices. Another party-centered line of attack came from the opposite perspective.

b   The Defense of Parties – And the Eclipse of the Mirroring Parliament

Antipartyism occupied a foundational place in the British debate on PR – not only among its champions, but even, as just analyzed, among those critics who were friendly to some of its ideals but who feared its results in practice. The PR movement was the locus for a number of complaints which chimed with the broader chorus of worries in mid-/late-Victorian culture about what was seen as the shift from "parliamentary supremacy" toward "the sovereignty of national parties."[314]

Even to many thinkers sympathetic to aspects of proportionalism, however, the hostilities to parties within PR advocacy went too far, becoming a fixation that hurt their cause.[315] As a result, in Britain defenders of the emerging party order tended to line up against PR.[316] Several of the justifications for party which they crafted in the last four decades of the nineteenth century directly challenged key tenets of the Harean movement. Hence, though it has not generally been recognized in studies of the development of modern British party politics,[317] it was in part via combating the Harean perspective that the first full defenses of the modern party were articulated. This subsection takes up a few major themes in the apologetics of party which were catalyzed to some degree by the challenge of PR.

The first accusation to which defenders had to respond was that parties lowered the level of ability and wisdom in political life. Apologists for cohesive, disciplined parties tended not to dispute that Hare- and Fawcett-style recriminations applied to some MPs. They simply treated this as unworrying. The aspiration to a group of more than 600 high-

---

[314] Angus Hawkins, *British Party Politics, 1852–1886* (Houndmills, Basingstoke, 1998), 268. Also J. F. Stephen, "Parliamentary Government [1]," *CR*, 23 (1873): 1–19; James Anthony Froude, "Party Politics," *FM*, 10 (1874): 1–18.

[315] Frisby, "Next Reform Bill," 242; Meredith, *Proportional Representation in Ireland*, xv–xvi.

[316] This is in direct contrast to what would become the standard embrace of parties by Continental proportionalists: Rosanvallon, *Le peuple introuvable*, ch. 5; Kelsen, *Essence and Value of Democracy*, 71–3.

[317] The exception to this rule is Parsons, *Thomas Hare and Political Representation*, ch. 5.

minded, freethinking MPs was, they believed, fantastical, and in any case a recipe for fruitless jabbering rather than enlightened, purposive discussion. As early as 1857, a short but striking article laid out the template that later backers of strong party organization would follow in countering claims that it diminished political competence.[318] Parties, argued the unidentified author, rendered parliaments more capable and effective bodies because they solved the problem of leadership. Parties made it such that "the character of Parliament" became "an impress of the chiefest men," "the few and the able." If one believed, as anyone with a modicum of faith in popular government was bound to do, that whatever the limitations of the public's grasp of complex issues it was capable of identifying effectual leaders, then the "practice of party Government" was indispensable, for it squared the circle of popular consent with "the influence of the best and the wisest, who are necessarily the few." Instead of the "inharmonious" anarchy of competing claims to set the parliamentary agenda from "second-rate intelligence[s]" posturing as so many "individual unit[s]" of political judgment, "Party Government" facilitated deference to "superior mind[s]" who had been "naturally elevated" as the "choicest champion of the principles" for which they stood. On this view, strong parties achieved two great goods: they secured assent to proper leadership from the horde of undistinguished but potentially fractious MPs, and they provided a structure by which these few true leaders could be held accountable to their following in the electorate.[319]

While Hare and the more ardent foes of party in the proportionalist tradition had little time for these sentiments, other STV supporters did assent to some of this analysis. These moderates did not warm to "party government" if by this term is meant an acceptance of the dominance of two parties as something like a perennial truth about representative systems – they did not believe that there was anything natural about a bimodal clustering of opinions,[320] nor that it was permissible to leave holders of "eccentric" or "abnormal" views without spokesmen in Parliament. But they could make their peace with chastened and more open party organizations. For these reformists about party, the precondition for achieving an

---

[318] E.g. T. H. S. Escott, "The Radical Programme: Machinery," *FR*, 34 (1883): 290–7; Bryce, *American Commonwealth*, vol. 2, 28.

[319] Anon., "Independent Voting and Party Government," *SR*, 3 (1857): 191–2.

[320] As ever, there are exceptions: both Droop and Dodgson thought an assembly characterized by a bifurcation between Liberals and Conservatives could be in "correspondence" to "the state of opinion in the country" and yet still supported versions of PR: Droop, *Political and Social Effects*, 18; Duncan Black, "The Central Argument in Lewis Carroll's 'The Principles of Parliamentary Representation,'" *Papers on Non-Market Decision Making*, 3 (1967): 1–17.

acceptable brand of party ties was to stop the cliques that ran the party machinery from seizing control over the selection of candidates. STV, to many authors, was a way of tempering top-down party dominance in the choice of candidates. Instead of having to meekly accept dictation from above about whom a Liberal had to vote for in order to keep out a Tory challenger, through the ability to rank-order candidates and transfer his vote down a series of options listed on his ballot the Liberal voter would be released from the moral blackmail of having to vote for whichever figure had been ordained to wear the party colors in their district rather than risk letting in the enemy.[321] Furthermore, in such a situation Liberals of a wider variety of opinions and character-types would be inclined to put themselves forward as candidates. Victorian PR, therefore, sought not to eradicate parties but to temper certain kinds of power which the oligarchies within them had claimed, and to open them up to a broader range of ideas and kinds of people. From being in a position to impose candidatures, they would now persist, so to speak, as precipitates of the free activity of like-minded citizens and politicians who had specific coordination and leadership needs. As one author wrote, the aim of STV's mechanisms of "transfer and elimination" was not to destroy the "legitimate influence and power" of party, but to remove the "irresponsible and absolute authority" bestowed on small "sets of persons" to curtail the appearance of "satisfactory candidate[s]" and enforce orthodoxy against "disloyal" candidates.[322]

In other words, the moderate-reformist strand of PR was oriented more toward freeing parties from top-down control and making them accessible to a diverse set of influences; it was not antiparty per se.[323] Whether such

---

[321] For proportionalists, the phenomenon familiar to plurality rule of a party being hurt by having too many candidates emblematized the irrationality of the whole system. The "obviously not fair" result, as Dodgson put it, "that the party should fail in bringing in their rightful number of Members" due to a "disarrangement of votes" among several candidates played for proportionalists something like the role that the price-stabilizing destruction of "overproduced" goods played for communists – as the latter exemplified the irrationality of capitalism, so the former exemplified the irrationality of plurality rule. Dodgson saw further than his contemporaries, though, to note that STV was not a perfectly reliable mechanism for addressing this problem; *Principles of Parliamentary Representation*, 192–4.

[322] Smith, "Parliamentary Reform: Minority Representation," 174–5. He continued: "The present system of election enables [a few persons] to reduce every member of their party to the dilemma of either supporting the candidate brought forward by the association or of risking the loss of the seat by schism." And see a rather heterodox Harean, the Christian Socialist J. Rigby Smith, on the goal of freeing "political party organizations" from their "abuses" so that they would function "not to crush individuality and to impose the will of a clique, but to develop it, and by skilful combination to make it effectual to the utmost degree"; Smith, *Personal Representation: A Simplification, Adaptation to the Ballot, and Defence of Mr. Hare's Scheme of Electoral Reform* (London, 1868).

[323] Compare the tone toward parties of figures such as J. P. Smith with, for example, Simone Weil's WWII-era *cri de coeur On the Abolition of All Political Parties*, trans. Simon Leys (New York, 2013).

fluid parties, eager to tolerate dissent and recognize true merit in all its varieties, would actually have been capable of solving the problems of leadership and organization identified by promoters of the strong party was unclear, to say the least. But the moderate STV vision of parties nonetheless proved satisfactory to many, including Mill. It has sometimes been a source of wonder that Mill could have been both an independent-minded philosopher and a reliable Liberal partisan.[324] In truth, however, for all the harsh words Mill directed toward the existing party system, he did not have a principled objection to parties as such. Indeed, he made it crystal clear that parties, suitably modified, would be a meaningful part of a Britain with PR. "The two great parties" would remain powerful, but they would have

> to put on their lists a number of people who, apart from party, would represent what I may describe as the various "isms." Now, we know very well that only three or four candidates put up for the representation. The candidates are frequently such men as no reasonable man would care to vote for, but, being compelled to vote there, or leave it alone, a great number of the electors vote simply for the Liberal or the Conservative, without reference to anything else, the candidates being the greatest noo-dles, who, having offended nobody, are what is known as respectable men, and, in the majority of cases, possess plenty of money. Under Mr. Hare's plan things will be different, because people's interests will be different, and their object will be to put upon their lists not only the best party men, but those who best represent ability and virtue all over the country. Liberals and Conservatives will then be represented by their best men, instead of, as frequently now, by their silliest, or by men of mediocre order.[325]

The more extreme antipartyist strains of PR, then, faced objections from both plurality rulers and from fellow proportionalists who placed their faith in improved party structures which reconciled leadership and coordination with freedom of choice and of thought. Apologists of party struck at Hare's antipartyism in another way, too: by claiming for themselves those key values of the PR movement, voluntary association and cooperation.[326] Francis Schnadhorst, the radical nonconformist and trailblazing Liberal party organizer, defended the much-maligned Liberal "caucus" on the

---

[324] Dennis Thompson, "Mill in Parliament: When Should a Philosopher Compromise?" in *J. S. Mill's Political Thought: A Bicentennial Reassessment*, ed. Nadia Urbinati and Alex Zakaras (Cambridge, 2007): 166–99.

[325] Mill, *Speech on Proportional Representation and Redistribution*, 241–2. And see Bruce Kinzer, "J. S. Mill and the Problem of Party," *JBS*, 21 (1981): 106–22.

[326] On the case for and against parties being treated as voluntary associations, see Nancy Rosenblum, *On the Side of Angels: An Appreciation of Parties and Partisanship* (Princeton, 2008).

grounds that – however top-down or tightly disciplined it appeared[327] – in reality it worked only because it could draw on the "voluntary zeal" of normal citizens and stimulate "the aid" of "voluntary workers."[328] Joseph Chamberlain, the great Radical-Liberal statesman and champion of the caucus, described the nature of party organization in similar ways. It was a free manifestation of the "watchful and intelligent interest" that led citizens dutifully to combine their efforts in pursuit of the common good. Chamberlain characterized parties as a manifestation of citizens' desire to come together in "political union[s] and organization[s]" that was continuous with the broader civic atmosphere of vital associationalism, and he clinched this characterization with the citation of a powerful authority: Tocqueville.[329] For optimists about the parties then budding under plurality rule, parties promised to bring the Englishman's cooperative instincts into the political sphere. As the suffrage expanded and Britain was more widely recognized to have entered a "democratic age," this Tocquevillian argument that parties were the kind of "intermediary associations" that allowed citizens who were weak and isolated on their own to act purposively together grew more compelling. Even some proportionalists accepted this apologia for parties.[330]

The portrait of their cooperative, collaborative nature gave endorsers of the disciplined party resources for rebutting another common criticism: that they suppressed diversity and shut out minority interests and opinions. The responses to this charge were not, at least not obviously, consistent. On the one hand, those who were bullish about party organization under plurality rule frequently waved off concerns about the inhospitality of the current representative regime to minority viewpoints and independent thought as inappropriate. At every level – from a local school board to a national cabinet – politics was a collective enterprise, and it was

---

[327] For a judgment that moderates but is sympathetic to complaints about the undemocratic domination of the "caucus," see Alan Ball, *British Political Parties: The Emergence of a Modern Party System*, second edition (Houndmills, Basingstoke, 1987), 30–1.

[328] Francis Schnadhorst, "The Caucus and Its Critics," *NC*, 12 (1882): 8–28, at 23. On Schnadhorst's impact as a party organizer, see Barry McGill, "Francis Schnadhorst and Liberal Party Organization," *JMH*, 34 (1962): 19–39.

[329] Chamberlain, "The Caucus," *FR*, 24 (1878), 740, 725. He quoted the key passages from *Democracy in America*'s chapter "On the Use That Americans Make of Associations in Civil Life" beginning "If men living in democratic countries had no right and no inclination to associate for political purposes, their independence would be in great jeopardy . . . "

[330] Smith, "Parliamentary Reform: Minority Representation," 174: "In the indiscriminate abuse poured upon the caucus, it often seems to be forgotten that co-operation is everything in politics, and that persons who take trouble and work in concert necessarily and legitimately secure a more extensive influence than their less energetic neighbours"; *Proportional Representation and British Politics*, 68–71.

intrinsic to collective endeavor that difference and independence could not be respected indefinitely, that a common line had eventually to be adopted and enforced.[331] This realist, deflationary stance toward inclusivity- or diversity-based concerns went hand-in-hand with a broader dualism about representation, wherein a two-party system was believed to adequately integrate the few lines of thought which were of any real significance to mass democracy.[332] The more sophisticated versions of such dualistic theses incorporated the themes of the previous section; instead of simply ignoring the existence of those currents of opinion that developed outside the main parties, authors such as Chamberlain asserted that the proper forum for them was the press, where they could offer proofs of their vitality before, if they were worthy, ultimately earning a presence on party platforms.[333] In a striking turn of phrase, the press was dubbed, on this perspective, the venue for *proportional representation of opinions*, whereas the Commons was the arena of *party contest*.[334] A final approach for downplaying the significance of worries that parties crushed diversity and imposed conformity capitalized on the perception of PR's "elitism." "Variety of opinion" was a luxury good, a fetish for the out-of-touch who could, unlike the mass of the people, afford to care about other objects than the fulfillment of the necessary business of the state and the carrying through of urgent reforms.[335]

---

[331] E.g. Gladstone, "Electoral Facts," *NC*, 4 (1878): 955–68; and especially Chamberlain, "The Caucus," 729, against the claims of "tyranny" from those would-be MPs who did not want to accept a common Liberal platform. Also Wilson, "The Caucus," 695–6, examining the way in which the authority of both Disraeli and Gladstone was invoked to justify party discipline in the late 1870s; and Salisbury, "Excerpt from An address to a Deputation of Conservative Associations," reprinted in Beattie, *English Party Politics*, vol. 1, 182–3.

[332] E.g. Dicey, "The Paralysis of the Constitution," *CR* 88 (1905): 305–16; Lowell, *Government of England*, vol. 1, 512, vol. 2, 84. The studies of Lowell, the late-nineteenth-/early-twentieth-century American political scientist and Harvard president, remain illuminating compendia of English thought about parties in the second half of the Victorian period.

[333] "The nice balance of parties which some people affect to desire, means stagnation in public business. In this country the minority is always represented on the platform and in the press"; Chamberlain, "A New Political Organization," *FR*, 22 (1877), 130.

[334] In the public sphere, any man can "gain a hearing for any views that he pleases to utter. Once committed to the press, they must take their chance in the great struggle for existence ... Without any elaborate devices, by the mere nature of the case, every opinion gets itself represented, as it ought to be represented, in proportion to the number and ability of its believers. Then again, we have the advantage that in this council everybody can talk at once, and about all conceivable subjects. Parliament is unluckily a body of finite powers, and a very narrow allowance of time"; Leslie Stephen, "Our Rulers," 290.

[335] Chamberlain, "The Caucus," 735, and his speech at the National Federation of Liberal Associations, 1877, quoted in Robert Spence Watson, *The National Liberal Federation from Its Commencement to the General Election of 1906* (London, 1907), 8.

But diminishing the relevance of anxieties about diversity and inclusivity was not the only Chamberlainite attitude on these questions. In other moments, champions of the new party machinery were keen to claim these values as their own. Laments that party activity reduced the space of free thought or constrained the development of opinion were, they argued, simply mistaken. To Chamberlain, fears that the party "distorted" or "manufactured" views to suit its needs expressed a condescending, unrealistically low view of the capacity of the average person to form his own beliefs.[336] Furthermore, Chamberlain and his allies countered, it was empirically untrue that party organizations were "stifling" influences on public opinion; rather, they were cooperative associations open to all who would take the time to come and express their convictions.[337] Any "creed of Liberalism" that gained strength within the Liberal party association was not an artifact of the ex ante imposition of "doctrinaire propositions," but emerged from the innumerable interactive and deliberative processes in party forums and through the negotiation of different perspectives that inevitably occurred in the carrying-out of the party's functions.[338]

These rebuttals to charges of the homogenizing, antideliberative impact of the plurality-rule party system led to a broader denial of any conflict between this system and the respect for pluralism. Presaging much mid-twentieth-century political science, most Victorian defenders of party government saw it as a method for channeling pluralism, not quashing it. The interests of minority groups, the strongly held convictions of small movements, the heterodox opinion that generates a following – these were already able to exert an influence on party organizations. To put it another way, parties were only able to maintain themselves because, far from being mechanisms for the enforcement of the narrow orthodoxies of a stratum of elites, they sought and received input from a diverse range of groups in society.[339] Later, the beginnings of the success of the Labour party would

---

[336] "One wonders at the frame of mind of those who have contrived to persuade themselves that the great bulk of the English people is so feeble, so ignorant, and so foolish, as to fall an easy prey to the first professional politician or wire-puller who comes round the corner"; "The Caucus," 735.

[337] "Its organisation is so free and so open, and so dependent upon voluntary work," that "its life is not produced by its machinery; its machinery is the expression of its life"; Henry Crosskey, "The Birmingham Liberal Association and Its Assailants," *MM*, 39 (1878): 151–57, at 151.

[338] It was only through the Liberal Association that "every Liberal has the opportunity of persuading his fellow member if he can, that he is right in his interpretation of the principles of Liberalism"; ibid., 152. Also Chamberlain, "The Caucus," 725–6, 730.

[339] As elsewhere on the antiproportionalist side, Shaw-Lefevre was paradigmatic: "In the conflict for power both parties endeavour to extend themselves in the direction of their opponents, so as to embrace as wide a number of adherents as it compatible with their cohesion as a party ... It follows

demonstrate to the satisfaction of many observers that the plurality-rule status quo was not a constraint rigged in favor of a duopoly of ossified party ideologies, but in fact was accessible to new ideas and interests.[340] Even before Labour had begun winning elections regularly, the dramatic changes which the main parties had undergone since the First Reform Act lent support to those who dismissed fears of the tyrannical character of parties and affirmed parties' responsiveness to the range of voices and interests that constituted public opinion.[341]

Defenders of the party system had to fend off a last, related charge: that parties were antideliberative entities. Especially from the 1880s onward, antiproportionalists recast strong parties as indispensable instruments of a deliberative polity. For one thing, parties were now lauded for preventing the deterioration of politics into a series of personal rivalries and battles over patronage; parties, which were built on a consensus to advance certain causes and principles, provided an antidote to such fates.[342] For another, parties brought average citizens into the fold of debate on public affairs in a more consequential way than the passive encounter with opinions expressed in the press; the concrete dilemmas of allegiance and mobilization which parties presented to citizens, and the opportunities for participation which they provided, were the only ways to meaningfully democratize political life.[343]

A two-tiered account of the deliberative character of British politics often implicitly structured defenses of party of this sort. Within the public sphere broadly conceived, it was vital that there be outlets for the sprawling jumble of interests and opinions present in their complex modern society; if new ideas could not be promulgated, if the needs of certain segments of the population could not hope to attract public attention, then society

---

also that neither party is likely to be so predominant as to be able to tyrannize over the other, and any attempt to do so would cause a defection of its supporters at the point nearest to the opposite party, for the benefit of the other side ... It is a matter of common experience that any interest or section has influence on an election in proportion to its real strength, and the party which puts itself into an attitude of hostility to any such section is certain to feel it in the contest. Thus the Catholic party in England, though it is unable to secure a special representation, has very great influence in the elections, and any attempt to deal in a hostile spirit with it would be resented and would have a marked result at elections. Party action, indeed, lends itself to the protection of small minorities and of special interests even to a greater degree than is always consistent with the public welfare"; "Representation of Minorities," 726, 729–30.

[340] E.g. MacDonald, *Socialism and Government*, vol. 1, 130.

[341] For a summation of these shifts in the midst of an apology of two-partyism, see Sidney Low, *The Governance of England* (London, 1904), 124–6.

[342] E.g. Chamberlain, "New Political Organization," 126–7; John MacCunn, *Ethics of Citizenship* (Glasgow, 1894), 131–2.

[343] E.g. T. H. S. Escott, "The Future of the Radical Party," *FR*, 34 (1883): 1–11.

would become at once static and unjust. But with regard to politics in the narrower sense of *governance* – the fulfillment of the administrative activities of the state and the resolution of those questions which had emerged as pressing matters of national concern – what it meant to be ruled in a deliberative manner was that there be (a) criticism of the government's conduct and (b) opposition within Parliament that could arouse the vigilance of the country and ensure that no proposals were enacted that might flout the deliberate will of the public.[344] The performance of these functions was what parties supplied. As Arthur Balfour, the Conservative statesman and quondam Prime Minister, wrote at the end of his life, summing up the lessons he had learned from serving in Britain's first era of mass democracy: "the only kind of organization natural to a free assembly, and sufficiently flexible to be in touch with public opinion, is organization by Party."[345] These notions were, of course, not created ex nihilo upon the arrival of mass suffrage.[346] But by the late-Victorian period they had become infused with democratic norms and a democratic vocabulary. Drawing from an older Whig defense of loose intraparliamentary parties an image of the practical, epistemic, and moral functions that opposition in the assembly served,[347] these purposes were now attributed to parties which did as much of their work outside Parliament as within it. They were, moreover, increasingly couched in terms of democratic values such as accountability to the electorate and the consent of the governed.[348]

This account of party government was far from the mirroring or microcosmic ideals of mid-Victorian liberalism. The change wrought by this defense of the two-party system can be summed up as a shift from the *descriptive representative* to the *devil's advocate* as the key player in representative government. While both descriptive representation and devil's advocacy are connected with a notion of how deliberation should operate, the difference between them with regard to the conceptualization

---

[344] Low's *Governance of England* excellently summed up this two-tiered perspective, for he embraced the multiplicity of ways in which it was possible to "giv[e] publicity to a subject" in the public sphere while defending the satisfactoriness of the two-party system in the legislative-electoral sphere; Low, *Governance of England*, chs. 5, 7.

[345] Balfour, "Introduction," to Bagehot, *The English Constitution* (London, 1927), vii, xii.

[346] For a remarkable mid-1850s defense of critical, adversarial two-partyism as the basis of free deliberative government, see Anon., "Parliamentary Opposition," *ER*, 101 (1855): 1–22. On the *longue-durée* history and metamorphosis of the idea, see Thomas Hockin, "The Roles of the Loyal Opposition in Britain's House of Commons: Three Historical Paradigms," *PA*, 25 (1971): 50–68.

[347] E.g. Henry Reeve, "Earl Grey on Parliamentary Government," *ER*, 108 (1858): 271–97.

[348] Contrast the importance which Graham Wallas believes "consent" was playing in political discourse in his time with the abeyance of this idea in the authors in Chapters 1–2; Wallas, *Human Nature in Politics*, ch. 2

of the representative system was fundamental. The former, as we have explored at length, was underpinned by a *sociological* logic. The latter, on the other hand, derived from a logic of *competition for power*: the disciplined party acted to win greater popular approval than its rivals, but happily the manner in which it did so – criticizing their ideas, offering counterproposals, appealing to neglected constituencies – also served some deliberative and epistemic ends. But ensuring that legislative decisions not be taken without being subjected to criticism, and that an alternative stable of members be ready to assume office should the current occupants lose favor, was in many ways a thinner ideal than the traditional liberal aspiration for the Commons to be a "mirror" or "express image" of the nation.

This is not to suggest that politicians and commentators were all aware of the extent of the shift. Ramsay MacDonald, for instance, espoused tenets continuous with the older descriptive heritage and the newer formula of democratic party government side by side. Some thinkers, though, did perceive clearly the growing discrepancy between novel democratic and traditional descriptivst ideals. Not coincidentally, one great critic of mid-Victorian "mirroring" parliaments would emerge, decades later, as not only a prominent antiproportionalist but also a great theorist of the "English Party System of Government."[349] The Dicey of the 1890s onward was deeply skeptical toward aspects of the party system, which he felt had considerable "vices" and worked "less satisfactorily" than was often imagined. In particular, he had a distaste for "the increasing rigidity of party discipline."[350] But he believed that the "working of English parliamentary government" was dependent on cohesive parties with a robust extra-parliamentary dimension. "Popular government" was possible only with "two leading and opposed parties" which criticized and combated one another and which stood before the electorate to gain consent for alternative sets of principles and policies. The combination of (a) devil's advocacy as the operating principle of a legislature oriented on a two-party axis with (b) the ratification of a governing party by the whole people in contested elections – these were the foundations, as well as the horizons, of a functional modern representative democracy.[351]

The distance between the underlying premises of the plurality-rule party democracy with which the later Dicey was grappling and the currents of liberal mirroring that he had criticized in an earlier phase of his career

---

[349] Dicey, "Memorandum on English Party System of Government (1889)," in *General Characteristics*, 37–58.

[350] Dicey, "English Party Government," *QR*, 210 (1909): 604–27, at 615, 621.

[351] Dicey, *Law of the Constitution*, lxix. Also Sidgwick, *Elements of Politics*, ch. 29.

appears most clearly through the sense of disintegration pervading his writing on party government. For Dicey's burst of theorizing on party democracy was spurred by his belief that the "conditions essential to [its] good working" were crumbling.[352] How did Dicey respond to this crisis of the representative system?

Victorian mirrorers had reacted to perceptions of the inadequacies of the Commons by attempting to correct its composition and to restore its status as truly representative of the nation. Dicey, by contrast, now turned to the referendum, the cardinal technique of *nonparliamentary* democracy, in order to remedy the defects of the electoral-representative sphere.[353] While it is often thought that Dicey's frustrations with the rise of collectivism and the movement for Irish Home Rule led him to become disillusioned with democracy,[354] in reality Dicey remained steadfastly democratic throughout his life. The shift that he underwent lay, on the contrary, in widening the scope of what he considered antagonistic to democracy. In his thirties, being a democrat meant opposing the view "that Parliament should be a mirror" of society; in his sixties and onward, defending democracy meant transcending the confines of "modern parliamentary government."[355] "The sovereignty of the nation" within the framework of "constitutional government," he now argued, required "an appeal to the people" such that the whole electorate ratified or rejected legislation concerning constitutional matters.[356]

This shift from Parliament to the people did not mean that deliberation fell out of sight. Quite the contrary: Dicey, if anything, became more of a deliberativist in his later years. But the nature of deliberation had changed. His call to displace the representative assembly was not anchored in a priori convictions in favor of direct democracy or any freestanding zest for participation; as Chapter 3 showed, the young Dicey had believed that a country governed by a legislature returned on manhood suffrage was fully democratic. Instead, his change of heart, he argued, merely reflected the fact that the capacity and standing of legislatures as deliberative bodies had diminished; they had undergone, he stated bluntly, an "eclipse."[357] Experience had revealed that claims that the Commons was the privileged

---

[352] Dicey, "English Party Government," 623.
[353] For Dicey's understanding of the referendum, see Rivka Weill, "Dicey Was Not Diceyan," *Cambridge Law Journal*, 62 (2003): 474–94.
[354] Bernard Hibbitts, "The Politics of Principle: Albert Venn Dicey and the Rule of Law," *Anglo-American Law Review*, 23 (1994): 1–31.
[355] Dicey, "Democracy in Switzerland," 143.
[356] Dicey, *Law of the Constitution*, xciii; "Democracy in Switzerland," 143.
[357] Dicey, "Will Parliamentary Government Be Permanent?," 73.

deliberative site, the locus of fine reasoning and informed exchange which made it the engine of a broader deliberative polity, were outdated. Fundamental changes that had occurred after his 1867 peak of confidence in a democratic Commons had stripped the idea of the augustness of "Parliamentary argument" of credibility.[358] The installation of such measures as the guillotine and the closure to curtail the abuse of the House's freedom of discussion as a means of obstruction;[359] the subordination of individual MPs to central party directives; the transfer of ever more power and responsibility from the membership as a whole to the government, giving the Cabinet near-complete control of the House and an ability to push through even very unpopular bills; the explosion of government business, beyond what the Commons was able to handle directly, as the state's activities expanded – these developments had reduced the "authority and prestige of representative government" as classically conceived.[360] The appointment of a government from among the legislature's members, which had been one of several functions of the Commons on Bagehot's accounting,[361] was now the entirety of its action, since the Cabinet concocted legislation with increasing independence and enforced its passage from on high with the backing of the party apparatus.[362] In light of this state of affairs, there was little ground for faith that the Commons was fit to reason collectively on important matters, or that any particular piece of legislation conformed to the wishes of the electorate.

In such circumstances, the only hope for the nation to be either well-governed or self-governed was to have the electorate directly approve or invalidate pieces of constitutional legislation. Hence, the referendum was needed. The use of this device would focus the entirety of the public's attentions on "a single, a clear ... a distinct issue," without discrete questions being "mixed and muddled up together" as normal party politics necessitated; it would establish an interval wherein citizens "can know, all that has been urged for it by its advocates and by its opponents"; it would generate a verdict free of the "intimidat[ions] and corrupt[ions] that tainted an assembly's proceedings"; the "People's Veto" (as Dicey named

[358] Dicey, "Ought the Referendum to Be Introduced into England," *CR*, 57 (1890), 502.

[359] "The House of Commons has ceased to be the home of free debate. The closure and the guillotine are necessities, but they diminish the dignity of the House"; Dicey, "The Political Situation: 'On the Brink of an Abyss'," 779–85. The closure (or "cloture") and the guillotine are parliamentary procedures by which the government can put an end to debate; on their development in the late-nineteenth/early twentieth century, in particular to deal with the obstruction of the Irish Nationalist contingent, see C. D. Allin, "The Position of Parliament," *PSQ*, 29 (1914): 214–43.

[360] Dicey, "Will Parliamentary Government Be Permanent?," 73.

[361] Bagehot, *English Constitution*, 289.   [362] Dicey, *Law of the Constitution*, lvi.

his desired version of the referendum) enabled true "deliberation."[363] The referendum alone was able not only to "give to the nation its full authority, but also to enable the nation to express its will in a rational manner."[364] From this perspective, the wrongness of PR advocacy consisted not only in the specific practical harms that PR threatened to visit upon Parliament[365] – after all, according to Dicey, there was not much farther for the current Commons to fall. PR advocacy was also harmful because it perpetuated the idea that making the Commons a "true mirror of the country" could yield any significant benefits at a time when such Parliament-centric visions of politics needed to be replaced by more radical democratic alternatives.[366]

Despite his landmark theorizations of the referendum and trenchant analysis of the passing of classical parliamentarianism, Dicey did not himself go far toward providing a new political philosophy for the twentieth century. Such an outlook, instead, was to be found in a diverse medley of New Liberal, pluralist, Idealist, and Fabian theories that flourished in the decades just before and after the turn of the century.[367] Important differences notwithstanding, at heart these schools shared a common core. They embraced democracy as the only legitimate political system for a modern society. But they doubted whether the young democratic state could fulfill its grand promise of ruling in accord with the will of the people while also respecting the rule of law, providing for the welfare of the mass of citizens in an industrialized society, and meeting the formidable challenges of governing a complex modern society, economy, and Empire. And, in grappling with this set of problems, they left much of the worldview of Victorian liberalism's mirroring parliamentarianism behind.

---

[363] Dicey, "English Party Government," 626–7; "Democracy in Switzerland," 137; *Law of the Constitution*, xcii.

[364] Dicey, "Unionists and the Lords," 703. Also Dicey, "The Referendum [I]," *NR*, 23 (1894): 65–72.

[365] He did believe these harms would be considerable, though; see Dicey, *Law of the Constitution*, lxvi-lxxiii.

[366] Lubbock, "Proportional Representation," 140; Dicey, *Law of the Constitution*, lxvi.

[367] E.g. David Weinstein, "Nineteenth and Twentieth-Century Liberalism," in *The Oxford Handbook of the History of Political Philosophy*, ed. George Klosko (Oxford, 2011): 414–35; Stapleton, *Political Intellectuals and Public Identities*, ch. 2; Michael Freeden, *The New Liberalism: An Ideology of Social Reform* (Oxford, 1978).

Conclusion

In 1866, Henry Vere Hobart, an important proponent of STV and a future governor of Madras, lamented the great "diversity of meaning" among the proposals for getting the country "duly represented in Parliament."[1] More than four decades later, in much altered electoral circumstances, Ramsay MacDonald observed that "a century of discussion has not yet settled in practice" the question of representation.[2] The Victorian pursuit of mirroring representation gave rise to as much conflict and diversity as existed in the pluralistic society whose faithful reflection they sought to carry into the assembly. In the end, not even "the great political doctrine of modern times," as Hare declared his system to be,[3] was capable of resolving one of the richest and widest-ranging debates about representation in history.

In part, this persistence of disagreement about the norms and institutions of representative government reflected the divided nature of Victorian society; as one scholar wrote, "no country in the world endured so many battles over social, political, and religious issues as England in the nineteenth century,"[4] and naturally such battles raged with special acuity around the crucial matter of political representation. But it also had much to do with the very nature of the problems of representation. The great virtue of studying the Victorian controversy about representative institutions is to acquaint us with a range of responses to these problems, and to illuminate the major trade-offs and fault-lines between them.

This book has argued that the ideal of the mirroring Commons was the polestar for a sprawling Victorian discussion about political representation. It has shown, further, that the meaning of mirroring was a closely contested question, and that this contest can be understood as a dispute between three major schools of thought and their votaries.

---

[1] Hobart, "Parliamentary Reform," 259. [2] MacDonald, *Socialism and Government*, vol. I, 127.
[3] Hare, *Election of Representatives*, 205.
[4] A. W. Brown, *The Metaphysical Society: Victorian Minds in Crisis* (New York, 1947), 267.

The first of these was the *variety of suffrages*. This crop of reformers comprised adherents to a wide range of parties and programs, drawing together mainstream thinkers and politicians such as Bagehot and the Third Earl Grey, authentic radicals such as G. J. Holyoake, and sui generis eccentrics such as George Harris. What united them was the belief that for Britain to have a mirroring Parliament it would have to recover and apply a principle that they judged to have been lost in the 1832 Reform Act: to wit, that a just system of representation required a variety of qualifications for the vote across a range of dissimilar constituencies in order to generate an assembly that accurately reflected their diverse society. This project of engineering a system of representation that allocated to the nation's various groups their "due weight" in the legislature was anchored in the view that the application of a single, uniform set of electoral rules across the nation produced illiberal class rule. In particular, they feared that under uniform universal suffrage – democracy – the legislature would be monopolized by the majority, and thus the polyphony of modern British society in all its registers would be muffled by the dominance of a single class. Importantly, it was fundamental to the enterprise of tailoring a variegated set of electoral rules to accurately reflect the "classes, interests, and opinions" that a set of sociological judgments had to precede and guide the design of electoral arrangements. These institutional prescriptions were crowned with a robust moral vision, the central element of which was a sophisticated theory of deliberation as the engine of social progress, and of the deliberative assembly as the keystone of a liberal society of reason-giving.

Two *democratic* responses to this tradition of nondemocratic mirroring emerged. The first, emblematized by authors such as John Boyd Kinnear and Lord Houghton and persisting into later Idealist currents, accepted the values of the variety-of-suffrages school, but denied that they were threatened by uniform universal suffrage. In fact, they claimed, the working class was itself a kaleidoscope of differing ideas and sentiments, and so its full enfranchisement would not appreciably threaten the diversity of thought in political life or the vitality of deliberation in Parliament. A second, more radical branch, epitomized by the young A. V. Dicey, took the extraordinary step of rejecting the mirroring ideal altogether. It argued that the attempt to make representative institutions conform to a particular image of society was intrinsically arbitrary and unfair. Instead, the only basis for legitimate parliamentary government was a system of equal, uniform voting rights which did not sort citizens antecedently into contestable categories based on discriminations about the groups to which they belonged and the respective importance of these groups.

A third theory found both of the foregoing positions inadequate; it would come to shape the future of political representation not merely in Britain, but across the globe. This was *proportional representation*, which in the Victorian context meant the single transferable vote championed by Thomas Hare and John Stuart Mill. Like Dicey and radical democrats, supporters of PR believed the group-based sociological criteria which underlay the variety-of-suffrages approach to writing electoral rules were arbitrary and violated the fundamental rights of the elector. Relatedly, they categorically rejected the idea of virtual representation, on which the traditional mirroring school depended. But unlike Dicey, Victorian proportionalists were devoted to constructing a Commons that would mirror the nation. To accomplish this goal in a way that was in keeping with their dismissal of the methods of the variety-of-suffragists, Hare and his followers revolutionized what it meant to achieve a mirroring assembly. Far from the communitarian bent of variety-of-suffragism, PR advocates now identified mirroring with the exact translation of the aggregate of individual preferences into parliamentary seats. Consequently, they set out to devise a system that offered the greatest possible measure of liberty and empowerment to the elector; in a word, they sought mirroring through individual freedom. For all of its individualism, Victorian PR was "democratic" in only a reluctant and conflicted way; Hare and many of his disciples abjured universal suffrage and advanced a number of other ideas that struck contemporaries as "elitist." Victorian PR's institutional innovations were inspired by a remarkable program to improve the personnel in Parliament and to purify and elevate British political culture. Naturally, these proposals did not go unopposed. Objections came especially from traditional mirrorers, who stayed faithful to a group-based, sociological understanding of representation against PR's individualistic proceduralism; from democratic defenders of an agonistic public sphere, who perceived PR's dissolution of the local constituency as nothing less than a recipe for society's stagnation; and from champions of the nascent mass parties and other forms of extra-parliamentary democracy that took root as the century came to a close.

The issues which animated the clash between this trio of visions remain with us, in some cases in strikingly similar form. For "Victorian" dilemmas still course through the politics of modern democracies. Should the representative system be oriented around the participation of individuals on an equal basis or should it aim for some sort of balance or reflection of social groups? And if the latter, how should we adjudicate rival claims about the kinds of group differences which warrant special provision? How should

the activity of legislatures interact with forms of mobilization and deliberation in society at large? What range of choice should be afforded to the
elector? How ought we to understand, and govern in accordance with,
"public opinion"? Which kinds of parties facilitate and which impede the
engagement of citizens with public affairs and the exchange of diverse
viewpoints? Indeed, the Victorian way of framing and responding to these
problems shapes much of how we wrestle with constitutional and representative perplexities in the present.[5]

The relevance of the contest between plurality rule and the array of PR
systems is not hard to find: we still live under these structures, and we still
argue over their relative merits. There is some danger, however, that the
variety-of-suffrages outlook may appear unduly distant. After all, few
political beliefs have been as widely held in Europe and America over the
last half-century as that we live, and are fortunate to live, in democracies[6] –
and yet Bagehot and his ilk upheld their theory precisely in opposition, and
as an alternative, to democracy. Undoubtedly, we are in many respects
more egalitarian than authors such as Bagehot, Greg, or Grey were.
Nevertheless, we also frequently hear that disillusion with democracy is
growing. Much of this restlessness or dissatisfaction seems to stem from
a sense that arrangements based on equal electoral power do not, in fact,
ensure adequate representation. As in the Victorian era, this perception has
sparked the promulgation of some radical programs that promise to do
a better job than standard electoral democracy of capturing the truth about
the condition of interests and opinions in society.[7] More tellingly still, both
citizens and political theorists have expressed concern that universal suffrage *tout court* does not yield a fair representation of social diversity, and
have argued that electoral law should build in provisions founded on
a group-based sociology in order to be more responsive to facts about the
salient divisions in society. Calls for quotas and special constituencies – the
basic tools in the variety-of-suffragist toolbox – have been issued on behalf
of a range of different groups, and such mechanisms of descriptive

---

[5] This is one way in which the familiar claim that the nineteenth-century English invented liberalism
still rings true; see e.g. Norberto Bobbio, *Liberalism and Democracy*, trans. Martin Ryle and Kate
Soper (New York, 2005).

[6] E.g. Quentin Skinner, "The Empirical Theorists of Democracy and Their Critics: A Plague on Both
Their Houses," *PT*, 1 (1973): 287–306; John Dunn, *Setting the People Free: The Story of Democracy*
(London, 2006).

[7] E.g. Harry Brighouse and Marc Fleurbaey, "Democracy and Proportionality," *JPP*, 18 (2008): 1–19;
Eric Posner and Glen Weyl, "Voting Squared: Quadratic Voting in Democratic Politics, *Vanderbilt
Law Review*, 68 (2015): 441–500. Even claims to capacitarian rule that resemble Lowe and Guizot
have been resurrected: e.g. Jason Brennan, *Against Democracy* (Princeton, 2016).

representation have been instituted by many modern governments in a range of contexts and for a variety of purposes.[8] Yet the question of "quotas," as the history of British representation illustrates, did not need to wait for modern democracy to appear, and it has in no way been settled by our entry into a democratic era. Thus, while democracy stands as a kind of umbrella ideal above contemporary public discourse and political theory, what the Victorians called the clash between "true liberalism" and the unmodified "rule of numbers" is hardly behind us. Perhaps W. E. H. Lecky, the historian-philosopher who kept his faith with the variety of suffrages even at the century's end, will look prescient for warning that, although democracy would "for a considerable time, dominate in all civilised countries," something more in the spirit of the old system of "class representation" might "in some future stage of the world's history . . . be largely revived."[9]

Yet much, of course, has also changed between their day and our own, and in the end it may be in these areas of divergence, rather than in the many points of overlap, that the Victorian theory of mirroring representation challenges us most. One such point of difference has just been noted – that all, or nearly all, participants in contemporary debates regard themselves as democrats, whereas it was rather the inverse in the period this book has covered. But I want to conclude by touching on another, somewhat ineffable but more profound gap between the Victorians and the present day. Although many of the nineteenth-century dilemmas about how to constitute and conceptualize political representation endure, it is hard not to feel that the wider *Weltbild* in which these dilemmas were embedded in Victorian times has passed. Far more than the hegemony of "democracy," which obscures continuities with the past at least as much as it picks out distinctive features of our current polities, it is the disappearance of this underlying moral substrate that most starkly separates us from the Victorians. A kind of disenchantment marks off the twenty-first from the nineteenth century, especially when it comes to representative institutions. Theoretical puzzles about, and political fights over, the forms of liberal government carry on today in lively and sometimes bitter

---

[8] For just a small sampling of this literature, see e.g. Mala Htun, "Is Gender Like Ethnicity? The Political Representation of Identity Groups," *Perspective in Politics*, 2 (2004): 439–58; Mona Krook and Diana O'Brien, "The Politics of Group Representation, Quotas for Women and Minorities Worldwide," *Comparative Politics*, 42 (2010): 253–72; Rochana Bajpai, *Debating Difference: Group Rights and Liberal Democracy in India* (Oxford, 2011); David Canon, "Electoral Systems and the Representation of Minority Interests in Legislatures," *Legislative Studies Quarterly*, 24 (1999): 331–85.

[9] Lecky, *Democracy and Liberty*, vol. I, 256, 264.

fashion. But who now believes, as the authors examined here believed, that getting these forms right will guarantee progress and lead to the continual discovery of new truths? That if only an assembly with the right composition rules over us, we will be secure from social and intellectual "stagnation"? That if only our electoral arrangements ensure the elector's "liberation" and provide him with "a magnificent field of choice," then public morality will be purified, collective decisions rendered sacrosanct, and the crème de la crème elevated naturally to positions of power? Or, conversely, that if only the design of constituencies derives from a proper account of "really organic" communities, then we will enjoy a public sphere simultaneously contestatory, educative, and integrative? That, in short, the "most critical change[s]," certain to rejuvenate "the whole body politic," were at stake in conflicts over the structures of representation?[10] We continue, naturally, to discuss the respective merits of different electoral systems, but we no longer see the choice between them, as the Victorian disputants did, as either the source of the most sweeping societal regeneration or a fatal blow to the most valuable aspects of our political culture.[11]

Perhaps the difference between the assumptions and motivations of Victorian and contemporary political thought shines through most clearly on the subject of deliberation. Anglophone political theory is currently as interested in deliberation, and as hostile to the supposition that liberal governance can be reduced to the mere aggregation of preferences, as at any point since the Victorian era. But the contemporary analysis of deliberation is both less grounded in political realities and less ambitious than its forerunner. That is to say, modern deliberative democrats lack the Victorian confidence that deliberation can successfully be rooted in the best version of the representative institutions under which they actually live.[12] Similarly, they operate (perhaps wisely) without the great expectations about the transformative, world-altering character of political deliberation that the Victorians harbored. Even the most hopeful of political theorists today has nothing like Bagehot's or Grey's or Hare's certainty that

---

[10] Collier, *Representation of Minorities*, 20.

[11] Alan Ryan's breezy dismissal of "Mill's enthusiasm" for "Hare's scheme" as "scarcely justifiable on rational grounds" still stands as a testament to just how wide the gulf is between Victorian and contemporary political thought; Ryan, *J. S. Mill* (London, 1974), 192.

[12] The preponderance of interest in mini-publics and other small-scale, experimental settings suggests that many theorists today have not managed to sustain the optimism about mass democracy's compatibility with deliberative politics that animated the moderate democrats of Chapter 3; see e.g. Simone Chambers, "Rhetoric and the Public Sphere: Has Deliberative Democracy Abandoned Mass Democracy?," *PT*, 37 (2009): 323–50.

from the wellspring of a deliberative system of representation would necessarily flow a great stream of benefits, from scientific advance to social cohesion to the enlightenment of the citizenry.

We ask, then, many similar questions to those raised in Victorian days: about the right composition of the membership of political bodies, the use of quotas, the clash between the claims of the individual and the group, the balance to be struck between conflict and consensus, the relationship between legislatures and other venues for the formation of public opinion, and so on. But we do so without the surrounding set of moral, social, and epistemological premises and beliefs that invested the nineteenth-century battles over these issues with such urgency and meaningfulness. Faced with the Victorian debate about mirroring representation, perhaps our task today is less to give superior answers to the questions we share with this earlier period than it is to interrogate more deeply our own reasons for cherishing (or rejecting) the various programs and traditions of representative government that vie for our allegiance.

Bibliography

For the sake of economy, I have maintained the system of abbreviations used throughout. I have also refrained from giving a separate listing of the many individual works of Walter Bagehot and John Stuart Mill that have been discussed, as for both of them I have cited from the standard multivolume modern editions of their Collected Works [CW]. In general, where relevant collections of the works of an author are available, I have named here only the collection rather than listing a separate entry for each particular work of the author that I have cited. Finally, specific entries from Hansard and the ODNB are omitted here.

Reference Works

Hansard's Parliamentary Debates, Third Series
Oxford Dictionary of National Biography, Online Edition

Primary Sources

[Anon.] *Observations on the British Constitution, and on the Proposed Improvement of Our Parliamentary Representation* (Edinburgh, 1831).
[Anon.] "Parliamentary Opposition," *ER*, 101 (1855): 1–22.
[Anon.] "Independent Voting and Party Government," *SR*, 3 (1857): 191–2.
[Anon.] *The Franchise: What Shall We Do to It?* (London, 1858).
[Anon.] *Parliamentary Reform* (London, 1867).
[Anon.] *Student's Handbook to the University and Colleges of Oxford* (Oxford, 1913).
"A Moderate Liberal." "Can Any Class Be Trusted?" *NR*, 2 (1884): 799–806.
"A Reformer." *A View of Parliamentary Reform* (Wallingford, 1867).
Acton, John Emerich Edward Dalberg, First Baron. *The History of Freedom and Other Essays*, ed. John Neville Figgis and Reginald Vere Laurence (London, 1907).
Alison, Archibald. "The Influence of the Press," *BM*, 36 (1834): 373–91.
  Essays Political, Historical, and Miscellaneous, 3 vols. (Edinburgh, 1850).
Allin, C. D. "The Position of Parliament," *PSQ*, 29 (1914): 214–43.

Andrae, Poul. *Andrae and His Invention: The Proportional Representation Method, A Memorial Work*, trans. Vaughn Meisling (Copenhagen, 1926).

Aris, Reinhold. "Proportional Representation in Germany," *Politica*, 2 (1937): 433–45.

Arnold, Matthew. *Irish Essays and Others* (London, 1882).

Austin, John. *A Plea for the Constitution*, second edition (London, 1859).

Aytoun, William Edmonstoune. "Reform Measures of 1852," *BM*, 71 (1852): 369–86.

Bagehot, Walter. *Essays on Parliamentary Reform* (London, 1883).

"Note of 18 Feb, 1859, to 'Parliamentary Reform'," *The Works and Life of Walter Bagehot*, ed. Mrs. Russell Barrington (London, 1915), vol. 3: 164–76.

The Collected Works of Walter Bagehot, 15 vols., ed. Norman St. John-Stevas (Cambridge, MA, 1965–86).

Bailey, Samuel. *Questions in Political Economy, Politics, Morals, Metaphysics, Polite Literature, and Other Branches of Knowledge* (London, 1828).

Essays on the Pursuit of Truth and the Progress of Knowledge, second edition (London, 1844).

Baily, Walter. *A Scheme for Proportional Representation* (London, 1869).

Proportional Representation in Large Constituencies (London, 1872).

Becker, Lydia. "Female Suffrage," *CR*, 1 (1867): 307–16.

"The Political Disabilities of Women," in *Before the Vote Was Won: Arguments for and against Women's Suffrage 1864–1896*, ed. Jane Lewis (London, 1987): 118–40.

Beales, Edmond, W. R. Cremer, G. J. Holyoake, et al. *Representative Reform: Report of the Committee Appointed by the Conference of Members of the Reform League, and Others, on Mr. Hare's Scheme of Representation, held 28th February, & 7th & 21st March, 1868* (London, 1868).

Belloc, Hilaire and Cecil Chesterton. *The Party System* (London, 1911).

Bentham, Jeremy. *Plan of Parliamentary Reform, in the Form of a Catechism* (London, 1817).

Anarchical Fallacies, Being an Examination of the Declaration of Rights Issued during the French Revolution, in *The Works of Jeremy Bentham*, 11 vols., ed. John Bowring (Edinburgh, 1838–43), vol. 2: 489–534.

Bentham's Theory of Fictions, ed. C. K. Ogden (New York, 1932).

Blanc, Louis. *Questions d'aujourd'hui et de demain*, 2 vols. (Paris, 1873).

Bodichon, Barbara. *Reasons for and against the Enfranchisement of Women* (London, 1869).

Bosanquet, Bernard. "The Reality of the General Will," in *The British Idealists*, ed. David Boucher (Cambridge, 1997): 130–41.

Bosanquet, S. R. *Eirenicon: Toleration, Intolerance, Christianity, Christian Unity, the Church of England and Dissent* (London, 1867).

Boundary Commission (England and Wales). *Report of the Boundary Commissioners for England and Wales, 1885*, 2 vols. (London, 1885).

Boutmy, Émile. *Essai d'une Psychologie politique du Peuple anglais au XIXe siècle* (Paris, 1902).

Brodrick, George Charles. "The Utilitarian Argument against Reform, as Stated by Mr. Lowe," in *Essays on Reform* (London, 1867): 1–26.

Political Studies (London, 1879).

Brougham, Henry, Lord. *Inaugural Discourse of Henry Brougham, Esq., MP: On Being Installed Lord Rector of the University of Glasgow* (Glasgow, 1825).

"France," *The British and Foreign Review*, 1 (1835): 492–512.

"French Parties and Politics," *ER*, 61 (1835): 123–7.

Contributions to the Edinburgh Review by Henry Lord Brougham, 2 vols. (London, 1856).

The British Constitution: Its History, Structure, and Working (London and Glasgow, 1861).

Works of Henry Lord Brougham, 11 vols. (Edinburgh, 1873).

Brown, William Jethro. *The New Democracy: A Political Study* (London, 1899).

Bryce, James. *The American Commonwealth*, second edition, 2 vols. (London, 1889).

Buckalew, Charles. *Proportional Representation: Or, the Representation of Successive Majorities in Federal, State, Municipal, Corporate, and Primary Elections*, ed. John Freeze (Philadelphia, 1872).

Buckle, Henry Thomas. "Mill on Liberty," *FM*, 59 (1859): 509–42.

Burke, Edmund. *Select Works of Edmund Burke*, 4 vols. (Indianapolis, 1990).

Further Reflections on the Revolution in France, ed. Daniel Ritchie (Indianapolis, 1992).

Miscellaneous Writings, ed. Francis Canavan (Indianapolis, 1999).

Calvert, Frederick. *The Representation of Minorities* (London, 1881).

Carlyle, Thomas. *On Heroes, Hero-Worship, and The Heroic in History* (London, 1841).

Cartwright, John. *Legislative Rights of the Commonalty Vindicated; or, Take Your Choice!*, second edition (London, 1777).

Chamberlain, Joseph. "A New Political Organization," *FR*, 22 (1877): 126–34.

"The Caucus," *FR*, 24 (1878): 721–41.

The Radical Programme, ed. D. A. Hamer (Brighton, 1971).

Chapman, John. "Politics, Sociology, Voyages, and Travels," *WR*, 41 (1872): 519–38.

Charles I. *His Majesties Answer to the XIX Propositions of Both Houses of Parliament* (London, 1642).

Christophle, François-Marie-Jules. *De la représentation proportionnelle* (Paris, 1887).

Church, Richard William. "Mill on Liberty," in *Liberty: Contemporary Responses to John Stuart Mill*, ed. Andrew Pyle (South Bend, 1994): 210–54.

Clifford, W. K. *The Ethics of Belief and Other Essays*, ed. Timothy Madigan (Amherst, 1999).

Cole, Henry Warwick. *The Middle Classes and the Borough Franchise* (London, 1866).

Coleridge, Samuel Taylor. *On the Constitution of Church and State, According to the Idea of Each: with Aids toward a Right Judgment on the Late Catholic Bill* (London, 1830).

The Political Thought of Samuel Taylor Coleridge, ed. R. J. White (London, 1938).

Collier, Robert. *Representation of Minorities* (London, 1868).

Congreve, Richard. *Essays Political, Social, and Religious* (London, 1874).

Constant, Benjamin. *Political Writings*, ed. Biancamaria Fontana (Cambridge, 1988).

Cooper, Anthony Ashley, Earl of Shaftesbury. *Two Seasonable Discourses Concerning This Present Parliament* (Oxford, 1675).

Cosgrove, Richard. *The Rule of Law: Albert Venn Dicey, Victorian Jurist* (London, 1980).

Courtney, Leonard. "Political Machinery and Political Life," *FR*, 20 (1876): 74–92.

"The Representation of Minorities," *NC*, 6 (1879): 141–56.

"The Seats Bill," *FR*, 37 (1885): 26–36.

Cox, Homersham. *The British Commonwealth: or a Commentary on the Institutions and Principles of British Government* (London, 1854).

The Institutions of English Government: Being an Account of the Constitution, Powers, and Procedure, of Its Legislative, Judicial, and Administrative Departments, with Copious References to Ancient and Modern Authorities (London, 1863).

Cracroft, Bernard. "The Analysis of the House of Commons, or Indirect Representation," in *Essays on Reform* (London, 1867): 155–90.

Essays, Political and Miscellaneous, 2 vols. (London, 1868).

Creasy, Edward Shepherd. *The Text-Book of the Constitution. Magna Charta, The Petition of Rights, and the Bill of Rights, with Historical Comments, and Remarks on the Present Political Emergencies* (London, 1848).

Crosskey, Henry. "The Birmingham Liberal Association and Its Assailants," *MM*, 39 (1878): 151–57.

Dicey, Albert Venn. "The Balance of Classes," in *Essays on Reform* (London, 1867): 67–84.

"Democracy in Switzerland," *ER*, 171 (1890): 113–45.

"Ought the Referendum to Be Introduced into England," *CR*, 57 (1890): 489–511.

"Alexis de Tocqueville," *NR*, 21 (1893): 771–84.

"The Referendum [I]," *NR*, 23 (1894): 65–72.

"Unionists and the House of Lords," *NR*, 24 (1895): 690–704.

"Will the Form of Parliamentary Government Be Permanent?" *Harvard Law Review*, 13 (1899): 67–79.

Lectures on the Relation between Law and Public Opinion in England during the Nineteenth Century (London, 1905).

"The Paralysis of the Constitution," *CR* 88 (1905): 305–16.

"English Party Government," *QR*, 210 (1909): 604–27.

"The Political Situation: 'On the Brink of an Abyss'," *NC*, 67 (1910): 779–85.

Introduction to the Study of the Law of the Constitution, eighth edition (London, 1915).

General Characteristics of English Constitutionalism: Six Unpublished Lectures, ed. Peter Raina (Bern, 2009).

Dobbs, Archibald. *General Representation, On a Complete Readjustment and Modification of Mr. Hare's Plan* (London, 1871).

Dodgson, Charles Lutwidge [Lewis Carroll]. *The Pamphlets of Lewis Carroll, Volume Three: The Political Pamphlets and Letters of Charles Lutwidge Dodgson*, ed. Francine Abeles (New York, 2001).

Donisthorpe, Wordsworth. *Individualism: A System of Politics* (London, 1889).

Droop, Henry Richmond. *On the Political and Social Effects of Different Methods of Electing Representatives* (LSE Selected Pamphlets, 1869).

"On Methods of Electing Representatives," *Journal of the Statistical Society of London*, 44 (1881): 141–202.

Dupont-White, Charles Brook. *Le Rôle et la liberté de la presse* (Paris, 1866).

"Introduction" to J. S. Mill, *Le Gouvernement représentatif*, trans. Dupont-White, third edition (Paris, 1877): v–xlviii.

Dupriez, Léon. *L'organisation du suffrage universel en Belgique. Vote plural, vote obligatoire et représentation proportionnelle* (Paris, 1901).

Dutcher, Salem. *Minority or Proportional Representation: Its Nature, Aims, History, Processes, and Practical Operation* (New York, 1872).

Duvergier de Hauranne, Prosper. "La démocratie et le droit de suffrage," *Revue des deux mondes*, 74 (1868): 608–43, 785–821.

Eardley-Wilmot, John Eardley. *Lord Brougham's Acts and Bills, from 1811 to the Present Time . . .* (London, 1857).

A Safe and Constitutional Plan of Parliamentary Reform (London, 1865).

Edgeworth, Francis Ysidro. *Mathematical Psychics: An Essay on the Application of Mathematics to the Moral Sciences* (London, 1881).

Escott, Thomas Hay Sweet. "The Future of the Radical Party," *FR*, 34 (1883): 1–11.

"The Radical Programme: Machinery," *FR*, 34 (1883): 290–7.

Fawcett, Henry. *Mr. Hare's Reform Bill Simplified and Explained* (Westminster, 1860).

The Leading Clauses of a New Reform Bill (Cambridge, 1860).

"Mr. Mill's Treatise on Representative Government," *MM*, 4 (1861): 97–102.

"Proportional Representation, from the Last Speech of the Right Hon. Henry Fawcett, MP, Delivered to His Constituents at Hackney, October 13, 1884," (Earl Grey Pamphlets Collection, 1884).

Fawcett, Millicent Garrett. "Proportional Representation," *MM*, 22 (1870): 376–82.

Home and Politics, third edition (London, 1894).

"The Electoral Disabilities of Women," in *The Subjection of Women: Contemporary Responses to John Stuart Mill*, ed. Andrew Pyle (Bristol, 1995): 223–35.

Figgis, John Neville. "William Warburton," in *Typical English Churchmen from Parker to Maurice*, ed. William Collins (London, 1902): 215–56.

Finer, Herman. *Fabian Tract No. 211: The Case against Proportional Representation* (Westminster, 1924).

Fisher, J. Francis. *The Degradation of Our Representative System and Its Reform* (Philadelphia, 1863).

Flaugergues, Pierre-François. *De la représentation nationale et principes sur la matière des élections* (Paris, 1820).

Freeman, Edward. *The Growth of the English Constitution from the Earliest Times* (London, 1872).

Frisby, Alfred. "The Next Reform Bill," *FR*, 32 (1882): 241–54.

Froude, James Anthony. "Party Politics," *FM*, 10 (1874): 1–18.

Gergonne, Joseph Diaz. "Arithmétique Politique. Sur les élections et le système représentatif," *Annales de Mathématiques*, 10 (1820): 281–8.

Gibbons, Philip Arnold. *Ideas of Political Representation in Parliament, 1660–1832* (Oxford, 1914).

Girardin, Émile de. *Force ou Richesse: Questions de l'année 1864* (Paris, 1865).

Gladstone, William Ewart. "The Declining Efficiency of Parliament," *QR*, 99 (1856): 521–70.

Speeches on Parliamentary Reform in 1866 (London, 1866).

"Electoral Facts," *NC*, 4 (1878): 955–68.

Gleig, George Robert. "The Reform Bill," *BM*, 99 (1866): 650–72.

Godwin, William. *Enquiry Concerning Political Justice, and Its Influence on General Virtue and Happiness*, 2 vols. (London, 1793).

Graham, William. *English Political Philosophy from Hobbes to Maine* (London, 1907).

Granier de Cassagnac, Adolphe. *L'empereur et la démocratie moderne* (Paris, 1860).

Green, T. H. "Parliamentary Reform," Speech of 25 February 1868, in *The Collected Works of T. H. Green*, ed. Peter Nicholson, 5 vols. (Bristol, 1997), vol. 5: 232–6.

Greg, Percy. "Redistribution: Right and Wrong Directions," *NR*, 2 (Feb. 1884): 807–23.

Greg, William Rathbone. "Difficulties of Republican France," *ER*, 92 (1850): 504–33.

"Representative Reform [1]," *ER*, 96 (1852): 452–508.

"The Expected Reform Bill," *ER*, 95 (1852): 213–80.

"Parliamentary Purification," *ER*, 98 (1853): 566–624.

"French Judgments of England," *ER*, 103 (1856): 558–90.

"Representative Reform [2]," *ER*, 106 (1857): 254–86.

"The Achievements and the Moral of 1867," *NBR*, 47 (Sept. 1867): 205–56.

Enigmas of Life (London, 1872).

Rocks Ahead: Or, The Warnings of Cassandra (London, 1874).

Grey, Albert, the Fourth Earl. *Mr. Albert Grey, MP, and the Redistribution of Seats* (Earl Grey Pamphlets, 1880).

"Proportional versus Majority Representation," *NC*, 16 (1884): 935–64.

Grey, Henry George, the Third Earl. *Parliamentary Government, Considered with Reference to Reform*, second edition (London, 1864).

Guizot, François. *Discours Académiques, suivis de divers essais de philosophie littéraire et politique* (Paris, 1861).

Histoire de la civilisation en Europe, suivie de Philosophie politique: de la souveraineté, ed. Pierre Rosanvallon (Paris, 1985).

The History of the Origins of Representative Government in Europe, trans. Andrew R. Scoble (Indianapolis, 2002).

Hall, Robert. *An Apology for the Freedom of the Press, and for General Liberty*, seventh edition (London, 1822).

Hallam, Henry. *The Constitutional History of England, from the Accession of Henry VII to the Death of George II*, sixth edition, 2 vols. (London, 1850).

Hare, Thomas. *The Machinery of Representation*, first edition (London, 1857).
  The Machinery of Representation, second edition (London, 1857).
  A Treatise on the Election of Representatives, Parliamentary and Municipal, first edition (London, 1859).
  "Representation in Theory and Practice," *FM*, 61 (1860): 188–204.
  "Representation of Every Locality and Intelligence," *FM*, 61 (1860): 527–43.
  A Treatise on the Election of Representatives, Parliamentary and Municipal, second edition (London, 1861).
  "Ideal of a Local Government for the Metropolis," *MM*, 7 (1863): 441–7.
  The Election of Representatives, Parliamentary and Municipal: A Treatise, third edition (London, 1865).
  "Mr. Hare's Electoral System: A Grouping of Parliamentary Electors that Combines a Just and Equal Distribution of Seats and the Free Expression both of Individual and Public Opinion with the Smallest Degree of Disturbance from Corrupt Influences," in *Transactions of the National Association for the Promotion of Social Science, Manchester Meeting, 1866*, ed. George Hastings (London, 1866): 202–8.
  "Minority Representation in Europe," *Journal of Social Science*, 3 (1871): 185–91.
  "On the Suggestions Afforded by the Application of the Cumulative Vote and by the Other Incidents of the School Board Elections," *Sessional Proceedings of the National Association for the Promotion of Social Science*, 4 (1871): 215–35.
  The Election of Representatives, Parliamentary and Municipal: A Treatise, fourth edition (London, 1873).
  "John Stuart Mill," *WR*, 45 (1874): 122–59.
  "A Note on Representative Government," *FR*, 18 (1875): 102–7.
  "The Reform Bill of the Future," *FR*, 23 (1878): 75–84.
  "The Coming Steps in Representation," *FR*, 37 (1885): 216–22.
  "Individual Responsibility in Representative Government," 4 (1886): 350–8.

Harris, George. *The True Theory of Representation in a State: Considered More Especially in Relation to the Proposal of the Government for the Extension of the Suffrage* (London, 1852).
  The True Theory of Representation in a State: Or, the Leading Interests of the Nation, Not the Mere Predominance of Numbers, Proved to Be Its Basis (London, 1857).
  The Autobiography of George Harris, LL.D., F.S.A. (London, 1888).

Harrison, Frederic. "The Religion of Inhumanity," *FR*, 13 (1873): 677–99.
  "The Revival of Authority," *FR*, 13 (1873): 1–26.
  Order and Progress (London, 1875).
  Tennyson, Ruskin, Mill, and Other Literary Estimates (London, 1899).

Haynes, Edmund Sidney Pollock. *The Decline of Liberty in England* (London, 1916).

Hazlitt, William. *Selected Writings*, ed. Jon Cook (Oxford, 1981).

Fugitive Writings, ed. A. R. Waller and Arnold Glover (London, 1904).

Hearn, William Edward. *The Government of England: Its Structure and Its Development*, second edition (London, 1866).

Hegel, Georg Wilhelm Friedrich *Political Writings*, ed. Laurence Dickey and H. B. Nisbet (Cambridge, 1999).

Herbert, George. "Liberty and Socialism," in *Herbert Spencer and the Limits of the State*, ed. Michael Taylor (Bristol, 1996): 95–126.

Heywood, John. *The Representation of Minorities: A Practical Plan* (Bristol Selected Pamphlets, 1884).

Hoag, Clarence and George Hallett. *Proportional Representation* (New York, 1926).

Hobart, Henry Vere. "Parliamentary Reform," *MM*, 13 (1866): 259–72.

Hobbes, Thomas. *Elements of Law*, ed. J. C. A. Gaskin (Oxford, 1994).

On the Citizen, ed. Richard Tuck (Cambridge, 1998).

Hobhouse, Leonard Trelawny. *Liberalism and Other Writings*, ed. James Meadowcroft (Cambridge, 1994).

Holyoake, George Jacob. *The Workman and the Suffrage. Letters to the Right Honourable Lord John Russell, M.P., and the "Daily News"* (London, 1859).

The Liberal Situation: Necessity for a Qualified Franchise. A Letter to Joseph Cowen, Jun. (London, 1865).

Working-Class Representation: Its Conditions and Consequences (Birmingham and London, 1868).

The Last Trial for Atheism in England: A Fragment of Autobiography, fourth edition (London, 1871).

The History of Co-Operation in England: Its Literature and Its Advocates, 2 vols. (London, 1875–79).

Hostile and Generous Toleration: A New Theory of Toleration (London, 1886).

Hoskins, James Thornton. *A Modification of Mr. Hare's Scheme for the Election of Representatives*, second edition (London, 1860).

Humboldt, Wilhelm von. *The Sphere and Duties of Government*, trans. Joseph Coulthard (London, 1844).

Humphrey, Arthur Wilfrid *A History of Labour Representation* (London, 1912).

Humphreys, John H. *Proportional Representation: A Study in Methods of Election* (London, 1911).

Hutton, Richard Holt. "The Political Character of the Working Classes," in *Essays on Reform* (London, 1867): 27–44.

Criticisms on Contemporary Thought and Thinkers, 2 vols. (London, 1894).

Ilbert, Courtenay. *Parliament: Its History, Constitution, and Practice* (London, 1911).

Inglis, Robert. *Parliamentary Reform. Substance of the Speech Delivered in the House of Commons, on Saturday, the 17th December, 1831* (London, 1832).

James, Edmund. "An Early Essay on Proportional Representation," *Proceedings of the American Philosophical Society*, 34 (1895): 468–71.

Jeffrey, Francis and Henry Brougham, "Parliamentary Reform," *ER*, 17 (1811): 253–90.

Jevons, William Stanley. *The State in Relation to Labour* (London, 1882).

Kebbel, T.E. "The Spirit of Party," *NC*, 11 (1882): 378–88.

Kelsen, Hans. *General Theory of Law and State* (New Brunswick, 2006).

The Essence and Value of Democracy, trans. Brian Graf (Lanham, 2013).

King, Joseph. *Electoral Reform: An Inquiry into Our System of Parliamentary Representation* (London, 1908).

Kinnear, John Boyd. *Principles of Reform: Political and Legal* (London, 1865).

"Practical Considerations on the Representation of Minorities," *FR*, 4 (1866): 49–64.

Knatchbull-Hugessen, Edward Hugessen. "Redistribution of Political Power," *MM*, 27 (1872): 67–76.

Kyllman, Max. "Mr. Hare's System of Personal Representation," reprinted from the 'Examiner and Times,' of October 2nd, 1866 (LSE Selected Pamphlets, 1866).

la Grasserie, Raoul de. *De la représentation proportionnelle de la majorité et des minorités* (Paris, 1889).

Laboulaye, Édouard René de. *L'état et ses limites, suivi d'essais politiques sur Alexis de Tocqueville, l'instruction publique, les finances, le droit de pétition, etc.*, fifth edition (Paris, 1871).

Laski, Harold. *Authority in the Modern State* (New Haven, 1919).

The Foundations of Sovereignty and Other Essays (New York, 1921).

Lecky, W. E. H. *The History of European Morals from Augustus to Charlemagne*, 2 vols. (London, 1876).

Democracy and Liberty, 2 vols. (London, 1896).

Introduction to Democracy and Liberty, Reprinted from the Cabinet Edition (London, 1899).

The Map of Life: Conduct and Character (London, 1901).

Lewis, George Cornewall. "Marshall on the Representation of Minorities," *ER*, 100 (1854): 226–35.

"History and Prospects of Parliamentary Reform," *ER*, 109 (1859): 264–92.

Dialogue on the Best Form of Government (London, 1863).

An Essay on the Influence of Authority in Matters of Opinion, second edition (London, 1875).

Lindsay, Alexander Dunlop, First Baron. *The Essentials of Democracy* (London, 1929).

Locke, John. *Two Treatise of Government*, ed. Peter Laslett (Cambridge, 1960).

A Letter Concerning Toleration, in *A Letter Concerning Toleration and Other Writings*, ed. Mark Goldie (Indianapolis, 2010): 1–68.

Lowenstein, Karl. "Militant Democracy and Fundamental Rights [1]," *APSR*, 31 (1937): 417–32.

Lorimer, James. *Political Progress Not Necessarily Democratic: or Relative Equality the True Foundation of Liberty* (Edinburgh, 1857).

"Mr. Mill on Representative Government," *NBR*, 35 (1861): 534–63.

Constitutionalism of the Future, or Parliament the Mirror of the Nation (Edinburgh, 1865).

Low, Sidney. *The Governance of England* (London, 1904).

Lowe, Robert. "Reform Essays," *QR*, 123 (1867): 244–77.

Speeches and Letters on Reform, with a Preface by the Right Hon. R. Lowe, MP (London, 1867).

Lowell, A. Lawrence. *The Government of England*, 2 vols. (New York, 1908).

Lowes-Dickinson, Goldsworthy. *The Development of Parliament during the Nineteenth Century* (London, 1895).

Lubbock, John. "Proportional Representation," *NC*, 15 (1884): 703–13.

Representation (London, 1885).

"Proportional Representation," in *The Pamphlets of Lewis Carroll, Volume Three: The Political Pamphlets and Letters of Charles Lutwidge Dodgson*, ed. Francine Abeles (New York, 2001): 140–4

Lubbock, John, Leonard Courtney, Albert Grey, and John Westlake. "Proportional Representation: Objections and Answers," *NC*, 17 (1885): 312–20.

Ludlow, John Malcolm. "Mr. Hare's Scheme of Parliamentary Representation," *CR*, 9 (1868): 80–97.

Ludlow, John Malcolm, Frederick Denison Maurice, and Charles Kingsley. *Politics for the People* (London, 1848).

Lytton, Robert. "Report by Mr. Lytton, Her Majesty's Secretary of Legation, on the Election of Representatives for the Rigsraad," printed in *Personal Representation, Speech of John Stuart Mill, Esq., MP, Delivered in the House of Commons May 29, 1867, with an Appendix Containing Notices of Reports, Discussions, and Publications on the System in France, Geneva, Germay, Belgium, Denmark, Sweden, The Australian Colonies, and the United States.*, second edition (London, 1867): 17–42.

Macaulay, Thomas Babington. *Critical and Historical Essays*, fifth edition, 2 vols. (London, 1848).

The Miscellaneous Writings of Lord Macaulay, 2 vols. (London, 1860).

MacCunn, John. *Ethics of Citizenship* (Glasgow, 1894).

Six Radical Thinkers: Bentham, J. S. Mill, Cobden, Carlyle, Mazzini, T. H. Green (London, 1907).

MacDonald, Ramsay. *Socialism and Government*, 2 vols. (London, 1909).

Mackinnon, W. A. *On the Rise, Progress, and Present State of Public Opinion, in Great Britain and Other Parts of the World* (London, 1828).

Mackintosh, James. "Universal Suffrage," *ER*, 31 (1818): 165–203.

"Parliamentary Reform," *ER*, 34 (1820): 461–501.

Maine, Henry. *Popular Government: Four Essays* (London, 1885).

Maitland, Frederic William. *A Historical Sketch of Liberty and Equality: As Ideals of English Political Philosophy from the Time of Hobbes to the Time of Coleridge* (Indianapolis, 2000).

Marshall, James Garth. *Minorities and Majorities: Their Relative Rights* (London, 1853).

Martin, Arthur Patchett. *Life and Letters of the Right Honourable Robert Lowe, Viscount Sherbrooke*, 2 vols. (London, 1893).

Marvell, Andrew. *An Account of the Growth of Popery and Arbitrary Government in England* (Amsterdam, 1675).

Marx, Karl. *The Marx-Engels Reader*, ed. Robert Tucker (New York, 1978).

Selected Writings, ed. Lawrence Simon (Indianapolis, 1994).

Maurice, Frederick Denison. "The Suffrage, Considered in Reference to the Working Class, and to the Professional Class," *MM*, 2 (1860): 89–97.

The Workman and the Franchise (London, 1866).

May, Erskine. *Democracy in Europe: A History*, 2 vols. (London, 1877).

Meredith, James Creed. *Proportional Representation in Ireland* (Dublin, 1918).

Mill, James. *Political Writings*, ed. Terence Ball (Cambridge, 1992).

Mill, John Stuart. *The Collected Works of John Stuart Mill*, 33 vols., ed. J. M. Robson (Toronto, 1963–91).

Milnes, Richard Monckton, Lord Houghton. "On the Admission of the Working Classes as Part of Our Social System; and Their Recognition for All Purposes as Part of the Nation," in *Essays on Reform* (London, 1867): 45–66.

Montalembert, Charles Forbes René de. *L'avenir politique de l'Angleterre*, fifth edition (Paris, 1857).

Morin, Antoine. *De la question électorale dans le canton de Genève* (Geneva, 1867).

Morley, John. *Modern Characteristics* (London, 1865).

Critical Miscellanies, 3 vols. (London, 1886).

Nineteenth-Century Essays, ed. Peter Stansky (Chicago, 1970).

Morrison-Bell, Clive. "Proportional Representation – What Is It?," *NC*, 73 (1913): 1122–30.

Naville, Ernest. *La Patrie et les Partis* (Geneva, 1865).

On the Theory and Practice of Representative Elections (London, 1872).

La pratique de la représentation proportionnelle (Earl Grey Pamphlets, 1882).

Newman, John Henry. *A Letter Addressed to His Grace the Duke of Norfolk, on Occasion of Mr. Gladstone's Recent Expostulation* (London, 1875).

Ostrogorski, Moisei. "Introduction of the Caucus into England," *PSQ*, 8 (1893): 287–316.

"Les Origines des associations politiques et des organisations de parti en Angleterre," *Revue Historique*, 52 (1893): 259–97.

Democracy and the Organization of Political Parties, trans. Frederick Clarke, 2 vols. (London, 1902).

Paley, William. *The Principles of Moral and Political Philosophy*, ed. D. L. Le Mahieu (Indianapolis, 2002)

Parker, Henry. *Observations upon Some of His Majesties Late Answers and Expresses* (London, 1642).

Peel, Robert. Speech of 3 March 1831, in *The Emergence of British Parliamentary Democracy in the Nineteenth Century*, ed. J. B. Conacher (New York, 1971): 27–32.

Pelletan, Eugène. *Les droits de l'homme* (Paris, 1858).

Pitt, William, the Younger, *The Speeches of the Right Honourable William Pitt in the House of Commons*, 4 vols. (London, 1806).

Pochin, Henry Davis. *A Plan of Parliamentary Reform* (London, 1866).

"Political Euclid." *The Reform Problem: Its True Solution* (London, 1866).

Pollock, Frederick. "Liberty, Equality, Fraternity," *FM*, 8 (1873): 86–97.

Prévost-Paradol, Lucien-Anatole. *Nouveaux Essais de politique et de littérature* (Paris, 1862).

La France Nouvelle, second edition (Paris, 1868)

Priestley, Joseph. *Priestley's Writings on Philosophy, Science, and Politics*, ed. John Passmore (New York, 1965).

Political Writings, ed. Peter Miller (Cambridge, 1993).

Rae, W. Fraser. "Political Clubs and Party Organization," *NC*, 3 (1878): 908–32.

Ritchie, David George. *Principles of State Interference: Four Essays on the Political Philosophy of Mr. Herbert Spencer, J. S. Mill, and T. H. Green* (London, 1891).

Natural Rights: A Criticism of Some Ethical and Political Conceptions (London, 1895).

"Social Evolution," *International Journal of Ethics*, 6 (1896): 165–81.

"Evolution and Democracy," in *Ethical Democracy: Essays in Social Dynamics*, ed. Stanton Coit (London, 1900): 1–29.

"The Rights of Minorities," in *The British Idealists*, ed. David Boucher (Cambridge, 1997): 142–55.

Reeve, Henry. "Earl Grey on Parliamentary Government," *ER*, 108 (1858): 271–97.

Reid, Andrew, ed. *Why I Am a Liberal: Being Definitions and Personal Confessions of Faith by the Best Minds of the Liberal Party* (London, 1885).

Renouvier, Charles Bernard. *Science de la morale*, 2 vols. (Paris, 1869).

Rousseau, Jean-Jacques. *The Social Contract and Other Later Political Writings*, ed. Victor Gourevitch (Cambridge, 1997).

Rose, J. Holland. *The Rise of Democracy*, second edition (London, 1904).

Russell, Lord John, *An Essay on the History of the English Government and Constitution from the Reign of Henry VII to the Present Time*, first edition (London, 1821).

An Essay on the History of the English Government and Constitution from the Reign of Henry VII to the Present Time, second edition, "greatly enlarged" (London, 1823).

Letter to the Electors of Stroud: On the Principles of the Reform Act, third edition (London, 1839).

An Essay on the History of the English Government and Constitution from the Reign of Henry VII to the Present Time, third edition (London, 1865).

An Essay on the History of the English Government and Constitution from the Reign of Henry VII to the Present Time, fourth edition (London, 1866).

Russell, Edward Richard. *Minority Representation* (London, 1883).

"The Electoral Future," *CR*, 47 (1885): 250–65.

Salisbury, Robert Arthur Talbot Gascoyne-Cecil, Third Marquess. "The Theories of Parliamentary Reform," in *Oxford Essays, Contributed by Members of the University* (London, 1858): 52–79.

"The Value of Redistribution: A Note on Electoral Statistics," *NR*, 4 (1884): 145–62.

"Excerpt from an Address to a Deputation of Conservative Associations," in *English Party Politics* (London, 1970), ed. Alan Beattie, vol. 1: 182–3.

Lord Salisbury on Politics, A Selection of His Articles in the Quarterly Review, 1860–1883, ed. Paul Smith (Cambridge, 1972).

Saripolos, Nicolas. *La Démocratie et l'élection proportionnelle: étude historique, juridique, et politique*, 2 vols. (Paris, 1899).

Schnadhorst, Francis. "The Caucus and Its Critics," *NC*, 12 (1882): 8–28.

Schloesser, Henry. *Fabian Tract No. 153: The Twentieth Century Reform Bill* (London, 1911).

Schmitt, Carl. *The Crisis of Parliamentary Democracy*, trans. Ellen Kennedy (Cambridge, MA, 1988).
Constitutional Theory, trans. Jeffrey Seitzer (Durham, 2008).
Senior, Nassau. "Lewis on Authority in Matters of Opinion," *ER*, 91 (1850): 508–58.
Seymour, Edward Adolphus, Duke of Somerset. *Christian Theology and Modern Skepticism* (London, 1872).
Shaw-Lefevre, George. "The Representation of Minorities," *CR*, 45 (1884): 714–33.
"The Crusade for Proportional Representation," *FR*, 37 (1885): 202–15.
Sidgwick, Henry. *The Elements of Politics*, second edition (London, 1897).
The Development of European Polity (London, 1903).
Sieyès, Emmanuel-Joseph, the Abbé. *Political Writings*, ed. Michael Sonenscher (Indianapolis, 2003).
Sismondi, Jean Charles Léonard de. *Examen de la constitution française* (Paris, 1815).
Études sur les constitutions des peuples libres (Paris, 1836).
Smith, J. Parker. *University Representation* (London, 1883).
"Parliamentary Reform: Minority Representation," *WR*, 121 (1884): 163–75.
Smith, J. Rigby. *Personal Representation: A Simplification, Adaptation to the Ballot, and Defence of Mr. Hare's Scheme of Electoral Reform* (London, 1868).
Smith, Goldwin. *Essays on Questions of the Day, Political and Social*, second edition (London, 1897).
Snowden, Philip. Speech in "The Witness of Europe for PR" *Representation*, 6 (1913): 94–118.
Southey, Robert. *Essays, Moral and Political*, 2 vols. (London: John Murray, 1832).
Spencer, Herbert. "Parliamentary Reform: The Dangers, and the Safeguards," *WR*, 17 (1860): 486–507.
Stapleton, Augustus. *Suggestions for a Conservative and Popular Reform* (London, 1850).
Stephen, James Fitzjames. "Journalism," *CM*, 6 (1862): 52–63
"Liberalism," *CM*, 5 (1862): 70–83.
"Parliamentary Government, in Two Papers" *CR*, 23 (1873): 1–19, 165–81.
Liberty, Equality, Fraternity, ed. Stuart Warner (Indianapolis, 1993).
Stephen, Leslie. "On the Choice of Representatives by Popular Constituencies," in *Essays on Reform* (London, 1867): 85–126.
"Reform," *MM*, 15 (1867): 529–36.
"Our Rulers – Public Opinion," *CM*, 21 (1870): 288–98.
"Social Macadamisation," *FM*, 6 (1872): 150–68.
Essays on Freethinking and Plainspeaking (London, 1873).
"Order and Progress," *FR*, 17 (1875): 820–34.
"The Value of Political Machinery," *FR*, 18 (1875): 836–52.
Life of Henry Fawcett, third edition (New York, 1886).

Social Rights and Duties, 2 vols. (London, 1896).

The English Utilitarians, 3 vols. (London, 1900).

Studies of a Biographer, 4 vols. (London, 1902).

Sterne, Simon. *On Representative Government and Personal Representation* (Philadelphia, 1871).

Taine, Hippolyte. *Du suffrage universel et de la manière de voter* (Paris, 1872).

Tocqueville, Alexis de. *Souvenirs* (Paris, 1999).

Democracy in America, trans. Arthur Goldhammer, 2 vols. (New York, 2004).

Trevelyan, George Otto. "A Few Remarks on Mr. Hare's Scheme of Representation," *MM*, 5 (1862): 480–6.

Voltaire, François-Marie Arouet de. *Treatise on Tolerance and Other Writings*, ed. Simon Harvey (Cambridge, 2000).

Wallas, Graham. "The American Analogy," *Independent Review*, 1 (1901): 505–16.

Human Nature in Politics, ed. Sugwon Kang (New Brunswick, 1981).

Ware, William Robert. *The Machinery of Politics and Proportional Representation* (London, 1872).

Watson, Robert Spence. *The National Liberal Federation from Its Commencement to the General Election of 1906* (London, 1907).

Weber, Max. *Political Writings*, ed. Peter Lassman and Ronald Speirs (Cambridge, 1994).

The Vocation Lectures, ed. David Owen and Tracy Strong, trans. Rodney Livingstone (Indianapolis, 2004).

Wells, H. G. *In the Fourth Year: Anticipations of a World Peace* (London, 1918).

West, Julius. *Fabian Tract No. 168: John Stuart Mill* (London, 1913).

Williams, J. Fischer. *Proportional Representation and British Politics* (London, 1914).

The Reform of Political Representation (London, 1918).

Wilson, Edward. "The Caucus and Its Consequences," *NC*, 4 (1878): 695–712.

Secondary Literature; Contemporary Political Theory and Social Science

Amy, Douglas. "The Forgotten History of the Single Transferable Vote in the United States," *Representation*, 34 (1996): 13–20.

Arnstein, Walter. *The Bradlaugh Case: A Study in Late Victorian Opinion and Politics* (Oxford, 1965).

Artz, Frederick. "The Electoral System in France during the Bourbon Restoration, 1815–30," *JMH*, 1 (1929): 205–18.

Austen-Smith, David and Jeffrey Banks. "Monotonicity in Electoral Systems," *APSR*, 85 (1991): 531–7.

Baehr, Peter. *Caesarism, Charisma, and Fate: Historical Sources and Modern Resonances in the Work of Max Weber* (New Brunswick, 2008).

Baer, Marc. *The Rise and Fall of Radical Westminster, 1780–1890* (Houndmills, Basingstoke, 2012).

Bailyn, Bernard. *The Ideological Origins of the American Revolution* (Cambridge, MA, 1967).

Bajpai, Rochana. *Debating Difference: Group Rights and Liberal Democracy in India* (Oxford, 2011).

Ball, Alan. *British Political Parties: The Emergence of a Modern Party System*, second edition (Houndmills, Basingstoke, 1987).

Ball, Terence. "Introduction" to James Mill, *Political Writings*, ed. Ball (Cambridge, 1992): xi–xxiii.

Barber, Kathleen. *Proportional Representation and Electoral Reform in Ohio* (Columbus, 1995).

  A Right to Representation: Proportional Election Systems for the Twenty-First Century (Columbus, 2000).

Barker, Rodney and Xenia Howard-Johnston, "The Politics and Political Ideas of Moisei Ostrogorski," *PS*, 23 (1975): 415–29.

Barzun, Jacques. "Bagehot as Historian," introduction to Bagehot, *CW*, vol. 3: 23–40.

Bastid, Paul. *L'avènement du suffrage universel* (Paris, 1948).

Baum, Bruce. "Freedom, Power, and Public Opinion: J. S. Mill on the Public Sphere," *HPT*, 22 (2001): 501–24.

Beales, Derek. *The Political Parties of Nineteenth-Century Britain* (London, 1971)
  "The Electorate before and after 1832: The Right to Vote and the Opportunity," *PH*, 11 (1992): 139–50.

Beattie, Alan. "1867–1906, Introduction," in *English Party Politics*, ed. Beattie, 2 vols. (London, 1970).

Beer, Samuel. "The Representation of Interests in British Government: Historical Background," *APSR*, 51 (1957): 613–50.

  British Politics in the Collectivist Age (New York, 1965).

Beiner, Ronald. *What's the Matter with Liberalism?* (Berkeley, 1992).

Beitz, Charles. *Political Equality: An Essay in Democratic Theory* (Princeton, 1989).

Bellamy, Richard. "T. H. Green and the Morality of Victorian Liberalism," in *Victorian Liberalism: Nineteenth-Century Political Thought and Practice*, ed. Bellamy (London, 1990): 131–51.

Benoit, Kenneth. "Which Electoral Formula Is the Most Proportional? A New Look with New Evidence," *Political Analysis*, 8 (2000): 381–8.

Bergounioux, Alain and Bernard Manin. *Le régime social-démocrate* (Paris, 1989).

Best, Geoffrey. *Mid-Victorian Britain, 1851–1875* (London, 1971).

Bevir, Mark. "Republicanism, Socialism, and Democracy in Britain: The Origins of the Radical Left," *Journal of Social History*, 34 (2000): 351–68.

Biagini, Eugenio. *Liberty, Retrenchment, and Reform: Popular Liberalism in the Age of Gladstone, 1860–1880* (Cambridge, 1992).

  "Introduction: Citizenship, Liberty, and Community," in *Citizenship and Community: Liberals, Radicals, and Collective Identities in the British Isles, 1865–1931*, ed. Biagini (Cambridge, 1996): 1–17.

"Liberalism and Direct Democracy: John Stuart Mill and the Model of Athens," in *Citizenship and Community: Liberals, Radicals, and Collective Identities in the British Isles, 1865–1931*, ed. Biagini (Cambridge, 1996): 21–44.

British Democracy and Irish Nationalism, 1876–1906 (Cambridge, 2007).

Biagini, Eugenio and Alastair Reid. "Currents of Radicalism, 1850–1914," in *Currents of Radicalism: Popular Radicalism, Organised Labour, and Party Politics in Britain, 1850–1914*, ed. Biagini and Reid (Cambridge, 1991): 1–19.

Birch, A. H. *Representative and Responsible Government: An Essay on the Constitution* (London, 1964).

Representation (London, 1971).

Black, Anthony. *Guild and State: European Political Thought from the Twelfth Century to the Present* (New Brunswick, 2003).

Black, Duncan. "The Central Argument in Lewis Carroll's 'The Principles of Parliamentary Representation'," *Papers on Non-Market Decision Making*, 3 (1967): 1–17.

A Mathematical Approach to Proportional Representation: Duncan Black on Lewis Carroll, ed. Iain McLean, Alistair McMillan, and Burt Monroe (New York, 1996).

Blais, André. "Introduction," to *To Keep or to Change First Past the Post? The Politics of Electoral Reform*, ed. Blais (Oxford, 2008): 1–6.

Blais, André, with Agnieska Dobrzynska and Indridi Indridason. "To Adopt or Not to Adopt Proportional Representation: The Politics of Institutional Choice," *BJPS*, 35 (2005): 182–90.

Blake, Robert. *Disraeli* (London, 1966).

Blewett, Neal. "The Franchise in the United Kingdom: 1885–1918," *Past & Present*, 32 (1965): 27–56.

Bobbio, Norberto. *Liberalism and Democracy*, trans. Martin Ryle and Kate Soper (New York, 2005).

Bogdanor, Vernon. *What Is Proportional Representation?* (Oxford, 1984).

"The Liberal Party and the Constitution," *Journal of Liberal History*, 54 (2007): 46–52.

Bonham, James and William Rehg. "Introduction," to *Deliberative Democracy: Essays in Reason and Politics*, ed. James Bonham and William Rehg (Cambridge, MA, 1997): ix–xxx.

Boucher, David. "Introduction," to *The British Idealists*, ed. Boucher (Cambridge, 1997): viii–xxxiii.

"David George Ritchie," *The Scottish Idealists, Selected Philosophical Writings*, ed. Boucher (Exeter, 2004): 159–61.

"Introduction" to *The Scottish Idealists, Selected Philosophical Writings*, ed. Boucher (Exeter, 2004): 1–22.

Bourke, Richard. *Empire and Revolution: The Political Life of Edmund Burke* (Princeton, 2015).

Bragues, George. "Prediction Markets: The Practical and Normative Possibilities for the Social Production of Knowledge," *Episteme*, 6 (2009): 91–106.

Brennan, Geoffrey and Alan Hamlin. "On Political Representation," *BJPS*, 29 (1999): 101–27.

Brennan, Jason. *Against Democracy* (Princeton, 2016).

Briggs, Asa. "National Bearings," ed. Briggs (London, 1962): 288–303.

"The Local Background of Chartism," in *Chartist Studies*, ed. Briggs (London, 1962): 1–28.

The Age of Improvement, 1783–1867, second edition (London, 2000).

Brighouse, Harry and Marc Fleurbaey. "Democracy and Proportionality," *JPP*, 18 (2008): 1–19.

Brock, Michael. *The Great Reform Act* (London, 1973).

Bromund, Ted. "Uniting the Whole People: Proportional Representation in Great Britain, 1884–5, Reconsidered," *HR*, 74 (2001): 77–94.

Brown, A. V. *The Metaphysical Society: Victorian Minds in Crisis* (New York, 1947).

Brown, Mark. "Citizen Panels and the Concept of Representation," *JPP*, 14 (2006): 203–25.

Brown, Philip. *The French Revolution in English History* (London, 1918).

Buchan, Alastair. *The Spare Chancellor: The Life of Walter Bagehot* (London, 1959).

Buel, Richard, Jr. "Democracy and the American Revolution: A Frame of Reference," *William & Mary Quarterly*, 21 (1964): 165–90.

Burn, W. L. "The Fancy Franchises," *PA*, 8 (1954): 240–5

Burns, J. H. "J. S. Mill and Democracy [II]," *PS*, 5 (1957): 281–94.

Burrow, John. "Sense and Circumstances: Bagehot and the Nature of Political Understanding," in Stefan Collini, Donald Winch, and Burrow, *That Noble Science of Politics: A Study in Nineteenth-Century Intellectual History* (Cambridge, 1983): 161–82.

Whigs and Liberals: Continuity and Change in English Political Thought (Oxford, 1988).

Butler, David. "Electoral Reform," *PA*, 57 (2004): 734–43.

Caine, Barbara. *Victorian Feminists* (Oxford, 1992).

Canon, David. "Electoral Systems and the Representation of Minority Interests in Legislatures," *Legislative Studies Quarterly*, 24 (1999): 331–85.

Cannon, John. *Parliamentary Reform, 1640–1832* (Cambridge, 1973).

Caramani, Daniele. *Elections in Western Europe since 1815: Electoral Results by Constituencies* (New York, 2000).

Carey, John, and Andrew Reynolds. "The Impact of Electoral Systems," *Journal of Democracy*, 22 (2011): 36–47.

Carstairs, Andrew. *A Short History of Electoral Systems in Western Europe* (London, 1980).

Casey, James. "Republican Courts in Ireland, 1919–1922," *Irish Jurist*, 5 (1970): 321–42.

Chadwick, Mary. "The Role of Redistribution in the Making of the Third Reform Act," *HJ*, 19 (1976): 665–83.

Chamberlin, John and Paul Courant. "Representative Deliberations and Representative Decisions: Proportional Representation and the Borda Rule," *APSR*, 77 (1983): 718–33.

Chambers, Simone. "Rhetoric and the Public Sphere: Has Deliberative Democracy Abandoned Mass Democracy?" *PT*, 37 (2009): 323–50.

Chase, Malcolm. *Chartism: A New History* (Manchester, 2007).

Christin, Olivier. *Vox Populi: Une histoire du vote avant le suffrage universel* (Paris, 2014).

Claeys, Gregory. "Justice, Independence, and Industrial Democracy: The Development of John Stuart Mill's Views on Socialism," *JP*, 49 (1987): 122–47.

"General Introduction. The Chartist Movement: A Brief History," in *The Chartist Movement in Britain, 1838–1850*, 6 vols., ed. Claeys (London, 2001), vol. I: xix–xxxviii.

Clark, J. C. D. *English Society, 1688–1832* (Cambridge, 1985).

"Introduction," to Burke, *Reflections on the Revolution in France: A Critical Edition* (Stanford, 2001).

Clarke, P. F. "Electoral Sociology of Modern Britain," *History*, 57 (1972): 31–55.

Clive, John. *Macaulay: The Shaping of the Historian* (Cambridge, MA, 1987).

Cohen, Joshua. "Deliberation and Democratic Legitimacy," *Deliberative Democracy: Essays in Reason and Politics*, ed. James Bonham and William Rehg (Cambridge, MA, 1997): 67–92.

"Procedure and Substance in Deliberative Democracy," in *Deliberative Democracy: Essays in Reason and Politics*, ed. James Bonham and William Rehg (Cambridge, MA, 1997): 407–37.

Deliberative Democracy, ed. Elster (Cambridge, 1998): 185–231.

Colaiaco, James. *James Fitzjames Stephen and the Crisis of Victorian Thought* (New York, 1983).

Cole, Alistair and Peter Campbell, *French Electoral Systems and Elections since 1789* (Aldershott, 1989).

Cole, G. D. H. *Chartist Portraits* (London, 1965).

Cole, Matt. "Party Policy and Electoral Reform: A Survey of Developments, Motives, and Prospects," *British Elections & Parties Review*, 9 (1999): 72–86.

Colomer, Joseph. "On the Origins of Electoral Systems and Political Parties: The Role of Elections in Multi-Member Districts," *Electoral Studies*, 26 (2007): 262–73.

Collini, Stefan. "The Idea of 'Character' in Victorian Political Thought," *TRHS*, 35 (1985): 29–50.

Public Moralists: Political Thought and Intellectual Life in Britain, 1850–1930 (Oxford, 1993).

Conti, Gregory. "James Fitzjames Stephen, John Stuart Mill, and the Victorian Theory of Toleration," *HEI*, 42 (2016): 364–98.

Conti, Gregory and William Selinger, "Reappraising Walter Bagehot's Liberalism: Discussion, Public Opinion, and the Meaning of Parliamentary Government," *HEI*, 41 (2015): 264–91.

"The Other Side of Representation: The History and Theory of Representative Government in Pierre Rosanvallon," *Constellations*, 23 (2016): 548–62.

Cook, Chris. *The Routledge Companion to Britain in the Nineteenth Century, 1815–1914* (London, 2005).

Coull, Gavin. "The Third Earl Grey, the Coming of Democracy, and Parliamentary Reform, 1865–67," *Durham University Journal*, 87 (1995): 11–22, 185–94.

Cowling, Maurice. *1867: Disraeli, Gladstone, and Revolution* (Cambridge, 1967).

Cox, Gary. "The Development of a Party-Orientated Legislature in England, 1832–1918," *BJPS*, 16 (1986): 187–216.

Cox, Gary and Scott Morgenstern, "The Increasing Advantage of Incumbency in the United States," *Legislative Studies Quarterly*, 18 (1993): 495–514.

Craiutu, Aurelian. "Guizot's Elitist Theory of Representative Government," *Critical Review*, 15 (2003): 261–84.

 Liberalism under Siege: The Political Thought of the French Doctrinaires (Lanham, 2003).

Crick, Bernard. *Democracy: A Very Short Introduction* (Oxford, 2002).

Crossman, R. H. S. "Introduction," to Bagehot, *The English Constitution*, ed. Crossman (London, 1963).

D'Alimonte, Roberto. "The New Italian Electoral System: Majority-Assuring but Minority-Friendly," *Contemporary Italian Politics*, 7 (2015): 286–92.

Dawson, Christopher. "Democracy and the British Tradition," *Dublin Review*, 212 (1943): 97–103.

Dickinson, H. T. "The Representation of the People in Eighteenth-Century Britain," in *Realities of Representation: State Building in Early Modern Europe and European America*, ed. Maija Jansson (Houndmills, Basingstoke, 2007): 19–44.

Dijn, Annelien de. "Aristocratic Liberalism in Post-Revolutionary France," *HJ*, 48 (2005): 661–81.

Dovi, Suzanne. *The Good Representative* (Oxford, 2007).

Downs, Anthony. *An Economic Theory of Democracy* (New York, 1957).

Drescher, Seymour. *Tocqueville and England* (Cambridge, MA, 1964).

Driver, C. H. "Walter Bagehot and the Social Psychologists," in *The Social & Political Ideas of Some Representative Thinkers of the Victorian Age*, ed. F. J. C. Hearnshaw (London, 1933): 194–221

Dryzek, John. "Legitimacy and Economy in Deliberative Democracy," *PT*, 29 (2001): 651–69.

 "Difference Democracy: The Consciousness-Raising Group Against the Gentlemen's Club," in *Democratizing Deliberation: A Political Theory Anthology*, ed. Derek Barker, Noëlle McAfee, and David McIvor (Dayton, 2012): 57–82

Dryzek, John and Simon Niemeyer. "Representation," in Dryzek, *Foundations and Frontiers of Deliberative Governance* (Oxford, 2010): 42–65.

Dummet, Michael. *Voting Procedures* (Oxford, 1984).

 Principles of Electoral Reform (Oxford, 1997).

Duncan, Graeme "John Stuart Mill and Democracy," in *John Stuart Mill's Social and Political Thought, Critical Assessments*, ed. G. W. Smith, 4 vols. (London, 1998), vol. 2: 69–87.

Duverger, Maurice. *Political Parties: Their Organization and Activity in the Modern State*, trans. Barbara and Robert North (New York, 1963).

Dworkin, Ronald. *Freedom's Law: The Moral Reading of the American Constitution* (Oxford, 1996).

Easton, David. "Walter Bagehot and Liberal Realism," *APSR*, 43 (1949): 17–37.

Edwards, David. "Toleration and Mill's Liberty of Thought and Discussion," in *John Stuart Mill's Social and Political Thought, Critical Assessments*, ed. G. W. Smith, 4 vols., (London, 1998), vol. 3: 334–58.

Edwards, Ruth. *The Pursuit of Reason*: The Economist, *1843–1993* (London, 1993).

Elster, Jon. "The Market and the Forum," in *The Foundations of Social Choice Theory*, ed. Elster and Aanund Hylland (Cambridge, 1986): 103–32.

"Introduction," to *Deliberative Democracy*, ed. Elster (Cambridge, 1998): 1–18.

Emerson, P. J. *The Politics of Consensus: For the Resolution of Conflict and the Reform of Majority Rule* (Belfast, 1994).

Ensor, R. C. K. *England 1870–1914* (Oxford, 1936).

Estlund, David. *Democratic Authority: A Philosophical Framework* (Princeton, 2008).

Evans, Eric. *The Great Reform Act of 1832*, second edition (London, 1994).
Parliamentary Reform in Britain, c. 1770–1918 (Abingdon, 2013).

Farrell, David. *Comparing Electoral Systems* (Houndmills, Basingstoke, 1997).

Fladeland, Betty. "Our Cause Being One and the Same," in *Slavery and British Society, 1776–1846*, ed. James Walvin (London, 1982): 69–99.

Fletcher, Ian Christopher. "'This Zeal for Lawlessness': A. V. Dicey, *The Law of the Constitution*, and the Challenge of Popular Politics," *PH*, 16 (1997): 309–29.

Foote, Geoffrey. *The Labour Party's Political Thought: A History* (Houndmills, Basingstoke, 1997).

Fontana, Biancamaria. *Rethinking the Politics of Commercial Society: The Edinburgh Review 1802–1832* (Cambridge, 1985).

Freeden, Michael. *The New Liberalism: An Ideology of Social Reform* (Oxford, 1978).
"The New Liberalism and Its Aftermath," in *Victorian Liberalism: Nineteenth-Century Political Thought and Practice*, ed. Richard Bellamy (London, 1990): 175–92.

Furet, François. *Revolutionary France, 1770–1880*, trans. Antonia Nevill (Oxford, 1992).

Gallagher, Michael. "Comparing Proportional Representation Electoral Systems: Quotas, Thresholds, Paradoxes, and Majorities," *BJPS*, 22 (1992): 469–96.

Garey, Alva Edward. *Proportional Representation* (MA Thesis, University of Wisconsin, 1920).

Gargarella, Roberto. "Full Representation, Deliberation, and Impartiality," in *Deliberative Democracy*, ed. Jon Elster (Cambridge, 1998): 260–80

Garrard, John. "Democratization in Britain," in *European Democratization since 1800*, ed. Garrard, Vera Tolz, and Ralph White (Houndmills, Basingstoke, 2000): 27–49.

Garsten, Bryan. "Representative Government and Popular Sovereignty," in *Political Representation*, ed. Ian Shapiro, Susan Stokes, Elisabeth Jean Wood, and Alexander Kirshner (Cambridge, 2009): 90–110.

Gash, Norman. *Politics in the Age of Peel: A Study in the Technique of Parliamentary Representation, 1830–1850* (New York, 1971).

Sir Robert Peel: The Life of Sir Robert Peel after 1830, second edition (London, 1988).

Gauchet, Marcel. "La Droite et la gauche," in *Les Lieux de Mémoire*, ed. Pierre Nora, 3 vols. (Paris, 1984–92), vol. 3: 395–467.

La condition politique (Paris, 2005).

Ghosh, Peter. "Gladstone and Peel," in *Politics and Culture in Victorian Britain: Essays in Memory of Colin Matthew*, ed. Ghosh and Lawrence Goldman (Oxford, 2006): 45–73.

Goldie, Mark. "Introduction" to John Locke, *A Letter Concerning Toleration and Other Writings*, ed. Goldie (Indianapolis, 2010): ix–xxiv.

Goldman, Lawrence. "The Social Science Association, 1857–1886: A Context for Mid-Victorian Liberalism," *EHR*, 101 (1986): 95–134.

(ed.) *The Blind Victorian: Henry Fawcett and British Liberalism* (Cambridge, 2003).

Science, Reform, and Politics in Victorian Britain: The Social Science Association 1857–1886 (Cambridge, 2004).

Greiff, Pablo de. "Deliberative Democracy and Group Representation," *Social Theory and Practice*, 26 (2000): 397–415.

Griffin, Ben. "Women's Suffrage," in *Languages of Politics in Nineteenth-Century Britain*, ed. David Craig and James Thompson (Houndmills, Basingstoke, 2013): 168–90.

Griffin, C. M. "L. T. Hobhouse and the Idea of Harmony," *JHI*, 35 (1974): 647–61.

Griffiths, A. Philips and Richard Wollheim, "How Can One Person Represent Another?" *Aristotelian Society*, 34 (1960): 187–224.

Griffiths, P. C. "Pressure Groups and Parties in Late-Victorian England," *Midland History*, 3 (1976): 191–205.

"The Caucus and the Liberal Party in 1886," *History*, 61 (1976): 183–97.

Grofman, Bernard. "Should Representatives Be Typical of Their Constituents?" in *Representation and Redistricting Issues*, ed. Grofman, Arend Lijphart, and Robert McKay (Lexington, 1982): 97–100.

Guerrero, Alexander. "Against Elections: The Lottocratic Alternative," *Philosophy and Public Affairs*, 42 (2014): 135–178.

Guillin, Vincent and Djamel Souafa. "La réception de Stuart Mill en France," *La vie des idées* (2010) [www.laviedesidees.fr/La-reception-de-Stuart-Mill-en.html].

Guinier, Lani. "The Representation of Minority Interests: The Question of Single-Member Districts," *Cardozo Law Review*, 14 (1993): 1135–74.

Gunn, J. A. W. "Influence, Parties and the Constitution: Changing Attitudes, 1783–1832," HJ, 17 (1974): 301–28.

Gutmann, Amy and Dennis Thompson. *Why Deliberative Democracy?* (Princeton, 2004).

Habermas, Jürgen. "Popular Sovereignty as Procedure," in Habermas, *Between Facts and Norms: Contributions to a Discourse Theory of Law and Democracy*, trans. William Rehg (Cambridge, MA, 1996): 463–90.

On the Pragmatics of Social Interaction, trans. Barbara Fultner (Cambridge, MA, 2001).

Hain, Peter. *Proportional Misrepresentation* (Hants, 1986).

Halévy, Élie. *The Growth of Philosophic Radicalism*, trans. Mary Morris (Boston, 1955).

Histoire du socialisme européen (Paris, 2006).

Hamburger, Joseph. "James Mill on Universal Suffrage and the Middle Class," *JP*, 24 (1962): 167–90.

James Mill and the Art of Revolution (New Haven, 1963).

Macaulay and the Whig Tradition (Chicago, 1972).

"The Whig Conscience," in *The Conscience of the Victorian State*, ed. Peter Marsh (Syracuse, 1979): 19–38.

"Individuality and Moral Reform: The Rhetoric of Liberty and the Reality of Restraint in Mill's *On Liberty*," in *John Stuart Mill's Social and Political Thought, Critical Assessments*, ed. G.W. Smith, 4 vols., (London, 1998), vol. 2: 402–45.

Hamer, D. A. *John Morley: Liberal Intellectual in Politics* (Oxford, 1968).

"Introduction," to *The Radical Programme*, ed. Hamer (Brighton, 1971): vii–xliv.

Hanham, H. J. *Elections and Party Management: Politics in the Time of Disraeli and Gladstone* (London, 1959).

ed. *The Nineteenth-Century Constitution, Documents and Commentary* (Cambridge, 1969).

Harling, "The State," in *A Companion to Nineteenth-Century Britain*, ed. Chris Williams (Oxford, 2004): 110–23.

Harris, Jose. *Civil Society in British History: Ideas, Identities, Institutions* (Oxford, 2003).

Harrison, Brian and Patricia Hollis, "Chartism, Liberalism, and the Life of Robert Lowery," *EHR*, 82 (1967): 503–35.

Hart, Jenifer. *Proportional Representation: Critics of the British Electoral System, 1820–1945* (Oxford, 1992).

Harvie, Christopher. "Ideology and Home Rule: James Bryce, A. V. Dicey, and Ireland, 1880–1887," *EHR*, 91 (1976): 298–314.

The Lights of Liberalism: The University Liberals and the Challenge of Democracy (London, 1976).

Harvie, Christopher and H. C. G. Matthew. *Nineteenth-Century Britain: A Very Short Introduction* (Oxford, 2000).

Hawkins, Angus. "'Parliamentary Government' and Victorian Political Parties, c. 1830–1880," *EHR*, 104 (1989): 638–69.

British Party Politics, 1852–1886 (Houndmills, Basingstoke, 1998).

Victorian Political Culture, "Habits of Heart and Mind" (Oxford, 2015).

Hayward, Jack, ed. *The Crisis of Representation in Europe* (London, 1996).

Hazareesingh, Sudhir. *Intellectual Founders of the Republic: Five Studies in Nineteenth-Century French Republican Political Thought* (Oxford, 2001).

Heesom, Alan. "'Legitimate' *versus* 'Illegitimate' Influences: Aristocratic Engineering in Mid-Victorian Britain," *PH*, 7 (1988): 282–305.

Henriques, Ursula. *Religious Toleration in England, 1787–1833* (Toronto, 1961).

Hermens, F.A. "L'erreur proportionnaliste et le régime parlementaire," *Revue politique et parlementaire*, no. 163 (1935): 429–57.

"Political Science and Proportional Representation," *Social Science*, 15 (1940): 5–19.

Herrick, Francis. "The Reform Bill of 1867 and the British Party System," *Pacific Historical Review*, 3 (1934): 216–33.

"The Origins of the National Liberal Federation," *JMH*, 17 (1945): 116–29.

"The Second Reform Movement in Britain, 1850–1865," *JHI*, 9 (1948): 174–92.

Hewitt, Martin, ed. *An Age of Equipoise? Reassessing Mid-Victorian Britain* (London, 2017).

Hibbitts, Bernard. "The Politics of Principle: Albert Venn Dicey and the Rule of Law," *Anglo-American Law Review*, 23 (1994): 1–31.

Hill, Roland. *Lord Acton* (New Haven, 2000).

Hillbruner, Anthony. "Emerson: Democratic Egalitarian," *Communication Studies*, 10 (1959): 25–30.

Hilton, Boyd. *The Age of Atonement: The Influence of Evangelicalism on Social and Economic Thought, 1785–1865* (Oxford, 1986).

A Mad, Bad, & Dangerous People, England 1783–1846 (Oxford, 2006).

Himmelfarb, Gertrude. "Introduction," to John Emerich Edward Dalberg Acton, *Essays on Freedom and Power*, ed. Himmelfarb (Boston, 1948): xv–lxvi.

Hockin, Thomas. "The Roles of the Loyal Opposition in Britain's House of Commons: Three Historical Paradigms," *PA*, 25 (1971): 50–68.

Hoppen, K. Theodore. "Roads to Democracy: Electioneering and Corruption in Nineteenth-Century England and Ireland," *History*, 81 (1996): 553–71.

The Mid-Victorian Generation (Oxford, 1998).

Houghton, Walter. *The Victorian Frame of Mind* (New Haven, 1957).

Humberstone, T. L. *University Representation* (London, 1951).

Htun, Mala. "Is Gender Like Ethnicity? The Political Representation of Identity Groups," *Perspective in Politics*, 2 (2004): 439–58.

James, Michael. "Public Interest and Majority Rule in Bentham's Democratic Theory," *PT*, 9 (1981): 49–64.

James, Michael Rabinder. *Deliberative Democracy and the Plural Polity* (Lawrence, 2004).

"The Priority of Racial Constituency over Descriptive Representation," *JP*, 73 (2011): 899–914.

"Two Concepts of Constituency," *JP*, 77 (2015): 381–93.

Jenkins, T. A. *Parliament, Party, and Politics in Victorian Britain* (Manchester, 1996).

Johnston, Neil. "The History of the Parliamentary Franchise," *Research Papers of the House of Commons Library* [https://researchbriefings.parliament.uk/Rese archBriefing/Summary/RP13-14#fullreport].

Johnston, R. J. "Seats, Votes, Redistricting, and the Allocation of Power in Electoral Systems," in *Choosing an Electoral System: Issues and Alternatives*, ed. Arend Lijphart and Bernard Grofman (New York, 1984): 59–69.

Jones, Andrew. *The Politics of Reform, 1884* (Cambridge, 1972).

Jones, H. S. "John Stuart Mill as Moralist," *JHI*, 53 (1992): 287–308.

"Political Uses of the Concept of 'Representation': How the French Debated Electoral Reform, c. 1880–1914," *Redescriptions*, 4 (2000): 15–36.

Victorian Political Thought (New York, 2000).

Jones, Paul. "Jesus Christ and the Transformation of English Society: "The 'Subversive Conservatism' of Frederick Denison Maurice," *Harvard Theological Review*, 96 (2003): 205–28.

Jones, Richard Wyn and Robert Scully. "Devolution and Electoral Politics in Scotland and Wales," *Publius*, 36 (2006): 115–34.

Judge, David. "Introduction," to *The Politics of Parliamentary Reform*, ed. Judge (Guildford and King's Lynn, 1984): 1–8.

Representation: Theory and Practice in Britain (London, 1999).

Kahan, Alan. *Aristocratic Liberalism: The Social and Political Thought of Jacob Burckhardt, John Stuart Mill, and Alexis de Tocqueville* (Oxford, 1992).

Liberalism in Nineteenth-Century Europe: The Political Culture of Limited Suffrage (Houndmills, Basingstoke, 2003).

Kemp, Betty. "Crewe's Act, 1782," *EHR*, 68 (1953): 258–63.

Kent, Christopher. *Brains and Numbers: Elitism, Comtism, and Democracy in Mid-Victorian England* (Toronto, 1978).

Kern, Paul. "Universal Suffrage without Democracy: Thomas Hare and John Stuart Mill," *Review of Politics*, 34 (1972): 306–22.

Keyssar, Alex. *The Right to Vote: The Contested History of Democracy in the United States* (New York, 2000).

Kinzer, Bruce. "J. S. Mill and the Problem of Party," *JBS*, 21 (1981): 106–22.

Kinzer, Bruce, Ann Robson, and John Robson. *A Moralist In and Out of Parliament: John Stuart Mill at Westminster 1865–1868* (Toronto, 1992).

Knights, Ben. *The Idea of the Clerisy in the Nineteenth Century* (Cambridge, 1978).

Krook, Mona and Diana O'Brien. "The Politics of Group Representation, Quotas for Women and Minorities Worldwide," *Comparative Politics*, 42 (2010): 253–72.

Krouse, Richard. "Two Concepts of Democratic Representation: James and John Stuart Mill," *JP*, 44 (1982): 509–37.

Kymlicka, Will. *Multicultural Citizenship: A Liberal Theory of Minority Rights* (Oxford, 1996).

Laborde, Cécile. *Pluralist Thought and the State in Britain and France, 1900–25* (London, 2000).

Lakeman, Enid. *How Democracies Vote*, third edition (London, 1970).

Landemore, Hélène. "Deliberation, Cognitive Diversity, and Democratic Inclusiveness: An Epistemic Argument for the Random Selection of Representatives," *Synthese*, 190 (2013): 1209–31.

　Democratic Reason: Politics, Collective Intelligence, and the Rule of the Many (Princeton, 2013).

Lang, Sean. *Parliamentary Reform, 1785–1928* (London, 1999).

Langford, Paul. *A Polite and Commercial People: England, 1727–1783* (Oxford, 1992).

Larsen, Timothy. *Friends of Religious Equality: Nonconformist Politics in Mid-Victorian England* (Rochester, 1999).

Lefort, Claude. *Democracy and Political Theory*, trans. David Macey (Cambridge, 1988).

LeQuesne, A. L. "Carlyle," in LeQuesne, George Landow, Stefan Collini, and Peter Stansky. *Victorian Thinkers* (Oxford, 1993): 1–101.

Lijphart, Arend. *Electoral Systems and Party Systems: A Study of Twenty-Seven Democracies, 1945–1990* (Oxford, 1994).

　Patterns of Democracy, Government Forms and Performance in Thirty-Six Countries, second edition (New Haven, 2012).

Lippincott, B. E. *Victorian Critics of Democracy* (Minneapolis, 1938).

List, Christian. "The Discursive Dilemma and Public Reason," *Ethics*, 116 (2006): 362–402.

Lively, Jack and John Rees. "Introduction," to *Utilitarian Logic and Politics*, ed. Lively and Rees (Oxford, 1978): 1–52.

Loewenberg, Gerhard. *On Legislatures: The Puzzle of Representation* (New York, 2011).

Lord, Robert. "The Parliaments of the Middle Ages and the Early Modern Period," *Catholic Historical Review*, 16 (1930): 125–44.

Mackie, Thomas and Richard Rose. *The International Almanac of Electoral History*, second edition (London, 1982).

McRae, Kenneth. "Contrasting Styles of Democratic Decision-Making: Adversarial versus Consensual Politics," *IPSR*, 18 (1997): 279–95.

Manin, Bernard. "On Legitimacy and Political Deliberation," trans. Elly Stein and Jane Mansbridge, *PT*, 15 (1987): 338–68.

　The Principles of Representative Government (Cambridge, 1997).

Mansbridge, Jane. "A Deliberative Theory of Interest Representation," in *The Politics of Interest: Interest Groups Transformed*, ed. Mark Petracca (Boulder, 1992): 32–57.

　"Should Blacks Represent Blacks and Women Represent Women? A Contingent 'Yes,'" *JP*, 61 (1999): 628–57.

　"What Does a Representative Do? Descriptive Representation in Communicative Settings of Distrust, Uncrystallized Interests, and

Historically Denigrated Status," in *Citizenship in Diverse Societies*, ed. Will Kymlicka and Wayne Norman (Oxford, 2000): 99–123.

"Rethinking Representation," *APSR*, 97 (2003): 515–28.

"Quota Problems: Combating the Dangers of Essentialism," *Politics & Gender*, 1 (2005): 622–38.

Mantena, Karuna. *Alibis of Empire: Henry Maine and the Ends of Liberal Imperialism* (Princeton, 2010).

Marongiu, Antonio. *Medieval Parliaments: A Comparative Study*, trans. S. J. Woolf (London, 1968).

Mather, F. C. "Introduction," to *Chartism and Society*, ed. Mather (London, 1980): 9–46.

Matthew, H. C. G. "Rhetoric and Politics in Great Britain, 1860–1950," in *Politics and Social Change in Modern Britain: Essays Presented to AF Thompson*, ed. P. J. Waller (Sussex, 1987): 34–58.

"Introduction" to *The Gladstone Diaries: with Cabinet Minutes and Prime-Ministerial Correspondence, vol. 10: Jan. 1881–June 1883* (Oxford, 1990): xxvii–cxcii.

Gladstone, 1809–1898 (Oxford, 1997).

McCormick, John. *Machiavellian Democracy* (Cambridge, 2011).

McGill, Barry. "Francis Schnadhorst and Liberal Party Organization," *JMH*, 34 (1962): 19–39.

McGowen, Randall and Walter Arnstein, "The Mid-Victorians and the Two-Party System," *Albion*, 11 (1979): 242–58.

McWilliam, Rohan. "Radicalism and Popular Culture: the Tichborne Case and the Politics of 'Fair Play,' 1867–1886," in *Currents of Radicalism: Popular Radicalism, Organised Labour, and Party Politics in Britain, 1850–1914*, ed. Eugenio Biagini and Alastair Reid (Cambridge, 1991): 44–64.

Michels, Robert. *Political Parties*, trans. Eden and Ceder Paul (New York, 1962).

Miller, J. Joseph. "J. S. Mill on Plural Voting, Competence, and Participation," *HPT*, 24 (2003): 647–66.

Milton-Smith, John. "Earl Grey's Cabinet and the Objects of Parliamentary Reform," *HJ*, 15 (1972): 55–74.

Mitchell, Leslie. *The Whig World, 1760–1837* (London, 2005).

Moore, David. *The Politics of Deference: A Study of the Mid-Nineteenth-Century English Political System* (Hassocks, 1976).

Moulin, Leo. "Les origines religieuses des techniques électorales et délibératives modernes," *Politix*, 11 (1998): 117–62.

Müller, Jan-Werner. "The Triumph of What (If Anything)? Rethinking Political Ideologies and Political Institutions in Twentieth-Century Europe," *Journal of Political Ideologies*, 14 (2009): 211–26.

Nässtrom, Sofia. "Review Article: Where Is the Representative Turn Going?" *EJPT*, 10 (2011): 501–10.

Nelson, Eric. *The Royalist Revolution: Monarchy and the American Founding* (Cambridge, MA, 2014).

Nicholson, Peter. *The Political Philosophy of the British Idealists: Selected Studies* (Cambridge, 1990).

"The Reception and Early Reputation of Mill's Political Thought," in *The Cambridge Companion to Mill*, ed. John Skorupski (Cambridge, 1998): 464–96.

Norman, Edward. *The Victorian Christian Socialists* (Cambridge, 1987).

Norris, Pippa. "The Politics of Electoral Reform in Britain," *IPSR*, 16 (1995): 65–78.

Norton, Philip. *The Constitution in Flux* (Oxford, 1982).

"The House of Commons, 1911–49" in *A Short History of Parliament: England, Great Britain, the United Kingdom, Ireland & Scotland*, ed. Clyve Jones (Woodbridge, 2009): 271–82.

Nozick, Robert. *Anarchy, State, and Utopia* (New York, 1974).

O'Leary, Cornelius. *The Elimination of Corrupt Practices in British Elections, 1868–1911* (Oxford, 1962).

O'Leary, Patrick. *Sir James Mackintosh: The Whig Cicero* (Aberdeen, 1989).

Qvortrup, Mads. "A. V. Dicey: The Referendum as the People's Veto," *HPT*, 20 (1999): 531–46.

Page, Scott. *The Difference: How the Power of Diversity Creates Better Groups, Firms, Schools, and Societies* (Princeton, 2007).

Parkinson, John and Jane Mansbridge, ed. *Deliberative Systems: Deliberative Democracy, at the Large Scale* (Cambridge, 2012).

Parry, J. P. *Democracy and Religion: Gladstone and the Liberal Party, 1867–1875* (Cambridge, 1986).

The Rise and Fall of Liberal Government in Victorian Britain (New Haven, 1993).

"The Impact of Napoleon III on British Politics, 1851–1880," *TRHS*, 51 (2001): 147–75.

Parsons, Floyd. "*Ignis Fatuus* vs. *Pons Asinorum*: William Gladstone and Proportional Representation, 1867–1885," *PH*, 21 (2002): 374–85.

Thomas Hare and Political Representation in Victorian Britain (Houndmills, Basingstoke, 2009).

Pasquino, Pasquale. "Emmanuel Sieyès, Benjamin Constant et le 'Gouvernement des Modernes'," *Revue française de science politique*, 37 (1987): 214–28

"Sur la théorie constitutionnelle de la monarchie de Juillet," in *Guizot et la culture politique. François Guizot et la culture politique de son temps*, ed. Marina Valensie (Paris, 1991): 111–28.

Pateman, Carole. *Participation and Democratic Theory* (Cambridge, 1970).

Pelling, Henry. *Social Geography of British Elections, 1885–1910* (London, 1967).

Pennock, J. Roland. *Democratic Political Theory* (Princeton, 1979).

Pettit, Philip. "Varieties of Public Representation," in *Political Representation*, ed. Ian Shapiro, Susan Stokes, Elisabeth Jean Wood, and Alexander Kirshner (Cambridge, 2009): 61–89.

Phillips, Anne. *The Politics of Presence* (Oxford, 1995).

"Democracy and Representation: or, Why Should It Matter Who Our Representatives Are?" in *Feminism and Politics*, ed. Phillips (Oxford, 1998): 224–40.

Phillips, John and Charles Wetherell, "The Great Reform Act of 1832 and the Political Modernization of England," *American Historical Review*, 100 (1995): 411–36.

Pickering, Parul. "Peaceably If We Can, Forcibly If We Must: Political Violence and Insurrection in Early-Victorian Britain," in *Terror: From Tyrannicide to Terrorism*, ed. Brett Bowden and Michael Davis (St. Lucia, Queensland, 2008): 113–33.

Pitkin, Hanna. *The Concept of Representation* (Berkeley, 1967).

Plotke, David. "Representation Is Democracy," *Constellations*, 4 (1997): 19–34.

Pocock, J. G. A. *Virtue, Commerce, and History: Essays on Political Thought and History, Chiefly in the Eighteenth Century* (Cambridge, 1985).

Pole, J. R. *Political Representation in England and the Origins of the American Republic* (Berkeley, 1966).

Pombeni, Paolo. "Starting in Reason, Ending in Passion: Bryce, Lowell, Ostrogorski, and the Problem of Democracy," *HJ*, 37 (1994): 319–41.

Pogge, Thomas. "Self-Constituting Constituencies to Enhance Freedom, Equality, and Participation in Democratic Procedures," *Theoria*, no. 99 (2002): 26–54.

Porritt, Edward. *The Unreformed House of Commons: Parliamentary Representation before 1832*, revised edition, 2 vols. (Cambridge, 1909).
  "Barriers Against Democracy in the British Electoral System," *PSQ*, 26 (1911): 1–31.

Porter, Theodore and Dorothy Ross. "Introduction," to *The Cambridge History of Science, vol. 7: The Modern Social Sciences*, ed. Roy Porter and Theodore Porter, Ross (Cambridge, 2003): 1–10.

Posner, Eric and Glen Weyl, "Voting Squared: Quadratic Voting in Democratic Politics, *Vanderbilt Law Review*, 68 (2015): 441–500.

Price, Roger. *Napoleon III and the Second Empire* (London, 1997).

Pugh, Martin. *The March of the Women: A Revisionist Analysis of the Campaign for Women's Suffrage, 1866–1914* (Oxford, 2000).

Quinault, Roland. "1848 and Parliamentary Reform," *HJ*, 31 (1988): 831–51.

Quincy, Keith. "Samuel Bailey and Mill's Defence of Freedom of Discussion," *The Mill Newsletter*, 21 (1986): 4–18.

Rawls, John. *The Law of Peoples: with the "Idea of Public Reason Revisited"* (Cambridge, MA, 2001).

Reeve, Andrew and Alan Ware, *Electoral Systems: A Comparative and Theoretical Introduction* (London, 1992).

Reeves, Richard. *John Stuart Mill: Victorian Firebrand* (London, 2007).

Rehfeld, Andrew. *The Concept of the Constituency: Political Representation, Democratic Legitimacy, and Institutional Design* (Cambridge, 2005).
  "On Quotas and Qualifications for Office," in *Political Representation*, ed. Ian Shapiro, Susan Stokes, Elisabeth Jean Wood, and Alexander Kirshner (Cambridge, 2009): 236–68.

"Representation Rethought: On Trustees, Delegates, and Gyroscopes in the Study of Political Representation and Democracy," *APSR*, 103 (2009): 214–30.

"The Concepts of Representation," in *APSR*, 105 (2011): 631–41.

Reitan, E. A. *Politics, Finance and the People: Economical Reform in England in the Age of the American Revolution, 1770–1792* (Houndmills, Basingstoke, 2007).

Richter, Melvin. *The Politics of Conscience: T. H. Green and His Age* (Cambridge, MA, 1964).

Riker, William. "The Two-Party System and Duverger's Law: An Essay on the History of Political Science," *APSR*, 76 (1982): 753–66.

"Electoral Systems and Constitutional Restraints," in *Choosing an Electoral System: Issues and Alternatives*, ed. Arend Lijphart and Bernard Grofman (New York, 1984): 103–10.

Roach, John. "Liberalism and the Victorian Intelligentsia," *Cambridge Historical Journal*, 13 (1957): 58–81.

Roberts, Matthew. "Resisting Arithmocracy: Parliament, Community, and the Third Reform Act," *JBS*, 50 (2011): 381–409.

Roberts, Peter. "The Tudor Origins of the Grant of Parliamentary Representation to English Universities in 1604," *Parliaments, Estates & Representation*, 26 (2006): 35–44.

Rosanvallon, Pierre. *Le Moment Guizot* (Paris, 1985).

"Préface: Le Gramsci de la bourgeoisie," in François Guizot, *Histoire de la civilisation en Europe, suivie de Philosophie politique: de la souvereaineté*, ed. Rosanvallon (Paris, 1985).

"Guizot et la Révolution française," in *Guizot et la culture politique de son temps*, ed. Marina Valensie (Paris, 1991): 59–68.

"Guizot et la question du suffrage universel au XIXe siècle," in *Guizot et la culture politique. François Guizot et la culture politique de son temps*, ed. Marina Valensie (Paris, 1991): 129–46.

Le sacre du citoyen: Histoire du suffrage universel en France (Paris, 1992).

Le peuple introuvable: Histoire de la représentation démocratique en France (Paris, 1998).

La démocratie inachevée: Histoire de la souveraineté du peuple en France (Paris, 2000).

Counter-Democracy: Politics in an Age of Distrust (Cambridge, 2008).

La légitimité démocratique: Impartialité, reflexivité, proximité (Paris, 2008).

Le bon gouvernement (Paris, 2015).

Rosenblum, Nancy. *On the Side of Angels: An Appreciation of Parties and Partisanship* (Princeton, 2008).

Rubinstein, David. "Millicent Garrett Fawcett and the Meaning of Women's Emancipation, 1886–99," *VS*, 34 (1991): 365–80.

Ryan, Alan. *J. S. Mill* (London, 1974).

Sabbadini, Lorenzo. "Popular Sovereignty and Representation in the English Civil War," in *Popular Sovereignty in Historical Perspective*, ed. Richard Bourke and Quentin Skinner (Cambridge, 2016): 164–86.

Salmon, Philip. "The English Reform Legislation," in *The History of Parliament, vol. 1: The House of Commons, 1820–1832*, ed. D. R. Fisher (Cambridge, 2009): 374–412.
  "The House of Commons, 1801–1911," in *A Short History of Parliament: England, Great Britain, the United Kingdom, Ireland & Scotland*, ed. Clyve Jones (Woodbridge, 2009): 249–70.
Saunders, Ben. "Estlund's Flight from Fairness," *Representation*, 46 (2010): 5–17.
Saunders, Robert. "The Politics of Reform and the Making of the Second Reform Act, 1848–67," *HJ*, 50 (2007): 571–91.
  Democracy and the Vote in British Politics, 1848–1867 (Farnham, 2011).
  "Democracy," in *Languages of Politics in Nineteenth-Century Britain*, ed. David Craig and James Thompson (Houndmills, Basingstoke, 2013): 142–67.
Schapiro, J. S. "John Stuart Mill, Pioneer of Democratic Liberalism in England," *JHI*, 4 (1943): 127–60.
Schauer, Frederick. *Free Speech: A Philosophical Enquiry* (Cambridge, 1982).
Schultz, Bart. *Henry Sidgwick: Eye of the Universe* (Cambridge, 2004).
Schwartzberg, Melissa. "Epistemic Democracy and Its Challenges," *ARPS*, 18 (2015): 187–203.
Scott, Joan Wallach. "Parité," in *The French Republic: History, Values, Debates*, ed. Edward Berenson, Vincent Duclert, and Christophe Prochasson (Ithaca, 2011): 182–8.
Searle, G. R. *The Liberal Party: Triumph and Disintegration, 1886–1929* (Houndmills, Basingstoke, 1992).
Selinger, William. *Parliamentarism: From Burke to Weber* (Cambridge, 2019).
  "Fighting Electoral Corruption in the Victorian era: An Overlooked Dimension of Mill's Political Thought," *EJPT* (forthcoming).
Seymour, Charles. *Electoral Reform in England and Wales: The Development and Operation of the Parliamentary Franchise: 1832–1885* (New Haven, 1915).
Shepherd, John. *Currents of Radicalism: Popular Radicalism, Organised Labour, and Party Politics in Britain, 1850–1914*, ed. Biagini and Reid (Cambridge, 1991): 187–213.
Shklar, Judith. "The Liberalism of Fear," in *Liberalism and the Moral Life*, ed. Nancy Rosenblum (Cambridge, MA, 1989).
  American Citizenship: The Quest for Inclusion (Cambridge, 1995).
Sisson, C. H. 'The Case of Walter Bagehot', in *The Avoidance of Literature*, ed. Michael Schmidt (Manchester, 1978): 349–438.
Skinner, Quentin. "The Empirical Theorists of Democracy and Their Critics: A Plague on Both Their Houses," *PT*, 1 (1973): 287–306.
  Liberty before Liberalism (Cambridge, 1998).
  "Hobbes on Representation," *European Journal of Philosophy*, 13 (2005): 155–84.
  "A Genealogy of the Modern State," *Proceedings of the British Academy*, 162 (2009): 325–70.
Smart, Paul. "'Some Will Be More Equal than Others': J. S. Mill on Democracy, Freedom and Meritocracy," Archiv für Rechts- und Sozialphilosophie, 76 (1990): 308–23.

Smith, Francis Barrymore. *The Making of the Second Reform Bill* (Cambridge, 1966).

"The View from Britain, I: 'Tumults Abroad, Stability at Home'," in *Intellectuals and Revolution: Socialism and the Experience of 1848*, ed. Eugene Kamenka and Smith (London, 1979): 94–120.

Smith, Graham and Corinne Wales, "Citizens' Juries and Deliberative Democracy," *PS*, 48 (2000): 51–65.

Smith, K. J. M. *James Fitzjames Stephen: Portrait of a Victorian Rationalist* (Cambridge, 1989).

Smith, Michael. "Parliamentary Reform and the Electorate," in *A Companion to Nineteenth-Century Britain*, ed. Chris Williams (Oxford, 2004): 156–73.

Smith, Paul. "Introduction," to *Lord Salisbury on Politics, A Selection of His Articles in the Quarterly Review, 1860–1883*, ed. Smith (Cambridge, 1972): 1–109.

"Introduction," to Bagehot, *The English Constitution*, ed. Smith (Cambridge, 2001): vii–xxvii.

Soltau, Roger. *French Political Thought in the Nineteenth Century* (New Haven, 1931).

Somervell, D. C. *English Thought in the Nineteenth Century* (London, 1929).

Southgate, Donald. *The Passing of the Whigs, 1832–1886* (London, 1962).

Spain, Jonathan. "Trade Unionists, Gladstonian Liberals, and the Labour Law Reforms of 1875," in *Currents of Radicalism: Popular Radicalism, Organised Labour, and Party Politics in Britain, 1850–1914*, ed. Eugenio Biagini and Alastair Reid (Cambridge, 1991): 109–33.

Squires, Judith. "Group Representation, Deliberation, and the Displacement of Antinomies," in *Democratic Innovation: Deliberation, Representation, and Association*, ed. Michael Saward (London, 2000): 93–105.

St. John-Stevas, Norman. "The Political Genius of Walter Bagehot," introduction to Bagehot, *CW*, vol. 5: 35–159.

Stapleton, Julia. "English Pluralism as Cultural Definition: The Social and Political Thought of George Unwin," *JHI*, 52 (1991): 665–84.

"Introduction," to *Liberalism, Democracy, and the State in Britain: Five Essays, 1862–1891*, ed. Stapleton (Bristol, 1991): 7–40.

"Introduction," to *Group Rights: Perspectives since 1900*, ed. Stapleton (Bristol, 1995): ix–xxxix.

"James Fitzjames Stephen: Liberalism, Patriotism, and English Liberty," *VS*, 41 (1998): 243–63.

Political Intellectuals and Public Identities in Britain since 1850 (Manchester, 2001).

Starzinger, Vincent. *The Politics of the Center, France and England, 1815–1848* (London, 1991).

Stasavage, Daniel. "Representation and Consent: Why They Arose in Europe and Not Elsewhere," *ARPS*, 19 (2016): 145–62.

Stedman Jones, Gareth. *Languages of Class: Studies in English Working Class History, 1832–1982* (Cambridge, 1983): 90–178.

Steed, Michael. "The Evolution of the British Electoral System," in *Adversary Politics and Electoral Reform*, ed. S. E. Finer (London, 1975): 35–54.

Still, Jonathan. "Political Equality and Election Systems," *Ethics*, 91 (1981): 375–94.

Sugden, Robert. "Free Association and the Theory of Proportional Representation," *APSR*, 78 (1984): 31–43.

Sykes, Leslie. *Proportional Representation: Which System?* (Leicester, 1990).

Szpiro, George. *Numbers Rule: The Vexing Mathematics of Democracy, from Plato to the Present* (Princeton, 2010).

Ten, C. L. "The Liberal Theory of the Open Society," in *The Open Society in Theory and Practice*, ed. Dante Germino and Klaus von Beyme (The Hague, 1974): 142–63.

"Democracy, Socialism, and the Working Classes," in *The Cambridge Companion to Mill*, ed. John Skorupski (Cambridge, 1998): 372–95.

Tholfsen, Trygve. "The Origins of the Birmingham Caucus," *HJ*, 2 (1959): 161–84.

Working Class Radicalism in Mid-Victorian England (London, 1976).

Thompson, Dennis. *John Stuart Mill and Representative Government* (Princeton, 1976).

"Mill in Parliament: When Should a Philosopher Compromise?" in *J. S. Mill's Political Thought: A Bicentennial Reassessment*, ed. Nadia Urbinati and Alex Zakaras (Cambridge, 2007): 166–99.

Thompson, James. "Modern Liberty Redefined," in *The Cambridge History of Nineteenth-Century Political Thought*, ed. Gareth Stedman Jones and Gregory Claeys (Cambridge, 2011): 720–47.

British Political Culture and Idea of Public Opinion, 1867–1914 (Cambridge, 2013).

Tideman, Nicolaus. "The Single Transferable Vote," *The Journal of Economic Perspectives*, 9 (1995): 27–38.

Tilby, A. Wyatt. *Lord John Russell: A Study in Civil and Religious Liberty* (New York, 1931).

Tuck, Richard. *Philosophy and Government, 1572–1651* (Cambridge, 1993).

The Sleeping Sovereign: The Invention of Modern Democracy (Cambridge, 2016).

Tucker, Jennifer. *Nature Exposed: Photography as Eyewitness in Victorian Science* (Baltimore, 2005).

Tulloch, Hugh. *James Bryce's American Commonwealth: The Anglo-American Background* (Woodbridge, 1988).

Turner, Michael J. "Political Leadership and Political Parties, 1800–46," in *A Companion to Nineteenth-Century Britain*, ed. Chris Williams (Oxford, 2004): 125–39.

Todorov, Tzvetan. "Du culte de la différence à la sacralisation de la victime," *Esprit*, 6 (1995): 90–102.

Tripp, Aili Mari and Alice Kang. "The Global Impact of Quotas: On the Fast Track to Increased Female Legislative Representation," *Comparative Political Studies*, 41 (2008): 338–61.

Tyler, Colin. *Idealist Political Philosophy: Pluralism and Conflict in the Absolute Idealist Tradition* (London, 2006).

Urbinati, Nadia. "Representation as Advocacy: A Study of Democratic Deliberation," *PT*, 28 (2000): 758–86.

Mill on Democracy: From the Athenian Polis to Representative Government (Chicago, 2002).

Representative Democracy: Principles and Genealogy (Chicago: 2006).

Urbinati, Nadia and Mark Warren, "The Concept of Representation in Contemporary Democratic Theory," *ARPS*, 11 (2008): 387–412.

Varouxakis, Georgios. *Victorian Political Thought on France and the French* (Houndmills, Basingstoke, 2002).

Varouxakis, Georgios and Paul Kelly, "John Stuart Mill's Thought and Legacy: A Timely Reappraisal," in *John Stuart Mill – Thought and Influence: The Saint of Rationalism* (New York, 2010): 1–18.

Verba, Sidney, Kay Schlozman and Henry Brady. *Voice and Equality: Civic Voluntarism in American Politics* (Cambridge, MA, 1995).

Vieira, Mónica Brita and David Runciman, *Representation* (Cambridge, 2008).

Vincent, John. *The Formation of the Liberal Party, 1857–1868* (London, 1966).

von Arx, Jeffrey Paul. *Progress and Pessimism: Religion, Politics, and History in Late-Nineteenth-Century Britain* (Cambridge, MA, 1985).

Wahrman, Dror. *Imagining the Middle Class: The Political Representation of Class in Britain, c. 1780–1840* (Cambridge, 1995).

Waldron, Jeremy. *Law and Disagreement* (Oxford, 1999).

"The Core of the Case against Judicial Review," *Yale Law Journal*, 115 (2006): 1346–406.

Political Political Theory: Essays on Institutions (Cambridge, MA, 2016).

Walkland, S. A. "Parliamentary Reform, Party Realignment, and Electoral Reform," in *The Politics of Parliamentary Reform*, ed. David Judge (Guildford and King's Lynn, 1984): 37–53.

Walton, John. *The Second Reform Act* (London, 1996).

Chartism (London, 1999).

Warner, Stuart. "Foreword," to J. F. Stephen, *Liberty, Equality, Fraternity*, ed. Warner (Indianapolis, 1993): ix–xxiv.

Warren, Mark. "Citizen Representatives," in *Designing Deliberative Democracy*, ed. Mark Warren and Hilary Pearse (Cambridge, 2008): 50–69.

Wasson, Ellis. "The Spirit of Reform, 1832 and 1867," *Albion*, 12 (1980): 164–74.

"The Great Whigs and Parliamentary Reform, 1809–1830," *JBS*, 24 (1985): 434–64.

Weil, Simone. *On the Abolition of All Political Parties*, trans. Simon Leys (New York, 2013).

Weill, Rivka. "Dicey Was Not Diceyan," *Cambridge Law Journal*, 62 (2003): 474–94.

Weinstein, David. *Utilitarianism and the New Liberalism* (Cambridge, 2007).

"Nineteenth and Twentieth-Century Liberalism," in *The Oxford Handbook of the History of Political Philosophy*, ed. George Klosko (Oxford, 2011): 414–35

West, Julius. *A History of the Chartist Movement* (Boston and New York, 1920).

Weston, Corrine. *The House of Lords and Ideological Politics: Lord Salisbury's Referendal Theory and the Conservative Party, 1846–1922* (Philadelphia, 1995).

Williams, Melissa. "Burkean 'Descriptions' and Political Representation: A Reappraisal," *Canadian Journal of Political Science*, 29 (1996): 23–45.

Voice, Trust, and Memory: Marginalized Groups and the Failings of Liberal Representation (Princeton, 1998).

"The Uneasy Alliance of Group Representation and Deliberative Democracy," in *Citizenship in Diverse Societies*, ed. Will Kymlicka and Wayne Norman (Oxford, 2000): 124–52.

Wilson, Alexander. "The Suffrage Movement," *Pressure from without in early Victorian England*, ed. Patricia Hollis (London, 1974): 80–104.

Wilson, Francis. *A Theory of Public Opinion* (Chicago, 1962).

Winch, Donald. "The Cause of Good Government," in Stefan Collini, Winch, and John Burrow, *That Noble Science of Politics: A Study in Nineteenth-Century Intellectual History* (Cambridge, 1983): 91–126.

Winter, James. "The Cave of Adullam and Parliamentary Reform," *EHR*, 81 (1966): 38–55.

Wishy, Bernard. "Introduction" to John Stuart Mill, *Prefaces to Liberty*, ed. Wishy (Boston, 1959): 1–33.

Wisler, Dominique. "Ernest Naville ou l'invention de la représentation proportionnelle" (2008) [www.researchgate.net/publication/280977838].

Wolff, Robert Paul. "Beyond Tolerance," in Wolff, Barrington Moore, and Herbert Marcuse, *A Critique of Pure Tolerance* (Boston, 1965): 3–52.

Woodward, Llewellyn. *The Age of Reform, 1815–1870*, second edition (Oxford, 1962).

Wright, Julian and H. S. Jones. "A Pluralist History of France?," in *Pluralism and the Idea of the Republic in France*, ed. Wright and Jones (Houndmills, Basingstoke, 2012): 1–22.

Wright, T. R. *The Religion of Humanity: The Impact of Comtean Positivism on Victorian Britain* (Cambridge, 1986).

Young, G. M. *Today and Yesterday* (London, 1948).

"The Greatest Victorian," in *Victorian Essays* (Oxford, 1962): 116–28.

Young, Iris Marion. "Justice, Inclusion and Deliberative Democracy," in *Deliberative Politics: Essays on Democracy and Disagreement*, ed. Stephen Macedo (Oxford, 1999): 151–8.

Inclusion and Democracy (Oxford, 2000).

Zaller, John. *The Nature and Origins of Mass Opinion* (Cambridge, 1992).

Index

Page numbers in *italics* refer to footnotes.

IDEAS IN CONTEXT

Edited by David Armitage, Richard Bourke, Jennifer Pitts, and John Robertson

CPSIA information can be obtained
at www.ICGtesting.com
Printed in the USA
LVHW082355091121
702925LV00012B/663

9 781108 450959